Private International Law, Art and Cultural Heritage

Private International Law, Art and Cultural Heritage

Christa Roodt

Lecturer, University of Glasgow, UK and Professor Extraordinaria, University of South Africa

EE Edward Elgar PUBLISHING

Cheltenham, UK • Northampton, MA, USA

Published by
Edward Elgar Publishing Limited
The Lypiatts
15 Lansdown Road
Cheltenham
Glos GL50 2JA
UK

Edward Elgar Publishing, Inc.
William Pratt House
9 Dewey Court
Northampton
Massachusetts 01060
USA

A catalogue record for this book
is available from the British Library

Library of Congress Control Number: 2014954953

This book is available electronically in the **Elgar**online
Law subject collection
DOI 10.4337/9781781002162

MIX
Paper from
responsible sources
FSC® C013056

ISBN 978 1 78100 215 5 (cased)
ISBN 978 1 78100 216 2 (eBook)

Typeset by Columns Design XML Ltd, Reading
Printed and bound in Great Britain by T.J. International Ltd, Padstow

Contents

Acknowledgements vi
List of abbreviations vii
Table of cases x
Table of legislation xviii

1. The role of private international law in the protection of art and cultural objects 1
2. Restitution: Complexities and opportunities introduced by private international law 67
3. Taking a full turn: Both inwards and outwards 108
4. Adjudicatory authority and its limits 161
5. Title laundering in complex 'lock' jurisdictions 224
6. Deciding claims for restitution of Nazi spoliated art on their merit: Towards value rationality 250
7. Towards the equalisation of claims based on public and private law 289
8. Realising the potential of private international law to settle claims to art and cultural heritage 339

Bibliography 349
Index 377

Acknowledgements

I am grateful to a number of people without whom this book would never have been written.

Thanks are due to Professor Nick Pearce and Professor Gillian Doyle in the School of Culture and Creative Arts at Glasgow University who assisted me in many tangible ways and offered their encouragement. Professor David Carey Miller conducted many discussions and teaching sessions with me. He offered numerous suggestions for the improvement of the text. He offered mentorship, friendship and co-authorship of the article on which Chapter 5 is based. He was also instrumental in the appointment of research assistant Nadine Burrath, a Master of Laws graduate. She offered enthusiastic and high-quality research support.

Two groups of people deserve a special word of thanks. First, the staff of UNIDROIT, and specifically Frédérique Mestre, Bettina Maxion and Marina Schneider extended their help to me in 2012. Secondly, the first intake of students on the Art Law and Business MSc Programme run by Christie's Education in conjunction with the University of Glasgow (2013–2014) proved to be a remarkable and rich testing ground for many of the ideas contained in the book.

I am grateful to Professor Sophia Tang who assisted me in many different ways at the inception of this project. Mariki Rudolph offered her unstinting support throughout its completion. Edward Elgar staff and an anonymous reviewer also deserve my gratitude.

The encouragement of loved ones and friends has made all the difference. I owe you a great debt of thanks.

The research was concluded on 31 July 2014. All errors that remain in the text are mine alone.

Abbreviations

General

AAM	American Association of Museums
AAMD	Association of Art Museum Directors
ADR	Alternative Dispute Resolution
ALR	Art Loss Register
AMAAA	Ancient Monuments and Archaeological Areas Act 1979
ARPA	Archaeological Resources Protection Act of 1979
BADV	Federal Office for Central Services and Unresolved Property Issues
BGBl	Bundesgesetzblatt or Federal Law Gazette
BGH	Bundesgerichtshof (Germany)
BGHZ	Entscheidungen des Bundesgerichtshofes in Zivilsachen or Decisions of the Federal Court in Civil Matters
CCPIA	Cultural Property Implementation Act
CJEU	Court of Justice of the European Union
CPR	Civil Procedure Rules (England)
CPTA	Federal Act on the International Transfer of Cultural Property 2003 (Switzerland)
DCFR	Draft Common Frame of Reference
DCMS	Department for Culture, Media and Sport
ECJ	European Court of Justice
EFTA	European Free Trade Association
FSIA	Foreign Sovereign Immunities Act of 1976
HCCAC	Hague Choice of Court Agreements Convention
ICC	International Chamber of Commerce
ICDR	International Centre for Dispute Resolution
ICOM	International Council of Museums

ICPRCP	Intergovernmental Committee for Promoting the Return of Cultural Property to Its Countries of Origin or Its Restitution in Case of Illicit Appropriation
IFAR	International Foundation for Art Research
IFSA	Immunity from Seizure Act of 1965
ILA	International Law Association
INTERPOL	International Criminal Police Organization
ITAP	Ministerial Advisory Panel on the Illicit Trade in Cultural Objects
JCC	Conference on Jewish Material Claims against Germany or Jewish Claims Conference
LCIA	London Court of International Arbitration
NAGPRA	Native American Graves Protection and Repatriation Act of 1990
NHPA	National Historic Preservation Act
NSPA	National Stolen Property Act
NYC	1958 New York Convention for the Recognition and Enforcement of Foreign Arbitral Awards
PCA	Permanent Court of Arbitration
QLTR	Queen's and Lord Treasurer's Remembrancer
TFEU	Treaty on the Functioning of the European Union
UK	United Kingdom of Great Britain and Northern Ireland
UNESCO	United Nations Educational, Scientific and Cultural Organisation
UNIDROIT	International Institute for the Unification of Private Law

Publications

AJCL	American Journal of Comparative Law
BYBIL	British Yearbook of International Law
CILSA	Comparative and International Law Journal of Southern Africa
ETS	European Treaty Series
IALR	International Arbitration Law Review
ICLQ	International and Comparative Law Quarterly
IJCP	International Journal of Cultural Property
JPIL	Journal of Private International Law

LQR	Law Quarterly Review
OJ C	Official Journal of the European Union, Information and Notices
OJ L	Official Journal of the European Union, Legislation
UNTS	United Nations Treaty Series
YBPIL	Yearbook of Private International Law

Table of cases

Argentina

Blue Ridge Investments, LLC v Republic of Argentina 12-4139-cv (2d Cir 2013), Court of Appeals for the Second Circuit 215

Australia

Aerospatiale Holdings Australia Pty Ltd and Eurocopter International Pacific Ltd v Elspan International Pty Ltd. et al., Supreme Court of NSW, Common Law Division, 14 August 1992, (1992) 28 NSWLR 321 217
John Pfeiffer Pty Ltd v Rogerson (2000) 172 ALR 625 96
McKain v RW Miller & Co (SA) Pty Ltd (1991) 174 CLR 1 96

Canada

Case of the Vessel Marquis de Somereuils 1812: Stewart's Vice-Admiralty Reports for Nova Scotia 1803–1813, 482 117
Hunt v T&N plc [1993] 4 SCR 289 311
R v Heller (1983) 27b Alta LR 2d 346 (Prov Ct); (1984) 30 Alta LR 2d 130 QB ... 128
Tolofson v Jensen (1994) 120 DLR 4th 289 96

Denmark

Arnamagnaean Institute v Ministry of Education 1966 UfR 22; 1971 UfR 299 313

European Court of Human Rights

Beyeler v Italy (Application no 33202/96), 2002 ECHR 462, 28 May 2002 306
Kozacioglu v Turkey [GC] (Application no 2334/03), 19 February 2009 1
Nordstrom-Janzon and Nordstrom Lehtinen v The Netherlands (Application no 28101/95), 27 November 1996 203
Sud Fondi Srl c Italia (Application no 75909/01), 20 January 2009 306
Suda v Czech Republic (Application no 1643/06), 28 October 2010 202
Suovaniemi and Others v Finland (Application no 31737/96), 23 February 1999 203

European Court of Justice

Case 120/78 Cassis de Dijon [1979] ECR 649 ....139, 140
Case 48/71 EC Commission v Italy [1972] ECR 527 ....7, 137
Case 7/68 EC Commission v Italy [1969] CMLR 1 ....7, 137–138
Case 7/78 R v Thompson [1978] ECR 2247, [1979] 1 CMLR 47 138
Case 72/83 Campus Oil [1984] ECR 2727 138
Case 8-74 Procureur du Roi v Benoît and Gustave Dassonville [1974] ECR 837 138
Case C- 281/02 Owusu v Jackson [2005] ECR I-1383 ....174, 187
Case C-120/95 Decker [1998] ECR I-1831 138
Case C-185/07 Allianz SpA and Generali Assicurazioni Generali SpA, formerly Riunione Adriatica di Sicurtà SpA v West Tankers Inc, The Front Comor [2009] ECR I-663 (Grand Chamber) 206
Kalfelis v Schroder C-189/87 [1988] ECR 5565 172
Rudolf Gabriel C-96/00 [2002] ECR I-6367 172

France

Federal Republic of Nigeria v Alain de Montbrison, Cour de Cassation, judgment of 20 September 2006 125
Frias v Pinchon 1886 Clunet 593 ....40, 225, 330
La Chartreuse v Cavagna, Cour de Cassation, 18 December 2003, (2004) ASA Bull 796 204
X v Banque Privée Edmond de Rothschild Arrêt no 983 du 26 septembre 2012 (11-26.022), Cour de Cassation, Première chambre civile 203
Rouen Municipal Council decision, session of 19 October 2007; Administrative Tribunal of Rouen (judgment of 27 December 2007); Administrative Court of Appeal in Douai (judgment of 24 July 2008) 79

Germany

Allgemeine Versicherungsgesellschaft v E.K., BGH, 22 June 1972 0 II ZR 113/70; BGHZ 59 332
Arabic Republic of Egypt v Antiques Dealer, Higher Regional Court of Berlin, judgment of 16 October 2006, 10 U 286/05, NJW 2007 705 332
Land Reform I case, Federal Constitutional Court, judgment of 23 April 1991, 1 BvR 1170/90, 1174/90, 1145/90, NJW 1991 1597 332
Peter Sachs v Stiftung Deutches Historisches Museum Landgericht, Berlin, 10 February 2009, 19 O 116/08; Berlin Higher Regional Court 28 January 2010, 8 U 56/09; BGH 16 March 2012, v. ZR 279/10 ....269–271, 274, 286
University of Leipzig v Germany represented by the Federal Office that deals with Restitution Affairs and Unsolved Property Questions Berlin Administrative Court 26 May 2011, VG 29 K 126.09 ....272, 284–285
Upper Regional Court (Oberlandesgericht) Hamm, Rechtsprechung zum Wiedergutmachungsrecht 1954, 41 BverwG VIZ 2000, 94 279

Hong Kong

FG Hemisphere Associates LLC v Democratic Republic of Congo [2009] 1 HKLRD 410 (Court of First Instance); [2010] 2 HKLRD 66 (CA); FACV 5-7/ 2010 (Ct of Fin al Appeal) 214

Italy

Atleta di Fano case, Tribunal of Sciacca, 9 January 1963, Foro Italiano, 1963, I, 1317; Tribunal of Pesaro, Order of 12 June 2009, No 2042/07 RGNR; Tribunal of Pesaro, Order of 10 February 2010, No 2042/07 RGNR; Court of Cassation, 18 January 2011, No 6558; Third Criminal Chamber of the Supreme Court 3 May 2012 ....75, 293
Republic of Ecuador v Danusso Civil and District Court of Turin, First Civil Section 4410/79; Court of Appeal of Turin Second Civil Section 593/82; 18 Rev dir int priv proc 625 (1982) 240, 305, 313–314
Stato Francese v Ministero Italiano per I beni culturali e ambientali e De Contessini Livio, Decision of the Tribunal of Rome on 27 June 1987; Court of Appeal in Rome on 6 July 1992; Court of Cassation (Sez I) 24 November 1995, No 12166 ....240, 290

The Netherlands

Batz-sur-Mer Madonna with Child Re Raad v OvJ, Hoge Raad (Criminal Division) 18 January 1983, NJ (1983) 1402, Nr 445 313
Bredius case, Hoge Raad, 16 Maart 1990, NJ (1991) 575 84

Switzerland

India v Credit Agricole Indosuez (Switzerland) SA, Swiss Federal Supreme Court, 8 April 2005, BGE 131 III 418 292
N de N c/N et al., Swiss Federal Supreme Court, 28 May 1998 SJ 1999 I 1 314
Türkische Republik v Kanton Basel-Stadt, Basel Trial Court judgment 16 August 1993; Basel Court of Appeal, 18 August 1995; Swiss Supreme Court, 22 May 1996 314

United Kingdom

Air Foyle Ltd v Center Capital Ltd [2004] ILPr 15 230
Attorney-General of New Zealand v Ortiz [1982] 3 All ER 432; [1983] 2 All ER 93 (HL) 40, 65, 66, 162, 292, 305, 307–311, 315, 316, 335
Bakwin and Erie International Trading Co Inc v Sotheby's, 22 November 2005 (unreported)(QBD) 199–200
Blair v Curran [1939] 62 CLR 464 210
Bumper Development Corporation v Commissioner of Police for the Metropolis [1991] 1 WLR 1362; [1991] 4 All ER 638 (CA) 95, 194, 228, 305, 312

Cammell v Sewell [1860] 8 WR 639 ....93, 227, 230
City of Gotha and the Federal Republic of Germany v Sotheby's and Cobert Finance SA transcript, unreported case no 1997/G/185, 9 September 1998, QBD..... 93, 105, 227, 244–245, 262
Commings v Heard (1869) LRQB 4 669 189
Edgerly v Bush (1880) 81NY199...244
Ferrexpo v Gilson [2012] EWHC 721 174
Fiona Trust v Privalov [2007] 1 Lloyd's Rep 391 (CA).......................................205
Government of the Islamic Republic of Iran v The Barakat Galleries Ltd [2007] EWHC 705 (QB); [2009] 1 QB 22 (CA) 88, 100, 245, 295–296, 309–310, 316–318, 327–328
Halsey v Milton Keynes General NHS Trust [2004] 1 WLR 3002 (CA) 53, 151–152
Her Majesty's Attorney-General v Trustees of the British Museum [2005] EWHC 1089 (Ch)...15, 265
Huntington v Attrill [1893] AC 150...292
Johnson v Gore Wood [2002] 2 AC 1 190
King of Italy v Marquis Cosimo de Medici Tornaquincy 34 TLR 623 (Ch 1918)..292
Kingdom of Spain v Christie's 1986 WLR 1120..20, 334
Konkola Copper Mines v Coromin [2005] EWHC 898 174
Kuwait Airways Corporation v Iraqi Airways Co [2002] 2 AC 883 103
Lanes Group Plc v Galliford Try Infrastructure Ltd [2011] EWHC 1679 (TCC) 190
Lord Advocate v University of Aberdeen & Budge 1963 SC 533 ....40, 86, 289
Love v Baker (1665) 1 Ch Cas 67 206
Maharanee Seethadevi Gaekwar of Baroda v Wildenstein [1972] 2 QB 283 81
Marcq v Christie Manson and Wood Ltd, t/a Christie's [2002] EWHC 2148, [2003] EWCA Civ 731, [2004] QB 286 (CA)..100
Midgulf International Ltd v Groupe Chimiche Tunisien [2010] EWCA Civ 66....205
Premium Nafta Products Ltd v Fili Shipping 2007 UKHL 40.............................205
Princess Paley Olga v Weisz [1929] 1 KB 718 (CA)..............................33, 103, 318
R v Ghosh [1982] QB 1053 303
R v Tokeley-Parry [1999] Crim LR 578..300–302
Re Anziani Herbert v Christopherson [1930] 1 Ch 407..93
Reichhold Norway ASA v Goldman Sachs International [2000] 1 WLR 173 (CA) 186
RTZ v Connolly [1998] AC 854...184
Sovarex SA v Romero Alvarez SA [2011] EWHC 1661 (Comm) 209–210
Spiliada Maritime Co v Cansulex [1987] AC 460 ....82, 184, 310
Todd v Armour (1882) 9R 901 230
Ust-Kamenogorsk Hydropower Plant JSC (Appellant) v AES Ust-Kamenogorsk Hydropower Plant LLP (Respondent) [2013] UKSC 35 206
West Tankers Inc v Allianz Spa & Another [2011] EWHC 829 (Comm).......206, 210
Winkworth v Christie Manson and Woods Ltd [1980] Ch 496............40, 93, 95, 227, 229–230, 232–233, 235–236, 239, 244–245
Yukos Capital SarL v OJSC Rosnef Oil Company [2011] EWHC 1461 (Comm) 210

United States

Alsdorf v Bennigson, No 04 C 5953, 2004 WL 2806301 (ND Ill 2004); No B168200; 2004 WL 803616 (Cal Ct App 2004); S124828; 2004 Cal Lexis 6903 (Cal 2004); S124828; 2005 Cal Lexis 13370 (Cal 2005) 163, 217
Altmann v Republic of Austria, 142 F Supp 2d 1187 (C D Cal 1999); 317 F3d 954 (9th Circuit 2002); 327 F3d 1246 (9th Circuit 2003); 123 S Ct 2129 (2003); 539 US 987 (2003); 335 F Supp 2d 1066 (C D Cal 2004).......90, 182–183, 185, 192, 214, 258
Asahi Metal Industry Co. v Superior Court of California, 480 US 102 (1987) 181
Austria v Altmann, 541 US 677 (2004)....................................26, 50, 101, 183, 259
Autocephalous Greek-Orthodox Church v Goldberg & Feldman Fine Arts, Inc, 717 F Supp 1374 SD Ind 1989); 917 F2d 278 (7th Circuit 1990); 112 S Ct 377 (1992) 28, 98–99, 178, 239
Bakalar v Vavra and Fischer, 619 F3d 136 (2d Circuit 2010); 819 FSupp 2d 293 (SDNY 2011); 500FApp'x 6, 8 (2d Cir 2012); No 12-1160, 2013 WL1993864 (US 2013) 89, 238, 266
Bakoss v Certain Underwriters at Lloyd's of London Issuing Certificate No 0510135, 707 F3d 140 (2d Circuit 2013) 151
Bennigson v Alsdorf, (Cal Supr Ct 16 June 2003) (unreported), aff 'd, No B168200...163, 164, 216–217
Byblos Bank Europe, SA v Sekerbank Turn Anonym Syrket, 885 NE2d 191 (2008) 190
Cassirer v Kingdom of Spain, 461 F Supp 2d 1157(C D Cal 2006)....... 104, 182, 185
Charrier v Bell, 498 So 2d 753 (1986) 78
Chasidei Chabad v Russian Federation 466 F Supp 2d 6 (2006); 528 F3d 934 (DC Circuit 2008) 102, 105, 182, 187, 188
Chromalloy Aeroservices Inc v ARE 939 F Supp 907 (DDC 1996) 207
Corporación Mexicana de Mantenimiento Integral v Pemex-Exploración y Producción No 10 Civ 206 (AKH), 2013 WL 4517225 (SDNY 27 August 2013) 209
Crow Creek Sioux Tribe v Brownlee, 331 F3d 912 (17 June 2003) 178–179
Detroit Institute of Arts v Ullin, ED Michigan (31 March 2007) ...149, 246, 274–275
DeWeerth v Baldinger 836 F2d 103 (2d Circuit 1987); 108 S Ct 2823 (1988); 486 US 1056 (1988); 804 F Supp 539 (SDNY 1992); 38 F3d 1266 (2d Circuit NY 1994); 115 S Ct 512 (1994) 187, 241
Dunbar v Seger-Tomschitz, 615 F3d 574 (5th Circuit 2010) 230, 275
Goodman v Searle, Complaint (N D Ill 17 July 1996) (No 96 – 6459) 101
Grosz v The Museum of Modern Art, 772 F Supp 2d 473 (SDNY 2010); 403 Fed Appx 575 (2d Circuit 2010); 132 S Ct 102; 181 L Ed 2d 30 (2011) 28, 98, 246, 275
Gulf Oil Corpn v Gilbert, 330 US 501 (1946) 184–185
Helicopteros Nacionales de Colombia v Hall, 466 US 408 (1984) 180
In re Holocaust Victim Assets Litigation I, 105 F Supp 2d 154 275
In re: Robert M Mardirosian, No BD-2007-012 199–200
International Shoe v Washington, 326 US 310, 316 (1945) 180, 184

Ipitrade International SA v Federal Republic of Nigeria, 465 F Supp 824 (DDC 1978) 214
Jeanneret v Vichey, 541 F Supp 80 (SDNY 1982); 693 F2d 259 (2d Circuit 1982) 187, 334
Laker Airways Ltd v Sabena, Belgian World Airlines, 731 F2d 909 (DC Circuit 1984) 926-27 ....187, 189
Leonard Malewicz v City of Amsterdam, 517 F Supp 2d 322 (2007); 362 F Supp 2d 298 (DDC 2005) 105, 182
Menzel v List, 267 NYS 2d 804, 809 (NY Sup Ct 1966); 279 NYS2d 608 (NY App Div 1967); 246 NE2d 742 (NY 1969) 105, 246–247, 276
Mirvish v Mott, 18 NY3d 510 (2012) 247–248
Museum of Fine Arts, Boston v Claudia Seger-Tomschitz, 623 F3d 1 (1st Circuit 2010) 275
Museum of Modern Art and Guggenheim Foundation v Schoeps, 603 F Supp 2d 273 (SDNY 2009) 274
O'Keeffe v Snyder, 83 NJ 478, 416 A2d 862 870 (NJ 1980) 246
Orkin v Taylor, 487 F3d 734 (9th Circuit 2007); 128 S Ct 491 ....96, 255
Perkins v Benguet Consolidated Mining Co., 342 US 437 (1952) 180
Peru v Johnson, 720 F Supp 810 (C D Cal 1989) sub nom Peru v Wendt, 933 F2d 1013 (9th Circuit 1991) 322–323
Piper Aircraft Co v Reyno, 454 US 235 (1981) 185
Princz v Federal Republic of Germany 26 F3d 116, 1176 (DC Circuit 1994) 258
Pueblo of San Ildefonso v Daniel Ridlon and Regents of the University of California, 103 F3d 936 (10th Circuit 1996) 178
Republic of Croatia v The Marquess of Northampton 1987 Settlement, 610 NYS2d 263 (NY App Div 1994); 84 NY2d 805 (NY 1994) 322
Republic of Lebanon v Sotheby's, 561 NYS 2d 566 AD 1 Dept 1990 187
Republic of Turkey v The Metropolitan Museum of Art, 762 F Supp 44 (SDNY 1990) 187, 323
Rosenberg v Seattle Art Museum, 70 F Supp 2d 1163 (D Wash 1999); 124 F Supp 2d 1207 (D Wash 2000) 262
Schlaifer Nance & Co v Estate of Andy Warhol, 764 F Supp 43, 46 (1991)
Schultz v US, 540 US 1106 (2004) 153, 217
Seetransport Wiking Trader Schifffahrtsgesellschaft GmbH and Co Kommanditgesellschaft v Navimpex Centrala Navala and Uzinexportimport, 989 F2d 572 (2d Circuit 1993), 1994 XIX YbCA 812 Kunstsammlungen zu Weimar v Elicofon, 536 F Supp 829 (EDNY 1981); 678 F2d 1150 (2d Circuit 1982) 1151 205
Schoeps v Museum of Modern Art, 594 F Supp 2d 461 (SDNY 2009) 42, 274
Shaffer v Heitner, 433 US 186, 201, 97 S Ct 2569, 53 L Ed 2d 683 (1977) 169
Solomon R Guggenheim Foundation v Lubell, 77 NY 2d 311 (1991) 28, 73, 187, 239, 244, 246
Toledo Museum of Art v Ullin, 477 F Supp 2d 802 (ND Ohio 2006) 149, 274–275
Turkey v OKS Partners, 1994 US Dist LEXIS 17032 (D Mass 1994) 323
US v An Antique Platter of Gold, 991 F Supp 222 (SDNY 1997); [1999] USCA2 301; 184 F3d 131 (2d Circuit 1999) 88, 305
US v An Arcaic Etruscan Pottery Ceremonial Vase Late 7th Century BC, No 1:96-cv-09437 (SDNY 1997) 87

US v Gerber, 999 F2d 1112 (7th Circuit 1993); 510 US 1071 (1994)......................87
US v Hollinshead, No 10970 (SD Cal 14 March 1973); 495 F2d 1154 (9th Circuit 1974)..65, 187, 305, 321, 326
US v Mardirosian, 602 F3d 1 (2010)..199, 200, 241
US v McClain, 545 F2d 658 (1978); 593 F2d 658 (1979); 444 US 918 (1979) 671 .... 65, 305, 321–323, 326
US v Melnikas, 9292 F Supp 276 (SD Ohio 1996)...87
US v One Oil Painting Entitled 'Femme En Blanc' by Pablo Picasso, 362 F Supp 2d 1175 (C D Cal 2005) 163, 216
US v Portrait of Wally, A Painting by Egon Schiele, No 99-CV-09940 (SDNY filed July 29, 2010); 105 F Supp 2d 288 (SDNY 2000); No 99 Civ 9940, 2000 WL 1890403 (SDNY December 28,2000); No 99 Civ 9940 (MBM), 2002 WL 553532 (SDNY April 12, 2002)...50, 164, 178, 253
US v Pre-Columbian Artifacts and the Republic of Guatemala, 845 F Supp 544 (ND Ill 1993)..323
US v Quarrel, 310 F3d 664 (10th Circuit 2002)...87
US v Schultz, 333 F2d 393 (2d Circuit 2003); 178 F Supp 2d 445 (2002)......40, 298, 321–326, 328
Vineberg v Bissonnette, 529 F Supp 2d 300 (DRI 2007) 92, 272, 274
Von Saher v Norton Simon Museum of Art at Pasadena, 592 F3d 954 (9th Circuit 2010)...102, 276, 278
Wertheimer v Cirker's Hayes Storage Warehouse, Inc., 752 NYS 2d 295 (Sup Ct 2002) 28
World-Wide Volkswagen Corp. v Woodson, 444 US 286 (1980)..................162, 180
Yale University v Pierre Konowaloff (D Conn 20 March 2014)............................32

International Law Cases

Application of the Convention on the Prevention and Punishment of the Crime of Genocide, (Bosnia and Herzegovina v Serbia and Montenegro), Judgment of 26 February 2007, ICJ Rep (2007)..121
Case concerning the Temple of Preha Vihear (Cambodia and Thailand), judgment of 15 June 1962, ICJ Reports (1962) 10
Certain Property (Liechtenstein v Germany), Preliminary Objections, Judgment of 10 February 2005, ICJ Rep (2005)..121
Factory at Chorzow (Ger v Pol) 1928 PCIJ, Series A, No 9 (July 26)......................68
Partial Award – Central Front, Eritrea's Claims 2, 4, 6, 7, 8 and 22, 28 April 2004 118

Nuremberg

Nuremberg Decision 6 FRD 69 (1946–1947)..258

Arbitration Cases and Awards

Bakwin and Erie International Trading Co Inc v Sotheby's (2005) 6 ArbLR 83....200

BP Exploration Co (Libya) Ltd v Government of the Libyan Arab Republic, 10 October 1973 and 1 August 1974, 53 ILR (1979) 297 202
Fomento de Construccuones y Contratas SA v Colon Container Terminal SA, 14 May 2001, ATF 127 III 279, [2001] ASA Bulletin 544.................................219
ICC Interim Award, Case no 4695 of 1984, XI YbCA (1986) 149.........................202
Majken Hofmann, Anna Lokrantz, Maria Müller, Andreas Müller Hofmann und Lena Müller Hofmann v Republic of Austria (21 November 2005) <www.bslaw.com/altmann/Zuckerkandl/Klage/284724.doc> 50, 153–154, 191–192, 259
Maria v Altmann, Francis Gutmann, Trevor Mantle, George Bentley, and DDr. Nelly Auersperg v Republic of Austria (15 January 2006) <http://bslaw.com/altmann/Klimt/award.pdf> 153, 191–192
Ministry of Defense of the Republic of Egypt v Chromalloy Aeroservices Inc., Cairo Court of Appeal, 5 December 1995, Rev Arb (1998) 723....................207
Société Européenne d'Etudes et d'Entreprises (S.E.E.E.) v Yugoslavia, 2 July 1956, 86 (1959) JDI 1074 222
Texaco Overseas Petroleum Co (TOPCO) & California Asiatic Oil Co (Calasiatic) v Government of Libyan Arab Republic, Preliminary Award (27 November 1975) and Award on the Merits (17 January 1977), 17 ILM (1978) 1 202
World Duty Free v Kenya ICSID Case No ARB/00/7 335

Table of legislation

Australia

Protection of Movable Cultural Heritage Act 1986 ....297, 320

Austria

Bundesgesetz über die Rückgabe von Kunstgegenständen aus den Österreichischen Bundesmuseen und Sammlungen BGBl I 181/1998 267
Nullification Act of 1946 267
Schiedsrechts-Änderungsgesetz 2006 202

Belgium

Belgian Civil Code, Art 2279(2) 242
Private International Law Code (*Code de droit international privé*) 16 July 2004 ....249, 345
Art 88 239
Art 90 ....68, 242–243
Art 92 ....68, 243
Art 127(7) 243

Canada

Cultural Property Export and Import Act of 1985 ....4, 297

Egypt

Law 117 on the Protection of Antiquities of 1983 (Egypt)......40, 86, 289, 324

European Union

Maastricht Treaty, Consolidated version 31 August 1992, 1992 OJ C 224 136
Treaty Establishing the European Economic Community, 25 March 1957, 298 UNTS 3...................135
Treaty of Amsterdam, 10 November 1997, OJ C 340 136
Treaty of Lisbon, 17 December 2007, OJ C 306/01 135
Art 167 136
Treaty on the Functioning of the European Union, 9 May 2008, OJ C 115/47 ....8, 135–137
Art 30 137
Art 36...........137, 138, 141, 143–144, 146
Art 81(1) 135
Art 114 145

Conventions

1980 Rome Convention on the Law Applicable to Contractual Obligations, Consolidated version [2005] OJ C334/1.......245, 332
Convention on Jurisdiction and the Recognition and Enforcement of Judgments in Civil and Commercial Matters, Council Decision 2007/712/EC of 15 October 2007 ....167, 170

Directives
Council Directive (EEC) 93/7 of 15 March 1993 on the return of cultural objects unlawfully removed from the territory of a member state OJ L 74/74, 27.3.93 ....7–8, 143, 144–147, 160, 175–176, 235, 294–295, 319
Art 1(1) 225
Art 4 147
Art 4(5) 17
Art 4(6) 196
Art 5 ....144, 235
Art 7 146
Art 7(4)................................147, 176
Art 9(1) 146
Art 12 147
Art 15 147
Directive 2001/38/EC of the European Parliament and of the Council of 5 June 2001, OJ L 187/43, 10.7.2001 ....143, 175, 294
Directive 2014/60/EU of the European Parliament and of the Council of 15 May 2014 on the Return of Cultural Objects Unlawfully Removed from the Territory of a Member State and amending Regulation (EU) No 1024/2012 (Recast) OJ EU L159/1, 28.5.2014 ....7–8, 143–148, 176, 225–226, 235, 295, 319, 337
Art 5.............................146, 196, 235
Art 5(4) 146
Art 8 146
Art 10 146
Art 12 148
Art 13 295
Art 16 147
Directive 96/100/EC of the European Parliament and of the Council of 17 February 1997 (L 60/59, 1.3.1997)..................143, 175, 294

Regulations
Council Regulation (EC) No 1210/2003 of 7 July 2003 concerning certain specific restrictions on economic and financial relations with Iraq and repealing Regulation (EC) No 2465/96, OJ L 169/6, 8.7.2003 119
Council Regulation (EC) No 1215 of 2012 of the European Parliament and of the Council of 12 December 2012 on Jurisdiction and the Recognition and Enforcement of Judgments in Civil and Commercial Matters OJ 2012 L351/1, 20.12.2012 ....81–82, 147–148, 170–171, 173, 176–177, 186, 206–207
Art 25 176
Art 29 167
Art 33 187
Council Regulation (EC) No 44/2001 of 22 December 2000 OJ L 12/1 16.1.2001...........................81, 170
Art 27–28 167
Art 31 57
Council Regulation (EEC) No 3911/92 of 9 December 1992 on the export of cultural goods, OJ L 395, 31.12.1992 1–5, replaced by Council Regulation (EC) No 116/2009 (codified) of 18 December on the export of cultural goods, OJ L 39/1 (2009)........8, 141, 143, 296
EC Regulation 562/2006 of the European Parliament and of the Council of 15 March 2006 establishing a Community Code on the rules governing the movement of persons across borders (Schengen Borders Code)...............................296, 329
Art 23 296

Drafts and Proposals
Draft European Parliament Legislative Resolution on the Proposal for a Regulation of the European Parliament and of the Council on Jurisdiction and the Recognition and Enforcement of Judgments in Civil and Commercial Matters (Recast), 15 October 2012 (A7-0320/2012) 175
Proposal for a Regulation of the European Parliament and of the Council on Jurisdiction and the Recognition and Enforcement of Judgments in Civil and Commercial Matters COM (2010) 74 8 Final (Recast)...................175

France

Loi No 2002-323 du 6 mars 2002 relative à la restitution par la France de la dépouille mortelle de Saartjie Baartman à l'Afrique du Sud 79
Loi No 2010-501 du 18 mai 2010 visant à autoriser la restitution par la France des têtes maories à la Nouvelle-Zélande et relative à la gestion des collections JO No 114, 19 May 2010..............................79
French Civil Code (*Code Civile*) 21 March 1804, Arts 2268, 2269, 2279 227
French New Code of Civil Procedure
Art 1458 204
Art 1511 157

Germany, including former Occupied Zones in Germany

Act to Implement the UNESCO Convention of 14 November 1970 on the Means of Prohibiting and Preventing the Illicit Import, Export and Transfer of Ownership of Cultural Property and to Implement the Council Directive 93/7/EEC of 15 March 1993 on the Return of Cultural Objects Unlawfully Removed from the Territory of a Member State (*Gesetz zur Ausführung des UNESCO-Übereinkommens vom 14. November 1970 über Maßnahmen zum Verbot und zur Verhütung der rechtswidrigen Einfuhr, Ausfuhr und Übereignung von Kulturgut und zur Umsetzung der Richtlinie 93/7/EWG des Rates vom 15. März 1993 über die Rückgabe von unrechtmäßig aus dem Hoheitsgebiet eines Mitgliedstaats verbrachten Kulturgütern) 18. Mai 2007* (BGBl. I 757, Nr 21 2547)...7, 143, 145, 196, 235, 319, 331, 294
Arbitration Act of 1998, Book 10 of the German Civil Code of Procedure (*Zivilprozessordnung ZPO*) 202
German Civil Code (BGB)...............260 270–271, 273, 285
Art 138 para 1 333
Art 221 para 11.3..........................245
Law No 59, British Military Government for Germany – *Britisches Kontrollgebiet – Amtsblatt der Militarregierung Deutschland* No 28, S.1169 ....280, 282, 284
Law No 59, US Military Government for Germany, 10 November 1947 – *Amerikanisches Kontrollgebiet – Amtsblatt der Militarregierung Deutschland, Ausgabe* G, S. 1 – 12 Fed. Reg. 7983 (29 November 1947)........................259, 266, 282
Regulation No 120 of the French High Command in Germany, 10 November 1947, *Amtsblatt des französischen Oberkommandos in Deutschland* No 119 of 14 November 1947 266

Rückerstattungsanordnung BK/O (49) 180 der Alliierten Kommandantur Berlin betreffend die Rückerstattung feststellbarer Vermögensgegenstände an Opfer der nationalsozialistischen Unterdrückungsmaßnahmen (vom 26. Juli 1949, VOBl. für Groß-Berlin I S. 221) 270

Italy

Consolidated Act for Cultural Heritage and the Environment, Law decree no 490 of 25 October 1999 .....4, 14
Code of Cultural Property of 2004......................................4, 14
Italian Civil Code (*Codice civile*) *Regio Decreto* 16 March 1942
Art 174 14
Arts 822-828 14
Arts 1153-1157 ....95, 229
Law No 218 of 1995 *Riforma del sistema italiano di diritto internazionale privato* 58, 94
Protection of Items of Artistic or Historical Interest, Law No 1089 of 1939................................4, 289

Iran

Legal Bill regarding Prevention of Unauthorized Excavations and Diggings of 1979 ....289, 316

Mexico

Federal Law on Archaeological, Artistic and Historic Monuments and Zones Act of 1972...................322

The Netherlands

Dutch Civil Code
3:86a 97
3:86b 97
3:87 97
3:87a 97
3:99(2) 225
4:123 84
4:134 84
Former Dutch Civil Code 227
Dutch Code of Civil Procedure, Art 1054(2)..................................157

New Zealand

Antiquities Act 1975 308

Portugal

Decree-Law No 27633 of 1937 230
Law No 13 of 1985..........................230

Russia

Decree on a Moratorium on the Return of Cultural Valuables Displaced in WWII, State Duma of the Federal Assembly of the Russian Federation, 21 April 1995, Russian Federation Collection of Legislation, 1995, No 19, Item 1721 32
Federal Law on Cultural Valuables Displaced to the USSR as a Result of WWII, 15 April 1998, no 64-FZ, Russian Federation Collection of Legislation, 1998, No 16, Item 1879 ....33, 77
Russian Civil Code, Art 1208...........273

South Africa

National Heritage Resources Act of 1999 305

Spain

Spanish Civil Code, Art 464............227

Switzerland

Federal Act on the International Transfer of Cultural Property of 20 June 2003 (SR 44.1).........297, 313
Federal Private International Law Act of 18 December 1987...................239
Art 148(1) 273
Art 187(1) 157
Swiss Civil Code 10 December 1907 33
Arts 930–934 252

Taiwan

Arbitration Act of 1998 219

Turkey

Conservation of Cultural and Natural Property Law No 2863, Official Gazette 23/07/1983 no 18113.....4, 273
Regulation on the Classification, Registration and Admission to Museums of Movable Cultural and Natural Assets Requiring Preservation of 2009....................4
Private International Law Code, Art 7 273

United Kingdom

Ancient Monuments and Archaeological Areas Act 1979 ....6, 87, 303
Arbitration (Scotland) Act of 2010...205
Arbitration Act (England and Wales) 1996 ....194, 201–202, 206
Civic Government (Scotland) Act 1982..................................86, 328
Customs and Excise Management Act 1979 329
Dealing in Cultural Objects (Offences) Act 2003 ......8, 301, 302, 303, 327, 328, 329
Export Control Act of 2002 329
Export of Objects of Cultural Interest (Control) Order 2003 329
Holocaust (Return of Cultural Property) Act 2009 ....67, 265, 268
Iraq (UN Sanctions) Order 2003, 12 June 2003 119
Limitation Act 1980....96, 231, 245, 262
Money Laundering Regulations 2007 97
Powers of Criminal Courts (Sentencing) Act 2000 302
Prescription and Limitation (Scotland) Act 1973 273
Sale of Goods (Amendment) Act 1994 229
Sale of Goods Act 1979 ......38, 101, 229
State Immunity Act 1978 215
The British Museum Act 1963 15
The Human Tissue Act (UK) 2004 ....59, 67
The Return of Cultural Objects Regulations 1994 ....8, 319
Theft Act 1968 c 60 (Eng) 300–302
Treasure Act 1996 (England and Wales) 86
Treasure (Designation) Order 2008 ...86

United States

Alternative Dispute Resolution Act 1998 (28 US Code 651) 151
Archaeological Resources Protection Act of 1979 (16 US Code 3–6) 86-87, 179, 303
California Code of Civil Procedure ...86, 102, 218
Certain Pre-Columbian Sculpture or Murals to Be Seized and Returned at the Expense of the Country of Origin (19 US Code 2091–2095) 320
Convention of Cultural Property Implementation Act (19 US Code 2601–2613).........6, 133, 298–299, 323–326

Diversity of Citizenship (28 US Code 1332) 165, 179
Foreign Sovereign Immunities Act 1976 (28 US Code 1602–1611) 105, 164, 181, 183, 187–188, 215, 320
Immunity from Seizure Act of 1965 (22 US Code 2459) 181–183
Instructions for the Government of Armies of the United States in the Field (Lieber Code), 24 April 1863, promulgated as General Orders No 100 in 1863 (Washington 1898: Government Printing Office) 47
National Historic Preservation Act (16 US Code 470aa–470mm)....6, 179, 303
National Museum of the American Indian Act 1989 Pub.L. 101–85 .78
National Stolen Property Act (18 US Code 2314–2315) ...200, 320–327, 331, 337
Native American Graves Protection and Repatriation Act 1990 (25 US Code 3001–3013)....6, 59, 78, 150, 178-179

CONVENTIONS, TREATIES AND MODEL PROVISIONS

Convention on International Trade in Endangered Species of Wild Fauna and Flora, 3 March 1973 306
Charter of the International Military Tribunal at Nuremberg, annexed to the London Agreement on War Criminals, 8 August 1945, vol 82 No 251 UNTS 279 257
Convention (IV) Respecting the Laws and Customs of War on Land and its Annex of Regulations, The Hague, 18 October 1907, TS 539.................................117, 256
Convention Concerning the Protection of the World Cultural and Natural Heritage, 16 November 1972, 1037 UNTS 151......................116
Convention for the Protection of Human Rights and Fundamental Freedoms (European Convention on Human Rights), 4 November 1950 203
Final Act of the Bretton Woods Conference, 1944 257
Final Act of the Paris Conference on Reparations, 1945...................257
Hague Convention for the Protection of Cultural Property in the Event of Armed Conflict, 14 May 1954, 249 UNTS 215........................116
Hague Convention IX concerning Bombardments by Naval Forces in Time of War, 18 October 1907, 36 Stat. 2351 47
Inter-Allied Declaration against Acts of Dispossession Committed in Territories under Enemy Occupation and Control, 5 January 1943...............................122, 257
International Covenant on Economic, Social and Cultural Rights, 16 December 1966, 993 UNTS 3.....3, 136
Model Provisions on State Ownership of Undiscovered Cultural Objects 25, 114, 128, 160, 329–331, 338
Second Protocol of the Hague Convention for the Protection of Cultural Property in the Event of Armed Conflict, 1954, 26 March 1999........................118, 122, 258
Treaty on Good-Neighbourliness, Partnership and Cooperation between the FRG and USSR, 9 November 1990, 30 ILM 504 76
Treaty on Mutual Assistance in Criminal Matters, 9 November 1982, US-Italy, 24 ILM 1536....34, 308

Treaty on Mutual Assistance in Criminal Matters, US–Italy, 3 May 2006 34
Treaty of Peace with Finland, 10 February 1947, vol 48 No 746 UNTS 183 257
UNESCO Convention on the Means of Prohibiting and Preventing the Illicit Import, Export and Transfer of Ownership of Cultural Property, 14 November 1970, 823 UNTS 231; 10 ILM 289......7, 45, 92, 123, 235, 259, 291
UNESCO Convention on the Protection and Promotion of the Diversity of Cultural Expressions, 20 October 2005, CLT-2005/Convention Diversite-Cult Rev 2–3, 48, 123, 139
UNESCO's Universal Declaration on Cultural Diversity, Paris, 2 November 2001 (2002) 47 ILM 57 3
UNIDROIT Convention on Stolen or Illegally Exported Cultural Objects, 24 June 1995, 34 ILM 1330 .....2, 4, 25, 97, 113, 123, 125, 163, 168, 193, 232, 259, 306
United Nations Universal Declaration of Human Rights 13
Vienna Convention on the Law of Treaties, 23 May 1969, vol 1155 UNTS 331........................124, 132
Washington Treaty on the Protection of Artistic and Scientific Institutions and Historic Monuments, 15 April 1935, 167 LNTS 289 47

UN General Assembly

A/Res/48/15 on the Return or Restitution of Cultural Property to the Countries of Origin of 2 October 1993...........................113
A/Res/60/147 Basic Principles and Guidelines on the Right to a Remedy and Reparation for Victims of Gross Violations of International Human Rights Law and Serious Violations of International Humanitarian Law of 16 December 2005 263
A/Res/66/180 Strengthening Crime Prevention and Criminal Justice Responses to Protect Cultural Property, especially with regard to its Trafficking of 30 March 2012 22
A/Res/67/80 on the Return or Restitution of Cultural Property to the Countries of Origin of 12 March 2013 113
A/Res/68/186 Strengthening Crime Prevention and Criminal Justice Responses to Protect Cultural Property, especially with regard to its Trafficking of 11 February 2014 22

UN Security Council

Resolution 661 (1990) of 6 August 1990.................................118-119
Resolution 686 (1991) of 2 March 1991 118
Resolution 1483 (2003) of 22 May 2003 118–120

1. The role of private international law in the protection of art and cultural objects

1. INTRODUCTION

Art and cultural objects form separate classes of objects that speak to the human condition and that mirror the life conditions of individuals and communities. Humans tend to develop a deep sense of personal attachment to antiquities.

Art is notoriously difficult to define. It has been called an 'unimaginable resource' that can, in the drive to make everything visible, extinguish sight.[1] It is nonetheless evident that art bestows gifts on many. The free and joyous activity that produces art can transform experience or alleviate suffering. It can enhance direct, immediate experience, push us to see, as if for the first time.[2] Its effects may provide a bulwark against an oppressive social order[3] or prompt us to seek co-operation.[4]

Art is particularly hard to define for purposes of interpreting relevant legislation such as export regulations and procedures.[5] The architectural heritage may qualify to be treated as having more than commercial value, for instance,[6] but when is a sculpture an ornament, a fixture, a fitting or an integral part of an architectural structure?

---

1 J Baudrillard, *The Conspiracy of Art* (tr A Hodges) (The MIT Press 2005) 65.

2 LB Gilkey, 'Can Art Fill the Vacuum' in D Apostolos-Cappadona (ed), *Art, Creativity and the Sacred* (Continuum 1996) 187, 188–89.

3 TW Adorno, *Minima Moralia: Reflections from Damaged Life* (tr by D Redmond 2005, Suhrkamp Verlag 1951) aphorism 143.

4 L Tolstoy, *What Is Art?* (tr A Maude 1898, The Brotherhood Publishing Company) 210.

5 E.g. Canova's sculpture 'The Three Graces', which is ensconced in a domed temple at Woburn Abbey (1814–1817). See SE Bush, 'The Protection of British Heritage: Woburn Abbey and The Three Graces' (1996) 5 IJCP 269.

6 *Kozacioglu v Turkey* [GC] (Application no 2334/03), 19 February 2009, 72; Preamble § 18 of the 2005 UNESCO Convention on the Protection and

'Cultural objects' embody archaeological, ethnological or historical information about the creative process and the identity of the group responsible for its production. A cultural object may form part of the functions of the life process of society,[7] and produce cultural identity at the same time. Identity may have a local or sub-state group focus,[8] and is not reserved for the nation state (which can be defined in several different ways).[9]

Cultural objects are defined by the significance they have for states and for sub-national groups.[10] Particular value systems ascribe subjective importance to the specific interest that attaches to cultural objects. The special status of these objects is linked to the human need for roots.[11] What a community or group recognises as part of its identity, and as representative of its symbolic continuity beyond its contingent existence, helps to identify that group. The significance of an object is not determined by the recognition achieved beyond that state or group.

Cultural objects tend to operate as repositories of knowledge that endure from generation to generation.[12] Consumer goods may attain

---

Promotion of the Diversity of Cultural Expressions, 20 October 2005, CLT-2005/Convention Diversite-Cult Rev <http://www.unesco.org/fileadmin/MULTIMEDIA/HQ/CLT/CLT/pdf/conventiontext_og_civilsociety_en.pdf> accessed 25 February 2014; entry into force in 2007.

7 GH Hartman, *The Fateful Question of Culture* (Columbia University Press 1997) 56, in response to H Arendt, *Between Past and Present* (The Viking Press 1961) 208.

8 K Last, 'Cultural Pluralism and the Return of Cultural Heritage' in S Tierney (ed), *Accommodating Cultural Diversity* (Ashgate 2007) 124–25.

9 In practice, it is up to national courts to decide whether an entity falls under the definition of a state in a particular situation. See N van Woudenberg, *State Immunity and Cultural Objects on Loan* (Martinus Nijhoff 2012) 20.

10 Meaning adopted in the 1995 UNIDROIT Convention on Stolen or Illegally Exported Cultural Objects, 24 June 1995, 34 ILM 1330; entry into force 1 July 1998, <http://www.unidroit.org/instruments/cultural-property/1995-convention> accessed 24 February 2014.

11 For more, see S Weil, *The Need for Roots* (Routledge 2002) 41, 51.

12 For more, see P Gerstenblith, 'Identity and Cultural Property: The Protection of Cultural Property in the United States' (1995) 75 Boston University Law Review 559, 569–70; F Francioni, 'Culture, Heritage and Human Rights: An Introduction' in F Francioni and M Scheinin (eds), *Cultural Human Rights* (Martinus Nijhoff 2008) 1, 6; F Francioni, 'Beyond State Sovereignty: The Protection of Cultural Heritage as a Shared Interest of Humanity' [2004] Michigan JIL 1209, 1221.

iconic status, embodying cultural identity.[13] Education can further both the significance and the level of appreciation shown for these objects.

The 'culture' in 'cultural objects' can be understood as the distinctive spiritual, material, intellectual and emotional features of society or groups – a force that co-determines what is created – such as art – and what is assimilated – lifestyle, ways of living together, value systems, traditions and beliefs.[14] The universality and dynamic thrust of the concept of 'culture' challenges us, for it prompts us to develop '... all sides of our humanity ... and ... all parts of our society'.[15] The implication of the coexistence of different cultures,[16] which requires a dialogue of parity among the cultures of the world,[17] is inescapable. Because culture makes 'identity' conceivable but also gives expression to our humanity, it fosters more than mere belonging. In fact, its identity-providing role is rather less important than its capacity to foster human connection and solidarity despite difference.[18] An assumption that the drive for identity ends in political harmony (or that political harmony is attainable at all) is false. Such a drive can undermine the very co-operation that cultural objects inspire, justifying obliteration of the identity of the 'other'. A dialogue of parity is only possible if diverse cultural values are accommodated; if value does not depend on the role which they are assigned to fulfill and where preference plays no part.

The technique of legal definition differs across legal systems. In practice, there are different domestic systems of definition in relation to cultural objects. An enumeration system makes specific mention of each type of item that it proposes to protect (e.g. the Netherlands). A

---

[13] E.g. the 1960s British Mini, or the 1950s German Volkswagen.

[14] Preamble to UNESCO's Universal Declaration on Cultural Diversity, Paris, 2 November 2001 (2002) 47 ILM 57.

[15] M Arnold, *Culture and Anarchy* (Cambridge 1935) 11.

[16] Objectives of the UNESCO Convention on the Protection and Promotion of the Diversity of Cultural Expressions (n 6); Art 15 of the International Covenant on Economic, Social and Cultural Rights, 16 December 1966, 993 UNTS 3; UN Committee on Economic, Social and Cultural Rights, *General Comment 21: Right of Everyone to Take Part in Cultural Life* 42 UN Doc E/C. 12/GC21 (21 December 2009); and the cultural heritage agendas of UNESCO and UNIDROIT.

[17] R Pannikar, *Cultural Disarmament: The Way to Peace* (John Knox Press 1995) 34.

[18] A Appiah, 'Cosmopolitanism: Ethics in a World of Strangers' in LV Prott (ed.) *Witnesses to History: A Compendium of Documents and Writings on the Return of Cultural Objects* (Unesco Publications 2009) 95, 109; Pannikar (n 17) 34.

categorisation system provides a very general description of what is to be protected (e.g. Germany). A classification system extends protection to a specific object only when a specific administrative decision is made to that effect (e.g. the UK). Various combinations of these systems are in operation across the world.[19] Italy combines categorisation with classification.[20] Turkey combines extensive listing in respect of some property but categorises other kinds of property.[21] Canada combines an inventory-based approach with administrative orders.[22]

Some states protect classes of artefacts that are unique to their national histories and that have considerable historic and artistic merit. They can be 'the centerpieces of active cultures and religions, illustrations of the changing patterns of aesthetics, anthropological records of previous societies, beautiful and desirable items which confer prestige on their owners, or commodities in the international art market'.[23] While the objects that states feel constrained to protect are frequently old, the tendency in the majority of national laws to define protected categories of objects by age means that the artistic or historical significance of modern art remains unaccounted for.

With the challenges and the differences in the technique of definition in mind, it is understandable that an objective definition of cultural objects is difficult to provide *in abstracto*.[24] In no more than a very general sense, therefore, the term 'cultural objects' can be understood to mean the physical remains of the past, man-made objects that are of

[19] For more, see LV Prott and PJ O'Keefe, *Law and the Cultural Heritage Vol. 3 Movement* (Professional Books 1984–1989) 26–30. National laws are available from the UNESCO Database of National Cultural Heritage Laws.

[20] Among others Protection of Items of Artistic or Historical Interest, Law No. 1089 of 1939; Consolidated Act for Cultural Heritage and the Environment, Law Decree No. 490 of 25 October 1999; Code of Cultural Property of 2004.

[21] Among others Conservation of Cultural and Natural Property Law No. 2863, Official Gazette 23/07/1983 no 18113; Regulation on the Classification, Registration and Admission to Museums of Movable Cultural and Natural Assets Requiring Preservation of 2009.

[22] Among others Cultural Property Export and Import Act of 1985, Consolidated Statutes of Canada, Chapter c 51 RSC 1985; Cultural Property Export Control Regulation; Order Establishing a Canadian Export Control List.

[23] LJ Borodkin, 'The Economics of Antiquities Looting and a Proposed Legal Alternative' (1995) *Columbia Law Review* 377.

[24] UNIDROIT Secretariat, Explanatory Report to the 1995 Unidroit Convention on Stolen or Illegally Exported Cultural Objects (2001) 3 Uniform Law Review 476, 496.

archaeological, historical, pre-historical, artistic, scientific, literary or technical interest.

2. CULTURAL HERITAGE LAW: NO STANDARD DEFINITION OF 'CULTURAL HERITAGE' POSSIBLE

Cultural heritage law is a conceptual framework in the form of a legal category that reflects trends and developments of international cultural law and its interactions with other fields of law.[25] It emerged as a new, separate category of law in 1990.[26] The cultural component of 'cultural heritage' is capable of carrying a composite meaning that embraces the tangible results of cultural activities, the processes of artistic and scientific creativity, and the ways of life of groups and communities.[27] As such, it conveys a meaning that is wider than 'cultural objects'. The term[28] is sufficiently wide to capture other markers of national or group identity, such as intangibles, language, traditional cultural expressions, folklore, genetic resources and intellectual property. In other words, the learning processes, traditions, knowledge and skills which were inherited from past generations, and which provide the identity that communities desire to transmit to future generations are included.[29]

This study considers the national and international law that makes cultural heritage law in the narrower respect of the tangible results of creative endeavour. These are corporeal and moveable objects that deserve to be maintained, cherished, preserved and bestowed.[30]

---

[25] V Vadi, *Cultural Heritage in International Investment Law and Arbitration* (CUP 2014) 23.

[26] LV Prott, 'Problems of Private International Law for the Protection of the Cultural Heritage' V *Recueil des Cours* (The Hague 1989) 214ff; A Chechi, *The Settlement of International Cultural Heritage Disputes: Towards a Lex Culturalis?* (unpublished PhD Thesis EUI 2011) 247ff supports a new taxonomy.

[27] Vadi (n 25) 19.

[28] For more on terminology, see Vadi (n 25) 24–29. The term 'cultural heritage' was officially adopted by the United Nations Educational, Scientific and Cultural Organization (UNESCO) in the 1972 Convention for Protection of the World Cultural and Natural Heritage <http://whc.unesco.org/en/convention text/> accessed on 30 June 2014. It includes 'cultural property', and its use is in line with current treaty practice.

[29] Francioni (n 12) 6; Vadi (n 25) 19.

[30] LV Prott and PJ O'Keefe, *Law and the Cultural Heritage Vol 1* (Professional Books 1984–1989) 7.

The challenges posed by cultural heritage law highlight the importance of the scope of the definition of cultural heritage (to the extent that legal norms can define the notion without reference to other disciplines).[31] It is important to establish control of the process of definition, for purposes of ensuring that a particular object is covered by the law concerned. Legal definitions necessarily reflect the cultural values of the drafter and the social constructions of categories of material culture. Minority cultures may be sidelined when the significance which the possessor ascribes to an object is different from the claimant's perspective.[32] It could mean the difference between protection and the failure to protect.

3. PROTECTION AND THE FAILURE TO PROTECT

3.1 Cultural Priorities in the US, the EU and the UK

National laws set their own cultural priorities and offer only one definition among many possibilities. They cannot supply a standard definition. What a single domestic legal system can accomplish when offering diverse definitions is to limit overlaps between different sets of rules for different types of cultural property. US law offers a fine example of a legal system that relies on various treaties, laws and policies to identify particular objects of material culture that are worthy of legal protection.[33] Cultural property stolen from a museum or a religious or secular public monument or similar institution, which is documented as appertaining to the inventory of that institution, represents a category for

---

[31] L Casini, '"Italian Hours": The Globalization of Cultural Property Law' (*Jean Monnet Working Paper 10*, September 2010) <http://centers.law.nyu.edu/jeanmonnet/papers/10/101101.pdf> accessed 24 February 2014.

[32] Last (n 8) 124, 126.

[33] US federal statutes define designated archaeological material (Cultural Property Implementation Act (CCPIA), Pub L 97-446, Title III, 96 Stat. 2350 (1983), 19 US Code 2601–2613); archaeological resources (Ancient Monuments and Archaeological Areas Act 1979); cultural items (Native American Graves Protection and Repatriation Act (NAGPRA), 25 US Code 3001–3013 (2000)); historical property and resources (National Historic Preservation Act (NHPA), 16 US Code 470aa–470mm (2000)); as well as commemorative works and objects of cultural heritage, 18 US Code Appx § 2B 1.5. P Gerstenblith, 'Recent Developments in the Legal Protection of Cultural Heritage' in N Brodie, MM Kersel, C Luke and K Walker Tubb (eds), *Archaeology, Cultural Heritage and the Antiquities Trade* (University Press of Florida 2006) 68, 75.

purposes of the implementation of Article 7(b) of the UNESCO Convention on the Means of Prohibiting and Preventing the Illicit Import, Export and Transfer of Ownership of Cultural Property.[34] Endangered archaeological and ethnological materials designated by the President subject to determinations by the Cultural Property Advisory Committee[35] form an independent category for purposes of implementing Article 9 of the UNESCO Convention. Bilateral treaties set out importation restrictions, provisions with regard to seizure if they have been violated, and provisions for the return of specific archaeological and ethnographic materials to their territory (whether state or sub-state).[36]

The EU concept 'cultural treasures'[37] signifies protective regimes that derogate from free movement in the internal market.[38] The internal market consists of a space without internal frontiers in which persons, goods, services and capital move freely as the Treaty on European Union envisages, but the EU allows exceptions for restrictions imposed for the protection of national treasures possessing artistic, historic or archaeological importance.

---

[34] 14 November 1970, 823 UNTS 231; 10 ILM 289.

[35] M Papa-Sokal, 'The US Legal Response to the Protection of the World Cultural Heritage' in N Brodie, MM Kersel, C Luke and K Walker Tubb (eds), *Archaeology, Cultural Heritage and the Antiquities Trade* (University Press of Florida 2006) 36, 44–45.

[36] A list of states is available at <http://www.unesco.org/eri/la/convention.asp?KO=13039&language=E> accessed 25 February 2014.

[37] The definition ought to be uniform but the nomenclature differs in the context of export controls (e.g. 'Kulturgut' in German; 'patrimonio nazionale' in Italian). The definition is considerably wider in Greece, Italy, Cyprus and Spain, than in other EU Member States. The ECJ did not define the concept when it considered the compatibility of a governmental measure of protection of cultural property with free trade requirements in Case 7/68 *EC Commission v Italy* [1969] CMLR 1 (ECJ) and Case 48/71 *EC Commission v Italy* [1972] ECR 527.

[38] Member States define their own national treasures. The definition in Directive 93/7/EEC has been adapted by Directive 2014/60/EU for the future. See Council Directive 93/7/EEC of 15 March 1993 on the Return of Cultural Objects Unlawfully Removed from the Territory of Member States Council Directive (EEC) 93/7 of 15 March 1993 on the return of cultural objects unlawfully removed from the territory of a member state OJ L 74/74, 27.3.93 (with amendments in 1997 and 2001); Directive 2014/60/EU of the European Parliament and of the Council of 15 May 2014 on the Return of Cultural Objects Unlawfully Removed from the Territory of a Member State and amending Regulation (EU) No 1024/2012 (Recast) OJ EU L159/1, 28.5.2014.

The commercial value of cultural objects may appreciate with time.[39] The UK confined its use of the term 'cultural property' to the items referred to in instruments of EU law for purposes of the application of the 1970 UNESCO Convention.[40] Whereas age and minimum financial value of certain types of objects used to function as criteria in EU law, this approach has now been revised. The scope of application of the new Directive 2014/60/EU[41] extends to cultural objects that are classified or defined by the Member States as a cultural treasure. Directive 2014/60/EU now acknowledges that it should be possible for Member States to return cultural objects other than those classified or defined as national treasures provided that they respect the relevant provisions of the TFEU, as well as cultural objects unlawfully removed before 1 January 1993.[42]

Any special law would define the field of its application. In instances where claims for return are not based on special laws or international instruments, the question of classification may well remain unanswered.[43] In England and Scotland, the concepts of treasure and buried ownerless property are defined in common law and legislation, but no special definition exists for cultural objects otherwise.[44] The 2003 Cultural Objects (Offences) Act does not attempt to add national definition, and nor do the Waverley Criteria, which are the Export Regulations that prevent cultural objects of monetary value exceeding the limits of the Open General Export Licence from leaving the country if a matching

---

39 B Demarsin, 'The Third Time Is Not Always a Charm: The Troublesome Legacy of a Dutch Art Dealer: The Limitation and Act of State Defences in Looted Art Cases' (2010) 28 Cardozo Art and Entertainment Law Journal 255, 257; A Hawkins, 'A Tale of Two Innocents: Creating an Equitable Balance between the Rights of Former Owners and Good Faith Purchasers of Stolen Art' (1995) 64 Fordham Law Review 49, 50.

40 Regulation 116/2009 of 18 December 2008, OJ L 39/1 (2009); Council Directive (EEC) 93/7 of 15 March 1993 (n 38).

41 Directive 2014/60/EU (n 38).

42 Recital 10.

43 B Schönenberger, *The Restitution of Cultural Assets* (Eleven International Publishing 2009) 42.

44 Return of Cultural Objects Regulations 1994, SI No 501 of 1994 as amended by SI No 1719 of 1997; SI 3972 of 2001. The implications of introducing limitation rules for cultural objects have been considered. Scottish Law Commission Discussion Paper on Prescription and Title to Moveable Property No 144 (Edinburgh 2010) Chapter 4; DL Carey Miller, DW Meyers and AL Cowe, 'Restitution of Art and Cultural Objects: A Re-Assessment of the Role of Limitation' [2001] Art Antiquity and Law 1, 11.

offer can be raised domestically.[45] The decision to grant a licence rests with the Reviewing Committee on the Export of Works of Art.[46] Export of works of art older than 50 years is governed by the Import, Export and Customs Powers (Defence) Act of 1939 and requires a licence. The absence of a register for corporeal moveables is unlike the position in Germany, where registered cultural objects qualify for protection against removal.[47]

Demarcation difficulties increase the risk of litigation for innocent dealers and traders in the legitimate art market.[48] A claim in respect of a cultural treasure based on an international instrument or an EC Directive would be guided by the categories enumerated therein. It is up to national courts to recognise these categories in international cases and to decide whether a sufficient interest has been established for purposes of a claim.

3.2 Different Situations Call for Protection

Protection by the state or an institution of the state could be called for in a number of different situations.[49] A state may seek to protect the rights of an owner of the object, e.g. to enable deprived owners to enforce their rights by recovering stolen objects. A state may seek to ensure physical continuance of the object, e.g. by preventing its destruction or deterioration, even while in the hands of a private owner, because of the heritage value of the object. In the capacity of custodian of the cultural heritage for the community it derives from, a state may seek to protect access to an object by requiring its display and preventing its exportation.

The underground market is a factor in the movement of art and cultural objects. The tentacles of the illicit trade reach into the cultural life of communities in developed and developing economies alike. Cultural

---

[45] Waverley Committee Report, RA Butler 6 September 1952, Report of a Committee appointed by the Chancellor of the Exchequer HMSO 1952.

[46] Export permission was refused in respect of 'The Three Graces' by Canova in 1994 (n 5), and export of 'Portrait of Everhard Jabach and family' by Charles Le Brun (1619–1690) was barred until 6 May 2014. <https://www.gov.uk/government/news/painting-deemed-national-treasure-may-leave-uk> accessed 11 March 2014.

[47] European Commission, *Study Report on Preventing and Fighting Illicit Trafficking in Cultural Goods in the European Union*, 10 October 2011, 190–94, 248–249 <http://ec.europa.eu/home-affairs/doc_centre/crime/docs/Report%20 Trafficking%20in%20cultural%20goods%20EN.pdf> 194 accessed 12 March 2014.

[48] Carey Miller et al. (n 44) 10–11.

[49] Prott (n 26) 235.

trafficking displaces art and cultural objects. Traffickers may try to evade claims by relocating the object, and their success in doing this may erode respect for the law. Protection may require return of cultural objects that have been retained unlawfully,[50] or of parts of cultural sites that had been removed during armed conflict.[51]

The unethical, immoral trade tends to be illegal in the source state,[52] but this is not necessarily the case in every market state.[53]

3.3 Failing to Protect

States may fail to protect cultural objects or to regulate trafficking because they benefit from the illegal or illicit trade. Ambiguity in a particular state policy can mean that cultural objects that were taken abroad without a permit are sought out and claimed, while objects with historical and archaeological significance to certain ethnic groups are left unguarded.[54] States have the capacity for white-collar crime and state control of their own citizens and museums.[55] States may also assume a deliberate stance based on a national policy to confiscate cultural property belonging to particular segments of society. Turning against their own citizens and museums, they may use their strength to enforce private property rights to expropriate art. Expropriation can be achieved,

---

[50] E.g. cultural objects excavated contrary to the law or excavated legally but unlawfully retained; see Clause 4 of the State Ownership of Undiscovered Cultural Objects. Text supplied in M Frigo, 'Model Provisions on State Ownership of Undiscovered Cultural Objects – Introduction' [2011] Uniform Law Review 1044.

[51] E.g. *Case Concerning the Temple of Preha Vihear (Cambodia and Thailand)*, judgment of 15 June 1962, Merits, ICJ Reports (1962) 6ff.

[52] Source states are rich in cultural materials for which there is a world market, but local demand for cultural materials keep the prices low. Examples include Mexico, India and Guatemala.

[53] Market states are economically strong and the demand for cultural objects is high. Examples include the US and the UK.

[54] AJG Tijhuis, *Transnational Crime and the Interface between Legal and Illegal Actors: The Case of the Illicit Art and Antiquities Trade* (Wolf Legal Publishers 2006) 161; A Efrat, 'Getting Governments to Co-operate against Looting: Insights from the American and British Experience' <http://portal.idc.ac.il/facultypublication.publication?PublicationID=2874&FacultyUserName=YXNpZg==> accessed 24 February 2014, comparing the position of the US and Britain in respect of the UNESCO Convention.

[55] E.g. *Kommerziele Koordinierung* (KoKo) combined state control, state intelligence and white collar crime in East Germany in the 1970s and 1980s, and benefited from art crime among other things. Tijhuis (n 54) 160, 172.

through military or other means, without any existing or even alleged legitimate purpose. It is also possible to delay and obstruct dispute settlement by grossly unfair and unethical methods. Sheer indifference in respect of physical preservation and evasion of return procedure can also do much harm. The indifference to the cultural heritage of those under their control meant that the occupying powers remained blatantly inactive when the antiquities scattered along the 'Old Silk Road' became coveted prizes in the international race for ancient Buddhist treasures. As Confucians who despised Buddhism, the prejudice of the Chinese officials allowed iconoclastic Moslems to proceed unchecked to damage frescoes, sites and treasures from Chinese Turkestan.[56] The tide has turned. Chinese authorities have been building global solidarity by means of international scientific involvement and participation in respect of, for instance, part of the Buddhist treasures that lie preserved in the time capsule of painted sculptures, murals, wooden architecture and relics of the Silk Road at the Mogao caves at Dunhuang.[57]

It is widely conceded that cultural objects deserve special treatment, and yet in practice, general commercial law rules are readily given extended application. The commercial imperative is discussed next.

4. COMMERCIAL IMPERATIVE

4.1 Trading on the Art Market

Today's art market is a multibillion dollar industry.[58] It consists in a 'myriad, often over-lapping, subspecialties that may be limited by region

---

[56] P Hopkirk, *Foreign Devils on the Silk Road: The Search for the Lost Cities and Treasures of Chinese Central Asia* (OUP 1980) 24, 31. For a photographic record of the Nepalese tragedy involving the looting of Buddha statues during the 1980s, see J Schick, *The Gods Are Leaving the Country* (Orchid Press 1999).

[57] Its 735 caves are cut into a cliff located 25 km southeast of Dunhuang. Cave construction began in 366 CE and continued for another thousand years. The National Library of China based in Beijing, national libraries of the UK and France, the Russian Academy of Sciences and the Mellon Foundation in the US are all in collaboration with the Dunhuang Academy on the 'Digital Dunhuang' Project. For more, see <http://www.expo2010.cn/expo/english/eu/nc/ct/userobject1ai12652.html> accessed 23 July 2014.

[58] D Chappell and K Polk, 'Unravelling the "Cordata": Just How Organized Is the International Traffic in Cultural Objects?' in S Manacorda and D Chappell (eds), *Crime in the Art and Antiquities World* (Springer 2011) 99, 101.

(e.g. Asian or North-American), by date (mediaeval, contemporary), by medium (paper, bronze) or by form (paintings, furniture) ... and archaeological and ethnographic materials ... [which] their countries of origin consider cultural heritage ...'.[59] The sale of works of art in the arena of the art market is an important commercial activity in many states, although a relatively small number of dealers are involved and there are significantly fewer works compared to the number of fungible goods in international trade.[60] The art trade makes an economic and cultural contribution which governments cannot ignore.[61]

The trade in art is also an intercontinental, transnational trade. The art trade readily crosses national borders, and has done so ever since the recorded development of the art market.[62] The 1680s saw the repeal of a law that banned the importation of paintings into England. There was then a great influx of paintings from the Lowlands, where significantly large numbers of people invested in pictures and paintings.[63] Today, London is at the global centre of cultural trade in European, South Asian and Middle Eastern art.[64] Most years, New York has the largest sales turnover in the world. This market focuses on Canadian, North American and South American art. Beijing claimed first place in 2012,[65] but it generally functions as a secondary national centre for the Asian trade in the primary location of Hong Kong. Emerging markets such as Iran, India and China have national markets that serve national developmental aims.[66] A self-sustaining national market was established in China in the 1990s,[67] but today, China has one of the fastest-growing art and antiquities auction sectors in the world.[68] While domestic business will dominate the Chinese

---

59 CC Coggins, 'A Licit International Traffic in Ancient Art: Let There Be Light' (1995) 4 IJCP 61, 65–66.

60 Gerstenblith (n 12) 569; JH Merryman, 'Cultural Property, International Trade and Human Rights' (2001) 19 Cardozo Arts and Entertainment 51, 52.

61 Efrat (n 54).

62 Schönenberger (n 43) 27; P Watson, *From Manet to Manhattan* (Random House UK 1992) 46.

63 Watson (n 62) 49.

64 I Robertson, *A New Art from Emerging Markets* (Lund Humphries 2011) 78.

65 S Blanc, 'New Fronts Open in Chinese Art Market as Records Fall' *API* (11 October 2013).

66 Robertson (n 64) 14.

67 Robertson (n 64) 76.

68 JL Graham, 'Art Exchange: How the International Art Market Lacks a Clear Regulatory Framework' in V Vadi and HEGS Schneider (eds), *Art, Cultural Heritage and the Market: Legal and Ethical Issues* (Springer 2014) 323.

art market for the foreseeable future, China has also opened its doors more widely to Sotheby's and Christie's. Sotheby's boasts a joint venture with a state-run company, and Christie's won a licence in 2013 to become the first international auction house to operate independently in China.

4.2 A Globalised Capitalist Art Market

The commodities trade in liberal capitalist societies are characterised by the commercial imperative that, in principle, the *bona fide* purchaser of a moveable thing should get a good title regardless of provenance. It is a matter of the market context facilitating easy title in order to promote commerce in many parts of the world.[69] Ordinary business norms may be appropriate to the transfer and exchange of many forms of art, but the protection of museum pieces, pieces obtained on the black market, and some forms of indigenous cultural heritage require different rules and approaches.[70]

Capitalism demands a continued readjustment of the self and what the self produces in response to the market.[71] This feature is most prominent at art fairs, where art is a globally traded commodity and the art market is largely unfettered. Different considerations are supposed to come into play where cultural heritage is concerned, but mechanisms that keep unbridled self-interest in check are absent in capitalist markets. The commercial imperative is insensitive to the importance of transmission of culture to current and future generations; or to the need for controlling the free movement of objects whose preservation is under threat; or to the outflow of cultural materials. When alteration can improve the marketability of a piece, capitalism will not be constrained by the risk of damage. The increased competition for sales by auction houses in the emerging markets is not necessarily seen as a bad thing. Yet, what the duties of market participants are, ought to be an active concern.

---

69 C Roodt and D Carey Miller,'Vitium Reale in Private Law and Private International Law' (2013) 10 TDM Special Issue 1.

70 The Western paradigm tends to confine itself to cultural rights that are 'indispensable for his dignity and the free development of his personality' by virtue of Art 22 of the United Nations Universal Declaration of Human Rights. Indigenous cultural property claims do not necessarily share this worldview. K Kuprecht and K Siehr, 'International Trade in Moveable Tangible Cultural Heritage of Indigenous Peoples: A European Perspective' in CB Graber, K Kuprecht and JC Lai (eds), *International Trade in Indigenous Cultural Heritage* (Edward Elgar 2012) 246, 269–70.

71 E Fromm, *To Have or To Be?* (Continuum 2002) 147–54; L Wilde, *Global Solidarity* (Edinburgh University Press 2013) 116.

The art market can be at odds with culture. The value of certain cultural items far exceeds any possible market valuation. Other items may have no market value but may be highly deserving of national and international regulation and protection.[72] Both the most significant and the least significant of these items may constitute evidence of vanishing ways of life. In addition, notwithstanding the recognition given to cultural diversity at the international level, the major supporters of free trade and trade liberalisation construe exceptions in respect of trade in culture restrictively. Restrictions on free trade in state cultural policy are not necessarily any easier to reconcile with the commercial imperative. The World Trade Organization is not particularly responsive to indigenous interests,[73] and the EU is vulnerable to the illicit trade in cultural objects.[74] Even if a human rights imperative in respect of tangible heritage could enable restitution in principle, restitution is incidental at best to any finding such a body might make[75] because restitution claims are not within the reach of free trade institutions.

4.3 Constraining the Commercial Imperative

At this point in its evolution, the art market is highly organised but largely unregulated. High prices attract and encourage roguish and criminal behaviour. The likelihood of buying cultural objects and works of art that have been stolen, looted or misappropriated in another jurisdiction, is high.

Public and private law contain provisions that contain and limit the commercial imperative and affect title issues. Public law may subject a particular object to inalienability, restricted transfer, indefeasible title, imprescriptibility or public domain rules,[76] as is the case in several

---

[72] Vadi (n 25) 20.

[73] CB Graber, K Kuprecht and JC Lai (eds), 'The Trade and Development of Indigenous Cultural Heritage: Completing the Picture and a Possible Way Forward' in *International Trade in Indigenous Cultural Heritage* (Edward Elgar 2012) 463, 493.

[74] Study Report (n 47) 100–104; A Koush, 'Fight Against the Illegal Antiquities' Traffic in the EU: Bridging the Legislative Gaps' (Bruges Political Research Papers Series 2011).

[75] IF Gazzini, *Cultural Property Disputes: The Role of Arbitration in Resolving Non-Contractual Disputes* (Transnational Publishers Inc. 2004) 50.

[76] E.g. Arts 822–828 of the Italian Civil Code of 1942; Consolidated Act for Cultural Heritage and the Environment, Law decree no 490 of 25 October 1999 (Italy); Art 174 of the Italian Code of Cultural Property of 2004 (criminal forfeiture). In general A Jakubowski, 'Return of Illicitly Trafficked Cultural

European states. The status of inalienability is irreversible in a number of jurisdictions.[77] For instance, the absence of a statutory mechanism for restitution in museum laws may mean that the museum in question is barred from initiating restitution, or that authorisation to transfer ownership or dispose of public collections will be withheld.[78]

Domestic public law frameworks that pay due attention to illegal export and import could catch looted objects that may otherwise be evidentially out of reach for a court.[79]

Private international law is called upon to assert its role in the international market for art and antiquities where most purchasers conglomerate and where prices are set.[80] As a potential legal constraint in respect of the commercial imperative, it operates alongside the constraints imposed by law in other areas. It rubs shoulders with public international law, which extends protection to antiquities and cultural objects by virtue of broad international accord. It is subject to inevitable adjustments to the relative stability of private law in recognition of extreme circumstances that prevailed during the Holocaust, or the Soviet Russian 'trophy' looting post-World War II. Additionally, museum policy may disregard the title position to effect repatriation or restitution.

Much work remains to be done to systematize national law, international civil procedure and international law. Systematisation in respect of the role and effects of private international law is a relatively unchartered area, but a better understanding of this global lens can improve the level of regulation in a demanding legal context. Private

---

Objects Pursuant to Private International Law: Current Developments' in The Illicit Traffic of Cultural Objects in the Mediterranean (EUI Working Papers 2009) 137, 139.

[77] M Cornu and M Renold, 'New Developments in the Restitution of Cultural Property: Alternative Means of Dispute Resolution' (2010) 17 IJCP 1, 9–10.

[78] The British Museum Act of 1963 barred the British Museum from restituting Old Master drawings in its possession (*Her Majesty's Attorney-General v Trustees of the British Museum* [2005] EWHC 1089 (Ch)). Legislative action had to be taken.

[79] S MacKenzie, 'The Market as Criminal and Criminals in the Market: Reducing Opportunities for Organised Crime in the International Antiquities Market' in S Manacorda and D Chappell (eds), *Crime in the Art and Antiquities World* (2011 Springer) 69, 73.

[80] P Watson, 'Convicted Dealers: What We Can Learn' in N Brodie, MM Kersel, C Luke and K Walker Tubb (eds), *Archaeology,Cultural Heritage and the Antiquities Trade* (University Press of Florida 2006) 93, 94; Tijhuis (n 54) 176.

international law does not determine its relation with other legal phenomena internally all by itself. Both the general theory of law and the theory of international law are well placed to contribute.

The responsibilities of participants in the art market are easily assumed to be similar to the responsibilities of participants in the commodities market.[81] To counter this default position, it is necessary to consider not only the law. First of all, the effect of non-legal factors such as ideology on compliance with rules and duties can be significant. Secondly, acquisition standards and the duties of market participants do not derive only from law. A normative ideal constrains the commercial imperative and shapes the responsibilities of market participants even when legislation is absent. The normative ideal is hard to identify, given that various different ideologies are likely to compete in a global setting. Moreover, moral standards cannot be legislated into existence. The relationship between private international law and the broader ethical framework will ultimately require closer definition. Its implications for private international law is addressed under 7.6 below.

5. THE CONTEXT IN WHICH PRIVATE INTERNATIONAL LAW MEETS CULTURAL HERITAGE LAW

5.1 Lodging Civil Claims

The true owner (whether individual, museum or business) or the source state may institute a civil law suit[82] to obtain restitution or return of an object that has been traded after it has been stolen, looted, excavated or smuggled into another jurisdiction.

Claims brought by foreign source states for archaeological objects they believe were removed in violation of patrimony or export laws will frequently be brought in a market state or in an intermediary (transit) jurisdiction, where the nature of the claim will be determined by private international law. There has also been a sharp increase since the Cold War has ended in the number of legal claims brought by heirs of Holocaust victims whose art works were looted or misappropriated by

---

[81] J Ulph and I Smith, *The Illicit Trade in Art and Antiquities* (Hart 2012) 13–15, 271.

[82] S MacKenzie, 'Illicit Deals in Cultural Objects as Crimes of the Powerful' (2011) 56 Crime Law Social Change 133, 146.

Nazis. Either the claimant or the defendant may base their argument on private international law.

A defendant with prior knowledge of an impending claim can, prior to the court becoming seised, relocate a cultural object with a view to avoiding the establishment of jurisdiction based on the location of the object when the court is seised.[83] As such, protection encompasses interim measures that are designed to prevent action to evade a return procedure after the unlawful removal of a cultural object from the territory of a particular state.[84]

5.2 Art Crime and Theft

Art crime refers to diverse acts which constitute crimes punishable by law provided they are reported and the offenders are apprehended. These acts may include art thefts and confiscations, damage and deceit, but art crime is closely linked also to the movement and outflow of cultural materials. Thus, these activities encompass clandestine excavation and illegal export[85] (discussed under 6.2 below).

Art theft is frequently motivated by greed. It may provide bartering means and improve social standing.

A comparatively small number of thefts registered with the Art Loss Register (ALR) and Interpol are from museums.[86] The disappearance of seven iconic pieces from the Kunsthal Museum in Rotterdam on 16 October 2012 counts among the biggest art thefts in Dutch history. The perpetrators have been convicted and sentenced, and must pay 18 million euros to the paintings' insurers, but the actual pieces have not been found.[87] This past decade has seen the disappearance and dramatic recovery of, e.g., 'Boy in a Red Vest' by Cezanne, 'Poppy Field at Vetheuil' by Claude Monet and 'Blossoming Chestnut Branches' by Vincent van

---

[83] L Gillies, 'The Conflict of Laws as a Technique of Demand Side Regulation in Claims for the Recovery of Cultural Objects' [2015] JPIL (forthcoming).

[84] E.g. Art 4(5) of Council Directive (EEC) 93/7 of 15 March 1993 (n 40).

[85] M Durney and B Proulx, 'Art Crime: A Brief Introduction' (2011) 56 Crime Law and Social Change 115.

[86] Durney and Proulx (n 85) 121. This may have to do with assumptions made about museum security systems.

[87] A Holligan, 'Dutch Art Theft Suspects Offer Paintings for Deal' *BBC News Europe* (13 August 2013). Among them are 'Tete d'Arlequin' by Picasso, and 'Femme devant une fenetre ouverte, dite la fiancee' by Gauguin.

Gogh. These paintings were stolen in 2008 from the private collection of EG Buhrle in Zürich and recovered before attempted sale by the thief.[88]

Like wealthy dwellings, museums are vulnerable to the activities of insiders such as curators.[89] Designer theft[90] and art-napping[91] have also occurred. Virtuoso and commissioned thefts deliver art to corrupt dealers, fences or middlemen, to be sold on.[92]

Works of art and cultural objects can be easy to conceal and move. Even parent works that are readily identifiable and therefore unmarketable may be disguised through partitioning, which could improve the marketability of the fragments at the same time. Smaller treasures are easily transportable and concealable, setting the scene for a deceptive transnational sale.[93] Once stolen, a work of art or cultural object may remain undiscovered for years, and may be hidden away deliberately, in storage sites, until it is deemed to be ripe for sale.

Most crimes never meet with criminal punishment. Deprived owners may prefer civil action. Private investigators may negotiate deals on the basis of rewards offered for recovery. The line between paying a ransom to criminals and paying a reward for information that leads to recovery is easily blurred.[94]

---

[88] A Oliver and D Baker, 'Pictured: The Dramatic Moment Police Stopped Suspected Art Thief at Gunpoint and Recovered a Stolen £68.3 million Cezanne' *Mail Online* (12 April 2012); A Vincent, '10 Most Wanted Missing Paintings' *The Telegraph* (London 25 July 2013).

[89] For more on 'insider' thefts and the facilitating interface, see Tijhuis (n 54) 150–52, 157, 177–78.

[90] Designer theft is the commissioned theft of selected works of art for later delivery through smuggling networks. N Palmer, 'Recovering Stolen Art' (1994) 47 Current Legal Problems 215, 216. Tijhuis (n 54) 204 highlights the absence of empirical evidence confirming that art is stolen on the order of rich collectors.

[91] Art-napping is the capture of works of art for future ransom from either the owner or the insurer for the safe return of the objects (Tijhuis (n 54) 151). The National Museum in Stockholm refused to pay a ransom for three paintings by Rembrandt and Renoir in 2001 (T Grandell, 'Ransom Demand for Stolen Pictures' *The Guardian* (2 January 2001)) but the Tate allegedly paid to have two stolen Turners returned (G Rayner, 'Lord Myners Faced Questions over £3m Ransom for Stolen Turners' *The Telegraph* (28 February 2009)).

[92] Tijhuis (n 54) 154.

[93] G Carducci, 'The Growing Complexity of International Art Law: Conflict of Laws, Uniform Law, Mandatory Rules, UNSC Resolutions and EU Regulations' in BT Hoffman (ed) *Art and Cultural Heritage: Law, Policy and Practice* (CUP 2006) 68.

[94] Durney and Proulx (n 85) 121; A Mostrous, 'The Murky World of the Art Detective' *The Times* (9 August 2014).

Private international law assumes importance in the context of the extra-territorial effect of sales of art. Sellers and purchasers are entitled to the certainty that their transactions are not only legal but will be respected locally and overseas, where sales laws may be different. Private international law also requires analysis when decision-makers must confront the differing treatment of post-theft transactions in various different jurisdictions for the purpose of settling restitution claims.

5.3 Trafficking in Illicitly Obtained Antiquities

News updates about illicit excavation and export of antiquities and archaeological materials are numerous[95] and cultural trafficking has spiralled out of control.[96] For example, tomb-raiding, relic smuggling and trading are rampant in China[97] where bureaucratic corruption is rife.[98] Unprofessional clandestine excavations are disrespectful of reporting standards. Antiques traffickers deface artefacts when this renders them less recognisable or easier to smuggle.[99] Pottery and sculpture may be reduced to fragments or disguised as cheap souvenirs or modern material. Murals are cut into blocks. The ease with which cultural materials transit across certain strategic borders in intermediary or transit states[100] is an additional worrying factor.

Traffickers devise many different ways by which to erase, cover and convert the illicit origins of objects, and present them as ready to be sold legally at destination. They have been known to conceal sites, obtain

---

[95] The American Society of International Law provides regular updates, e.g. M Durney et al., 'Art and Antiquities Trafficking News Notes for May 2010–October 2010' (2010) 1 Cultural Heritage and Arts Review 57. The ICJP and International Lawyer also supply chronicles and reports.

[96] Among many others see Ministerial Advisory Panel on Illicit Trade, Department for Culture, Media and Sport, 7th Report, December 2000; C Alder and K Polk, 'The Illicit Traffic in Plundered Antiquities' in P Reichel (ed), *Handbook of Transnational Crime and Justice* (Sage Publications 2005); SRM MacKenzie, *Going, Going, Gone: Regulating the Market in Illicit Antiquities* (Institute of Art and Law 2005); Tijhuis (n 54).

[97] D Barboza, G Bowley and A Cox, 'A Culture of Bidding: Forging an Art Market in China' *The New York Times* (28 October 2013).

[98] S Shiu-Hing Lo, *The Politics of Cross-Border Crime in Greater China: Case Studies of Mainland China, Macao and Hong Kong* (ME Sharpe 2009) 23.

[99] I.e. export or import without the required authorisation.

[100] E.g. Hong Kong, Singapore, Thailand and Finland.

false permits to order excavation and export,[101] and forge provenance[102] in locations where this could increase commercial value[103] or where opportunities exist for documented provenance to be generated.[104] Falsified documentation enables eventual sales to be made to purchasers in good faith.[105] Traffickers and dealers may also buy back objects at auction on the 'open market' to ensure objects have a specious provenance, and title can be laundered in this way.[106]

Clandestine removal and illegal export of previously undiscovered archaeological objects and other artefacts virtually guarantee that the objects will be damaged or even destroyed. When antiquities are looted directly from ancient habitation areas and burial sites, the loss of meaning and integrity (provenience)[107] is irreparable[108] because information about the excavation site and original context is lost. The removal of antiquities from the place they are found at in the source state poses issues for completion of historical record and for the preservation and restoration of cultural identity. With information on the find spot of the item in their excavation missing, the cultural affiliation of the object remains undecided, and the inherent value lodged in the historic, cultural and scientific information is irreparably injured.[109] Reconstruction of the past then relies on piecing together the identities and location of local contacts, middlemen, procurers, transporters, dealers and criminals.[110] Moreover, if the origin of an object is not immediately apparent, a dealer

---

101 *Kingdom of Spain v Christie's* 1986 WLR 1120 (further circulation of Goya's 'La Marquesa de Santa Cruz' prevented by the granting of the declaration sought by Spain that the export permit had been forged).

102 E.g. the Sevso Treasure, which purportedly came from the Lebanon, but which was moved under fake export licences. P Watson and S Todeschini, *The Medici Conspiracy* (Public Affairs 2006) 82.

103 Chappell and Polk (n 58) 105.

104 Switzerland's lax laws of import and export have long made it into a global warehouse and convenient trading post along the way. Several legal loopholes have now been closed, not least by the promulgation of the Federal Act on the International Transfer of Cultural Property of 2005.

105 Ulph and Smith (n 81) 258.

106 Term is explained below.

107 Chappell and Polk (n 58) 101; P Gerstenblith, 'The Public Interest in the Restitution of Cultural Objects' (2001) 16 Conn J Int L 197, 207, 245.

108 Gerstenblith (n 107) 203; Watson and Todeschini (n 102) 172–73.

109 Gerstenblith (n 107) 199.

110 Coggins (n 59) 70.

or intermediary may pose as owner when transferring for value. Depriving the source state in this manner detracts from everyone's understanding of local and regional history.[111] International quarrels about provenience become likely.

It is to be regretted that the aesthetic value of the vast majority of unprovenanced objects, such as the decorated pottery from Apulia,[112] is used to compensate for lack of context. Information about scientific and historical context was considerably muted in the case of the Crosby Garret Helmet, which was found in Cumbria, England. Sensationalism can foster indifference to archaeological interests on the part of market players.[113] The relationship between the aesthetic and economic spheres can also put pressure on business practice.

Most source states have not documented and excavated all their important sites, and need to do more to prevent further unsupervised and illegal excavations of sites on public or private land to supply objects to the art market. Such activities may be a last survival strategy for impoverished local people. Vulnerable sites are made all the more vulnerable by conflict, war, revolution or political distress.[114] Paradoxically, however, looting and destruction may continue long after hostilities have dissipated,[115] as the ongoing losses of cultural heritage in Cambodia and Afghanistan illustrate.

5.4 Co-mingling of Licit and Illicit Trade

The illicit trade is embedded within the licit art and antiquities trade. The trade tends to be open and licit in the major commercial centres, but the legitimate market intersects with the illegal market. Reliable data is hard

---

[111] DC Lane, DG Bromley, RD Hicks and JS Mohoney, 'Time Crime: The Transnational Organization of Art and Antiquities Theft' (2008) 24 Journal of Contemporary Criminal Justice 243, 255; Cornu and Renold (n 77) 18.

[112] More than 88 percent of Apulian pottery has no provenance. R Elia, 'Analysis of the Looting, Selling, and Collecting of Apulian Red-figure Vases: A Quantitative Approach' in N Brodie, J Doole, and C Renfrew (eds), *Trade in Illicit Antiquities: the Destruction of the World's Archaeological Heritage* (Cambridge 2001) 145.

[113] Chappell and Polk (n 58) 101; Gerstenblith (n 107) 207, 245; <http://www.bbc.co.uk/news/uk-england-cumbria-11287093> accessed 7 March 2014.

[114] J Dietzler, 'On "Organized Crime" in the Illicit Antiquities Trade: Moving Beyond the Definitional Debate' (2013) 16 Trends in Organized Crime 329, 340; Tijhuis (n 54) 135–37.

[115] Tijhuis (n 54) 136.

to come by, but the link is undeniable[116] and the flows in the licit and illicit markets intermix.[117] It is fair to say that the art and antiquities market is grey.[118] Lines blur as a result of the movement, given that the identity which a cultural object fosters may change, and so may its status, category, function, physicality and meaning.[119] The status and function of art and cultural objects may change not only with time, but also simply on account of being smuggled.[120] The same activity may have a different status, depending on the jurisdiction and the characteristics of the objects.[121] The status of an object may prove hard to verify in cross-border transfers that rely on a multidimensional network of trade, travel, banking, multinational entities and international regulatory bodies.

In combination with an acquisition-at-any-price culture, the co-mingling of legitimate sales with illicit transnational trade practices provide cover for those who wish to evade criminal responsibility. That scope exists for organised criminals[122] to take advantage of the grey market was evident from the unsystematic excavations perpetrated in Italy to support the masterminds, dealers and middlemen of the Medici conspiracy. Not only are powerful dealers in a position to evade the legal obstacles of evidence and proof associated with criminal prosecution, but middlemen may confound law enforcement efforts by converting the status of the object or by navigating the applicable law in civil claims.[123]

---

[116] OW Muscarella, *The Lie Became Great: The Forgery of Ancient Near Eastern Cultures* (Styx 2000) 1–29; Watson (n 80) 95; T Davis, 'Supply and Demand: Exposing the Illicit Trade of Cambodian Antiquities through a Study of Sotheby's Auction House' (2011) 56 Crime Law and Social Change 155ff; Tijhuis (n 54) 157.

[117] MacKenzie (n 79) 72.

[118] B Bowman, 'Transnational Crimes against Culture: Looting at Archaeological Sites and the "Grey" Market in Antiquities' (2008) 24 Journal of Contemporary Criminal Justice 225.

[119] N Pearce, 'From Relic to Relic' [2013] Journal of the History of Collections 1, 3, 13 on the skull of Confucius; Schönenberger (n 43) 17 and Cornu and Renold (n 77) 17 on the Zuni Pueblo tribe and natural disintegration of certain objects.

[120] C Roodt, 'Restitution of Art and Cultural Objects and Its Limits' (2013) 46 CILSA 286, 291.

[121] Tijhuis (n 54) 129, 156.

[122] MacKenzie (n 79) 69. In respect of forms of organised crime, see UN General Assembly Resolutions 66/180 and 68/186 on Strengthening Crime Prevention and Criminal Justice Responses to Protect Cultural Property, especially with regard to its Trafficking, A/Res/66/180 of 30 March 2012 and A/Res/68/186 of 11 February 2014.

[123] MacKenzie (n 82) 136.

5.5 Demand, Supply and Regulation in the Illicit Trade in Cultural Objects

Market participants keep the cycle of demand and supply going.[124] Looters are driven by desperation and poverty to find objects and evade controls; smugglers by prospects for gain;[125] middlemen by the exceptional incentives offered by the art trade;[126] and collectors, who are part of the social elite, by their insatiable appetite for rare pieces of human history and the ancient contents of sites that can manifest their own wealth and enhance their status.[127] Soaring prices incentivise smuggling and trade; after all, resale on the black market is always an option.[128] Investors and cultural institutions with vast purchasing power contribute to driving up the demand for cultural material. Unscrupulous dealers tempt looters to offer antiquities to the market, while they entice collectors to invest. They have few qualms about passing on missing links in provenance to private and public collections that represent portals of entry to the legitimate world of trade in art. The purchaser's belief that an object is 'unique' enables a distinct market to form.

Finite, scarce and fragile objects are prizes in the quest for an instant personal history. The sense of belonging they provide contributes to the commoditisation of these objects.

Any remedies for non-compliance with acceptable standards of behaviour must be appropriate, while the effect of non-compliance-inducing factors should not be underestimated.

It would be erroneous to assume that an economic demand and supply approach necessarily condones the illicit trade. Demand and supply theory does not sit comfortably with measures that impede the free movement of legitimate antiquities, but it also values whatever adds to the value of an object – which includes a certified provenance for pieces. Unfortunately, while having to pay a high monetary value for the piece in question may ensure an interest in their physical protection, high yields

---

124 S Hutt, 'Cultural Property Law Theory' in JR Richman and MP Forsyth (eds), *Legal Perspectives on Cultural Resources* (AltaMira Press 2004) 17; JD Murphy, 'The People's Republic of China and the Illicit Trade in Cultural Property: Is the Embargo Approach the Answer?' [1994] IJCP 227, 234.

125 Murphy (n 124) 227, 229.

126 N Brodie, 'Pity the Poor Middlemen' (1998) 3 Culture without Context 7.

127 Chappell and Polk (n 58) 104, 111.

128 A Preston, 'Art Theft: Who's in the Frame? Why Steal a Priceless Masterpiece When It's Almost Impossible to Sell?' *Daily Mail Online* (9 February 2013).

may also expose the archaeological record to harm. Additionally, source states tend to be permanently deprived of the long-term economic benefits of the cultural objects.[129] An economic demand and supply approach is suitable when provenance is complete, databases for stolen cultural objects have been checked and authenticity has been confirmed. It is unsuitable, however, where sales continue amid cultural tensions or conflict, and when internet technology obstructs regulation.

Criminologists have studied the dynamics of the art trade with a view to devising models for improving regulation and the efficiency of law enforcement. Among other approaches, it has been suggested that 'sector vulnerability' is useful. 'Sector vulnerability' requires the rate of the illicit trade in cultural objects to be seen as connected to demand, supply, regulation and competition.[130] Market reduction approaches operate on the basis that restriction of demand at the end-point of the market will reduce the supply.[131] Market entry can be controlled by means of a strong regulatory component that keeps in check both the supply and demand sides of the trade. Routine activity theory draws attention to recurrent and prevalent adaptive activities of individuals and populations in specific social formations at a micro-level.[132] Recurrent patterns of activity in any particular market can affect or corrode other sectors of the economy.[133] Although opinion differs on whether routine activity theory is directly suitable to structural analysis of a transnational market,[134] the components which the theory identifies help to explain why criminal activity occurs. Whatever the motivation may be, art crime occurs when three factors converge: a suitable target; a motivated offender; and absence of effective guardianship or surveillance.[135]

Preliminary studies show that the route by which looted and misappropriated art and antiquities is taken depends upon their original location,

---

[129] Bowman (n 118) 225; Durney and Proulx (n 85) 125.

[130] MacKenzie (n 79) 75.

[131] S MacKenzie, 'Identifying and Preventing Opportunities for Organized Crime in the International Antiquities Market' in S Manacorda (ed), *Organized Crime in Art and Antiquities* (2009 International Scientific and Professional Advisory Council of the UN Crime Prevention and Criminal Justice Programme) 41; Gerstenblith (n 107) 211.

[132] Lane et al. (n 111) 244–45.

[133] Lane et al. (n 111) 245.

[134] Lane et al. (n 111) 244–45; contrast Dietzler (n 114) 336.

[135] L Cohen and M Felson, 'Social Change and Crime Rate Trends: A Routine Activity Approach' 1979 (44) American Sociological Review 588; Durney and Proulx (n 85) 127.

market demand and low levels of checks and security in carefully chosen transit states.[136]

The legitimate economy could be strengthened if source states ensured that these objects continue to fulfill their social roles and safeguarded opportunities for scientific research. They would be wise to adopt export licensing systems, impose reporting duties and reward those who report finds in order to regulate the supply. Source states do not control the reduction of market demand in market states, and many lack sufficient capacity for law enforcement. Nonetheless, they can also take steps to increase the likelihood of foreign courts recognising and applying the concepts and property categories in their laws that are affected by crime. They can enact clear state ownership laws ('vesting laws'). National ownership laws that are not predicated on common law preclude owners from acquiring title to antiquities found in the ground by providing that objects found after the entry into force of the relevant statute are the property of the state concerned. Vesting laws affect the marketability of looted antiquities among respectable dealers; because claims to these objects remain open under the 1995 UNIDROIT Convention on Stolen or Illegally Exported Cultural Objects,[137] no time limit applies. The new Model Provisions on State Ownership of Undiscovered Cultural Objects promote the recognition of the validity of sovereign title claims under foreign vesting laws.

6. RELEVANCE AND ROLE OF PRIVATE INTERNATIONAL LAW IN CONTROLLING CROSS-BORDER MOVEMENT AND TRADE

The cross-border transfer of scarce cultural objects is likely if demand is high. The demand for antiquities vastly exceeds the shrinking legitimate supply. Suppliers (looters, dealers, middlemen) use or avoid the law in cross-border deals to advance their position in the market. Against this backdrop, the role which private international law can play to re-script the demand and supply cycles of the trade deserves investigation.

---

136 Lane et al. (n 111) 257.

137 See n 10.

6.1 Prerequisites for Achieving Justice[138]

Under 5.1 above, the context in which civil claims are lodged was outlined. To succeed, pathways to justice are needed. Jurisdiction grounds that allow a national court to be seised and ADR facilitate justice. In case of a claim for restitution, the adjudicator requires an opportunity to receive and consider, on its merits, a request for return or restitution of an object that was retained or removed unlawfully. Jurisdiction in respect of confiscation or expropriation actions by the state within its own territory comes within the purview of the act of state doctrine and foreign immunity laws. A narrow interpretation of the exceptions to foreign immunity and the act of state defence can preclude a hearing on the merits.[139]

Depending on how a court deploys mechanisms such as classification and the public policy exception, choice of law method can grant (or preclude) an opportunity to rule on the merits of the case, and to enable (or disable) value-based decision-making. Once the object has been identified and the whereabouts of the possessor have been established, choice of law method can select among the potentially applicable legal systems one which recognises that crime voids the title transfer, or that the object bears an indelible taint until it is restored.[140]

If proceedings are pending in respect of a cultural object, it will be kept safe for the duration of the trial. The object will be detained and prevented from being removed unless anti-seizure legislation demands application. A court other than the one that has jurisdiction over the merits of the claim may be approached for provisional and protective measures that may apply extra-territorially.[141]

Restitution may be vital for the reconstitution of identity, among many other things.[142] In the context of restitution claims, the 1995 UNIDROIT Convention indicates that a balance must be struck between numerous interests that condition the rules that could be applied and the risk of their impairment. The Convention demands the return of objects that

---

[138] For more on conflicts justice, material justice, systemic justice and global justice, and the need to ensure justice in respect of ordering, norms and rights, see A Mills, *The Confluence of Public and Private International Law* (CUP 2010) 17ff, 303.

[139] *Austria v Altmann* 541 US 677–700 (2004). For more, see 6.3. Also Chapter 2 sub 6.4; and Chapter 4.

[140] Chapter 5 returns to this aspect.

[141] For more on these aspects, see van Woudenberg (n 9); Gillies (n 83).

[142] Chechi (n 26) 33.

have been stolen, but requires that the requesting or source state demonstrates any of the following interests: the physical preservation of the object or of its context; the integrity of a complex object; the preservation of information of, e.g., a scientific or historical character; or the traditional or ritual use of the object by a tribal or indigenous community.

The success of a restitution claim may depend on the recognition and application of provisions of public law designed to safeguard access to the object in question. Public display may be required and export prohibited. When the foreign provision claims application, the adjudicator requires an opportunity to check if mutual recognition would encroach on any forum interest and whether it would be internationally acceptable.[143]

The hurdles posed by the commercial imperative and the risk that the special nature of the object in question might go unrecognised, have been referred to above. Title laundering is an additional hurdle that will need to be identified.

6.2 Title Laundering

It has been observed that criminal activities involving art and clandestine excavation of antiquities have little in common.[144] Art theft and clandestine excavation of antiquities differ in that clear title to art pre-exists the theft; with respect to previously undiscovered antiquities buried in the ground, the source state frequently assumes the status of legal owner only once state ownership legislation takes effect. By that point the crime may long be done and the context of the find damaged or destroyed.[145] However, closer inspection reveals this differentiation to be inaccurate. Obvious commonalities include the attraction that both types of crime exert on those who are motivated by economic gain, and the fuel that revolution, war, conflict and state repression can provide for these activities.[146] In addition, both are associated with a willingness to launder title. Where it can be proven that an object has been stolen, the object has to undergo the additional extra step of acquisition in good faith in a jurisdiction that protects good faith for laundering to be accomplished.[147] Laundering may be accomplished through time limitations in respect of

---

[143] Chapter 7 returns to this aspect.
[144] Dietzler (n 114) 332; Tijhuis (n 54) 132–33.
[145] Carducci (n 93) 77.
[146] Tijhuis (n 54) 161.
[147] Tijhuis (n 54) 187–88.

the period within which an allegation of true ownership and a claim for restitution of the object must be brought before a court.[148] Goods circulate more freely if the prior title of the owner is extinguished after a relatively short prescription period.[149] A purchaser in good faith obtains security of title through adverse possession,[150] prescriptive doctrines (including the 'laches' defence),[151] and estoppel,[152] since title is considered to have been transferred. Recovery is normally by means of claims in civil courts, where characterisation can give inadvertent support to laundering.

Those adept at title laundering distinguish between intermediary or transit states and end points in a transaction chain.[153] Title laundering is facilitated when the status of a work of art or cultural object as stolen cannot be verified when crossing a border. Communication difficulties and lack of information exchange between market states and source states are common and will cause an object to be treated, for practical purposes, as a smuggled object only, as opposed to an object that had been stolen before it was exported. Smugglers benefit if regulation is lacking, criminal repercussions are limited, ratification of pertinent conventions such as the 1970 UNESCO Convention is delayed, EU law is ineffective, and policing in the end point is inadequate.[154]

The blurring of the distinction between licit and illicit trade facilitates title laundering further. Global legal diversity means that the legal status of objects depends on the jurisdiction in which trade takes place. There may be differences in crime definitions, laws and reporting duties as well

---

[148] E.g. the reason why Robert Hecht was not successfully prosecuted for his part in the Medici Conspiracy in 2012, and why the heirs of George Grosz failed when they sued to have his works returned (*Grosz v The Museum of Modern Art*, 772 F Supp 2d 473 (SDNY 2010); 403 Fed Appx 575 (2nd Circuit 16 December 2010); 132 S Ct 102; 181 L Ed 2d 30 (2011)).

[149] G Reichelt, 'International Protection of Cultural Property' [1985] Uniform Law Review 42, 105ff, (reprinted as Study LXX Doc 1 Unidroit 1986); Prott and O'Keefe (n 19) 396ff.

[150] Carducci (n 93) 69.

[151] *Solomon R Guggenheim Foundation v Lubell* 77 NY 2d 311 (1991); *Wertheimer v Cirker's Hayes Storage Warehouse, Inc.*, 752 NYS 2d 295 (Sup Ct 2002).

[152] *Autocephalous Greek Orthodox Church of Cypus v Goldberg and Feldman Fine Arts, Inc.*, 717 F Supp 1374 (SD Ind 1989) 1388.

[153] E.g. the UK. See Koush (n 74) 16.

[154] Tijhuis (n 54) 191, 203.

as in respect of property law, statutory limitations and evidentiary law.[155] No wonder the statistics about the volume and the value of art theft and the art trade are unreliable.[156]

The rectification of wrongful activity by means of civil remedies demands that we identify situations in which the law is liable to be used as a laundering device. Identification of opportunities for laundering will help more fully to realise the potential of private international law to constrain the illicit trade in cultural objects. Even when those opportunities are identified, the adjudicator's commitment to basing his or her decision on value rationality, may be challenged. Attention returns to this aspect under 7.6 below.

6.3 Legal Systems in a Lock

Criminological theories about the difficulty of distinguishing between the licit and the illicit trade tend to focus on the absence and evasion of regulation more than on the part played by particular jurisdictions and the effect of the passing of time in those jurisdictions. This study puts the primary focus on civil law, highlighting how private international law acts alongside other legal disciplines (commercial law, property law, public international law, human rights law and criminal law) to realize its role in respect of constraining the commercial imperative when purchasers and borrowers fall short of the minimum standards of ethical acquisition and collection in cross-border trade. Theories that account for title laundering, such as the 'lock' theory and the progression theory, are particularly relevant to this study.

The 'lock' model entails a description of the laundering mechanism, whereas the progression model enables study of the connections between activities and components in the 'lock' model at different stages of the trade. Both models enable analysis of title-laundering and leave room to discover how foreign law would affect the outcome of a case.

Tijhuis has developed a theory in respect of complexities associated with making a proper distinction between licit and illicit activities.[157] This theory is significant because it accommodates private international

---

[155] Durney and Proulx (n 85) 125, 127. For example, not all countries that report to Interpol record thefts by the type of object stolen. Many countries report by the circumstances of the theft.

[156] N Brodie, 'Congenial Bedfellows? The Academy and the Antiquities Trade' (2011) 27 Journal of Contemporary Criminal Justice 408, 411; Tijhuis (n 54) 137–39.

[157] Tijhuis (n 54) 129, 143ff.

law rules and devices, and allows room in which it is possible to show how they sustain the 'lock' mechanism. He distinguishes between the 'interface typology' developed by Passas,[158] which can describe the mechanism of laundering the illicit art and antiquities trade, and the 'lock model', which he designed to explain the mechanism of entry into the licit market and its various parts.[159] Individuals, companies, organisations and jurisdictions are different parts that combine variously to form 'locks' that transform the legal status of a certain activity. Examples of locks that 'launder' or clean title in a stolen object include an individual dealer who brokers deals with foreign purchasers on behalf of the Nazi regime; an individual who mediates between the robbers in one jurisdiction and the good faith purchasers in another; and a jurisdiction that remains on the outside of Conventions and lacks a proper regulatory framework and law enforcement. Lack of regulation and specialist policing in certain jurisdictions help those jurisdictions to operate as locks;[160] while lax and tight regulation in different jurisdictions can combine to contribute to the formation of a lock.[161] While open-border contexts where the political and economic infrastructure is weak may attract sellers,[162] the complex interface of private law, private international law and treaty law as applied by states provides cover for traffickers and powerful dealers participating in global networks. Traffickers take advantage of the fact that title can be transferred in some jurisdictions in dubious circumstances. They may navigate the applicable law and launder title in ways that pre-empt civil claims. If provenance is not complete and apparent, a dealer or intermediary may pose as owner when transferring for value. If the origin of an artefact is disputed or it is unknown when excavation and export occurred, it cannot be established if laws that seem relevant will apply.

Locks are created when a jurisdiction provides a refuge for good faith purchasers, and private international law rules and devices sustain the mechanism. This is relevant in respect of a large number of unprovenanced pieces that are being traded post-excavation or after illicit

---

[158] N Passas, 'Cross-border Crime and the Interface between Legal and Illegal Actors' (2003) 16 Security Journal 19. Symbiotic interfaces include facilitating, outsourcing, co-opting, reciprocity and legal interactions.

[159] Tijhuis (n 54) 99ff, 191.

[160] Tijhuis (n 54) 187.

[161] Tijhuis (n 54) 162–65, 202–3 highlight case studies of sales of art and antiquities taken from France, by dealers, receivers and auction houses in the Netherlands and Belgium.

[162] Dietzler (n 114) 339.

exportation. If a trafficked object has been exported and absorbed into the international market, successful litigation implies proof of ownership and the enforceability of the claim. If a cultural object were stolen or misappropriated at any point, its ownership record is defective. The provenance argument relies on fact and inference based on intellectual, physical or forensic proof, or on scholarly deduction regarding the security of the chain of title. In legal discourse, provenance refers to record of title.[163] At the same time, it does not equate to legality. Provenance is synonymous with legality only if a secure chain of provenance leads back to the moment of manufacture. The effect of a defect in the provenance on the purchaser will depend on which system of law is applicable and which legal family that system belongs to.

The progression model permits analysis of the sequence and connections between different jurisdictions. Felson has cautioned against underestimating how crime co-operation interacts with legitimate activities. He maintains that the problematic behaviour, the way in which events and behaviours are linked, their sequence, and the settings where actors meet in a criminal and organised market, warrant more attention than the groups that may be involved.[164] The progression model builds on Felson's system. In addition to the separate factors that connect supply and demand settings and events, the progression model distinguishes between the mechanisms associated with transit, facilitation and trade, which may or may not come into play: (a) the theft by the looters at the site concerned; (b) the transit by smugglers at airports, ports or border checkpoints; (c) the possible facilitation of the transit at border checkpoints, ports, universities, museums, or embassies by means of forged documentation, laundering, corrupt officials, curators, academics and valuers who are complicit in the trade; and (d) the sale conducted by

---

[163] 'Provenance' discloses much more than ownership in curatorial discourse. Collection history, publication and exhibits are included. Among many other things, it also provides an account of changing artistic tastes and collecting priorities, a record of social and political alliances, and an indication of economic and market conditions influencing the sale or transfer of the work in question. <http://www.ifar.org/provenance_guide.php> accessed 24 February 2014. 'Provenience' would feature prominently in empricial archaeological discourse, whereas constructivist approaches are concerned with more than the origin or find spot of a cultural object.

[164] M Felson, 'The Ecosystem for Organized Crime' (*HEUNI Paper No 26*, 20 October 2006) <http://www.heuni.fi/material/attachments/heuni/papers/6Ktmwqur9/HEUNI_papers_26.pdf> accessed 24 February 2014.

dealers, purchasers, collectors at places such as homes, hotels and museums.[165]

This approach suggests that researchers and policy-makers ought to focus on the progression of the trade from source state to market state at different stages. It enables them to analyse the role, sequence and setting of parts of the trade that work on their own or together.[166] The basic sequence of the progression can be 'analysed microscopically as individual ecosystems'. The links between the 'ecosystems' can be mapped.[167] The progression model can help direct available law enforcement capacity to the stage of the trade in which a particular jurisdiction participates.[168] It also allows room for considering the role played by private international law in the progression of the trade.

6.4 Sovereign Acts of Expropriation or Confiscation Can Promote 'Lock' Formation

It is unlikely that the validity of state confiscations pursuant to national laws (which may qualify as sovereign acts of state) can be successfully challenged within the territory of the expropriating state. When the objects that were confiscated by the state turn up in another jurisdiction – they could be resold abroad for foreign currency, or they could be sold to a private owner who is abroad – testing the validity of these acts of state is possible. If the court recognises state ownership in these circumstances, the restitution action fails.[169]

Examples include the nationalisation of art collections during the Russian Revolution of 1917 and the more recent nationalisation laws passed by the Russian Duma in 1995 and 1997. A Federal Law on a Moratorium on the Return of Cultural Valuables Displaced in World War II of 1995[170] applies to acts which occurred before the First Protocol to the Hague Convention for the Protection of Cultural Property entered into force. It confirms Russia's position on war reparations. The Federal Law

---

165 Dietzler (n 114) 338.

166 Dietzler (n 114) 329ff.

167 Dietzler (n 114) 340.

168 Dietzler (n 114) 338.

169 Schönenberger (n 43) 141. E.g. *Yale University v Pierre Konowaloff*, No. 3:09-cv-00466, stayed (D Conn 1 November 2011); granting summary judgment (D Conn 20 March 2014).

170 Decree of the State Duma of the Federal Assembly of the Russian Federation, 21 April 1995, Russian Federation Collection of Legislation, 1995, No 19, Item 1721.

on Displaced Cultural Valuables of 1998[171] was then passed in order to nationalise displaced cultural property located on Russian territory. The constitutional court forced the President to sign the law into operation. As was indicated, a restitution claim will fail if a foreign court recognises Russian state ownership as created in terms of these contentious laws.[172] The theft and subsequent entry of Nazi spoliated art into the global art trade also introduced cross-border elements into dispute resolution processes that highlight several jurisdictional and normative aspects of restitution.

The 'lock' mechanism can engage jurisdictions that provide a refuge for good faith purchasers of confiscated objects. Switzerland frequently offered a reliable outlet. Articles 930–934 of the Swiss Civil Code[173] extend favourable treatment to the possessor of a corporeal moveable, and if the possessor acquired in good faith and on the conviction that he or she would become owner, their rights are protected even if the transferor lacked authority to make the transfer. Moreover, several Swiss art professionals who were linked to top officials in the Nazi Party were willing to launder stolen art. Ordinary commercial or criminal law rules proved too general to deal effectively with claims based on confiscation, forced sales and sales at an undervalue.

Jurisdictions that extend recognition to state ownership based on expropriation may also form a lock. Such recognition can be extensive. For instance, courts are unlikely to question title in the wake of expropriation of the property of Russian nationals carried out by the Bolsheviks.[174]

Other laws can supply technical defences that impose limits on restitution claims, preventing them from being heard on their merits. For instance, there are legal systems that protect acquisition in bad faith after a certain length of time to draw a line under the matter, e.g. France and Germany.[175] Statutory limitations tend to feature when the court classifies the cause of action (discussed below in 7.3).

---

[171] Federal Law, 15 April 1998, no 64-FZ, Russian Federation Collection of Legislation, 1998, No 16, Item 1879.

[172] AB Sargent, 'New Jurisdictional Tools for Displaced Cultural Property in Russia' [2010] Yearbook of Cultural Property Law 167, 173.

[173] The Code dates from 10 December 1907.

[174] See *Princess Paley Olga v Weisz* [1929] 1 KB 718 (CA) (nationalisation by the Soviet regime after the Russian Revolution).

[175] Schönenberger (n 43) 140.

6.5 Criminal Law and Private International Law: Differences of Scope

Criminal proceedings and co-operation treaties in criminal matters can result in the return of objects to their state of origin. For instance, Italy requested assistance from the US to obtain the return of the 'Atleta di Fano' (also known as 'Victorious Youth' or the Getty Bronze) in 2010, after an Italian forfeiture action was instituted in Pesaro. The Treaty on Mutual Assistance in Criminal Matters between Italy and the US[176] appeared to be relevant, given that states do not automatically recognise and apply foreign criminal sanctions enacted in respect of illicit import and trade in stolen and illegally imported or excavated objects. This Treaty empowers federal district courts to execute requests to serve and produce documents, execute searches and seizures, take testimony and enables transnational forfeiture. Nonetheless, co-operation was ruled out due to the fact that Italy, the requesting state, itself never successfully prosecuted the offenders. The statutory limitation period had run out at the time.[177]

It is frequently assumed that a clear distinction between the scope of criminal law and of private international law of the forum state suffices.[178] Consequently, the effect of the two disciplines on each other is seldom questioned. It is submitted that the potential of private international law can only be realized in disputes involving art and cultural objects if the various stages of the illicit trade, and the involvement of crime networks at various points in the trade, are firmly kept in view.

6.6 Risk of Underestimating Private International Law

The effect of private international law argument in litigated art and heritage claims has received independent scholarly attention.[179] Prott predicted in 1990 that cultural heritage law would profoundly impact

---

[176] Treaty on Mutual Assistance in Criminal Matters, US–Italy, 24 ILM 1536, signed 9 November 1982; entry into force 13 November 1985; Treaty on Mutual Assistance in Criminal Matters, US–Italy, signed on 3 May 2006.

[177] A Lanciotti, 'The Dilemma of the Right to Ownership of Underwater Cultural Heritage: The Case of the "Getty Bronze"' in S Borelli and F Lenzerini (eds), *Cultural Heritage, Cultural Rights, Cultural Diversity: New Developments in International Law* (Nijhoff Publishers 2012) 301, 325.

[178] Lanciotti (n 177) 316.

[179] E.g. WW Kowalski, 'Restitution of Works of Art Pursuant to Private and Public International Law' 2001 (288) *Recueil des Cours* (The Hague 2002) 212–13; M Anton, *Handbuch Kulturgüterschutz und Kunstrestitutionsrecht/*

choice of law and its limits.[180] Private international law was never expected to make a huge contribution to cultural heritage law, and expectations have remained low.[181] The situation is partly due to the baffling, perplexing side of private international law. Its technical concepts and arguments can add to the risk of uncertainty and unsatisfactory results in litigation.[182] Its reputation is not improved by the scholarly capacity for pallid, uncritical scholastic language. The assertion or denial of title, and trade in general, depend on the application of a determinate body of law, and this implies that choice of law rules (conflicts rules) will be applied when disputes arise.[183] However, the logic of private international law argument can become overpowering and relentless[184] when a small number of multilateral choice of law rules are fixated upon in the international art market. As long as the Organon of Logic operates on the basis of rules that are nationally conceived, contradictions and ethical questions cannot be satisfactorily solved. Paradoxically, to regard its scheme of logic as complete is to make it harder to see what private international law can offer in respect of the protection of art and cultural objects.

Both private international law and cultural heritage law are in search of comprehensive models and guiding principles to counter the illicit trade of art and antiquities. Both disciplines aspire to managing global legal diversity in a context of intermingling private and public law. The private international law argument, when offered, determines the rights of cultural institutions, owners, possessors, dealers and traffickers. Work of

---

Illegaler Kulturgüterverkehr (Handbuch Kulturguterschutz und Kunstrestitutionsrecht) (De Gruyter 2010), Vols 3 and 5; E Jayme, 'Globalization in Art Law: Clash of Interests and International Tendencies' (2005) 38 Vanderbilt Journal of Transnational Law 927; S Symeonides, 'A Choice-of-Law Rule for Conflicts Involving Stolen Cultural Property' (2005) 38 Vanderbilt Journal of Transnational Law 1177; M Lee, 'A Choice of Law Dilemma: The Conflict and Reconciliation of Laws Governing Cross-Border Transfers of Stolen Art' [2008–2009] Cardozo Public Law Policy and Ethics Journal 719, 724; K Siehr, 'International Art Trade and the Law' VI (243) *Recueil des Cours* (The Hague 1993) 9; Jakubowski (n 76) 137; Gillies (n 83).

180 Prott (n 26) 214; Jakubowski (n 76) 137, 138.

181 E.g. Last (n 8) 123.

182 E.g. Prott (n 26) 214; Chechi (n 26) 92, 105–6; Jakubowski (n 76) 137.

183 M Whincop and M Keyes, *Policy and Pragmatism in the Conflict of Laws* (Ashgate 2001) 108.

184 FK Juenger, 'Conflict of Laws: A Critique of Interest Analysis' (1984) 32 AJCL 1.

this nature is already far advanced in Germany, for instance,[185] but consistent work is required if we are to improve our understanding of its interaction and impact on cultural heritage law, on the one hand, and its capacity to offer market participants and adjudicators support in building global solidarity and welfare.

Private international law makes control measures available at the point of market demand. The practical control which private international law can offer as a regulatory tool for market states is considered next. It is vital to highlight how it can draw the cycles of supply and demand into closer alignment with ethical aspirations that contribute to a secure society.

7. WHAT PRIVATE INTERNATIONAL LAW CAN OFFER CULTURAL HERITAGE LAW

7.1 The International Dimension

Demand drives the looting of cultural material, feeds the black market and sustains the outflow of cultural materials.[186] There are a large number of unprovenanced pieces being traded post-excavation or after illicit exportation. States struggle to adapt their legislation and provide appropriate standards for acquisition and trade. The popular doctrinal conception of sovereign national legal systems – at once competing for application and arbitrating that conflict – cannot constrain the commercial imperative. Conceived as a series or a set number of separate national conflicts rules that draw on national sources that invite competing representations of law, the method is supremely hostile to international norms and suppresses the public law dimension of the subject.[187] In order to exert control at the demand side of the market,[188] it must be possible to identify jurisdictions that operate as part of locks. The national conception cannot hope to keep up with the spectacular globalisation which cultural trafficking has undergone in recent decades.

---

[185] Anton (n 179).

[186] Durney and Proulx (n 85), 125; C Forrest, *International Law and the Protection of Cultural Heritage* (Routledge 2010) 156.

[187] Mills (n 138) 3, 12, 243; F Rödl, 'Regime-Collisions, Proceduralised Conflict of Laws and the Unity of the Law: On the Form of Constitutionalism beyond the State' in R Nickel (ed), *Conflict of Laws and Laws of Conflict in Europe and Beyond* (Intersentia 2010) 263, 266–7.

[188] Rödl (n 187) 268.

Private international law was originally conceived as part of a universal law of nations. It was regarded as a set of secondary legal norms aimed at global legal ordering.[189] Conceived as an 'internationalised' discipline that posits an international system, the subject can assume a unique role and function at the interface of universal norms and national norms. Its potential for unity comes from solving conflict by a higher ranking order, from simplifying the complex choices associated with international claims brought by private individuals or states.

7.2 At the Point of Classification

In international cases, classification is supposed to determine whether a particular issue is subject to the applicable law at all (it will be so only if it relates to the substance of the dispute). Depending on the classification, different legal systems could claim application. Is the underlying category the transfer of property or is it restitution? The type of claim instituted in international disputes depends on being classified into a particular type – the cause of action could be non-contractual (delictual/tortious) or penal, a matter of transfer of real rights, a contractual obligation, a personal injury and so forth.[190]

Courts frequently use the property transaction as a basis for classification when art has crossed jurisdictional lines after having been stolen. When classified as a matter of proprietary transfer, legal diversity permeates the definitions, methods and conditions for valid transfer of title, levels of abstraction, approaches to organisation, and remedies for protection.[191] Civilian jurisdictions differentiate between the contract directed at the transfer of rights and the actual transfer of a right from a transferor to a transferee by way of conveyance. If real rights can be transferred independently of any underlying legally recognised reason (*causa*) to pass the real right – as German law allows by virtue of the *Abstraktionsprinzip* – the system of transfer of real rights is abstract. If ownership can pass on mere delivery, an illegal contract cannot destroy the valid conveyance.[192] In causal systems, which require a valid underlying basis for transfer (a valid agreement *in rem* or a 'real/proprietary contract' such as a sale), an illegal or invalid contract means the act of

---

189 Mills (n 138) 72, 117.

190 D Shapiro, 'Repatriation: A Modest Proposal' (1998) 31 International Law and Politics 95, 100.

191 Jakubowski (n 76) 140.

192 LPW van Vliet, 'Transfer of Movable Property' in JM Smits (ed), *Elgar Encyclopedia of Comparative Law* (Edward Elgar 2006) 730.

conveyance will be void or voidable, depending on the circumstances. On this basis of ownership, the seller would be in a position to claim back what has been sold. Austrian and Swiss law fall into this category.[193] There may also be a requirement of a proper or constructive delivery. Some sale codes are based on consensual conveyance. This is the rule in s 17 of the UK Sale of Goods Act. Ownership passes when the parties intend for it to pass, regardless of what may be agreed in respect of delivery or payment. The default position in terms of s 18 is that property passes when the contract is made.[194] The differences between consensual systems and *traditio* systems are less stark than they seem at first; fictitious *traditio* and exceptions to the requirement of *traditio* have brought them closer together.[195]

Classification determines the effect of the passage of time on the claim; classified as a matter of substance, the same connecting factor and the same law will determine its effect. The connecting factor is a localising agent. It can relate to a person (domicile, habitual residence, nationality), a legal person (place of the central administration of a business when a contract was concluded), or the place of an event (place of contracting, place of performance, place of breach, place of wrongful action, place of damage).

This level of detail is hardly necessary to know, however, if the decision-maker were to treat classification as a step towards making a value-based decision. Ultimately, it is the value-judgement which the applicable legal system permits to be made in respect of restitution that is pertinent in claims involving art and cultural objects. In addition, if the decision-maker were to treat the distinction between substance and procedure in private international law as fluid and permeable[196] rather than as a hard and fast line, a value-judgement can be facilitated. In English private international law practice, the basic distinction between substance and procedure leads, in one and the same case, to the application of rules belonging to different legal systems to the merits of the case and the conduct of the proceedings. Whereas matters of substance are governed by the law of the cause (the applicable law), matters of procedure are governed by the law of the forum (the court hearing the case). The basic substance/procedure distinction is widely

[193] Van Vliet (n 192) 731.

[194] Van Vliet (n 192) 730; LPW van Vliet, *Transfer of Movables in German, French, English and Dutch Law* (Arts Aequi Libri 2000) 111.

[195] Van Vliet (n 192) 731.

[196] R Garnett, *Substance and Procedure in Private International Law* (OUP 2012) 3.

assumed to be a matter of classification for purposes of traditional common law. The European Civil Law Model holds firmly to the dichotomy on the basis that differences in the nature of legal rules justify differences in their application in space. Rules that determine parties' rights and the merits of their arguments clearly differ from rules that support the smooth running of the court machinery. This model permits ready acceptance that the forum follows its own procedural rules in service of process, pleading and evidence, and allows the law of the cause to determine rights and liabilities. Thus, as in matters of procedure, it is to be expected that all evidentiary aspects will be subject to the law of the court hearing the case. At the same time, foreign procedural law can be taken cognizance of where procedural issues come into play.

A broad view of the scope of procedure leads to many foreign cases being decided on local procedural grounds, which, depending on classification, could include statutory limitations. Whereas a modest and functional definition of 'procedure' keeps procedural encroachments upon substance to a minimum, an over-inclusive definition fosters legal uncertainty. An over-inclusive definition of 'substance' bears a different kind of cost, namely that of proof of foreign law.

Expedience is the most commonly cited modern rationale for the distinction.[197] The forum court draws the distinction for its own protection, for it cannot devote all its effort to adopting wholescale every intricate procedural rule of another state, even if that state's law governs the substance or merits of the dispute in hand. Nonetheless, the forum court is free to determine for itself how far it may go, without unduly inconveniencing itself, in applying the rules of the foreign legal system.[198] If this freedom of the court to follow its own rules or the rules of a foreign court in matters of procedure, provided those rules are compatible with the authority and structure of the forum,[199] is underplayed, claims involving art will not proceed to the merits stage. This obstacle poses a hindrance in many claims involving Nazi spoliated art, but the potential for merit-based decision-making inheres in the classification mechanism. This potential is at the disposal of adjudicators of cases involving cultural objects.

---

[197] Garnett (n 196) 10.

[198] WW Cook, 'Characterization in the Conflict of Laws' (1941) 51 Yale Law Journal 191, 201.

[199] AV Levontin, *Choice of Law and Conflict of Laws* (AW Sijthoff 1976) 121–22.

7.3 At the Point of Application of Foreign Public Law

The effect of a cross-border transfer of a tangible cultural object could be that the original owner loses ownership rights;[200] that the object loses its special status through non-recognition of the laws that are designed to prevent an object from crossing the boundary of public into private ownership;[201] or that the state of origin might fail to enforce its export controls.[202] Enforcement of import and export controls is polemical as a normative basis for international regulation, since a court may require a state to establish a property right in order to bring a claim. Common law, or an umbrella statute that vests ownership of undiscovered archaeological material in the state, represents a more readily accepted basis for a restitution claim. The *lex situs* rule, which refers to the law of the place where the object is situated at the time of transfer and which tends to dominate in questions of title transfer, can render the inalienability of a cultural object ineffective.[203] This result can be prevented if the forum court were to decide to apply foreign public law protective of archaeological finds,[204] export and import regulations for cultural heritage,[205] and statutory declarations of state ownership of undiscovered antiquities that have left the state (vesting law).[206] The recognition or application of a state claim to property will have the same effect as restitution of the

---

[200] *Winkworth v Christie Manson and Woods Ltd* [1980] Ch 496.

[201] *Frias v Pinchon* 1886 Clunet 593.

[202] *Attorney-General of New Zealand v Ortiz* [1983] 2 All ER 93 (HL), affirming *Attorney-General of New Zealand v Ortiz* [1982] 3 All ER 451 (CA).

[203] E.g. *Frias v Pinchon* (n 201). For more, see MA Renold, 'The International Protection of Archaeological Heritage: Questions of Private International Law and of Legal Harmonization' <http://biblio.juridicas.unam.mx/libros/7/3457/18.pdf> accessed 11 June 2014, 297, 298–99.

[204] Archaeological finds in Scotland belong to the Crown and are allocated to museums on the basis of their written claims. Museums may make ex gratia payments to finders. Scottish Archaeological Finds Allocation Panel, *Treasure Trove in Scotland – a Code of Practice* (Scottish Government 2008); *Lord Advocate v University of Aberdeen & Budge* 1963 SC 533.

[205] *Attorney-General of New Zealand v Ortiz* [1983] 2 All ER 93 (HL), affirming *Attorney-General of New Zealand v Ortiz* [1982] 3 All ER 451 (CA); (English conflict of laws espouses that foreign penal legislation will not be recognised and enforced in an English forum).

[206] E.g. Egyptian Law 117 on the Protection of Antiquities of 1983. Art 6 declares all antiquities discovered in Egypt after 1983 to be the property of the Egyptian government, and which makes private ownership or possession of such objects illegal. *US v Schultz*, 333 F2d 393 (2nd Circuit 2003) *cert denied Schultz v United States*, 540 US 1106 (2004).

objects that were removed from its territory. Private international law has the potential to co-ordinate diverse national standards in the context of restitution claims based on vesting laws (see Chapter 7 below).

7.4 Taking Account of Policy Interests in Choice of Law Method

The intensification of connections between and among individuals, societies and economies provoke interpenetration of categories and interests – be they specific, general or international. Public interests embodied in legislation affect the choice of law process or push out the 'private' in private international law. To the extent that the classic divisions between public and private law relationships are blurring, the distinction between private and public international law comes to resemble an unrealistic principle of organisation. The notion of a global or transnational public sphere, and the overlap between international regimes and activities of state and non-state actors, support this idea.

The pressure of global legal diversity may be alleviated by the type of conflicts rule applied, or by allowing the policy underlying the rule to shape the outcome of its application. A choice of law rule indicates merely the legal system which is to supply the substantive relief or remedy sought in the particular case. Choice of law rules do not direct the forum to a particular substantive provision or decisional norm. They are not supposed to be directly concerned with the substantive outcome of disputes.[207] Nonetheless, the legal relationship does not exist as an objective factor isolated from national interests and policies.

Orthodox multilateral private international law rules are frequently over-estimated and permitted to instil fixed conceptions of what counts as 'rule' and what counts as 'exception'. When this happens, these rules fail to promote value-based decision-making and produce mere instrumentalist or formulaic rulings.

Policy and value judgements shape private international law method especially in the US. The capacity of private international law to promote the role of law in the maintenance of a secure society can be explored more directly where substantive rules and their underlying policies enjoy prominence in conflicts theories, as is the case in the US. Federal choice of law is absent because federal institutions have withdrawn from this

---

[207] JM Carruthers, *The Transfer of Property in the Conflict of Laws* (OUP 2005) §1.03.

matter. The individual states are not in any position to provide impartial conflicts rules that would serve a federal system.[208]

While the US Constitution continues to have a low impact on choice of law, American conflicts thinking brings public interests squarely in view in private international law method. This tendency disturbs the multilateral method, on which European choice of law is predicated.

One way in which the US conflicts system takes public interests and policies underlying substantive rules into account, is by way of governmental interest analysis.[209] Although eventually settled out of court in 2009, *Schoeps v Museum of Modern Art*[210] illustrates the effect of interest analysis in the context of a claim to a Picasso painting, 'Boy Leading a Horse'. The painting had allegedly been transferred by a Jewish banker to his wife as a wedding gift in 1927. It was sent to Switzerland in 1933 and consigned to a Jewish art dealer in Switzerland in 1934, allegedly in response to Nazi duress. In 1936 it was sold on to an art dealer who bequeathed it to the Museum of Modern Art in New York. While the transfer of title in Germany could have been conceived as a consequence of duress to which German law could arguably apply as the *lex loci delicti*, New York law was held to have a more significant relationship to the parties and the painting. The court did not enquire into the quality of the causal link between Nazi persecution and the transfer of the work as it might have done, had it considered the potentially applicable laws to be German and Swiss law. New York law prevailed because the painting was shipped to New York immediately upon concluding the sale in 1936, remained there for more than seventy years, and was the property of a major cultural institution in New York. The interim transfer was considered to have been made at a temporary *situs*, meaning that Switzerland's interest in the application of its law was less compelling. The *lex situs* rule, which typifies many questions of title transfer, did not determine the outcome therefore.

7.5 At the End of the Choice of Law Process: Public Policy Exception

The public policy exception is an exception to the reference by a conflicts rule to a foreign legal system. This exception may prevent the

---

208 J Basedow, 'Internal and External Conflicts, Federalism and Market Regulation: Federal Choice of Law in Europe and the US – a Comparative Account of Interstate Conflicts' (2008) 82 Tulane Law Review 2119, 2125.

209 SC Symeonides, 'The American Choice-of-Law Revolution: Past, Present and Future' (Martinus Nijhof 2006) 15–24.

210 *Schoeps v Museum of Modern Art*, 594 F Supp 2d 461 (SD NY 2009).

selected law from applying and may clear the way for the law of the court to apply. Public policy is a fluid concept that derives from domestic, regional and international law. It evolves along with a particular state's legal and social norms. The exception operates as a 'safety valve' that bars the application of an otherwise competent foreign law when it conflicts with a more fundamental public policy of the forum. It operates defensively in its traditional (common law) role as a 'weapon of last resort'. It is employed at the end of a forum's choice of law process.

The public policy exception defines the outer limits of the tolerance of difference enabled by choice of law rules. When global, national, private, object and market interests compete or clash, this device enables the adjudicator to put the protective values of the forum first. It marks the point at which a court may refuse to support pluralism.[211]

Limits that could signal non-application of the foreign law are found in public interests and the social order of the forum (e.g. expropriation, confiscation of the property of alien nationals or money laundering); in the regulation of the national economy (e.g. import and export regulations); in morality (e.g. handling stolen property or illicit trading in cultural property); or in public law intervention in international transactions (e.g. currency legislation). When the potentially applicable foreign law does not conform with fundamental rights conceptions, the displacing role of the public policy exception intensifies.[212]

In turn, local public policy is also subject to limits. For instance, it is constrained by the norms of international law. These limits prevent it from undermining justice pluralism. In a federal system, it has a lesser role because of stronger obligations of mutual respect. Whether the public policy exception is invoked ought to be subject to considerations of proximity and relativity: the proximity or connection between the state and the dispute, and the severity of the breach of public policy.[213]

Theoretically, when the public policy exception is invoked, what remains of the applicable law should be applied. In practice, local law is applied (because the forum uses appropriate local provisions in lieu). Ideally, if an ethical dimension is to assume relevance, the law that best advances global welfare should be applied (see 7.6. below).

In figure-ground perception, the policy position can function either as 'figure' or as 'ground'. In the multilateral choice of law method, the multilateral choice of law rule will necessarily function as 'figure',

---

211 Mills (n 138) 191.

212 B Fauvarque-Cosson, 'Comparative Law and Conflict of Laws – Allies or Enemies?' (2001) 49 AJCL 407, 409–10.

213 Mills (n 138) 191, 306–7.

leaving the public policy exception to form the ground. Perception can shift. The public policy exception can function as the 'figure' when it is conceived as a 'rule' that attends to the substantive content of the applicable law to check if the content is detestable, or when it is regarded as an exceptional choice of law rule that prioritises the local law of the forum as embodied in its public law. Perceiving the policy position as 'figure', a court may protect a vital state interest in the social order. The multilateral choice of law rule becomes 'ground' and its role can be qualified in accordance with this perception. Public policy asserts itself in this 'positive' way, when unilateral or mandatory rules are used to override choice of law rules prior to their application, or where the court insists on the application of a law that would not be applicable otherwise (forum law or even foreign law).[214] Arguably there are in-between possibilities, depending on public policy laws and public interests (wider in meaning than 'laws') where the application of the relevant choice of law rule is qualified, that are better suited to respond to a particular state policy.

In New York, for instance, courts do not permit the state to be used as a haven for stolen cultural property; their interpretation of the *lex situs* rule is qualified in accordance with this priority. Chapter 5 illustrates how the choice of law methods play out in disputes involving stolen cultural objects when a global lens is applied. Mutual recognition of the exclusive reference to forum law produces a new type of unilateralism that can ultimately foster co-operation between nations, build international solidarity and make room for the comity of nations (in the sense of respect and recognition of the legislative, executive and judicial acts of a foreign government). Even where the *lex fori* is the only point of reference, made at the end of the choice of law process, global welfare is served when mutual recognition of forum law follows. The result is similar to having applied the unilateral method (see 6.2 above).[215] In Europe, it is conceivable that protective national rules could qualify for application provided they are re-characterised and do not infringe on European law.

While the consistent legal treatment of international cases of the same type is an unachievable goal, it is the pursuit of the goal that keeps the method on track. Without it, theoretical and methodological approaches in private international law can be over-estimated, and the orthodox multilateral private international law rules will be treated as something

---

[214] *Regazzoni v Sethia* [1958] AC 301 (HL). TC Hartley, *International Commercial Litigation: Text, Cases and Materials on Private International Law* (CUP 2009) 514.

[215] Directive 2014/60/EU, Recital 6.

other than the manifestations of international norms they are. Fixed conceptions of what counts as 'rule' and what counts as exception pose obstacles on the way towards consistent treatment.

7.6 When Ethics Demand a Place Alongside Private International Law

Museums, galleries and collectors should only be acquiring material with reliable documentation that confirms that the object had left its country of origin before a legal prohibition of export was enacted in that country or otherwise in accordance with the law. In practice, however, collectors frequently fail to make contact with foreign authorities before they acquire objects. Ethics cannot be legislated, nor concern for the market forced, but ethics have a bearing on the standards applicable to the acquisition of pieces lacking a discoverable, documented or complete provenance. Ideally, a secure chain of title leads all the way back in time to the date of manufacture, production or excavation.

Many states adopted legislation to regulate state ownership and export in the mid-twentieth century.[216] For those that did not, the international 'cut-off' date for the trans-border movement of pieces without a proper collecting history would be 1970.[217]

The highest aspirations of society are found in commitments to support provenance research, development of databases that facilitate independent searches, norms (hard law) and codes of conduct. It is desirable to make full use of the law to control and to rein in market activity, when ethics so require. Ultimately, there are legal and non-legal factors that facilitate the global and widespread illicit trafficking of art and cultural objects. Factors such as legal diversity can affect the chain of ownership, but there may be non-legal factors that encourage problematic behaviours. Realism demands keeping both the legal and the non-legal factors in view, in order that behaviours can be modified and adverse effects countered.

---

216 P Craddock, *Scientific Investigation of Copies, Fakes and Forgeries* (Elsevier 2009) 21.

217 1970 UNESCO Convention on the Means of Prohibiting and Preventing the Illicit Import, Export and Transfer of Ownership of Cultural Property 14 November 1970, 823 UNTS 231; 10 ILM 289. MM Miles, *Art as Plunder: The Ancient Origins of Debate about Cultural Property* (CUP 2008) 355.

Ethical action may not be legally required in every jurisdiction. The standards of due diligence[218] differ across jurisdictions[219] and depend on whether criminal or civil remedies are being pursued. Nonetheless, due care never ceases to be an option. The potential buyer may always choose to consult a commercial, international or state-run database.[220] It will always be vitally important to enable those buyers, dealers and auction houses that take responsibility for the art market to conduct searches and run checks before buying or selling. Given that there are market participants who choose to take responsibility for the market, database checks are one of the best ways in which to control the spill-over effects of the market onto source states.

Since the problem of dubious acquisition practices has an ethical dimension, the most suitable response is through a normative ideal that can bring market activity into alignment with a framework that keeps unbridled self-interest in check. This is so because non-legal standards affect compliance with legal obligations. As was stated above, acquisition standards and the duties of market participants do not derive only from law. In fact, the notion that the law is the source and origin of these behavioural standards deserves to be challenged.

It is essential to draw attention also to the limits of the law. For instance, relevant international instruments do not provide standard autonomous definitions of undesirable conduct. They cannot ensure adequate support for curators and museums. They cannot guarantee the safety of archaeological sites. They cannot compel the public and private sector of the state parties to devise successful multi-jurisdictional art loss

---

[218] Principle 2.3 of the Code of Ethics of the International Council of Museums (ICOM) 1986 as amended refers to the duty to discover the full history of an item since discovery or production. The glossary refers to '[t]he requirement that every endeavour is made to establish the facts of a case before deciding a course of action, particularly in identifying the source and history of an item offered for acquisition or use before acquiring it'.

[219] See Chapter 2, sub 4.2.2.

[220] E.g. the INTERPOL Stolen Art and Antiquities Database; London Stolen Arts Database; Leonardo Database (specialist police database of stolen works of art used by the Italian police art and heritage protection squad, which is also the largest European database); International Observatory on Illicit Traffic in Cultural Goods (ICOM) (designed to counter the lack of centralized information on illicit traffic in cultural goods; operational since July 2013, and funded for 3 years). WWII provenance research resources include the Art Loss Register; Central Registry of Information on Looted Cultural Property, 1933–1945, administered by the Commission for Looted Art in Europe; and the Lost Art Internet Database.

registers.[221] No convention can make up or substitute for an inefficient cultural policy at home. The law cannot even impose a permanent illegal status on an item. It can only proscribe particular behaviour[222] such as theft, looting, forced sale, unprofessional and unsystematic excavation and illegal export as defined in domestic legislation.

Never are the limits of law more evident than in the countless uprooted and fragmented lives lived in communities in states at war or caught in circumstances of social and economic upheaval. All 'markers of culture' are affected by conflict.[223] Culture is under perpetual threat and its fruits traded willy-nilly. Modern conflicts directly open new sources of cultural heritage for looting, as the conflicts in Palestine, Afghanistan, Iraq, Egypt and Syria demonstrate.[224] The ways in which cultural objects are sometimes destroyed are indicative of a cultural heritage crisis.[225] The destruction of the Bamiyan Buddhas in Afghanistan in March 2001 at the hands of the Taliban was a particularly disturbing example that flies in the face of the basic principle that cultural property has partial immunity from seizure.[226] The 1954 Hague Convention for the Protection of Cultural Property in the Event of Armed Conflict[227] is protective of cultural diversity. It requires the safeguarding of cultural property during

---

221 Siehr (n 179) 279.

222 K Alderman, 'The Ethical Trade in Cultural Property: Ethics and Law in the Antiquity Auction Industry' [2008] ILSA Journal of International and Comparative Law 1, 13.

223 Ulph and Smith (n 81) 258.

224 E.g. M Bogdanons, 'The Casualties of War: The Truth about the Iraq Museum' (2005) 109 American Journal of Archaeology 477; J Halperin, 'Egypt's Malawi Museum Ransacked' *The Art Newspaper* (21 August 2013); T Ghose, 'Syria's Civil War Imperils Nation's Rich Archaeological Treasures' *NBC News* (4 September 2013).

225 Gerstenblith (n 33) 78–83.

226 The first statement with actual legal force was Instructions for the Government of Armies of the United States in the Field (Lieber Code), 24 April 1863, promulgated as General Orders No 100 in 1863 (Washington 1898: Government Printing Office); Regulations annexed to 1899 Hague Convention II and 1907 Hague Convention IV Concerning the Law and Customs of War on Land (Arts 27 and 56); Hague Convention IX concerning Bombardments by Naval Forces in Time of War, 18 October 1907, 36 Stat. 2351 (Art 5); Washington Treaty on the Protection of Artistic and Scientific Institutions and Historic Monuments (Roerich Pact), 15 April 1935, 167 LNTS 289; entry into force 26 August 1935.

227 The Hague, 14 May 1954.

occupation or during war, but recognises that the cultural damage wrought during World War II proved the inadequacy of existing rules.[228]

Tolstoy concluded *What Is Art* with a profound realisation concerning the enormity of the task of art: 'Art should cause violence to be set aside. And it is only art that can accomplish this.'[229]

He noted sombrely that when art fails to fulfil its task, co-operation is obtained only through law courts and law enforcement agencies. This perspective has some bearing on the method adopted for purposes of this inquiry. Art and cultural objects possess the capacity to promote a shared sense of community in a pluralist world.[230] To the extent that they reach past the physical aspects of being human to encourage 'intercultural respect' that makes 'a culture of peace',[231] they are an inspiration in the search for dispute resolution.

7.7 Global Solidarity: How Does Private International Law Contribute?

Global solidarity is built on a normative ideal with a moral aim located in the cultural sphere.[232] Illicit trafficking and unethical trade in cultural objects and looted art is a global issue that requires co-ordinated international action. The achievement of the normative ideal, whether by legal or by non-legal means, presupposes the development of key human potentials, including the potential for rationality and for mutual respect and co-operation. At the international level, the same human potentials are required – rationality, mutuality and realizing that the welfare of a single state is connected to the welfare of every state.

The ideal of solidarity points towards a demanding step-up in rational decision-making, because its achievement requires value-rationality.[233]

---

[228] Gazzini (n 75) 3.

[229] Tolstoy (n 4) 210.

[230] PM Bator, 'An Essay on the International Trade in Art' (1982) 34 Stanford Law Review 275, 307; E Jayme, 'Neueste Entwicklungen im Internationalen Kunstrecht' in *Kunst im Recht* (Graz Jurisprudential Faculty 2004) 15; Van Woudenberg (n 9) 15–16; JP Fishman, 'Locating the International Interest in Intranational Cultural Property Disputes' (2010) 35 The Yale Journal of International Law 347, 389, 393.

[231] UNESCO Convention on the Protection and Promotion of the Diversity of Cultural Expressions (n 11).

[232] Wilde (n 71) 64–67, 105.

[233] For more on the difference between instrumental and value rationality, see Wilde (n 71) 119–20, 191ff.

Value-rationality refers to ethical action taken irrespective of the prospects of success; acting in accordance with mutuality even when the prospects of success are low, and even when private fairness and convenience indicate otherwise.

The ways in which claims for restitution of trafficked objects and of stolen, looted or misappropriated cultural objects are dealt with can either exacerbate the problems associated with the ethics deficit in acquisition practices, or can strengthen global solidarity and the aspirations embodied in instruments of international policy. The settlement of claims in the spirit of global solidarity requires insight into the options for dispute resolution and demands a step-up in the approaches and methods that prevail today.

In the light of the above, the true measure of the success of any method that purports to have something to contribute to cultural heritage law, is its ability to promote impeccable, clear acquisition standards; foster a deeper commitment to value-based rationality; and control the spill-over effects of the market demand onto source states. Private international law offers tools that can prove useful here, but then these tools are to be used advisedly. If the adjudicator succumbs to pure techniques of law and artificial procedural considerations that confine the scope for value-based decision-making, these tools will come to nought. Pure technique deserves to be questioned, and with consistency.[234] Legal instrumentalism poses as big a hurdle to protection, as the complex nature of art and cultural objects and the co-mingling of the licit and the illicit trade do. Sustained systematic academic scrutiny must identify why value choices fall by the wayside and suggest ways in which to counter practices that preclude proper consideration of values.

Choice of law methods can work in tandem with public law and public international law when the perspective on the interaction between different systems of civil justice draws on global welfare.[235] This opportunity

---

[234] A Carty, *Philosophy of International Law* (Columbia University Press 2007) questions the use of legal technique and instrumental decision-making in public international law. Arguably, it is vital to make room for the ethical dimension of society in public international law also, given that pure techniques of law limit the scope for value-based decision-making.

[235] For more on the significance of global solidarity and welfare in private international law, see H Muir Watt, 'Choice of Law in Integrated and Interconnected Markets: A Matter of Political Economy' (2003) 9 Columbian Journal of European Law 383, 405. For more on the significance of these concepts in international relations and in public international law, see Wilde (n 71) and Carty (n 234) (Chapter 8) respectively.

arises when the classification mechanism is applied, in the context of the public policy exception, and when policy and substantive interests and values must be accommodated.

The avoidance of value-based decisions by classification – e.g. classifying statutory limitations or prescription as a matter of procedure to be governed by the law of the forum – generates pressure in an area where global solidarity is sorely needed. This tendency affects the success of claims involving Nazi spoliated art.

The post-war restitution cycle, which was intended to address the Nazi spoliation in Europe in the 1940s and 1950s, had a strict national legal thrust. German and Austrian post-war laws repudiated all spurious 'transactions' of this era, including art 'deals' that were made to appear legal. These repudiations came soon enough after World War II ended, and never qualified for protection as acts of state.[236] It has been argued that a new openly moral and policy-based cycle of restitution was born after 1989.[237] Since then it has been recognised that compliance with the law could not always function as a precondition to restitution.[238] If a more openly policy-oriented and ethics-driven approach to restitution processes were to take root, the meaning of 'restitution' would extend to instances in which the legal obstacles in the way of return must be overcome.[239] This understanding seems accurate. Legal grounds for confiscations and the obstacles they presented to restitution were already being addressed in different post-war municipal laws at the end of World War II.[240] In special regulations for the return of Nazi-induced losses in Austria, Germany and Switzerland, return was indicated regardless of good faith or adverse possession.[241] The criteria and procedures of the national mediation commissions that operate in five EU Member

---

[236] *Republic of Austria v Altmann*, 541 US 677, 682 (2004); *Majken Hofmann, Anna Lokrantz, Maria Müller, Andreas Müller Hofmann und Lena Müller Hofmann v Republic of Austria* (Nov. 21, 2005)(Arbitral award in German) <www.bslaw.com/altmann/Zuckerkandl/Klage/284724.doc> accessed 24 February 2014; *US v Portrait of Wally*, 2002 US District LEXIS 6445, 25ff; Schönenberger (n 43) 202–3.

[237] Tijhuis (n 54) 2–3.

[238] W Veraart and L Winkel, 'An Introduction to Dilemmas of Post-War Restitution in Europe' in W Veraart and L Winkel (eds), *The Post-war Restitution of Property Rights in Europe* (Rvp Press 2011) 1; Cornu and Renold (n 77) 15.

[239] Veraart and Winkel (n 238) 2; Schönenberger (n 43) 228.

[240] Schönenberger (n 43) 201ff.

[241] Schönenberger (n 43) 221.

States[242] signal significant progress in this regard, even if their recommendations are ad hoc and case-by-case.

Mutuality may pose an issue in an action to recover moveable property in another state when the forum state reserves its position on the application of foreign public law.[243] As Chapter 7 demonstrates, global solidarity counters the non-recognition argument. Source states, market states and states that operate at both ends of the spectrum can build global solidarity by their willingness to harmonize their responses in the interest of global welfare. Arguably, this willingness is less a matter of legal obligation than it is of human potential for co-operation for purposes of the effective control and counter-action of the illicit trade.

The potential of private international law to contribute to global solidarity deserves to be utilised alongside that of international law and criminal law, and in addition to money-laundering regulations and administrative procedures concerned with import and export controls.[244] Private international law does not take the place of other manifestations of global solidarity, such as social movements that are informed about global issues. Specifically, it does not purport to supplant the solidarity that is built on a normative ideal with a moral aim located in the cultural sphere. Private international law could never achieve more than the voluntary return of an unprovenanced cultural object could. For example, two artefacts that belong to the 'Benin Bronzes' collection[245] were returned to the King of Benin in Nigeria in 2014, after the heir discovered more about their role in Britain's colonial history, namely that the testator had taken part in the British Punitive Expedition at Benin in 1897.[246]

Ultimately, Tolstoy is right about the law being but an external means. Our interior lives can accomplish so much more.[247] Yet, the external protection offered by the law may strengthen the ethical framework and the solidarity that precedes it. It may also create a more favourable

---

242 Meeting of Five European Committees, Symposium in the Peace Palace in The Hague, 26/27 November 2012, <http://www.restitutiecommissie.nl/en/committees.html> accessed 25 February 2014.

243 See Chapter 7.

244 Among others Forrest (n 186) 219; Ulph and Smith (n 81) 101–45 (controls in the UK).

245 For more, see <http://www.britishmuseum.org/explore/highlights/highlight_objects/aoa/b/benin_plaque_oba__europeans.aspx> accessed 20 July 2014.

246 AFP, '"Looted" Nigerian Art Returned to Traditional Ruler' *South African Courier* (23 June 2014).

247 Tolstoy (n 4) 210.

environment for 'cultural diplomacy'. This concept includes the mutual understanding that art and culture foster, as well as the global understanding that collaborative excavation and research projects, exhibitions, loans, and knowledge exchange can offer.[248] Italian soldiers took the Obelisk of Aksum (3 BCE) from Ethiopia in 1937. It was due to be returned under an agreement reached in 1947. Regrettably however, it remained in Rome for 68 years, to be restituted only in 2005. Clearly, cultural diplomacy stands no chance if co-operation and mutuality are lacking.[249]

An appreciation of the wider context for dispute resolution helps to provide perspective on what private international law can offer. Because litigation is not always the best procedure for return, and restitution frequently depends on value-based decision-making, the use of alternative dispute resolution mechanisms (ADR) has gained more prominence.[250]

8. WIDENING THE FOCUS TO ENCOMPASS DISPUTE RESOLUTION

8.1 ADR

Courts are not always regarded as ideal fora to decide disputes involving art and heritage, because there are discrepancies between state law and practice and irreducible differences between different legal families and legal cultures which domestic choice of law rules can struggle to overcome. A 'national' private international law could mean that the systemic effects of applying certain conflict rules become amplified and adaptations hard to make. The protection and enforcement of state (sovereign) interests may distort the process of dispute resolution and the

---

[248] Kuprecht and Siehr (n 70) 270; I Stamatoudi, *Cultural Property Law and Restitution* (Edward Elgar 2011) 208.

[249] Wilde (n 71) 105, 117ff. For examples, see <http://www2.mcdonald.cam.ac.uk/projects/iarc/culturewithoutcontext/issue10/watson.htm> accessed 24 February 2014 (return of the head of Amenhotep III to Egypt); S Knapton, 'Smuggled Ancient Sculpture Returns to Egypt' *The Telegraph* (19 December 2008).

[250] M Granovsky, 'A Permanent Resolution Mechanism of Cultural Property Disputes' (2008) 8 Pepperdine Dispute Resolution Law Journal 25; AL Bandle and S Theurich, 'Alternative Dispute Resolution and Art-Law – a New Research Project of the Geneva Art-Law Centre' (2011) 6 Journal of International Commercial Law and Technology 28.

outcome of an international judicial ruling may not be what communities and groups would regard as just.

Claims for return are frequently resolved extra-judicially.[251] Negotiation and mediation have made their mark. For instance, the settlement of the intra-national dispute between St Gallen and Zürich over the territorial removal of books, paintings, manuscripts and astronomical instruments during times of war suggests that the cumulative application of various different techniques for dispute resolution enabled an amicable solution to be found.[252] Mediation by the Swiss Confederation resulted in restitution in the form of a long-term loan, a donation, the production of a replica, and there was formal recognition of the importance of certain objects to the identity of the counter-party. State-run mediation can offer wide-ranging solutions which may include the continuance of an existing business or professional relationship or an agreement to take some action without any existing legal obligation to do so.[253] The jurisdictional scope within which judges operate does not permit such unconventional remedies. Typical hurdles in litigation may be overcome because special mediation processes take account of highly specific subject matter, and of commercial, cultural, ethical, historical, moral, religious and spiritual aspects.

The nature of the remedy that the claimant seeks in a dispute over ownership and possession gives some indication of the most appropriate dispute resolution mechanism to be followed. Independent mediation (which is not state-run) seeks to resolve disputes on an informal basis by a neutral intermediary who assists the parties to identify common ground. Successful independent mediation may yield a settlement agreement with tangible outcomes that can be enforced under contract law.[254] It is vital to identify the best stage at which to mediate. If it is embarked upon too

---

[251] See the database set up by the Art-Law Centre of the University of Geneva under the name *ArThemis*, <http://unige.ch/art-adr> accessed 24 February 2014.

[252] Cornu and Renold (n 77) 12, 18.

[253] *Halsey v Milton Keynes General NHS Trust* [2004] 1 WLR 3002 (CA) 3008–9 (mediation in a damages suit).

[254] JC Wichard and WB Wendland, 'Mediation as an Option for Resolving Disputes between Indigenous/Traditional Communities and Industry Concerning Traditional Knowledge' in BT Hoffman (ed), *Art and Cultural Heritage: Law, Policy and Practice* (CUP 2006) 477.

early, the parties will be insufficiently informed about each other's cases; if it starts too late, high costs may already have been incurred.[255]

If the form of the mediation in question focuses on the needs and interests of the parties (e.g. if facilitative mediation is used), future relationships and goals are considered to be more important than redress of past conduct.[256] The goal may be different in evaluative or transformative mediation.

The capacity for dispute resolution through ADR and by having recourse to an international tribunal is weakened to an extent by being consent-based. Consent may be absent when gaps become apparent in the provenance of the work after its acquisition in good faith, and non-compliance with the outcome entails no sanction.[257] In the event of non-compliance with the outcome of independent mediation, contract-based court action would be necessary.

If a state entity is involved, consent is a moot point. If the parties are bound into state-run mediation, their autonomy to choose any ADR option is curtailed. The accountability structures for state entities may not permit them to opt out of the mediation and enforcement of the agreement against a state-entity is unlikely to end up in a state court.

8.2 Arbitration

Arbitration of claims to cultural property has been an appealing possibility for commentators ever since the 1990s.[258] Over the last decade, more sustained and critical work has been done in respect of this form of dispute settlement.[259] Arbitration is no panacea, however. The purchaser

---

255 Lord Jackson, *Review of Civil Litigation Costs: Final Report* (1st edn, The Stationery Office 2010).

256 N Palmer, 'Litigation: The Best Remedy?' in International Bureau of the Permanent Court of Arbitration (Hrsg.)(ed.) *Resolution of Cultural Property Disputes* (The Hague 2004) 113.

257 A Chechi, 'Some Reflections on International Adjudication of Cultural Heritage-Related Cases' (2013) 10 TDM Special Issue 1, 7.

258 EI Gegas, 'International Arbitration and Resolution of Cultural Property Disputes' (1997) 13 Ohio State Journal on Dispute Resolution 129, 151ff; E Sidorsky, 'The 1995 Unidroit Convention on Stolen or Illegally Exported Cultural Objects: The Role of International Arbitration' (1996) 5 IJCP 19.

259 Gazzini (n 75) 50; BW Daly, 'The Potential for Arbitration of Cultural Property Disputes: Recent Developments at the Permanent Court of Arbitration' [2005] Law and Practice of International Courts and Tribunals 261; N Palmer, 'Arbitration and the Applicable Law in Resolution of Cultural Property Disputes' in International Bureau of the Permanent Court of Arbitration (ed), *Resolution of*

of a cultural object may suddenly be caught 'between' different adjudicatory procedures if the true owner institutes a suit while there is an arbitration agreement between the purchaser and the seller. The court and the arbitral tribunal adhere to the rules and conventions of decidedly different legal spheres.

A new international court that has compulsory jurisdiction in respect of cultural heritage disputes has been a point of discussion. Although many commentators have supported this idea, a new treaty is highly unlikely to be achieved. The implications of jurisdictional rules and challenges in domestic courts retain their relevance and deserve to be kept in view. Chapter 4 elaborates on these themes. Research on culturally sensitive principles has also moved beyond the question of the appropriate mechanism of dispute resolution.

8.3 Culturally Sensitive Principles to be Considered by Courts, International Tribunals and Arbitral Venues

Approaches that restrain the uncritical application of ordinary business norms to transactions involving cultural objects have been identified. In an effort to offer a path through the dense and complex terrain of an unstructured international legal order, these approaches have been integrated into a set of culturally sensitive principles deriving from common rules of adjudication.[260] The application of these common rules and their dissemination is expected to yield a composite body of law – the *lex culturalis* – that will enhance the protection of cultural heritage. Since it is the intention of a *lex culturalis* to help prevent the uncritical application of ordinary business norms to transactions involving cultural objects, it draws on dispute resolution mechanisms and substantive uniform law. The willingness to keep in view developments at the cross-over of private international law and ADR qualifies as a strength of the *lex culturalis*.

The *lex culturalis* is supposed to be able to reconcile 'all moral, historical, cultural, financial and legal interests'.[261] In this regard, it is important to keep inflated expectations in check. An integrated body of cultural law, predicated on uniform law that obliges purchasers to seek

---

Cultural Property Disputes (The Hague 2004) 291; E Varner, 'Arbitrating Cultural Property Disputes' (2012) 14 Cardozo Journal of Conflict Resolution 477.

260 Chechi (n 26) 202, 317–18.

261 Chechi (n 26) 204.

export documents and ensure a clean chain of title, may be as unattainable as world peace. A global regulatory regime that is premised on a uniform and integrated world law has not been achieved. Not even the simple proposition contained in the erstwhile Draft Convention Providing All Uniform Law on the Acquisition in Good Faith of Corporeal Movables, that '[t]he transferee of stolen movables cannot invoke his good faith', made it to convention-status.[262] An overarching special private international law regime for portable cultural objects remains out of reach also. Modern attempts to avoid the very broad *lex situs* rule and its connecting factor are partly motivated by the perceived need for non-application of 'cumbersome' private international law rules in claims involving art and cultural objects. However, while it is easy to agree with the non-application of the *lex situs* rule, it is unrealistic to envisage a body of principles that can reconcile 'all moral, historical, cultural, financial and legal interests'.[263]

Differences in the civil justice systems of states may have an even greater impact than any choice of law rule on the success of claims based on foreign law. The intersection between private international law, ADR, arbitration and culturally sensitive principles by which disputes deserve to be settled invites dedicated development. This work will be facilitated if the yardsticks for measuring impact and success can be agreed. Arguably, as stated earlier, it would be important to promote impeccable, clear acquisition standards; encourage regulatory frameworks that control the spill-over effects of the market onto source states; and foster a deeper commitment to value-based rationality.

Value-based action is evident also from voluntary return. In respect of indigenous cultural heritage, this may be the only option available[264] by which the profound disempowerment of communities who are alienated from their own culture can be overcome.

9. SCOPE

The scope of this book is narrowly focused on claims for return arising from the unlawful removal and theft of material, portable culture. This delineation follows that of the first report by the Cultural Heritage Law

262 Art 11 of the Draft Convention Providing All Uniform Law on the Acquisition in Good Faith of Corporeal Movables, reprinted in 1975 (1) Uniform Law Review 66.

263 Chechi (n 26) 204.

264 Graber et al. (n 73) 493.

Committee of the International Law Association in 2000, which limits the understanding of cultural heritage to tangible goods. The examples used derive from the accumulated material heritage of humankind: e.g. fine art, archaeological materials, indigenous artwork, sacral objects or human remains, art and cultural objects that were stolen, looted, misappropriated or confiscated during armed conflict or in peace time. Restitution, the obstacles to restitution and refusals to make restitution are highlighted in order to illustrate the relationship between arguments in support of restitution and those of private international law.

The analysis covers claims to title or to transfer of title in respect of art and cultural objects that have incomplete or indeterminable provenance, but ostensibly excludes analysis of crimes such as art fraud, forgery, unauthorised commercial reproduction, false attribution, vandalism and iconoclasm. Also excluded are disputes over donations, matters of insurance and indemnity, restoration or confidentiality clauses, and artist representation, copyright and moral rights, reproduction or access rights.[265]

This study is confined to proprietary issues linked to the unlawful removal, theft and restitution of portable material. The competence of a court other than the one that has jurisdiction over the merits of the claim to grant provisional and protective measures to safeguard the object and the rights of the claimant is regulated in secondary law at EU level. The relevant provision has not played a significant role in the management of cross-border litigation,[266] and therefore this aspect has not been covered. Much more significant is the sharp increase in litigated cases that concern the tension between the right of the lender and the borrower to immunity from seizure in the transnational exchange of art, and the need of the borrowing state, where the art is located, to give effect to its own mandatory civil and criminal law provisions.[267] However, the contractual dimension is not highlighted as a separate category that determines the

---

[265] E.g. JB Prowda, *Visual Arts and the Law* (Lund Humphries 2013).

[266] Art 31 of Council Regulation (EC) No 44/2001 of 22 December 2000 OJ L 12/1 16.1.2001 (the Judgments Regulation).

[267] The implementation of the European Agenda for Culture, the Council Work Plan for Culture 2011–2014 highlighted the importance of intercultural dialogue, and established a priority area on 'Cultural heritage, including mobility of collections' (OJ C 325, 2.12.2010, 1). Meetings held within the framework of the Open Method of Coordination resulted in a Report on Improving the Means of Increasing the Mobility of Collections (OMC Expert Working Group on the Mobility of Collections, *Final Report and Recommendations to the Cultural Affairs Committee on Improving the Means of Increasing the Mobility of Collections* (June 2010) 7–8, available at http://www.lending-for-europe.eu/

applicable law for purposes of this book. The theory and practice of anti-seisure and anti-suit in the context of art loans are outside the scope of this work.

This book is not concerned with voluntary transfers of ownership where the right *in rem* is attributed in a contract.[268] In fact, the law applicable to contractual obligations is relevant only[269] in so far as the choice of law remit of arbitrators is concerned. Their remit necessitates reference to the private international law rules governing contracts in the Rome I Regulation on the law applicable to contractual obligations.[270] The conflict's rules for non-contractual obligations in the Rome II Regulation on the law applicable to non-contractual obligations[271] would be relevant in respect of a claim for damages in respect of a moveable object.[272] Property choice of law rules will determine whether a claimant has sufficient title to sue in conversion, but for EU member states the Rome II Regulation may apply to the wrongdoing itself.[273] These EU choice of law rules, and their effects on the legislation of the Member States and the systems that used to be in place in those Member States,[274] are not directly relevant for ownership and restitution claims, and fall outside the scope of this work.

The outcome of litigation depends on constellations of facts that may relate to the illicit excavation of previously undiscovered archaeological items; newly discovered cultural material regardless of whether it forms part of the cultural heritage of indigenous peoples; the quality of justice delivered during dispute settlement in claims involving Nazi spoliated art;

---

fileadmin/CM/internal/OMC/OMC_Mobility_of_Collections_Report_Rome_7_July10.pdf).

268 As in Italian law for example. See Law no 218 of 1995 *Riforma del sistema italiano di diritto internazionale privato.*

269 Gazzini (n 75) 63.

270 Regulation (EC) No 593/2008 of the European Parliament and of the Council of 17 June 2008 on the law applicable to contractual obligations (Rome I) OJ L 177, 04.07.2008, 6.

271 Regulation (EC) No 864/2007 of the European Parliament and of the Council of 11 July 2007 on the law applicable to non-contractual obligations (Rome II) OJ L 199, 31.07.2007, 40.

272 The jurisdictional ground which the Recast Regulation now provides for is discussed in detail in Chapter 4.

273 Ulph and Smith (n 81) 249–50.

274 E.g. TD Czigler and I Takacs, 'The Law Applicable to Contracts in the European Union' (2012) 20 The California International Law Journal 21.

their connection to the passage of time[275] and the 'Vergangenheits-bewältigung'. This work does not explore the existence of a right to the protection of cultural property, or map the search for independent, supplementary or alternative paths to obtaining restitution in these cases.[276] Its focus is confined to claims to tangible cultural heritage, on the understanding that it is a violation of property rights that can come within the protection of the ECHR if such a community is deprived of an object that formed part of its ancestral, cultural and religious environment and gave tribal life meaning, after the Convention took effect.[277] Western jurisprudence and common law concepts fail to define the right that has been infringed in these circumstances. Considered with reference to the individual right to 'the peaceful enjoyment of [his] possessions' when the individual right of private property and the public interest in the conservation of cultural objects need to be accommodated,[278] cultural objects are to be protected like any other moveable object. The claims brought by indigenous peoples may be in respect of human remains.[279] Human remains represent the only category of indigenous cultural property considered in legislation in the UK and the US.[280] Nonetheless, neither one of these legal systems contains all-encompassing solutions which a UN Declaration may envisage in this category.[281]

---

[275] Veraart and Winkel (n 238) 7.

[276] Gazzini (n 75) 48; Kuprecht and Siehr (n 70) 247–48.

[277] T O'Donnell, 'The Restitution of Holocaust Looted Art and Transitional Justice: The Perfect Storm or the Raft of Medusa?' (2011) 22 Eur J Int Law 49, 69.

[278] Art I of the First Protocol to the European Convention for the Protection of Human Rights and Fundamental Freedoms.

[279] K Kuprecht, 'Human Rights Aspects of Indigenous Cultural Property Repatriation' in K Odendahl and PJ Weber (eds), *Kulturgüterschutz – Kunstrecht – Kulturrecht: Festschrift für Kurt Siehr* (Baden-Baden 2010) 191, 192.

[280] The Human Tissue Act (UK) of 2004 regulates the storage, use and disposal of human bodies, organs and tissue and provides for the transfer of human remains from certain museum collections. The Human Tissue (Scotland) Act of 2006 deals with the donation of human tissue and its removal, retention and use following a post-mortem examination. The NAGPRA addresses repatriation of human remains and ownership of sacred objects and objects of cultural patrimony.

[281] Art 12 of the UN Declaration on the Rights of Indigenous Peoples, Resolution adopted at the 107th plenary meeting of the General Assembly, 13 September 2007, <http://www.un.org/esa/socdev/unpfii/documents/DRIPS_en.pdf>.

Development projects that threaten the built heritage[282] and the position in respect of the underwater heritage[283] have been covered in dedicated strands of the literature, and will not be analysed here.

10. METHOD

This work strives for increased international understanding, realism and putting comparative law and experience to proper use; the very same elements that Rabel identified in order to 'internationalize' private international law.[284] As long as private international law is treated as a series of separate national rules that draw on national sources,[285] it will be unable to support the orderly coexistence of distinct domestic legal systems.[286] It is not called on to 'ordinate' national legal systems, but to co-ordinate them – a more specialised function than merely to 'put into order'. Co-ordination is about the consistency of private international law as a whole. For present purposes, therefore, it is treated as an 'internationalised' discipline or international system that operates by national courts through national law. The method employed here is congruent with the aim of the work: to demonstrate how private international law can be applied as a global lens in order to achieve a worldwide perspective. The method requires keeping track of its interaction with public international law, international arbitration and dispute settlement,

---

282 E.g. T Scovazzi, B Ubertazzi and L Zagato (eds), *Il Patrimonio Culturale Intangibile nelle sue Diverse Dimensioni* (Guiffre 2012); S Theurich, 'Alternative Dispute Resolution in Art and Cultural Heritage – Explored in the Context of the World Intellectual Property Organization's Work' in K Odendahl and PJ Weber (eds), *Kulturgüterschutz – Kunstrecht – Kulturrecht: Festschrift für Kurt Siehr* (Baden-Baden 2010) 569, 573; MF Brown, 'Heritage Trouble: Recent Work on the Protection of the Intangible Cultural Property' (2005) 12 IJCP 40.

283 Respectively Chechi (n 26) and C Forrest and P Fletcher-Tomenius, 'The Protection of the Underwater Cultural Heritage and the Challenge to UNCLOS' (2000) 5 Art Antiquity and Law 125.

284 E Rabel, *The Conflict of Laws: A Comparative Study Vol. 4* (Ann Arbor, U Mich 1958) 97ff.

285 Mills (n 138) 3, 12.

286 C Roodt, 'Reflections on Theory, Doctrine and Method in Choice of Law' (2007) XL CILSA 76, 95, 101.

and cultural heritage law, and to articulate its relationship with ethics, ADR, soft law and EU law.[287]

Realism is a vital ingredient of this study. In the context of art crime, the analysis is informed by quantitative studies that correlate lootings with the appearance of categories of objects on the market.[288] The analysis of the theory and method of private international law seeks to highlight the risks of dogmatic compartmentalisation and methodological fundamentalism that is bent on finding a single workable conflicts method or category or connecting factor. Such conceptual splits can only lead to unpalatable outcomes.

International civil procedure and choice of law methodology have always been heavily reliant upon the trends that are notable across jurisdictions. Not only does information on the content of potentially applicable foreign legal systems assist in conflict situations and classification conflicts, but a functional approach to comparative law helps identify best practice on the basis of a comparative ethos.[289] This is a vital aspect in the pursuit of law that serves the aims of global welfare. Comparative law and private international law share the same origin: global legal pluralism.[290] Comparative law and experience should keep the researcher alive to the convergence of legal traditions on the acquisition of works of art.[291] Nonetheless, harmonised substantive law or centralised institutions are but one way of coping with legal diversity. Even if the great majority of states were to agree on common principles of substantive law, this would not automatically imply mutual recognition of their national regimes of cultural property protection.[292] Cultural heritage law has been left untouched by the progressive unification of private international law rules, which is foremost among the aims of the Hague Conference on private international law.[293] In any event, even if this area of law were harmonised, unification is a project that will never

---

287 DPF Arroyo, 'Private International Law and Comparative Law: A Relationship Challenged by International and Supranational Law' (2009) XI Yearbook of Private International Law 31, 62, 71.

288 Gerstenblith (n 107) 207–9 discusses several empirical studies.

289 E.g. Prott's comparative analysis of the major obstacles to successful restitution claims in national courts. Prott (n 26) 214.

290 Fauvarque-Cosson (n 212) 409.

291 Schönenberger (n 43) 252–53.

292 Siehr (n 179) 25.

293 Established as an inter-governmental organisation in 1955, with traditions dating back to 1893. Statute of the Hague Conference on Private International Law, 15 July 1955, UNTS 220 (123).

be completed.[294] Divergent judicial interpretations will always create new conflicts. The legal diversity that underlies many restitution claims can render justice pluralism inevitable. A decision can be based on strict law, ethics or on the facts of the case.[295] The principle of justice pluralism is revisited again in Chapter 6, where it is argued that acceptance of this principle turns access to justice into the overriding concern. Once access to justice is certain, adjudicators need to identify, and make the most of opportunities to make value-based decisions that limit the scope for criminal activity and maximise the protection of the object.

Fundamental rights norms and communautarisation shape and change both disciplines. Where the ECHR applies, the use of the public policy exception intensifies, necessitating even more extensive recourse to comparative method.[296] It has been argued that communautarisation in the context of the EU renders the differences and antagonisms between the methods, aspirations and respective dynamisms of these two disciplines more visible.[297] However, communautarisation can also be viewed as a factor that prompts private international law to make an outward turn. This aspect is revisited in Chapter 3.

11. OUTLINE

Chapter 1 introduces the role private international law can play in the protection of art and cultural objects. Among other things, these objects can be conceived of as part of national identity; as moveable artefacts susceptible to economic evaluation; as expressions of human creativity that possess intrinsic value; as objects of human rights in peacetime;[298] or as objects that claim special protection in the international law of armed conflict.[299] The nature, definition and status of these objects pose challenges in disputes that arise from international art sales. Post-theft,

---

294 Fauvarque-Cosson (n 212) 414.

295 Mills (n 138) 6.

296 Fauvarque-Cosson (n 212) 409–10.

297 J Kropholler, 'Die Vergleichende Methode und das Internationale Privatrecht' (1978) 77 Zeitschrift für Vergleichende Rechtswissenschaft 1; M Reimann, 'Comparative Law and Private International Law' in M Reimann/R Zimmermann (eds), *The Oxford Handbook of Comparative Law* (Oxford 2006) 1363, 1366; B Grossfeld, *The Strength and Weakness of Comparative Law* (Oxford 1990) 19.

298 FN Brodie, J Doole and P Watson, *Stealing History: The Illicit Trade in Cultural Material* (MacDonald Institute for Archaeological Research 2000) 11.

299 F Francioni, 'The Human Dimension of International Cultural Heritage Law: An Introduction' (2011) 22 EJIL 9, 9–10.

post-excavation or post-confiscation transactions on the art market frequently cross borders. Private international law can constrain the commercial imperative when the trade falls short of acquisition and collection standards. It can also offer support to cultural heritage law in restitution claims if the synergies that can arise between trafficking and the substance of the law applied in the jurisdictions that are used for laundering purposes can be anticipated. Commercial interaction on the art market, and the way in which traffickers and dealers position themselves in relation to the law, invite private international law to help identify appropriate forms of justice. The broader context within which private international law operates is informed by ethics and by dispute resolution processes. The scope and the method used in the book reflect these broad perspectives.

The pressure of global legal diversity demands solutions that are attuned to the international dimension of art and heritage claims that are based on ownership or possession of a thing. Chapter 2 considers the grounds, limits and international dimension of restitution. The categories of restitution claims are discussed and circumstances in which restitution would be inappropriate indicated. The perplexing problems introduced by private international law in claims for restitution are highlighted, together with the opportunities and the potential this discipline presents to facilitate restitution and dispute settlement by fulfilling its specialised co-ordination function.

Chapter 3 explores the turn(s) which private international law must make for its structure and method to respond appropriately to developments in cultural heritage law. Complex choices available in international cases must be simplified and drawn together with the help of a global lens that brings into better view customary international law, international conventions states enter into to prevent the transfer of stolen cultural objects, soft law, EU law and the ECHR.

That systems of civil justice differ is an important aspect of legal diversity and the obstacles it presents in claims for restitution brought by states, private actors, museums or groups. Jurisdictional rules and challenges control the venue in which a case proceeds. Litigation about where to litigate a claim involving a work of art or a cultural object carries a risk that the merits of the case may not be ventilated. Chapter 4 considers jurisdictional rules relied upon under the UNIDROIT Convention, in the EU, and in US courts. One of the challenges is to keep the consistency of private international law in mind. The chapter highlights the implications of forum-shopping and of the need for consistency of decision across international cases. The defendant may prefer artificial procedural arguments that steer the court away from value-based decision-making. Parties have scope to choose where to take their dispute, and the defendant may indicate that another court is more appropriate to exercise jurisdiction. The question of arbitration as a dispute resolution mechanism in cultural property disputes is investigated, and mechanisms that prevent the re-litigation of cases and wasting of judicial resources are considered. The main argument is that these mechanisms need to be used in ways that foster access to justice in claims for restitution.

Chapter 5 deals with the potential to use the structure and method of private international law to deter title laundering. Consigners of stolen or smuggled works of art and cultural objects are tempted to hide behind the good-faith purchase laws of certain European countries such as Italy and France and to argue that title was validly transferred. It is widely conceded that cultural objects deserve special treatment, and yet in practice general commercial law rules are given extended application and little or no due diligence is required. Courts have used the property transaction as a basis for classification when art was retained by a third party purchaser after having crossed jurisdictional lines post-theft. The effect of the passage of time on the claim will be referred to the same law if classified as a matter of substantive law. Choice of law method can be used to mark the fact of theft or the context of smuggling instead of fortifying the interests of the market and neglecting those of the cultural community in question. The structure and method of private international law enables jurisdictions to block transfer of defective title, to compensate for the oversimplification of the problems that arise in art transactions on account of the *lex situs* rule, and to ease tensions between private law and criminal law in the art markets in New York and London. Legal developments in the UK and specifically New York acknowledge the inherent taint or defect in a title to property which attaches to stolen goods until they are returned to the original owner. These developments demonstrate how private international law can support the objective of restitution embodied in pertinent international instruments.

Chapter 6 considers claims for restitution and the procedure-based argument for non-restitution of dispossessed Nazi spoliated art. Claimants may engage in jurisdictional trade when immunity legislation does not prevent this. The success of mediated claims to Nazi spoliated art in a number of European jurisdictions contrasts sharply with the low recovery rate through litigation in the US. When it comes to determining the venue for dispute resolution of Nazi-looted art cases, process and substance tend to interlink remarkably closely. Domestic and applicable law arguments provide scope for non-restitution in the context of the definition of a 'forced sale' and the *lex situs* rule. Procedural advantages in court may preclude a hearing on the substantive merits of the case. While courts may be a popular choice for this reason, this preference may also rule out value-based decisions that can take proper account of ethical considerations. Mediation committees in France, Germany, the Netherlands and the UK give advice that is value-based. Except for the Spoliation Advisory Panel in the UK, these committees do not draw a distinction between recommendations affecting public or private ownership. National developments in respect of restitution do not occur in isolation. The principle of international law that spoils of war can be claimed back by their country of origin if identified and found has long existed. Various peace treaties concluded from the seventeenth century onwards embody the idea of return or compensation.[300] This principle continues to affect global restitution practices, which indicate differences not only in respect of the treatment accorded to objects won in economic or colonial conquests and objects looted in armed conflicts, but also in respect just of the last-mentioned category. Practice has also been affected by policy changes and renewed interest in restitution to victims of the Holocaust since 1989. The chapter considers the reasons for these policy changes in greater detail.

Chapter 7 explores the application of foreign public law in sovereign claims that are accessory to private law in US, UK and German law. Ultimately, it is vital to cultivate international understanding and to foster mutual assistance in situations where foreign prevention and control measures and criminal sanctions cannot be applied directly to protect significant items of cultural heritage. International policy ought to be based on the need for mutual assistance when it comes to safeguarding against physical damage, dismemberment and decontextualisation, as much as against depriving states of the opportunity to do so. Civil forfeiture could be based on a violation of a criminal statute[301] and could provide a basis for the enforcement of accessory claims to trafficked cultural objects that are based on foreign public law.[302] A claim may also be based on private law.[303] Account may be taken of foreign public law by means of the recognition of the category of property that applies in the state in which the theft occurred and by whose law restitution would

---

300 Gazzini (n 75) 5.

301 *United States v Hollinshead*, 495 F2d 1154 (9th Circuit 1974); *US v McClain*, 545 F2d 658 (1978), *US v McClain*, 593 F2d 658 (1979), *cert denied*, 444 US 918 (1979) 671.

302 Per Staughton J in *Attorney-General of New Zealand v Ortiz* [1982] 3 All ER 432 at 451.

303 Jakubowski (n 76) 139.

be justified, or by way of novel ways of applying domestic law. Regardless of the legal basis of the claim, judicial consideration of the legal nature of state claims for the return of illicitly trafficked cultural objects is called for. The recognition by domestic courts of a public law category is a controversial issue in private international law.[304] Courts readily enforce the contract and delict claims brought by private parties, but they may be more hesitant to enforce foreign public law.[305] Value-based decisions depend on recognizing the capacity of private international law to relax the strict public policy objection to such a claim.

[304] Jakubowski (n 76) 140; AF Lowenfeld, 'Public Law and the International Arena: Conflict of Laws, International Law, and Some Suggestions for their Interaction' II (163) *Recueil des Cours* (Sijthoff & Noordhoff 1980) 311.

[305] Per Lord Denning MR in *Attorney-General of New Zealand v Ortiz* [1982] 3 All ER 456j–457.

2. Restitution: Complexities and opportunities introduced by private international law

1. INTRODUCING RESTITUTION CLAIMS[1]

Individuals, institutions, states and government authorities, communities, minorities and groups may claim or oppose restitution of an object which they would assert belongs to cultural heritage. The general public may also get involved because of their interest in museum displays.[2] On the supposition that different role occupants agree that an object constitutes part of cultural heritage, they may differ about whose cultural heritage it is. Their interests may overlap.

States may institute action on the basis of statutory measures designed to safeguard public and private rights in respect of cultural objects. It has to be determined which actors have the capacity to initiate the restitution claim, and to whom items in public collections may be returned.[3] Collectors and museums may claim an individual item based on prior ownership or may sue in the tort of conversion if the object can be located; the claim may be for the alleged wrongful retention of the object in question or it may follow a wrong that caused damage or destruction. A distinction between claims at law or in equity may apply. Special laws may be necessary to override the bar of inalienability that had been set up by law.[4]

---

1 This chapter develops the private international law aspects of restitution.

2 M Cornu and M Renold, 'New Developments in the Restitution of Cultural Property: Alternative Means of Dispute Resolution' (2010) 17 IJCP 1, 4.

3 Cornu and Renold (n 2) 8–10 re public domain legislation.

4 Holocaust (Return of Cultural Property) Act 2009; S 47 of The Human Tissue Act (UK) of 2004. The capacity to enter into long-term loans is not subject to the same limitation. The Board of Trustees of the British Museum does not require authorisation to return even the Parthenon Marbles on a long-term loan. Cornu and Renold (n 2) 8.

Policy or morals may offer parties more than solutions that are based on law.[5] While the law is not devoid of moral force, a claimant may be more willing to accept a museum offer for less than the fair market value of the work, for instance, if the museum were to undertake to set out the history of the piece in full including the circumstances in which the ancestor of the claimant acquired it and the circumstances of its confiscation by the Nazis. Ordinary criminal law is unsuitable in the context of government confiscations before and during World War II, and the same holds true for objects sold under duress.

This chapter starts by introducing the grounds for restitution (2. below). The categories in respect of which restitution claims may be brought that may be affected by private international law argument, are then set out (3. below). Repatriation claims deserve to be treated separately (4. below). The circumstances in which restitution would be inappropriate, are indicated (5. below). Private international law argument may fail to identify, name or remove obstacles to restitution (discussed under 6. below). These problems can be prevented. They should not be allowed to overshadow the potential of private international law to control impediments to states' restitution obligations and to rank norms where one norm interferes with the intended functioning of another norm (discussed under section 7 below).

2. LEGAL AND MORAL GROUNDS FOR RESTITUTION

Restitution may be made on the basis of various peace treaties that embody the idea of return or compensation;[6] customary international law;[7] special domestic legislation;[8] or it may be based on pertinent administrative decisions that remove an object from the public domain and result in a change of classification.[9] Law can provide the framework

---

[5] DPF Arroyo, 'Private International Law and Comparative Law: A Relationship Challenged by International and Supranational Law' (2009) XI Yearbook of Private International Law 31, 41.

[6] IF Gazzini, *Cultural Property Disputes: The Role of Arbitration in Resolving Non-Contractual Disputes* (Transnational Publishers Inc. 2004) 5.

[7] *Factory at Chorzow (Ger v Pol)* 1928 PCIJ, Series A, No 9 (July 26), 21.

[8] Arts 90 and 92 of the Belgian Code of Private International Law, OJ 27 July 2004 support re-vindication.

[9] Formal legal procedures may be needed to enforce an administrative decision in some instances.

for negotiation and dispute settlement in many cases. Nonetheless, it does not always make sense to confine restitution to instances where there is a mandatory legal obligation to make restitution. By the same token, while the distinction between voluntary restitution and a legal obligation may ordinarily carry weight,[10] it may be less important when the historic background and special circumstances of a case warrant non-legal interests to be taken into account by virtue of new legislation. The Cultural Property Originating from Occupied Territory Act of 2007 enabled the Netherlands to return items looted from Cyprus by Aydin Dikman in 2010, after Dutch courts had ruled against return at first. This Act prohibits the import and ownership of cultural property from a territory that was occupied in an armed conflict after 1959.

Obstacles to restitution that inhere in the law itself may justify non-restitution on the basis of a legal standard. When this is the case, a solution based on legal grounds would be less than ideal. A wrong may have been purged by time, and yet the cultural link between the state and a trafficked object might be indisputable and exclusive. A prior settlement can become amenable to review.[11] An individual museum or a private owner may decide in favour of voluntary return of objects that were subject to the systematic plunder perpetrated by agents of the Third Reich in Nazi-occupied territories.[12] Or, at the time, removal may have been lawful and based on the necessary consent, and yet historic views of justice and policy may undergo change and give scope to new facts that call for reopening cases that were settled in the post-war period.[13]

From a strictly legal point of view, restitution implies return of a cultural object to the legal owner claiming it, in accordance with what the

---

[10] JM Carruthers, *The Transfer of Property in the Conflict of Laws* (OUP 2005) § 5.12.

[11] As with the agreement concluded between France and Nigeria in 2002 concerning return by France of the Nok statues subject to a long-term loan. For more, see Cornu and Renold (n 2) 14.

[12] WW Kowalski, 'General Observations: Claims for Works of Art and Their Legal Nature' in International Bureau of the Permanent Court of Arbitration (ed), *Resolution of Cultural Property Disputes* (2004) 31; AM Ritchie, 'Victorious Youth in Peril: Analyzing Arguments Used in Cultural Property Disputes to Resolve the Case of the Getty Bronze' (2009) 9 Pepperdine Dispute Resolution Law Journal 325, 334.

[13] As the Dutch Advisory Committee on the Assessment of Restitution (Restitution Committee) interpreted the term 'novum' when it commenced its work in 2001. W Veraart and L Winkel, 'An Introduction to Dilemmas of Post-War Restitution in Europe' in W Veraart and L Winkel (eds), *The Post-war Restitution of Property Rights in Europe* (Rvp Press 2011) 5.

law prescribes. Restitutions of Nazi spoliated art that were based on strict law were limited however.[14] The search for a 'fair and just solution' is supported in several inter-governmental agreements and instruments of 'soft law'. 'Soft law' can either create special commissions or may designate ADR as preferable to litigation.[15] Adjudicators must decide whether the violation lodges in the taking itself or whether the taking of the object can be compensated in another way.[16] This question has implications for deciding whether physical restitution is the only way in which the harm perpetrated by the Nazis against European Jews can be undone.[17] Moral and policy factors can shape restitution rulings in this category.

Law and basic moral standards shape and inform each other. On its own, moral argument tends to lack legal force, and yet conventional property law struggles to do justice to the physical and metaphysical dimensions of cultural objects. While specious moral claims will only contribute to inefficiency in the process by which property is allocated, a single version of law-based truth can stifle the debate.[18] Rather than providing a corrective for the morality of society, the law ought to guard and keep open the path to justice. Satisfactory outcomes of disputes over ownership may depend on a 'higher law', located in fact-finding that establishes provenance.[19] An international commission of inquiry comprised of independent experts with professional credentials and moral authority may make a finding that has greater impact than a court ruling.

---

[14] See 3.3 below and Chapter 6.

[15] B Schönenberger, *The Restitution of Cultural Assets* (Eleven International Publishing 2009) 228; CC Coggins, 'A Licit International Traffic in Ancient Art: Let There Be Light' (1995) 4 IJCP 61, 76.

[16] HJ Steiner and DF Vagts, *Transnational Legal Problems: Materials and Text* (The Foundation Press Inc. 1986) 725.

[17] MJ Bazyler, 'Nuremberg in America: Litigating the Holocaust in United States Courts' (2000) 34 University of Richmond Law Review 1, 165; N Murphy, 'Splitting Images: Shared-Value Settlements in Nazi-Era Art Restitution Claims' (2009) 3 Florida Entertainment Law Review 1 (*Social Science Research Network*, 25 February 2010) <http://ssrn.com/abstract=1559373> accessed 24 February 2014.

[18] Schönenberger (n 15) 229.

[19] MJ Harris, 'Who Owns the Pot of Gold at the End of the Rainbow? A Review of the Impact of Cultural Property on Finders and Salvage Laws' (1997) 14 Arizona Journal of International and Comparative Law 224, 238.

The establishment of the facts is an indispensable component of peace-building,[20] whereas the significance of the property law that determines ownership or title recedes. An inquiry does not impinge on sovereign prerogatives and is less intrusive than a ruling issued by an international court.[21] The outcome of the inquiry could also feed into other mechanisms of dispute settlement. It could generate pressure to respect minimum standards of protection of cultural heritage.

3. CATEGORIES OF RESTITUTION CLAIMS THAT MAY FEATURE PRIVATE INTERNATIONAL LAW ARGUMENT

3.1 Stolen Art

Break-ins into museums and art heists tend to be well published, while the more mundane thefts of works by lesser known artists taken during ordinary household thefts are seldom considered newsworthy. In the stolen art category are the legendary thefts from the Isabella Stewart Gardner Museum in Boston in March 1990, when works by Vermeer, Rembrandt and Manet were stolen along with a finial and an ancient bronze beaker. Like 'Woman with a Fan' by Modigliani, which was stolen from the Musée d'Art Moderne de la Ville de Paris in May 2010, these works have not been recovered.[22] In 2002, it was discovered that 'Odalisque in Red Trousers' by Matisse, owned and displayed by the Caracas Museum of Contemporary Art, had been stolen and replaced with a copy that managed to pass as the delicate original for a significant period of time. When the thieves attempted to sell the original to undercover agents in Miami, it was recovered. Both were convicted on a charge of conspiracy to transport and sell stolen property; one of the thieves was also convicted on charges of interstate transportation of stolen property and possession of stolen property. Police returned the painting to

---

[20] A Chechi, 'Some Reflections on International Adjudication of Cultural Heritage-Related Cases' (2013) 10 TDM Special Issue 1, 9.

[21] Chechi (n 20) 8.

[22] KQ Seelye and T Mashberg, 'A New Effort in Boston to Catch 1990 Art Thieves' *New York Times* (18 March 2013).

the museum in 2014.[23] Private international law did not assume relevance in this instance, but it could have been relevant if the painting were sold post-theft. A court may then be called on to decide whether to establish and exercise jurisdiction in a civil claim for the restitution of the work; and whether title to the allegedly stolen property was, or could have been, validly transferred to a purchaser in good faith (see Chapter 5).

3.2 Stolen and Illegally Excavated/Exported Artefacts

A large number of unprovenanced pieces are being traded post-excavation and exported without the permission of the source state. If another jurisdiction were to recognise the property right established by the source state, restitution is possible; if not, the only viable claim may be for the violation of export law. Private international law can assume relevance where demand-side control is an issue, as Chapter 1 indicates. The agreement that was reached by Italy and the Metropolitan Museum of Art in 2006, when the Medici Conspiracy became public,[24] serves as a good example of restitution of objects in this category. However, this particular agreement stipulated that disputes arising thereunder are to be decided by an arbitral tribunal on the basis of the rules of Arbitration and Conciliation of the International Chamber of Commerce. Consequently, the first relevant question for private international law concerning jurisdiction was avoided in this instance. In many other cases in which title laundering occurs post excavation or by means of exportation, the relevant questions remain: where should the source state bring proceedings?; will the source state succeed with a restitution claim?

3.3 Cases Involving Nazi Spoliated Art

Cases involving seisure before, during and after World War II can be grouped into several distinct categories.[25] These may include degenerate

---

[23] AFP, 'Missing Matisse Thieves, a Cuban American Man and a Mexican Woman, plead guilty in Miami' <http://artdaily.com/news/58676/Missing-Matisse-thieves–a-Cuban-American-man-and-a-Mexican-woman–plead-guilty-in-Miami> accessed 25 July 2014.

[24] R Contel, G Soldan and A Chechi, 'Case Euphronios Krater and Other Archaeological Objects – Italy and Metropolitan Museum of Art' (*Art-Law Centre, University of Geneva,* June 2012) <https://plone.unige.ch/art-adr/cases-affaires/euphronios-krater-and-other-archaeological-objects-2013-italy-and-metropolitan-museum-of-art/case-note-2013-euphronios-krater-and-other-archaeological-objects/view> accessed 24 February 2014.

[25] Schönenberger (n 15) 5; 202–3.

art (i.e. modern and abstract work which Hitler and his regime believed to be a corrupt influence on the German people or an insult to German sentiment because natural form or artistic skill was deemed absent); looted or spoliated art (including works looted from unknown owners); and plundered or trophy art. In any of these categories, works stolen from Jewish families may have been returned but subsequently re-gifted or purchased by the state. Claims for restitution may be based on confiscation, forced sales and sales at an undervalue, all of which are associated with the involuntary losses that were incurred in exchange for export permits, exit visas, means of subsistence, and the taxes imposed for inciting violence during *Kristallnacht*.

Considered as a single broad category, Nazi spoliated art has little in common with simple art theft.[26] This category is also distinct from illicit excavation and export. Nonetheless, some legal questions are familiar, such as whether title to the allegedly stolen property was, or could have been, validly transferred to a purchaser in good faith.[27] Whether blanket restitution is in order cannot be settled with reference to ordinary commercial or criminal law rules. It is a question that deserves full investigation in the light of public international law or the public policy exception in private international law. The relationship between private international law and international expropriation law, and the relevance, in a restitution claim, of whether the property of a citizen or that of an alien national was confiscated, are discussed in greater detail under 6.4 below.

Post-expropriation sales may have occurred in the occupied territories or in non-occupied territories, giving scope for choice of law argument. Sales in non-occupied territories after families had escaped from Germany raise related questions. A decision may also be required as to whether the fair market value or the compensatory payment that had already been made must be taken into account once again when physical restitution is demanded in a state court.[28] The law–equity distinction has not been imported into private international law, and consequently the

---

[26] E.g. KA Falconer, 'When Honour Will Not Suffice' (2000) 21 University of Pennsylvania Journal of International Economic Law 383, 423.

[27] E.g. *Solomon R Guggenheim Foundation v Lubell* 77 NY2d 311 317–18 (1991).

[28] K Lubina and H Schneider, 'Pringsheim, Provenance and Principles: A Case Study on the Restitution of Nazi Looted Art and Compensatory Payments' in K Odendahl and PJ Weber (eds), *Kulturgüterschutz – Kunstrecht – Kulturrecht: Festschrift für Kurt Siehr* (Baden-Baden 2010) 161ff; JA Kreder, 'Reconciling Individual and Group Justice with the Need for Repose in Nazi-Looted Art

equitable basis for claims to restitution in a particular domestic legal system is relevant primarily in domestic litigation. Nonetheless, it is conceivable that jurisdiction may be established in a court that requires parties to act in accordance with its equitable principles, or that the demand for restitution in view of past injustice may become so strong that even statutory limitations are suspended or court judgments reviewed.[29] After all, a sense of unlawfulness or moral discontent may continue to linger despite the good faith defence. This theme is explored in more depth in Chapter 6.

4. WHEN RESTITUTION IS CONTENTIOUS, INAPPROPRIATE OR UNLIKELY TO SUCCEED

When the desire to control cultural property is absent, or where intangible heritage is in issue, restitution is inappropriate. People from the Rai Coast in Papua New Guinea forgo claims, for instance, because they regard their cultural material as being more productive when in circulation.[30] A modern nation in the same geographical space where an ancient civilisation used to be may have the desire to control cultural objects that were buried by an ancient civilisation, but restitution is no less contentious in these circumstances. For instance, there is no universal agreement that Greeks should be permitted to lay claim to Athenian, Byzantine or Ottoman artefacts. The claim of the Greek government to the Parthenon Marbles is pending in the 1978 UNESCO Intergovernmental Committee for Promoting the Return of Cultural Property to Its Countries of Origin as *Greece v British Museum*, without the likelihood of it being settled.[31] The Cultural Heritage Law Committee of the International Law Association proposed a Principle of Repose at the Berlin Conference in 2004.[32] Cultural material that has reposed in the territory of a state for at least 250 years is proposed to be exempt from return to its place of

---

Disputes: Creation of an International Tribunal' (2007) 73 Brooklyn Law Review 155, 206.

29 Veraart and Winkel (n 13) 2.

30 MF Brown, 'Heritage Trouble: Recent Work on the Protection of the Intangible Cultural Property' (2005) 12 IJCP 40, 47.

31 In general, see JH Merryman, 'Thinking about the Elgin Marbles' [1985] Michigan Law Review 1881, 1915–1921; JH Merryman, *Thinking about the Elgin Marbles* (2d edn Kluwer 2009); M Papa-Sokal, 'Beyond the Nationalist-Internationalist Polarisation in the Protection of the Archaeological Heritage' (2009) 14 Art Antiquity and Law 237.

32 <http://www.ila-hq.org/> accessed 25 February 2014.

origin. The state where cultural material is located when the claim is made is to consider, in good faith, any requests from the requesting state for loan of such cultural material, unless the size or condition of the object or its extraordinary significance to the state where the object is presently located, precludes a loan.

It is conceivable that the history of a particular piece could be so convoluted as to make it impossible to establish the facts and the find spot. When this is the case, the item could be unfit to be restituted. Ever since the 1960s Italy has tried to recover the Atleta di Fano (Greek 'Bronze Statue of a Victorious Youth').[33] The statue is believed to have been looted when the Romans conquered Greece.[34] The statue was lost in the Adriatic Sea in antiquity when the ship that was carrying it to the Roman Empire sank. It was found by chance; smuggled into an Italian seaside village; hidden in a bathtub and a field; and smuggled into and hidden in Brazil. It surfaced in London; was later conserved in Germany; and was purchased as soon as J. Paul Getty died, in Boston, by the Getty Museum.[35] The Getty has justified non-return on different grounds, including the time that it took to lodge the claim; the uncertainty over whether the find spot of the object was in international waters or not; and the care the object receives at the hand of the Getty.[36] The fishermen who found the Atleta neither reported the find, nor did they hand it over to the authorities.[37] Because the statue originated in ancient Greece, the claim faces difficulty: there was no proof that the find spot was within the territorial boundary of Italy (that the fishing boat was Italian does not bear much weight), and the object had but a brief and concealed stay in Italy.[38]

---

33 Attributed to Lyssippus, personal sculptor of Alexander the Great (fourth c. BCE). Cf Getty catalogue at <http://www.getty.edu/art/gettyguide/artObject Details?artobj=8912> accessed 7 March 2014.

34 The case started in the Tribunal of Sciacca, 9 January 1963, Foro Italiano, 1963, I, 1317, but several rulings have since followed, including Third Criminal Chamber of the Supreme Court, 3 May 2012.

35 Tribunal of Pesaro, Order of 10 February 2010, No 2042/07 RGNR, 8.

36 A Lanciotti, 'The Dilemma of the Right to Ownership of Underwater Cultural Heritage: The Case of the "Getty Bronze"' in S Borelli and F Lenzerini (eds), *Cultural Heritage, Cultural Rights, Cultural Diversity: New Developments in International Law* (Nijhoff Publishers 2012) 301, 302.

37 Tribunal of Pesaro, Order of 12 June 2009, No 2042/07 RGNR, 10, 14.

38 A Chechi, R Contel and MA Renold, 'Case Victorious Youth – Italy v. J. Paul Getty Museum' Platform ArThemis <http://unige.ch/art-adr> Art-Law Centre, University of Geneva, October 2011.

From whom the object is taken (be it a nation, a sub-group or an individual) can assume great importance. The existence of legal personality and the requirements of standing constitute preliminary issues that can make or break an international case. Communal property or collective ownership of a community is often not legally recognised. Where the claim is brought by a community, the request for return has to be made through the state. Appropriation and transfer by a caretaker or member of that community may breach tribal or customary law, but if that custom is not protected in law or officially recognised by the nation concerned, the appropriation may not be considered unlawful and the sale may be taken to have been concluded in good faith. Oral evidence may be the only way in which ownership can be proved in court, but is not permissible in every court. The uncertainties that plague the need to establish a property right and whether others will recognise it add significantly to the legal uncertainty that already surrounds the significance of art and cultural objects. These difficulties are compounded further when the status of art and cultural objects differs at the level of domestic (national or subnational) and international law.[39]

Restitution claims may reach an international impasse if cultural objects were taken during wartime. Whereas the Allies did not formulate a coherent policy on the restitution of cultural assets from the start of World War II,[40] the Soviet government had devised concrete restitution plans in 1943. Lists of objects that would be equivalent to those lost in museums in Germany and other states, including Austria, Italy and Finland, were drawn up.[41] Today, Russian and German opinion in respect of restitution of art taken from Germany diverges sharply.[42] Germany's claims are brought on the basis of international laws of war and a bilateral treaty on co-operation,[43] while Russia claims compensatory

---

[39] Cornu and Renold (n 2) 10; K Last, 'Cultural Pluralism and the Return of Cultural Heritage' in S Tierney (ed), *Accommodating Cultural Diversity* (Ashgate 2007) 123, 132; Schönenberger (n 15) 45.

[40] AB Sargent, 'New Jurisdictional Tools for Displaced Cultural Property in Russia' [2010] Yearbook of Cultural Property Law 167, 170. George Stout had devised a plan of wartime conservation in a pamphlet in 1942. He worked at the Department of Conservation and Technical Research, Fogg Art Museum, at the time, and the plan was not official policy.

[41] Sargent (n 40) 170.

[42] 'Merkl and Putin View Exhibition of Disputed Art' (*BBC News Europe*, 22 June 2013) <http://www.bbc.co.uk/news/world-europe-23001274> accessed 24 February 2014.

[43] Treaty on Good-Neighbourliness, Partnership and Cooperation between the FRG and USSR, 9 November 1990, 30 ILM 504.

restitution (restitution-in-kind) and the right to retain cultural property as war reparations based on customary international law.[44] There is also federal legislation[45] that is widely considered to be contrary to international law.[46]

Repatriation claims deserve to be distinguished from claims for restitution in the context of global restitution practices. The section that follows indicates why.

5. REPATRIATION CLAIMS

Repatriation efforts by indigenous peoples are frequently part of a broader movement of decolonisation, addressing past injustices in order to ensure the continuity, revival and survival of their cultural identity.[47] Independence has also stimulated claims for the repatriation of items of cultural significance to independent states.[48] Claims for repatriation[49] of human remains are distinguishable from cases concerning cultural heritage because the issues intermingle with indigenous peoples' rights and human rights, including the right to self-determination.[50] Disputes tend to be settled upon identification of the ethnic group most closely affiliated to the dead person, or of his or her 'homeland'.[51] Ethnic identity, predicated on cultural affiliation, supplies the link between the community and the object.

---

44 Sargent (n 40) 172–3.

45 Federal Law, 15 April 1998, no 64-FZ, Russian Federation Collection of Legislation, 1998, No 16, Item 1879.

46 Sargent (n 40) 173.

47 C Bell and RK Paterson, 'Introduction' in C Bell and RK Paterson (eds), *Protection of First National Cultural Heritage: Laws, Policy, and Reform* (UBC Press 2009) 3.

48 Last (n 39) 134.

49 On the meaning of the term 'repatriation', see Last (n 39) 128.

50 C Forrest, *International Law and the Protection of Cultural Heritage* (Routledge 2010) 165; JAR Nafziger, 'The Protection and Repatriation of Indigenous Cultural Heritage in the United States' in C Bell and RK Paterson (eds), *Protection of First Nations Cultural Heritage: Laws, Policy, and Reform* (UBC Press 2009) 110, 138–39.

51 *Bonnichsen v US*, 969 F Supp 614 (D Or 1997); 969 F Supp 628 (D Or 1997); 217 F Supp 2d 1116 (D Or 2002); affirmed and remanded by 367 F3d 864 (9th Circuit 2004) (connection between Holocene human skeleton and modern Native American tribe difficult to prove).

These claims tend to be moral rather than legal. Legal rights feature during the negotiation process to set the parameters of any agreements reached or conditions for return.[52]

Regulations adopted under the Native American Graves Protection and Repatriation Act of 1990 (NAGPRA) address repatriation of human remains and ownership of sacred objects and objects of cultural patrimony owned by the culturally affiliated tribe. The disposition of Native American items discovered or excavated, either inadvertently or intentionally, on federal lands after 16 November 1990 differs from the rules in respect of repatriation of Native American objects in possession of federal agencies and museums.[53] NAGPRA provides notification and inventory procedures pursuant to which Indian human remains and funerary objects unearthed on federal lands must be repatriated to the appropriate Indian Tribe if cultural affiliation is shown or can be proved. In other words, NAGPRA obliges US federal agencies and federally funded museums to make repatriations unless the human remains are found outside of federal and tribal lands, or cultural affiliation remains unproven.[54] Repatriation may be delayed if a specific scientific study remains to be completed or if there are multiple requests and the museum or federal agency cannot determine the most appropriate claimant. Repatriation regulations do not contain a limiting date.[55] Prior to NAGPRA, American Indian tribes were not always required to prove that the burial remains were those of their ancestors.[56]

Returns have gathered pace since 1989.[57] Several voluntary returns have been made to communities and to heirs. Preserved tattooed heads of Maori people have been returned to Te Papa Tongarewa Museum in New Zealand.[58] When similar decisions were successfully challenged in

---

[52] Last (n 39) 134–35.

[53] 43 CFR §§ 10.3(a) & 10.4(a) (1995); 43 CFR §§ 10.8-10.10 (1995) respectively.

[54] 25 USC 3005.

[55] National Museum of the American Indian Act of 1989 (Pub.L. 101-185) and NAGPRA.

[56] *Charrier v Bell*, 498 So 2d 753 (1986).

[57] 1989 Vermillion Accord on Human Remains, an international agreement on the treatment of human remains adopted by the World Archaeological Congress. <http://www.worldarchaeologicalcongress.org/site/about_ethi.php#code2> accessed 25 February 2014.

[58] Scottish museums have returned more than twenty heads. The University of Aberdeen returned nine heads in January 2007. NGW Curtis, 'Thinking about the Right Home: Repatriation and Marischal Museum, University of Aberdeen'

French courts,[59] the French Parliament passed legislation to confirm that Maori heads no longer form part of French museums' collections, in order to facilitate their return.[60] The mortal remains of persons of Khoikhoi descent have been the subject of negotiations for repatriation to South Africa on different occasions. A French museum returned the remains of Sara Baartman after a poem inspired a single article French law.[61] An administrative decision that reversed the status of inalienability of the human remains[62] could have facilitated the return, but it was not forthcoming at the time. The repatriation of her remains, and burial at a gravesite in the Eastern Cape near the place of her birth, connects with the prevailing ideology of reconciliation and nation building of the South African government, to counterbalance the misdeeds that occurred during the colonial past.

An Austrian museum repatriated the remains of Klaas and Trooi Pienaar in 2012, after having de-accessioned and changed their classification from cultural artefacts to human remains. Their remains were smuggled out of South Africa into Austria by an Austrian anthropologist in 1909.[63] South Africa's liberation heritage encompasses the human remains of Khoi who had been the subject of scientific study or exhibition during the colonial era and of Khoi leaders who 'had died in undignified circumstances in foreign lands'.[64]

Arguably, the restitution of Nazi spoliated art shares common ground with the repatriation of human remains in respect of the ethical, emotive

---

in M Gabriel and J Dahl (eds), *UTIMUT – Past Heritage Future Partnerships: Discussions on Repatriation in the 21st Century* (IWGIA/NKA 2008) 44.

59 Rouen Municipal Council decision, session of 19 October 2007, was anulled by the Administrative Tribunal of Rouen (judgment of 27 December 2007). The Administrative Court of Appeal in Douai upheld this decision (judgment of 24 July 2008).

60 Art 1, *Loi No 2010-501 du 18 mai 2010 visant à autoriser la restitution par la France des têtes maories à la Nouvelle-Zélande et relative à la gestion des collections* JO No 114, 19 May 2010.

61 France acceded to President Mandela's request for the return of the mortal remains of Sara (Saartjie) Baartman to South Africa on 6 March 2002 by virtue of *Loi No 2002–323 du 6 mars 2002 relative à la restitution par la France de la dépouille mortelle de Saartjie Baartman à l'Afrique du Sud.*

62 Cornu and Renold (n 2) 9, 11.

63 C Rassool, 'Human Remains, the Disciplines of the Dead and the South African Memorial Complex' <http://sitemaker.umich.edu/politics.of.heritage/files/rassool_human_remains.doc> 17–18 accessed 24 February 2014.

64 C Goko, 'Khoi Chief's Bones Back in SA Next Year' (*Business Day*, 14 May 2013) <http://www.bdlive.co.za/national/2013/05/14/khoi-chiefs-bones-back-in-sa-next-year> accessed 24 February 2014.

dimension of the repatriation claim and the opportunity which return offers to 'remember' and to educate the public about human dignity.[65]

Objects that were removed from human remains can be difficult to classify. The Glasgow City Council repatriated a Lakota (Native American) artefact known as the Ghost Dance Shirt, which the city of Glasgow obtained from George Crager in 1891. The Lakota tribe believed that their Ghost Shirts would protect them against bullets in battle, but some 150 Native Americans died during the last battle of the American Indian Wars, the 'Wounded Knee' Massacre of 29 December 1890. One of the Ghost Shirts was removed from the body of a warrior killed in battle immediately after. Thirteen months after the massacre, the Kelvingrove Museum purchased the Shirt from Crager, who was the Lakota interpreter for Buffalo Bill Cody's Travelling Wild West Show.[66] The tribal claim was rebuffed in 1995, but in 1999, it succeeded. The Wounded Knee Survivors Association received the Ghost Shirt on behalf of the Blackfoot tribe, who donated a replica of the Shirt to the Museum.[67]

The remaining sections of this chapter turn to restitution claims. The complexities introduced by private international law and the opportunities it offers for value-based decisions are set out.

6. COMPLICATIONS AND OPPORTUNITIES WHICH PRIVATE INTERNATIONAL LAW INTRODUCES IN RESTITUTION CLAIMS

6.1 Choice of Jurisdiction and Forum-Shopping – a Complication of Procedure

Different civil justice systems affect the success of any claim based on a foreign law. Legal diversity cuts across procedural aspects. Consequently, even the application of the same national law in every court based on the same connecting factor cannot ensure the same result in a claim based on

---

65 Schönenberger (n 15) 51–52; 184; 236–37; C MacLachlan, 'A Long Road Home' (2010) XV Art Antiquity and Law 275, 277.

66 The show ran between November 1890 and February 1891.

67 M O'Neill, 'Repatriation and Its Discontents: The Glasgow Experience' in E Robson, L Treadwell and C Gosden (eds), *Who Owns Objects?: The Ethics of Collecting Cultural Property* (Oxbow 2006) 105; Carruthers (n 10) §§ 5.11–5.12.

foreign law.[68] The convenience of the defendant and the speedy conclusion of the trial may weigh more than an advantageous sales law when a particular national court must be chosen.[69]

The identification of the appropriate forum to hear the dispute is determined by jurisdictional rules and choices between state courts within the national legal sphere. These rules and choices determine whether the court has regulatory authority in respect of persons, property and activities and whether the court should exercise jurisdiction when authority is found to exist. Some jurisdiction rules rely on connecting factors to determine whether a court should exercise jurisdiction. The connecting factor which Council Regulation (EC) No 44/2001 of 22 December (the Judgments Regulation) and its successor, Regulation 1215/2012 (EU) of 12 December 2012 (the Recast Regulation),[70] rely on to create general jurisdiction (i.e. jurisdiction irrespective of the particular claim) is the domicile of the defender. Jurisdiction may also be based on a specific factual connection between the cause of action and the forum (proximity). Examples include the place of performance of the obligation in question; the place where goods are delivered; the place where a service is performed; and the place where a harmful event that gave rise to damage occurs or may occur.

In the EU, the bases of jurisdiction under the Judgments Regulation will always apply. States cannot revert to their national private international law rules. The EU adopted new rules on jurisdiction that provide a jurisdiction ground for claims to cultural objects between EU Member States in the Recast Regulation. In an action for restitution of a cultural object there could be more than one forum without there being one that is more natural and appropriate, or clearly inappropriate. England, Scotland and other Commonwealth jurisdictions generally apply the more appropriate forum test. In Australian private international law, the 'clearly inappropriate forum test' sets a higher threshold for declining jurisdiction.[71]

---

68 *Maharanee Seethadevi Gaekwarof Baroda v Wildenstein* [1972] 2 QB 283 (Indian princess residing in France instituted proceedings against an American art dealer resident in France when he came to England for the Ascot races).

69 K Siehr, 'International Art Trade and the Law' VI (243) *Recueil des Cours* (The Hague 1993) 9, 48–49.

70 Council Regulation (EC) No 44/2001 of 22 December 2000 OJ L 12/1 16.1.2001; Council Regulation (EC) No 1215 of 2012 (hereafter Recast Regulation) OJ 2012 L351/1, entry into force 10 January 2015.

71 A Reed, 'Venue Resolution and Forum Non Conveniens: Four Models of Jurisdictional Propriety' (2013) 22 Journal of Transnational Law and Contemporary Problems 369.

Forum-shopping is not prohibited. Litigants are motivated to obtain procedural advantages or to seek out the venue of convenience under the substantive law that will best serve their interests.[72] Freedom of contract allows parties to limit legal uncertainty and risk by way of choice of court clauses.[73] A choice of court agreement is permitted in the EU Judgments Regulation[74] and in the US.[75] However, parties may not always be free to designate a neutral court. Article 19 of the Hague Choice of Court Convention allows states to declare that their courts will not exercise jurisdiction over a dispute that has no connection with their courts.

While EU law and common law recognise choice of court agreements, they also limit the freedom to forum-shop to an extent. The common law has long relied on *forum non conveniens*, an apparently a-political, deferential doctrine of comity that permits a court to decline jurisdiction on the grounds that another forum is the appropriate forum and that considerations of justice require that the dispute be resolved by that forum.[76] It would be undesirable to exercise jurisdiction if a litigant commenced proceedings at a particular venue because this places the opponent in the worst possible legal or practical position. Forum-shopping is not supposed to enable the claimant to vex, harass or maximise the inconvenience and expense of the opposing party.

If the choice of forum is based on the likelihood of restitution in terms of the applicable law in claims involving art or cultural objects, the risk

---

[72] Gazzini (n 6) 53; A Chechi, *The Settlement of International Cultural Heritage Disputes: Towards a Lex Culturalis?* (unpublished PhD Thesis EUI 2011) 203.

[73] In general, see Council Regulation (EC) No 1215 of 2012, OJ 2012 L351/1, entry into force 10 January 2015; Hague Choice of Court Agreements Convention of 30 June 2005, <http://www.hcch.net/index_en.php?act=conventions.text&cid=98> accessed 25 February 2014; D Sancho Villa, 'Jurisdiction over Jurisdiction and Choice of Court Agreements: Views on the Hague Convention of 2005 and Implications for the European Regime' (2010) 12 Yearbook of Private International Law 399.

[74] Case C-159/97 *Trasporti Castelletti Spedizione Internazionali SpA v Hugo Trumpy SpA* [1999] ECR I-1597 § 50.

[75] *MS Bremen v Zapata Off-Shore Co*, 407 US 1 (1972).

[76] *Spiliada Maritime Co v Cansulex* [1987] AC 460, 476. In Scotland, an equivalent basis is found in Rule 2(i) of Schedule 8 to the Civil Jurisdiction and Judgments Act 1982.

exists that the adjudicator may not acknowledge the special nature of cultural heritage. Inconsistency of decisions could then become inescapable.[77]

Different jurisdictional rules and the rules on recognition and enforcement of judgments are designed to control the risk of parallel jurisdiction in international disputes, and bring the risk of irreconcilable judgments or contrasting recommendations under better control. Determining which adjudicator's ruling is final and enforceable can pose problems, because this may not be apparent until all proceedings are concluded. Finality is of importance for litigation concerning art and cultural objects and property crime. Chapter 4 explores this issue in more depth.

6.2 Choice of Law Methods and Their Effect on Substance

6.2.1 Two principal methods

The terms 'unilateralism' and 'multilateralism' describe the two principal methods by which courts or legislatures choose the law governing cases that have contacts with more than one state. The terms denote two different types of rule: a rule that selects a legal system to apply, and a rule that ordains when the legal system it originates from applies.

In response to the question of which law governs the legal relationship in question, Savigny posited a methodological metaphor in 1849.[78] He indicated that international disputes could be solved by starting with the ubiquitous essence of the private legal relationship, which supposedly has a spatial seat in the world that can be discovered through logic and reason. The method reveals which law from among the potentially applicable laws should apply to a particular question. The multilateral method connects the cause of action to a particular location or territory (e.g. the *situs* or the principal place of business of an individual). The category the legal relationship belongs to is determined (classification), and then linked to the applicable law by means of a legal concept or localising agent upon which a choice of law or jurisdiction rule is based (a connecting factor).[79] The connecting factor refers to the link between an event, transaction, thing or a person and a legal system. This

---

[77] Chechi (n 72) 203.

[78] FK von Savigny, *Private International Law, and the Retrospective Operation of Statutes: A Treatise on the Conflict of Laws, and the Limits of Their Operation in Respect of Place and Time* (Guthrie trans) (2nd rev edn) (Edinburgh, T & T Clark 1880). Commentary by FK Juenger, 'General Course on Private International Law' IV (193) *Recueil des Cours* (The Hague 1985) 123, 159.

[79] Von Savigny (n 78) 28, 43, 108.

multilateral method became an influential conflictual method that represents the basic allocation at the heart of choice of law in Europe today.

Unilateralism reinforces the public law dimension of private international law. The method is predicated on the assumption that a private international law problem (i.e. a conflicts decision) can be solved with reference to the substantive law rules found in domestic law, rather than with reference to the legal relationship at stake.[80] Because this method focuses on an examination of purposes and policies of substantive rules, it can identify scope rules or priority rules that operate based on public interests of the forum expressed in a domestic statute such as, e.g., a Museum Act or a Heritage Protection Act. Such a law could claim application in an international case by virtue of the spatially conditioned internal rules it contains.[81] An evaluation of the policy behind the rule will reveal that it is 'space conditioned' – that is, if the very anatomy of every legal provision does not impose this already. The policy will reveal the scope.[82]

Unilateral rules apply to international disputes not on account of any choice of law rule, but because their nature and content demand their application. Their nature and content delimit the spatial reach of the *lex fori* so that the scope of application of its provisions is apparent.[83] Typically, they give no indication of when foreign law applies. For purely domestic purposes, their 'incompleteness' hardly presents an issue. The

---

80 TG Guedj, 'The Theory of the Lois de Police, A Functional Trend in Continental Private International Law – a Comparative Analysis with Modern American Theories' (1991) 34 AJCL 661, 665; P Hay, 'Comments on Self-Limited Rules of Law in Conflicts Methodology' (1982) 30 AJCL Supplement 129, 135.

81 *Bredius* case, Hoge Raad, 16 Maart 1990, NJ (1991) 575 (proceedings to amend the bequest of an art collection to a Dutch museum for purposes of public display in the Prinsengracht in The Hague by a Monegasque testator, so as to allow the collection to move to another location in The Hague). The ruling preceded the revocation of the Dutch Museum Act 1925 by way of an amendment of the Dutch Civil Code, 4: 123; 4: 134.

82 AV Levontin, *Choice of Law and Conflict of Laws* (AW Sijthoff 1976) 149; Guedj (n 80) 667.

83 CF Forsyth, *Private International Law* (5th edn, Juta 2012) 9; FK Juenger, 'The Problem with Private International Law', Centro di studi e ricerche di diritto comparato e straniero: saggi, conferenze e seminari, No 37 (Rome 1999) 2–3 <http://www.cisg.law.pace.edu/cisg/biblio/juenger1.html> accessed 29 March 2014.

vast majority of domestic rules fall into this category. From an international point of view, however, their 'incompleteness' is more obvious, for they cannot answer the question as to when foreign law would apply.

Savigny was aware of the effect of unilateral conflicts rules.[84] He defined them as laws that seek to protect moral values or that 'rest on reasons of public interest, whether these relate to politics, organisation of the state or political economy'. There is no English common law equivalent to the priority rule except in the very broad sense of rules that pull against multilateral rules, and that compensate for the inequality among individual legal systems. In English common law, it is the public policy exception that can block the application of a foreign rule that is otherwise applicable or chosen to decide a particular issue, when this rule is, or through its application becomes, unacceptable to the forum.

Unilateral rules can also be understood as prioritising governmental policies and interests in cross-border relationships between parties. The policy-based functional approach found in the Second Restatement of Conflict of Laws is an example in point,[85] which is intended to lead to the elaboration of newly principled rules.[86] The method takes into consideration policies of the forum, of foreign states, and of the particular field of law; it marries policies of substantive law with conflicts principles.

Giving scope to underlying policies in substantive law, rather than to the multilateral method and classification, was a prominent tendency during the American conflicts revolution.[87] While the term 'revolution' is an overstatement, it does convey that classification receded into the background, and that something new was brought into view.[88]

The view that courts apply their own law more effectively, accurately and justly than any foreign law, was a well-defended position during the conflict revolution. To this day, substantive policy continues to preclude

---

[84] Von Savigny (n 78) 76.

[85] Restatement of the Conflict of Laws (Second), Washington D.C. 1971 § 6.

[86] Hay (n 80) 135.

[87] FK Juenger, 'The Problem with Private International Law' in J Basedow et al. (eds), *Private Law in the International Arena: From National Conflict Rules Towards Harmonization and Unification: Liber Amicorum Kurt Siehr* (TMC Asser Press 2000) 289. AA Ehrenzweig, 'A Counter-Revolution in Conflicts Law? From Beale to Cavers' (1966) 80 Harvard Law Review 377, coined the phrase.

[88] SC Symeonides, 'The American Choice-of-Law Revolution in the Courts' 298 *Recueil des Cours* (The Hague 2002) 431; R Michaels, 'The New European Choice-of-Law Revolution' (2008) 82 Tulane Law Review 1607.

the application of foreign law, when the public policy exception is called upon. There is further opportunity for this method to minimise normative clashes if mutual recognition is extended to rules of foreign law without the need for recourse to a rigid multilateral conflicts rule. This opportunity arises in the context of claims instituted by states, public entities and private persons based on treasure legislation,[89] rules of common law dealing with buried ownerless property (*bona vacantia*)[90] or vesting laws.[91] For example, in England and Wales, all buried ownerless property with a certain precious metal content vests in the Crown by virtue of the Treasure Act 1996. Finds must be reported to the Crown, which has the right to acquire treasure. In the Treasure (Designation) Order 2008, the narrow scope of this category has been extended to include prehistoric finds. If an object is conferred on a museum, archaeological analysis and public display become possible.[92] In Scottish practice, ownerless goods fall to the Crown, represented by the Queen's and Lord Treasurer's Remembrancer (QLTR). The QLTR may claim all artefacts of historical interest, including precious metal objects or wooden objects. In practice, only those objects deemed to be of archaeological value are claimed against payment of the market value of the find as reward if the find is retained. While the English treasure legislation and the Scots principle of *bona vacantia* do not seem to have much in common with vesting laws that are consistent with a state ownership declaration, they can be classed together from a global perspective that illuminates them as spatially conditioned internal rules that delineate the sphere of application of the domestic law. US legislation that vests ownership of archaeological resources found on federally owned or controlled lands (i.e. public and Native American Lands) belongs to the same class. The Archaeological Resources Protection Act of 1979 (ARPA)[93] was created to protect archaeological sites in the US against unlicensed excavation,

---

[89] E.g. the Treasure Act 1996.

[90] See *Lord Advocate v University of Aberdeen and Budge* [1963] SC 533 (St Ninian's treasure belongs to the Crown); principles applying in respect of lost or abandoned property as codified in ss 67–73 of the Civic Government (Scotland) Act 1982.

[91] Law 117 on the Protection of Antiquities of 1983 (Egypt); see Chapter 7.

[92] Newly discovered archaeological material that does not qualify as treasure and embedded objects belong to the landowner, unless those rights give way to the rights of someone with superior title before the limitation period expires. Finds may be assigned to a finder if classed as lost or abandoned.

[93] 16 US Code 470aa–470mm (2000). See P Gerstenblith, 'Schultz and Barakat: Universal Recognition of National Ownership of Antiquities' (2009) XIV Art Antiquity and Law 21, 22.

removal and damage,[94] but has been applied to resources stolen from foreign states on several occasions.[95] ARPA contains public law provisions that confer authority on the federal government, and it provides criteria and procedures pursuant to which a 'federal land manager' may issue excavation permits for federal lands and for notification of Indian Tribes if permits may result in harm to Indian cultural or religious sites. ARPA prohibits the sale, purchase, exchange and transport in interstate or foreign commerce of any archaeological materials taken in violation of any state or local law. The requirements in respect of the granting of permits extend to all public and Indian land.[96] Convictions for archaeological materials removed from a Native American Indian site located on private land have also been upheld.[97]

Considering that the modern concept of the unilateral method is associated with legislative provision, few commentators would be so bold as to identify rules of common law in respect of buried ownerless property as unilateral conflicts rules at this point.

Public bodies and states may institute claims based on public law when the issue concerns the exercise of governmental power (acts *jure imperii*). Public law is its own unilateral scope rule, for its operation cannot be anything but territorially confined. If sufficient numbers of states were to recognise the cultural heritage law of foreign states – which essentially comprises a set of scope rules because they determine that the scope of their own application is domestic – greater consistency of international decisions could be achieved. However 'incomplete' rules that define their sphere of application may be, this does not mean that they lack all capacity to minimise normative clashes.

The unilateral method is inherently limited if it is unknown when excavation and export had occurred, or where the find spot of a cultural object is. In these circumstances, it cannot be established if laws that

---

94 *US v Gerber*, 999 F2d 1112 (7th Circuit 1993), *cert denied*, 510 US 1071 (1994).

95 *US v Melnikas*, 9292 F Supp 276 (SD Ohio 1996)(manuscripts); *US v An Arcaic Etruscan Pottery Ceremonial Vase Late 7th Century BC*, No 1:96-cv-09437 (SDNY 24 March 1997); Chechi (n 72) 79–80.

96 Permit requirements under the Ancient Monuments and Archaeological Areas Act 1979 (AMAAA) in England are at the discretion of the Secretary of State, and relate only to scheduled monuments or protected areas.

97 *US v Gerber*, 999 F2d 1112 (7th Circuit 1993); *US v Quarrel*, 310 F3d 664 (10th Circuit 2002).

seem relevant will apply.[98] In *United States v An Antique Platter of Gold*[99] the court ordered forfeiture of an illegally imported ancient gold phiale dating from 400 BCE in Sicily. The customs officials were deceived concerning the origin of the phiale due to fraudulent declarations as to the provenance of the piece in the customs import documents. The defendant had made a false declaration that it had originated from Switzerland and a false valuation had been submitted. As such, the officials did not know they were entitled to hold the phiale on the basis of Italian ownership laws. Because the material misrepresentations justified the forfeiture order, the court did not need to confront either the title question or the recognition of the relevant Italian law.[100]

When the relevant dates and find spot are known, unilateral rules can provide ready support for restitution claims. The implication of extending recognition to foreign state ownership laws that render illicitly excavated objects stolen upon export is investigated in depth in Chapter 7.

Methodological divergence between multilateral and unilateral conflicts rules in private international law is a matter of degree rather than a strict dichotomy. The fact that they do not stand in strict opposition affects basic conceptions of what constitutes the 'rule' and what constitutes the 'exception' in the application of choice of law. Methodological divergence offers great scope for legal argument in support of restitution, provided any fixed ideas about the exception and the rule are removed.

Whereas unilateral rules are clearly based on national norms, multilateral rules can be considered manifestations of international norms. Nonetheless, significant legal diversity affects the starting point and proof of multilateral choice of law rules, and this presents a potential complication that has cost implications.

6.2.2 Legal diversity in respect of the procedural treatment of foreign law

Rights of possession and ownership of a cultural object can be treated as domestic substantive law issues; as issues that are subject to the law of the court or its treatment of foreign law; or as peculiar facts that are governed by the current location of the moveable. English courts approve of the classical multilateral conflicts method in property which refers to what is valid and effective by the law of the *situs*, as other Member States

---

98 *Government of the Islamic Republic of Iran v The Barakat Galleries Ltd* [2007] EWHC 705 (QB).

99 *US v An Antique Platter of Gold,* 991F Supp 222 (SDNY 1997), affirmed, 184 F3d 131 (2nd Circuit 1999).

100 Cornu and Renold (n 2) 16–17.

of the EU do, but the procedural treatment of foreign law is marked by legal diversity. Differences are apparent in respect of theory, the rules governing pleading and proof, the result of a failure to prove, and the approaches adopted by a review court.[101]

Courts in Civil Law jurisdictions consider themselves bound to apply domestic choice of law rules. They apply these rules *suo motu*. Thus, the choice of law rules or the parties' choice of law may require the court to apply the substantive law of a foreign state to the facts presented in a case, unless there are reasons that exclude such application. In jurisdictions where the application of the choice of law rules depends on whether the parties plead it, courts will generally apply the *lex fori*. If one of the parties raises the choice of law issue or there is a contractual choice of law clause, the procedural treatment of foreign law assumes relevance, and the content has to be pleaded and proved. Such a facultative approach is evident in English courts.[102] Their pragmatism manifests in a desire to avoid the risk of error or misapplication of the foreign law.[103] Foreign law will govern a claim based on ownership if it is pleaded and proved.

In the US, Rule 44.1 of the Federal Rules of Civil Procedure requires parties to give notice of their intention to raise foreign substantive private law. The court may engage in its own research on this point and may determine issues that were not raised by the parties. The ruling of the court is treated as a ruling on a question of law. In practice, federal judges tend to rely heavily on expert witnesses. Most state jurisdictions have adopted the Rule 44.1 approach, but some of them rely on the judicial notice concept or adhere to the common law method of proving foreign law.[104] Judges do not frequently intervene to introduce foreign law into litigation. The testimony of duelling experts, and the relative persuasiveness of one foreign law expert over the other can affect the outcome of a case.[105]

---

[101] TC Hartley, 'Pleading and Proof of Foreign Law: The Major EU Systems Compared' (1996) 45 ICLQ 271, 272.

[102] M Whincop and M Keyes, *Policy and Pragmatism in the Conflict of Laws* (Ashgate 2001) 15–16.

[103] S Lalani, *Doubt Develops Where Certainty Ceases: Foreign Law in Domestic Courts* (PhD Thesis, University of Lausanne 2011) 6 (unpublished).

[104] MJ Wilson, 'Demystifying the Determination of Foreign Law in US Courts: Opening the Door to a Greater Global Understanding' (2011) 46 Wake Forest Law Review 887, 901.

[105] E.g. *Bakalar v Vavra and Fischer*, 619 F3d 136 (2d Circuit 2010); *Bakalar v Vavra and Fischer*, 819 FSupp 2d 293 (SDNY 2011) aff'd, 500FApp'x

Litigation expenses can be expected to escalate if questions of fact and law are intricate or expert testimony is required in respect of the law. Courts find ways to avoid foreign law altogether. For instance, a dismissal on procedural grounds precludes the hearing of foreign law claims. If the foreign law issues are not sufficiently raised or briefed, a court may simply use domestic law.[106]

6.2.3 Justice pluralism – accommodating ethics

Where a conflicts situation arises in an international dispute, every substantive law rule is subject to 'conflicts justice' (the justice of the conflict of laws).[107] Neither 'conflicts justice' nor 'substantive justice' exists in splendid isolation of the ethical considerations that are so pertinent in art and heritage cases. Ethical considerations include the circumstances of the loss, the fate of former owners, and efforts made to claim objects back. The 'safety valve' provided by the public policy exception enables a value-judgement that alleviates the tension between conflicts justice and material justice.[108]

6.3 Classification

6.3.1 Complicating factor?

Having made the initial decisions concerning the dispute resolution process and the establishment of jurisdiction, substantive rights and obligations can be determined. Which law is supposed to govern the merits of the case? The common situation of a diversity factor in any assertion or denial of ownership to art works leads to the vigorous contestation of choice of law. Who owns art depends on whose law applies, and the applicable law depends, in turn, on the choice of law rule. Reliance on a conflicts rule leads to a variety of different answers depending on whose law applies to a legal dispute, since this rule determines whether the purchaser in good faith receives good title, and whether reacquisition is an option.

In a claim for the return of a cultural object, the European conflicts tradition will utilise classification or characterisation to identify the

---

6, 8 (2d Cir 2012), *cert denied* No 12-1160, 2013 WL1993864 (US 2013); *Altmann v Austria*, 142 F Supp 2d 1187, 1210. For more, see Wilson (n 104) 887.

[106] Wilson (n 104) 891, 897.

[107] G Kegel, 'The Crisis of Conflict of Laws' II *Recueil des Cours* (The Hague 1964) 95, 184.

[108] Chechi (n 72) 101.

applicable law. Classification determines the legal system that governs the legal question, and therefore also the outcome of restitution claims instituted by businesses, dealers or collectors, or cultural institutions with differing domiciles. The court will need to classify the cause of action into a particular type – non-contractual (delictual/tortious) or penal, a matter of transfer of real rights, a contractual obligation, a personal injury or something else.[109]

Opinions differ on what precisely is classified – whether it is the facts, the cause of action or claim, or a legal rule. The composite entity of the claim draws from the facts on which the claim is based; the legal rule transforms the facts into a cause of action.[110] The causes of action and type of claim may differ depending on where proceedings are instituted.

In German law, the action of delivery of the *res*, known as an *Eigentumsherausgabeanspruch* (*rei vindicatio*), lies against the possessor. If the action succeeds, the possessor loses the right to possession to the owner.[111] The German *Abstrakzionsprinzip*[112] tends to provoke unjust enrichment claims as a corrective device for the fact that ownership can pass on mere delivery.[113]

In Scots law, deprived owners claim delivery (a vindicatory action based on proof of a right of ownership), *spuilzie* (a remedy by which to obtain restoration of possession in the circumstances of an unauthorised deprivation but which does not require proof of ownership) or multiple-poinding (two or more claimants claim property held by a third party).[114]

In England, the main civil law mechanism for obtaining the return of tangibles is conversion.[115] Conversion is available in respect of an intentional dealing with goods that is seriously inconsistent with the possession or right to immediate possession of another person. In principle, a possessor is liable on the basis of a refusal to restore in response to a demand to do so, and commits a separate tort on each

---

[109] D Shapiro, 'Repatriation: A Modest Proposal' (1998) 31 International Law and Politics 95, 100.

[110] Levontin (n 82) 136.

[111] § 985 BGB.

[112] See Chapter 1.

[113] TW Bennett, 'Choice of Law Rules in Claims of Unjust Enrichment' (1990) 39 ICLQ 136, 139.

[114] G Maher and B Rodger, *Civil Jurisdiction in the Scottish Courts* (W Green 2010) §13.01–§13.06.

[115] J Ulph and I Smith, *The Illicit Trade in Art and Antiquities* (Hart 2012) 263.

instance of refusal.[116] Two or more claimants bring their claim in respect of property held by a third party by way of inter-pleader.

In US law, an original owner or person with a right of possession who brings an action for restitution of personal property (i.e. the physical return of objects under conversion (denial of title) *in lieu* of damages or criminal prosecution of the possessor[117]), files for replevin or detinue in different states.[118]

While a deprived owner may have personal or proprietary remedies at their disposal against end-users in transit states or in end-point states, the fundamental question as to what the underlying category might be remains to be answered. The very title of the UNESCO Convention, on the Means of Prohibiting and Preventing the Illicit Import, Export and Transfer of Ownership of Cultural Property, prompts a choice between transfer of property or its restitution. There are separate conflicts rules for transfer of property and for contractual obligations and non-contractual obligations[119] by which to identify the substantive law rule, but no separate choice of law rule has crystallised in respect of restitution claims.[120] Theoretically, restitution claims may be proprietary, contractual, or in equity (in Anglo-American common law systems). They may encompass several legal issues.[121] Characterisation is directed at each particular issue which may arise. Prior to the identification of the applicable law, the issue may be classified as proprietary if: that issue is title to an object that has been transferred voluntarily; as restitution if that issue is unjust enrichment; as equitable in Anglo-American common law

---

116 DL Carey Miller, 'Title to Art: Developments in the USA' (1995) 1 Scottish Law and Practice Quarterly 115, 122.

117 The claimant must prove ownership at the time of loss of possession; that the object was lost without his or her agreement or consent, and that the defendant is in wrongful possession of the object. *Vineberg v Bissonnette*, 529 F Supp 2d 300 (DRI 2007) 17. Schönenberger (n 15) 61.

118 P Gerstenblith, 'The Public Interest in the Restitution of Cultural Objects' (2001) 16 Conn J Int L 197, fn 1.

119 Enrichment actions either supplement other remedies or they seek to correct or undo a situation such as the passing of title. For this reason, it has been argued that they do not deserve a separate category for conflict of laws purposes. Bennett (n 113) 167.

120 G Carducci, 'The Growing Complexity of International Art Law: Conflict of Laws, Uniform Law, Mandatory Rules, UNSC Resolutions and EU Regulations' in BT Hoffman (ed), *Art and Cultural Heritage: Law, Policy and Practice* (CUP 2006) 68, 70; G Panagopoulos, *Restitution in Private International Law* (Hart 2000) 159.

121 E.g. Panagopoulos (n 120).

systems; or a hybrid of these.[122] Clearly each of these issues is capable of attracting a choice of law rule when falling within the scope of a recognisable rule, or to call for a new choice of law rule altogether. In practice however, new choice of law rules fail to garner support. While logic would expect that any new problem of characterisation would be solved with reference to the cause of action, the causes of action and their associated choice of law rules form a closed list[123] and theoretical and conceptual unity requires treating the issue as a single issue.[124] Only a small number of pre-existing choice of law rules determine the solutions.[125] The conflicts rule enjoys greater pre-eminence than do the legal categories in the ruling.[126]

The multilateral method appears to be simple enough, but the basic question of 'which law applies?' can sprout complications. For instance, should the forum court consider applying a foreign category that could undermine return to the owner? Which part of the foreign law does the adjudicator take into account in order to obtain an answer? Whether proprietary, delictual, equitable or otherwise, classification points to different choice of law rules and the content of the governing law indicated by the rule will likely differ. These potential classifications are considered in more detail in turn.

6.3.2 A proprietary classification

If the validity of transfer of title to moveable property relates to property rather than contract, and the property transaction is a basis for classification, the *lex situs* determines whether title passes. The transfer of title to moveables (category) is governed by the law of the country in which the moveable object was physically located when title is alleged to have been created, modified or terminated.[127]

The *lex situs* is the connecting factor that points in the direction of the law to be applied whenever classification is based on the property

---

[122] Panagopoulos (n 120) 62–105.
[123] E.g. Panagopoulos (n 120).
[124] Panagopoulos (n 120) 37–44.
[125] Bennett (n 113) 142.
[126] Bennett (n 113) 143.
[127] *Cammell v Sewell* [1860] 5 H & N 728, 29 LJ Ex 350, 6 Jur NS 918, 8 WR 639, 2 LT 799; *Re Anziani Herbert v Christopherson* [1930] 1 Ch 407; *Winkworth v Christie Manson and Woods Ltd* [1980] Ch 496; *City of Gotha and the Federal Republic of Germany v Sotheby's and Cobert Finance SA* transcript, unreported case no 1997/G/185, 9 September 1998, QBD. E Rabel, *The Conflict of Laws: A Comparative Study Vol. 4* (Ann Arbor, U Mich 1958) 40.

transaction, or that 'allocates' a legal relationship to a particular legal system which may confirm transfer of title to a *bona fide* purchaser or not.[128]

Legal systems rely on very different epistemic frameworks in the area of personal and moveable property. Assuming that a matter is classified as proprietary, do the conditions for the valid transfer of title refer to delivery or constructive delivery of the object; a legal cause or a valid contract; consensual conveyance; or an abstract real contract?[129] The *lex situs* rule also determines if title passes by abstract or causal approaches to the transfer of ownership, i.e. delivery or mere agreement.[130]

The *lex situs* rule has been the subject of systematic study.[131] In public international law, the rule does not set a minimum standard as many other rules of international law do. It has a special status in defining an element in a public international law rule in matters involving title to property. Some legal systems impose limits based on policy on the *lex situs* rule. Domestic law may also delineate the scope of the *lex situs* rule.[132]

The determination of the law governing proprietary rights may be considered to be crucial in private title-based claims for the return of

---

[128] For more on the position in England and Scotland, see EB Crawford and JM Carruthers, *International Private Law: A Scots Perspective* (3rd edn, W Green 2010) 523; JJ Fawcett and JM Carruthers, *Cheshire, North & Fawcett Private International Law* (14th edn, OUP 2008) 1212; L Collins et al. (gen eds), *Dicey, Morris and Collins on The Conflict of Laws* (14th edn, Sweet & Maxwell 2006) Rule 24 1164; Carruthers (n 10) 79. For more on the position in the US, see L Frey, 'Bakalar v Vavra and the Art of Conflicts Analysis in New York: Framing a Choice of Law Approach for Moveable Property' (2012) 112 Columbia Law Review 1055.

[129] LV Prott, 'Problems of Private International Law for the Protection of the Cultural Heritage' V *Recueil des Cours* (The Hague 1989) 214, 269.

[130] Collins (n 128) § 24-006. A contract may relate to the transfer of a thing (*realvertrag*); see DL Carey Miller, *The Acquisition and Protection of Ownership* (Juta 1986) § 9.2.2.3.

[131] Carruthers (n 10); M Lee, 'A Choice of Law Dilemma: The Conflict and Reconciliation of Laws Governing Cross-Border Transfers of Stolen Art' [2008–2009] Cardozo Public Law Policy and Ethics Journal 719; HLE Verhagen, *Conflit Mobile bij Roerende Zaken: Assimilatie of Transformatie* (Kluwer 2007); C Staker, 'Public International Law and the *Lex Situs* Principle in Property Conflicts and Foreign Expropriations' (1987) 58 BYBIL 151.

[132] E.g., Art 51(2) of Law no 218 of 1995 *Riforma del sistema italiano di diritto internazionale privato* provides that the acquisition and loss of proprietary rights are governed by the *lex situs* rule unless the attribution of a right *in rem* derives from a contract.

cultural objects, but there is no denying that the rule displays instability. In part, this is because *situs* is contingent on market valuations.[133] Legal diversity also contributes to the instability. It complicates the distinction between the licit and the illicit trade and may enable title laundering.[134] Unprovenanced cultural objects may change hands many times prior to the filing of a lawsuit for recovery. A transferor who does not own the object may move it through an intermediate jurisdiction that permits good title to pass even if it were to transpire later that the object had been stolen.[135] If title is transferred in a location whose law does not permit restitution and which purges a title from vices, or if the object transits through a civil law jurisdiction,[136] a good faith possessor has the opportunity to divest the owner of legal title.[137] Multiple cross-border resales involving all manner of intermediaries and at least one civil code that protects the good-faith purchaser enable an item to enter the legal market as soon as the *lex situs* deems the purchaser to be in good faith.[138] Compliance with non-demanding good-faith purchaser standards[139] and short prescription periods further enable title to objects of dubious provenance to be laundered.[140]

The scope of the conflicts rule for property poses an uncertainty. The scope of the rule is potentially affected by whether there is a right to make a claim; whether the dispossessed owner or the good-faith purchaser bears the risk of loss of cultural objects; the legal consequences of alleged abandonment of title; whether the purchaser's state of mind is

---

[133] Whincop and Keyes (n 102) 110.

[134] Gazzini (n 6) 55, 206; C Roodt and D Carey Miller,'Vitium Reale in Private Law and Private International Law' (2013) 10 TDM Special Issue 1.

[135] K Siehr, 'The Protection of Cultural Heritage and International Commerce' [1997] IJCP 304, 305–7; SRM MacKenzie, *Going, Going, Gone: Regulating the Market in Illicit Antiquities* (Institute of Art and Law 2005) 6; Ulph and Smith (n 115) 5; Cornu and Renold (n 2) 14.

[136] N Palmer, 'Recovering Stolen Art' (1994) 47 Current Legal Problems 215, 249.

[137] *Winkworth v Christie Manson and Woods Ltd* [1980] Ch 496; Arts 1153–1157 Italian Civil Code. The potential intermediate status of Italian law was not considered by Slade J.

[138] P Lalive, 'A Disturbing International Convention: The UNIDROIT Convention on Cultural Objects' in LV Prott (ed), *Witnesses to History: A Compendium of Documents and Writings on the Return of Cultural Objects* (Unesco Publications 2009) 29, 30.

[139] *Bumper Development Corporation Ltd. v Commissioner of Police of the Metropolis and Others* [1991] 1 WLR 1362 CA (1991).

[140] Gazzini (n 6) xxiii.

relevant; what standard of due diligence applies; the pertinacity with which the claimant has to pursue his/her claim in that law; and by whether adverse possession, statutory limitation periods, and prescriptive doctrines apply. The difficulties associated with classification extend to the possible suspension or extinction of an owner's right of action, and due diligence may affect the position. This aspect requires separate treatment before other classifications are discussed.

6.3.3 An owner's right of action – due diligence

The time within which action can be brought depends upon technical rules of prescription or limitation and of acquisition in good faith, which differ greatly among legal families and systems.[141] A claim for restitution fails if the possessor raises the objection of a statutory limitation or of prescription successfully.

Generally, the time period to file suit commences to run as soon as the purchaser takes possession. Section 3(1) of the English Limitation Act of 1980 limits actions in respect of further conversions after six years from the date on which the cause of action accrued in respect of the original conversion.

In California, the statutory limitation has been taken to commence at the point of conversion,[142] but as from 1983 the period runs from the moment of actual discovery. This approach is more favourable to owners.

If the statutory limitations or rules of prescription were to be classified as pertaining to procedure, the law of A could apply; but classified as pertaining to substance, the law of B could apply. The narrow concept of procedure that is limited to the rules that regulate the mode and conduct of court proceedings has wide appeal.[143] However, when prescription is

---

141 Schönenberger (n 15) 111–37; European Commission, *Study Report on Preventing and Fighting Illicit Trafficking in Cultural Goods in the European Union*, 10 October 2011, <http://ec.europa.eu/home-affairs/doc_centre/crime/docs/Report%20Trafficking%20in%20cultural%20goods%20EN.pdf> 100–104 accessed 12 March 2014.

142 E.g. *Orkin v Taylor*, 487 F3d 734 (9th Circuit 2007); 128 S Ct 491 (claim to 'Vue de l'Asile et de la Chapelle de St. Remy' was considered to come under the Californian three-year statutory period for the discovery rule; period was taken to have commenced at the auction sale in 1963, namely the point of conversion).

143 On the position in Australia, see *John Pfeiffer Pty Ltd v Rogerson* (2000) 172 ALR 625, 651; *McKain v RW Miller & Co (SA) Pty Ltd* (1991) 174 CLR 1, 26–27; on the Canadian position, see *Tolofson v Jensen* (1994) 120 DLR 4th 289 (that there is no justification for regarding any limitation rule as procedural even if it does not extinguish the substantive right).

regarded as a question of title, a foreign *lex causae* is potentially applicable if the *lex situs* is employed as the connecting factor. That law may bar or extinguish the claim, and the forum court may decide to follow the template of the foreign law.[144]

The relevance, meaning and scope of good faith and due diligence vary across legal families and legal cultures,[145] and this difference also affects the right to bring a claim.

In civil law legal systems, concepts of good faith and due diligence are pertinent. Due diligence can be an indicator of good faith (e.g. when the purchaser investigates the ownership history or provenance of an object prior to buying it) or a criterion in establishing it (when a dispossessed owner makes an effort to locate and recover his or her property).[146] The Netherlands has codified in its domestic law due diligence beyond what the ratification of the 1995 UNIDROIT Convention requires.[147] Good faith cannot be invoked and transfer is invalid for certain objects. Acquisition of stolen property in good faith is possible only at public auctions in German law, or if a holder's certificate is produced in Greek law.[148] In the Anglo-American common law legal systems, these concepts feature in the application of statutory limitations but play no role in the acquisition of property. For instance, the discovery rule of US law has both a positive and a negative effect on the owner, who is protected against the running of statutory limitations and prescription, but who is also obliged to obtain knowledge of the whereabouts of his property.[149] In England and Wales, acquisition of stolen property in good faith is also required in criminal law, namely in the Money Laundering Regulations 2007.

---

144 For instance, the law of prescription in Scotland extinguishes rights, but in English law, the underlying obligation still exists after the statutory limitation period has lapsed. The limitation only provides a defence to the action. S Wilson, 'Prescription and Limitation of Actions in Scotland and England in Relation to Dispute Resolution in Construction Contracts' (2001) 15 ELR 122, 123.

145 European Commission, *Study Report* (n 141) 104–8.

146 European Commission, *Study Report* (n 141) 105.

147 Arts 4.1 and 4.4 of the 1995 UNIDROIT Convention on Stolen or Illegally Exported Cultural Objects, 24 June 1995, 34 ILM 1330; entry into force 1 July 1998. <http://www.unidroit.org/instruments/cultural-property/1995-convention> accessed 24 February 2014; Dutch Civil Code 3:86a; 3:86b; 3:87; 3:87a.

148 European Commission, *Study Report* (n 141) 104, 107.

149 S Symeonides, 'A Choice-of-Law Rule for Conflicts Involving Stolen Cultural Property' [2005] Vand J Transnat'l Law 1177, 1192.

Time limits are not necessarily a purely instrumental technicality. They protect against inevitable inaccuracy in reconstructing history when the hearing proceeds on the merits.[150] If a specialist tribunal were to assume jurisdiction, it is possible that no limitation period would apply.[151] Changing the method of dispute resolution can, therefore, neutralise aspects that make private international law unpopular. The problem can be fixed where it arises, however. The classification by which the applicable law permits a decision on the merits to be made can be identified as the applicable law. Classification can enable value-based decision-making, without changing the method of dispute resolution.

6.3.4 Authority to transfer ownership lacking: Non-contractual (delict/tort) classification

If the purported transfer of a thing by a person who is not the owner, or who lacks the authority to transfer ownership, is classified as pertaining to delict/tort rather than to the transfer of ownership, a US court may characterise a multi-jurisdictional art and antiquities dispute by the nature of the harm suffered by the plaintiff, and apply the law with the most significant relationship with the cause of action. The *lex loci delicti commissi* rule enables a forum court to apply the law of the place where the object was located at the time of the wrongdoing. The law of the place where the delict or tort occurred may either be the law of the state where the object has been taken, or the law of the state where the object is wrongfully held by the tortfeasor.[152] There may be fortuitous or deliberate connections with a variety of potentially applicable laws when cultural objects have passed across jurisdictional lines.

In *Autocephalous Greek-Orthodox Church v Goldberg & Feldman Fine Arts Inc*[153] an art dealer had bought four Kanakariá mosaics, prised from the sixth century apse of a Greek-Orthodox Church located in Northern Cyprus. This occurred sometime between 1976 (two years after Turkish

---

150 *Grosz v The Museum of Modern Art*, 772 F Supp 2d 473 (SDNY 2010), aff'd 403 Fed Appx 575 (2nd Circuit 2010), *cert denied* 132 S Ct 102; 181 L Ed 2d 30 (2011).

151 *Brear v James Hardie and Co Pty Ltd* (2000) 50 NSWLR 388 (NSWCA) (law of the cause applied to bar the action; but the statutory regulation of the specialist tribunal on dust diseases could arguably constitute an overriding mandatory rule).

152 *Charash v Oberlin College*, 14 F3d 291 (6th Circuit 1994).

153 *Autocephalous Greek-Orthodox Church v Goldberg & Feldman Fine Arts Inc*, 717 F Supp 1374 (SD Ind 1989) aff'd 917 F2d 278 (US Court of Appeals 7th Circuit 1990) (No 89-2809) *cert denied* 112 S Ct 377 (1992).

occupation of Northern Cyprus) and 1979 (when the theft was reported). The transaction was concluded in the free port area of Geneva airport in 1988. The Church instituted a replevin action in a court in Indiana. The court characterised the action as a matter of tort and the court weighed the substantive rules of Swiss law and Indiana law before deciding to apply Indiana law and the Indiana statute of limitations.[154] The court modified the traditional interpretation of the *lex loci delicti commissi* rule which would have pointed towards Swiss law as the law that has 'the most significant contact' with the acquisition.[155] The mosaics remained in the free port area and never passed through Swiss customs; did not enter Swiss commerce; and were on Swiss soil for a brief period of four days. The modification of the *lex loci delicti* rule enabled the court to escape the standard rule that shows little connection with the action.[156] The Church succeeded with its claim for the return of the mosaics. If the *lex situs* had been applied, Swiss law would have determined the validity of the title transfer, and the case would have presented a near-perfect example of laundered title. The Federal Act on the International Transfer of Cultural Property of 2005[157] has now changed the opportunity structure for title laundering.

The choice of law analysis employed in *Goldberg* reflects the tension between the security of title in international commerce and global protection through recovery.[158] It is uncertain whether the court preferred a home-bound approach because the law of Indiana is easier to understand and apply correctly,[159] or whether the court pursued a policy goal of restitution.[160] It may have adapted existing law in the light of an 'international' private international law paradigm.

---

[154] *Autocephalous Greek-Orthodox Church v Goldberg & Feldman Fine Arts Inc*, 717 F Supp 1394–95.

[155] *Autocephalous Greek-Orthodox Church v Goldberg & Feldman Fine Arts Inc*, 717 F Supp 1394.

[156] *Autocephalous Greek-Orthodox Church v Goldberg & Feldman Fine Arts Inc*, 717 F Supp 1393.

[157] *Systematische Rechtssammlung* no 444.1 *Bundesblatt* (2003) 4475.

[158] TW Pecoraro, 'Choice of Law in Litigation to Recover National Cultural Property: Efforts at Harmonization in Private International Law' [1990] Virginia Journal of International Law 1, 10; Q Byrne-Sutton, 'The Goldberg Case' (1992) 1 IJCP 151; DL Crowell, '*Autocephalous Greek-Orthodox Church of Cyprus v Goldberg & Feldman Fine Arts Inc*: Choice of Law in the Protection of Cultural Property' (1992) 27 Texas International Law Journal 173ff.

[159] Byrne-Sutton (n 158) 151, 159.

[160] Pecoraro (n 158) 1.

6.3.5 Common law classification as conversion (wrongful interference with possession)

A common law tort action imposes strict liability for a wrongful interference with the right to possession of a chattel (conversion). Conversion consists of any act of willful interference, without lawful justification, with another's chattel in a manner inconsistent with their possession or their right to immediate possession. There is authority for the view that conversion exists when a defendant intentionally exercises exclusive control over the claimant's chattel without his consent.[161] Conversion can be committed in various different ways, including by buying or selling or refusal to deliver up on demand. If an auctioneer innocently offers a stolen painting for sale in one of its auctions, and sells the painting or offers it as security for when payment fails, it could be liable for conversion under English law.[162] As a strict liability tort that is indifferent to causation, innocence or due diligence does not normally constitute a defence.[163] An innocent converter may seek contribution against the initial converter.[164] The innocent purchaser of stolen goods is at the receiving end of the harshest effects of this tort. If an undiscovered archaeological item had been discovered after the commencement of a state ownership law that vests title thereof in the state, and the conversion took place thereafter, the source state is in a position to obtain restitution.[165]

6.3.6 A conceptual device with potential

In claims arising from theft, classification should pose no difficulty. Simple theft or dispossession with the intention to deprive the owner permanently is universally recognised as a crime for which criminal sanction is sought;[166] so is dealing in stolen goods.[167] The legal scenario

---

[161] S Douglas, 'The Nature of Conversion' (2009) 68 Cambridge LJ 198 at 199, 209.

[162] Ulph and Smith (n 115) 186 disagree with the ruling in *Marcq v Christie Manson and Wood Ltd, t/a Christie's* [2002] EWHC 2148, [2003] EWCA Civ 731, [2004] QB 286 (CA) (to the effect that the auction house was not liable when it returned it to the ostensible seller).

[163] Douglas (n 161) 217.

[164] Douglas (n 161) 223.

[165] *Government of the Islamic Republic of Iran v The Barakat Galleries Ltd* [2009] 1 QB 22 (CA) § [143]–[150].

[166] JH Merryman, 'A Licit International Trade in Cultural Objects' (1995) 4 IJCP 13, 18–19.

[167] P Gerstenblith, 'Recent Developments in the Legal Protection of Cultural Heritage' in N Brodie, MM Kersel, C Luke and K Walker Tubb (eds),

is relatively straightforward if an original owner is deprived of an object.[168] A thief does not acquire title to the property he or she steals, and civil proceedings cannot change this. In addition, limitation periods do not generally apply to actions instituted against thieves.[169] This is not to say that legal systems are in full agreement as to when an object has been stolen,[170] because subtle differentiation can be made between a disposer who is not entitled to dispose and a thief.

While criminal conduct could be of direct concern to private international law, as pointed out in Chapter 1, it does not pose a classification problem.

Domestic criminal law governs crime. But suppose the object is stolen while it is being transported across the territories of several states, which law governs then? Criminal conduct gives scope to the public policy exception, which introduces flexibility into the method in civil proceedings. The application of foreign law raises an issue where contracting parties intend to skirt the law (discussed further under 7. below). *Fraus legis* can eliminate the whole of choice of law in favour of the law of the forum. Even if rather extreme, its effect is similar to that of the public policy exception. However, this device operates mainly in family and contractual relationships in choice of law. Whether the scale and intensity of looting and trafficking justify such a radical elimination in the trade and sale of cultural objects is discussed in Chapter 5.

Classification alters the status of ownership and affects the right of possession, but if treated as a conceptual device, it provides a powerful way for ensuring value-based decisions that optimise the legal protection of cultural objects at the demand-end. This is not to deny that questions of application of foreign law and choice of law are significantly more expensive to pursue than the alternatives offered by criminal law. Litigation expenses escalate if legal questions are intricate.[171]

Archaeology, Cultural Heritage and the Antiquities Trade (University Press of Florida 2006) 68, 81.

[168] Last (n 39) 123.

[169] E.g. s 4 of the Sale of Goods Act (England and Wales).

[170] Siehr (n 69) 60. Also Chapter 5.3 below.

[171] The settlement in *Goodman v Searle*, Complaint (ND Ill 17 July 1996) (No 96 – 6459) barely covered litigation expenses. Settlement prior to litigation is therefore far more preferable. Access to justice and legal fees posed problems in *Austria v Altmann*, 541 US 677 (2004).

6.4 Applying the Public Policy Exception to Sovereign Acts

Von Saher v Norton Simon Museum of Art in Pasadena[172] concerned an action brought by a US citizen against a US museum over oil paintings by Lucas Cranach the Elder, which were located in the US. The court had to determine the validity of appropriations made by the Dutch and Soviet governments. Russia had auctioned off nationalised works of art in the late 1920s and the Norton Simon Museum contended that Russia had illegally expropriated the paintings the museum had acquired from the Stroganoff family. Von Saher contended, on the other hand, that she was entitled to the works which the Jewish collector Jacques Goudstikker had bought before the Holocaust because the Dutch government would have restituted the paintings to her in 2006 if it had not sold them to Stroganoff-Scherbatoff in the early 1960s. The case exhibited an overwhelming number of domestic connections, yet it assumed a distinctly international flavour.[173] While the decision turned on the permissibility of California extending its statutory limitations in a field where federal action had already been taken in this instance, public policy may have played a more prominent role in a different constitutional (e.g. non-federal) and jurisprudential context.

The general principles of international law require courts to recognise governmental expropriations at the international level when such actions do not violate international law.[174] Whereas the legal basis for recognition is found in the act of state doctrine in common law (i.e. the notion that common law courts do not sit in judgement of the acts of the government of another state), in civil law legal systems it hinges on the principle of territoriality.[175]

---

[172] *Von Saher v Norton Simon Museum of Art at Pasadena*, 592 F3d 954 (9th Circuit 2010) held unconstitutional Cal. Code. Civ. Proc. § 354.3, which took effect on 1 January 2003. The US Supreme Court declined von Saher's petition for review on 27 June 2011.

[173] B Demarsin, 'The Third Time Is Not Always a Charm: The Troublesome Legacy of a Dutch Art Dealer: The Limitation and Act of State Defences in Looted Art Cases' (2010) 28 Cardozo Art and Entertainment Law Journal 255, 299.

[174] *Chasidei Chabad v Russian Federation* 466 F Supp 2d (2006) (orthodox Jewish organisation cannot recover Library containing sacred manuscripts seized in the aftermath of the Bolshevik Revolution and during World War II by the Russian Federation because owner is a national of taking state). The appellate court reversed this ruling, see *Chasidei Chabad v Russian Federation* 528 F3d 934 (DC Circuit 2008) at 939.

[175] Schönenberger (n 15) 143.

The relationship between the act of state doctrine, sovereign immunity, private international law, choice of law and jurisdiction is a source of perennial confusion and uncertainty. Sovereign immunity is a principle of international law, but the act of state doctrine is not.[176] The implications of state sovereignty, the separation of powers and the comity of nations must be understood in the constitutional and jurisprudential context in which complex factual and legal questions of a transnational nature are to be decided. Jurisprudential borrowing is a bad idea, even among common law jurisdictions. Outcomes are predicated on factors unique to the jurisdiction in question.[177]

In England, the jurisprudential origins of state immunity and the act of state doctrine are closely related – and strongly influenced – by the notion of comity and respect for the territorial sovereignty of other states. The judiciary has always been at pains to refrain from conducting a state's foreign affairs, involving itself in those affairs, or bringing into jeopardy the conduct of such affairs. Issues that can put the international relations of states in jeopardy, where the parties before the court are not those states themselves or representatives from those states, are not the province of the court to decide.[178] The link between the public policy exception and the act of state defence is evident in English law. That courts will not enforce laws which are contrary to the public policy of the *lex fori* is borne out in cases[179] that confirm that acts of foreign governments executed within their territory that are in patent breach of public international law will not be enforced.[180] Nonetheless, the toleration for difference can also be remarkably extensive.[181]

On the continent, the principle of territoriality means that the validity of expropriations are determined by the *lex situs* at the time of the expropriation, and this domestic act creates state ownership that other states recognise and respect.[182] The systematisation of the principle of territoriality is a matter for debate – it can be regulated under public or private international law – but it remains clear that *ordre public* operates

---

[176] FA Mann, *Foreign Affairs in English Courts* (Clarendon Press 1986) 164; M Alderton, 'The Act of State Doctrine: Questions from Validity to Abstention from Underhill to Habib' [2011] Melbourne Journal of International Law 1, 3.

[177] Alderton (n 176) 3.

[178] Ibid.

[179] E.g. *Kuwait Airways Corporation v Iraqi Airways Co* [2002] 2 AC 883.

[180] Alderton (n 176) 14.

[181] See *Princess Paley Olga v Weisz* [1929] 1 KB 718 (CA) (nationalisation by the Soviet regime after the Russian Revolution).

[182] Schönenberger (n 15) 143.

here and can preclude the application of the choice of law rule.[183] *Ordre public* operates as an escape device in civil law systems to override the application of foreign law when that law is deemed to be sufficiently objectionable or incompatible with national public law and policy interests. It is territorial in application.

Courts do not seek to identify the law governing a right of restitution of confiscated property, but the nationality of the victim of expropriation is relevant. In expropriations affecting nationals, the act of state doctrine urges foreign courts not to examine the validity of a taking of a cultural object under the public policy of the forum or under international law.[184] The only legal issue is that of compensation because the context is domestic.[185] The public policy exception is likely to preclude the application of the *lex situs*[186] if the state expropriates the property owned by non-citizens without compensation within its territory.[187] The seizure of Jewish property by the Nazi regime is an international expropriation due to the citizenship factor. Jewish persons were not the only victims of Nazi ideology, but the Nazis committed clear violations of international law when they acquired the property of Jews who were denied German citizenship or stripped of their citizenship under the 1935 Nuremberg Laws.[188] The art and antiquities collections belonging to non-practising Jews and converts were not always spared.[189]

Works in the category of degenerate art, by Jewish artists or that formed part of Jewish collections, would make the issue an international one. German artists and artists of other nationalities were also affected. Degenerate art that was purged by decree from German public collections was considered to have been 'legally' seized by the Nazis from public museums because these confiscations did not discriminate on the basis of religion or race. Restitution claims lodged by state museums in Germany are unlikely to succeed, therefore. Where degenerate works belonged to nationals, the legal context is domestic. Compensation is the only legal issue arising.[190]

---

[183] Schönenberger (n 15) 143.

[184] Steiner and Vagts (n 16) 725; Schönenberger (n 15) 34; Gerstenblith (n 118) 236.

[185] Staker (n 131) 155, 239; Schönenberger (n 15) 200, 203.

[186] Staker (n 131) 219–20.

[187] Staker (n 131) 221.

[188] *Cassirer v Kingdom of Spain*, 461 F Supp 2d 1157, 1165 (C D Cal 2006).

[189] Lubina and Schneider (n 28) 161ff.

[190] Staker (n 131) 151, 155, 239.

The act of state doctrine is a substantive rule of law created in the US. It can preclude a court from adjudicating on the merits of a case once a foreign sovereign is haled into court; it is not a jurisdictional limit on the court.[191] It derives from the separation of powers in the US Constitution. Deference applies in respect of a foreign official act of state in the territory of the foreign state. For fear of interfering with the conduct of foreign relations by the executive, the judiciary will not question the official acts of a foreign state.[192] The doctrine is connected with public international law, for it is understood that the defence does not apply where the acting state violated any of its treaty obligations.[193] While takings in breach of general international law may go unquestioned, this is unlikely when a treaty governs the matter.[194]

Nazi expropriation policies and actions do not necessarily constitute sovereign actions that attract the act of state defence and preclude the court from adjudicating on the merits,[195] more particularly where the takings occurred in the occupied territories. If a government frustrates an owner's efforts to recover property when there is a final ruling that favours recovery, US courts consider international law to have been violated. Federal jurisdiction is conferred on the basis of the 'retaking' or 'second taking' of the property; sovereign immunity is not deemed a viable defence.[196]

UK courts may deal with this situation simply by extending the principle by which they will not enforce laws which are contrary to the public policy of the *lex fori*.[197]

---

191 *Malewicz v City of Amsterdam*, 517 F Supp 2d 322, 337 (DDC 2007).

192 I.e. not just the action of a state official or the act of a political party that happens to control the state, and it must be a state that still exists, otherwise there would be no foreign relations problem in questioning its acts.

193 *Menzel v List* 267 NYS 2d 804, 812 (NY Sup Ct 1966); Gerstenblith (n 118) 236.

194 A Aust, *Handbook of International Law* (2nd ed CUP 2010) 147.

195 *Menzel v List* 267 NYS 2d 804, 812 (NY Sup Ct 1966) (Chagall painting confiscated by *Einsatzstab Reichsleiter Rosenberg* (ERR) from an apartment in Brussels, Belgium; case between two individuals; no state involvement).

196 *Chasidei Chabad v Russian Federation* 528 F3d 934 (DC Circuit 2008) (expropriations of both Archive and Library of sacred manuscripts in the aftermath of the Bolshevik Revolution and during World War II did not preclude federal jurisdiction under the expropriation exception in the FSIA. Library owned by worldwide religious movement).

197 *City of Gotha and the Federal Republic of Germany v Sotheby's and Cobert Finance SA*, unreported case no 1997/G/185, 9 September 1998, QBD.

7. CONCLUSION

Restitution and anti-restitution movements coexist. Old and new conceptions of relevant facts and policy coexist. There is no presumptive right of restitution. Both 'rights-based arguments' and moral arguments have their place. Supranational standards may be found in contemporary international instruments or transnational law, but practice remains uneven. Differences in national outlook can be rather striking. The law needs to be ascertained on a case-by-case basis, and legislative amendments to enable restitution to take place can take time.

Restitution may be made for consideration, subject to conditions, or be part of broader co-operation measures.[198]

Against this backdrop, the complications traditionally associated with private international law can overshadow any existing potential it has for value-based decision-making in respect of restitution. If choice of law rules are cast in a national straitjacket, they will fail to live up to their function in disputes in which the menace of title laundering jeopardise a restitution action. Organised criminals, thieves, fences and handlers avoid jurisdictions that protect the title of the original owner, and launder title in jurisdictions where the *lex situs* rule can support their activities. Criminal law enforcement is territorial, and the norms intended for ordinary commerce or trade in commodities rehabilitate offenders. Consequently, smugglers can take advantage of the law to strengthen their position.

If classification is treated as anything but a conceptual device, it becomes overwhelmingly complex. It simplifies matters considerably when it is conceived as a gateway to the 'safety valve' of the public policy exception at the interface of domestic and international law. The two principal methods in choice of law seem dogmatically complex and mutually exclusive, but they offer an interesting choice between 'rule' and 'exception'. As in figure-ground perception, their difference is but a matter of degree.

---

198 E.g. agreement of 21 February 2006 between Italy and the Metropolitan Museum of Art. Any dispute under the agreement is to be decided by an arbitral tribunal on the basis of the rules of Arbitration and Conciliation of the ICC. Italy waived the right to civil or criminal action. R Contel, G Soldan and A Chechi, 'Case Euphronios Krater and Other Archaeological Objects – Italy and Metropolitan Museum of Art' <https://plone.unige.ch/art-adr/cases-affaires/euphronios-krater-and-other-archaeological-objects-2013-italy-and-metropolitan-museum-of-art/case-note-2013-euphronios-krater-and-other-archaeological-objects/view>, accessed 30 July 2014.

In the context of restitution claims, private international law also co-ordinates diverse national standards contained in legal provisions concerning archaeological finds or export regulations or ownership declarations in respect of finds of certain objects of national importance (vesting law). Foreign public law protective of cultural heritage is applied in the court of the forum, but not by virtue of a multilateral choice of law rule. The analysis of the movement, trade and protection of art and cultural objects is significantly simplified if courts extend recognition to rules that define their own sphere of application. The recognition of state claims that depend on state ownership of undiscovered antiquities leaving state borders will have the same effect as restitution of the objects that were removed from its territory.

While jurisprudential borrowing may lead to a muddled application of state and sovereign immunity, scope remains for the public policy exception to minimise normative clashes between global, national, private, object and market interests, and to shape outcomes.[199] This exception alleviates the pressure of global legal diversity and the tension between conflicts justice and material justice.[200] After all, it is able to facilitate value-based decision-making in cases of private and state theft, looting and trafficking of art and cultural objects.

---

[199] E Jayme, 'Globalization in Art Law: Clash of Interests and International Tendencies' (2005) 38 Vanderbilt Journal of Transnational Law 927, 929.

[200] Chechi (n 72) 101.

3. Taking a full turn: Both inwards and outwards

1. INTRODUCTION

Conflicts that arise as a result of a foreign element in a dispute become more frequent on account of the pressures of globalisation. These pressures give rise to conflicts between different levels of regulation, different structures of norm-production, and different cross-cultural backgrounds.[1] Claims to art and cultural objects could engage different sources of normativity, e.g. universal norms and national law; different norm-producing structures, e.g. different venues that are available in cross-border conflicts; and actors in the national, international and federal context with different interests and identities.

No wonder then that claims involving art and cultural objects present both 'traditional' and 'new' complexities.[2]

Normative conflicts may arise due to multiple sources of law, e.g. between different international conventions, codifications, transnational principles, customs and trade usages.[3] Conflicts may be evident between substantive rules and rules pertaining to procedure; between various choice of law rules; between substantive rules found in treaties that support restitution and priority rules found in domestic law; between the priority rules of the forum and the priority rules of a third state; or between a conflicts rule and a scope rule that stipulates when the law of X applies to an agreement concerning Y. The inter-mix of different types of rules, e.g. choice of law rules, scope rules, priority rules contained in forum statutes, foreign public law and jurisdiction rules (in respect of

---

[1] C Roodt, 'Reflections on Theory, Doctrine and Method in Choice of Law' (2007) XL CILSA 76, 80.

[2] G Carducci, 'The Growing Complexity of International Art Law: Conflict of Laws, Uniform Law, Mandatory Rules, UNSC Resolutions and EU Regulations' in BT Hoffman (ed), *Art and Cultural Heritage: Law, Policy and Practice* (CUP 2006) 68, 72.

[3] B Fauvarque-Cosson, 'Comparative Law and Conflict of Laws – Allies or Enemies?' (2001) 49 AJCL 407, 425.

consolidation, third-party joinder, impleader or intervention[4]) creates opportunities to find legal loopholes and results in legal uncertainty.[5] The mechanisms embedded in different structures of norm-production may encourage rulings that conflict with each other. The first question of law, 'who decides', must be confronted head-on when national courts, international tribunals and non-confrontational alternatives in dispute settlement[6] interact or compete across the principal hubs of the art market.

It may not always be possible to predict if the property model will control disposition and trade, or if it will recede into the background.[7] The Critical Heritage Studies Movement positions heritage studies not so much in relation to law, but in relation to public history, memory studies, museology, cultural heritage, tourism studies, architecture and planning, conservation, cultural geography, sociology, cultural policy, anthropology, archaeology and ethnomusicology, artistic research and artistic practices. Legal diversity can combine with differences in ethical standards in archaeology and conservation, for instance, raising new complexities.

Legal uncertainty may result in less than satisfactory outcomes and contributes to inconsistency across international cases.[8]

The chapter analyses two interfaces that are significant in respect of legal diversity in disputes involving art and cultural objects: first, where domestic law and private international law interact, and second, where private international law interacts with public international law and EU law.

An inward turn is necessary to uncover the essentials. The supposed 'neutrality' of the discipline has become too closely associated with the structure and function of multilateral conflict rules. The traditionalist conviction that choice of law needs to be 'value-neutral' in order to reduce the likelihood of the court relying on subjective values in conflicts

---

4 These rules may extend to intra-national conflicts between indigenous and settler communities, which are not covered in this work. On intra-national conflicts, see JP Fishman, 'Locating the International Interest in Intranational Cultural Property Disputes' (2010) 35 The Yale Journal of International Law 347.

5 IF Gazzini, *Cultural Property Disputes: The Role of Arbitration in Resolving Non-Contractual Disputes* (Transnational Publishers Inc. 2004) 53.

6 The extent to which these demonstrate a preference for a particular legal family or culture may differ.

7 K Alderman, 'The Human Right to Cultural Property' [2011] Michigan Journal of International Law 69.

8 H Hartung, 'The Holocaust and World War II Looted Art: Arbitrated between Great Dreams and Reality' in The International Bureau of the Permanent Court of Arbitration (ed), *Resolution of Cultural Property Disputes* (The Hague 2004) 327, 331.

rules to justify the application of forum law, is easily distorted into a paradigm in which there is no room for substantive interests and material justice and which precludes an outward turn in the discipline.

An outward turn is necessary to incorporate and co-ordinate public law interests hitherto applied exclusively by way of an exception to the multilateral rule. Conceptions of the public good, as found in public law, are just as relevant in international litigation as are considerations of private fairness and convenience. Private international law brims with ideas and theories of international ordering when regulatory systems come into conflict in private disputes. Private international law imposes national or federal limits on the authority of state regulators, and functions as a system of rights protection in the relations between the state and individuals at the same time.[9] Its public, international dimension supports the achievement of optimal co-ordination between and among different legal frameworks in the interest of global welfare.

The federal dimension is highly relevant for the EU, where the harmonisation of private international law has moved forward in leaps and bounds,[10] but where property law has not formed part of the trend. Presumably, differences in respect of the definitions, methods and conditions for transfer, levels of abstraction, approaches to organisation, and remedies for protection would make harmonisation difficult to achieve.

A reference to public policy necessarily encompasses the public policy of both the Member State and that of the EU (which includes the ECHR).[11] Nationalist conceptions cannot simply be replaced by freedom of movement and commercial dealings that favour good faith purchasers in title disputes.[12] Full account must be taken of the volume of the flow of objects of cultural, historical, ethnological and artistic value from source states into intermediary and market states in the argument for freedom of movement.[13]

---

9 A Mills, *The Confluence of Public and Private International Law* (CUP 2010) 206–8.

10 E.g. jurisdiction and applicable law in contractual and non-contractual obligations.

11 DPF Arroyo, 'Private International Law and Comparative Law: A Relationship Challenged by International and Supranational Law' (2009) XI Yearbook of Private International Law 31, 60.

12 Arroyo (n 11) 57.

13 LV Prott, 'Problems of Private International Law for the Protection of the Cultural Heritage' V *Recueil des Cours* (The Hague 1989) 215, 235.

Private international law offers parties a useful negotiating tool in disputes over ownership, possession, return, restitution and possible compensation. It can inform and strengthen a particular legal position, but it can also be a flexible bargaining tool.

2. PRIVATE INTERNATIONAL LAW: CO-ORDINATION WITH A VIEW TO DISPUTE SETTLEMENT AND RESTITUTION

2.1 Where Domestic Law and Private International Law Interact

Various taxonomies attempt to categorise the interests – global, national, private, public, object, market – that intermingle at the meeting point between private international law and cultural heritage law. The search for workable theories has oscillated between the standards propounded by nationalism and internationalism. The long-standing debate about who owns the past and the scope of domestic laws in this debate have separated the 'cultural internationalists' from the 'cultural nationalists'.[14]

Cultural property nationalists attribute a national character to objects independent of their location and ownership. Nations and the descendants of ancient civilisations are regarded as having an inalienable interest in their cultural property, and adherents argue in favour of the legitimacy of national export controls and demands for restitution.[15] The nationalists accord primacy to the interests of source states and support control by the culture that produced the object even if the means for proper conservation practices are hard to find.

The internationalists attach great meaning to the notion of the 'cultural heritage of mankind'.[16] Preservation of and access to objects of artistic, archaeological, ethnological or historical interest are highly regarded as 'components of common human culture, whatever their places of origin or present location, independent of property rights or national jurisdiction'.[17] Utilitarian arguments associated with cultural property internationalism originated in the concern for the safety of the common cultural

---

[14] E.g. JH Merryman, 'Two Ways of Thinking about Cultural Property' [1986] AJIL 831; JH Merryman, 'The Public Interest in Cultural Property' [1989] California Law Review 339, 355ff.

[15] E.g. Merryman (n 14) 831; Preamble to the 1970 UNESCO Convention.

[16] 1954 Hague Convention for the Protection of Cultural Property in the Event of Armed Conflict 249 UNTS 240 (1956).

[17] Merryman (n 14) 831.

heritage endangered by war. These arguments have been used, however, to indicate how national restrictions on the sale and export of cultural materials contribute to the growing black market in art and antiquities.[18] Internationalists argue that source nations are under a duty to allow sale, export and import of cultural objects for the sake of preservation and access.[19] Some among them propose a radical reduction in export restrictions.[20] They criticise what they see as the 'blind' return in response to export embargoes by source nations, and oppose the automatic enforcement of foreign export laws.[21] They are also wary of the unquestioning enforcement of state ownership legislation, tending to assume that state ownership laws are export regulations in disguise[22] or grant source states the power to determine whether movement is legitimate and not.[23]

These arguments are attractive where the antiquities in question have been assimilated in the culture of the place of location after export; the connection with the country of origin has become tenuous; and conservation, documentation and preservation practices are of a low standard in the country of origin. These arguments lose some of their appeal where tension between group rights and the nation prevent the state from satisfying citizens' claims to the protection of cultural heritage. If tensions remain at this basic level, it is unreasonable to expect national controls of outflow to be relaxed.

---

18 PM Bator, 'An Essay on the International Trade in Art' (1982) 34 Stanford Law Review 275, 315, 318. C Vitale, 'The Protection of Cultural Heritage between the EU Legal Order and the Global Legal Space' in E Chite and BG Mattarella (eds), *Global Administrative Law and EU Administrative Law: Relationships, Legal Issues and Comparison* (Springer Verlag 2011) 211, 219.

19 Bator (n 18) 287; Merryman (n 14) 831; JH Merryman, 'Thinking about the Elgin Marbles' [1985] Michigan Law Review 1881, 1915–1921; WG Pearlstein, 'Buying and Selling in Today's Market' (2012) 3 Spencer's Art Law Journal 2.

20 CC Coggins, 'A Licit International Traffic in Ancient Art: Let There Be Light' (1995) 4 IJCP 61, 63, 67 insists that export controls are counter-productive.

21 Coggins (n 20) 64.

22 Merryman (n 14) 363; Bator (n 18) 348–49; KE Yasaitis, 'National Ownership Laws as Cultural Property Protection Policy: The Emerging Trend in *United States v Schultz*' (2005) 12 IJCP 95, 99.

23 JH Merryman and JAR Nafziger, 'The Private International Law of Cultural Property in the United States' (1994) 42 AJCL Supplement 221, 237.

The dualistic nationalist-internationalist conception of the scope of movement of antiquities cannot adequately explain the present state of private international law in respect of moveable cultural property.[24] It does not represent an accurate reflection of the spirit of the law and the policy that underlies it.

The 1995 UNIDROIT (Rome) Convention on Stolen or Illegally Exported Cultural Objects[25] is primarily concerned with the question of return of stolen or illegally excavated objects to the original owner, be it a nation, a private person or a legal person. Articles 5 and 6 promote the enforcement of export controls of countries of origin where these exist, implying that such restrictions are valid and legitimate.[26] Archaeological objects need not be designated by the state in order to enjoy the protection of the Convention. Unregistered and uninventoried objects also qualify for return.

Statutes that assert state ownership in the vestiges of the past are in line with the UN General Assembly Resolutions recommending that states adopt or strengthen the necessary protective legislation with regard to their own heritage and that of other peoples.[27] Inventories of museum collections should include not only the items on display, but ideally also a photographic record of items held in storage. States are encouraged to require photographic documentation of each object brought to light during excavations to be made available to national authorities, as per a clause in excavation permits.

Source states can maximise their chances to succeed with state ownership claims by means of clear regulation that creates a presumption

---

[24] The human dimension of international cultural heritage law and the current threat against the archaeological heritage also remain unaccounted for. See M Papa-Sokal, 'Beyond the Nationalist-Internationalist Polarisation in the Protection of the Archaeological Heritage' (2009) 14 Art Antiquity and Law 237, 238, 265; F Francioni, 'The Human Dimension of International Cultural Heritage Law: An Introduction' (2011) 22 EJIL 9.

[25] 1995 UNIDROIT Convention on Stolen or Illegally Exported Cultural Objects, 24 June 1995, 34 ILM 1330; entry into force 1 July 1998. <http://www.unidroit.org/instruments/cultural-property/1995-convention> accessed 24 February 2014.

[26] Chapter III resonates with Art 1(b).

[27] UN General Assembly Resolutions on the Return or Restitution of Cultural Property to the Countries of Origin A/Res/48/15 of 2 November 1993; A/Res/67/80 of 12 March 2013.

that possessors of undocumented items have stolen those items.[28] The Model Provisions on State Ownership of Undiscovered Cultural Objects support this idea.[29] Casting doubt on the seller's title necessarily raises fears of lawsuits by the state of origin.[30]

The stark dichotomy between the nationalist and internationalist views also misses the point that every cultural heritage policy is imbued with elements from both sides.[31] The main pitfalls of 'cultural property internationalism' include the convenient hide-out it provides for the appropriation of poor nations' heritage that flows out into wealthy countries, links with commercial interests, and the legitimising of private collecting of antiquities.[32] In turn, 'cultural property nationalism' provides an easy excuse for inadequate blanket conservation measures, and suffers from the distasteful history of Nazi control over supposedly 'Aryan' artwork which was perpetrated in the name of nationalism.[33]

For present purposes, the most fundamental objection against the dichotomous view is its failure to ameliorate the normative conflicts that may arise between legal rules. The internationalists dismiss the need for market states to enforce foreign export control legislation and public domain legislation, without differentiating between the two categories.[34] The effect of export controls on property rights in foreign jurisdictions[35] and the categories of objects that may be legally traded and/or exported[36] deserve more systematic attention. The rule that claims application, and

---

[28] C Forrest, 'Strengthening the International Regime for the Prevention of the Illicit Trade in Cultural Heritage' (2003) 4 Melbourne Journal of International Law 592 sub V.

[29] M Frigo, 'Model Provisions on State Ownership of Undiscovered Cultural Objects – Introduction' [2011] Uniform Law Review 1044.

[30] M Papa-Sokal, 'Beyond the Nationalist-Internationalist Polarisation in the Protection of the Archaeological Heritage' (2009) 14 Art Antiquity and Law 237, 265.

[31] Papa-Sokal (n 30) 245.

[32] Papa-Sokal (n 30) 272.

[33] G Mihan, *Looted Treasure: Germany's Raid on Art* (Alliance Press 1944) 7; MJ Harris, 'Who Owns the Pot of Gold at the End of the Rainbow? A Review of the Impact of Cultural Property on Finders and Salvage Laws' (1997) 14 Arizona Journal of International and Comparative Law 224, 238.

[34] Bator (n 18) 280 n. 8 makes an express declaration in this regard; N Mealy, 'Mediation's Potential Role in International Cultural Property Disputes' (2011) 26 Ohio State Journal on Dispute Resolution 169, 177.

[35] Papa-Sokal (n 30) 259–60.

[36] J Ulph and I Smith, *The Illicit Trade in Art and Antiquities* (Hart 2012) 264.

the interests that underpin this rule, must be considered in the context of claims for return of smuggled objects, or objects that were sold in contravention of state ownership legislation.[37] It is an encouraging sign that, despite great differences in regard to both method and analysis, rulings in respect of undiscovered and unrecorded finds are converging in the US and the UK. The convergence is discussed in detail in Chapter 7.

2.2 Where Private and Public International Law Meet

Private international law rules are not universally agreed in the way that the rules of public international law are. This obvious difference means that efforts to abstract a supposed hierarchy between public international law and private international law cannot but fail.[38] It would be more realistic to posit that their interaction is marked by subtle affinity, so that theoretical perspectives on private international law that remain blind to the aspiration embodied in international norms deserves closer scrutiny. This subtle affinity is evident from several observations.

First, the international ordering established by rules of private international law to reduce conflict between regulatory systems replicates norms of public international law. Just as the full faith and credit clause in the US Constitution poses a basic minimum standard, the minimum standard does not necessitate the adoption of particular jurisdiction rules; states determine the rules within the outer limits set thereby.[39] Secondly, public international law is of relevance in all states, regardless of their socio-economic, cultural, political or religious histories,[40] as a type of 'applicable law'. Certain rules of private international law have the status of rules of public international law. They operate within the framework set by public international law; they also define international norms.[41] In turn, customary international law, treaties and soft law enrich the international dimension in which these disciplines meet up in civil claims for restitution. There are many horizontal contacts between private international law and public international law in this context, where there

---

37 Papa-Sokal (n 30) 238, 256, 260ff.

38 H Jokela, 'Internationalism in Private International Law' in DS Clark (ed), *Comparative and Private International Law Essays in Honor of John Henry Merryman on his Seventieth Birthday* (Duncker & Humblot 1990) 395, 397.

39 Mills (n 9) 242.

40 RY Jennings, 'Universal International Law in a Multicultural World' in M Bos and I Brownlie (eds), *Liber Amicorum for the Rt Hon Lord Wilberforce* (Clarendon Press 1987) 39, 40.

41 Mills (n 9) 24.

is potential for 'confluence'. Thirdly, dissonant decisions by domestic courts in international questions is of interest to both disciplines to the extent that they are concerned with the principles underlying the allocation of regulatory authority between states.[42]

2.3 Wartime: International Law of Armed Conflicts and Military Occupation

The exemption of cultural objects from the consequences of acts of war was contemplated in the sixteenth century, but the development of a principle that private property should not be plundered did not develop then. The principle took shape in the seventeenth century, when Grotius asserted that '… what is captured during an unjust war is to be restored, and not only by the captors [those who have taken property], but by others, into whose hands they have anyhow come'.[43] The first protections for cultural property that were enacted beyond national attempts were developed in the context of the plunders and spoils of armed conflicts and military occupation.[44] The idea of a separate category underpinned a commitment to keep in check the appropriation of war booty. The concept of a 'cultural heritage of all mankind' reflects a common concern and commitment to preserve, protect and keep safe art, religious and cultural property that warranted special treatment during wartime.[45] If plundered property was identified and located, it had to be restored to its country of origin. International protections of cultural property do not appoint the international community as titleholder of cultural heritage.[46] The principle that the looting of works of art transgresses the laws and customs of war showed signs of becoming established by the beginning of the nineteenth century. In 1812, a Canadian court held that objects of artistic value aboard a ship bound from Italy to Philadelphia during military hostilities between the US and England had to be returned to the

---

[42] Mills (n 10) 228.

[43] Hugonis Grotii, *De Iure Belli et Pacis* 1625 Book III Section XVI (John W Parker 1853) 281–82.

[44] Gazzini (n 5) 1.

[45] A Chechi, *The Settlement of International Cultural Heritage Disputes: Towards a Lex Culturalis?* (unpublished PhD Thesis EUI 2011) 30, 125.

[46] Used first in the Hague Convention of 1954, The Hague Convention for the Protection of Cultural Property in the Event of Armed Conflict, 14 May 1954; entry into force 7 August 1956; 249 UNTS 215. It appears also in the 1972 Convention Concerning the Protection of the World Cultural and Natural Heritage, 16 November 1972; entry into force on 17 December 1975; 1037 UNTS 151.

owner because they were protected from seizure during war.[47] This bold judicial statement declared that arts and sciences were entitled to protection in times of war, because of the common interest of all. Nonetheless, states and national legal norms carry most of the responsibility for the protection of the cultural heritage within their own territories and within territories occupied in wartime.[48]

As was indicated in Chapter 1, the list of international instruments relevant to the legal protection of cultural objects in wartime is extensive. The 1907 Hague Convention on the Laws and Customs of War on Land[49] reaffirmed and expanded on the principle that wartime plunder was prohibited, without an attempt to regulate the return of stolen property. It forbade the seizure and destruction of foreign cultural property in occupied war territories, except when military necessity required this, and provided for compensation when its provisions were violated.[50] Necessity is a general limitation to any use of force in self-defence, or to the conduct of hostilities. However, it can be pleaded to exonerate a state from responsibility.

Among the various codes applicable to wartime is the 1954 Hague Convention for the Protection of Cultural Property in the Event of Armed Conflict,[51] which requires the safeguarding of cultural property during occupation or during war. If parties have not signed up to the 1954 Hague Convention, customary international law will affect the private international law argument.[52] Plunder, destruction or damage of cultural objects violates customary international law recognising them as a special protected category in wartime. In order to be considered a rule of customary law, a rule needs to be based on a widespread, repetitive and

---

[47] *Case of the Vessel Marquis de Somereuils* 1812: Stewart's Vice-Admiralty Reports for Nova Scotia 1803–1813, 482; K Chamberlain, 'Holocaust Art Claims and Public International Law' (2008) 13 Art Antiquity and Law 351.

[48] P Gerstenblith, 'The Public Interest in the Restitution of Cultural Objects' (2001) 16 Conn J Int L 197, 201, 211; Chechi (n 45) 124.

[49] Art 23 of the Convention (IV) Respecting the Laws and Customs of War on Land and Its Annex of Regulations, The Hague, 18 October 1907, The Hague, 18 October 1907, TS 539; entry into force 26 January 1910.

[50] Arts 46, 47, 53, 56.

[51] The Hague, 14 May 1954.

[52] This was the finding of the Eritrea/Ethiopia Claims Commission. The Commission was established under the Algiers Peace Agreement of December 2000 to resolve the complaint in respect of the 'Stela of Matara'. Ethiopia felled the Stela of Matara when it was at war with Eritrea, between 1998 and 2000. Partial Award – Central Front, Eritrea's Claims 2, 4, 6, 7, 8 and 22, 28 April 2004 § 13.

virtually uniform practice of states that are actively involved in a particular practice or field. The practice must also be accepted as a legal obligation to act that way (*opinio juris*); not as mere courtesy or pragmatism.[53] Not all categories of cultural state property qualify for protection as customary international law, however. For the majority of categories, a virtually uniform acceptance as would be evident from what the states that are involved in a particular practice do and say is bound to be lacking.

The likely outcome of customary international law argument could affect the parties' choice of dispute resolution mechanisms.

2.3.1 Ad hoc measures adopted in modern conflicts

In emergency situations, the UN Security Council may adopt *ad hoc* rules of international law to stem illicit trafficking in cultural property and to restore cultural objects to their nations of origin. A striking example presented itself when the First Gulf Conflict caused a massive cultural crisis. After April 2003, which was when coalition forces invaded Iraq, the looting of archaeological sites escalated. There were no US plans in place to protect Iraq's cultural and archaeological heritage against bombing and post-war looting in accordance with the Second Protocol of the 1954 Hague Convention for the Protection of Cultural Property in the Event of Armed Conflict 1999.[54] The US became a member of the 1954 Hague Convention in 2009, but it did not adopt the Protocols. US forces took no action against looting civilians and Iraqi snipers who used heritage sites for military operations in direct breach of the First Protocol 1949 Geneva Convention. The international community responded with a declaration of nullity of transactions creating ownership in cultural objects originating from Iraq.[55] Several UN Security Council instruments were adopted[56] to order the return of property to Kuwait[57] and Iraq.[58] The trade or transfer of cultural objects suspected of illegal

---

[53] N van Woudenberg, *State Immunity and Cultural Objects on Loan* (Martinus Nijhoff 2012) 33ff, 43.

[54] The Hague, 26 March 1999; entry into force in 2004. For status table see <http://www.icrc.org/ihl.nsf/INTRO/590> accessed 25 February 2014.

[55] B Schönenberger, *The Restitution of Cultural Assets* (Eleven International Publishing 2009) 225.

[56] Ibid.

[57] Resolution 686 (1991) of 2 March 1991 ordered the return of property to Kuwait.

[58] Resolution 661 (1990) of 6 August 1990; Resolution 1483 (2003) of 22 May 2003 (adopted in terms of Article 48 of the UN Charter). The latter ordered

removal was prohibited. The measures have retrospective effect and may be extended by the Security Council or by the implementing state.[59] The special law is binding on all UN Member States by virtue of the UN Charter.[60]

The measures adopted by the Security Council exemplify a special restitution law that has the effect of declaring previous grounds for property transfer null and void. Illegal appropriation and transfer of cultural objects by the occupying power, and the failure to return objects that had been transferred illegally, would infringe this mandatory rule.

At the EU level, the measures in respect of Iraqi property were implemented by way of Council Regulation 1210/2003 of 7 July 2003.[61] Council Regulation 1210/2003 prohibits the import or introduction, export or removal from Iraq, as well as the dealing in Iraqi cultural property. Its effects extend to any international agreement signed, any contract concluded, or any licence or permit granted before its entry into force.[62] The Regulation has direct effect in the legal systems of the Member States and coexists with the UN Security Council Resolution 1483. If return is effected in accordance with the Security Council Resolution, the prohibitions under Regulation 1210 cease to apply.[63]

Many nations implemented Resolution 1483 (2003) by means of administrative measures. The US have had sanctions in place for the removal of materials from Iraq since 1990, and merely left them to continue in an extended form.[64] The UK implemented this Resolution by way of the Iraq (UN Sanctions) Order 2003 of 12 June 2003. Article 8 prohibits the importation and exportation of cultural objects illegally removed from any location in Iraq after 6 August 1990, and declares the legality of the removal under UK law or any other law to be immaterial. The fact that documentation verifying the ownership of museums had

---

the return of Iraqi cultural property removed from cultural institutions in Iraq since the adoption of Resolution 661.

59 Carducci (n 2) 81.

60 Francioni (n 24) 14.

61 Council Regulation (EC) No 1210/2003 of 7 July 2003 concerning certain specific restrictions on economic and financial relations with Iraq and repealing Regulation (EC) No 2465/96, OJ L 169/6, 8.7.2003.

62 Art 14.

63 Carducci (n 2) 81.

64 P Gerstenblith, 'Recent Developments in the Legal Protection of Cultural Heritage' in N Brodie, MM Kersel, C Luke and K Walker Tubb (eds), *Archaeology, Cultural Heritage and the Antiquities Trade* (University Press of Florida 2006) 68, 81.

been compromised or destroyed, complicates the prosecution and conviction under looting and theft statutes. The legal position of Iraqi institutions and owners is eased somewhat by a reversal of the burden of proof. It has shifted away from the person alleging bad faith on the purchaser's part onto the possessor, so that diligence at the time of acquisition can be assessed.

Because the main objective of Resolution 1483 (2003) was to prevent the illegal trade in these objects,[65] this instrument does not contain any direct cause of action for restitution. Fortunately, because Iraq has declared itself to be the owner of all antiquities lost on its territory, the state is able to claim return of its cultural heritage.

2.3.2 The ICJ may rule on aspects of confiscation

The principal judicial organ of the United Nations, the International Court of Justice (ICJ), was established by the United Nations Charter in 1945.[66] The primary function of the ICJ is to adjudicate in disputes brought before it by states, and to provide authoritative, influential advisory opinions on matters which international organisations, agencies and the UN General Assembly may refer to it. Its jurisdiction extends to cultural heritage disputes in inter-state controversies[67] but it has not built up a credible record of settling international cultural heritage disputes.[68]

First, its 1962 finding on Cambodia's entitlement to restitution in the *Merits (Cambodia v Thailand)* case[69] was incidental to the delimitation of borders between the two states. Ultimately, the ruling did not restore peace to the area. Cambodia filed for an interpretation of the 1962 judgment in 2011.

A claim in respect of the confiscation by Czechoslovakia in 1945 of a painting by the seventeenth-century Dutch artist Pieter van Laer[70] was the

---

[65] Schönenberger (n 55) 226–27 indicates the uncertainty over who should lodge a restitution claim.

[66] Art 92 of the UN Charter, 24 October 1945, 1 UNTS XVI; J van Haersolte-van Hof, 'The Revitalization of the Permanent Court of Arbitration' [2007] NILR 395.

[67] Gazzini (n 5) 51.

[68] A Chechi, 'Some Reflections on International Adjudication of Cultural Heritage-Related Cases' (2013) 10 TDM Special Issue 1, 3–5.

[69] Judgment of 15 June 1962, ICJ Rep 1962.

[70] 1599–c. 1642. The painting is titled 'A Roman Lime Quarry'.

subject of several suits.[71] In *Certain Property (Liechtenstein v Germany)*[72] the ICJ held it lacked jurisdiction *ratione temporis* to decide the dispute, as the issue concerned facts that had taken place long before 1980, which is when the European Convention for the Peaceful Settlement of International Disputes of 29 April 1957 entered into force between Liechtenstein and Germany. Consequently, it could not find that Article 1 of the 1957 Convention applied to the painting in question.

The link between the intention to destroy a group and the destruction of cultural objects that belong to it may seem self-evident, but the ICJ held that the obliteration of traces of life and culture of the Muslim population did not constitute genocide in *Bosnia and Herzegovina v Serbia and Montenegro*.[73]

The pitfalls of international litigation include uncertain outcomes.[74] State consent to the jurisdiction of an international court determines the functioning and effectiveness of that court to a large extent. States may also decide not to comply with judicial rulings.[75]

2.4 Restitution Claims to Nazi Spoliated Art in International Law

The theft and counter-theft which the Axis and the Allies engaged in during World War II sparked the renewal of international efforts to protect cultural objects against destruction and vandalism in times of war. Most peace treaties contain clauses on restitution of war booty, of which cultural objects were a popular kind, but they find no application in the context of the Nazi era. The Nazi art confiscation programme was a systematic plunder perpetrated against European Jews, rather than a general destruction associated with more common military action.[76] As

---

[71] Czechoslovakia was an allied country during World War II. Courts in Czechoslovakia and Germany rejected the claim. In *Prince Hans-Adam II of Liechtenstein v Germany* (Application no 42527/98, 21 July 2001), the ECtHR held that the exclusion of jurisdiction in post-war Germany was not unreasonable.

[72] *Certain Property (Liechtenstein v Germany)*, Preliminary Objections, Judgment of 10 February 2005, ICJ Rep (2005).

[73] *Application of the Convention on the Prevention and Punishment of the Crime of Genocide, (Bosnia and Herzegovina v Serbia and Montenegro)*, Judgment of 26 February 2007, ICJ Rep (2007); but findings of the International Criminal Tribunal for the Former Yugoslavia recognise the connection.

[74] Chechi (n 68) 4–5.

[75] Chechi (n 68) 7.

[76] E.g. *Application of the Convention on the Prevention and Punishment of the Crime of Genocide, (Bosnia and Herzegovina v Serbia and Montenegro)*,

such, it deserves to be distinguished from the general category of plunder in war.[77] Nonetheless, it has also been argued that pertinent provisions of the 1907 Hague Convention[78] deserve to be treated as peremptory norms in international law (*jus cogens*) in cases of breach and could apply,[79] because typical cases of wartime plunder of cultural objects were originally classified as a *delicta juris gentium* (an international crime).

With the Declaration of London in 1943, Allied nations imposed a responsibility on states to return displaced property, and called on neutral states to undertake restitution.[80] The Declaration included the right to declare invalid both transfers by open looting and by means that were purportedly effected voluntarily and seemingly legal. It publicly disavowed the protection of anyone who acquired looted works of art in good faith. The underlying principle was simple: no one ought to benefit from unlawful acts.[81] This aspect is significant because it adopts a position on a question that private international law is called on to determine. Chapter 6 provides further analysis of this issue, and explores the potential application of the Second Protocol to the 1954 Hague Convention for the Protection of Cultural Property in the Event of Armed Conflict in the context of Nazi spoliated art.[82]

The public international law doctrine of state immunity operates as a direct limitation on jurisdiction and attachment of state property in litigation. If the plea succeeds, it prevents courts from exercising jurisdiction over the state. Nazi expropriation policies and actions do not necessarily constitute sovereign actions that preclude the court from

---

Judgment of 26 February 2007, ICJ Rep (2007), §§ 335–44 (recognising the systematic destruction of religious buildings as an international crime but declining to consider these acts as constituting evidence of the specific intent to commit genocide).

77 Hartung (n 8) 330; KA Falconer, 'When Honour Will Not Suffice' (2000) 21 University of Pennsylvania Journal of International Economic Law 383, 423.

78 Arts 46, 47, 56.

79 Hartung (n 8) 333.

80 Inter-Allied Declaration against Acts of Dispossession Committed in Territories under Enemy Occupation and Control (London, 5 January 1943), <http://www.lootedartcommission.com/inter-allied-declaration> accessed 24 February 2014. The Declaration was signed by 17 governments and the French National Committee.

81 Chamberlain (n 47) 353.

82 The Hague, 26 March 1999; entry into force in 2004. For status table see <http://www.icrc.org/ihl.nsf/INTRO/590> accessed 24 February 2014. The US and the UK have not ratified it.

adjudicating on the merits, however. Other dispute resolution fora are not precluded from hearing a case either.

2.5 Peacetime Solutions: UNESCO and UNIDROIT Treaties

States look to international conventions in their attempt to prevent the cross-border transfer of stolen cultural objects, to manage the problems caused by different conceptions of property rights and ownership, and to bring the unpredictability of the normative content of the applicable law identified by a choice of law rule under control. Two influential UNESCO cultural heritage conventions are concerned with the protection of moveable cultural objects. Both of them are contemporary peacetime treaties that grant signatory states a right to restrict trade of designated items of cultural significance, even if privately owned, thus potentially impacting peacetime looting and destruction of archaeological sites. Foremost is the 1970 UNESCO Convention on the Means of Prohibiting and Preventing the Illicit Import, Export and Transfer of Ownership of Cultural Property,[83] and the other is the 1995 UNIDROIT (Rome) Convention on Stolen or Illegally Exported Cultural Objects.[84] The 2005 UNESCO Convention on the Protection and Promotion of the Diversity of Cultural Expressions[85] is silent on the restitution of tangible heritage.

The UNESCO Convention is meant to be a broad framework for inter-governmental collaboration. Individuals and businesses are entitled to claim restitution only where the law of the state party in question permits this.[86] The UNIDROIT Convention is a mixed instrument that contains both international and private law principles to fill the gaps and remedy the weaknesses of the UNESCO Convention.[87] States are duty-bound to avoid entering into conflicting treaty obligations and contributing to an actual collision of such obligations by Article 26 of the Vienna

---

[83] Art 13 of the 1970 UNESCO Convention on the Means of Prohibiting and Preventing the Illicit Import, Export and Transfer of Ownership of Cultural Property, 14 November 1970, 823 UNTS 231; 10 ILM 289; entry into force on 24 April 1972.

[84] See n 25.

[85] 2005 UNESCO Convention on the Protection and Promotion of the Diversity of Cultural Expressions, 20 October 2005, CLT-2005/Convention Diversite-Cult Rev <http://www.unesco.org/fileadmin/MULTIMEDIA/HQ/CLT/CLT/pdf/conventiontext_og_civilsociety_en.pdf> accessed 25 February 2014.

[86] Art 13(c).

[87] NR Lenzner, 'The Illicit International Trade in Cultural Property: Does the UNIDROIT Convention Provide an Effective Remedy for the Shortcomings

Convention on the Law of Treaties.[88] States that are party to both instruments must avoid contributing to 'normative tension' between these two instruments.

National legislative schemes that incorporate the UNESCO and UNIDROIT instruments[89] maximise the opportunities for the jurisdictions concerned to discourage the illicit trade and encourage restitution. Any gaps remaining are to be filled by general private international law rules that remain applicable alongside these instruments.[90]

The effectiveness of international and national protections turns on prevention and control, direct sanctions and rights, and restitution.[91] The effectiveness of the provisions contained in the cultural conventions closely depends on how well-respected and closely followed these instruments are. These aspects are assessed in turn.

2.5.1 Prevention and control

UNESCO drafted the 1970 Convention on Prohibiting and Preventing the Illicit Import, Export and Transfer of Cultural Property in response to concerns about illegal trade and transfer of cultural heritage from source nations and experts. It is a document of intent that aims to improve 'international cooperation towards preserving cultural treasures that … are of importance to the nations whence they originate'. It is also set on improving 'international understanding of our common heritage'.[92] It directs signatory states towards the adoption of preventative measures against illicit trade at the domestic level. These measures include setting up national services to ensure protection; creating inventories of important objects; export certificates; import controls; penal and administrative sanctions; awareness activities; and rules governing the conduct of curators, collectors and antique dealers.[93]

Signatory states are encouraged to protect the cultural property located inside their borders by means of registers or monitoring of movement.

---

of the UNESCO Convention?' (1994) 15 University of Pennsylvania Journal of International Business 469, 491; DL Carey Miller, DW Meyers and AL Cowe, 'Restitution of Art and Cultural Objects: A Re-Assessment of the Role of Limitation' [2001] Art Antiquity and Law 1, 9.

[88] Vienna Convention on the Law of Treaties, 23 May 1969, vol 1155 UNTS 331; entry into force 27 January 1980.

[89] E.g. New Zealand. Cf Protected Objects Amendment Act 2006.

[90] Carducci (n 2) 80.

[91] After the structure employed in Gazzini (n 5) 10ff.

[92] S Rep No 97-564 21 (1982).

[93] Arts 5–8.

They are to establish a system of export certificates to improve the effective enforcement of domestic export controls designed to counter illicit removals from the territory of a state party.

Article 7a encourages states to exert some control over the acquisitions policy of museums, insofar as this would be consistent with their domestic laws. Article 7(b)(i) prohibits importation of cultural objects stolen from the documented inventory of museums or religious or secular public monuments and subsequently exported. Specific procedures apply at diplomatic level for requests for the return of such inventoried cultural objects.

Article 9 creates a mechanism for signatories' urgent applications to the executive branch to prohibit the import of archaeological and ethnological material originating from a Contracting Party whose cultural patrimony is in jeopardy from pillage.[94] This provision does not relate to ownership or restitution claims but constitutes a preventative step in respect of such claims.

The Convention is a broadly construed framework which allows for discretion in its application.[95] As such, it is non-self-executing. There is ample room for the establishment and improvement of laws and mechanisms for implementation in several state parties.[96]

The 1995 UNIDROIT (Rome) Convention on Stolen or Illegally Exported Cultural Objects was an attempt to unify the private law aspects of international cultural property law, in the interest of finding a uniform solution to the problem of trafficking in stolen and/or illegally excavated or illegally exported cultural objects.[97] Objects exported illegally are to be restituted to the state of origin when cultural and scientific significance is demonstrable. Recovery under the UNIDROIT Convention does not depend on government intervention or state designation of property.[98]

The UNIDROIT Convention is the only cultural convention to consider claims for restitution brought by private individuals. Article 3 relies on

---

94 See in general J Church, 'Evaluating the Effectiveness of Foreign Laws on National Ownership of Cultural Property in US Courts' [1992] Columbia Journal of Transnational Law 179, 214, 223; J Church 'Evolving US Case Law on Cultural Property Disputes' [1993] IJCP 47, 56; KJ Warren, 'Perspectives of the Victims: Case Studies' in PM Messenger (ed), *The Ethics of Collecting Cultural Property* (University of New Mexico Press 1989) 17ff.

95 Gazzini (n 5) 7.

96 Cf the reason why Nigeria's claim to the Nok statutes failed in *Federal Republic of Nigeria v Alain de Montbrison*, Cour de Cassation, judgment of 20 September 2006.

97 Carey Miller et al. (n 87) 9.

98 Arts 1–2.

the common law presumption of *nemo dat quod non habet*[99] by placing the possessor under an obligation to return stolen property. A claim for the return of an object cannot be countered by acquisition in good faith. Therefore, innocent purchasers are not exempt. Because the Convention assumes that the current possessor of the object will have no legal right thereto, it does not take account of due diligence on the part of a good faith purchaser. The UNIDROIT Convention invites an assessment of good faith and due diligence in the compensation stage, when restitution is indicated. The more radical *nemo dat* alternative of the common law does not allow for compensation. This approach would have been cheaper and arguably also more effective in terms of the standard of care.

Article 3(2) considers an object unlawfully excavated or lawfully excavated but unlawfully retained as stolen. This aspect is considered the Convention's greatest gain.[100]

Restitution claims lodged in terms of the UNIDROIT Convention are subject to the discovery rule. A claim for restitution or return is timely made if brought within a general limitation period of 50 years, reduced to three years if knowledge of the location or the identity of the possessor of the cultural object is gained. This limitation also applies to claims relating to objects stolen from monuments or archaeological sites or from public collections. There is the possibility of extending the time limit to 75 years if a state stipulates this when it becomes bound by the Convention.[101] There is also a possibility to extend the limitations period in accordance with the national law of the adjudicating body when this is beneficial to claimants under Article 11. Concealment of the object in bad faith allows for this under Article 11(a)(ii). It is possible to conceal objects until the time limitation expires.[102] An extension could be crucial. The claim is barred absolutely 50 years after the theft. Article 11 rules out any defence of open possession as owner, with the result that the 50-year rule introduces a higher level of protection for the owner compared to many domestic legal systems. These provisions support the aim of the Convention to deter bad faith acquisition of illegally obtained cultural objects. However, if courts were to focus on the good or bad

---

[99] In a title contest involving moveable property, this rule gives preference to an original owner over a good-faith purchaser.

[100] Ulph and Smith (n 36) 53.

[101] Arts 3(3) and 3(4) of the UNIDROIT Convention.

[102] C Fox, 'The UNIDROIT Convention on Stolen or Illegally Exported Cultural Objects: An Answer to the World Problem of Illicit Trade in Cultural Property' [1993] American University International Law Review 225, 258.

faith of the possessor for purposes of interpreting Article 11, Article 3 would not fully achieve its purpose to have stolen objects returned.

As was indicated, the good faith of the purchaser is relevant for the question of potential compensation on return. In terms of Article 4(1), the possessor is entitled to fair and reasonable compensation provided that he or she neither knew nor ought reasonably to have known that the object was stolen and can prove that due diligence had been exercised when acquiring the object. Article 6(1) provides the same in respect of illegal exports. The compensation arrangement promotes provenance research and discourages acquisition of objects in suspicious circumstances. This feature of the UNIDROIT Convention signifies opposition to a no-questions-asked culture. An unusual location or time of the transaction, or signs of recent excavation, raise red flags that prompt further inquiry. Being so conducive to the international protection of cultural objects, it has found support among many civil law countries. The rules of evidence have been relaxed in favour of the owner. The burden of proof rests on the possessor even if he or she had acquired the object in good faith.[103]

Other specifics of what actions need to be taken are left to individual states. This includes whether or not insurance cover extends to a compensation claim against the true owner.

The UNIDROIT Convention has failed to attract a good number of contracting states.[104] Its structure and principles are simple but the areas of law they relate to highly intricate. These intricacies cover choice of law, the application of foreign public law, comparative civil law on sale and transfer of ownership, and international mutual legal assistance.[105] What constitutes due diligence or 'fair and reasonable compensation' is subject to discretion. 'Stolen/theft', 'possessor', and 'illegal export' remain undefined. Since legal systems may disagree on when an object

---

[103] BJ Tyler, 'The Stolen Museum: Have United States Art Museums Become Inadvertent Fences for Stolen Art Works Looted by the Nazis in World War II?' (1998–1999) 30 Rutgers Law Journal 464.

[104] P Valentin, 'The UNIDROIT Convention on the International Return of Stolen or Illegally Exported Cultural Objects' [1999] Art Antiquity and Law 107, 115.

[105] P Lalive, 'A Disturbing International Convention: The UNIDROIT Convention on Cultural Objects' in LV Prott (ed), *Witnesses to History: A Compendium of Documents and Writings on the Return of Cultural Objects* (Unesco Publications 2009) 29, 32.

has been stolen,[106] the absence of a definition leaves the door open to criticism that the language is not sufficiently clear to promote uniform interpretation. Moreover, its private law effect could be clarified. It is supposed to have self-executing status, as it is deemed to give rise to a direct right for a private party to bring an international law claim, regardless of whether the treaty requires incorporation or transformation into domestic law. However, Article 4 does not meet the standard of clarity and precision implied by this status[107] and there is a measure of doubt over whether the Convention reaches the issue of private law effect.[108] For illegally exported cultural property, the requesting state must prove that removal from its territory significantly impairs certain of its cultural interests.[109] This could be difficult to achieve in respect of unregistered finds. The Model Provisions on State Ownership of Undiscovered Cultural Objects provides a helpful model in this respect.

2.5.2 Sanctions

Article 8 of the 1970 UNESCO Convention invites state parties to impose penalties or administrative sanctions on anyone who infringes import and export controls that operate in that state or in respect of objects stolen from museums, religious or secular public monuments. Most states that provide such controls criminalise infringements; examples are unlicensed excavations, concealment of treasure belonging to the state *ex lege*, and the destruction of cultural objects. Few specify theft of a cultural object as an infraction.[110] These penalties and sanctions have limited territorial scope. Civil forfeiture may attach to infringements without the necessity of filing a civil action,[111] but the return of the disputed property may not necessarily be secured.[112] In this respect, its thrust differs from the 1995 UNIDROIT Convention.

---

106 See Chapter 2, 6.3.2; Falkoff, 'Mutually Beneficial Repatriation Agreements: Returning Cultural Patrimony, Perpetuating the Illicit Antiquities Market' (2008) 16 JL & Pol 165, 301.

107 Gazzini (n 5) 7.

108 K Odendahl, *Kulturgüterschutz: Entwicklung, Struktur und Dogmatik eines Ebenübergreifenden Normsystems* (Mohr Siebeck 2005) 178.

109 Art 5.

110 Gazzini (n 5) 18.

111 Gazzini (n 5) 19.

112 *R v Heller* (1983) 27b Alta LR 2d 346 (Prov Ct) upheld on procedural grounds (1984) 30 Alta LR 2d 130 QB.

The 1995 UNIDROIT Convention confronts the issue of restitution but it lacks sanctions due to its nature as a private and commercial law initiative which has an accessory function to the criminal law.

2.5.3 Restitution

The UNESCO Convention encourages states to consider restitution in respect of the transactions of public institutions and to entertain actions for the recovery of certain registered and inventoried artistic objects.[113] The formulation of this principle challenges private law rules and institutions. Bureaucracies respond differently, depending on resources, ideology and constituency.[114] Implementation has proved problematic in as far as the Convention relies on Member States to recognise the export prohibitions of the foreign state. The state of origin and the exact date of the illegal export must be known because the restitution mechanism requires both the requesting and requested states to be Contracting Parties to the Convention at the time of illegal export. Illegally excavated property is excluded. Moreover, Article 13 refers individuals who wish to bring restitution claims for privately owned items to national mechanisms. National rules of just compensation and time limitation apply unchanged.

The approach of the UNIDROIT Convention to restitution is much wider compared to the UNESCO Convention.[115] As indicated above, a good-faith purchaser who is able to show due diligence in the compensation stage is entitled to reasonable compensation.[116] It also relies on a complex formula for statutory limitations.[117] The Convention splits the private law issue concerning the return of stolen objects (Chapter II) and the public law issue concerning the return of illegally acquired, transferred and unlawfully exported cultural objects (Chapter III). The effort of covering these two widely different topics in one instrument resulted in a vague definition of 'cultural object'.[118] The Convention neutralises

---

113 Art 7(b)(i) of the UNESCO Convention.

114 A Efrat, 'Getting Governments to Co-operate against Looting: Insights from the American and British Experience' [2012] Journal of Art Crime Electronic Issue 31, 41 <http://portal.idc.ac.il/facultypublication.publication?PublicationID=2874&FacultyUserName=YXNpZg==>; accessed 25 March 2014.

115 Schönenberger (n 55) 78–79; Gazzini (n 5) 21.

116 Arts 4(1) and 6(2); Gazzini (n 5) 21.

117 Art 3(3), 3(6) and 5(5); Gazzini (n 5) 23.

118 E Sidorsky, 'The 1995 Unidroit Convention on Stolen or Illegally Exported Cultural Objects: The Role of International Arbitration' (1996) 5 IJCP 19, 31.

the traditional axiom of non-application of foreign public law when the object has considerable cultural importance (this is subject to interpretation), and its exportation compromises preservation interests, integrity of a complex object, and scientific or historic interests. This obstacle to restitution is given detailed treatment in Chapter 7. Affiliation and emotive interests are recognised in the context of the traditional or ritual use of an object by indigenous or tribal communities.

2.5.4 Status

The 1970 UNESCO Convention initially enjoyed limited ratification by states that regard transit of cultural objects to benefit their local interests. The tide has now turned. Many culture-rich countries, significant importing states, and several former centres of illicit traffic have now ratified. The total number of ratifications is 127. Recent ratifications include those by Belgium, the Netherlands, and Germany. Japan and the UK accepted the Convention in 2002. The UK made legislative provision that took effect on 30 December 2003.[119]

The 1995 UNIDROIT Convention aims to harmonise civil law and common law property principles to maximise the number of signatories. At 33, the number of contracting states remains low and the prevention of the illicit trade less than effective. It has proven difficult to persuade states to subscribe, given the issues with interpretation, the uncertainty about its private law effect, and the underlying compromise it strikes. Several art-importing or dealer-collector states stand to gain from the mutual international assistance and global solidarity envisaged by the Convention, yet only Italy, Spain, Portugal, Norway and Finland have ratified it. Major market states such as the US, the UK, Germany and Japan have not shown support. This is cause for grave disappointment. Switzerland, France and Russia signed, but have not ratified it. Nationalism, regional or sectoral self-interest and intellectual conservatism seem to induce passivity.[120]

---

[119] Acceptance creates the obligation to refrain from acts that would defeat the object and purpose of the Convention. <http://portal.unesco.org/la/convention.asp?KO=13039&language=E&order=alpha> accessed 25 February 2014; Cmnd 5500. The UK accepted the Convention on 1 August 2002. K Chamberlain, 'UK Accession to the 1970 UNESCO Convention' (2002) 7 Art Antiquity and Law 231, 239 indicates that internal effect was achieved when the legislative provision took effect. If ITAP is correct that new legislative provision was not needed, full accession would have been achieved on 1 November 2002 (three months following the deposit of the instrument of acceptance).

[120] Lalive (n 105) 29.

2.5.5 Standing

Neither the 1970 UNESCO Convention nor the 1995 UNIDROIT Convention has been a resounding success.[121] Both instruments have had to withstand a number of criticisms. Among the less serious criticisms levelled at the UNESCO Convention is that a uniform definition of cultural property is lacking. It depends on individual states to designate property they consider to be important for their archaeology, history, literature, art or science before protection.[122] The criticism against the scope for states to define the concept according to their own understanding is largely ill-conceived, considering that definitions of cultural property are necessarily dependent on context. Whether warranted or not, reservations ensued due to a perception that source states alone have the right to decide what constitutes illegally acquired cultural property under the terms of the Convention and thereby to force market states to return any such objects that enter their borders.[123] Reservations have been registered in respect of the provision that import, export or transfer of ownership effected contrary to the provisions of the Convention are to be considered illicit.[124] The precise meaning of 'illicit' is capable of raising contention. For instance, Guatemala considers illicit the import and transfer of ownership of cultural property effected contrary to the national provisions in force that are not in conflict with the provisions of the Convention. The position in respect of blanket export bans resulted in reticence on the part of the US.[125] The US entered a reservation upon ratification by which it retains the right to determine whether or not to impose export controls over cultural property; this is contrary to the requirement in Article 6 of the Convention that state parties are to prohibit the export of their cultural property without an export certificate.

The UNESCO Convention is also criticised for being confined to a small class of cases. Article 7(b) refers to 'property stolen from a museum or a religious or secular public monument or similar institution … provided that such property is properly documented as appertaining to the inventory of that institution'. While these are the very objects likely to be essential to the 'national estate', the cultural objects of minority

---

121 Valentin (n 104) 107ff; MJ Kelly, 'Conflicting Trends in the Flourishing International Trade of Art and Antiquities: *Restitutio in Integrum and Possessio Animo Ferungi/Lucrandi*' [1995] Dickinson Journal of International Law 31, 44ff.

122 Kelly (n 121) 44.

123 Mealy (n 34) 197.

124 Art 3 of the UNESCO Convention.

125 Merryman (n 14) 831, 845.

cultures may not be included in state designations, and sub-state groups may be without recourse if this is the case. Textual weaknesses hinder the achievement of its aims. Article 7 contains no international agreement in respect of the purchaser in good faith, who is protected under the civil law systems of many of the market and transit states; nor does this provision cover the unlawful taking of formerly unrecorded objects from archaeological sites. The less than satisfactory position is that the gap had to be filled by the UNIDROIT Convention.

It is a frequent criticism that cultural conventions do not apply retrospectively to art illegally imported or exported before entering into force.[126] Non-retroactivity applies to treaties in general and the principle enjoys the force of international customary law.[127] Thus, even if the UK were to ratify the 1995 UNIDROIT Convention tomorrow, the Convention would not apply in respect of objects stolen or illegally exported before this date. National laws and remedies apply in respect of items that have been underground for years before surfacing. Uncertainty about when excavation, discovery, acquisition or export took place complicates proof that the relevant legislative framework or convention applies. This limitation impacts harshly on indigenous peoples' repatriation claims. Dealer or market states benefit from the situation, but the relationship between domestic law and convention provisions are not open to change. Historical disputes that occurred prior to the entry into force of the conventions are left to diplomatic means and consensual dispute resolution mechanisms.[128]

There are a number of serious criticisms in respect of which improvement is possible. First, autonomous concepts are lacking. National courts determine the interpretations of 'good faith', 'due diligence', 'fair and reasonable compensation' and also ownership after return. Secondly, signatory states are able to avoid obligations because they remain free to control which parts of the Convention to incorporate into their domestic law, and to decide on how to do this.[129] Developing states generally struggle to adapt their national legal frameworks to conventional law or

---

[126] Art 7(b)(ii) of the UNESCO Convention; Art 10(1) and (2) of the UNIDROIT Convention.

[127] Art 28 of the 1969 Vienna Convention on the Law of Treaties.

[128] Chechi (n 45) 123, 203.

[129] A Parkhouse, 'The Illicit Trade in Cultural Objects: Recent Developments in the United Kingdom' in BT Hoffman (ed), *Art and Cultural Heritage: Law, Policy and Practice* (CUP 2006) 178, 180.

develop domestic preservation programmes,[130] and the standard of incorporation raises questions. In the US, nothing in the UNESCO Convention applies unless the CCPIA has implemented it. The standard of incorporation in US law has also given rise to questions. For example, the US has refused to allow the Convention to extend federal control over museums and institutions such as auction houses. The insistence that the states and local authorities regulate the obligation imposed on antique dealers to maintain proper records of acquisition and sale of antiques[131] effectively meant it was never implemented.[132] Thirdly, the enforcement mechanism of the UNESCO Convention calls on extensive administrative machinery in every state, and significant human and financial resources need to be dedicated to implementing the Convention. The Intergovernmental Committee for Promoting the Return of Cultural Property to its Countries of Origin or its Restitution in Case of Illicit Appropriation was not set up to ensure the centralised enforcement of the Convention.[133] Restitution depends exclusively on state action steered through diplomatic channels.[134] The Convention addresses the illicit trade in art by means of the channels of public international law,[135] and does not create any personal right of action for individual owners. No procedures for recovery have been set out. These shortcomings complicate actual enforcement. Moreover, sub-state groups cannot utilise the Convention unless the state acts on their behalf.[136] Fourthly, Article 7 resorts to a rather imprecise phrase, 'whenever possible', which creates the impression that the treaty is non-obligatory. Sanctions and mechanisms for transgressing states are poor and ineffective.[137] Retroactive application of the restitution clauses is excluded.[138]

---

[130] JD Murphy, 'The People's Republic of China and the Illicit Trade in Cultural Property: Is the Embargo Approach the Answer?' [1994] IJCP 227, 230.

[131] Art 10(a) of the UNESCO Convention.

[132] M Papa-Sokal, 'The US Legal Response to the Protection of the World Cultural Heritage' in N Brodie, MM Kersel, C Luke and K Walker Tubb (eds), *Archaeology, Cultural Heritage and the Antiquities Trade* (University Press of Florida 2006) 36, 50.

[133] Gazzini (n 5) 45.

[134] Arts 5, 6 and 7.

[135] Lenzner (n 87) 477; JM Carruthers, *The Transfer of Property in the Conflict of Laws* (OUP 2005) § 5.26.

[136] K Last, 'Cultural Pluralism and the Return of Cultural Heritage' in S Tierney, *Accommodating Cultural Diversity* (Ashgate 2007) 123, 133.

[137] Gazzini (n 5) 47–48.

[138] Report no 18, 9 ILM 1040 (1970).

From an international law perspective, the most serious criticism concerns the extent to which states party are supposed to give effect to foreign law regulating cultural property. The UNESCO Convention gives no clear direction in this regard.[139] Variation is allowed in domestic laws from one Contracting State to another. Legal diversity and difference in respect of what should and should not be protected hinders co-operation. Market nations seek to protect the free market of trade and generally oppose repatriation. For instance, in its 2000 report ITAP saw the range of stolen cultural objects under Chapter II as overly broad without the option of narrowing it down. The Convention contains no filter for provisions that serve no cultural aim. Article 13(d) states that parties 'recognize the indefeasible right of each State Party … to classify and declare certain cultural property as inalienable which should *ipso facto* not be exported, and to facilitate recovery of such property by the State concerned in cases where it has been exported.'[140] The importing state is required to facilitate the recovery and repatriation to the country of origin[141] without any ability to counter blanket export bans that widen the scope of the Convention.

The 1970 Convention was the catalyst for the subsequent adoption of numerous national laws to regulate illicit trade in trading countries that are not easily classifiable as source or market states.[142] Governments that support the art market do not want to be transit points for looted material.[143] International trade in objects in violation of domestic import and export restrictions is still treated as illicit. Given the reluctance to take any action that will curb a lucrative industry, this is a huge accomplishment. The Convention makes a bold statement about the obligation of wealthy Western nations to address illicit trading. Ratification of the UNESCO Convention by the US has not diminished or halted criticism of the Convention.[144] Acquisition of pieces that are not 1970 compliant (the year the UNESCO Convention took effect) is being

---

139 Papa-Sokal (n 132) 47.

140 For more, see MA Renold, 'The International Protection of Archaeological Heritage: Questions of Private International Law and of Legal Harmonization' <http://biblio.juridicas.unam.mx/libros/7/3457/18.pdf> accessed 11 June 2014, 297ff.

141 On the 'blank check' feature of the UNESCO Convention, see Merryman (n 14) 844–45; Fishman (n 4) 390.

142 E.g. Canada. For information on the status of the 1970 UNESCO Convention and an up-to-date list of parties, see <http://www.unesco.org/eri/la/convention.asp?KO=13039&language=E> accessed 25 February 2014.

143 ITAP 2000 paras 8–10.

144 Pearlstein (n 19) 2ff.

discouraged, but not all collecting museums in the US check for compliance. Some of them consider acquisition if the country of origin permits private ownership and a legal market exists in the materials in question.[145] Some codes of conduct detract from the UNESCO Convention standard.[146]

Importantly, however, and whatever its status in law, the Convention succeeds in highlighting the importance of approaches based on mutuality or solidarity with the human community. It also 'changed forever the ethical landscape of the museum world'.[147] Museums are ethically obliged not to acquire material illegally exported. Relevant professional organisations, including the UK Museums Association and ICOM, reflect this ethical standard in their respective codes of conduct.

2.6 EU law: Free Movement and Restrictions on Movement of Art

In the EU, private international law has assumed a specialist function, having gone through stages of coordination (1957–1992), co-operation (1992–1997), Community action (1997–2007) and beyond. Ever since the adoption of the Treaty Establishing the European Economic Community of 1957,[148] a border-free Europe in which direct competition between Member States stimulates economic growth has been high on the agenda. In 1997, Article 65 of the EEC Treaty determined that measures had to be taken in the field of judicial co-operation in civil matters having cross-border implications, in so far as necessary for the proper functioning of the internal market. The internal market became a reality in 1993. Amendments effected by the Treaty of Lisbon[149] entered into force on 1 December 2009. The EC Treaty is now known as the Treaty on the Functioning of the European Union (TFEU).[150] Presently, the legal basis for judicial co-operation in civil matters having cross-border implications is to be found in Article 81(1) of the TFEU. Rulings

---

145 Pearlstein (n 19) 11.

146 See the 2008 amendment to the Association of American Museum Directors' Guidelines, which provide for an object registry. Frequent amendments since 2001 accentuate the ethics deficit of the position the Guidelines adopt in respect of unprovenanced pieces.

147 N Brodie, J Doole and P Watson, *Stealing History: The Illicit Trade in Cultural Material* (MacDonald Institute for Archaeological Research 2000) 9.

148 Treaty Establishing the European Economic Community, 25 March 1957, 298 UNTS 3.

149 Treaty of Lisbon, 17 December 2007, OJ C 306/01.

150 TFEU, 9 May 2008, OJ C 115/47.

by courts in the EU Member States qualify for recognition and enforcement without the need for special procedures, but this is not necessarily the case elsewhere.

The introduction of a cultural component in the external and internal competence of the EU demonstrates that the EU is a social and cultural project in progress, and not just an economic instrument.[151] Article 151 of the 1992 Maastricht Treaty[152] provided a legal basis for promoting culture, as did the Treaty of Amsterdam,[153] with its stipulation that '[t]he Community shall contribute to the flowering of the cultures of the Member States, while respecting their national and regional diversity and at the same time bringing the common cultural heritage to the fore'. This same objective reappears in Article 167 of the Treaty of Lisbon of 2009,[154] which amended the Treaty on the Functioning of the European Union.[155] The EU must take measures to respect and promote the diversity of cultures, and its Member States must co-operate in the sphere of culture. The EU and Member States must foster co-operation also with third states and international organisations in the sphere of culture.

Cultural exchange has been high on the agenda in the EU ever since 2003.[156] The wider cultural dimension of the cultural component is not yet regulated in any coherent manner, and cultural actions are largely of an ad hoc nature. Measures adopted thus far have not aimed at the harmonisation of the laws and regulations relating to cultural property that forms part of the domestic law of the Member States.[157] Nonetheless even at this early stage, exchanges of cultural and historical objects from museum collections are included in the cultural actions of the Member States.

The majority of EU Member States have ratified the 1970 UNESCO Convention, but five states have not done so yet.[158] None of the instruments referred to above addresses repatriation claims on the part of Member States of the EU. Special measures were adopted to fill this gap

---

151 K Dittrich-von Wehring, 'Introduction' in R Fisher (ed.), *A Cultural Dimension to the EU's External Policies – from Policy Statements to Practice and Potential* (Amsterdam 2007) 3.

152 Maastricht Treaty, Consolidated version 31 August 1992, 1992 OJ C 224.

153 Treaty of Amsterdam, 10 November 1997, OJ C 340.

154 Treaty of Lisbon, 17 December 2007, OJ C 306/01.

155 TFEU, 9 May 2008, OJ C 115/47; 30 March 2013 OJ L 83/47.

156 Van Woudenberg (n 53) 214; Dittrich-von Wehring (n 151) 3.

157 Ulph and Smith (n 36) 16–17.

158 Austria, Ireland, Latvia, Luxembourg and Malta. France, Belgium and the UK have registered reservations.

(2.7.2 below). Restitution on account of the moral force of existing soft law is conceivable, however. More particularly, the legal position of objects in cultural exchanges may be affected.[159]

2.6.1 Cultural objects are 'goods' in free trade terms

The liberalisation of trade and the basic principle of the free circulation of goods in the EU in terms of Article 36 of the Treaty of Rome (TFEU)[160] imply the abolition of export and import restrictions within the EU. This step was taken in 1993 when a single market was achieved and internal borders were dismantled.[161] The Court of Justice of the EU, the judicial organ of the EU charged with the interpretation and application of EU law, has faced the task of determining whether cultural property constitutes 'goods'. In 1968 the ECJ (now CJEU) ruled in Case 7/68 *EC Commission v Italy (Re Export Tax on Art Treasures)*[162] that all articles possessing artistic or historic value are goods within the meaning of the EEC Treaty:

> [W]hatever may be the characteristics which distinguish them from other goods in commerce, [they] nevertheless share with those latter the characteristics of being able to be valued in money and so to be the object of commercial transactions.[163]

This exception did not allow states to impose onerous taxes on the exportation of objects that belong to the artistic, historical or archaeological heritage in order to discourage their exportation, without also ensuring protection.[164] Exportation may be prohibited but taxes on exportation were deemed to constitute a measure equivalent to a customs tax (Article 30 TFEU) which is not justified by Article 36 TFEU.[165]

---

159 E.g., Parliamentary Assembly of the Council of Europe, Resolution No 1205 on Looted Jewish Cultural Property of 4 November 1999, clause 15 calls for restitution and for consideration to be given to 'relaxing or reversing anti-seizure statutes which currently protect from court action works of art on loan'.

160 EEC Treaty Art 36 was replaced by EC Art 30 before TFEU Art 36 became applicable.

161 I Stamatoudi, *Cultural Property Law and Restitution* (Edward Elgar 2011) 112ff.

162 Case 7/68 *EC Commission v Italy* [1969] CMLR 1 (ECJ) [5].

163 Case 7/68 *EC Commission v Italy* [1969] CMLR 1 (ECJ) [5].

164 Case 7/68 *EC Commission v Italy* [1969] CMLR 1 (ECJ) [8].

165 Case 48/71 *EC Commission v Italy* [1972] ECR 527.

Regulations that contain export restrictions for cultural objects count among the exceptions to the principle of the free circulation of goods.[166] Articles 34 and 35 prohibit limitations on the import, export or goods in transit fixed by reference to quantitative criteria such as amount or value (also referred to as quotas or quantitative restrictions), or measures having equivalent effect between Member States. A complete ban on the import of a particular type of good is a quantitative restriction,[167] and so is any partial restraint on the free movement of goods. Import licence requirements may constitute measures having equivalent effect to quantitative restrictions, and may directly or indirectly, actually or potentially, hinder intra-Community trade.[168] Justification for any such measures is required in Article 36 TFEU, which is discussed next.

2.6.2 Restrictions must be justifiable with reference to Article 36 TFEU

The CJEU must preserve the proper functioning of the single market. To this end, it has the power to challenge measures adopted by the Member States of the EU to protect 'national treasures possessing artistic, historic or archaeological value' when these measures infringe on the rules concerning the free movement of goods. It interprets narrowly the list of derogations in Article 36 TFEU. The items on the list relate to non-economic interests.[169] This provision states that:

> [t]he provisions of Articles 34 and 35 shall not preclude prohibitions or restrictions on imports, exports or goods in transit justified on grounds of … public policy … [or] the protection of national treasures possessing artistic, historic or archaeological value ….

Public policy interests may provide a justification but the scope for this is exceedingly limited because public policy is narrowly construed.[170] It was successfully relied on in Case 7/78 *R v Thompson*,[171] in which the

---

[166] Conseil d'Etat, 7 October 1987, Ministre de la Culture/Consorts Genty, Dalloz 1988, jurisprudence 269 (affirmed administrative decision to deny an export permit in respect of medieval Chinese jar).

[167] As per Case 7/68 *Commission v Italy* [1969] CMLR 1 (ECJ).

[168] Case 8-74 *Procureur du Roi v Benoît and Gustave Dassonville* [1974] ECR 837.

[169] Case C-120/95 *Decker* [1998] ECR I-1831; Case 72/83 *Campus Oil* [1984] ECR 2727.

[170] C Kessedjian, 'Public Order in European Law' [2007] Erasmus Law Review 25.

[171] Case 7/78 *R v Thompson* [1978] ECR 2247.

relevant national rules that hindered trade in old coins were ruled to be acceptable.[172] Old collectors' coins in gold and silver were held to constitute 'goods and products' and not 'means of payment', because they were not in circulation as legal tender. Relevant UK law[173] prohibited the importation of Kruger gold coins and the exportation, melting down or destruction of silver-alloy coins minted in the UK before 1947, to prevent their destruction in another Member State even if they were no longer legal tender. The ECJ held that the coins were subject to the rules on the free circulation of goods. The ban was justified on grounds of public policy within the meaning of EC Article 30 (ex 36) because it stems from the need to protect the right to mint coinage, which is traditionally regarded as implicating the fundamental interests of the state.[174] To permit the movement of the coins to another Member State would be in breach of public policy.

National treasures have been partly defined in a number of instruments, but the ECJ/CJEU has not had occasion to lay down criteria to differentiate between a national treasure and a cultural object. The EU has ratified the Convention on the Protection and Promotion of the Diversity of Cultural Expressions,[175] which is the first international instrument to recognise the dual economic and cultural nature of cultural goods.

The notion of 'treasures' refers to objects of cultural importance for which the criteria differ across states and in regard to which overlapping classification among more than one state is possible. A 'national treasure' could include, for instance, items listed in the inventories of museums or libraries' conservation collections; pictures, paintings, sculptures; books; means of transport; or archives.

The movement and transfer of national treasures involve economic consequences, but they can also be assessed from a cultural non-economic perspective.[176] Because they signify the application of

---

172 Case 120/78 *Cassis de Dijon* [1979] ECR 649 (certain national rules which create obstacles to trade will be acceptable provided they satisfy the criteria laid down by the ECJ in this decision).

173 Import of Goods (Control) Order 1954; s 304(b) of the Customs and Excise Act 1952; and the Export of Goods (Control) Order 1970.

174 [1978] ECR 2247.

175 2005 UNESCO Convention on the Protection and Promotion of the Diversity of Cultural Expressions, 20 October 2005, CLT-2005/Convention Diversite-Cult Rev <http://www.unesco.org/fileadmin/MULTIMEDIA/HQ/CLT/CLT/pdf/conventiontext_og_civilsociety_en.pdf> accessed 25 February 2014.

176 Ulph and Smith (n 36) 16.

protective national regimes that derogate from the notion of free movement, they can be excluded from the process of market integration. However, any derogation that is claimed will fail if there is doubt about whether the pieces constitute national treasure or about whether there is a real risk to national treasure.

Derogations may not represent wrongful or arbitrary discrimination or a concealed restriction on trade between Member States.[177] National rules and practices that impact on the free circulation of goods within the European single market must satisfy the test of objective justifiability, strict necessity and proportionality. Any distinction must be made on an objective basis. The ECJ will allow national restrictions or bans to derogate from the principle of free movement of national treasures only to the extent that restrictions are necessary to achieve their protection. Thus, necessity for protection of a national treasure of artistic, historic or archaeological value (which must constitute an essential element of a broader totality of unremarkable or redundant objects) must be clear. Any justifiable quantitative restriction must respect the principle of proportionality. This means that a restriction must not go beyond what is necessary to achieve a stated objective; the state legislation imposed in order to satisfy a 'mandatory requirement of state' must be proportionate and the least restrictive measure possible.[178] States must use means that are capable of achieving the same end but which are less restrictive of intra-Community trade. If a measure goes beyond what is necessary, the claimed derogation will fail on account of a breach of Article 34.

The boundary between EU and Member State competence are not fully compatible or clear for all purposes.[179] The CJEU is not well placed to resolve disputes involving cultural objects that implicate interests that are still 'extraneous' to the overarching EU regime.[180] There are also serious and unique challenges to the protection of the cultural heritage associated with the abolition of customs checks and the eastern enlargement of the EU. Two compensatory measures, discussed next, were intended to fill the gaps left by the abolition of border checks, to bring the incidental increase foreseen in smuggling cultural objects under control, and to ease the consequences of free circulation of goods on cultural objects. The CJEU can be requested to settle disputes concerning their interpretation, but no decisions have been taken so far.

---

177 Art 36 and 1994 GATT Art XX. In general, Vitale (n 18) 216.

178 Case 120/78 *Cassis de Dijon* [1979] ECR 649 applies to Article 34 cases.

179 Stamatoudi (n 161) 120–33, 157.

180 Chechi (n 68) 7.

2.7 Secondary EU Law

2.7.1 EU Regulation (EEC) No 3911/92 of 9 December 1992 on the export of cultural goods, now Council Regulation (EC) No 116/2009

Regulation (EC) No 116/2009 on the export of cultural goods[181] contains restrictions on the movement of art in a global context. It is intended to halt the flow of cultural property from the EC with the impending abolition of borders and customs controls. The Regulation imposes uniform controls on the export of protected goods to non-member countries.[182] Export licences are required for the export of national cultural assets from Member States to a third state, and where national legislation protects the cultural treasures in question, the export licence may be refused. Member States impose different restrictions on the export of antiques and other cultural artefacts, and those restrictions – as well as related administrative procedures, such as the completion of declaration forms and the provision of supporting documents – are generally considered to be justified under Article 36 TFEU.

Fifteen categories of goods are listed in a Joint Annex as categories that are covered by such an export licence. The decisive criteria are age and minimum value. There is notable diversity across EU Member States in terms of export regulations and systems for controlling exit of cultural objects from the territory, the objects they cover, the value and age thresholds that apply and regulations controlling circulation within and

---

[181] Council Regulation (EEC) No 3911/92 of 9 December 1992 on the export of cultural goods, OJ L 395, 31.12.1992 1–5, replaced by Council Regulation (EC) No 116/2009 (codified) of 18 December on the export of cultural goods, OJ L 39/1 (2009). Several interim corrections were published; see Council Regulation (EEC) No 3911/92 of 9 December 1992 OJ L267, 19.10.1996, 30, amended by Council Regulation (EC) No 2469/96 of 16 December 1996 amending the Annex to Regulation (EEC) No 3911/92 OJ L 335, 24.12.1996, 9 and by Council Regulation (EC) No 974/2001 of 14 May 2001 amending Regulation (EEC) No 3911/92 OJ L 137, 19.5.2001, 10–11. Also Commission Regulation (EC) 752/93 of 30 March 1993 laying down provisions for the implementation of Council Regulation 3911/92 on the export of cultural goods, as amended by Commission Regulation (EC) 1526/98 of 16 July 1998, OJ L201/47 and Commission Regulation (EC) 656/2004 of 7 April 2004, OJ L104/50 (Corrigendum), OJ L 203, 8.6.2004/14 (656/2004).

[182] European Commission, *Free Movement of Goods: Guide to the Interpretation of Treaty Provisions Governing the Free Movement of Goods* (Luxembourg 2010) 28. <http://ec.europa.eu/enterprise/policies/single-market-goods/files/goods/docs/art34-36/new_guide_en.pdf> accessed 25 February 2014.

outside the EU.[183] For instance, the value thresholds between the EU and the UK have differed since 2003. Changes to the thresholds mean that whereas an export licence may be required under EU law, a UK export licence is not necessarily needed.[184] The licence must be presented to customs together with the export certificate. The requirement to present both could be an issue.

The export of any work outside of the categories specified in the Annex is governed by national rules of the Member State.[185] National regulatory divergences complicate and undermine compliance. The external export rules of an EU state of origin can be evaded if the object is transferred to another EU Member State prior to exporting it to a third state. Unscrupulous traffickers could move a work protected by the strict export control laws of Member State A via Member State B into a third state if B has more lenient export controls.[186] Certain states act as an interface for smuggled objects in respect of which theft cannot be proved. Operating as a 'lock' in the illicit trade on account of lax controls in respect of imports and exports, they become transit states.

Customs authorities do not necessarily prioritise the smuggling of cultural objects to third states. Their capacity for law enforcement is unequal across the EU, and it would be unwise to over-extend existing control regimes beyond any realistic prospect of enforcement. The World Customs Organization is developing tools for information-sharing amongst customs administrations, national and international agencies tasked with the protection of cultural heritage, and law enforcement agencies. Much remains to be done in this regard.

---

183 European Commission, *Study Report on Preventing and Fighting Illicit Trafficking in Cultural Goods in the European Union*, 10 October 2011, 190–94, 249 available at <http://ec.europa.eu/home-affairs/doc_centre/crime/docs/Report%20Trafficking%20in%20cultural%20goods%20EN.pdf> accessed 25 February 2014.

184 BT Hoffman, 'European Union Legislation Pertaining to Cultural Goods' in BT Hoffman (ed), *Art and Cultural Heritage: Law, Policy and Practice* (CUP 2006) 191.

185 Art 1 Regulation OJ L 39/1 (2009).

186 KA Short, 'Preventing the Theft and Illegal Export of Art in a Europe without Borders' (1993) 26 Vanderbilt Journal of Transnational Law 633; Gazzini (n 5) 12.

2.7.2 Council Directive 93/7/EEC of 15 March 1993 and Directive 2014/60/EU of 15 May 2014

Council Directive 93/7/EEC of 15 March 1993 on the return of cultural objects unlawfully removed from the territory of a Member State[187] was issued to 'counterbalance the establishment of the internal market and its impact on customs controls among Member States'.[188] The Directive was adopted when internal frontiers were abolished on 1 January 1993. It was intended to complement the Regulation in securing the return of cultural objects that have been removed from the territory of a Member State in violation of the Regulation. Its scope was restricted to cultural objects removed after 1 January 1993. Directive 93/7/EEC conferred a right of return in respect of cultural goods classified as 'national treasures possessing artistic, historic or archaeological value' and belonging to the categories referred to in its Annex or forming an integral part of public collections or inventories of ecclesiastical institutions. The Directive determines which items fall within its scope by means of a list of different categories of cultural goods that qualify for return to their native Member State, listed by age and by a certain value or financial threshold (e.g. archaeological objects more than one hundred years old; pictures and paintings executed by hand more than fifty years old and with a value of €150 000). Objects qualify when they either belong to one of the limited categories listed in the Directive, which are the same as those in the Annex attached to Council Regulation (EC) No 116/2009, or feature on the inventory of a public collection or ecclesiastical institution. The Annex supplies categories of object which may be classified as such[189] as an interpretive aid, and is not intended to define objects which rank as 'national treasures' within the meaning of Article 36 TFEU. In the absence of agreement in respect of the definition of a 'national treasure',[190] the interpretation could be wider for certain interest groups (e.g. source states), and narrower for others (e.g. dealers, collectors and market states). A wide interpretation could be incompatible with the notion of

---

[187] Council Directive (EEC) 93/7 of 15 March 1993 on the return of cultural objects unlawfully removed from the territory of a member state OJ L 74/74, 27.3.93 with amendment of the annex by Directive 96/100/EC of the European Parliament and of the Council of 17 February 1997 (L 60/59, 1.3.1997), and by Directive 2001/38/EC of the European Parliament and of the Council of 5 June 2001, OJ L 187/43, 10.7.2001.

[188] Carducci (n 2) 79–80.

[189] European Commission, *Free Movement of Goods* (n 182) 28.

[190] K Siehr, 'The Protection of Cultural Property: UNIDROIT Convention and EEC Instruments of 1992/93 Compared' (1998) 3 Uniform Law Review 677.

'European cultural heritage'.[191] Extending export restrictions to 'national heritage' that does not also qualify as a 'national treasure' is unjustified;[192] yet, defining a 'national treasure'[193] of artistic, historical or archaeological value obviously invites consideration of a wide variety of factors and a contextual assessment of the patrimony of the Member State concerned. Member States remain free to extend the application of the Directive to cultural objects not included in the Annex.

The return scheme contemplated in Directives 1993/7/EEC and 2014/60/EU is triggered by unlawful removal from national territory. The requesting Member State has to institute legal proceedings before the competent court in the requested Member State,[194] and that court then orders the physical return of the cultural object in question if the set preconditions have been met. The 1993/7/EEC Directive does not set out to protect national treasures, but a decision to return an object when a request was made under the Directive has an effect equivalent to enforcing another Member State's law protecting cultural treasures.[195] A repatriation claim for smuggled cultural objects under the Directive is analogous to Article 9 of the UNESCO Convention. However, whereas the UNESCO Convention applies to stolen items, the Directive applies regardless of any pre-existing theft.[196]

In practice, the peacetime Conventions and domestic criminal prosecution remain viable options for recovery actions, and the Member States prefer to use these options. Civil and criminal proceedings offer quicker and cheaper alternatives compared to the return proceedings provided for under the Directive.[197] Few claims have been brought under the Directive. States have blamed its infrequent application on the limited scope of the instrument; the short time allowed for instituting an action; the cost of applying the Directive; the difficulties of identifying the competent court in another Member State; and the unequal compensation ordered by

---

191 Vitale (n 18) 219.

192 A Biondi, 'The Merchant, the Thief and the Citizen: The Circulation of Works of Art within the European Union' (1997) 34 Common Market Law Review 1173.

193 In the sense of former Art 36 of the Treaty of Rome. Now Art 36 TFEU.

194 Art 5 of Council Directive (EEC) 93/7.

195 Stamatoudi (n 161) 143.

196 Clause 6(1). Carducci (n 2) 80 supports an amendment that would extend the operation of the Directive to theft.

197 Schönenberger (n 55) 81; Carey Miller et al. (n 87) 12; Stamatoudi (n 161) 156.

various national judges.[198] Differences in the meaning between core concepts, categories and thresholds, and a high level of administrative complexity obstruct co-operation and exchange of information.[199]

Law reform became inevitable when an attempt to codify Directive 93/7/EEC was withdrawn by the Commission.[200] A Working Group on Return of Cultural Goods was set up to identify problems and propose acceptable solutions.[201] It concluded its work in 2011. The Commission had several reports on the application of the Directive at its disposal. The fourth report[202] indicated that administrative co-operation among the national authorities had increased and pro-active Member States had started to take precautionary measures to prevent evasion of the return procedure. Nonetheless, certain problems persisted and a recast was unavoidable.

Directive 2014/60/EU[203] is intended to further the approximation of laws under Article 114 TFEU and the mutual recognition of relevant national laws. It is due to take effect on 19 December 2015. The scope of application is considerably simpler. Cultural objects classified or defined as national treasures would no longer have to belong to categories or comply with thresholds related to their age or financial value in order to qualify for return. The scope of application is extended to include any cultural object classified or defined by a Member State under national

---

198 *Report from the Commission to the Council, the European Parliament and the European Economic and Social Committee: Fourth Report on the Application of Council Directive 93/7/EEC on the Return of Cultural Objects Unlawfully Removed from the Territory of a Member State*, Brussels 30 May 2013 COM(2013) 0310 final, <http://eur-lex.europa.eu/LexUriServ/LexUriServ.do?uri=COM:2013:0310:FIN:EN:PDF> §4.1 accessed 25 February 2014.

199 *Report from the Commission to the Council, the European Parliament and the European Economic and Social Committee: Third Report on the Application of Council Directive 93/7/EEC on the Return of Cultural Objects Unlawfully Removed from the Territory of a Member State*, Brussels 30 July 2009 COM(2009) 408 final 8 (which covers 2004–2007).

200 Proposal for a Directive of the European Parliament and of the Council on the return of cultural objects unlawfully removed from the territory of a Member State (Codified version) COM(2007) 873 final, 11.1.2008, OJ C/282, 18.09.10.

201 *Third Report* (n 199) COM(2009) 408 final 9.

202 *Fourth Report* (n 198) COM(2013) 310 final.

203 Directive 2014/60/EU of the European Parliament and of the Council of 15 May 2014 on the Return of Cultural Objects Unlawfully Removed from the Territory of a Member State and amending Regulation (EU) No 1024/2012 (Recast) OJ EU L159/1, 28.5.2014.

legislation or administrative procedures as a national treasure possessing artistic, historic or archaeological value within the meaning of Article 36 TFEU. Directive 2014/60/EU now acknowledges in Recital 10 that it should be possible for Member States to return cultural objects other than those classified or defined as national treasures provided that they respect the relevant provisions of the TFEU, as well as cultural objects unlawfully removed before 1 January 1993.

Other improvements relate to the timescales for initiating return proceedings, for taking necessary measures to preserve an object or to prevent an action to evade the return procedure; better administrative co-operation and information exchange between central authorities; and shifting the burden of proof of the date and place of removal to the possessor.

Directive 93/7/EEC mirrored the UNIDROIT Convention in respect of the time limits that apply to return proceedings and the compensation that is due to the possessor if due diligence is found to have been exercised.[204] The same time limits are applicable under Directive 2014/60/EU.[205] Under Directive 93/7/EEC the duty to return ceased to apply one year after the requesting Member State became aware of the location of the object and the identity of the possessor, but this period has now been extended to three years.[206] The standard period remains at 30 years from the date of illegal exportation, but special protection arrangements under national law that stipulate a longer time limit are permitted in certain circumstances. Directive 2014/60/EU maintains the opportunity for taking necessary measures to preserve an object or to prevent an action to evade the return procedure.[207]

Article 10 of Directive 2014/60/EU contains a detailed stipulation in respect of due diligence that derives from Article 4.4 of the UNIDROIT Convention, but that does not appear in Directive 93/7/EEC. It provides that, in determining whether the possessor exercised 'due care and attention', consideration must be given to all the circumstances of the acquisition, in particular the provenance documentation, the requisite authorisations for removal by the law of the requesting Member State, the character of the parties, the price paid, whether the possessor consulted any accessible register of stolen cultural objects and any relevant information which he could reasonably have obtained, or took any other step which a reasonable person would have taken in the

---

204 Arts 7 and 9(1) of Directive 93/7/EEC.
205 Recital 17 and Art 10 of Directive 2014/60/EU.
206 Recital 14 and Art 8 of Directive 2014/60/EU.
207 Recital 13 and Art 5(4) and (5) of Directive 2014/60/EU.

circumstances. Directive 1993/7/EEC merely required proof that due care had been exercised upon acquisition for the payment of fair compensation.

Directive 93/7/EEC contemplated claims between states. The Member State in receipt of a request for the return of an unlawfully removed cultural object had a duty to repatriate objects that meet the criteria and procedures contained in the instrument. Member States were responsible for any ownership issues involving private natural or legal persons.[208] Nonetheless, civil and criminal proceedings for restitution were not precluded.[209] Consequently, parallel proceedings brought by both the requesting Member State and the owner of a previously stolen object were possible. EU Member States could request the return of cultural treasures in terms of the Directive, and the owner could institute proceedings in respect of a stolen object under the national laws of a Member State. This position is now confirmed by Article 16 of Directive 2014/60/EU. Private collectors or religious institutions deprived by theft will be able to bring recovery proceedings, and the jurisdictional grounds available in the improved Brussels regime may be employed for this purpose. The jurisdictional basis for an ownership action is found in Council Regulation (EC) No 1215 of 2012 of the European Parliament and of the Council of 12 December 2012 on Jurisdiction and the Recognition and Enforcement of Judgments in Civil and Commercial Matters (Recast).[210] Detailed analysis thereof is provided in Chapter 4.

By virtue of Article 12 of Directive 93/7/EEC, once return to the requesting State had taken place, the *lex originis* (the law of the requesting Member State) applied in relation to its ownership. Directive 93/7/EEC did not say whether it was the substantive law of the requesting State that applied or its private international law. For the purpose of deciding the validity of a property transfer, the law of the country where the object was situated could also apply. Views differed as to whether Directive 93/7/EEC impacted the conflicts rules of national legal systems. Some commentators were of the view that Directive 93/7/EEC did not affect the national legal systems' conflicts

---

[208] Art 4 of Directive 93/7/EEC.

[209] Art 15 of Directive 93/7/EEC.

[210] Council Regulation (EC) No 1215 of 2012, OJ 2012 L351/1, 20.12.2012. Art 7(4) confers special jurisdiction in respect of an owner's civil claim for recovery of an object defined in Council Directive 93/7 EEC (now Directive 2014/60/EU) in the courts for the place where the cultural object is situated at the time the court is seised (discussed in more detail in Chapter 4 below).

rules;[211] title acquired by a good faith purchaser from someone who was not the owner under the *situs* rule would stand if the object was located in a legal system that confers good title in such circumstances. Other commentators argued that the Directive was intended to achieve restitution; consequently the good faith of the purchaser is relevant only for the question of potential compensation on return.[212]

This question continues to have relevance, considering that Article 12 of Directive 2014/60/EU grants a requesting EU Member State the right to recover the costs and compensation paid from the persons responsible for the unlawful removal of a cultural object from its territory.

The Scottish Law Commission has indicated that the right of return under the Directive is unaffected if the possessor obtains good title by prescription.[213] More importantly, to the extent that the *lex situs* rule is unstable and susceptible to 'lock' formation that operates between certain transit and end-states in Europe (discussed in Chapter 5 below), this will enable traffickers to launder title. The real measure of success of the improved Directive 2014/60/EU will be the extent to which locks are prevented from forming. This would prove to be more feasible through return of stolen or illegally excavated or illegally exported cultural objects, than by way of the *lex situs* rule.

2.8 At the Cross-over into ADR

2.8.1 Litigation

National courts rule on the basis of disparate national regulations and standards.[214] Litigation is 'gladiatorial', expensive, time-consuming and unpredictable.[215] Culturally related interests are not specifically considered when the legal position of the parties is being determined. The pleading, proof and application of foreign law is an uncertain matter at best, considering that classification, methodology, rule and exception, domestic title and ownership rules, statutory limitation and prescription,

---

211 Carruthers (n 135) § 5.33–34; N Palmer, 'Recovering Stolen Art' (1994) 47 Current Legal Problems 215, 237.

212 G Carducci, *La Restitution Internationale des Biens Culturel et des Object d'Art: Droit Commun, Directive CEE, Conventions de l'Unesco et d'Unidroit* (LGDJ 1997) 408; Schönenberger (n 55) 221 n 1130.

213 Scottish Law Commission Discussion Paper on Prescription and Title to Moveable Property No 144 (Edinburgh 2010) § 4.6–§ 4.8.

214 Gazzini (n 5) 26–27.

215 K Sykes, 'Recovery of Stolen and Looted Works of Art: London December 10 1998' (1999) 4 Art Antiquity and Law 81.

and differences in civil litigation systems can present issues. The negative publicity of a public trial can impact severely on the marketability of the cultural object, which is likely to diminish if title or authenticity remains clouded or unresolved in the course of the trial. Even unmeritorious claims can affect marketability and value.[216]

Museums and cultural institutions may face a dilemma when they resort to private international law rules and legal defences based on private international law argument, without due regard for non-legal factors or ethical considerations.[217] They may be perceived as benefiting from the proceeds of a 'crime against humanity'[218] on the basis of a point of law.

Disputes in national courts and arbitral tribunals will be resolved by reasoned argument. If the conflict between the parties has escalated beyond a level where reason has any effect, consensus-building will be of little use. Other methods may need to be tried.

The potential for a claimant to cross over to a different dispute resolution process means it is wise to keep in view developments in respect of alternative dispute resolution mechanisms (ADR). ADR can exclude litigation-like procedures, choice of law analysis and technical defences that prevent the merits of the claim from being ventilated.[219]

In disputes concerning moveables, the possessor is in a strong position, not least because the object may be moved. The possessor may be disinclined to agree to ADR for that reason. Additionally, any likelihood of succeeding with a private international law argument in court may prompt a possessor to reject the recommendation of the mediator and pursue litigation. Consequently, it is useful to know whether governmental institutions and state entities lack the independence to opt out of state-run mediation, or whether a claimant has this freedom. Court rulings rank above recommendations in respect of their binding effect. The implications of conflicting rulings receive attention in Chapter 6 below.

---

216 Pearlstein (n 19) 57.

217 RK Paterson, 'Resolving Material Culture Disputes: Human Rights, Property Rights and Crimes against Humanity' [2006] Willamette International Law and Dispute Resolution 155, 159.

218 The term was introduced into the Nuremburg statute by Hersch Lauterpacht.

219 Statutory limitations constituted a technical defence that precluded arbitration because the statutory limitations had passed in *Toledo Museum of Art v Ullin*, 477 F Supp 2d 802 (ND Ohio 2006); *Detroit Institute of Arts v Ullin*, No 06-10333 2007 US Dist LEXIS 28364 (ED Michigan 31 March 2007).

2.8.2 Other options

Non-confrontational responses to requests and claims for return of cultural objects have received attention.[220] It is unfortunate that none of the existing treaties offers a comprehensive and efficient dispute settlement system.[221] With particular groups of cases, there may be a cultural bond or a very real emotive interest that may be broadly shared and respected.[222] The object might fulfill a strong identity-providing role.[223] Ethics underpinned by an affiliation interest will have an important role to play in such claims.[224] Principle 8 of the ILA Draft Principles for Cooperation in the Mutual Protection and Transfer of Cultural Material of 2004[225] reads as follows:

> If parties to a request for the return of cultural material are unable to reach a mutually satisfactory resolution of any dispute related to the request within a period of two years from the time of the request, they will attempt in good faith to resolve the dispute by consultation, mediation, conciliation, ad hoc arbitration or institutional arbitration.

The explanatory note accompanying the ILA Draft Principles states that ADR is preferable to litigation, and that where attempts to negotiate solutions to requests for return of cultural material are unsuccessful, parties ought to be 'required to stipulate ADR'. It is not clear who is to require this and by what authority, or whether this provision intends to impose a duty on national courts to refer parties to compulsory mediation.

Compulsory ADR schemes exist in Belgium and Greece, both of which are signatories to the Convention on Human Rights and Fundamental

---

220 E.g. ILA Draft Principles for Cooperation in the Mutual Protection and Transfer of Cultural Material of 2004, International Law Association, Cultural Heritage Law Committee Report, Berlin Conference 2004, 3 <www.ila-hq.org/> accessed 24 February 2014. Many other examples exist in the category of Nazi spoliated art.

221 E.g. Art 5.3 Unidroit Convention; NAGPRA in respect of repatriation on human remains; ILA Principles for Co-operation in the Mutual Protection and Transfer of Cultural Material, reprinted in 2006 IJCP 409; Schönenberger (n 55) 259–61.

222 As opposed to returns motivated by emotional extortion from outside pressure. Schönenberger (n 56) 251.

223 Schönenberger (n 55) 51.

224 M Cornu and M Renold, 'New Developments in the Restitution of Cultural Property: Alternative Means of Dispute Resolution' (2010) 17 IJCP 1ff.

225 International Law Association, Cultural Heritage Law Committee Report, Berlin Conference 2004, 3 <http://www.ila-hq.org/> accessed 25 February 2014.

Freedoms. Compulsory ADR has been deemed an unacceptable constraint on the right of access to court in England,[226] but it has been pointed out that mediation merely delays the trial briefly without interfering with the right to a fair trial.[227] An ADR agreement cannot be rescinded in California and federal district courts can require parties to mediate disputes.[228]

Of all the forms of ADR mentioned by ILA, mediation offers the greatest opportunity to take non-legal factors into account. It is also the most appropriate for the consideration of moral reasoning, ethics, and history.[229] Bargaining can lead to a compromise, as was the case with the Lydian Hoard.[230]

A pure fact inquiry may either be an adjunct to dispute settlement procedures, or an innovative dispute avoidance strategy. The clarification of the facts and the content of potentially applicable foreign law (which may form part of the enquiry) can prepare the way to peaceful settlement.[231] It can promote conciliation, the most unchartered of all the options mentioned in the ILA Draft.[232]

2.8.3 Is arbitration a form of ADR?

Whereas mediation squarely falls within the ambit of ADR, the position of arbitration is more ambiguous. The definition is important because it matters whether a process is arbitration for enforcement purposes. US courts are still grappling with state-law definitions of arbitration that are not easily reconciled with the federal conception of arbitration.[233]

---

[226] *Halsey v Milton Keynes General NHS Trust* [2004] 1 WLR 3002 (CA), 3007–8 (compulsory ADR would breach the right to a fair trial as it would amount to an unacceptable constraint on the right of access to justice).

[227] A Clarke, 'The Future of Civil Mediation' *Tribunals Judiciary* (8 May 2008) maintains that the *Halsey* decision was obiter in this regard; LJ Lightman, 'Mediation: An Approximation of Justice' *Tribunals Judiciary* (28 June 2007).

[228] S 652 of the Alternative Dispute Resolution Act of 1998 (28 USC).

[229] K Kuprecht and K Siehr, 'International Trade in Moveable Tangible Cultural Heritage of Indigenous Peoples: A European Perspective' in CB Graber, K Kuprecht and JC Lai (eds), *International Trade in Indigenous Cultural Heritage* (Edward Elgar 2012) 246, 267 refers also to customs and traditions of indigenous people.

[230] For more examples, see Gazzini (n 5) 60ff.

[231] Chechi (n 68) 8.

[232] Cornu and Renold (n 224) 10–13.

[233] The Alternative Dispute Resolution Act of 1998 (28 USC 651) includes arbitration. *Bakoss v Certain Underwriters at Lloyd's of London Issuing Certificate* No 0510135, 707 F3d 140 (2nd Circuit 2013) did not resolve the

'Arbitration' may describe a non-adversarial process that does not resolve the entire cause of action. For instance, the Boston Museum of Fine Arts proposed binding arbitration in order to consolidate the various claims in respect of a Flemish oil with a view to returning it to its true owner.[234]

In Europe, arbitration is more readily distinguishable from ADR processes. In England, ADR is actually understood as referring only to mediation by a third party, despite the formal definition in the glossary to the Civil Procedure Rules referring to methods of resolving disputes other than through the normal trial process.[235]

Arbitration deserves further scrutiny before a conclusion can be reached on what it has to offer in the context of ownership claims involving art and antiquities.

2.8.4 Arbitration

Scholars and commentators regularly recommend arbitration in art and cultural heritage disputes.[236] Proposals involving arbitration refer to a large variety of potential models for resolving such disputes.[237]

---

fundamental issue of whether state law or federal common law defines the term 'arbitration'. The states do not adopt a uniform approach to including or excluding non-adversarial ADR clauses in the definition.

234 K Siehr, 'Chronicles of 1 July 2000–31 December 2000' (2001) 10 IJCP 137, 149. Gazzini (n 5) 120.

235 *Halsey v Milton Keynes General NHS Trust* [2004] 1 WLR 3002 (CA), 3006 (claimant refused mediation for a damages claim against the NHS arising from the negligent treatment of her husband).

236 E.g. EI Gegas, 'International Arbitration and Resolution of Cultural Property Disputes' (1997) 13 Ohio State Journal on Dispute Resolution 129, 151ff; BW Daly, 'The Potential for Arbitration of Cultural Property Disputes; Recent Developments at the Permanent Court of Arbitration' [2005] Law and Practice of International Courts and Tribunals 261; Sidorsky (n 119) 19; N Palmer, 'Arbitration and the Applicable Law in Resolution of Cultural Property Disputes', in International Bureau of the Permanent Court of Arbitration (ed), *Resolution of Cultural Property Disputes* (The Hague 2004) 291; M Granovsky, 'A Permanent Resolution Mechanism of Cultural Property Disputes' (2008) 8 Pepperdine Dispute Resolution Law Journal 25; AL Bandle and S Theurich, 'Alternative Dispute Resolution and Art-Law – a New Research Project of the Geneva Art-Law Centre' (2011) 6 Journal of International Commercial Law and Technology 28.

237 These include the International Court of Justice, the Permanent Court of Arbitration (PCA), UNCLOS III, the International Commission on Holocaust Era Insurance Claims (ICHEI), or the Claims Resolution Tribunal of the Holocaust Victim Assets Litigation against Swiss Banks and other Swiss Entities. Gegas (n 236) 151–59; MO Wantuch and A Niethammer, 'Compensation for Nazi

Arbitration is an option for a local dispute[238] or for a dispute with international connections.[239] It may be conducted intra-nationally (as between two Swiss cantons) or internationally (as in a border dispute). International arbitration is an extrajudicial procedure that is transnational in nature.

In commercial arbitration, parties have greater control over the dispute resolution process compared to litigation. Basically, every decision apart from the outcome is theirs to make in commercial arbitration, including: (a) the rules of procedure that should apply to their case; (b) the applicable law or another set of rules or non-state law; (c) to have the arbitrator decide *ex aequo et bono* on the basis of fairness or as an *amiable compositeur* to restore the relationship between the parties;[240] (d) which specialists to appoint to adjudicate;[241] and (e) whether to publish the ruling and whether to anonymise it before publication.[242]

The parties may agree that equitable considerations ought to prevail in order that a mutually agreeable solution can be reached. This flexibility may appeal to parties from different cultural and linguistic backgrounds. Parties who agree on arbitration may select experts who have the requisite experience to pinpoint the cultural significance of an object (Article 5(3) of the UNIDROIT Convention), trace its provenance, determine the date of excavation and/or export, and identify the applicable substantive law and matters determined thereby (e.g. standard for

---

Wrongdoing: The Case for an Integrated Approach' (2007) 12 *Art Antiquity and Law* 29, 55.

238 Examples of local arbitrations include *Schlaifer Nance & Co v Estate of Andy Warhol*, 764 F Supp 43, 46 (1991) re rights to license Warhol's artworks, name and likeness; also *Thomas Kinkade Co v White* No 10-1634 Appeal from the US District Court for the Eastern District of Michigan at Detroit 2 April 2013.

239 *Majken Hofmann, Anna Lokrantz, Maria Müller, Andreas Müller Hofmann und Lena Müller Hofmann v Republic of Austria* (21 November 2005)(Arbitral award in German) <www.bslaw.com/altmann/Zuckerkandl/Klage/284724.doc> accessed 24 February 2014; *Maria V Altmann, Francis Gutmann, Trevor Mantle, George Bentley, and Dr. Nelly Auersperg v Republic of Austria* (15 January 2006)(Arbitral award in German) *available at* <http://bslaw.com/altmann/Klimt/award.pdf> accessed 25 February 2014; *Liamco and Government of the Libyan Arab Republic*, 12 April 1977, Arbitration Tribunal, (1981) 20 ILM 1.

240 Palmer (n 236) 301; Schönenberger (n 55) 248.

241 E Varner, 'Arbitrating Cultural Property Disputes' [2012] *Cardozo Journal of Conflict Resolution* 477, 514–15.

242 If no agreement is in place, it depends on the rules that govern the operation of the tribunal.

due diligence and fair compensation). Lack of such expertise may mean that external expertise will need to be obtained at a cost. In addition, arbitration strives to accommodate or conciliate parties' views. Thus it offers non-conventional remedies that can ensure restorative justice[243] and create notable potential for settlement.[244]

In the US, arbitrators are not held to the same standard of judicial decorum that binds US federal judges and other members of the judiciary. In the eyes of the CJEU, the distinction between judge and arbitrator rests on the permanence of the office of judge, the state authority that underpins it, and the exercise of compulsory jurisdiction.[245] Arbitral awards are not necessarily substantiated by high-quality legal reasoning or reasons. The arbitrator may be a non-lawyer and lower standards apply compared to judicial decision.[246] Generally speaking, the coherence and consistency of the awards are less important from the perspective of adjudicators than are the interests of the parties and the circumstances of the individual case. Arbitrators are not required to have expertise in the governing substantive law, unless the case presents a particular legal issue; nor are they required to apply the same reasoning and solution in similar cases. The flexibility in respect of the application of the law sets the arbitrator apart from the state court judge.

The 1958 New York Convention for the Recognition and Enforcement of Foreign Arbitral Awards (NYC)[247] offers a common legal framework that eases enforcement of foreign arbitral awards[248] between physical or legal persons. The NYC applies to differences arising from a legal relationship, whether contractual or not, which are considered as commercial under national law.[249] The procedure for enforcement is determined by the national procedural law of the seat, but the conditions for

---

243 *Majken Hofmann, Anna Lokrantz, Maria Müller, Andreas Müller Hofmann und Lena Müller Hofmann v Republic of Austria* (Nov. 21, 2005)(Arbitral award in German) <www.bslaw.com/altmann/Zuckerkandl/Klage/284724.doc> accessed 24 February 2014; WIPO ADR Arbitration and Mediation Center, available at <http://www.wipo.int/amc/en/arbitration/case-example.html> accessed 24 February 2014.

244 S Theurich, 'Alternative Dispute Resolution in Art and Cultural Heritage – Explored in the Context of the World Intellectual Property Organization's Work' in K Odendahl and PJ Weber (eds), *Kulturgüterschutz – Kunstrecht – Kulturrecht: Festschrift für Kurt Siehr* (Baden-Baden 2010) 569, 574–75.

245 Case C-196/09 *Miles and Others* [2011] ECR I-0000 § 37.

246 Gazzini (n 5) 114.

247 Gazzini (n 5) 79.

248 Art I(1).

249 Art I(3).

enforcement and the grounds for the refusal of enforcement are determined by the NYC.[250] The enforcement bias of the NYC means that *prima facie* evidence of enforceability, combined with the production of formal documentary proof, are sufficient for enforcement where the party against whom enforcement is sought is unable to demonstrate that at least one ground of refusal listed in the NYC applies. There is no possibility at all for re-opening the merits for debate at the enforcement stage.[251]

2.8.4.1 Speed and fairness Arbitrators are intimately acquainted with the commercial market. They are not automatically disqualified by a business relationship with the parties before them if both parties are informed of the relationship in advance, or if the relationship is trivial. Procedural safeguards and protections available in court proceedings may be curtailed for the sake of efficiency. The only protections that apply are minimum requirements of procedural fairness[252] and the fundamental guarantees inferred from procedural public policy.[253]

Review, where available, tends to be conducted only in terms of fairness and public order. States do not assume any direct responsibility under human rights instruments for the conduct of arbitral proceedings; they assume subsidiary responsibility for the right to appeal, or to oppose the recognition and enforcement of awards that violate international private rights or procedural minima.[254]

The procedure is accelerated for reasons that may include lenient procedures; the tendency to restrict the intervention by local courts; and the relative simplification of choice of law, but it is necessary to take a closer look at whether arbitration can avoid the choice of law complications associated with litigation.

---

250 Arts IV and V.

251 Gazzini (n 5) 80–81.

252 T Schultz, 'Human Rights: A Speed Bump for Arbitral Procedures? An Exploration of Safeguards in the Acceleration of Justice' [2006] IALR 1, 7ff; *Boulois c/UNESCO*, Cour d'Appel de Paris (14e Ch A) 19 June 1998, Rev Arb (1999) 343, 344 (denial of justice under Art 6 ECHR if party is precluded from approaching a national court in respect of the nomination of an arbitrator when the other party witholds co-operation for this purpose); Gazzini (n 5) 112–17.

253 Procedural public policy affects the recognition and enforcement of foreign judgments and arbitral awards. Case C-7/98 *Krombach v Bamberski* [2000] ECR-I-1935 (if a ruling violates the right to a fair trial as espoused in Art 6 of the ECHR, the public policy requirement of the Brussels Convention is not met).

254 Gazzini (n 5) 115, 117.

2.8.4.2 Choice of law in arbitration In an international arbitration, the arbitrators face the conflict of laws question of 'which law applies' in addition to the question 'which system applies: the system that is used by domestic courts at their seat, or a different system?' Arbitrators do not derive their authority from a national system of law and, in respect of the substance of the dispute, they apply a conflict of laws system that differs from that applied by courts.[255] The arbitrator must take the contractual dimension of arbitral jurisdiction into account. Consequently, when they rule 'in accordance with the applicable law', their solutions are likely to be broadly consistent with the applicable law and with the standards of the trade. He or she enjoys a degree of discretion and flexibility because the *lex fori* is not compelling, nor is it possible to rely on a *lex fori* to supply choice of law rules.[256]

The arbitration procedure, the validity of the arbitration agreement, the legal capacity to consent to the arbitration, and the merits and finality of the award are not necessarily governed by the same law.[257]

With regard to the law governing the substance and merits of the case, an arbitral tribunal usually seeks to show that any solution based on national law meets an internationally accepted standard.[258] There is nothing to prevent an arbitrator from applying a national law because a large number of national legal systems have such rules, and consequently it would be acceptable to determine the merits by the laws of the opponent's nationality. Parties could also designate the 1995 UNIDROIT Convention as the law applicable to the merits of their dispute, or they may opt for the Unidroit Principles of international commercial contracts. In the absence of a designation in favour of the 1995 UNIDROIT Convention, however, arbitrators may not apply it. The parties must opt for it to apply and its application must accord with what the governing law allows.[259]

---

255 F de Ly, 'Conflicts of Law in International Arbitration – an Overview' in F Ferrari, S Kroll (eds), *Conflicts of Law in International Arbitration – an Overview* (Sellier 2011) 3; M Piers and J Erauw, 'Application of the UNCITRAL Principles of International Commercial Contracts in Arbitration' (2012) 8 JPIL 441.

256 Gazzini (n 5) 97.

257 V Heiskanen, 'Forbidding *Dépeçage*: Law Governing Investment Treaty Arbitration' (2009) 32 SuffolkTransnational Law Review 367.

258 E.g. Arbitral Award International Court of Arbitration of the Chamber of Industry and Commerce of the Russian Federation 83/2008, <www.unilex.org> accessed 24 February 2014. Piers and Erauw (n 255) 466.

259 Gazzini (n 5) 103.

The hope that the 1995 UNIDROIT Convention will contribute to an autonomous and more coherent case law in the area is still alive.[260] However, development in this direction has been slow.

If a specific choice of law clause is absent in respect of the arbitration agreement, and the arbitrators are not called upon to decide *ex aequo et bono* or as *amiable compositeur*, the award would have to be justifiable on the basis of applicable substantive law. The arbitrators have the freedom to apply a conflict of laws approach (rules of the court, personal law, law of the seat, *lex fori*), but they are also permitted[261] to use a substantive rule method, i.e. designate the applicable substantive law directly (*la voie directe*); consider all potentially applicable conflicts rules (e.g. seat and respective home countries) and decide which rule best matches the dispute before them; or apply the principles and usages of international trade. The seat of the arbitration will be taken into account when the applicable law is designated.[262]

If parties have expressly authorised the arbitral tribunal to do so, the arbitral tribunal could rule in accordance with principles of equity and good conscience as *amiable compositeur* or *ex aequo* under UNCITRAL Rules (United Nations Commission on International Trade Law).[263] As *amiable compositeur*, an arbitrator may modify strict rules of law if the parties have agreed. In the art world, codes and soft law abound, and strict law and doctrine may seem undesirable. Nonetheless, the parties resemble adversaries more than they resemble partners pursuing a joint venture.

Many arbitration statutes stipulate that arbitrators apply the law or the rules of law they deem appropriate.[264] The rules by which an institutional or ad hoc arbitration operate may provide further direction. For instance, under the most recent PCA Arbitration rules for mixed arbitrations, the Arbitral Tribunal will apply the rules of law designated by the parties as applicable to the substance of the dispute. However, failing designation by the parties, the arbitral tribunal applies the law which it determines to

---

260 Gazzini (n 5) 207.

261 This is not a universal position, though. The German ZPO § 1051 governs the determination of material applicable law, and requires the arbitrators to apply the state law with which the dispute is most closely connected. Cf also Art 187 of the Swiss Code in Private International Law.

262 Piers and Erauw (n 255) 446.

263 UNCITRAL Rules 2010 Amendment, Art 35.

264 Art 1511 of the French New Code of Civil Procedure (NCPC); Art 187(1) of the Swiss Federal Code on Private International Law; Art 1054(2) of the Dutch Code of Civil Procedure.

be appropriate, having regard to the terms of the agreement and relevant trade usages.[265]

Article 35 of the UNCITRAL Arbitration Rules 2010 embodies an approach whereby the arbitrator first searches for the most appropriate conflicts rule without being bound by the law of the seat. Thereafter, different techniques can be used to select the applicable substantive law. A comparative or cumulative method allows the arbitrator to analyse all the conflicts rules applicable to the dispute (e.g. seat and respective home countries). This method only works if the conflicts rules of the different jurisdictions are more or less similar. Another option is the method of the closest connection, which considers the weight given to the respective connecting factors rather than the conflict of laws rules of a national legal system. It is also possible to apply more than one regulatory system in conjunction (e.g. the Unidroit Principles in combination with a particular national law) and to apply a national law or transnational law.[266]

Reference to harmonised choice of law rules applied in courts in EU Member States[267] would be necessary before an arbitrator would be obligated to find for an implied choice of law or impose a condition that an express choice be clearly demonstrated.

When the parties have agreed that their contract be governed by the general principles of law, the arbitrator may take this to mean the general principles of most national legal systems.[268] Agreement that the general principles of law or the *lex mercatoria* govern their contract will entitle an arbitrator to apply the Unidroit Principles in reference to an equivalent type of rule.[269] The *lex mercatoria* is a controversial expression of internationalism (as opposed to conflictualism), which refers to an autonomous body of law (norms and dispute-settlement mechanisms) created by the international business community. The controversy about this body of law raged during the 1980s. Today, adjudicators verify that a provision appears in several sets of principles before concluding that it forms part of *lex mercatoria*. The parties may also specify the relevant

---

[265] Art 35. Art 21 of the 2011 ICC Arbitration Rules; Art 28(1) of the ICDR Arbitration Rules; Art 22(3) of the LCIA Arbitration Rules.

[266] Piers and Erauw (n 255) 447–52.

[267] Rome I Regulation on the law applicable to contractual obligations.

[268] *Liamco and Government of the Libyan Arab Republic*, 12 April 1977, Arbitration Tribunal, (1981) 20 ILM 1, 41. For more, see E Gaillard, 'General Principles of Law in International Commercial Arbitration – Challenging the Myths' (2011) 5 World Arbitration & Mediation Review 161.

[269] Piers and Erauw (n 255) 453, 455, 456.

principles of international law,[270] general principles of private international law,[271] or rules that are public in character.[272] A simple reference to the practices and customs in international trade or sound commercial practices may be regarded as too vague and could therefore result in the application of a precise set of rules (e.g. the Unidroit Principles).[273]

3. CONCLUSION

International cases present complex choices that require simplification with the help of a global lens. Private international law has the capacity to facilitate restitution and dispute settlement by fulfilling a highly specialised co-ordination function. For its structure and method to respond appropriately to developments in cultural heritage law, the inbuilt flexibility of private international law must be put to full use.

At the interface with domestic law, private international law can be used in market states to recognise foreign export control legislation and public domain legislation.

At the interface with public international law, private international law must work constructively alongside, for instance, customary international law, international conventions which states enter into to prevent the transfer of stolen and illegally exported cultural objects, and soft law.

At the interface with primary and secondary EU law, there has long been a lack of unity with respect to export regulations and systems for controlling exit of cultural objects from the territory of EU Member States. A border-free Europe complicates the monitoring of the movement of art and cultural objects within the EU. Circulation within and outside the EU has been subject to a complex system that has been open to exploitation.

This chapter has highlighted the effect, sanctions, status and standing of global and regional instruments that have been designed to prevent the

---

270 Which has been construed as a reference to the *lex mercatoria* and the general principles of law in Arbitral Award ICC 12111, 2003, <www.unilex.org> accessed 24 February 2014.

271 Piers and Erauw (n 255) 448.

272 Gazzini (n 5) 101–2 stresses that these are not excluded from the scope of the NYC as the nature of the law applied is not decisive. The NYC does not preclude the r/e of such an arbitral award as long as the subject matter is arbitrable and the award differentiates between physical and legal persons.

273 Arbitral Award ICC 12040, 2003, <www.unilex.org> accessed 24 February 2014; but cf Arbitral Award ICC 11256, 2003, <www.unilex.org> accessed 24 February 2014.

looting and destruction of cultural finds and archaeological sites and their unlawful removal from the territory of EU Member States. The 1970 UNESCO Convention was the catalyst for the adoption of numerous subsequent national laws to regulate illicit trade in trading countries. Slow to win the support of states, it is now a Convention to reckon with. The UNIDROIT Convention was intended to fill the gaps and remedy the weaknesses of the UNESCO Convention, but problems remain in a number of areas, including clarity of the language, definition of key terms, margin of discretion when it comes to due diligence, and the private law effect of this instrument. The requesting state must prove that removal from its territory significantly impairs certain of its cultural interests, but in respect of unregistered finds, this will prove difficult. The extent to which the Model Provisions on State Ownership of Undiscovered Cultural Objects can be helpful, will be explained in more detail in Chapter 7. The impact of Directive 93/7/EEC has been low in practice. A recast Directive, which will take effect in December 2015, is set to improve the legal position of Member States and private claimants.

The relationship between private international law and non-litigious dispute resolution is a vital part of the context in which private international law functions in art disputes today. Developments at the cross-over deserve to be kept in view. Non-confrontational responses exclude litigation-like procedures, choice of law analysis and technical defences that put obstacles in the way of deciding on the basis of the merits of the claim.

It is possible for a plaintiff to out-manoeuvre the usual private international law rules in international litigation. It is readily assumed that a choice of arbitration as the dispute resolution mechanism can achieve this. The aspiration of internationalism underlies all forms of international arbitration. An overly complex interaction of laws would negate this aspiration. Thus, choice of law can be a simpler matter for an arbitral tribunal than for a national court. Another strong attribute of arbitration in cultural heritage matters is the depth of the understanding which the arbitrator and the expert witness may offer on issues that affect the trade in art and cultural objects.

The nature of the remedy that the claimant seeks, gives some indication of the most appropriate mechanism to be followed. Restitution simple is not the only option in the quest to effect reconciliation. Chapter 4 returns to this theme and explores some of the fundamental questions that arbitration leaves unanswered in the complex setting of ownership and restitution disputes.

4. Adjudicatory authority and its limits

1. INTRODUCTION

The question of adjudicatory authority and how it is divided globally is closely related to the question of the power and authority of law. Private international law confronts the very first question of law: the power, authority, and potentiality of law, and the conditions of its exercise. Jurisdiction co-determines how normative existence is ordered.[1] From the perspective of international law, jurisdiction rules deal with the sources and limits of national legal authority.[2] The doctrine of jurisdiction 'stands somewhere on the borderline between international and municipal law and cannot be treated in isolation from either'.[3] Jurisdiction rules allocate regulatory authority between states at the horizontal level, thereby ordering the horizontal diversity which may arise when a legal issue is based on a decision or allocated to a legal system closely connected to those affected by it.[4] Public international law defines the extent of legitimate adjudicatory authority, and requires that the territorial connection be substantial in order to warrant the assertion of authority.[5] This requirement is not always satisfied.[6]

Interests in jurisdiction are varied. A plaintiff has an interest in obtaining relief; his or her opponent has an interest in what is convenient;

---

[1] S McVeigh (ed), *Jurisprudence of Jurisdiction* (Routledge-Cavendish 2007).

[2] A Mills, *The Confluence of Public and Private International Law* (CUP 2010) 107.

[3] FA Mann, 'The Doctrine of Jurisdiction in International Law' I (111) *Recueil des Cours* (The Hague 1964) 1, 23. Mills (n 2) 229 agrees. That public international law has relevance in respect of jurisdiction disputes in private international law is not a popular view.

[4] Mills (n 2) 107, 113.

[5] FA Mann, 'The Doctrine of International Jurisdiction Revisited after Twenty Years' III (186) *Recueil des Cours* (1984) 9, 29.

[6] M Keyes, 'The Suppression of State Interests in International Litigation' in S McVeigh (ed), *Jurisprudence of Jurisdiction* (Routledge-Cavendish 2007) 123, 125–56.

and state interests impact on jurisdictional principles and practices. For example, whereas the interstate judicial system of the US has an interest in the efficient resolution of disputes, particular sister states may share an interest in furthering substantive social policies.[7] A foreign state will necessarily have an interest in the resolution of the dispute in international litigation. In the common law legal system, courts are reticent to acknowledge foreign state interests in international cases; courts will weigh the interests of the forum and the foreign state only in extreme cases,[8] and may refuse to entertain the dispute.[9] The *Ortiz* case did not contain any political element, nor was there any conceivable trace of grounds for a public policy exception in the forum, and yet the Appeal Court held that an English court could not adjudicate on the enforcement of a statute that grants title to the Crown at the moment of unlicenced export.[10] When the Attorney General for the UK applied for an injunction to restrain the publication of the 'Spycatcher' memoir written by a former officer of the British Security Service,[11] the cause of action was confidentiality and the claim was framed by reference to personal injury or damage to property. Thus it had a private law character. Nonetheless, the 'central interest' of the UK in bringing the action was the maintenance of national security, which entailed an exercise of the prerogative of the Crown. The cause of action was thus held to be governmental in nature. The High Court of Australia held that the Australian courts did not have jurisdiction to deal with the claim.

A deprived party who wishes to institute legal proceedings in a national court will need to identify a court that is competent to decide the matter.[12] The question is whether the court regards itself as competent to hear and determine the dispute? Different legal traditions and legal systems offer a considerable variety of jurisdictional grounds for ownership and restitution claims, which need to be established before the merits of a claim for ownership or restitution can be met. A court may assume jurisdiction because a connection exists between the defendant

---

[7] These were the factors laid out in *World-Wide Volkswagen Corp. v Woodson*, 444 US 286 (1980).

[8] Keyes (n 6) 123.

[9] Keyes (n 6) 124–45, 127.

[10] *Attorney-General of New Zealand v Ortiz* [1982] 3 All ER 432.

[11] *Attorney-General (United Kingdom) v Heinemann Publishers Australia Pty Ltd.* (1988) 165 CLR 30.

[12] CMV Clarkson and J Hill, *The Conflict of Laws* (4th edn, Oxford 2011) 70ff; I Stamatoudi, *Cultural Property Law and Restitution* (Edward Elgar 2011) 102–4.

(individual, business or institution) and the court for a number of reasons: because the substance of the claim is connected with the court; because the court is located where the events that gave rise to the claim occurred; because of where the cultural object is situated at the time of the suit; because of where the art or cultural object was attached or arrested; or because the parties entered into a valid choice of court agreement when they agreed to transfer ownership. The court will be competent if the defendant has submitted to the jurisdiction of the court in which the claimant initiated the proceedings. Private international law rules determine whether the prerequisites for jurisdiction have been met.

Assuming that jurisdiction exists, the next question is whether the court, in the exercise of its state authority, will decline to hear the dispute.[13] In cases with a transnational dimension, there is always a prospect of multiple proceedings before courts in different states. Private international law rules determine the success or failure of a challenge to the exercise of jurisdiction.[14] In applying these rules, the judiciary does not necessarily engage openly with the interest on the part of the foreign state in the resolution of the dispute in question. A choice in favour of another dispute resolution procedure such as arbitration could potentially complicate matters further if a court refuses to stand down or seeks to intervene in the process.

This chapter focuses on the venue of proceedings and the implications of this choice. Arbitration and litigation are treated as two ways of administering justice. When the stakes are high, the willingness to incur higher litigation costs increases and the interest in other fora for dispute resolution wanes. However, if both parties are reluctant to litigate, they may be able to agree on an arbitrator.

The first part of this chapter is dedicated to the issue of the existence of jurisdiction. The practices of courts of the signatory states of the 1995 UNIDROIT Convention on Stolen or Illegally Exported Cultural Objects, US courts, and EU Member State courts are considered. If the defendant

---

[13] Keyes (n 6) 123.

[14] Factual background in *Bennigson v Alsdorf*, (Cal Supr Ct 16 June 2003) (unreported), aff 'd, No B168200; 2004 WL 803616 (Cal Ct App 15 April 2004) (defendant's contacts with California insufficient to justify assertion of personal jurisdiction), review granted, S124828; 2004 Cal Lexis 6903 (Cal 28 July 2004), dismissed pursuant to notice of settlement, S124828, 2005 Cal Lexis 13370 (Cal 30 Nov 2005); *Alsdorf v Bennigson*, No 04 C 5953; 2004 WL 2806301 (ND Ill 2004) (granting a six-month stay awaiting resolution of *Bennigson v Alsdorf*); *US v One Oil Painting Entitled 'Femme en Blanc' by Pablo Picasso*, 362 F Supp 2d 1175 (C D Cal 2005).

refuses to submit, or challenges the existence or the exercise of jurisdiction, the national court that is seised of the case must decide whether it will decline to hear the case or grant an application for a stay in favour of the courts of the foreign state. This aspect makes up the second part of this chapter. The third part is dedicated to the wider and more fundamental choice between seizing a national court, or opting for an alternative method by which to resolve the dispute. When judicial procedures interlock, legal uncertainty is exacerbated. Claimants who seek the recovery of artworks wrongfully seized by the Nazi regime have the prospect of significant advantages when a US court establishes jurisdiction.[15] This state of affairs will be considered in detail.

2. PRIVATE INTERNATIONAL LAW RULES CAN BE 'OUT-MANOEUVRED'

Jurisdictional rules and choice of law rules are designed to manage the competing claims of respective legal systems to resolve a particular claim.[16] When substantive mandatory forum legislation is applicable, the forum would be inclined to determine that jurisdiction exists and to exercise it. Arguably, a vesting law, public domain rules or an anti-seizure statute can claim application, and would constitute substantive mandatory forum legislation. If such a provision were to determine the scope of its own application, as it is likely to, its application may affect a multilateral conflicts rule. In practice, however, the role that forum state interests play in the determination and exercise of jurisdiction tends to be obscure in common law legal systems. It is safe to state only that the

[15] E.g. *US v Portrait of Wally, A Painting by Egon Schiele*, No 99-CV-09940 (SDNY filed July 29, 2010). K Siehr, 'Commercial Transactions and the Forfeiture of State Immunity under Private International Law' (2008) 13 Art Antiquity and Law 339; K Chamberlain, 'Holocaust Art Claims and Public International Law' (2008) 13 Art Antiquity and Law 351; CA Caprio, 'Artwork, Cultural Heritage Property, and the Foreign Sovereign Immunities Act' [2006] Uniform Law Review 285; JP Fishman, 'Locating the International Interest in Intranational Cultural Property Disputes' (2010) 35 The Yale Journal of International Law 347; L Fielder Redman, 'The Foreign Sovereign Immunities Act: Using a "Shield" Statute as a "Sword" for Obtaining Federal Jurisdiction in Art and Antiquities Cases' 31 (2008) Fordham Int'l LJ 781, 782; LM Kaye, 'Avoidance and Resolution of Cultural Heritage Disputes: Recovery of Art Looted during the Holocaust' [2006] Willamette Journal of International Law and Dispute Resolution 243, 264ff.

[16] Keyes (n 6) 132.

issue of mandatory forum rules highlights the relevance of applicable law in questions on jurisdiction.

In a common law legal system, courts may altogether refuse to entertain a dispute in which foreign state interests are strongly represented,[17] and they are likely to avoid discussing, weighing and applying state interests.[18] Jurisdiction in England and Australia is under-theorised because a theoretical framework is deemed to be unnecessary for purposes of addressing the 'procedural' and 'practical' questions that adjudicatory competence invites. Pragmatic formalism and assumptions about the role of the judge in an adversarial system combine with the perceived constitutional restraints on the functions of the judiciary (e.g. separation of powers and parliamentary sovereignty) to suppress the articulation and evaluation of state interests.[19] Consequently, such interests may disturb the international adjudicatory order and potentially also the protection of cultural heritage.

Jurisdiction rules in US law take account not only of convenience, fairness to the parties, and service, but importantly, of state interest. State interests must be articulated and evaluated, because a court may not refuse to hear a case arising under foreign law unless to do so would violate a fundamental principle of justice, good morals or a deep-rooted tradition. Sufficient justification must exist. Furthermore, a court may apply forum law only if this is not arbitrary or fundamentally unfair.[20] The Full Faith and Credit Clause of the US Constitution[21] affects how courts apply the laws of other states when deciding cases based on diversity jurisdiction[22] or with parties, events, or property in more than one state.

Because various different jurisdictional grounds exist and opponents may seize different courts, parallel litigation is a practical reality. If more than one adjudicator asserts jurisdiction in the same case, conflicting decisions may follow. A variety of definitions of parallel litigation apply to a wide range of situations in which disputes, which are linked in some way, are brought before different adjudicators.[23]

---

17 Keyes (n 6) 127, 129.

18 Keyes (n 6) 130.

19 Keyes (n 6) 123, 129–31.

20 *Allstate Ins Co v Hague*, 449 US 302 (1980) 313.

21 Art IV, Section 1.

22 Diversity of Citizenship, 28 US Code 1332.

23 G Cuniberti, 'Parallel Litigation and Foreign Investment Dispute Settlement' (2006) 21 ICSID Review Foreign Investment Law Journal 381, 382.

Courts in the seat of the arbitration may act in an interventionist manner in relation to arbitration proceedings for a wide variety of reasons. A court would be justified in interfering with a tribunal that has impeded a party's due process. Court involvement may be expected in the arbitral reference in any of three stages. Before arbitration commences, the court may uphold the arbitration agreement, issue directions on the commencement of the arbitral reference and assist with the appointment or removal of arbitrators or protect the assets from dissipation. After the commencement, the court may assist the parties and the arbitral tribunal in its function of gathering evidence, challenging and removal of arbitrators, granting or enforcing interim measures, or enforcing orders made by the arbitral tribunal. Once the arbitral award has been handed down, the court may be requested to recognise and enforce it, remit it to the arbitral tribunal, or entertain proceedings to nullify it or set it aside. Additionally, it may be expected where the prejudicial effect of an arbitrator's order on the rights of one of the parties needs to be undone. In complex multi-party transnational disputes, however, things may be a lot less neat, and the simple enforcement of an arbitral agreement between two parties seldom solves all the issues. Judicial procedures may interlock. For instance, a good-faith possessor could institute a contractual proceeding against the intermediary and a civil declaratory proceeding against the dispossessed owner to establish his right based on prescriptive acquisition.[24] There are even greater potential risks if tripartite proceedings interlock. For instance, a deprived owner could institute a claim against a good faith possessor or intermediary seller in a national court, but the good faith possessor may institute proceedings against the intermediary seller with a view to the rescission of the sale in an arbitration. The owner would be better able to identify the defendant if the related claim is settled first, and settlement of the related claim may well be required for a cause of action to accrue. At the same time, however, awaiting the outcome of the related proceeding could be to the detriment of the owner.[25] Furthermore, the judiciary may fail to support the arbitration or judicial interference can occur because of a poorly conceived legislative framework or inadequate arbitral laws. When this

---

[24] IF Gazzini, *Cultural Property Disputes: The Role of Arbitration in Resolving Non-Contractual Disputes* (Transnational Publishers Inc. 2004) 196.

[25] Gazzini (n 24) 196.

happens, there is bound to be tactical manoeuvering, delays and inefficiency.[26] This situation was averted in the EU, but a lengthy period of legal uncertainty was caused by proposals for reform of the Judgments Regulation that lost sight of the dire consequences of treating litigation and arbitration as equals. They cannot be treated thus, because arbitral tribunals lack inherent jurisdiction.

National courts have means at their disposal by which to structure and co-ordinate parallel proceedings in the same dispute so as to avoid inefficiency, delay and conflicting decisions. These means include consolidation, third-party joinder, impleader or intervention. In addition, the first filed rule (*lis pendens* or 'pending proceedings') features prominently in EU private international law instruments[27] to control parallel proceedings filed in different Member States (discussed under 5. below). The court second seised must give up its right to adjudicate in favour of the court first seised. The powers of an arbitral tribunal, on the other hand, are generally confined to the immediate parties. Co-ordination may be called for when awards may conflict, or when an award may conflict with a decision, yet the parties involved would need to consent before a tribunal would be in a position to endeavour to structure or co-ordinate the procedures.[28] In interlocking proceedings between a court and a tribunal, it is uncertain whether the adjudicator must give up the right to hear the case if *lis pendens* is established and the proceedings were filed in another forum first.[29]

For purposes of this chapter, parallel proceedings are treated as a fact of transnational dispute resolution. It deserves to be controlled in the interest of ordering the horizontal diversity that marks regulatory authority in accordance with due process, the rule of law and standards of fairness.

---

[26] C Roodt, 'Conflicts of Procedure between Courts and Arbitral Tribunals in Africa: An Argument for Harmonization' (2010) 25 Tulane European and Civil Law Forum 65, 67.

[27] Among others, Art 21 of the Lugano Convention on Jurisdiction and the Recognition and Enforcement of Judgments in Civil and Commercial Matters, 30 October 2007 (EU, Denmark, Iceland, Norway and Switzerland); See attachment to Council Decision 2007/712/EC of 15 October 2007; Arts 27–28 of Regulation (EC) 44/2001; Art 29 of the Recast Regulation.

[28] Gazzini (n 24) 143, 152, 179ff.

[29] C Roodt 'Border Skirmishes between EU Courts and Arbitral Tribunals: Finality in Conflicts of Competence' (2011) 13 Yearbook of Private International Law 91; Gazzini (n 24) 197.

3. THE EXISTENCE OF JURISDICTION

3.1 The 1995 UNIDROIT Convention: Jurisdictional Grounds in Signatory States

The 1995 UNIDROIT Convention on Stolen or Illegally Exported Cultural Objects[30] regulates jurisdiction and enforcement of judgments within the ambit of the Convention in signatory states.[31] The Convention facilitates claims for restitution of stolen cultural objects or return of illegally exported cultural objects. Ordinary judicial channels are available in respect of restitution claims. Article 8 recognises the competence of the authorities of the *res situ* alongside that of the authorities designated by national and regional jurisdiction rules.[32] None of the bases of jurisdiction available under other jurisdictional regimes, including the Brussels regime and those of the US discussed hereafter, are precluded. Because this jurisdictional basis coexists with grounds that are found in other legislation, a claim may be brought before the courts or other authorities that have competence under the rules in force in Contracting States, and before the courts or other competent authorities of the Contracting State where the cultural object is located.

This provision is likely to improve enforcement. First, where a cultural object is offered for sale by an auction house or dealer domiciled in state A while it is physically located in state B, the dispossessed owner may institute action in the courts of the state of location (state B). If the state of location is bound by the UNIDROIT Convention but the state where the auction house or the seller is domiciled is not, the owner would be in a more favourable position than he otherwise would. Secondly, the state of location will not have to impose another state's judgment ordering return, but will be able to rely on the judgment of its own courts. Thirdly, if an action is brought in a state other than where the object is located, the dispossessed owner or state may apply for provisional measures in the courts of the state of location of the cultural object in order to prevent auction, sale or export as well as to ensure the general integrity and safety of the object.[33] This is necessary to prevent an object from

[30] The 1995 *UNIDROIT* Convention on Stolen or Illegally Exported Cultural Objects, 24 June 1995, 34 ILM 1330; entry into force 1 July 1998. <http://www.unidroit.org/instruments/cultural-property/1995-convention> accessed 24 February 2014.

[31] Stamatoudi (n 12) 102–4.

[32] Gazzini (n 24) 23.

[33] Art 8(3) of the UNIDROIT Convention.

disappearing before the judgment for the restitution or return of a cultural object can be enforced. The Convention also permits the intervention of another court if the *lex fori* or a choice of court agreement permits this.[34] The 2005 Hague Choice of Court Agreements Convention sets common rules on jurisdiction for cross-border civil and commercial litigation and for the enforcement of orders only for this particular head of jurisdiction. The EU and the US intend to ratify it in an attempt to improve the effectiveness and legal certainty of choice of court agreements in international commerce.[35]

Claimants who wish to proceed with an ownership or restitution claim in respect of a cultural object or a piece of art will be in position to choose between general, special and alternative grounds of jurisdiction. They may have the option to proceed in the court of the place where an object is located, but it is a basic feature of this area of law that more than one legal system may provide a forum and the substantive law to resolve a dispute. Thus, some degree of forum-shopping is to be expected.

States that have not ratified the 1995 UNIDROIT Convention cannot avail themselves of this complementary jurisdictional ground. It follows that a separate inquiry would need to be lodged in order to ascertain whether courts for the place where a cultural object is located in the UK and the US are competent to assume and exercise jurisdiction. Traditional jurisdiction rules grant courts in England, Scotland and Wales exclusive jurisdiction over proceedings that have as their subject-matter rights *in rem*, whatever the domicile of the defendant. US courts have jurisdiction over property, including personal property, located within their territory, if it provides minimum contacts among the forum state, the defendant and the litigation.[36]

An interesting development occurred at EU level along a line similar to that of the Convention, when the Judgments Regulation was being revised for courts of the EU Member States. The courts of the place where the object is located is competent to hear civil proceedings concerning rights *in rem* or possession in moveable property. This jurisdiction is available in respect of moveable property in general and also for proceedings for the recovery of cultural objects by their owners. Developments at EU level are discussed next.

---

[34] DPF Arroyo, 'Private International Law and Comparative Law: A Relationship Challenged by International and Supranational Law' (2009) XI Yearbook of Private International Law 31, 41.

[35] Federal implementing legislation is expected in the US.

[36] *Shaffer v Heitner*, 53 L Ed 2d 683 (1977).

3.2 EU Rules on Civil and Commercial Jurisdiction

3.2.1 The Brussels/Lugano regime

EU Member States rely on a rule-based allocation of jurisdiction in civil and commercial matters. The relevant rules form part of the so-called 'Brussels/Lugano regime' which has been embodied in the 1968 Brussels Convention on Jurisdiction and the Enforcement of Judgments in Civil and Commercial Matters; its successor Regulation 44/2001 of 22 December 2000 (hereafter the 'Judgments Regulation'[37]); and its successor Regulation 1215/2012 (EU) by the European Parliament and of the Council of 12 December 2012 (hereafter the 'Recast Regulation').[38] These successive sets of rules are designed to further the ideal of an internal market by promoting the free circulation of judgments within the EU and the mutual enforcement of judgments between EU Member States. The same rules regulate jurisdiction between the EU Member States and certain EFTA Member States (Denmark, Norway, Iceland and Switzerland).[39] For purposes of the Brussels regime, civil and commercial matters are given an autonomous interpretation that excludes a public authority acting in the exercise of its prerogatives.

The Brussels/Lugano regime facilitates judicial cooperation in EU Member States; its effect does not normally extend to third countries. An EU Member State applies traditional jurisdiction rules to decide jurisdiction if the defendant is not domiciled in an EU Member State and the Regulation does not apply.[40] Under the Judgments Regulation, domestic jurisdiction rules continue to apply in intra-UK cases and cases involving the UK and a non-EU state. The Recast Regulation changes the position as from 2015, in that no national rules of jurisdiction may be applied by EU Member States in relation to parties domiciled outside the EU in situations where the courts of a Member State have exclusive jurisdiction

---

[37] Council Regulation (EC) No 44/2001 of 22 December 2000 OJ L 12/1 16.1.2001, entry into force 1 March 2002.

[38] Council Regulation (EC) No 1215 of 2012 OJ 2012 L351/1, entry into force 10 January 2015.

[39] Agreement of 19 October 2005 between the EU and Denmark on jurisdiction and the recognition and enforcement of judgments in civil and commercial matters, in International Agreements OJ L 79/4, 21.03.2013 (entry into force on 1 July 2007); the 2007 Convention on Jurisdiction and the Recognition and Enforcement of Judgments in Civil and Commercial Matters, Council Decision 2007/712/EC of 15 October 2007.

[40] A Nuyts, 'Study on Residual Jurisdiction: General Report' (3 September 2007) <http://ec.europa.eu/civiljustice/news/docs/study_residual_jurisdiction_en.pdf> accessed 25 February 2014.

under the Recast Regulation or where such courts have had jurisdiction conferred on them by an agreement between the parties.

3.2.2 Jurisdiction of courts in EU Member States

The general rule, found in Article 2 of the Judgments Regulation, is that the defendant must be sued in his or her state of domicile. Persons domiciled in a Member State will be sued in the courts of that Member State whatever their nationality.[41] This principle means that, when deciding jurisdiction over other claims relating to immoveable or moveable property situated in England, e.g. a claim for breach of a condition of sale, the defendant's domicile is the starting point. It caters for the interest a defendant has in what is convenient, and ensures fairness towards them. Article 23 of the Judgments Regulation confers on parties the power to confer jurisdiction upon a forum that would not have jurisdiction otherwise, in which case the rule that the defendant must be sued in their country of domicile does not apply. The rules for specific jurisdiction differ from the general rule in Article 2(1) of the Judgments Regulation. The jurisdiction rules for contractual and non-contractual obligations harmonise the position with respect to claims brought in courts in the Member States of the EU. For instance, if the parties have a prior contractual relationship, the wrongful removal of a cultural object between jurisdictions may be considered to constitute a 'matter relating to contract' under Article 5(1). In matters relating to tort, delict or quasi-delict, the specific jurisdiction ground of Article 5(3) applies. The plaintiff may institute proceedings where a harmful event occurred to cause damage to an object, or may occur, which would be the place where the cultural object was wrongfully removed, provided the defendant's liability for such an event can be established.

Neither the Judgments Regulation nor the 1968 Brussels Convention contains a rule that the court where the corporeal object is situated has jurisdiction or that jurisdiction may be established by way of the seizure of property in that jurisdiction. Neither one of these instruments provides any specific jurisdiction rule for property questions or for the recovery of moveable property. The Brussels/Lugano regime does not permit a claimant to rely on the presence of a borrowed object in the territory of the court, or an attachment to found jurisdiction. A relevant nexus cannot be established in this way, because such jurisdiction is considered

---

[41] Art 2(1) of the Judgments Regulation.

exorbitant. A non-EU Member State court could possibly establish such jurisdiction.[42]

Under the Judgments Regulation, a claim in respect of ownership of a cultural object comes before a court under subject-matter jurisdiction provided for by rules set out in the Regulation. A civil claim for restitution of moveable objects or damages may be filed where criminal proceedings are taking place. The court seised of the criminal proceedings relating to dispossession of plaintiff may hear a restitution claim.[43] The place where criminal proceedings are taking place may well be the court for the place where objects are located.

Classification is unregulated in the Judgments Regulation. An English court may classify a restitution claim in respect of a moveable tangible object as one for wrongful interference with proprietary rights (conversion) and apply the special jurisdiction rule for tort. However, Article 5(3) could only apply to an *in personam* claim in tort in the courts of the place where the cultural object was removed wrongfully and provided the defendant's liability for the harmful event can be established.[44] It is conceivable that a foreign court could treat a restitution claim as coming within the scope of the rule for general jurisdiction. A German court may proceed on the basis of the general ground in Article 2(1).

Where the defendant is not domiciled in a Member State, Article 4 of the Brussels I Regulation refers the matter to Member States' residual jurisdiction. Absent a special jurisdiction rule for proprietary claims or restitutionary claims in the Judgments Regulation, a claimant who wishes to proceed in England would institute action in tort for conversion in terms of the common law regime of the CPR.[45] If moveable property was damaged in Scotland, an action for *spuilzie* may be brought.[46] However,

---

[42] G Maher and B Rodger, *Civil Jurisdiction in the Scottish Courts* (W Green 2010) 116–17.

[43] Art 5(4) of the Judgments Regulation; Art 5(4) of the Lugano Convention.

[44] *Kalfelis v Schroder* C-189/87 [1988] ECR 5565; *Rudolf Gabriel* C-96/00 [2002] ECR I-6367.

[45] CPR 6.36 permits a claimant to serve a claim from outside of the jurisdiction with the permission of the court if any of the grounds set out in § 3.1 of Practice Direction 6B apply. The grounds include if 'a claim is made in tort where damage was sustained within the jurisdiction'. The claimants need to satisfy the court that the object in question was located there and that it was damaged there; that there is both a serious issue to be tried on the merits and a good arguable case that the claim comes within § 3.1(9)(a).

[46] Rule 2(c) of Schedule 8 to the Civil Jurisdiction and Judgments Act.

in Germany, the claim would be based on ownership rights.[47] Article 5(1) of the Judgments Regulation will not be helpful in the context of restitution claims where no prior contractual relationship exists between the parties.

Differing classifications make forum-shopping more likely. This is to be expected until such time as the CJEU rules on the classification of restitution claims, or the Recast Regulation enters into operation (see 3.2.5 below).

Most Member State courts have jurisdiction, based on the location of property within their territory, to order provisional and conservatory measures concerning objects located there.[48] Application may be made to the court of an EU Member State, even if another Member State court has jurisdiction as to substance, and even when the defendant is domiciled in a non-EU state. Most Member State courts also have jurisdiction to adjudicate on the merits of a claim against the defendant owner of the object. In countries such as England, Scotland, Hungary, Spain, Sweden, Finland, Germany, the Netherlands, Austria, Poland and Portugal, this is a ground for specific jurisdiction which covers only property claims related to the object located within the territory. In other Member States, this is a ground for general jurisdiction, which allows any claim (including claims unrelated to the object) to be brought against the defendant. While Scottish and Hungarian courts depend on attachment or arrest of property to hear proprietary claims, in France, Luxembourg or Romania the location or arrest of property within the jurisdiction is not a basis of jurisdiction to adjudicate on the merits of the case as such, even for claims that seem to relate to such property.[49]

3.2.3 Prorogated jurisdiction under the Brussels regime

Parties stand to gain if they are spared pretrial or interlocutory motions to determine the correct forum. Jurisdiction (choice-of-court) agreements also secure tactical advantages for the plaintiff. Jurisdiction agreements that come within the scope of the Brussels regime are presumed exclusive unless parties expressly agree otherwise. The opposite position prevails in US law where jurisdiction clauses are presumed to be non-exclusive. Parties who are domiciled in a third country may also

---

47 The material law of Germany provides for damages claims in respect of the violation of ownership rights based on tort in § 823 BGB, but § 985 BGB provides a special basis for restitution claims, which is ownership. With thanks to Nadine Burrath for drawing my attention to this example.

48 Jurisdiction seemingly derives from Art 31 of the Judgments Regulation.

49 Nuyts (n 40) § 51.

enter into jurisdiction agreements, but if the chosen court is a non-Member State court, Article 23 does not apply. Courts in the European Judicial Area will use traditional domestic law to decide jurisdiction since the effect of the Judgment Regulation does not normally extend to third countries. Article 23(3) of the Judgments Regulation permits differential treatment of cases where one of the parties is an EU domiciliary and in cases where both are non-EU domiciliaries.

The effect of *Owusu v Jackson*,[50] which renders mandatory the application of Article 2 of the Judgments Regulation, has been controversial. English courts have tried to limit the effect of this ruling.[51] The case has potential to override a choice in favour of a third state court. The influential theory of reflexive effect, first propounded by Droz[52] and refined by several other scholars,[53] was neither approved nor rejected in *Owusu*. The doctrine was dismissed in an Irish case,[54] and parallel proceedings were permitted to continue in Ireland and the US because Article 2 did not permit the granting of a stay. The ruling allows entities domiciled in third states engaged in commercial disputes with parties domiciled in the EU, to sue EU-domiciled parties in their home jurisdiction irrespective of the fact that litigation has already been commenced in a non-EU jurisdiction. These entities will not be able to rely on proceedings already begun within their jurisdiction to overcome jurisdiction established under Article 2.

3.2.4 Revision of the Judgments Regulation

The process of revising the Judgments Regulation reached a point at the end of 2010 when it seemed likely that more opportunities would be established, under heads recognised in the Judgments Regulation, to bring a claim concerning rights *in rem* in moveable property before the courts of the EU Member States.[55] Separate draft provisions granted

---

50 Case C-281/02 *Owusu v Jackson* [2005] ECR I-1383.

51 *Konkola Copper Mines v Coromin* [2005] EWHC 898; *Ferrexpo v Gilson* [2012] EWHC 721.

52 G Droz, *Compétences Judiciaires et Effets des Jugements dans le Marché Commun* (Dalloz 1972) §§ 164–69.

53 Clarkson and Hill (n 12) 143; I Pretelli, The Proposal for a Regulation of the European Parliament and of the Council on Jurisdiction and the Recognition and Enforcement of Judgments in Civil and Commercial Matters (Recast) (EP Directorate-General for Internal Policies 2011) 23–24.

54 *Goshawk Dedicated and Others v Life Receivables Ireland Ltd* [2008] IEHC 90.

55 Proposal for a Regulation of the European Parliament and of the Council on Jurisdiction and the Recognition and Enforcement of Judgments in Civil and

non-exclusive jurisdiction to the courts of a given Member State on the ground that certain assets are located in the area where the court sits. Courts for the place of the *situs rei* were supposed, *a fortiori*, to be able to deal with proceedings related to possession and rights *in rem* in goods.[56] It was proposed that jurisdiction should also extend to owners who were non-EU domiciliaries.[57] They were to be sued before the courts of the Member State where their property was located regardless of the subject matter of the claim. To ensure access to court and the prevention of a denial of justice in relations with third states, necessity was put forward as an additional basis for jurisdiction.[58]

The European Parliament issued its Legislative Resolution on the Recast Proposal in October 2012.[59] The Resolution stipulated the jurisdictional ground in recovery cases and referred to the definition of a cultural object in Council Directive 93/7 EEC of 15 March 1993 on the Return of Cultural Objects Unlawfully Removed from the Territory of Member States.[60] The European Parliament Report contained no trace of any subsidiary jurisdiction rule, nor was necessity proposed as a basis for jurisdiction. However, the owner of an object that met the definition contained in Council Directive 93/7 EEC of 15 March 1993 could initiate civil proceedings for its recovery. Proposed Article 13a was to the effect that the owner of such an object should be able to initiate civil

---

Commercial Matters COM (2010) 74 8 Final (Recast); P Franzina,'The Proposed New Rule of Special Jurisdiction Regarding Rights In Rem in Moveable Property: A Good Option for a Reformed Brussels I Regulation?' (2011) 3 Diritto de Commercio Internazionale 789.

[56] Moveables designated 'corporeal and incorporeal property other than immovable property' in C von Bar et al. (eds), Study Group on a European Civil Code and the Research Group on EC Private Law *Principles, Definitions and Model Rules of European Private Law: Draft Common Frame of Reference* (Sellier 2009) (DCFR).

[57] Draft Arts 5(3)–(5) and 25.

[58] Draft Art 26. Conditions for its application had to do with the value of the property and the connection between the dispute and the court seised.

[59] Draft European Parliament Legislative Resolution on the Proposal for a Regulation of the European Parliament and of the Council on Jurisdiction and the Recognition and Enforcement of Judgments in Civil and Commercial Matters (Recast), 15 October 2012 (A7-0320/2012).

[60] Council Directive (EEC) 93/7 of 15 March 1993 on the return of cultural objects unlawfully removed from the territory of a member state OJ L 74/74, 27.3.93 with amendment of the annex by Directive 96/100/EC of the European Parliament and of the Council of 17 February 1997 (L 60/59, 1.3.1997), and by Directive 2001/38/EC of the European Parliament and of the Council of 5 June 2001, OJ L 187/43, 10.7.2001.

proceedings for the recovery of an object in one of the courts of the place where the object is situated when the suit is instituted, even where a state claim had been made under the Directive. Proposed Article 4a established special jurisdiction in respect of an owner's civil claim for recovery of an object that meets the definition in the courts for the place where the cultural object is situated at the time the court is seised.

3.2.5 A new Judgments Regulation (Recast Regulation)

The final and new form of the Judgments Regulation, known as the Recast Regulation,[61] enables the courts of Member States to hear such claims. The text of the Recast Regulation was finalised in December 2012. New article 7(3) renders Member State courts competent to try a claim or enforce a judgment involving a cultural object in respect of which another EU Member State, or a third state, has asserted ownership, if it is a civil claim for damages or a claim for restitution that is based on an act giving rise to criminal proceedings. The court seised of those proceedings has jurisdiction to the extent that its own law permits it to entertain civil proceedings. Recital 17 reiterates that an owner ought to be able to initiate civil proceedings for the recovery of an object covered by Council Directive 93/7 EEC (soon to be replaced by Directive 2014/60/EU), in a court for the place where the object is situated when the suit is instituted. New article 7(4) confers special jurisdiction in respect of an owner's civil claim for recovery of an object defined in Council Directive 93/7 EEC(Directive 2014/60/EU) in the courts for the place where the cultural object is situated at the time the court is seised. Judgments decided in respect of such an object in Lugano states and third states qualify for recognition and enforcement.

The Brussels regime operates on the basis of the understanding that the rules governing the formal validity of choice of court agreements are sufficient to guarantee real consent. The Recast Regulation provided greater clarity in this regard. The Recast Regulation expressly regulates the material validity of the choice of court agreement, which is to be tested with reference to the law of the chosen jurisdiction.[62] Choice of court agreements that nominate third state courts are not regulated.

A civil claim for recovery under Article 7(4) is brought *in personam* by the party claiming the right to recover in the place where the object is situated, against a defendant in another EU Member State. The court

[61] Council Regulation (EC) No 1215 of 2012, OJ 2012 L351/1, entry into force 10 January 2015.

[62] Recital 20 and Art 25 of the Recast Regulation.

seised will determine whether the object in question is moveable or not. Secondary EU law will inform its classification as a cultural object (discussed in Chapter 2) which must correspond with the basis of jurisdiction and the exclusive competence of the Member States in this regard.[63]

The claim should be based on ownership.[64] It is suggested that this right must be found to exist in the law of the Member State which classified the object as a national treasure prior to its unlawful removal or retention, in line with secondary EU law, and that the claimant must rely on that law in its claim for recovery.[65] Of course, traffickers stand to benefit greatly from the sheer difficulty of determining ownership without knowing if the object concerned was traded legally.

3.2.6 Enforcement of judgments in courts in EU Member States

Judgments in regard to moveables will probably be recognised and enforced if the object concerned were situated within the area of jurisdiction of the foreign court at the time of the proceedings. Judgments given in EU Member States are automatically enforced in other EU Member States and certain EFTA States by virtue of the Judgments Regulation. The new provisions of the Recast Regulation also provides that a judgment given in a Member State will be recognised in the other Member States without any specific procedure and, if enforceable in the member state of origin, will be enforceable in the other Member States without any declaration of enforceability. Grounds on which enforcement may be refused, are limited. Exceptions apply in certain specific cases, for example if a judgment is manifestly contrary to public policy.[66] If a judgment is produced by a third state court, then national law applies unless there are bilateral agreements in respect of the recognition and enforcement of such judgments.

In respect of art that belongs to publicly owned museums in debtor states, immunity regimes are relevant to the guarantee of return. These regimes can most often be found in immunity statutes that respond to international law rules. This is not necessarily true in all cases, and consequently, careful specification is necessary before immunity can be applied in a case. In the US, the scope of the immunity in federal and

---

[63] Maher and Rodger (n 42) 108; L Gillies, 'The Conflict of Laws as a Technique of Demand Side Regulation in Claims for the Recovery of Cultural Objects' [2015] JPIL (forthcoming).

[64] Recital 17 of the Recast Regulation.

[65] Gillies (n 63).

[66] Art 34ff of the Judgments Regulation.

New York statutes has required change in the wake of the Portrait of Wally debacle involving the temporary loss of immunity against criminal seisure. The litigation of the heirs against two museums ended only when the director of the Leopold Museum died.[67] He had unlawfully appropriated the painting for himself and was finally ordered to stand trial. Just days before the trial date of 26 July 2010, the Leopold Museum paid Lea Bondi's estate a settlement of USD 19 million for the painting.[68] Immunity was extended, but the museum community was shaken by the seizure and the lack of a guarantee that art on loan would be returned.[69]

3.3 Jurisdiction of US Courts

3.3.1 Minimum contacts

As a threshold matter, a US court may exercise jurisdiction over a person or company only where that entity has 'minimum contacts' with the particular state in which that court sits. These contacts may take the form of the commission of some act within the state, contracting for the provision of goods or services within the state, deriving some benefit from conducting business within the state, ownership of property, or placing an item in the stream of commerce with the intention that it be distributed within the state.[70]

Federal jurisdiction results from a grant or cession of jurisdiction by the state to the federal government, for lands owned or otherwise possessed by the federal government. Federal courts are competent to hear cases involving cultural objects and human remains. In *Pueblo of San Ildefonso v Daniel Ridlon and Regents of the University of California*,[71] the court concluded that the Pueblo staked a claim under NAGPRA to establish federal subject matter jurisdiction. In *Crow Creek Sioux Tribe*

---

[67] *US v Portrait of Wally, A Painting by Egon Schiele*, No 99-CV-09940 (SDNY filed July 29, 2010) <http://www.comartrecovery.org/sites/default/files/wally_SFX103_0.pdf> accessed 25 February 2014.

[68] Press release by the US Attorney for the Southern District of New York dated 20 July 2010.

[69] A O'Connell, 'Immunity from Seizure Study' (30 September 2005) <http://www.lending-for-europe.eu/fileadmin/CM/public/training/Antwerp/Immunity_from_Seizure_Paper_Anna_O_Connell.pdf> accessed 24 February 2014.

[70] 'The ABCs of Cross-Border Litigation in the United States' (*Crowell Moring*, 2008) <http://www.crowell.com/files/abc-guide-to-cross-border-litigation.pdf> accessed 24 February 2014.

[71] *Pueblo of San Ildefonso v Daniel Ridlon and Regents of the University of California*, 103 F3d 936 (10th Circuit 1996).

v Brownlee,[72] the Sioux tribe did not succeed with their claim that enforcement of the federal cultural protection statutes NAGPRA, ARPA and the National Historic Preservation Act (NHPA)[73] on the transferred lands injures tribal rights. The claim was dismissed for lack of standing and of subject matter jurisdiction.

Once any property within the exclusive jurisdiction of the US is no longer utilised by the government for governmental purposes, and the title or any interest therein is conveyed to private interests, the jurisdiction of the federal government ceases and jurisdiction reverts to the State.[74]

Federal subject-matter jurisdiction ('diversity jurisdiction') exists in cases where the opposing parties are non-US citizens (domiciliaries) or citizens of different states in the US. US district courts in the federal judiciary are authorised by federal law to hear civil cases of this nature.[75] The subject matter jurisdiction of the federal courts is not defined by the subject matter of the underlying dispute, but by who the litigants are. The amount in controversy must meet the minimum threshold.[76]

The subject-matter jurisdiction of state courts refers to the competence to decide the kind of controversy that is involved. The Due Process Clause of the 14th Amendment of the US Constitution imposes limits on the jurisdiction powers of states. The court is competent to enter a judgment binding on the particular defendant when there is subject matter jurisdiction and process was duly served on the defendant. Subject matter jurisdiction is not an alternative to personal jurisdiction. Both jurisdictional hurdles need to be cleared.

Personal jurisdiction may be extended to a defendant who is not physically present within the territory of the forum under so-called long-arm statutes. The state has the power to regulate any issues with minimum connections with the US in principle. Any challenge in respect of the jurisdiction of a court in the US under a state or federal long-arm statute has a constitutional dimension, because the due process clause of the US Constitution imposes limits. The protection afforded by the clause

---

72 *Crow Creek Sioux Tribe v Brownlee*, 331 F3d 912 (17 June 2003).

73 NHPA, 16 US Code 470aa–470mm (2000) sets out the procedures federal agencies must follow prior to a federal 'undertaking' to consider its impact on properties with historical value.

74 <www.constitution.org/juris/fedjur1.htm> accessed 25 February 2014.

75 Diversity of Citizenship, 28 US Code 1332.

76 The constitutional basis is found in Art III s 2.

extends to foreign defendants.[77] Courts may decline to exercise jurisdiction based on a long-arm statute if it would be inappropriate to hear the case. The due process test for personal jurisdiction in US courts comprises two components: a 'minimum contacts' analysis and a 'reasonableness inquiry' conducted on the basis of various relevant interests. Property in the jurisdiction provides minimum contact. The jurisdiction of any particular state extends to all persons and property located or found within its borders. Actions involving property can be brought in the court of the area where they are situated. Actions taken outside of the forum directed at persons or businesses within the forum, or actions that have consequences within the forum, may suffice. In terms of constitutional due process, the quality and nature of the forum-related activities of a non-resident must satisfy the minimum contacts test, so that 'the maintenance of the suit does not offend traditional notions of fair play and substantial justice'.[78]

To assert general jurisdiction in respect of a non-resident defendant on any cause of action, when the cause of action is not dependent on the relationship between the forum and the claim, the defendant must have extensive, systematic and continuous contacts with the state, or the corporation must have carried out continuous and systematic activities within the forum, such that a suit there on any claim is to be expected.[79] When such minimum contacts are found, the 'reasonableness' prong is rarely employed separately. The person or entity may be sued for any claim, and will therefore be subject to the jurisdiction of at least one court. Additionally, the state has a governmental interest in any person who acts on a continuous basis in its territory.

For specific jurisdiction in respect of non-residents, the cause of action must derive from the defendant's contact and the case must have a substantial connection with the non-resident's activity. A court must determine whether a defendant has 'purposefully availed' itself of the protections and benefits of the forum's law, and assess whether the exercise of jurisdiction would be reasonable in the circumstances.[80]

---

[77] A Bell, *Forum-shopping and Venue in Transnational Litigation* (OUP 2003) 145.

[78] *International Shoe v Washington*, 326 US 310, 316 (1945).

[79] *Perkins v Benguet Consolidated Mining Co.*, 342 US 437 (1952) (the 'doing business' standard); *Helicopteros Nacionales de Colombia v Hall*, 466 US 408 (1984) (choice of court clause in favour of Peruvian courts; no continuous and systematic contacts with courts in Texas).

[80] *World-Wide Volkswagen Corp. v Woodson*, 444 US 286 (1980). Bell (n 77) 146.

The circumstances must be such as that a party can 'reasonably expect to be haled into court in that state'.[81] This expectation may be hard to establish when one party is a foreign state or state entity.

3.3.2 Recognition and enforcement

The Full Faith and Credit Clause requires state and federal courts to respect judgments made by courts in other states as well as judgments made in foreign countries. The last decision in a line of inconsistent judgments is recognised for purposes of full faith and credit. Special provisions for recognition and enforcement of foreign judgments differ among individual states. US courts are not bound by the rendering country's concept of *res judicata*.[82] US courts decide for themselves whether a judgment can be classified as final. This has not affected the attraction of US courts.

Where a judgment is entered against a company that is majority-owned or controlled by a foreign state, the attachment of the company's assets is governed by the Foreign Sovereign Immunities Act (FSIA). This Act provides that the property of state agencies and instrumentalities are immune from attachment unless one of the specified exceptions applies (including, e.g., where the agency conducts business in the US or contractually waives attachment immunity). In addition, the assets of a state-owned company may be attached to enforce a judgment against the foreign state, at least where the company is subject to 'extensive control' by the state.

3.3.3 FSIA and IFSA

The jurisdiction-granting provisions of the Foreign Sovereign Immunities Act of 1976 (FSIA)[83] – the listed exceptions contained in sections 1605 to 1607 – have changed the face of art restitution cases brought in US federal courts. The most important exception listed in section 1605 for purposes of art restitution claims is the expropriation exception. It provides, in part, that foreign states do not have immunity from the jurisdiction of US federal and state courts in cases in which rights in property that was taken in violation of international law are in issue, and that property is present in the US in connection with a commercial activity carried on in the US.

---

[81] *Asahi Metal Industry Co. v Superior Court of California*, 480 US 102 (1987) (purposeful direction of the intent to sell the product in the forum).

[82] DP Stewart, 'Recognition and Enforcement of Foreign Judgments in the United States' (2010) 12 Yearbook of Private International Law 180, 189.

[83] FSIA, 28 US Code 1605 ff.

The FSIA strips US courts of subject-matter jurisdiction over most claims against foreign states, but claims that fall under any of the statute's exceptions are permitted to go forward.[84] Judicial practice in respect of the FSIA[85] and the Immunity from Seizure Act (FISA)[86] has allowed several cases to be brought against foreign states. The broad and extensive interpretation given to the immunity exceptions has enabled US nationals to proceed against foreign sovereigns. Foreign sovereign state-run museum-related activities of a commercial nature have been brought within the scope of the immunity exceptions, and alien nationals have been able to proceed before federal courts for restitution of art spoliated by the Nazis and not yet restituted.[87] Where subject-matter jurisdiction is found, personal jurisdiction follows as soon as the defendant has been properly served.[88]

While the Nazi party has not been treated as a sovereign or the ERR (Reichsleiter Rosenberg Taskforce) its agent for purposes of the act of state defence, US courts consider Nazi acts to be sovereign acts for purposes of gaining jurisdiction under the FSIA.[89]

The broad applications of the commercial activities and expropriation exceptions make a draw-card of international jurisdiction in the US. Some say they threaten to eclipse foreign sovereign immunity in US courts.[90] Used as a sword instead of a shield, sovereign immunity incentivises forum-shopping. Corrective legislation is in the offing, but regardless of this factor, low fees and other procedural advantages in

---

[84] Fishman (n 15) 355 note 35; Fielder Redman (n 15) 782.

[85] *Leonard Malewicz v City of Amsterdam*, 517 F Supp 2d 322 (2007) (contacts of City of Amsterdam with US were substantial; lending of art between museums is a commercial activity for purposes of the FSIA).

[86] IFSA 22 US Code 2459. *Leonard Malewicz v City of Amsterdam*, 362 F Supp 2d 298 (DDC 2005)(IFSA did not lend protection to the Stedelijk Museum).

[87] E.g. *Cassirer v Kingdom of Spain*, 461 F Supp 2d 1157 (C D Cal 2006); *Chasidei Chabad v Russian Federation* 528 F3d 934 (DC Circuit 2008).

[88] 28 USC 1330 (b).

[89] *Altmann v Republic of Austria*, 142 F Supp 2d 1187 (C D Cal 1999), affirmed and remanded by 317 F3d 954 (9th Circuit 2002), rehearing denied en banc, 327 F3d 1246 (9th Circuit 2003), stay granted pending petition for writ of certiorari, 123 S Ct 2129 (2003), *cert* granted in part by 539 US 987 (2003); affirmed on other grounds by 541 US 677 (2004); on remand to *Altmann v Republic of Austria*, 335 F Supp 2d 1066 (C D Cal 2004). B Schönenberger, *The Restitution of Cultural Assets* (Eleven International Publishing 2009) 206; Siehr (n 15) 345–46; AB Sargent, 'New Jurisdictional Tools for Displaced Cultural Property in Russia' 2010 Yearbook of Cultural Property Law 167, 175.

[90] Fielder Redman (n 15) 782.

litigation in US courts remain attractive for forum-shoppers. Once a US court has established jurisdiction, strong evidence-gathering powers in the form of orders for disclosure take effect. Parties have an opportunity to pursue interlocutory orders such as an injunction to 'freeze a situation' until a final decision is reached. The settlement rate is poor.[91]

The willingness of the bench to permit litigation in the face of the FISA and to dis-apply the Immunity from Seizure Act (IFSA), regardless of where the cultural objects are, have given rise to fears of foreign governments getting trapped into a US court. This situation could compromise cultural exchanges, including art loans.[92]

Defences against federal courts hearing a case involving a claim to art in the US may involve combinations of the exceptions contained in the FSIA, aspects of the FISA, the act of state doctrine (dealt with in Chapter 2), and *forum non conveniens* (analysed under 4. below).[93]

4. COURT MAY DECLINE TO HEAR THE DISPUTE IN THE EXERCISE OF ITS STATE AUTHORITY

Because various different jurisdictional grounds exist, litigants may seize different courts, and not all of them will necessarily exercise their jurisdiction and rule in a case. The Common Law and civilian traditions respond markedly differently to deciding whether to decline jurisdiction when litigation has been instituted in multiple fora.[94] Whereas the common law has always relied on judicial discretion regardless of whether the proceedings are between the same parties and/or concern the same cause of action, civilian systems and the Brussels regime utilise a

---

91 JA Nafziger and AM Nicgorski, *Cultural Heritage Issues: The Legacy of Conquest, Colonization and Commerce* (2009) 379.

92 Caprio (n 15) 285.

93 E.g. *Altmann v Austria* 317 F3d 954 (9th Circuit 2002) §§ 51–54. In *Austria v Altmann* 541 US 677 (2004) 677–700, the US Supreme Court adopted a narrow focus, electing to adjudicate on the issue of retrospectivity of the FSIA to the exclusion of *forum non conveniens*, lack of personal jurisdiction and whether the expropriation exception applied on the facts. The suggestion that the State Department could file suggestions of immunity clouded the issue with concerns over separation of powers.

94 N Andrews, *The Three Paths of Justice: Court Proceedings, Arbitration and Mediation in England* (Cambridge 2012) 228–35, 251.

rule-based method.[95] These differences are set out in more detail in the sections that follow.

4.1 Common Law and Civil Law Legal Systems

Generally speaking, a decision to decline jurisdiction or grant an application for a stay is dealt with by way of judicial discretion in common law legal systems.[96] The origins of the discretionary power are to be found in Scots law.[97] The original conception of *forum non conveniens* was that a case pending in a foreign court would factor into a wider *forum non conveniens* determination and that judicial discretion would determine the matter.[98] By the time it was received into English law,[99] a stay required the defendant to show that another forum was clearly more appropriate in the sense of having a more substantial connection to the case than the forum seised. The existence of concurrent or related proceedings in another forum that is claimed to be the natural forum may affect the assessment of the natural forum, particularly if those proceedings are bona fide.

The doctrine is employed not only at federal level in the US, but every US state has a doctrine that lets its courts stay actions if another court is shown to be more appropriate, to avoid duplicative litigation.[100] Judicial practice has developed in a federal context, rather than in an international context.

Forum non conveniens applies under the federal law standard to promote the achievement of the ends of justice. Where jurisdictional requirements have been met, the court declines the exercise because an

---

[95] C McLachlan, *Lis Pendens in International Litigation* (Hague Academy of International Law 2009) 49, 53.

[96] In general Clarkson and Hill (n 12) 102.

[97] AE Anton, *Private International Law* (2nd ed, W Green 1990) 212–18; JJ Fawcett and JM Carruthers, *Cheshire, North & Fawcett Private International Law* (14th edn, OUP 2008) 426.

[98] *Hawkins v Wedderburn* 4 Dunlop 854 (1842) Court of Session (litigation begun in England and then begun in Scotland between the same parties in the same case after the defendants had appeared and pled in England; claimants restrained).

[99] Received into English law in *Spiliada Maritime Co v Cansulex* [1987] AC 460, 476 and *RTZ v Connolly* [1998] AC 854. Fawcett and Carruthers (n 97) 428–43.

[100] *Forum non conveniens* was systematically recognised and used after *International Shoe v Washington*, 326 US 310, 316 (1945). See *Gulf Oil Corp v Gilbert,* 330 US 501 (1947).

adequate foreign court is available, relevant public and private interests weigh in favour of dismissal, and the plaintiff can reinstate the suit in that alternative forum without undue convenience or prejudice.[101]

The private interest factors considered by courts in the US refer to all the considerations that make the trial of a case easy, expeditious and inexpensive.[102] The public interest factors include the administrative impact in terms of congestion; the local interest in having a diversity trial in a forum that is at home with the law that governs the action; and the avoidance of conflicts problems or problems associated with the application of foreign law.[103] The factors that affect substantive justice include the lack of legal aid and the level of development and independence of the courts. The likelihood of a fair trial, and conflicts problems such as the likelihood of the foreign court applying a law which might be unjust or offensive, or of the final decision of the foreign court violating fundamental policy, retain relevance. Both procedural efficiency and the achievement of substantive justice have a role to play. In contrast, courts in England and Australia feel unsure about whether they can accurately assess issues of administrative convenience in an international context, and thus they prefer not to consider public interest factors affecting the convenience of the court in a *forum non conveniens* inquiry.[104]

The prospects of a defendant being granted a stay in a state court in the US depends on the state where the court is located.[105] Relevant factors may include, for instance, public policy, the relative burdens placed on the court systems, and how a change of the forum would affect each party's case.

In *Altmann v Austria*[106] the US court was requested to decline jurisdiction in the interests of justice on the basis of a *forum non*

---

101 *Piper Aircraft Co v Reyno*, 454 US 235 (1981); *Gulf Oil Corpn v Gilbert*, 330 US 501 (1946). Cf *Cassirer v Kingdom of Spain*, 461 F Supp 2d 1157 (C D Cal 2006). In general, Fielder Redman (n 15) 808.

102 *Gulf Oil Corpn v Gilbert*, 330 US 501 (1946) 508.

103 *Clerides v Boeing Co*, 534 F3d 623 (7th Cir 2008) 628 citing *Gilbert*, 330 US 501, 508–9 (1946).

104 *Lubbe v Cape PLC* [2000] 4 All ER 268, 287; M Davis, 'Time to Change the Federal Forum Non Conveniens Analysis' (2002) 77 Tulane Law Review 309, 371, 374.

105 Bell (n 77) 150.

106 *Altmann v Austria*, 142 F Supp 2d 1187, 1210 (the bar on account of the statute of limitations as well as the high filing fee were both considered relevant); 317 F3d 954 (limitations argument irrelevant as fraudulent concealment would toll the statute of limitations and the 1998 Austrian Federal Statute on the Restitution of Art Objects would permit the claim). The high filing fee was just

conveniens defence. The request did not succeed because Austria did not provide an adequate alternative forum for the plaintiff. Austria's failure to seek justice for Mrs Altmann soured international relations considerably.

The doctrine of *forum non conveniens* avoids giving offence to a foreign state when assuming jurisdiction[107] because it is possible to prioritise the convenience of the defendant over the interests of the forum or foreign state in having its own law applied, or the plaintiff's interests in a favourable applicable law. In English hands, however, the governing law was among the factors that affected the assessment of the natural forum,[108] even if public interest factors are generally regarded to be irrelevant.[109] It is unavoidable that mandatory forum rules will bring considerations relevant to the law to be applied to the fore in questions that concern the establishment and exercise of jurisdiction.

Civil Law courts rely on a rule-based system. With a few exceptions, whenever two different but equally competent courts are seised in the same dispute between the same parties regarding the same subject-matter or relief (*petitum*) and based on the same legal grounds (*causa petendi*), a *prior temporis* formula determines which court has the first opportunity to adjudicate the merits of the matter.[110] The simple rule of priority grants precedence to the court first seised to resolve conflicts of jurisdiction. It precludes the non-recognition of a judgment in the state where recognition is being sought on account of being irreconcilable with another judgment in the same dispute between the same parties.

The mandatory jurisdiction scheme of the Judgments Regulation leaves no room for judicial discretion.[111] The ECJ (now CJEU) outlawed discretion-based mechanisms in litigation involving the courts of EU Member States, although they continue to be used in intra-UK disputes and disputes involving the courts of third states. The new Recast Regulation provides for a discretionary *lis pendens* and related actions

---

one among several other relevant considerations, namely that Mrs Altmann was elderly, had lived in the US for 60 years, and absence of conflict of laws issues other than the statute of limitations.

[107] See *Reichhold Norway ASA v Goldman Sachs International* [2000] 1 WLR 173 (CA); ILA *Final Report on Lis Pendens and Arbitration*, Report of the Seventy-Second Conference, Toronto, 2006, <www.ila-hq.org> §§ 2.5–2.7; 2.12–2.13, accessed 24 February 2014.

[108] Bell (n 77) 152.

[109] *Lubbe v Cape PLC* [2000] 4 All ER 268, 281.

[110] BM Cremades and I Madalena, 'Parallel Proceedings in International Arbitration' (2008) 24 Arbitration International 3; ILA *Final Report on Lis Pendens and Arbitration* (n 107) §§ 2.8ff; 2.16.

[111] Case C-281/02 *Owusu v Jackson* [2005] ECR I-1383.

provision in relation to third states. The Recast Regulation will allow the courts of a member state, on a discretionary basis, to stay the proceedings and eventually dismiss the proceedings in situations where a court of a third state has already been seised either of proceedings between the same parties or of a related action at the time the EU court is seised.[112]

The first filed rule applies only to parallel proceedings commenced within the US, between a federal and a state court or between two or more state courts. It has no application in transnational cases.[113]

4.2 Jurisdictional Challenges in US Courts

The defendant who mounts a challenge to jurisdiction is put to considerable expense and inconvenience. Interlocutory jurisdictional skirmishes require time and effort. This may induce a settlement offer, but it may also win the defendant more time to develop its defence on the merits.[114] Compared to a counterpart in the EU, the position of the defendant is more uncertain in the US. The bases of jurisdiction in EU law are more specific by far. Nonetheless, despite the frequency of jurisdictional skirmishes in US courts,[115] the US court system is one of the most attractive for litigating disputes for the return of cultural objects to their countries of origin.[116]

A jurisdictional challenge will not stand if the taking of property was in violation of international law. For example, in *Chasidei Chabad v Russian Federation*,[117] federal jurisdiction under the FSIA was held to have been conferred. The expropriations of both Archive and Library sacred manuscripts belonging to Chabad, an orthodox umbrella entity, by

---

[112] Art 33 of the Recast Regulation.

[113] *Laker Airways Ltd v Sabena, Belgian World Airlines*, 731 F2d 909 (DC Circuit 1984) 927.

[114] Bell (n 77) 147.

[115] Bell (n 77) 145.

[116] E.g. *United States v Hollinshead*, 495 F2d 1154 (9th Circuit 1974); *Jeanneret v Vichey*, 541 F Supp 80 (SDNY 1982); rev'd and remanded 693 F2d 259 (2nd Circuit 1982); *DeWeerth v Baldinger*, 836 F2d 103 (2nd Circuit 1987) *cert denied* 108 S Ct 2823 (1988); 804 F Supp 539 (SDNY 1992); 38 F3d 1266 (2nd Circuit NY 1994); 115 S Ct 512 (1994); *Autocephalous Greek-Orthodox Church v Goldberg & Feldman Fine Arts Inc*, 717 F Supp 1374 (SD Ind 1989) aff'd 917 F2d 278 (7th Circuit 1990) *cert denied* 112 S Ct 377 (1992); *Republic of Lebanon v Sotheby's*, 561 NYS 2d 566 AD 1 Dept 1990; *Republic of Turkey v The Metropolitan Museum of Art*, 762 F Supp 44 (SDNY 1990); *Solomon R Guggenheim Foundation v Lubell* 77 NY 2d 311 (1991). Fishman (n 15) 355.

[117] *Chasidei Chabad v Russian Federation* 466 F Supp 2d 6 (2006).

the Nazis during World War II and by the Soviets in the aftermath of the Bolshevik Revolution, were found to have been perpetrated in breach of international law.[118] However, because the Library was in the hands of Russia or citizens of Russia (1920–1921), principles of international law were found not to apply to it. The act of state defence was also upheld in respect of the Library. The appellate court *Chasidei Chabad v Russian Federation*[119] expanded the jurisdictional reach of the FSIA, and reversed with respect to the Library. A 'retaking' had taken place in 1991–1992 when the Soviet Union became the Russian Federation.[120] The act of state was held not to apply. The claim that there was a taking for purposes of jurisdiction is held to the 'substantial and non-frivolous claim' standard. It does not have to be determined on the merits.[121] Jurisdiction under the FSIA is now opening up to cultural property that was taken physically and retaken politically.[122]

5. DIFFERENT CONCEPTIONS OF FINALITY OF JUDGMENTS (*RES JUDICATA*) PREVAIL

Finality of outcome is attained on account of the conclusive and preclusive effects of *res judicata*.[123] The positive or conclusive *res judicata* effect of an arbitral award concerns the effect of decisions contained in an award in other proceedings, be it between the same parties or between different parties. The preclusive or negative effect of *res judicata* of an arbitral award concerns the prevention of further litigation on a matter resolved in a prior arbitral award. The difference has also been described in terms of the formal and material aspects of finality. The formal aspect of *res judicata* obviates a repetitious lawsuit, based on the public policy interest of the finality of trial. Its material aspects differ widely in different legal traditions, however. In Dutch law, for instance, its material effect is that neither the claimant nor the

---

118 *Chasidei Chabad v Russian Federation* 466 F Supp 2d 6 (2006) 19–20.

119 *Chasidei Chabad v Russian Federation* 528 F3d 934 (DC Circuit 2008).

120 *Chasidei Chabad v Russian Federation* 528 F3d 934 (DC Circuit 2008) 944; 953–54.

121 Sargent (n 89) 175.

122 For more, see Sargent (n 89) 187.

123 LG Radicati di Brozolo, 'Res Judicata' in Post Award Issues ASA Special Series no 38 2011, Chapter 7; LG Radicati di Brozolo, 'Res Judicata in International Arbitral Awards' (*Social Science Research Network*, 15 April 2011) 2 <http://ssrn.com/abstract=1842685> accessed 25 February 2014.

defendant is permitted to dispute the decisions material to the final outcome of a decision in a subsequent lawsuit on a different issue.[124]

It is possible to classify jurisdictions in accordance with their conception of finality.

Predictably, Common Law courts rely on an inherent judicial discretion to manage parallel adjudication in multiple forums. A court would allow actions to proceed simultaneously 'until a judgment is reached in one which can be pled as *res judicata* in the other'.[125] The broad-scope concept of the Common Law does not insist that the parallel proceedings occur between the same parties and/or concern the same cause of action.[126] A court may ignore previous judgments if no one complains of being vexed or harassed by the re-ventilation of the same claim (or issue).[127] In rule-based systems of the German-Continental civil-law system, *res judicata* has a narrow scope that is limited to when the same dispute between the same parties and regarding the same subject-matter or relief (*petitum*) and the same legal grounds (*causa petendi*) is brought before another forum.[128] Most civilian legal systems apply the test of identity of action in an earlier and final judgment (or arbitral award) in a strict fashion.[129] Under German civil procedure, which is situated on the strict end of the Civil Law continuum, parties are entitled to have any case tried *de novo* until the highest authority has spoken within the narrow confines of *res judicata*.[130] Since the Civil Law conception accepts that *res judicata* concerns the public interest, some Civil Law jurisdictions require courts to take previous judgments into account on their own initiative.[131]

A pragmatic Common Law conception of *res judicata* has been shown to be more cost-effective than the Continental counterpart.[132] This is

---

124 M Bos, *A Methodology of International Law* (TMC Asser 1984) 186; Y Sinai, 'Reconsidering *Res Judicata*: A Comparative Perspective' (2011) 21 Duke Journal of Comparative and International Law 353ff.

125 *Laker Airways Ltd v Sabena, Belgian World Airlines*, 731 F2d 909 (DC Circuit 1984) 926–27.

126 *Commings v Heard* (1869) LRQB 4 669, 673 ('When once a matter has been decided between parties, the parties ought to be concluded by the adjudication' *per* Lush J); Sinai (n 124) 385; ILA *Final Report on Lis Pendens and Arbitration* (n 107) §§ 2.13 2.5–2.7 2.12–2.13.

127 Sinai (n 124) 363.

128 Cremades and Madalena (n 110) 3.

129 McLachlan (n 95) 112–30.

130 Sinai (n 124) 384, 386.

131 Sinai (n 124) 385.

132 Sinai (n 124) 385.

because non-formalistic approaches to enforceability that are based on a looser or more encompassing definition of finality will aid the enforcement of the judgment or award. The interests of both the parties and the public are served by decisions that qualify to be recognised and enforced.[133]

The last-in-time rule applicable to sister state judgments in the US is not automatically applicable to foreign court judgments. Courts are reluctant to apply the rule to a last-in-time judgment that departs from *res judicata* principles by permitting a party to relitigate the merits of an earlier judgment.[134]

Except for the decision to withdraw a claim or discontinue the proceedings, plaintiffs are not free to determine the competence *ratione materiae* of the court to adjudicate a dispute; nor can they impose the procedure by which the court adjudicates.[135]

Religious law systems[136] frequently practice non-finality. This model is a non-starter in secular legal systems that depend on finality of trial.

6. OUT-OF-COURT SETTLEMENTS

When the stakes rise, the willingness to incur higher litigation costs increases and the interest in ADR wanes. The social costs of litigation can be minimised through out-of-court settlements based on choice of law rules. When they settle, parties still incur some litigation cost but it is usually much lower than the cost of going to trial.[137] Mainstream conflicts scholarship tends to avoid the area of 'jurisdictional trade',[138]

---

133 *Johnson v Gore Wood* [2002] 2 AC 1 at 31A–D *per* Lord Bingham, quoted with approval in *Lanes Group Plc v Galliford Try Infrastructure Ltd* [2011] EWHC 1679 (TCC) at § 45.

134 E.g. *Byblos Bank Europe, SA v Sekerbank Turn Anonym Syrket* 885 NE2d 191 (2008) 194.

135 Gazzini (n 24) 142.

136 Andrews (n 94) 228–35, 251; Sinai (n 124) 353ff.

137 N Murphy, 'Splitting Images: Shared-Value Settlements in Nazi-Era Art Restitution Claims' (2009) 3 Florida Entertainment Law Review 1 (*Social Science Research Network*, 25 February 2010) <http://ssrn.com/abstract=1559 373> accessed 25 February 2014.

138 MJ Whincop and M Keyes, *Policy and Pragmatism in the Conflict of Laws* (Ashgate 2001) 128.

but it remains an undeniable reality.[139] The cost of litigation can be avoided without a choice of law clause in circumstances that are conducive, such as where a bilateral treaty is in existence.[140]

7. INTERNATIONAL ARBITRATION: A SERIOUS OPTION?

As a method for settling disputes involving cultural objects, arbitration hardly counted during the 1990s.[141] It has since been considered more seriously. Recent empirical research done in the US[142] reveals that most respondents believe arbitration to be 'better, faster and cheaper than litigation'. Arbitration was favoured by factors such as the ability to choose arbitrators with particular qualifications and the relative confidentiality of arbitration provided appropriate redactions are made.

The mixed international arbitration involving Altmann and Austria[143] illustrates the involvement of one state party and one private party in an international arbitration. Maria Altmann filed a claim against the Austrian government in 1998 for the return of six Gustav Klimt pieces valued at

---

[139] C Roodt, 'State Courts or ADR in Nazi-era Art Disputes: A Choice "More Apparent Than Real?"' (2012) 3 Cardozo Journal of Conflict Resolution 421, 455.

[140] Cf agreement of 21 February 2006 between Italy and the Metropolitan Museum of Art, reached when the Medici Conspiracy became public. R Contel, G Soldan and A Chechi, 'Case Euphronios Krater and Other Archaeological Objects – Italy and Metropolitan Museum of Art' (Art-Law Centre, University of Geneva, June 2012) <https://plone.unige.ch/art-adr/cases-affaires/euphronios-krater-and-other-archaeological-objects-2013-italy-and-metropolitan-museum-of-art/case-note-2013-euphronios-krater-and-other-archaeological-objects/view> accessed 24 February 2014.

[141] K Siehr, 'International Art Trade and the Law' VI (243) *Recueil des Cours* (The Hague 1993) 9, 25.

[142] TJ Stipanovic and JR Lamare, 'Living with ADR: Evolving Perceptions and Use of Mediation, Arbitration and Conflict Management in Fortune 1,000 Corporations' (*SSRN working paper*, 19 February 2013) <http://ssrn.com/abstract=2221471> accessed 24 February 2014.

[143] *Majken Hofmann, Anna Lokrantz, Maria Müller, Andreas Müller Hofmann und Lena Müller Hofmann v Republic of Austria* (21 November 2005)(Arbitral award in German) <www.bslaw.com/altmann/Zuckerkandl/Klage/284724.doc> accessed 24 February 2014; *Maria V Altmann, Francis Gutmann, Trevor Mantle, George Bentley, and Dr. Nelly Auersperg v Republic of Austria* (15 January 2006)(Arbitral award in German) <http://bslaw.com/altmann/Klimt/award.pdf> accessed 25 February 2014.

approximately USD 150 million.[144] The Klimt paintings were located in Austria and the defending institution was domiciled in Austria, but the advertisements for exhibitions held in Austria were distributed in the US. Action was first instituted in Austria. The filing fee owed to the Austrian court was calculated as a percentage of the recoverable amount, and was out of Altmann's reach.[145] Altmann then sued in the US. Litigation in the US was more affordable and the action was not time barred. This action lasted seven years. When, at last, litigation in the US reached a dead-end and the parties agreed to arbitration in 2006, the matter was swiftly concluded by an Austrian arbitration panel in two separate arbitrations.[146] While this is an encouraging precedent involving arbitration in the context of restitution, arbitration followed only after Austria became unwilling to risk another failure in court. Had *ad hoc* arbitration been tried first, there may have been a strategic deviation into litigation in the US courts.

Arbitration would be suitable when parties have a large differential in power, but arbitration is readily utilised for cross-border sales or loan agreements involving works of art.[147]

---

144 *Altmann v Republic of Austria*, 142 F Supp 2d 1187 (C D Cal 1999) affirmed and remanded by 317 F3d 954 (9th Circuit 2002) rehearing denied en banc, 327 F3d 1246 (9th Circuit 2003) stay granted pending petition for writ of certiorari, 123 S Ct 2129 (2003), cert granted in part by 539 US 987 (2003) aff'd on other grounds by 541 US 677 (2004) on remand to *Altmann v Republic of Austria*, 335 F Supp 2d 1066 (C D Cal 2004).

145 It came to USD 1.6 m because the amount in controversy was approximately USD 135 m (see *Altmann v Austria*, 317 F3d 954 (9th Circuit 2002) § 11). Mrs Altmann sought a reduction. The adjustment came to USD 133 000 (*Altmann v Republic of Austria*, 142 F Supp 2d 1187 (C D Cal 1999) 1197) but to USD 350 000 (541 US 677 (2004) 688). Mrs Altmann would have been able to recover the filing fee and other legal fees if she prevailed. However, Austria lodged an appeal against the reduction.

146 *Maria V Altmann, Francis Gutmann, Trevor Mantle, George Bentley, and Dr. Nelly Auersperg v Republic of Austria* (15 January 2006)(Arbitral award in German) <http://bslaw.com/altmann/Klimt/award.pdf> accessed 25 February 2014. The restitution of the sixth painting, a portrait of Amalie Zuckerkandl, was rejected in a separate arbitration (*Majken Hofmann, Anna Lokrantz, Maria Müller, Andreas Müller Hofmann und Lena Müller Hofmann v Republic of Austria* (21 November 2005) (Arbitral award in German), <www.bslaw.com/altmann/Zuckerkandl/Klage/284724.doc.> accessed 24 February 2014).

147 N Palmer, 'Arbitration and the Applicable Law', in International Bureau of the Permanent Court of Arbitration (ed), *Resolution of Cultural Property Disputes* (The Hague 2004) 291.

7.1 Global Instruments and Systems for Arbitration

The drafters of the UNIDROIT Convention encouraged the use of arbitration.[148] By virtue of Article 8(2) a claim for restitution may be submitted to arbitration. Article 8 permits claims in respect of stolen, illegally excavated and unlawfully exported objects to be submitted to any other competent authority in the country where the cultural object is located, or any court or other competent authority in arbitration. This provision addresses the issue of restitution but it does not answer the question of ownership once a cultural object is returned.

The impact of Article 8 on dispute resolution choices has not been noticeable, but one must remain mindful that the mere option to arbitrate a dispute can facilitate settlement. The failure to settle allows a full merits hearing in respect of the legal contention and for the outcome to be published. While the lack of guidance on the design of arbitration procedures could partly be to blame,[149] the Venice Court of National and International Arbitration (VENCA) was established in 1998 to work in areas such as restitution, which the most important arbitral institutions do not cover. Unfortunately, the 1998 VENCA Rules of Arbitration are not suited to non-contractual disputes.[150] Non-profit companies such as ArtResolve are the only bodies with tailor-made procedural rules specifically designed for private dispute settlement for matters of title and provenance,[151] but even ArtResolve refers clients to the UNCITRAL arbitration rules.

Draft principle 8 of the 2004 ILA principles for co-operation in the mutual protection and transfer of cultural material concerns requests for the return of cultural material that remains unsolved after two years from the time of the request. UNESCO expanded its present role in the formation of mediation and arbitral panels when the Intergovernmental Committee for Promoting the Return of Cultural Property to Its Countries of Origin or Its Restitution in Case of Illicit Appropriation (ICPRCP) was

---

148 UNIDROIT Secretariat, Explanatory Report to the 1995 Unidroit Convention on Stolen or Illegally Exported Cultural Objects, 32; E Sidorsky, 'The 1995 Unidroit Convention on Stolen or Illegally Exported Cultural Objects: The Role of International Arbitration' (1996) 5 IJCP 19, 33–34.

149 A Chechi, *The Settlement of International Cultural Heritage Disputes: Towards a Lex Culturalis?* (unpublished PhD Thesis EUI 2011) 115.

150 Gazzini (n 24) 205.

151 'ArtResolve : The Art Claims Dispute Resolution Service', <http://www.artresolve.org/> accessed 24 February 2014.

established. Its mandate was strengthened in 2005.[152] Institutions that lack the resources to engage in protracted ADR are encouraged to approach UNESCO for monetary and professional assistance. After an unsuccessful initial request, other requests are likely to be barred for a certain period.

The 1958 New York Convention for the Recognition and Enforcement of Foreign Arbitral Awards (NYC)[153] facilitates the recognition and enforcement of arbitral awards made in the territory of another Contracting State, subject only to specific reservations[154] and limited exceptions.[155] National divergences cause inconsistent application of the NYC,[156] but arbitration remains attractive from an enforcement perspective, considering that there is no equal worldwide mechanism for the enforcement of judicial orders granted in civil and commercial claims. All foreign judgments require enforcement[157] beyond what the narrow sphere of application of the 2005 Choice of Court Agreements Convention would include after it enters into force.[158]

The same tribunal may conduct concurrent hearings of disputes involving the same parties if they consent.[159]

---

152 ICPRCP, *Draft Declaration of Principles Relating to Cultural Objects Displaced in Connection with the Second World War* (2009) and rules of procedure for mediation and conciliation to facilitate restitution of cultural property (ICPRCP, July 2010, CLT-2010/CONF.203/COM.16/7); Chechi (n 149) 111–12.

153 Concluded 10 June 1958; 9 USCA §§ 201–8. Compare Art 8 of the UNCITRAL Model Law on International Commercial Arbitration, first adopted on 21 June 1985 (UN Doc. A/40/17, Annex I), and amended in 2006 by UNCITRAL's report on the work of its 39th session (UN Doc. A/61/17 Annex I).

154 Any awards made in a foreign state come within the purview of Article I(3). Switzerland recognises and enforces all arbitral awards issued by arbitral tribunals seated outside Switzerland. States may limit their recognition and enforcement to awards issued in other Contracting States or in non-Contracting States that grant reciprocal treatment application of the Convention.

155 Art V of the NYC.

156 Gazzini (n 24) 81.

157 *Bumper Development Corporation v Commissioner of Police for the Metropolis* [1991] 1 WLR 1362; [1991] 4 All ER 638 (CA); RK Paterson, 'The "Curse of the London Nataraja"' (1996) 5 *IJCP* 330. A large judgment for costs was successfully enforced in favour of the plaintiffs.

158 <http://www.hcch.net/> accessed 24 February 2014.

159 E.g. s 35(1)(b) of the Arbitration Act (England and Wales) of 1996.

Some bodies offer both administered and non-administered arbitration, e.g. the ICC and the UNCITRAL Model Law and Rules. Judicial intervention is unlikely when institutional rules and processes apply, because these rules will have passed judicial scrutiny.[160] Administered arbitration may save cost and time, but the adequacy of these institutional rules must be judged separately and with reference to each individual case in complex cases. Commercial arbitrations that rely on UNCITRAL Arbitration Rules may involve the Permanent Court of Arbitration (PCA), since its role is not limited to inter-state disputes and these arbitrations are relatively independent from a national legal system. The role of the PCA has been steadily expanding in respect of mixed arbitrations ever since 1976. Among several sets of rules that have been developed for use in the PCA system are the 1993 Optional Rules for Arbitrating Disputes between Two Parties of Which One Is a State,[161] which contain a fall-back for the appointment of the arbitrators.[162] The PCA Arbitration Rules of 2012[163] are designed for disputes involving at least one state, state-controlled entity, or international organisation. The new Rules consolidate four sets of PCA procedural rules from the 1990s.[164] They also take account of the 1976 UNCITRAL Arbitration Rules, the 2010 revisions to the UNCITRAL Arbitration Rules, and the PCA's experience with its own procedural rules. Model clauses that parties may consider inserting in treaties, contracts, or arbitration agreements, whether for existing or future disputes, appear in the annex to the new Rules. It would be important, for instance, to ensure that protective orders can be obtained from local courts. The parties may have failed to elect a clause in respect of protective orders, and the arbitrators are not competent to order attachment of the object in this instance.[165]

---

[160] E Varner, 'Arbitrating Cultural Property Disputes' (2012) 14 Cardozo Journal of Conflict Resolution 477, 500.

[161] Effective 6 July 1993.

[162] J van Haersolte-van Hof, 'The Revitalization of the Permanent Court of Arbitration' [2007] NILR 395 400–401.

[163] Effective as of 17 December 2012. See <http://www.pca-cpa.org/showfile.asp?fil_id=2054> accessed 24 February 2014; PCA Arbitration Rules 2012 (Permanent Court of Arbitration, 17 December 2012) <http://www.pca-cpa.org/showfile.asp?fil_id=2054> accessed 24 February 2014.

[164] The Optional Rules for Arbitrating Disputes between Two States (1992), the Optional Rules for Arbitrating Disputes between Two Parties of Which Only One Is a State (1993), the Optional Rules for Arbitration between International Organizations and States (1996), and the Optional Rules for Arbitration between International Organizations and Private Parties (1996).

[165] Sidorsky (n 148) 45.

7.2 Secondary EU Law

Council Directive 93/7/EEC of 15 March 1993[166] permits disputes between the requesting Member State and the possessor or holder to be resolved in arbitration.[167] Article 5 of Directive 2014/60/EU[168] stipulates that the central authorities of the Member States must act as intermediary between the possessor and/or holder and the requesting Member State with regard to return. To that end, the competent authorities of the requested Member State may facilitate the implementation of an arbitration procedure, in accordance with the national legislation of the requested Member State and provided that the requesting Member State and the possessor or holder consent formally. The procedure is without prejudice to any litigation. Arbitration proceedings in terms of secondary EU law have not been used to date.

7.3 Non-legal Factors in Arbitration: A Promised Advantage of Arbitrating Restitution and Ownership Claims

The question arises whether commercial arbitration systems can lead in non-contractual disputes between two private parties or privately owned museums, until UNESCO and other suitable bodies become fully active in this regard.[169] The arbitration model is designed to avoid potential national court bias and ensure effectiveness and speed. The broad scope of party autonomy promises to accommodate the variable and differentiated needs and goals of the parties. It allows them to determine what rules or guidelines are to be used, and to designate an institution or identify rules that are suited to their claim.[170]

Depending on the agreement of the parties, an arbitrator may be duty-bound to take account of non-legal factors or ethical considerations

---

[166] Art 4(6).

[167] Art 4(6).

[168] Directive 2014/60/EU of the European Parliament and of the Council of 15 May 2014 on the Return of Cultural Objects Unlawfully Removed from the Territory of a Member State and amending Regulation (EU) No 1024/2012 (Recast) OJ EU L159/1, 28.5.2014.

[169] T Orford, '"Sending It Back" – the Role of Law and the Cultural Patrimony Debate' <http://www.artright.co.za/media/cms_page_media/37/Sending%20Art%20Back%20by%20Toby%20Orford.pdf> accessed 3 November 2012.

[170] Palmer (n 147) 301.

that may not necessarily engage a court.[171] The difference between deciding as *amiable compositeur* or *ex aequo*[172] is that an *amiable compositeur* decides the dispute according to law and legal principle, but may modify the effect of certain non-mandatory legal provisions. This route represents the option to mitigate the strict effect of legal rules to avoid inequitable results and to apply the law in a flexible manner.[173] The support of the law is never wholly irrelevant. The means of resolution remains dependent on the applicable legal system or the relevant institutional rules when gaps need to be filled. If the arbitrator acts as *amiable compositeur*, effect may be given to an arbitral agreement that is invalid technically; a particular national law may be applied but some provisions of that law can be avoided; the general principles of law may be applied alongside special rules; or unique interpretations can be provided for the case at hand. There is no superior authority that could sanction departures from strict legal provisions and case law.[174]

There is a risk that a party with something to gain from a stricter application of the law may be willing to resort to a national court where the agreement between the parties does not exclude the right to strict application.

Dispute settlement *ex aequo et bono* is a decisive step in the direction of a delocalised arbitration. The decision is taken in accordance with moral principles. The parties indicate their intention not to be bound by any principle of national law. Disregard for mandatory provisions of law is permitted but international public policy has to be respected at all times. Arbitral tribunals ought to be able to respond to requests from indigenous groups to apply customary law if the parties have empowered them to decide *ex aequo et bono*. However, little is known about arbitrating indigenous cultural property claims.[175] Settlement opportunities arise more frequently in arbitration. Stark win-lose results that are

---

[171] E.g. when a possessor benefits from the proceeds of a crime against humanity on the basis of a point of law. See RK Paterson, 'Resolving Material Culture Disputes: Human Rights, Property Rights and Crimes against Humanity' [2006] *Willamette International Law and Dispute Resolution* 155, 159.

[172] For more, see C Bühring-Uhle, L Kirchhoff and G Scherer, *Arbitration and Mediation in International Business* (2nd revised edn, Kluwer Law International 2006) 40.

[173] Gazzini (n 24) 109.

[174] Gazzini (n 24) 106, 123.

[175] For more, see K Kuprecht and K Siehr, 'International Trade in Moveable Tangible Cultural Heritage of Indigenous Peoples: A European Perspective' in CB Graber, K Kuprecht and JC Lai (eds), *International Trade in Indigenous Cultural Heritage* (Edward Elgar 2012) 246, 267.

unavoidable in litigated claims could be avoided in arbitration,[176] as the title and possessory interests of two innocent parties may be balanced in ways that national courts do not easily conceive of. There are remedies besides specific performance, damages or injunctions. Collections can be divided. Title can be traded for a loan of the object in question or for loans of other works in the title holder's collection. Ownership can be awarded to the claimant on the condition that he or she pays the opposing party the difference in the price of a painting when its whereabouts should have been located, and the present value. Other conditions could include capacity-building exchanges or extending formal recognition of the importance of the object to cultural identity. It is possible to uncouple title and possession (or of ownership and rights of enjoyment and use). Cash settlement, donations or financial compensation could be feasible. All these remedies are available prior to arbitration as well.

Innovative future solutions may include dual nationality and collective ownership.[177]

7.4 Complexities of Arbitrating Art and Heritage Claims

7.4.1 Expertise can give rise to contention

The criterion of significant cultural importance is subjective.[178] Arbitration does not necessarily solve the issue of expertise, or make 'fairness' any more readily achievable. Arbitrator expertise could well mean that the arbitrator is partial to the object or the cultural interests in the object, and apt to neglect serving the interests of the parties.[179] Unfortunately, cultural independence on the part of any adjudicator, or a willingness to embrace 'cultural disarmament',[180] cannot be guaranteed.

7.4.2 Non-contractual nature of dispute

There is no material or formal impediment to arbitrating restitution cases involving moveable cultural objects.[181] It is widely believed that arbitration offers the most effective and equitable means of settling art and

---

[176] Varner (n 160) 523.

[177] M Cornu and M Renold, 'New Developments in the Restitution of Cultural Property: Alternative Means of Dispute Resolution' (2010) 17 IJCP 1, 18.

[178] In terms of Art 8(1) of the UNIDROIT Convention, the court where the object is located must establish this.

[179] Gazzini (n 24) 118–19.

[180] See introduction to Chapter 1.

[181] Gazzini (n 24) 132.

cultural heritage disputes.[182] This belief needs to be examined critically, however. Arbitration is a 'summary procedural mechanism devised primarily, albeit not exclusively, for contractual disputes …'.[183] Its suitability in bipolar contractual disputes is unquestioned,[184] but the adequacy of voluntary arbitration in the event of claims for the restitution of art and cultural objects deserves examination.

Whereas tort and unjust enrichment claims are amenable to arbitration under a submission agreement,[185] arbitration is unsuitable for resolving cases involving simple theft.[186] National courts assume responsibility for dispensing justice in disputes involving criminal offences and penalties, and these are not open to arbitration. The conciliatory aims of arbitration do not square with the public policy core impacted by crime.[187] In the event of deprivation by theft, conversion or looting, the extent of the relationship is bound to be confined to a restitution claim. When the dispute is entirely non-contractual or a pre-existing contractual relationship is non-existent, parties are likely to be less than keen to consent to arbitration.

The effects of creating a false impression of the title in valuable stolen works of art reverberated in courts in England and in the US, when Mardirosian, a retired Massachusetts lawyer, was convicted and disbarred for the theft of several Impressionist paintings in the Bakwin collection. The thief retained Mardirosian when he was charged with a gun-related crime, but he was killed after he had appointed the lawyer. Mardirosian

---

182 EI Gegas, 'International Arbitration and Resolution of Cultural Property Disputes' (1997) 13 Ohio State Journal on Dispute Resolution 129, 151ff; BW Daly, 'The Potential for Arbitration of Cultural Property Disputes; Recent Developments at the Permanent Court of Arbitration' [2005] *Law and Practice of International Courts and Tribunals* 261; Sidorsky (n 148) 19; Palmer (n 147) 291; N Palmer, 'Litigation: The Best Remedy?' in International Bureau of the Permanent Court of Arbitration (Hrsg.) (ed), *Resolution of Cultural Property Disputes* (The Hague 2004) 265; AL Bandle and S Theurich, 'Alternative Dispute Resolution and Art-Law – a New Research Project of the Geneva Art-Law Centre' (2011) 6 Journal of International Commercial Law and Technology 28; Varner (n 160) 480–85.

183 Gazzini (n 24) xxviii.

184 Gazzini (n 24) 159.

185 Gazzini (n 24) 129.

186 *Bakwin Eire International Trading Co Inc v Sotheby's*, 22 November 2005 (unreported); *US v Mardirosian*, 602 F3d 1 (2010) and *In re: Robert M Mardirosian*, No BD-2007-012.

187 Gazzini (n 24) 131.

was in possession of the paintings after his client's death, and succeeded in convincing his agent that he also had clear title.

The owner instituted recovery proceedings in England.[188] In order to allow the shipment of the paintings to the UK to proceed, the Art Loss Register maintained towards Sotheby's that the thief had clear title.

Arbitration in Switzerland was on the cards, but an English ruling questioned the competence of an arbitration tribunal to determine its own jurisdiction where the possessor exerted undue pressure on the owner.[189] An 'agreement' had been concluded between Mardirosian and the owner of the paintings involving the return of the stolen works. This 'agreement' purported to change the stolen status of six of the paintings by signing them over to Mardirosian, in exchange for the return of the most valuable piece. As such, it could not be said that the agreement had been freely concluded by both parties.[190] In truth, arbitration was unsuitable because the owner's free consent to arbitrate was absent, and arbitrability of a matter involving stolen property would have posed an insurmountable problem.

Mardirosian later argued that he subjectively believed he had clear title of six paintings further to his agreement with Bakwin that the seventh painting would be returned, and that he was unaware that the paintings in his possession qualified, in terms of the National Stolen Property Act, as having been stolen.[191] Criminal proceedings in the US resulted in a conviction on counts of possession, concealment, transportation and attempted sale of paintings allegedly stolen by a client.[192] Civil proceedings resulted in disbarment.[193] Proceedings to recover the costs of the return from him, are still ongoing.

The competence of a national court or arbitral tribunal may be questioned in legal proceedings; courts will not always defer to the arbitral tribunal to decide its own competence to decide. *Erie International Trading Company Inc v Sotheby's* illustrates the resolve of the English courts to determine the validity of an arbitration agreement for

---

188 *Bakwin Eire International Trading Co Inc v Sotheby's*, 22 November 2005 (unreported).

189 *Bakwin Eire International Trading Co Inc v Sotheby's*, 22 November 2005 (unreported); [2005] 6 ArbLR 83.

190 *Bakwin and Erie International Trading Co Inc v Sotheby's*, 22 November 2005 (unreported); *US v Mardirosian*, 602 F3d 1 (2010) and *In re: Robert M Mardirosian*, No BD-2007-012.

191 NSPA, 18 US Code 2315; *US v Mardirosian*, 602 F3d 1 (2010) 8.

192 *US v Mardirosian*, 602 F3d 1 (2010).

193 *In re: Robert M Mardirosian*, No BD-2007-012.

themselves, and to retain jurisdiction to grant a stay under s 10 of the Arbitration Act 1996 or refuse it under s 9(4).[194]

Even where a prior contractual relationship existed, the parties would be unlikely to be interested to preserve it.[195] In addition, an arbitration agreement is readily regarded as a contractual waiver of the jurisdiction of courts in France, which is the most radical jurisdiction when it comes to the scope of the powers enjoyed by the arbitral tribunal.[196]

7.4.3 State arbitrations and consensual jurisdiction

Consent is a foundational requirement of arbitration. State consent is required for an arbitration agreement concluded between states. Consensual jurisdiction in inter-state disputes was the basis on which the PCA has been functioning since 1932.

7.4.4 Default arbitration model

Notwithstanding provocative ideas in regard to a default international commercial arbitration model that treats arbitration as the natural mode for solving international commercial disputes,[197] states have not progressed far in this direction. Mandatory arbitration started to develop in the US in the 1970s. At first it denoted instances where arbitration was identified as the only means for dispute resolution in standard form contracts entered into by big corporations.[198] These clauses were pre-prepared. They promoted the efficiency of commerce, but were not negotiated on an equal footing.

If arbitration is imposed by law instead of by the parties' own choice, courts would be able to compel it directly. Replevin actions do not feature among the civil actions that are subject to mandatory non-binding arbitration.[199]

---

[194] *Erie International Trading Co Inc v Sotheby's*, 22 November 2005 unreported (QBD); (2005) 6 ArbLR 83.

[195] Gazzini (n 24) 124.

[196] The NYC offers no autonomous definition of arbitrability. Agreements to arbitrate disputes that are non-arbitrable under domestic law need not be honoured (Art II) nor awards rendered pursuant to them enforced (Art V).

[197] G Cuniberti, 'Beyond Contract – the Case for Default Arbitration in International Commercial Disputes' (2008) 32 Fordham Int'l LJ 417.

[198] JR Sternlight, 'Creeping Mandatory Arbitration: Is It Just?' [2004/2005] 57 Stan LR 1631, 1637.

[199] E.g. Illinois Supreme Court Rule 86; Rules governing the Courts in the State of New Jersey 4:21A.

7.4.5 Choice of procedural law

The explanatory note accompanying the ILA Draft Principles for Cooperation in the Mutual Protection and Transfer of Cultural Material of 2004[200] states that a pre-existing set of rules or rules and procedures of the parties' own invention may be used.

In the absence of an agreement by the parties on the procedural law of the arbitration, procedural complications may arise and cause delays.[201] There are various options, which include the law of the seat of the arbitral tribunal;[202] the law of the state where the arbitration takes place;[203] the law designated or devised by the arbitral tribunal;[204] the procedural law of the *lex causae*;[205] or in a mixed arbitration, international law.[206]

7.4.6 Breach of waiver of right to a court hearing

A voluntary waiver or restriction on the right of access to court does not offend the fair trial provision, provided the arbitration agreement is lawful and unequivocal.[207] By choosing voluntary arbitration in an unequivocal manner and without contravening any public interest, the parties waive their right to a public hearing as guaranteed by Article 6(1)

---

[200] International Law Association, Cultural Heritage Law Committee Report, Berlin Conference 2004, 3 <http://www.ila-hq.org/> accessed 25 February 2014.

[201] Gazzini (n 24) 140–42 (example unlikely given that theft or conversion are non-arbitrable).

[202] *BP Exploration Co (Libya) Ltd v Government of the Libyan Arab Republic*, 10 October 1973 and 1 August 1974, 53 ILR (1979) 297.

[203] S 1042(3) of the German Arbitration Act of 1998, Book 10 of the *Zivilprozessordnung* (German Civil Code of Procedure (ZPO)).

[204] E.g. before 1 July 2006, s 587(1) of the Austria Arbitration Act of 1983 applied in the absence of an agreement by the parties that the rules of the arbitral institution apply. Thereafter, by virtue of s 594(1) of the ZPO, of which the *Schiedsrechts- Änderungsgesetz* 2006 forms part, non-mandatory law applies, and in the absence of non-mandatory law, the arbitrators are free to conduct the proceedings at their discretion. T Lörcher, G Pendell and J Wilson (eds), *CMS Guide to Arbitration* Vol 1 (4ed CMS Legal Services EEIG 2012), sub 'Austria' (D Karollus-Bruner) § 6.2.1 <http://eguides.cmslegal.com/arbitration> accessed 24 February 2014. Cf also s 33(1) of the Arbitration Act (England and Wales) of 1996.

[205] ICC Interim Award, Case no 4695 of 1984, XI YbCA (1986) 149, 151ff.

[206] *Texaco Overseas Petroleum Co (TOPCO) & California Asiatic Oil Co (Calasiatic) v Government of Libyan Arab Republic*, Preliminary Award 27 November 1975 and Award on the Merits 17 January 1977, 17 ILM (1978) 1, 8.

[207] *Suda v Czech Republic* (Application no 1643/06), 28 October 2010 (choice of tribunal must be clear and unambiguous).

of the 1950 European Convention for the Protection of Human Rights[208] and Article 14(1) of the 1966 International Covenant on Civil and Political Rights.[209] The waiver should be reviewed carefully to ensure the claimant is not subject to any constraint when entering into the agreement to arbitrate.[210] The aim pursued must be legitimate, e.g. the pursuit of extra-judicial settlement by means of arbitration, and the means employed must be proportionate.[211] So, arbitration constitutes an acceptable limitation on the right of access to justice even if national courts cannot guarantee the enjoyment of all the Article 6 protections.[212] However, there are limits on the power of courts to direct parties against their will to use arbitration.

Depending on the agreement to arbitrate, court proceedings can be stayed permanently and parties may waive their right to approach a court to decide.[213] However, the right to a court hearing is not always expressly excluded in the arbitration agreement or in the domestic arbitration legislation of the seat court. A party who initially agreed to an arbitration clause may decide to litigate. What is the legal effect of proceeding in court after an arbitral tribunal is already considering the case? Is the court competent to decide or has its competence been ousted? This issue could become more complicated, e.g. can a unilateral split jurisdiction clause that gives one party the right to choose between a state court and an arbitral tribunal be enforceable or does it infringe the right of access to court?[214]

By virtue of the doctrine of *compétence-compétence*, the arbitral tribunal is competent to decide on its own jurisdiction, including any objections with respect to the existence or validity of the arbitration

---

208 Convention for the Protection of Human Rights and Fundamental Freedoms (European Convention on Human Rights) signed on 4 November 1950; entry into force 3 September 1953.

209 *Suovaniemi and Others v Finland* (Application no 31737/96), 23 February 1999 (waiving the right to an independent and impartial tribunal is permissible, provided the waiver is voluntary and it is done in the light of the behaviour of the party after the fact). Gazzini (n 24) 73.

210 *DeWeer v Belgium* (1980) 2 EHRR 439 § 49.

211 Gazzini (n 24) 74.

212 *Nordstrom-Janzon and Nordstrom Lehtinen v The Netherlands* (Application no 28101/95), 27 November 1996.

213 Gazzini (n 24) 73.

214 *X v Banque Privée Edmond de Rothschild* Arrêt no 983 du 26 Septembre 2012 (11-26.022), Cour de Cassation, Première Chambre Civile.

agreement[215] and the standard (*prima facie* or otherwise) to be used for that purpose. There are national variations in application. The doctrine changes colour depending on the context. In the Continental tradition, the doctrine is a *prior temporis* mechanism (first filed) that grants arbitrators the first opportunity to examine their own jurisdiction and make a ruling, be it interim or final, before courts are permitted to review jurisdiction.[216] The negative effect of *compétence-compétence* prioritises the ruling of the arbitrators on their competence to decide: they are the first judges of their own jurisdiction, and court control is postponed to the enforcement or set aside stage.[217] In addition, an arbitration agreement is readily regarded as a contractual waiver of the jurisdiction of courts in the most radical, in terms of the scope of the powers enjoyed by the arbitral tribunal, namely France.[218] The court must declare itself incompetent to decide, unless the arbitration agreement is manifestly null or manifestly inapplicable. If there is both a choice of court and an arbitration agreement in the agreement, the arbitral tribunal decides which one prevails.[219]

An arbitration agreement does not exclude the jurisdiction of the court altogether in the English model, but justifies a stay of the court proceedings until the arbitral award is issued. Once the award is issued, the court may revisit all the work done by the arbitral tribunal. A freely chosen and exclusive arbitration agreement constitutes a waiver of the

---

215 Cf e.g. UNCITRAL Rule 23; LCIA Arbitration Rule 23.1; ICC Rules Art 6(3) and (4).

216 CH Petrus, 'Spanish Perspectives on the Doctrines of Kompetenz-Kompetenz and Separability: A Comparative Analysis of Spain's 1988 Arbitration Act' (2000) 11 American Review of International Arbitration 396, 402–3.

217 E Gaillard and Y Banifatemi, 'Negative Effect of Competence-Competence: The Rule of Priority in Favour of the Arbitrators' in E Gaillard and D di Pietro (eds), *Enforcement of Arbitration Agreements and International Arbitral Awards: The New York Convention in Practice* (Cameron 2008) 257, 260.

218 Art 1458 French New Code of Civil Procedure. TE Carbonneau, 'Judicial Approbation in Building the Civilization of Arbitration' (2009) 113 Penn State Law Review 1343, 1355; S Brekoulakis, 'The Negative Effect of Compétence-Compétence: The Verdict Has to Be Negative' (2009) 2 Austrian Arbitration Review 237; P Gillies and A Dahdal, 'Waiver of a Right to Arbitrate by Resort to Litigation, in the Context of International Commercial Arbitration' (2007) 2 Journal of International Commercial Law and Technology 221.

219 *La Chartreuse v Cavagna*, Cour de Cassation, 18 December 2003 (2004) ASA Bull 796.

right of access to court, but the waiver is not absolute.[220] An application to a foreign court for a declaration that an arbitration agreement does not exist, constitutes a repudiation of the arbitration agreement.[221]

The minimalist tradition of *compétence-compétence* leaves courts free to assume jurisdiction concurrently where the jurisdiction of the arbitral tribunal is challenged on the basis that an arbitration agreement is void, or when it is claimed that the wider agreement of which the arbitration agreement forms part, is null and void. In terms of the Arbitration (Scotland) Act, recourse to court proceedings cannot be precluded in an arbitration agreement.[222] Prior to this modernisation of Scots arbitration law, the jurisdiction of the court has never been considered as 'ousted' by an arbitration agreement in Scotland.

The NYC does not specify the law governing the validity of arbitration agreements. The effect of waiver cannot be assumed to be uniform. While public justice (domestic court procedure) focuses on correctness, private justice is more concerned with finality and efficiency in the settlement of disputes.[223] A wide construction of implied waiver appears to be justified when a state that concluded an arbitration agreement is signatory to the NYC. In a mixed arbitration, a state's consent to arbitration constitutes a waiver of any right of immunity from jurisdiction in respect of the proceedings.[224] A waiver of immunity from execution of an arbitral award must be express.[225] Examples can be found where state consent to arbitration included both a waiver of immunity against jurisdiction and against execution.[226]

---

[220] *Fiona Trust v Privalov* [2007] 1 Lloyd's Rep 391 (CA), conf'd in *Premium Nafta Products Ltd v Fili Shipping* [2007] UKHL 40.

[221] *Midgulf International Ltd v Groupe Chimiche Tunisien* [2010] EWCA Civ 66.

[222] S 10 (2) Arbitration (Scotland) Act of 2010.

[223] T Schultz, 'Human Rights: A Speed Bump for Arbitral Procedures? An Exploration of Safeguards in the Acceleration of Justice' [2006] IALR 1, 16.

[224] Art 1(2) of the PCA Arbitration Rules 2012.

[225] Art 9 of the Resolution adopted by the Institute of International Law, 'Arbitration between States, State Enterprises, or State Entities, and Foreign Enterprises', September 1989. It is known as the 1989 Santiago de Compostela Resolution. Its scope is restricted to immunity from jurisdiction.

[226] For decisions on arbitration clauses that refer to ICC rules, see Gazzini (n 24) 90–91. Also *Seetransport Wiking Trader Schifffahrtsgesellschaft GmbH and Co Kommanditgesellschaft v Navimpex Centrala Navala and Uzinexport-import*, 989 F2d 572 (2nd Circuit 1993), 1994 XIX YbCA 812, 815.

7.4.7 Competence to issue anti-suit injunctions

An anti-suit injunction is an order to enjoin the commencement or continuation of legal proceedings brought in a foreign jurisdiction, i.e. compelling a party not to commence or continue such proceedings.[227] This *in personam* remedy has been used in common law legal systems as a mechanism by which to enforce the choice of forum. The CJEU ruled in the notorious *West Tankers* case[228] that an anti-suit injunction cannot be permitted to restrict the obligation of a national court competent under the Judgments Regulation to assert the jurisdiction it has under that instrument; nor can it be permitted to strip a court of the power to rule on its own jurisdiction under the Regulation and on the applicability of the Judgments Regulation to the dispute brought before it. The discretion which common law legal systems afford the judiciary in the EJA to order an anti-suit injunction ultimately interferes with the power of the foreign court to determine its own jurisdiction. The furore that followed the ruling was in part caused by the narrow definition the ECJ gave to the exclusion of arbitration in the Judgments Regulation. The Recast Regulation has now firmed up the exclusion of arbitration. The clarification of the scope of the exclusion of arbitration from the purview of this instrument was timely and the restoration of the precedence of Article II(3) of the NYC over the Judgments Regulation was highly necessary.[229]

While injunctive relief in relation to foreign proceedings within the Brussels/Lugano space is impermissible under the Regulation and Convention, it survives in respect of proceedings in third state courts, outside the Brussels Regulation/Lugano regime. The Supreme Court of the United Kingdom has confirmed the power of English courts, which is long-standing and well recognised, to restrain foreign proceedings brought in violation of an arbitration agreement.[230] This power exists even where no arbitration is afoot or in contemplation. It is conferred in the Arbitration Act 1996, and has not been removed from the courts.

Anti-suit injunctions are capable of producing serious conflicts between courts, but US courts permit their use in exceptional circumstances which outweigh the threat to judicial restraint and comity posed

---

227 First issued by the Courts of Chancery in England in *Love v Baker* (1665) 1 Ch Cas 67; statutory backing was eventually afforded in England.

228 Case C-185/07 *Allianz SpA and Generali Assicurazioni Generali SpA, formerly Riunione Adriatica di Sicurtà SpA v West Tankers Inc, The Front Comor* [2009] ECR I-663 (Grand Chamber).

229 Recital 12.

230 *Ust-Kamenogorsk Hydropower Plant JSC (Appellant) v AES Ust-Kamenogorsk Hydropower Plant LLP (Respondent)* [2013] UKSC 35.

by anti-suit injunctions.[231] The fairness of the trial may demand their use; the arbitration agreement may have been forged; or a recalcitrant party may fail to respect a review of the question of arbitrability of a particular matter and persist with the arbitration.[232] Views about whether anti-suit injunctions issued by arbitral tribunals create problems of compatibility with EU law and with the Judgments Regulation and the Recast Regulation, can be expected to continue to diverge. EU procedural law places a high premium on mutual trust. Ultimately, however, the pursuit of uniformity in the EU can result in an unpalatable unevenness of mechanisms in the international dimension of private international law.[233]

7.4.8 *Res judicata* and enforcement of the arbitral award

The underpinnings and precise scope of the doctrine of *res judicata* in arbitration are seldom subject to elaborate theoretical scrutiny. The approach tends to be pragmatic.[234] State law and practice in respect of the enforcement of arbitral awards differ widely, and *res judicata* adds another variable to the equation.

It is possible to differentiate between positive enforcement of arbitral awards and indirect enforcement. An arbitral award may be annulled by the court of the place where the award had been made, but be enforced elsewhere.[235] Positive enforcement may be called for if an arbitral tribunal has set aside the ownership claim of a state, but the state is temporarily in possession of the item in question. Positive enforcement may also be required in the wake of restitution proceedings against a state with respect to items in its public collection.[236] Arbitration laws frequently grant *res judicata* authority to arbitral awards handed down in their seat, thus barring the parties from obtaining another decision in the same dispute.

Recognition of an arbitral award under the NYC is in no way precluded by institutional arbitration or a denationalised procedure in international commercial arbitration. The party who enforces the arbitral

---

231 *TSMC N Am v Semiconductor Mfg Inl Corp*, 161 Cal App 4th 581 (Cal App 1st Dist 2008).

232 McLachlan (n 95) 251.

233 P Shine, 'The Treatment of Non-EU Nationals before Domestic Courts of Member States' (2010) 9 Chinese Journal of International Law 451, 471.

234 Radicati di Brozolo (n 123).

235 *Ministry of Defence of the Republic of Egypt v Chromalloy Aeroservices Inc.*, Cairo Court of Appeal, 5 December 1995, Rev Arb (1998) 723; but see *Chromalloy Aeroservices Inc v ARE* 939 F Supp 907 (DDC 1996).

236 Gazzini (n 24) 95.

award first under the NYC has the advantage of *res judicata*, and the party who succeeds to get the award annulled or set aside first will prevail if the vacatur realises international private rights. These are the negative implications of the award, which can be tantamount to indirect enforcement.[237]

Some jurisdictions resort to hard law rather than to guidelines and discretion to avoid contradictory decisions in their legal order. Legislative provisions to the effect that judicial precedent binds the arbitral tribunal are found in Switzerland and Mexico. In these states, *res judicata* embodies procedural *ordre public*.

A vacatur that does not realise international private rights can mean that the enforcing court will react to the perceived injustice. When it would be fundamentally unfair to defer to the judgment of a foreign court that sets aside an arbitral award handed down in its territory, US courts may decide to recognise that award. Such an unusual and extreme circumstance arose, for instance, when a federal district court in the Southern District of New York confirmed an ICC award in favour of Commisa, a Mexican subsidiary of a US firm, against Mexican state oil company Pemex. Pemex challenged the jurisdiction of the arbitral panel on the basis that, inter alia, the Mexican court's decision deprived it of jurisdiction. The arbitrators ruled that they had jurisdiction and proceeded to hear the merits. Commisa won the arbitration and sought confirmation of the award granted in Mexico City under the Panama Convention (the Inter-American Convention on International Commercial Arbitration), whereas Pemex applied for nullification in Mexico. When Pemex rescinded the contract (it had a right to administrative rescission), Commisa challenged the constitutionality of the administrative rescission in litigation. While this move did not affect the merits of the case, it carried a certain risk. Instituting action in a court could be interpreted as opting out of the arbitral system; the court procedure was an annulment procedure after all. Commisa's challenge failed, yet the court that was requested to recognise and execute the arbitral award held that the prior administrative and constitutional judgment had a *res judicata* effect that barred the arbitral award from being executed. This judgment was taken after examining the non-performance of the contract and the administrative rescission by Pemex had been denied. Also, the limitation period applying to administrative rescission disputes in Mexican law was amended in 2007 from ten years to 45 days. In 2009 such disputes were

---

[237] C Roodt, 'Reflections on Finality in Arbitration' (2012) 2 De Jure 485, 505; Gazzini (n 24) 94.

declared non-arbitrable.[238] The court decided that administrative rescission was inarbitrable and the arbitral award was set aside at the arbitral seat.[239] By the time the Mexican court vacated the award, the right of the US firm to pursue its claim in litigation had been extinguished by a statute of limitations which would bind the court that would hear the case.

In this instance, the US District Court declined to defer to the nullifying judgment given by the Mexican court. The retroactive application of a law 'that was not in existence at the time the parties' contract was formed' to invalidate an award combined with denying the winning party the right to pursue its claim in any other forum. This combination violated the basic notions of justice in the US. To prevent this from happening, the US District Court reconfirmed the award and granted enforcement.

If a claimant commences court proceedings with respect to the legality of the termination of a contract in the face of an arbitration clause while the arbitration is under way, there is the risk that the arbitration can be jeopardised. The right to arbitration may be considered as having been waived if the other party responds at court. The arbitration would not proceed if the right has been waived, regardless of whether the administrative rescission is arbitrable or not.

State parties possess strong litigating power, which they may use in court battles about venue. They may wear their opponent down with arguments involving the competence of the arbitral tribunal or conditions precedent. In jurisdictions where *res judicata* is not a procedural *ordre public* principle, it may help the parties to 'fortify' the *res judicata* effect of an award by excluding appeal and review of the award on the merits by a national court, and by including issue estoppel in the determination of finality.[240] In Common Law jurisdictions, issue estoppel is a particular application of the general rule of public policy that there should be finality in litigation. Issue estoppel precludes a party from relitigating an issue previously decided in other proceedings, even if the cause of action is not identical. It is justified where a fact or law is alleged or denied when its existence was a matter necessarily decided by the prior

---

[238] L Shore, 'US District Court Confirms Arbitral Award against Pemex That was Nullified at Its Seat' in Herbert Smith Freehills, Arbitration Notes (18 September 2013) 1.

[239] *Corporación Mexicana de Mantenimiento Integral v Pemex-Exploración y Producción*, No 10 Civ 206 (AKH), 2013 WL 4517225 (SDNY 27 August 2013).

[240] *Sovarex SA v Romero* [2011] EWHC 1661 (Comm).

judgment, decree or order.[241] How a court defines an 'issue' will inform how broadly or narrowly issue preclusion is to be applied in the subsequent action. In a small minority of common law jurisdictions, courts use the doctrine to prevent a party from raising issues in subsequent proceedings that could have been raised in earlier proceedings, but were not.[242] Suspending the adjudication of a related dispute has no ultimate *res judicata* effect.

While forced consolidation is a feature of some legal systems,[243] an arbitral tribunal will not usually impose a consolidation of causes or joinder of third parties when a party objects thereto. Arguably, there is utility in treating related claims holistically, so that consolidation deserves to be regulated directly in supranational arbitration rules.[244] The utility of such treatment must be balanced against the equality and freedom of the parties to nominate the arbitrators.[245] Parties are not likely to agree on a basic strategy by which parallel proceedings, consolidation, impleader, third party joinder and intervention could be managed, but it is advisable for them to do so. The case may not develop promptly and satisfactorily without such a technical procedural basis.

The wider the interpretation given to *res judicata* in international disputes, the less readily conflicts between courts and arbitrators will arise.[246] A wide construction of *res judicata* could control dilatory tactics to some extent when international private rights are under threat; it may also counter abuse of process. Unfortunately, a wide construction will not be effective if *res judicata* and *lis pendens* are linked or *res judicata* constitutes procedural *ordre public*.

If different venues reach conflicting decisions on aspects such as compensation, the award that enjoys finality first will determine the amount to be paid. *Res judicata* and the doctrine of *compétence-compétence* will continue to have a role in determining finality.[247] Neither consolidation of related proceedings nor inter-adjudicatory co-ordination is an automatic feature of arbitration. Much depends on the

---

241 *Blair v Curran* [1939] 62 CLR 464, 532; *Yukos Capital SarL v OJSC Rosnef Oil Company* [2011] EWHC 1461 (Comm).

242 Roodt (n 237) 497.

243 Gazzini (n 24) 120, 162–63.

244 As is the case with Arts 7–10 of the ICC Arbitration and ADR Rules (2011). For more on consolidation, see Gazzini (n 24) 153–65.

245 Gazzini (n 24) 160.

246 Roodt (n 237) 510.

247 E.g. *West Tankers Inc v Allianz Spa & Another* [2011] EWHC 829 (Comm); *Sovarex SA v Romero Alvarez SA* [2011] EWHC 1661 (Comm).

initiative of the parties, and the level of respect which the national court in question shows with regard to the NYC in conflicts of competence with arbitral tribunals.

7.5 Disputes Involving Nazi Spoliated Art

The statutory limitations provisions of the 1995 UNIDROIT Convention mean that claims in respect of Nazi spoliated art fall outside the scope of the arbitration provision in Article 8(2).

Private ordering processes that depend to a high degree on party power may be suitable for parties who are eager to maintain their commercial relationship and are able to consent. In this category of claims, commercial arbitration (discussed above) is clearly unsuitable.[248] Detailed processes have been pondered, but none has yielded the fruit of an international arbitration framework. Owen Pell put forward an initial proposal on the basis that *in rem* jurisdiction of an exclusive tribunal was the only answer to the inefficient results of the US court system.[249] The basic premise of the proposal is that uniform rules, procedures and standards would benefit claimants, museums and other holders of Holocaust-looted art. Pell modified his initial proposal to propose the PCA as *the* forum with final authority[250] and with exclusive, compulsory control of Nazi spoliated art disputes.[251] A central registry was proposed for title registration.[252] The registration of a work would cut off or relinquish all claims against prior sellers or holders. After some defined

---

248 E.g. R Keim, 'Filling the Gap between Morality and Jurisprudence: The Use of Binding Arbitration to Resolve Claims of Restitution Regarding Nazi-Stolen Art' (2003) 3 Pepperdine Dispute Resolution Law Journal 295, 298 (in favour of 'the creation of international law or treaty arbitration as the forum to resolve claims of stolen art'); ILA Principles for Co-operation in the Mutual Protection and Transfer of Cultural Material, reprinted in 2006 IJCP 409.

249 C Pell, 'Using Arbitral Tribunals to Resolve Disputes Relating to Holocaust-Looted Art' in International Bureau of the Permanent Court of Arbitration (ed), *Resolution of Cultural Property Disputes* (The Hague 2004) 307.

250 Pell (n 249) 307, 309, 317, 320, 325.

251 Pell (n 249); OC Pell, 'The Potential for Mediation/Arbitration Commission to Resolve Disputes Relating to Artworks Stolen or Looted during World War II', (1999) 10 De Paul-LCA Journal of Art and Entertainment Law 10; OC Pell, 'Holocaust-Looted Art: Lost but Not Forgotten' (*UVA Lawyer*, fall 2002) <http://www.law.virginia.edu/html/alumni/uvalawyer/f02/opinion.htm> accessed 24 February 2014.

252 Pell (n 249) 316.

period, absent a claim, the tribunal would declare the object cleared, while works subject to claims would be referred to arbitration.[253] The qualifications, powers and functions of the arbitrators were set out.[254] Choice of law problems, inconsistent decisions on like claims, and jurisdictional problems were to be avoided by the Anglo-American law rule that a looter cannot pass good title. Rules of proof and evidence would facilitate settlements and assure that claimants are not unfairly disadvantaged by the passage of time.

The European Parliament considered Pell's proposal in 2003.[255] As part of his role in the committee on Legal Affairs and the Internal Market, the Belgian MEP Willy De Clercq recommended to the Commission that common principles had to be identified, first regarding a common cataloguing system for data on looted cultural goods and existing claims in respect thereof, for use by both public entities and private collectors; secondly regarding access to public or private archives that hold information on property identification and location; and thirdly regarding the determination of ownership or title, prescription, standards of proof, and rights to export or import of objects that had been recovered. He favoured dispute resolution mechanisms that would avoid lengthy and uncertain judicial procedures and take into account principles of fairness and equity, and a cross-border coordination administrative authority to deal with title disputes.[256]

Like Pell's proposal, De Clercq's recommendations were not implemented. The latest modification of secondary EU law does not bear the hallmarks of an efficient procedure for restitution of Nazi-looted art.

Pell's proposal has seen modifications that existing instruments and bodies,[257] including the NYC,[258] be utilised, or that a new International

---

253 Pell (n 249) 317.

254 Pell (n 249) 317–24.

255 WCEH De Clercq, *Report on a Legal Framework for Free Movement within the Internal Market of Goods Whose Ownership Is Likely to Be Contested* (2002/2114(Ini) (2003), Eur. Parl. Doc. A5-0408/2003), recommending that the European Parliament examine the plausibility of an EU-led title-clearing mechanism.

256 *Report* (n 255) 6.

257 Pell (n 249) 307–8, 316; J Mullery, 'Fulfilling the Washington Principles: A Proposal for Arbitration Panels to Resolve Holocaust-Era Art Claims' 2010 Cardozo Journal of Conflict Resolution 643, 672.

258 E.g. I Barker, 'Thoughts of an Alternative Dispute Resolution Practitioner on an International ADR Regime for Repatriation of Cultural Property and Works of Art', in BT Hoffman (ed), *Art and Cultural Heritage: Law, Policy and Practice* (CUP 2006) 483, who recommends the NYC.

Tribunal with limited but exclusive jurisdiction be established in a new international arbitration agreement.[259]

The scope of Pell's model illustrates great ambition but its credibility has been marred by a number of problematical features. The proposed power of the tribunal, the PCA, to determine the *res judicata* effect of prior rulings is highly problematical.[260] Many parties will have incurred high litigation costs in order to obtain final determinations of ownership, and will refuse to subject to a centralised commission or tribunal functioning under the auspices of the PCA. A new arbitration procedure would erode the public policy interest in the conclusiveness of legal proceedings. It would permit a party to claim more than once against an opponent, or give a defendant more than one opportunity to make use of the same line of defence in the same matter. Kreder suggests that the new international agreement, or the NYC, would attribute *res judicata* effect to its awards,[261] but the other proposals do not indicate what effect is to be given to the recognition and enforcement of foreign judgments and arbitral awards, estoppel by *res judicata*, or issue estoppel. Conflicting decisions and differences in the mechanisms by which legal traditions accord finality would require more careful treatment.

Pell's proposal envisages roles for adjudicators, mediators, advocates, advisors, legal assistants and auctioneers. Staff who work for the Tribunal are supposed to assess how claims would be handled, provide auction services, and draft settlement agreements for the division of proceeds.[262] These services would be provided in the shadow of sanctions against museums and dealers who fail to co-operate with the tribunal.[263]

With regard to the proposal for a new international arbitration treaty, the time pressures of Nazi spoliated art claims make it seem unrealistic to expect to find a solution for settlement in such a mechanism.[264] Binding common standards under the auspices of a central institution imply, at a minimum, a binding international protocol, special statutory regulations and agreement on where to set it up. No global common standard of

---

259 KA Falconer, 'When Honour Will Not Suffice' (2000) 21 University of Pennsylvania Journal of International Economic Law 383; Mullery (n 257) 643; JA Kreder, 'Reconciling Individual and Group Justice with the Need for Repose in Nazi-Looted Art Disputes: Creation of an International Tribunal' (2007) 73 Brooklyn Law Review 155.

260 Pell (n 249) 320.

261 Kreder (n 259) 210. Contra Pell (n 249) 316, 319.

262 Pell (n 249) 323.

263 Pell (n 249) 323.

264 Murphy (n 137) 13.

public international law has been identified for Holocaust art cases.[265] A small number of non-participating jurisdictions can weaken a new international treaty significantly if they are central to the success of the tribunal.[266] An international alternative will not necessarily be any less costly or time-consuming than litigation would be.[267]

The *Altmann* case illustrates how fundamental access to justice is in this category of claims, and how arbitration simplified matters for the parties not only with respect to choice of law, but also as to issues of procedure. Three government-appointed Austrian judges presided in the arbitration. The parties did not exclude the application of the domestic restitution law of Austria in their arbitration agreement. Austrian procedural and substantive law supplied legal criteria for the arbitration. Austrian law was the curial law of the seat, the law applicable to the arbitration procedure (*lex arbitri*), and the law governing the arbitral tribunal. Domestic restitution law determined the outcome. Another advantage of the arbitration was a reduced risk of an abusive plea of sovereign immunity.[268] Sovereign immunity is typically unavailable as a defence to the contracting state in arbitration between a state and a foreign private enterprise.[269] Austria was initially unwilling to arbitrate in the *Altmann* case, but upon learning that it was unprotected by sovereign immunity in litigation, it consented to arbitration.

Whereas waiver of sovereign immunity is unavailable in litigation, it is implicit in mixed arbitration where one party is private and the other is a

---

[265] H Hartung, 'The Holocaust and World War II Looted Art: Arbitrated between Great Dreams and Reality' in The International Bureau of the Permanent Court of Arbitration (ed), *Resolution of Cultural Property Disputes* (The Hague 2004) 327, 333.

[266] B Demarsin, 'Let's Not Talk about Terezín: Restitution of Nazi Era Looted Art and the Tenuousness of Public International Law' (2011) 37 Brooklyn Journal of International Law 120, 167–68.

[267] JF Sawka, 'Reconciling Policy and Equity: The Ability of the Internal Revenue Code to Resolve Disputes Regarding Nazi-Looted Art' (2009) 17 University of Miami International and Comparative Law Review 1, 16; Barker (n 258) 483, 484, 486.

[268] Gazzini (n 24) 81–84; 207.

[269] *Ipitrade International SA v Federal Republic of Nigeria*, 465 F Supp 824 (DDC 1978); *FG Hemisphere Associates LLC v Democratic Republic of Congo* [2009] 1 HKLRD 410 (court of first instance); [2010] 2 HKLRD 66 (CA); FACV 5-7/2010 (Ct of Final Appeal) (consent to arbitration is a waiver of immunity against jurisdiction). Also Art 1(2) of the PCA Arbitration Rules 2012; Art 9 of the Resolution adopted by the Institute of International Law, 'Arbitration Between States, State Enterprises, or State Entities, and Foreign Enterprises', September 1989 (known as the 1989 Santiago de Compostela Resolution).

state or state entity that does not claim sovereign immunity. Having acquiesced in arbitration, states cannot invoke their immunity from jurisdiction to bar arbitration proceedings.[270] In other words, an agreement by the state to submit a dispute to arbitration is an implied waiver of a state's immunity from jurisdiction for the purpose of arbitration proceedings. Entering into an arbitration agreement is tantamount to voluntary self-restriction on the exercise of the prerogatives of sovereignty. The sovereign state is bound to the undertakings it has made.[271] The implied waiver extends to judicial proceedings that are connected thereto or conducted in support of the arbitral proceedings, as well as *exequatur* proceedings in respect of the arbitral award where this is required for purposes of execution of the award.[272]

Wide agreement on substantive principles by which to resolve disputes involving Nazi spoliated art is unlikely in most disputes. International policies in this area have not always been sufficiently clear and firm.[273] Consequently, the focus has shifted to procedure and legal access.

In Europe, compelling private parties into arbitration of Nazi spoliated art disputes would risk a breach of the Article 6(1) safeguards in respect of the right to a public hearing of the European Convention for the Protection of Human Rights. Compulsory arbitration of this category of claims has also turned out to be less attractive for the US. Ambassador SE Eizenstat, who led the Prague Holocaust Era Assets Conference in 2009, was opposed to the idea of compulsory arbitration for Nazi spoliated art disputes. Ambassador Douglas Davidson announced in November 2012 that binding arbitration has proved to be a non-starter and that the US will be examining options involving public/private partnerships.[274]

---

[270] *Blue Ridge Investments, LLC v Republic of Argentina* 12-4139-cv (2d Cir 2013), Court of Appeals for the Second Circuit (Argentina waived its foreign sovereign immunity pursuant to two separate and independent exceptions to the immunity from suit provided by the Foreign Sovereign Immunities Act: (1) the implied waiver exception described in 28 US Code 1605(a)(1), and (2) the arbitral award exception described in 28 US Code 1605(a)(6)).

[271] *Texaco Overseas Petroleum Co (TOPCO)* case (n 206).

[272] S 9 of the 1978 State Immunity Act; *travaux preparatoires* of 1976 FSIA 28 US Code 1602–1611; S 177 (2) of the 1987 Swiss Private International Law Act; Gazzini (n 24) 84–86.

[273] Sawka (n 267) 12.

[274] E Campfens, 'Impression of the Symposium "Fair and Just Solutions?"' (*Advisory Committee on the Assessment of Restitution Applications for Items of Cultural Value and the Second World War*, 3 December 2012)

A large number of soft law instruments and codes of conduct promote recourse to non-judicial fora and ADR in preference to litigation.[275] Several jurisdictions rely on mediation in national committees.[276] The triumph of mediation in the resolution of Nazi spoliated art disputes is likely to affect the incidence of arbitration in ownership and restitution disputes.[277]

It is reasonable to expect that claimants would want to avoid high transaction costs in art restitution claims by settling. It has already been demonstrated that to settle is the most economically efficient course of action in Nazi spoliated art restitution claims.[278] However, Nazi-looted

---

<http://www.restitutiecommissie.nl/en/impression_of_the_day.html> accessed 24 February 2014.

[275] Principle VIII, IX and XI *Washington Conference Principles on Nazi-Confiscated Art*, 30 November–3 December 1998; Parliamentary Assembly of the Council of Europe, Resolution No 1205 on Looted Jewish Cultural Property of 4 November 1999, clause 16 <http://assembly.coe.int/main.asp?Link=/documents/adoptedtext/ta99/eres1205.htm> accessed 24 February 2014; *Vilnius Forum Declaration on Holocaust Era Looted Cultural Assets*, Vilnius, Lithuania, 3–5 October 2000 <http://www.lootedartcommission.com/vilnius-forum> accessed 24 February 2014; ICOM's new mediation programme for museums; 'Prague Holocaust Era Assets Conference: Terezin Declaration' (*US Department of State*, 30 June 2009) <http://www.state.gov/p/eur/rls/or/126162.htm> accessed 24 February 2014; ICPRCP, *Draft Declaration of Principles Relating to Cultural Objects Displaced in Connection with the Second World War* (2009) and rules of procedure for mediation and conciliation to facilitate restitution of cultural property (ICPRCP, July 2010, CLT-2010/CONF.203/COM.16/7); ILA Draft Principles for Cooperation in the Mutual Protection and Transfer of Cultural Material of 2004, International Law Association, Cultural Heritage Law Committee Report, Berlin Conference 2004, 3 <www.ila-hq.org/> accessed 24 February 2014.

[276] Meeting of Five European Committees, Symposium in the Peace Palace in The Hague, 26/27 November 2012; see <http://www.restitutiecommissie.nl/en/committees.html> accessed 24 February 2014.

[277] Stipanovic and Lamare (n 142) 44.

[278] Examples include *US v One Oil Painting Entitled 'Femme en Blanc' by Pablo Picasso*, 362 F Supp 2d 1175 (C D Cal 2005); *Bennigson v Alsdorf*, (Cal Supr Ct 16 June 2003) (unreported), aff'd, No B168200; 2004 WL 803616 (Cal Ct App 15 April 2004) (affirming the insufficiency of the defendant's contacts with California to justify assertion of personal jurisdiction), review granted, S124828, 2004 Cal Lexis 6903 (Cal 28 July 2004), dismissed, S124828, 2005 Cal Lexis 13370 (Cal 30 Nov 2005) (dismissing the case pursuant to notice of settlement). Also *Alsdorf v Bennigson*, No 04 C 5953, 2004 WL 2806301 (ND Ill 2004) (granting a six-month stay awaiting resolution of *Bennigson v Alsdorf*). In general Murphy (n 137) 23–26.

art cases do not settle at the expected rate.[279] Possible explanations include party expectations; information asymmetries; and the unique and indivisible nature of the object in question.[280] Settlement will not be a priority for parties who regard the law as the more powerful moral argument. Litigation remains a popular choice in the US and elsewhere.[281] When gaps become apparent in the provenance of an art work, a party may prefer to pursue court action for its competency to determine ownership, and an ADR agreement may be rescinded for this reason.[282]

7.6 Parallel Proceedings before a Court and an Arbitral Tribunal

Conflicting rulings may result if a limited arbitration clause subjects only a few selected issues in the dispute concerning a cultural object to arbitration.[283] If the arbitration clause is too narrow to cover all the matters in dispute, the arbitration proceedings in respect of the arbitrable portion of the claims may run parallel to judicial proceedings.[284]

Arbitral tribunals and courts are not equivalent in the work they do in respect of commercial and civil disputes. Their difference goes beyond the standing to request preliminary rulings from the CJEU under Article 234 EC. To put arbitral tribunals on an equal footing with courts is to misunderstand both the origin of their jurisdiction, which is consensus, and their private, individualised, and *ad hoc* nature. The risk of conflicting awards exists in spite of the arbitrator's best efforts to come up with an enforceable award. Conflicting rulings and awards are possible, not on account of any formal rebuttal of mechanisms by which to manage parallel proceedings in multiparty arbitration, but on account of the

---

279 Gazzini (n 24) 57–58 (enumerating some of the costs of a typical art restitution action); Sawka (n 267) 33; Murphy (n 137) 22, 26.

280 Whincop and Keyes (n 138) 129; Murphy (n 137) 27–29.

281 Stamatoudi (n 12) 189–90; Roodt (n 139) 421.

282 Falconer (n 259) 425.

283 *Schlaifer Nance and Co., Inc.* raised claims in respect of the same licensing agreement with the Warhol Foundation in arbitration and in federal court (e.g. *Schlaifer Nance & Co v Estate of Andy Warhol*, 764 F Supp 43, 46 (1991)).

284 E.g. *Aerospatiale Holdings Australia Pty Ltd and Eurocopter International Pacific Ltd v Elspan International Pty Ltd. et al.*, Supreme Court of NSW, Common Law Division, 14 August 1992, (1992) 28 NSWLR 321, Yearbook XIX (1994) 635.

fundamental nature of arbitration.[285] In some instances, concurrent processes can be avoided if the tribunal or the court orders a stay. Judicial proceedings may be stayed pending the completion of arbitration proceedings that are likely to settle questions of fact pertinent to non-arbitral claims; pending the determination of the existence or validity of the arbitration clause or waiver of the right to arbitrate; or when a party seeks to enforce a valid arbitration clause for the same subject-matter. The execution of an award may be stayed pending annulment proceedings.[286] Arbitrators may also stay proceedings, although express provisions in this regard are scarce.[287] Staying jurisdiction to allow the court first seised to establish its jurisdiction on the basis of *lis pendens* differs from suspending the adjudication of a related dispute. The first filed rule anticipates a positive conflict of competence to decide the same dispute where the parties, the subject-matter, and the cause of the action are the same. *Res judicata* is eventually established because the authority that is second seised is definitively excluded. The arbitrator has a completely different perspective on ordering stays in related proceedings. Arbitrators will order a stay if all the parties request it jointly; if only one party requests it, the arbitrator will use discretion rather than act on the basis of any hard and fast rule. In the large majority of jurisdictions, the only criteria for priority would be the date of the delivery of the final award and the generic public policy exception.[288]

Generally speaking, arbitrators ensure some degree of co-ordination of related arbitration proceedings, but they use much less intrusive mechanisms than courts to do so.[289] The Swiss and Taiwanese legislative frameworks offer a different model. If the law of the seat avoids contradictory decisions in the same legal order by means of a legislative provision that judicial precedent binds the abitral tribunal, *res judicata* is part of procedural *ordre public*. In Switzerland, *lis pendens* and *res judicata* apply to arbitral tribunals when a court was seised first. *Lis pendens* qualifies as a jurisdictional mechanism and not a procedural one. Failure to apply it to resolve conflicts between court rulings and arbitral

---

[285] Gazzini (n 24) 152ff; 182.

[286] Gazzini (n 24) 192 provides a collection of examples of cases.

[287] S 1281.2(c) of the California Code of Civil Procedure.

[288] Gazzini (n 24) 200–201.

[289] Gazzini (n 24) 186ff; C Roodt, 'Autonomy and Due Process in Arbitration: Recalibrating the Balance' European Journal of Law Reform 2011–13 (Special Issue) 413; Cremades and Madalena (n 110) 1.

awards would infringe public policy.[290] After the famous *Fomento* case,[291] the date an adjudicating authority is first seised determines the priority between a conflicting award and decision, but clear prerequisites apply. The court proceedings must be filed first in a foreign court within the European Judicial Area; the action must have the same subject matter between the same parties; the foreign court's decision must be enforceable in Switzerland; and the foreign court's decision must be due within reasonable time without foreseeable delay with the application of a prima facie standard of review of the validity of the arbitration agreement. If a summary examination of the arbitration agreement does not permit the court to make a finding on this, the court must decline jurisdiction. Taiwanese law has a similar feature. Conflicts between an award and a prior decision constitute a specific ground for non-recognition or vacatur of the decision or award issued by the authority that was second seised.[292]

Utmost caution is advised when choosing between different mechanisms for dispute resolution.[293]

8. CONCLUSION: COURTS AND ARBITRAL TRIBUNALS AS VENUES

Identifying an appropriate venue for proceeding with a claim in respect of ownership and restitution of an art object or a cultural object is an important first step in seeking a litigated solution. Private international law rules determine whether that court will hear the case, grant an application for a stay, decline jurisdiction in favour of the courts of another country, and whether a challenge to jurisdiction can succeed. Adjudicatory competence invites 'procedural' and 'practical' questions that are not always supported by robust theoretical or jurisprudential

---

290 The interface of the *lis pendens* principle and *compétence-compétence* is regulated in Art 9 and Art 186 PILA. Art 186(1bis) gives precedence to *compétence-compétence.*

291 *Fomento de Construccuones y Contratas SA v Colon Container Terminal SA*, 14 May 2001, ATF 127 III 279, [2001] ASA Bulletin 544; Interim Report of the International Arbitration Committee of the International Law Association, Berlin Conference, London, 2004, 826–61, <http://www.ila-hq.org/en/committees/index.cfm/cid/19> § 4.5; § 4.36; § 4.37 accessed 25 February 2014. Gazzini (n 24) 197, 200.

292 E.g. Art 40(9) of the Taiwanese Arbitration Act of 1998.

293 Gazzini (n 24) 67.

frameworks in every jurisdiction. Nonetheless, the opportunity for value-based decision-making is the aspiration to strive for. Legal access is paramount in questions about jurisdiction. The EU has now added to the jurisdictional bases contained in the Brussels regime. This amendment supports access to justice in disputes involving art and cultural objects, and constitutes a step in the right direction.

Depending on the rules applied by the forum, the proceedings may not reach the merits, or the court may proceed to hear arguments on the merits. A significant state interest in the application of mandatory rules may result in the establishment and exercise of jurisdiction. This situation may create an opportunity to engage with the protection of the object in question, even if the theoretical basis of jurisdiction is open to question.

Arbitrating claims involving ownership and restitution of art and cultural objects is an option that is fraught with risk. Conditions are rarely conducive to making arbitration a viable alternative to court adjudication in claims to cultural objects, and the practical advantages may be more limited than is usually postulated.

Claims involving stolen, looted and misappropriated art and cultural objects may raise arbitrability issues. Moreover, where power is asymmetrical or where complex multi-party non-contractual disputes are at stake, resolution may depend on the very legal technicalities that ADR seeks to avoid. These disputes tend to start off as traditional bi-polar disputes, yet could turn into complex multiparty non-contractual disputes. The technical rules that are required for efficient management make the arbitration into litigation by a different name. The practical advantages of arbitration become very limited in such cases.[294]

Parties may have agreed about arbitrating their dispute, but they may not have agreed the procedures. Where parties do not agree on procedures for themselves, and have not referred to an arbitration institution in the arbitration clause, there may be delays and complications along the way.

One of the great supposed advantages of arbitration is the freedom of the parties to choose their own decision makers instead of dealing with the randomness of the judicial system. This advantage can prove to be illusory. Very little information is known about how arbitrators or institutions have performed in arbitrations, and this affects both the new entrants to the system of international arbitration and experienced users. Additionally, the experts identified to adjudicate may turn out to be partial on account of their expertise.

---

[294] Gazzini (n 24) 207.

The *Altmann* arbitration was necessary to reach finality in the case. Finality appears to provide an argument in favour of arbitration. Nonetheless, the concept can be misleading. There is considerable scope for parties to address the implications of *res judicata* in their agreement or terms of reference for their agreement, in order to foreclose relitigation of the subject matter of the dispute.[295]

Reaching wide agreement on substantive principles by which to resolve disputes involving Nazi spoliated art has proved difficult. Much hesitation has accompanied international policies in this area. As a consequence, the emphasis has now shifted towards procedure and legal access. Ultimately, it is more important to safeguard access to justice than to promote any single form of dispute resolution above others. Access to justice is best effectuated if filing fees are kept within reason and time bars that encourage claimants to forget rather than ensure legal access are not enforced.

Private international law continues to have relevance in international arbitration procedures.[296] Arbitral tribunals have greater freedom in respect of selecting the law applicable to the merits of the case compared to the judiciary.[297] Since the potential scope of choice of applicable rules is wider compared to litigation, the risk associated with leaving choice of law undecided is more limited. The *Altmann* case demonstrated that arbitration can simplify the dispute resolution process. Loss of the right of judicial appeal makes closure possible sooner. Nonetheless, the procedural effects of arbitration agreements and the global regulation of competence can raise jurisdictional complications in art and heritage claims.

When more than one venue is seised with a case, there is potential for one norm to interfere with the intended functioning of another norm. The implications of the doctrine and practice of *compétence-compétence*, *lis pendens* and *res judicata* are not the same across every jurisdiction. Domestic or regional conditioning plays an important role in how each of these concepts function.

Arbitrators lack inherent jurisdiction. Jurisdictional challenges may result in the involvement of national courts in arbitrations between

---

[295] Radicati di Brozolo (n 123) 23.

[296] F de Ly, 'Conflicts of Law in International Arbitration – an Overview' in F Ferrari, S Kroll (eds), *Conflicts of Law in International Arbitration – an Overview* (Sellier 2011) 3.

[297] Gazzini (n 24) 96; M Piers and J Erauw, 'Application of the UNCITRAL Principles of International Commercial Contracts in Arbitration' (2012) 8 JPIL 459.

private parties and business. A party may commence suit on a different continent, while an arbitration is under way, basing his claim on the material invalidity of the arbitration agreement. The courts could be engaged more frequently, and for much longer than is desirable or beneficial, if the parties failed to agree on steps that would contain this type of situation.[298] Tribunals have limited functional powers. All original and third parties must consent to consolidation, impleader, third-party joinder or intervention because the arbitral tribunal has no real power to order consolidation and joinder. Institutional arbitration rules are becoming increasingly dense and more complex, yet they do not necessarily make adequate provision for the management of pernickety parallel proceedings and multi-party disputes. It takes but one dissenting voice to derail the proceedings, and the lack of any pre-existing contractual relationship makes dissent more likely. Even if the technicalities could be resolved, this is possible only as between the original arbitrating parties.[299]

The 'judicialisation'[300] of arbitration brings with it time and cost implications, combined with more formality and less flexibility.[301]

Tellingly, lower costs and cycle time used to be among the leading reasons that counted in favour of arbitration up until the 1990s, but the comparative cost of arbitral proceedings has ceased to be a compelling argument in its favour. Cost-benefit analyses are popular[302] but seldom illuminate the interaction between ADR and litigation. To be useful, the complexities associated with multiple simultaneous proceedings that address the same substantive challenges to an arbitral award need to be addressed. Such an analysis would need to include also the conflicts of competence that arise when a national court and an arbitral tribunal take a different view of the validity of the arbitration agreement. There may also be concurrent enforcement and annulment actions in different NYC contracting states, which will make it hard to isolate the respective costs associated with different methods of dispute resolution (e.g. court fees,

---

298 30 years in the case of *Société Européenne d'Etudes et d'Entreprises (S.E.E.E.) v Yugoslavia*, 2 July 1956, 86 (1959) JDI 1074; case concluded in the Cour d'appel Rouen, France, 13 November 1984. <http://www.newyorkconvention1958.org/index.php?lvl=notice_display&id=119> accessed 24 February 2014.

299 Gazzini (n 24) 208, 210.

300 Gazzini (n 24) 118.

301 Gazzini (n 24) 118.

302 E.g. Sidorsky (n 148) 34–37.

translation costs, expert witnesses, compensation, conservation costs and the costs of recognition and enforcement of the order in question).

While there is scope for making the argument that arbitration simplifies choice of law in dispute resolution, procedurally it offers the respondent an extended choice of delaying tactics. Indeed, arbitration can be more onerous than litigation, and it does not guarantee the achievement of neutrality and speed. As such, it is unlikely to emerge as a superior mechanism that simplifies dispute resolution when ownership and restitution claims are instituted in respect of stolen or illegally exported objects. Practical indications of the viability of arbitration in the art and antiquities sector are also rather limited at this stage.

5. Title laundering in complex 'lock' jurisdictions*

1. INTRODUCTION

In later *ius commune* development concerning purchases from someone who does not own what is sold,[1] the view that moveables cannot be pursued (*mobilia non habent sequelam*)[2] came to compete with that axiom of property law expressed in the maxim that nobody can transfer a greater right than she owns (*nemo plus iuris transferre potest quam ipse habet*).[3] The policy basis of the former is the perceived commercial imperative that, in principle, the *bona fide* purchaser of a moveable thing, in a normal market context, should get a good title regardless of provenance. The latter prevents the *bona fide* purchaser from acquiring title if the transferor did not have title to convey, or from claiming compensation when restitution is made to the owner. The tension between the two positions is reflected in the range of solutions of modern European law concerning whether and when the prior title of the owner is extinguished or his action for restitution is barred.[4]

Legal systems tend to reflect a preference between these two approaches in corporeal moveable property title issues in general.[5] A few

* This chapter develops the idea, argument, examples and conclusion contained in C Roodt and DL Carey Miller, 'Vitium Reale in Private Law and Private International Law' (2013) 10 TDM Special Issue 1.

[1] P Stein, 'Jus Commune and Its Demise' (2004) 25 Journal of Legal History 161ff.

[2] L J van Apeldoorn, 'Mobilia Non Habent Sequelam' (1932) 11 Tijdschrift voor Rechtsgeschiedenis 132.

[3] *Digesta Iustiniani* D.50.17.54 credits the Roman jurist Ulpian (c. 170–223). See Ulpian, *Commentary on the Praetor's Edict* Book 46.

[4] G Reichelt, 'International Protection of Cultural Property' [1985] Uniform Law Review 42, 105ff.

[5] Study Group on a European Civil Code and the Research Group on EC Private Law in C von Bar et al. (eds), *Principles, Definitions and Model Rules of European Private Law: Draft Common Frame of Reference* (Sellier 2009) DCFR VIII-4:101ff.

legal systems make exceptions for cultural moveables.[6] Others apply specific rules that safeguard the public interest associated with different public and private rights by means of restricted transfer, indefeasible title, imprescriptability or public domain rules.[7] Cultural objects merit special treatment, but general commercial law rules are readily extended to proprietary rights in these objects,[8] even when smuggling is suspected. The Duke of Frias donated a silver ciborium to Burgos Cathedral in Spain subject to its inalienability, and the donation was considered valid in terms of Spanish law; when the Duke instituted action in France because the cathedral transferred it to a person who sold it to a purchaser in good faith in France, this restriction was not recognised.[9] Inalienability was decided separately under every respective *lex rei sitae.* Likewise, smugglers may defeat inalienability rules by relying on the *lex situs* rule.[10] A state ownership rule could be recognised and applied in proceedings conducted abroad, but it would have no automatic extra-territorial application.

A value judgement is involved in attributing the epithet 'cultural' to an object.[11] An objective definition of the concept of 'cultural object' is difficult to provide *in abstracto*. Chapter 1 indicated that national laws and international instruments follow diverse approaches, techniques and concepts. EU Directives also rely on different approaches in respect of definition. Original statuary more than fifty years old would qualify as a cultural object under Article 1(1) of Council Directive 93/7 EEC on the Return of Cultural Objects Unlawfully Removed from the Territory of Member States,[12] but in terms of Directive 2014/60/EU, cultural objects

---

6 E.g. Dutch Civil Code 3: 99(2); commentary in DCFR VIII-4:102 n 13.

7 A Jakubowski, 'Return of Illicitly Trafficked Cultural Objects Pursuant to Private International Law: Current Developments' in The Illicit Traffic of Cultural Objects in the Mediterranean (EUI Working Papers 2009) 137, 139.

8 A Chechi, *The Settlement of International Cultural Heritage Disputes: Towards a Lex Culturalis?* PhD Thesis EUI (2012) 249; Jakubowski (n 7) 140.

9 *Frias v Pinchon* 1886 Clunet 593.

10 A Lanciotti, 'The Dilemma of the Right to Ownership of Underwater Cultural Heritage: The Case of the "Getty Bronze"' in S Borelli and F Lenzerini (eds), *Cultural Heritage, Cultural Rights, Cultural Diversity: New Developments in International Law* (Nijhoff Publishers 2012) 301, 314. Lanciotti goes on to argue in support of its application (at 315).

11 UNIDROIT Secretariat, Explanatory Report to the 1995 Unidroit Convention on Stolen or Illegally Exported Cultural Objects, (2001) 3 Uniform Law Review 476, 496.

12 Council Directive (EEC) 93/7 of 15 March 1993 on the return of cultural objects unlawfully removed from the territory of a member state OJ L 74/74,

classified or defined as national treasures would no longer have to belong to categories or comply with thresholds related to their age or financial value in order to qualify for return.[13] Clandestine excavation and illegal export are not marked and treated as mandatory substantive rules in common law courts (see Chapter 4), and where civil law judges have treated them as such,[14] the rulings have been subjected for not separating out criminal law from private international law.[15] Fortunately, the impact of substantive mandatory rules in Italian law has been recognised.[16]

Jurisdictions lacking regulation and law enforcement, or protective of good faith purchasers, provide scope to 'launder' illegal activities when title is transferred. Some criminological theories incorporate jurisdictions when offering explanations for the laundering mechanism.[17] The 'lock' theory[18] shows how a complex lock is created when proof is available that an object has been stolen (and the same applies where a statute vests ownership in a state and it can be proven that excavation and export occurred after it entered into force). For laundering to be accomplished, one extra step is required, namely acquisition in good faith in a jurisdiction that protects acquisition in good faith.[19] While it is trite that theft encroaches on ownership and possessory rights in fungible objects, choice of law can end up sustaining the laundering mechanism, and miss the mark in the process.

27.3.93 (amended 1997 and 2001). To qualify for return, the object must be classified among the national treasures under national legislation, and belong to the categories referred to in the Annex or form an integral part of public collections or inventories of ecclesiastical institutions.

[13] Directive 2014/60/EU of the European Parliament and of the Council of 15 May 2014 on the Return of Cultural Objects Unlawfully Removed from the Territory of a Member State and amending Regulation (EU) No 1024/2012 (Recast) OJ EU L159/1, 28.5.2014.

[14] Ordinanza 2010, 24.

[15] E.g. Lanciotti (n 10) 316.

[16] Ibid. The time is ripe for more work to be done to demonstrate the link between cultural heritage protection and the overriding mandatory provisions of the forum state indicated in Article 9(2) of the Rome I Regulation.

[17] E.g. the theories of M Felson, 'The Ecosystem for Organized Crime' HEUNI Paper No 26 in HEUNI 25th Anniversary Lecture (Helsinki: The European Centre for Crime Prevention and Control 2006), 8; and J Dietzler, 'On "Organized Crime" in the Illicit Antiquities Trade: Moving Beyond the Definitional Debate' (2013) 16 Trends in Organized Crime 329.

[18] AJG Tijhuis, *Transnational Crime and the Interface between Legal and Illegal Actors: The Case of the Illicit Art and Antiquities Trade* (Wolf Legal Publishers 2006). First highlighted in Chapter 1.

[19] Tijhuis (n 18) 187–88.

When stolen art moves across jurisdictional lines, municipal legal systems' rules are in constant interplay with jurisdictional and choice of law rules.[20] Strong commercial orientation may be evident in the law. Provisions dealing with the validity of title transfer will be favourably disposed to title laundering if the real vice of theft that attaches a title defect to a cultural object until it is returned to its true owner (*vitium reale*[21]) is not accounted for. The broad *lex situs* rule of private international law responds to commercial imperative, and oversimplifies the nature and extent of the problems affecting the choice of law argument.[22]

This chapter suggests that tensions between private law and criminal law and between conflicts justice and material justice are eased in the art markets of New York. This potential has also been deployed in England.[23] Based on this balancing trend, an owner or a state deprived by cross-border sale ought to be able to recover on the strength of *vitium reale* and the implications it has for choice of law method.

2. THE MENACE OF TITLE LAUNDERING

2.1 The Phenomenon

Title to works of art and antiquities that can be proved to have been stolen is easily 'laundered' in jurisdictions that favour acquisition by a *bona fide* purchaser[24] due to rules that permit title to pass from art dealers to purchasers even if the owner who sold the object to the dealer had been deprived through theft or looting. A number of continental European states extend protection immediately upon the conclusion of the transaction[25] or very soon after the sale.[26] Title can be lost by an

---

[20] A Kenyon and S MacKenzie, 'Recovering Stolen Art – Australian, English and US Law on Limitations of Action' (2001–2002) 30 Western Australian Law Review 233, 235.

[21] See 2.2 below.

[22] *Cammell v Sewell* [1860] 8 WR 639; *Winkworth v Christie Manson and Woods Ltd* [1980] Ch 496; *City of Gotha and the Federal Republic of Germany v Sotheby's and Cobert Finance SA* transcript, unreported case no 1997/G/185, 9 September 1998, QBD.

[23] Chechi (n 8) 101.

[24] LV Prott, 'Problems of Private International Law for the Protection of the Cultural Heritage' V *Recueil des Cours* (The Hague 1989) 215, 264.

[25] E.g. Spanish Civil Code Art 464.

[26] French Civil Code Arts 2268, 2269, 2279; Former Dutch Civil Code Art 2014.

owner because the purchaser does not have to prove the validity of the aforementioned transfers, and the position of the purchaser remains unaffected by subsequent notice that a link in the transfer chain is defective. The purchaser has no incentive to inquire into the provenance of art in such a system. It adds to the owner's peril if the court considers the legal rules that require to be classified in isolation. If the property transaction is used as a basis for classification, the integrity of the transaction chain, the conveyance history of the object, and the legal consequences of the operative facts and their context will go unchecked.[27] The burden of proof is on the claimant, who may need to prove that suspicious circumstances surrounding the transaction should have caused the purchaser to doubt the seller's authority to sell the property and to inquire about the property's origins.

The *lex situs* rule and its connecting factor, the law of the place where the moveable object was physically located when title is alleged to have been created, modified or terminated,[28] can purge an object of tainted title upon sale. Classed as a matter of title, possible prescription of the action would depend on the legal system indicated by the *lex situs* rule.[29] Compliance with non-demanding good-faith purchaser standards[30] and short prescription further enable title to objects of dubious provenance to be laundered.[31]

---

[27] WW Kowalski, 'Restitution of Works of Art Pursuant to Private and Public International Law' (2001) 288 *Recueil des Cours* (The Hague 2002) 218–22.

[28] L Collins et al. (gen eds), *Dicey, Morris and Collins on The Conflict of Laws* (14th edn, Sweet & Maxwell 2006) Rule 24 1164 with Second Cumulative Supplement (Sweet and Maxwell 2008) 149; E Crawford and J Carruthers, *International Private Law: A Scots Perspective* (3rd edn, W Green 2010) 523; JM Carruthers, *The Transfer of Property in the Conflict of Laws* (OUP 2005) 79; JJ Fawcett and JM Carruthers, *Cheshire, North & Fawcett Private International Law* (14th edn, OUP 2008) 1212.

[29] A particular domestic legal system may regulate this issue separately or hold a claim time-barred with reference to the law of the court if statutory limitations are considered a matter of procedure.

[30] *Bumper Development Corporation Ltd. v Commissioner of Police for the Metropolis* [1991] 1 WLR 1362 (CA).

[31] IF Gazzini, *Cultural Property Disputes: The Role of Arbitration in Resolving Non-Contractual Disputes* (Transnational Publishers Inc 2004) xxiii.

2.2 *Winkworth v Christie Manson and Woods Ltd*[32]

The *Winkworth* ruling illustrates the laundering of title to valuable Japanese miniature carvings or *netsuke*, at a time when these thefts increased sharply.[33] The original owner's title was extinguished by a post-theft sale to a purchaser who received good title in Italy. The purchaser later returned the objects to England to be auctioned off. When the owner filed proceedings against the seller and the auctioneer, the English court applied Italian domestic law. Italian private law permits a good-faith purchaser who bought from a thief or a seller who is not the owner to gain title immediately upon the conclusion of the transaction.[34] The stolen collection was already in Italy when the Italian purchaser acquired it. The court concluded that the acquirer in good faith prevailed over the original owner's title, even if the moveable was stolen.

The rule of *market overt* developed in the Middle Ages at a time when most goods were bought and sold at the local market.[35] The rule prevented the owner from pursuing the recovery of possessions sold in *market overt* because ownership was extinguished in favour of the good faith purchaser.[36] *Winkworth* was decided when English law still permitted the prior title of the rightful owner to be sacrificed, some fourteen years before the Sale of Goods (Amendment) Act 1994 abolished the rule.[37] *Nemo dat quod non habet* has applied more freely since the law reform took effect. If the seller does not possess legal title, ownership cannot be transferred; if an object was stolen or removed at some point in the transaction chain, this would be the case.[38]

The court did not address the case for a distinction of the carvings based on the cultural property factor, but treated the rule as an ideal rule

---

[32] See n 22.

[33] Auction prices reached £125 000 in 1991. See D Alberge, 'Stolen Ivory Miniatures Attract Pounds 15,000 Reward' *The Independent* (4 August 1993), illustrating how the market develops for certain objects.

[34] While there is no presumption in Italian law that the possessor is owner, Arts 1153–1157 of the Italian Civil Code permit the good faith purchaser to acquire title immediately if: (a) good faith existed when the thing is bought; (b) the transaction is capable of transferring ownership; and (c) the documents evidencing the sale are capable of transferring title. This feature of Italian law is noted in the DCFR (n 5) VIII-3:101 n 101.

[35] DJ Keenan and S Riches, *Business Law* (10th edn, Longman 2005) 347.

[36] S 22(1) of the Sale of Goods Act, 1979. Carruthers *The Transfer of Property* (n 28) § 8.27.

[37] Carruthers, *The Transfer of Property* (n 28) § 8.27.

[38] Kowalski (n 27) 218–22.

of international law. The *lex situs* rule was held to govern corporeal property that was transported across state boundaries. Two cases formed the authoritative basis of the decision: one regarding a horse stolen and sold in Ireland before the purchaser took it to Scotland;[39] the other a cargo of timber that was sold when the carrier was wrecked off the coast of Norway.[40] The Japanese carvings had been stolen in England, shipped abroad, resold and then returned to England, but counsel never linked the indelible *vitium reale* in Scots law to the transmission of the *netsuke*.[41] Legal systems that recognise the right of the owner who has been deprived by theft to recover, may do so on the basis that crime voids the title transfer,[42] or that a 'real vice' attaches to the thing until it is restored.[43] Scottish private law does not specifically protect cultural objects, but it extends protection to the deprived owner. Flawed title cannot be cleaned by any market transaction because the thief or transferor passes it on to all successive transferees in the transaction chain.[44] The window for any demonstration of good faith may be exceedingly narrow.[45] The legal position is not necessarily comparable across other mixed legal systems.[46] While the acquirer always has the

---

[39] *Todd v Armour* (1882) 9R 901.

[40] *Cammell v Sewell* [1860] 5 H & N 728 (original owner was voluntarily and lawfully dispossessed of his timber), confirmed in *Air Foyle Ltd v Center Capital Ltd* [2004] ILPr 15 and relied on in *Winkworth* (n 22) at 505F.

[41] *Winkworth* (n 22) at 506D–G. At 507B, Slade J described *Todd v Armour* as a fine example of the application of the principle in *Cammel*.

[42] Art 1 of Decree-Law No 27633 of 1937 and Art 31 of Law No 13 of 1985 render transactions in Portuguese territory concerning cultural objects originating in a foreign country null and void when effected in breach of legislation regulating alienation or exportation.

[43] DL Carey Miller, 'Title to Art: Developments in the USA' (1995) 1 Scottish Law and Practice Quarterly 115, 121.

[44] DCFR (n 5) VIII-3.101 n 103, n 130.

[45] I.e. where 20 years' negative prescription is pleaded. The Scottish Law Commission is undecided as to whether treasure is subject to negative prescription in Scots law (Scottish Law Commission, *Discussion Paper on Prescription and Title to Moveable Property No 144* (Edinburgh 2010) § 4.14–§ 4.15). If it is not, a *bona fide* third-party purchaser may face a claim from the Crown even after possession for 20 years. This would mean significant protection for state ownership in Scots law.

[46] In Louisiana, a purchaser may acquire clean title to stolen art if he or she has maintained unchallenged possession of the work. *Dunbar v Seger-Tomschitz*, 615 F3d 574 (5th Circuit 20 August 2010)(acquisitive prescription ran in respect of 'Portrait of a Youth' by Kokoschka under Louisiana law).

option of consulting a commercial, international or state-run database,[47] no central and complete registry for stolen art exists.

Counsel and Slade J overlooked the potential of the *vitium reale* concept of Scots law to preclude any laundering of title, by recognising that the 'real defect' of theft precludes subsequent acquisition provided the act of theft can be established. The potential intermediary status of Italian law in the circumstance of the case before it was not spared any thought,[48] despite the fact that recognition of wrongful acts that lead to displacement, undermines everyone's ownership of unique and special objects.[49] That the *netsuke* had been dealt with without the knowledge and consent of the owner, was considered insufficient to prevent the automatic application of the *lex situs* rule.

Winkworth would have won if the court had applied English law, because the limitation period on his claim had not run. Title accrues to a purchaser in good faith six years after the purchase,[50] barring recovery by the owner. No statutory limitation applies to recovery claims by a dispossessed owner if the acquisition was in bad faith; time only starts to run on the first good faith transfer of the stolen property. Later exercise of rights of ownership over the property of another (conversion) is presumed to relate to an earlier theft. The presumption obliges the purchaser to investigate whether the seller is passing on clean title.[51]

2.3 Responding to *Winkworth*

A narrow pursuit of the *lex situs* rule because it points towards application of a legal system that favours the possessor (as opposed to a skirting of the law) enables stolen works of art to continue to circulate. That multilateral conflicts rules are purportedly neutral in the sense of allocating a legal relationship to a legal system without favouring any particular outcome, does not necessarily help adjudicators reach impartial decisions. In an unconditioned form, the rule is of little use in ownership

---

[47] E.g. Art Loss Register; INTERPOL Stolen Art and Antiquities Database; London Stolen Arts Database; Lost Art Internet Database; 'Leonardo' Database.

[48] Carruthers, *The Transfer of Property* (n 28) §§ 8.38–40.

[49] G Carducci, 'The Growing Complexity of International Art Law: Conflict of Laws, Uniform Law, Mandatory Rules, UNSC Resolutions and EU Regulations' in B Hoffman (ed), *Art and Cultural Heritage: Law, Policy and Practice* (CUP 2006) 68, 76.

[50] The six-year time bar waters down the effect of Art 7 of the UNESCO Convention in England and Wales.

[51] S 4 of the Limitation Act 1980; Kenyon and MacKenzie (n 20) 241.

and restitution claims. The declaration made by Slade J, that the movement of the *netsuke* was irrelevant for the questions of transfer of title, went too far.[52] Yet the wider implications of the *Winkworth* ruling for the art world did not alarm everyone.[53] The judge found a connecting factor that serves the convenience, certainty and consistency required by commerce to be worthy of endorsement.[54] The *lex situs* rule protects the property title in the jurisdiction in which the object was acquired. Sale is possible even before the legal requirements of the previous *situs* have been met and purchasers cannot be lightly subjected to a duty to make further enquiries into the provenance or conveyance history of an object.

The systemic effects of the *lex situs* rule tend to remain obscure and unquestioned because the rule is so well established. Nonetheless, UNIDROIT and commentators realised that the mechanical recourse to the law of the last transaction by which acquisition of title is alleged, gives scope to title laundering,[55] resulting in havens for art thieves and their transferees.[56] The *lex situs* at the time of the alleged transfer indicates only if the previous possessor authorised the transfer of the object, and not if the original owner granted or withheld authorisation.[57] A purchaser need only investigate one law before proceeding.[58] The connection could be transitory.

The 1995 UNIDROIT Convention on Stolen or Illegally Exported Cultural Objects (hereinafter UNIDROIT Convention)[59] is primarily concerned with the question of return to the original owner, be it a private

---

52 At 514B.

53 DW Rowe, 'Stolen Property in the Conflict of Laws' [1980] Canterbury Law Review 71.

54 At 506B and at 513A–B.

55 Prott (n 24) 260ff; Reichelt (n 4) 91; N Palmer, 'Recovering Stolen Art' (1994) 47 Current Legal Problems 215, 249; I Stamatoudi, *Cultural Property Law and Restitution* (Edward Elgar 2011) 189–90; Chechi (n 8) 102–3.

56 M Lee, 'A Choice of Law Dilemma: The Conflict and Reconciliation of Laws Governing Cross-Border Transfers of Stolen Art' [2008–2009] Cardozo Public Law Policy and Ethics Journal 719, 722–23; Prott (n 24) 269; S Symeonides, 'Choice of Law in the American Courts in 2010: Twenty-Fourth Annual Survey' (2011) 59 AJCL 303, 362.

57 PA Lalive, *The Transfer of Chattels in the Conflict of Laws* (Clarendon Press 1955) 159.

58 D Fincham,'How Adopting the Lex Originis Rule Can Impede the Flow of Illicit Cultural Property' (2008) 32 Columbia Journal of Law and the Arts 111, 117.

59 UNIDROIT Convention on Stolen or Illegally Exported Cultural Objects, 24 June 1995, in force 1 July 1998; 34 ILM 1330.

person, a legal person or a nation. The *vitium reale* approach finds measured support in the common law presumption of *nemo dat quod non habet* adopted in Article 3 of the UNIDROIT Convention. In a title contest involving moveable property, an original owner has preference over a good faith purchaser so that a claim for the return of an object cannot be countered by acquisition in good faith. While the Convention's preference for stringent standards of diligence and compensation to the purchaser in good faith does not necessarily detract from a *vitium reale* approach, there is no presumption of bad faith on the part of the possessor in the absence of an export certificate. Moreover, the Convention does not prevent trade that is lawful under the *lex situs* by the calculated mischief of professional traffickers who specialise in the transnational removal of cultural objects. Organised criminals, thieves, fences and handlers launder title in jurisdictions where the *lex situs* rule can support their activities. Jurisdictions that protect the title of the original owner are used as intermediary or transit states. If the validity of the transfer of title is manipulated by means of technical compliance with one law to skirt another, the benefits under the Convention are extinguished and works of art tainted by the vice of theft continue to circulate.[60]

The *Winkworth* outcome would not have been different if the UNIDROIT Convention had been incorporated into English law at the time of the decision.[61] If the case had arisen in Italy post 2000, the outcome may have been different though.[62] The claim would clearly be international[63] in character and the policy that underpins the Convention may have had the effect of an 'anti-conflict' rule.

---

60 Carruthers *The Transfer of Property* (n 28) § 5.29.

61 Study LXX Doc 1 Unidroit 1986 16–17; Study LXX Doc 7 Unidroit 1988.

62 Italy ratified on 11 October 1999 and acceded on 1 April 2000 <http://www.unidroit.org/status-cp> accessed 24 February 2014. The Italian Movement of Goods of Cultural Interest Act Articles 2, 4 also accommodates restitution claims from an EU Member State when a cultural object was unlawfully moved there although the period permitted after knowledge of the location of the object and the identity of the possessor is very short (DCFR (n 5) VIII-3:101 n 135 4876).

63 Explanatory Report, UNIDROIT Convention, Study LXX Doc 51 2002 10.

2.4 EU and Global Instruments

The *lex originis* is recognised in the 1991 Basel Resolution adopted by the Institute of International Law.[64] The most popular alternative connecting factor is the *lex originis*[65] (i.e. the law of the place where it was created, found or discovered; the place of which the artist is a national; or the place depicted in a work of art). Many artists do not spend their lives in a single country, and the connection of the *lex originis* can become very uncertain.[66] 'Country of origin' refers to the country that designates the object as part of its cultural heritage or that classifies it as national treasure or includes it in a record on an ad hoc basis. However, an object with indisputable cultural significance may not be so designated, since not every state uses national inventories for designating objects as culturally significant. Some states adopt an export approach, and defer any decision until export.[67] A genuine cultural link may exist between the country and the object independent from any formal designation. Such a link may also be forged with an 'adoptive' state or a community that attributes value to the object[68] and the overlapping of claims is possible. The *lex originis* rule can correct some of the ills and uncertainties inherent in the *lex situs*,[69] but it will be anything but watertight in these circumstances, or if the find spot of an archaeological item is unknown or contested.

Article 2 of the Resolution states that 'transfer of ownership of works of art belonging to the cultural heritage of the country of origin shall be governed by the law of that country'. The country of origin is defined as the place with which the object has the closest cultural link. Article 3

---

[64] *Institute of International Law Yearbook Vol 64/II* (1992), 'International Sale of Works from the Angle of the Protection of the Cultural Heritage' 403.

[65] *Institute of International Law Yearbook Vol 56* (1975) Wiesbaden Resolution 'The Application of Foreign Public Law' 20th Commission, Res. 4, 551–53; Basel Resolution (n 64); E Jayme, 'Die Nationalität des Kunswerkes als Rechtsfrage' in G Reichelt (ed), *Internationaler Kulturgüterschutz* (Wien 1992) 7; S Symeonides, 'A Choice-of-Law Rule for Conflicts Involving Stolen Cultural Property' (2005) 38 Vanderbilt Journal of Transnational Law 1177, 1183–86.

[66] C Armbrüster, 'Private Law as an Instrument for the Protection of Cultural Property' (2013) 10 TDM Special Issue 1, 3.

[67] JD Murphy, 'The People's Republic of China and the Illicit Trade in Cultural Property: Is the Embargo Approach the Answer?' [1994] IJCP 227, 230.

[68] M Cornu and M Renold, 'New Developments in the Restitution of Cultural Property: Alternative Means of Dispute Resolution' (2010) 17 IJCP 1, 16–17.

[69] Carducci (n 49) 70.

provides that the *lex originis* governs the export of such works. This idea found its way into Council Directive 93/7/EEC on the return of cultural objects, which applies regardless of any theft. It does not focus on rights *in rem* in cultural objects and the *forum originis* enjoys no special status under the Directive or its successor, Directive 2014/60/EU. Article 5 of Directive 93/7/EEC establishes the competence of the national courts requested to rule on the merits of a claim for return. For the purpose of deciding the validity of an illegal transaction, the law of the country where the object used to be kept may apply, but 'return' is defined in a way that leaves the question of ownership to the choice of law rule of the court hearing the case (i.e. the competent court in the requested Member State).[70] Article 12 of the Directive provides that, after return, ownership of the cultural object is determined by the law of the requesting Member State (which is likely to be the law of the nation of origin or *lex originis*[71]).

Directive 93/7/EEC enables EU Member States to request the return of cultural treasures and the owner of a stolen object to institute civil proceedings in respect thereof.[72] This has had little impact on the title laundering situation. It has been suggested that extending its operation to theft in express terms would be advisable.[73]

Article 5 of Directive 2014/60/EU now makes direct reference to stolen materials and Article 10 creates an obligation to consult any databases of stolen cultural objects. These are positive changes that are likely to take matters forward.

The 1970 UNESCO Convention on the Means of Prohibiting and Preventing the Illegal Import, Export, and Transfer of Ownership of Cultural Property (hereinafter UNESCO Convention[74]) was in force when the *Winkworth* case was decided, but the UK only ratified it in 2002. Article 7(b)(i) of the UNESCO Convention encourages states to consider restitution to public institutions and entertain actions for the recovery of certain registered and inventoried artistic objects. A stolen object is effectively re-bought after the crime when just compensation is paid to the good faith purchaser from the state of origin under Article 7

---

70 Art 1.

71 E Jayme, 'Globalization in Art Law: Clash of Interests and International Tendencies' (2005) 38 Vanderbilt Journal of Transnational Law 937.

72 Art 15.

73 Carducci (n 49) 80.

74 Convention on the Means of Prohibiting and Preventing the Illicit Import, Export and Transfer of Ownership of Cultural Property, 14 November 1970, in force 24 April 1972; 823 UNTS 231.

of the UNESCO Convention. To the extent that it permits the transfer of defective title, it fails to lend support to a *vitium reale* approach and to due diligence as to provenance. While it calls for international co-operation and reciprocal understanding, states are generally unwilling to apply foreign law on these grounds.[75]

A uniform and integrated world law would overcome horizontal competition among states based on substantive and procedural diversity. This will help to prevent the uncritical application of ordinary business norms to transactions involving cultural objects.[76] There is, however, no treaty rule to the effect that transferees of stolen moveables cannot invoke good faith,[77] and harmonisation of substantive law remains elusive. If global diversity in title issues is managed by means of a method that allows title to be purged from vices as soon as the object is transferred in a particular jurisdiction, there is no hope of improving the standard of legal protection.

3. CHOICE OF LAW RULES AND CONTEXT

Conflicts rules are supposed to function in the abstract to designate the applicable municipal law. However, if they are wholly unconcerned with the chain of provenance and sequential sales that disguise provenance, the role of the law in the maintenance of a secure society is compromised. Decisions based on the *lex situs* rule will be anything but neutral in a context where intermediary states have such integral roles in trafficking networks specialising in the transnational removal of cultural objects.[78]

The *lex situs* rule defers to the relationship between the true owner and the purchaser in good faith,[79] while it disregards the relationship between owner and thief.[80] It assigns importance to the transaction chain, but because of how the validity of transfer is determined, it overlooks how crime affects the very practical human interests at stake.

---

75 Jakubowski (n 7) 141.

76 Chechi (n 8) 249.

77 Convention Providing All Uniform Law on the Acquisition in Good Faith of Corporeal Movables, 1975 (1) Uniform Law Review 66 (never entered into force).

78 See generally Prott (n 24) 268.

79 As in *Winkworth* (n 22) 513 C–F.

80 Carducci (n 49) 77; Carruthers, *The Transfer of Property* (n 28) § 8.18; LV Prott and PJ O'Keefe, *Law and the Cultural Heritage Vol. 3 Movement* (Butterworth 1989) 614.

Jurisdictions do not necessarily agree on when an object has been 'stolen'. German law draws a distinction between the acquisition of a stolen object from the thief,[81] and from a disposer who is not entitled to dispose of the thing. If the purchaser obtains possession from a disposer who is not entitled to dispose, acquisition of ownership in good faith is possible and the market factor enjoys priority.[82] Only acquisition from the thief precludes acquisition in good faith. The *vitium reale* concept, on the other hand, achieves an expanded definition of theft that includes any unlawful removal of cultural objects as a defect which, in principle, precludes subsequent acquisition. The expansion contributes towards preserving the law[83] and its role in the maintenance of a secure society that prevents safe havens for stolen or trafficked objects from flourishing.

4. USING STRUCTURE AND METHOD OF CHOICE OF LAW TO DETER TITLE LAUNDERING

Content-selecting conflicts rules are preferable when substantive rules diverge sharply and an important international policy demands consideration. An impressive list[84] of attractive specific conflicts rules for the art trade exists.[85] The law of the place where the object had been stolen features on the list, but the connection between the loss and the territory

---

[81] Ownership cannot be acquired on the basis of BGB §§ 932–34 if the thing which has been stolen from the owner goes missing or is otherwise lost.

[82] BGB § 929 and BGB § 392. *Kunstsammlungen zu Weimar v Elicofon*, 536 F Supp 829 at 839 (EDNY 1981); K Siehr, 'International Art Trade and the Law' VI (243) *Recueil des Cours* (The Hague 1993) 9, 60.

[83] Chechi (n 8) 289.

[84] Study LXX Doc 1 Unidroit 1986 20, 35–36 proposes, for lost or stolen goods, the intention of the parties and the law most closely connected; H Hanisch, 'Internationalprivatrechtliche Fragen im Kunsthandel' in A Dieckmann et al. (eds), *Festschrift für Wolfram Müller-Freienfels* (1986) 193, 215 proposes the *lex furti*; E Jayme, 'Die Nationalität des Kunswerkes als Rechtsfrage' in G Reichelt (ed), *Internationaler Kulturgüterschutz* (Wien 1992) 7 and the Institute of International Law propose the *lex originis* prior to the first illegal exportation in its Wiesbaden Resolution 'The Application of Foreign Public Law' 20th Commission, Res. 4 (1975) 56 *Institute of International Law Yearbook* (551–53) and Basel Resolution of 1991 (n 65); Symeonides (n 56) 1183–86 proposes the *lex originis* subject to clear exceptions.

[85] For an early effort to identify such discrete rules, see Reichelt (n 4) 91. Carruthers, *The Transfer of Property* (n 28) § 5.42 n 111 argues against such proliferation.

seems haphazard.[86] The *lex originis* also features on the list, and some commentators look to the application of the law of the source state to correct some of the ills and uncertainties inherent in the *lex situs*.[87] The *lex originis* focuses on simplicity and cultural connection.[88]

The assumption that the law of the country of origin is appropriate in art claims that are distinct from claims to cultural objects is not always borne out by the facts.[89] The identity of the artist often lies more central to art than his or her identity in respect of cultural property, and it may be both impossible and undesirable to judge the origin of a work of art in these situations.[90] The rule offers no assistance where orphaned works are concerned.[91] Assuming that the *lex originis* will provide the most effective protection to its cultural heritage may turn out to be false.[92] The law of the place of the domicile of the dispossessed owner might be taken to be the country of origin, but such a restriction on the *lex situs* will not necessarily discourage wrongdoers from passing title in jurisdictions with favourable *bona fide* acquisition rules. The method for determining the country of origin is not clear. An object may become assimilated in the culture of the place of location after export; thus the connection between the country of origin and the modern history of the object may be tenuous[93] and the claim of the country of origin slight.[94] Time limitations under the *lex originis* may be even shorter than those of the *lex situs*, and difficulty with the identification of the applicable law remain.[95]

---

86 C Armbrüster, 'Private Law as an Instrument for the Protection of Cultural Property' (2013) 10 TDM Special Issue 1, 3.

87 Carducci (n 49) 70.

88 L Frey, 'Bakalar v Vavra and the Art of Conflicts Analysis in New York: Framing a Choice of Law Approach for Moveable Property' (2012) 112 Columbia Law Review 1055, 1093.

89 As with the Egon Schiele drawing in *Bakalar v Vavra and Fischer*, 619 F3d 136, 2010 WL 3435375 (2nd Circuit 2010).

90 Frey (n 88) 1094.

91 *Ibid.*

92 As demonstrated in *Kunstsammlungen zu Weimar v Elicofon*, 536 F Supp 829 (EDNY 1981); 678 F2d 1150 (2nd Circuit 1982) 1151. See Jakubowski (n 7) 141.

93 JH Merryman, 'Thinking about the Elgin Marbles' [1985] *Michigan Law Review* 1881, 1915.

94 TW Pecoraro, 'Choice of Law in Litigation to Recover National Cultural Property: Efforts at Harmonization in Private International Law' [1990] Virginia Journal of International Law 1, 17.

95 Siehr (n 82) 75.

Alternative rules for cultural objects in transit[96] do not identify 'intermediate' and 'final' destinations of trafficking networks either. There is no ascertainable court to determine whether an object is in transit and the *forum* tends to apply its own law[97] without checking what theft may signal.

The easy transfer of stolen and looted art can be countered by, among other things, exceptions;[98] formulated exceptions;[99] or assessment of the diligence of the possessor during the acquisition.[100] The conditions for good faith[101] differ but its significance has not disappeared altogether.

A different category will change matters. On the premise that restitution of property is the underlying category, the connecting factor that indicates the applicable law for restitutionary issues could be the unjust factor.[102] The unjust factor is the circumstance that leads to receipt of a benefit at another's expense, in other words, what needs to be reversed or restituted. The unjust factor is either event-based or law-based. A forced transfer and an unconscientious receipt are event-based. It has been suggested that the law of the place with the closest and most real

---

96 E.g. the law of the place of destination; *Autocephalous Greek Orthodox Church of Cyprus v Goldberg and Feldman Fine Arts, Inc.*, 717 F Supp 1374 (SD Ind 1989) 1394–95; Art 101 of the Swiss Federal Statute on Private International Law of 18 December 1987; Art 88 of the Belgian PIL Code.

97 Carruthers, *The Transfer of Property* (n 28) § 1.28.

98 *Winkworth* (n 22) at 501. Carruthers *The Transfer of Property* (n 28) § 1.27, 1.46, 3.35; C Staker, 'Public International Law and the Lex Situs Principle in Property Conflicts and Foreign Expropriations' (1987) 58 BYBIL 151, 219.

99 Counsel for Mr Winkworth formulated an exception (at 510F) which the court declined (at 511C). The formulation was proposed to apply to 'movables that have been stolen from country A … and are then from country A removed without the owner's knowledge or consent and are then dealt with in country B without his knowledge and consent and are then returned voluntarily to country A'. It was suggested that the law of country A should determine whether the original owner is still the true owner of the movables.

100 The defence of neglect or omission to assert a right ('laches') encourages owners to be diligent in searching for stolen objects and database listings (*Solomon R Guggenheim Foundation v Lubell* 77 NY 2d 311 (1991)), but they also have the advantage of the heavy evidentiary burden imposed on the good faith purchaser (Kenyon and MacKenzie (n 20) 246–49).

101 MA Renold, 'Stolen Art: The Ubiquitous Question of Good Faith' in The International Bureau of the Permanent Court of Arbitration (ed), *Resolution of Cultural Property Disputes* (The Hague 2004) 251, 254ff.

102 G Panagopoulos, *Restitution in Private International Law* (Hart 2000) 159ff.

connection with the unjust factor ought to apply. When the law considers that restitution ought to be made, the law-based category applies and the legal system that is most closely connected with the alleged reason for restitution is identified.[103]

It has also been suggested that another connecting factor is at work, and that property rights in works of art ought to be governed by the law of the state that first banned export of a work of art in question, subject to exception in case of a vesting statute in respect of undiscovered objects.[104] Armbrüster maintains that a special connection exists between a work of art and an export ban, and that comity and international harmony of decision-making support such a choice.[105] This approach takes public interests into account.[106]

The main difficulty with these suggestions is the understanding, albeit unwritten, that conflicts rules form a closed list.[107] In addition, national court rulings display inconsistencies,[108] and recovery is not automatic in practice.[109] It would be undesirable to introduce a potential limitation that confines the claim to unjust enrichment. Application of the law that provides for an export ban is also likely to prove unpopular in cases where export controls are considered to be excessively broad in scope or stringent in their operation. Neither of these suggestions works when the find spot presents an issue.

It seems clear that hard and fast conflicts rules will not improve the level of protection of stolen and trafficked cultural objects. It would also

---

103 Panagopoulos (n 102) 168.

104 Armbrüster (n 86) 4.

105 Armbrüster (n 86) 5.

106 Pecoraro (n 94) 16.

107 E.g. Panagopoulos (n 102).

108 E.g. *Stato Francese v Ministero Italiano per i beni culturali e ambientali e De Contessini Livio*, Corte di Cass (Sez I) 24 November 1995, No 12166 (Italian purchaser of the French tapestries stolen from a public building in Lyon received protection depite the fact that the tapestries were inalienable under French law and under Italian law. Mutual recognition was not extended); *Republic of Ecuador v Danusso* Civil and District Court of Turin, First Civil Section 4410/79; Court of Appeal of Turin Second Civil Section 593/82; 18 *Rev dir int priv proc* 625 (1982) (Ecuadorian export ban in respect of a cultural item acquired in Ecuador recognised). Gazzini (n 31) 36; Siehr (n 82) 188–89; Prott (n 24) 266.

109 M Frigo, 'Ethical Rules and Codes of Honor Related to Museum Activities: A Complementary Support to the Private International Law Approach Concerning the Circulation of Cultural Property' [2009] IJCP 49, 60–61.

be undesirable to have a proliferation of conflicts rules[110] for a 'sub-category of property law' that is supposed to cover the discrete trade in art and cultural objects. Does the protection of private interests warrant the creation of a new regime?

The position in US law was rather uncertain for a time,[111] but today, a large majority of the states, even if *ad hoc*, favour the true owner. Thieves and swindlers are unable to pass good title because they do not have a right of ownership which can be transferred, as is the case with *nemo dat quod no habet*.[112] The provenance of the cultural object is generally valued more highly than the reputation of the merchant or intermediary. US courts are not shy to admit that policy shapes both the rules and the exceptions of conflicts rules. As indicated in Chapter 3,[113] they apply foreign substantive private law as the exception rather than as the rule, and revert to the application of forum law with great ease. The European conflicts system is more confined. It does not permit a multilateral reference rule to assume a public policy function. Rather, it allows an exception when the law that is indicated to apply encroaches on fundamental public policy considerations.[114] Classification, connection and the limits of the applicable law are supposed to inform the methodology. If choice of law structure and method are utilised to achieve a nuanced analysis, the risk of a proliferation of choice of law rules

110 Carruthers, *The Transfer of Property* (n 28) § 5.42 note 111.

111 See UCC § 2-403(1) (1991); E.g. *DeWeerth v Baldinger* 836 F2d 103 (2nd Circuit 1987) *cert denied* 108 S Ct 2823 (1988) (demand rule applied together with the due diligence of the owner rule; defendant retained the painting); 804 F Supp 539 (SDNY 1992) (inflexibility in respect of due diligence in making the demand under the demand and refusal rule of New York law); *DeWeerth v Baldinger* 24 F3d 416 (2nd Circuit 1994); 38 F3d 1266 (2nd Circuit NY 1994) *cert denied* 115 S Ct 512 (1994)(true owner required to make a diligent search for the stolen painting to prevent the statute of limitations from beginning to run).

112 E.g. *US v Mardirosian*, 602 F3d 1 (2010) 5–6 (possessor told family friend that he had legal title, and the ALR confirmed this to Sotheby's in order to safeguard the opportunity to seise the paintings when they reached London for auction).

113 Under 3.3.

114 L Raape, *Internationales Privatrecht* (5th edn, Verlag Franz Vahlen 1961) 90; M Martinek, 'The Seven Pillars of Wisdom in Private International Law: The German and the Swiss Experience with the Codification of Conflicts Law Rules' [2001] Chinese Yearbook of Private International Law and Comparative Law 15 § 4.2 <http://archiv.jura.uni-saarland.de/projekte/Bibliothek/text.php?id=221> accessed 24 February 2014.

disappears. This claim is investigated more closely with reference to structure and method of private international in Belgium, England and New York.

4.1 Nuances in the Belgian Code of Private International Law

Belgium is an active end- or destination point for the antiquities' trade because of the low risk of prosecution.[115] Nonetheless, owners have some legal protection when their moveable property has been stolen. They must exercise the *rei vindicatio*, if the transferee is in bad faith, within 30 years. *Rei vindicatio* also lies against the subsequent purchaser of the transferee in good faith within three years from the dispossession.[116] The Belgian Code of Private International Law[117] contains discrete new conflicts rules for objects that are officially considered to be part of a state's cultural heritage. The rules extend freedom and protection to the true owner or source state. The *lex originis* rule supplants the *lex situs* rule in respect of objects that come within the protective scope of public domain legislation (non-tradable cultural objects) but that are purchased in good faith abroad.[118] Other market states may well want to consider the ideas contained in the new rules.

Article 90 § 1 stipulates that, if an item which the state considers to be part of its cultural heritage were exported illegally in terms of that state's law at the time of removal,[119] the revindication is governed by its own law as at that time (*lex originis* or law of the item's provenance), or by the law of the place where the item is located at the time of revindication. The state may choose whichever option is most convenient. Under Article 90 § 2, the same protection may be extended to the possessor in good faith as is available under the law of the place where the item is located at the time of revindication, if the *lex originis* does not grant the possessor any protection. This alternative reference rule points the

---

[115] A Koush, 'Fight against the Illegal Antiquities' Traffic in the EU: Bridging the Legislative Gaps' *Bruges Political Research Papers* (December 2011) 14–16; Tijhuis (n 18) 128.

[116] Art 2279(2) of the Belgian Civil Code; DCFR VIII – 3:101 4872.

[117] Law of 16 July 2004 which holds the Code of Private International Law, Article 90, Belgian OJ 27 July 2004; in force from 1 October 2004.

[118] European Commission, *Study on Preventing and Fighting Illicit Trafficking in Cultural Goods in the European Union* (2011 final report) 107. Report available on http://ec.europa.eu/home-affairs/doc_centre/crime/docs/Report%20Trafficking%20in%20cultural%20goods%20EN.pdf.

[119] The retrospective application of the regulations of the claimant state is not permitted. Jakubowksi (n 7) 143.

international community in the direction of a more commonly held position on the transfer of ownership of cultural objects.[120]

Article 90 embodies the universal ideal of restitution and protection of cultural property and balances the rights of those who acted in good faith. When museums and collectors in Belgium resisted the introduction of these provisions into the new Private International Law Code, a time bar was introduced. Article 90 only applies from 1 October 2004 onwards, and claims from states that complied with Article 90 before that date are excluded.[121] Article 92 of the Belgian Private International Law Code is intended for stolen goods, but claims in respect of illicitly excavated objects may also be based on this provision. The original owner (and the state that has enacted a state ownership law) is offered an alternative reference rule. Revindication of a stolen object is governed, at the choice of the original owner, by the law of the state where the object was located when it disappeared, or by the law of the state where the object is located when the revindication action is brought. The rule implies that the owner knows where the object is to be found. If the law of the place where the object was located when it disappeared does not grant protection to the possessor in good faith, the possessor may invoke the protection offered by the law of the place where the object is located at the time of revindication.

Alternative reference rules enable the claimant to decide which law is applicable, but the defendant may claim the protection available under the law of the place where the object is situated. Choice of law method achieves a balancing of starkly opposing interests, but the formation of locks is not prevented thereby. The possessor may take advantage of the law at the point of destination, which may be integral to trafficking networks specialising in the transnational removal of cultural objects. The possessor may prefer a law that has been pre-selected on the basis of its capacity for title laundering.

Developments in English law have taken a very different turn.

---

[120] RM Collin, 'The Law and Stolen Art, Artifacts, and Antiquities' (1993) 36 Howard Law Journal 17, 24–25, 27; DL Crowell, 'Autocephalous Greek-Orthodox Church of Cyprus v Goldberg & Feldman Fine Arts Inc: Choice of Law in the Protection of Cultural Property' (1992) 27 Texas International Law Journal 173, 209.

[121] Art 127(7) of the Belgian Code of Private International Law; Jakubowski (n 7) 143.

4.2 Public Policy Status of the Limitations Provisions Used by English Courts

That the policy limits of the applicable law argument can assist was recognised in *Winkworth*.[122] Counsel for Mr Winkworth argued that broad considerations of policy have prompted US courts to protect the dispossessed owner whose property had been removed to another state without his consent.[123] European choice of law method gives effect to the substantive interests of the law when fundamental public policy considerations are threatened by the application of foreign law. However, the argument failed[124] because the court refused to accept that the owner's involuntary loss constituted grounds for an exception to the *lex situs* rule.[125] Slade J declared his willingness to take the escape route if any Italian provision were against what the English court could countenance,[126] but did not think an escape was warranted.

The duration and conditions of a prescriptive or limitation period may operate as aspects of public policy when the public policy interests of the forum are threatened; if this is the case, the *non*-application of the choice of law rule in question is justified. This device prevents time from affecting rights to stolen cultural objects.[127] *City of Gotha*[128] dealt with the English public policy status of the limitations provisions that apply to conversions by theft. The claim was for restitution of a tiny painting[129] looted during the Soviet occupation of Germany. The painting was located in Russia between 1946 and the mid-1980s and, briefly, in West Berlin from 1987 before being put on auction in London in 1992. The court found against the Panamanian company that consigned the work to

---

122 *Winkworth* (n 22) at 510D.

123 At 511G.

124 At 511H.

125 At 512D. Counsel relied on *Edgerly v Bush* (1880) 81NY199 (at 511H), which has no bearing on either cultural objects or on trafficking. The grounds for exceptional treatment (e.g. for goods in transit or where the purchaser did not act in good faith) were considered at 501.

126 At 514C–D.

127 In *Guggenheim Foundation v Lubell* (n 100), the mere lapse of time did not affect the respective possessory rights of the parties in a Chagall painting, and the Museum triumphed.

128 *City of Gotha and the Federal Republic of Germany v Sotheby's and Cobert Finance SA* transcript, unreported case no 1997/G/185, 9 September 1998, QBD.

129 'The Holy Family with Saints John and Elizabeth with Angels' (1603) by Joachim Wtewael.

Sotheby's, ruling that a thief who has fraudulently concealed the whereabouts of an artwork cannot have the benefit of a shorter limitation period. Moses J readily admitted that the conflicts method used was premised on reaching the desired result.[130] He recognised that *Winkworth* was not authoritative when the *lex situs* rule was contrary to English public policy embodied in the English Limitation Act of 1980. Because the vice of theft can be countered without necesssarily fixing on 'when' and 'where' it occurred, it was possible to see that the location of the painting did not prevent the court from noting that the claim was not time-barred under German law.[131] After all, commentators on the German Civil Code held the view that thieves, robbers and embezzlers could not count the period of possession by predecessors to their own advantage as part of the period of limitation. That the German limitation period runs irrespective of whether the claimant knows about the loss or is aware of the identity of the possessor, was acknowledged *obiter*. If the completion of the foreign limitation period rewarded thieves, transferees or other recipients of stolen property who were not in good faith, a conflict with English public policy arises.[132] That the limitation period in German law was longer than the period in English law did not justify subordinating the rights of the dispossessed owner to a possessor in bad faith. Since the exception for foreign limitation periods was not applied narrowly,[133] there was scope for finding that s 4 of the Limitation Act 1980 reflects English public policy against criminal gain.[134]

Gotha resonates with the progressive ruling in *Iran v Barakat Galleries Ltd.*[135] English courts seem increasingly willing to equate the sum of the rights of a foreign state in undiscovered objects to ownership in English law, and to relax the strict public policy objections to a claim based on state ownership legislation.[136]

New York courts adopt a unique approach, which is dealt with next.

---

130 § I.2(2).

131 § II.3 on Art 221 of the BGB (German Civil Code) and commentators' views.

132 Cf Art 2(1) of the Foreign Limitation Periods Act 1984; R Garnett, *Substance and Procedure in Private International Law* (OUP 2012) 274.

133 Kenyon and MacKenzie (n 20) 242–43. The general rule in s 1 of the Foreign Limitation Periods Act 1984 is that an English court will apply the limitation provision of the law of the cause.

134 The supplementary provisions of the 1980 Rome Convention were not relevant in this instance. The Rome I and Rome II Regulations are now broadly similar on the issue of limitation.

135 *Iran v Barakat Galleries Ltd* [2009] 1 QB 22 (CA).

136 Chechi (n 8) 106.

4.3 Combined Approach Used by New York Courts

As was explained under 4. above, the general position is that a thief cannot convey good title to a purchaser in good faith for value under common and statute law in the US.[137] Other parties further downstream cannot obtain clean title either. Time has been ruled insufficient to affect the respective possessory rights of the parties.[138] Against this backdrop, New York courts have devised a conflicts method that combines the choice of law process in respect of proprietary interests with policy grounds that inform the process and limit the application of the choice of law rule. This approach counters the problematic evasion of the law (*fraus legis*)[139] in a striking way, for it confronts the complex lock that enables the legal diversity factor combined with fraudulent intent and techniques used by dealers to launder title.[140]

New York law deploys several strategies to guard the state from becoming a haven for trafficking in art.[141] Artwork stolen during World War II belongs to the owner rather than to the possessor or innocent purchaser in good faith; the possessor bears the burden of proof that the art was not stolen; and the action accrues when the art is demanded back but refused.[142] The demand and refusal rule requires that a suit to recover

---

[137] Louisiana law is an exception (n 46).

[138] *Guggenheim v Lubell* (n 100) 318, 320 (burden of proving clean title rested on the purchaser; dispossessed owner has no duty to search diligently for missing art under the demand and refusal rule).

[139] If applied, the doctrine would mean that the forum court denies recognition to a valid act performed abroad if it were performed abroad with the intention to circumvent a prohibition in the law of the forum.

[140] Tijhuis (n 18) 202.

[141] P Lalive, 'A Disturbing International Convention: The UNIDROIT Convention on Cultural Objects' in LV Prott (ed), *Witnesses to History: A Compendium of Documents and Writings on the Return of Cultural Objects* (Unesco Publications 2009) 29, 29–30.

[142] The 'discovery' rule was first applied in *O'Keeffe v Snyder*, 83 NJ 478, 416 A2d 862 870 (NJ 1980) (concerning the weight of the burden of victim diligence). The early cases are *Menzel v List*, 267 NYS 2d 804, 809 (NY Sup Ct 1966), modified by *Menzel v List*, 279 NYS2d 608 (NY App Div 1967), rev'd by *Menzel v List*, 246 NE2d 742 (NY 1969). The action does not accrue when the wrongful act is committed, or when the whereabouts of the painting or identity of the possessor is discovered. More recently *Detroit Institute of Arts v Ullin*, 2007 US Dist LEXIS 28364 (ED Mich 31 March 2007)(action accrued in 1938); *Grosz v The Museum of Modern Art*, 772 F Supp 2d 473 (SDNY 2010), aff'd 403 Fed Appx 575 (2nd Circuit 2010), *cert denied* 132 S Ct 102; 181 L Ed 2d 30

stolen property be filed within three years of the original owner discovering its whereabouts, demanding its return, and being refused by the purchaser in good faith. The rule operates on the understanding that, as between the innocent victim and the purchaser in good faith, the equitable balance ought to favour the victim who had no choice in the matter over the purchaser, who had an opportunity to ascertain the provenance of the artwork,[143] or who could hire competent advisors.

Civil proceedings in New York are guided by the interest of a particular state in maintaining the integrity of the marketplace.[144] Theft signals the need to uncover the most significant relationship between the law and the cause of action. Due process requirements mean that the state in which the object ends up after having been voluntarily removed must recognise the ownership position prior to the move, but the provenance and conveyance history of an object be duly taken account of.[145] The art policies of the forum mediate the application of the *lex situs* rule[146] and preclude its application, unless the foreign law safeguards the position of the person who can claim clear title.[147]

Because the state must be prevented from being used as a marketplace for stolen or looted art, purchasers eager to maintain the *status quo* and to avoid liability must look after themselves. They have no choice but to use the opportunity to investigate provenance and innocent possessors.

Progressive courts prefer not to draw any distinction between theft and conversion. The Court of Appeals in *Mirvish v Mott*[148] recently ruled that the true owner has a right to claim a sculpture affected by conversion. Yulla, the widow of sculptor Jacques Lipschitz, had gifted it to her long-time companion, who had sold his interest in the work to Mirvish. Meanwhile, Yulla's son had sold it abroad. Mirvish alleged conversion, which ultimately prevented the relevant period being counted to the

---

(2011) (action time-barred on account of implicit refusal of demand; contesting possession signalled refusal, which allowed conversion and replevin claims to accrue).

143 *Menzel v List I* 267 NYS 2d 804, 809 (NY Sup Ct 1966); LM Kaye, 'Avoidance and Resolution of Cultural Heritage Disputes: Recovery of Art Looted during the Holocaust' [2006] Willamette Journal of International Law and Dispute Resolution 243, 259.

144 Chechi (n 8) 103–4; Symeonides (n 56) 362; Lee (n 56) 748, 754.

145 Lee (n 56) 730–1.

146 § 6(2) Restatement (Second) of Conflict of Laws Vol 1.

147 S Symeonides, 'The American Revolution and the European Evolution in Choice of Law: Reciprocal Lessons' [2008] Tulane Law Review 1741, 1746 n 25; Lee (n 56) 729.

148 *Mirvish v Mott*, 18 NY3d 510 (3 January 2012).

defendant's advantage. The court did not distinguish between theft and conversion, and regarded as irrelevant the expiry of statutory limitations to legal title.[149]

5. CONCLUSION

The cause of involuntary loss has a role to play in disputes concerning title to cultural objects. The solutions adopted by municipal systems in proprietary disputes are directed by distinctions regarding the legal nature of the property, the cause of loss of possession and the circumstances of acquisition. If the loss has been caused by theft, stricter principles ought to apply to protect the owner's rights in cultural objects. Extending the definition of theft to conversion, and refusing to permit time periods to render an object immune from recovery, will counteract title laundering insofar as domestic legal systems are concerned.

Private international law sustains the complex 'lock' mechanism that relies on strict compliance with the law designated by the *lex situs* principle to evade another law. This mechanism facilitates illicit trafficking, leaves art and cultural objects vulnerable to diverse national legal approaches, routinely supports the circulation of tainted works of art, and challenges the foundations of choice of law theory and practice. The aspiration to prevent easy marketplaces for art thieves, smugglers and their transferees is critical to any decision on the merits. It helps choice of law method to brace itself against the impact of dogmatic orthodoxy on the illicit trade in art, so as to preserve the integrity of transactions for all owners, not only some. Several alternative reference rules, modifications, exceptions and formulated exceptions have been proposed for title and limitations conflicts. Ultimately, result-selection is the only route to a desirable outcome. A policy choice is required in favour of the deprived party, who had no option but to succumb to the vice of theft. Once this functional choice is made, the method follows.

Chapter 5 has demonstrated the implications of a *vitium reale* approach, which counters an over-inclusive and unstable *lex situs* rule that bolsters the illicit trade of art and cultural objects. Legal systems acknowledge *vitium reale* in art litigation in different ways. All of them make use of the broad system and structure of private international law to support deprived parties or their descendants in circumstances of the enduring character of cultural property. None of them utilise fixed rules

---

149 *Mirvish v Mott* (n 148) 520.

or rigid modifications. A single-method strategy is bound to fail to constrain an over-inclusive *lex situs* rule that amplifies the illicit trade of cultural objects. It can only undermine the support which deprived parties require. English conflicts method demonstrates dis-applying foreign law that conflicts manifestly with fundamental principles of justice. Result-selection is enabled by a value-choice against dishonest purchasers and purchasers who do not investigate provenance. New York law conditions the *lex situs* rule when the dispossession of the original owner was involuntary and unlawful. The Code of Private International Law in Belgium provides new discrete rules for stolen and illegally exported art and cultural objects. The Code balances opposing interests in an interesting way that does not confine the claimant to one fixed *lex situs* formula. However, allowing the defendant to opt for the protection offered by the law of the location of the object when it disappeared, or when the action is brought, does nothing to break any lock that may form.

The strength of the *vitium reale* argument intensifies in respect of ownership and restitution claims involving Nazi spoliated art. Chapter 6 deals with restitution on the merits and procedure-based arguments for non-restitution in this category of art claims.

6. Deciding claims for restitution of Nazi spoliated art on their merit: Towards value rationality

1. INTRODUCTION

The 'Final Solution' demanded the deliberate extermination of the culture of European Jews who were in Nazi-occupied Europe during World War II.[1] The theft of paintings was 'relatively low on the totem pole of Nazi atrocities',[2] but the plundering of cultural property in possession of European Jews between 1933 and 1945 was a national policy that was given high priority.[3] Art was programmatically and methodically looted from German, French, Dutch, Austrian and Belgian Jews, and from Poles and Russians of any faith. This plunder occurred at the behest of Adolf Hitler, Reichsmarshall Hermann Göring and the Minister of Art and Culture, Alfred Rosenberg.[4] The Nazis considered the ideologically motivated looting a 'safeguarding' of art treasures.[5] Their main project was the pursuit of art which they considered valuable in a classical sense.

[1] 'Nazism' is widely understood as a political epithet that refers to 'Nationalsozialist' in *Nationalsozialistische Deutsche Arbeiterpartei*, led by Hitler from 1920. The word derives from the German form of the masculine proper name Ignatius, i.e. 'Ignatz'. See A Rabinbach and SL Gilman, *Third Reich Sourcebook* (University of California Press 2013) 4 note 3.

[2] K Platoni, 'The Ten Million Dollar Woman' (*East Bay Express*, 4 August 2004).

[3] MA Torsen, 'National Reactions to Cultural Property Looting in Nazi Germany: A Window on Individual Effort and International Disarray' [2005] EJCL 1, 3.

[4] H Feliciano, 'The Great Culture Robbery: The Plunder of Jewish-Owned Art' in A Beker (ed) *The Plunder of Jewish Property During the Holocaust: Confronting European History* (NY University Press 2001) 164, 165–66; H Feliciano, *The Lost Museum: The Nazi Conspiracy to Steal the World's Greatest Works of Art* (Basic Books 1997) 31–42.

[5] Order issued by Hermann Göring concerning the distribution of Jewish art treasures, 5 November 1940.

'Shopping catalogues' were put together so that Hitler could choose which artwork and furniture he desired from across Europe[6] for a Führer Museum in Linz, his hometown in Austria. Linz was set to become the cultural centre of Europe.[7] Various other museum collections were to be expanded, and the personal collections of the Nazi elite soon became impressive.[8] Modern and abstract works of art were collected for a different purpose. Hitler and his regime believed these works to corrupt the German people and insult German sentiment. 'Degenerate art' by Jews, non-Jews, German and non-German modern artists in public ownership in Germany was destroyed in order to eradicate their wider impact and democratic message. Approximately twenty thousand such works were impounded for an exhibition of 'Entartete Kunst', a defamatory public display scheduled to take place in 1937.[9] Many were traded or returned to the open market with the help of a few accredited dealers such as Hildebrand Gurlitt. Ideology and the profit motive clashed, however. The dealers were instructed to remove all reference to the museum provenances of the works that were going to be sold, and yet the provenances were needed to maximise the selling prices. Consequently, the instruction frequently went unheeded.[10] Sales on the Paris art market or in Switzerland yielded billions of dollars in proceeds which the Nazis used for their own financial benefit and for that of the Third Reich.[11]

Looted artworks and 'degenerate art' were dispersed widely and amidst uneven provenance practices.[12] Dealing became common soon after the

---

[6] Rosenberg's letter to Hitler accompanying albums of photographs of works of art stolen for Hitler's museum dated 16 April 1943; J Stengle, 'Photo Albums Related to Nazi Art Theft Unveiled' *Yahoo News* (28 March 2012).

[7] R Edsel, *The Monuments Men: Allied Heroes, Nazi Thieves, and the Greatest Treasure Hunt in History* (Center Street 2009) 12–14.

[8] See the first catalogue raisonné of the Göring painting collection, compiled by NH Yeide, *Beyond the Dreams of Avarice: The Hermann Goering Collection* (Laurel Publishing 2009).

[9] U Fleckner, 'Marketing the Defamed: On the Contradictory Use of Provenances in the Third Reich' in G Feigenbaum and I Reist (eds), *Provenance: An Alternative History of Art* (Getty Research Institute 2012) 137, 139.

[10] Fleckner (n 9) 145, 149.

[11] MJ Bazyler, 'Nuremberg in America: Litigating the Holocaust in United States Courts' (2000) 34 University of Richmond Law Review 1, 161; N Palmer, *Museums and the Holocaust: Law, Principles and Practice* (Institute of Art and Law Ltd 2000) 11.

[12] E.g. T von Stockhausen, 'The Failure of Provenance Research in Germany' in G Feigenbaum and I Reist (eds), *Provenance: An Alternative History of Art* (Getty Research Institute 2012) 124, 130–33.

war.[13] Officers, thieves and dealers who brokered deals on behalf of the Nazis were active both within Germany and in places like Paris, Switzerland and Italy.[14] Switzerland offered a well-placed outlet for the art trade as a vital component of a lock, for instance.

Protection for the good-faith purchaser in Swiss law has always offered refuge for keen buyers.[15] During the Nazi era, there were several art professionals in Switzerland who were linked to top officials in the Nazi Party and who were willing to launder stolen art. Private individuals, trusts and foundations, private museums, state museums and governments acquired these works with varying degrees of good faith.

The Russians lost many cultural treasures.[16] 'Trophy brigades' were dispatched from Moscow to collect art, archives and books to be transported back to the Soviet Union. Consequently, a large number of works appeared in Russia. The trophy brigades expedited their work when it became clear that the Allies were collecting Nazi art for purposes of making returns.[17] A complex mix of concern for artwork, opportunism and a desire to avenge the Nazi looting motivated the trophy hunts. Several works and collections were returned to the GDR between 1955 and 1960, but after 1960, the Soviet government publicly denied possession of any more trophy art, and cultural property is now retained as war reparations.[18] No agreement has been reached on the issue of restitution.[19] Allied forces who engaged in counter-theft contributed to making the past inaccessible to the generation who experienced the horror.

---

[13] E.g. 'Adele Bloch-Bauer I'; 'Adele Bloch-Bauer II'; 'Bücherwald'; 'Apfelbaum I'; 'Häuser in Unterach am Attersee' by Gustav Klimt (1862–1918); 'Femme en Blanc' and 'The Absynthe Drinker' by Pablo Picasso (1881–1973).

[14] Yeide (n 8) 14–15.

[15] Arts 930–934 of the Swiss Civil Code of 10 December 1907; D Carvajal, 'Wooing the Public to Recover' *New York Times* (19 March 2014).

[16] K Akinsha and G Kozlov with S Hochfield, *Beautiful Loot: The Soviet Plunder of Europe's Art Treasures* (Random House 1995).

[17] Akinsha and Kozlov (n 16) 79, 121; AB Sargent, 'New Jurisdictional Tools for Displaced Cultural Property in Russia' 2010 Yearbook of Cultural Property Law 167, 171.

[18] JM Henckaerts and L Doswald-Beck, *Customary International Humanitarian Law Vol I Rules* (International Committee of the Red Cross 2005) 137–38; Akinsha et al. (n 16) 43–51; Sargent (n 17) 171–72.

[19] Akinsha et al. (n 16) 243–59; S Evans, 'Merkl and Putin View Exhibition of Disputed Art' *BBC News Europe* (22 June 2013).

Collectively, the looted works of art constitute an enormous 'world museum', which is oddly reminiscent of Hitler's last will. Hitler also had in place a detailed plan for the cultural re-appropriation of works of art taken from Germany and dispersed throughout the world,[20] which he did not have the time to bring to fruition.

Notwithstanding Allied restitution initiatives and the compensation paid by West Germany, future generations continue to be affected by the injustice suffered by the persecuted families.[21] The scale and intensity of this massive property transfer and trade in the proceeds of war crimes exceeded anything that had gone before. The liquidation of entire families, towns and villages has proven difficult to rectify. Those who were exterminated could not apply for restitution; those who escaped could not always file applications for restitution or compensation before the deadlines expired. Many claims continued to simmer underneath the surface of Cold War tensions.[22]

Chance finds continually remind Europe of its unfinished business. They challenge states, both individually and as a community. When the media learnt about the art hauls that were discovered in the dwellings of the son and heir of the leading art dealer, Hildebrand Gurlitt, it made international headlines.[23] Hildebrand Gurlitt engaged in business with the

---

[20] 'Kümmel Report' (a complete list of German art work that had been removed since 1500 and that, being of Aryan origin, qualified to be returned to Germany). For more, see Feliciano, *The Lost Museum* (n 4) 24–30.

[21] E.g. *US v Portrait of Wally*, 105 F Supp 2d 288 (SDNY 2000); *US v Portrait of Wally*, No 99 Civ 9940, 2000 WL 1890403 (SDNY December 28, 2000); *US v Portrait of Wally*, No 99 Civ 9940 (MBM), 2002 WL 553532 (SDNY April 12, 2002); *US v Portrait of Wally, A Painting by Egon Schiele*, No 99-CV-09940 (SDNY filed July 29, 2010).

[22] LH Nicholas, *The Rape of Europa: The Fate of Europe's Treasures in the Third Reich and the Second World War* (Alfred Knopf 1994); B Demarsin, 'Let's Not Talk about Terezín: Restitution of Nazi Era Looted Art and the Tenuousness of Public International Law' (2011) 37 Brooklyn Journal of International Law 117; HN Spiegler, 'Recovering Nazi-Looted Art: Report from the Front Lines' (2001) 16 Connecticut Journal of International Law 297, 301.

[23] *Focus* magazine first reported the discovery on 3 November 2013. See 'Meisterwerke zwischen Müll – Fahnder entdecken in München Nazi-Schatz in Milliardenhöhe' *Focus Online* (4 November 2013) <http://www.focus.de/kultur/kunst/nazi-raubkunst-meisterwerke-zwischen-muell-fahnder-entdecken-kunstschatz-in-milliardenhoehe_aid_1147066.html> accessed 25 February 2014. The investigative journalism on the part of *Der Spiegel* contributed to shedding light on Germany's inaction and the wider implications of this inaction. See e.g. 'Legal Issues Complicate Munich Art Treasure Trove Find' (*Spiegel Online International*, 18 November 2013) <http://www.spiegel.de/international/germany/

Nazis. Assigned to recycle and sell these pieces for hard currency abroad, he brokered deals on their behalf after 1933. German authorities had been investigating tax evasion since February 2012 and had taken the works into custody pending the outcome of their investigation. They were slow to make any public announcement of the art haul, but having made it, return was swiftly made.[24] Germany's failure to take efficient steps to clarify the provenance of the works, and to identify Nazi loot publicly, caused an outcry. The press condemned Germany for its secrecy.[25] Altogether six claimants have come forward to date, and recent media reports claim that between forty and fifty works are implicated.[26]

Gurlitt's son inherited possession of the artworks from his father more than thirty years ago. A true owner's claim for restitution of the artworks may be time-barred by the German courts, even if possession was in bad faith.[27] A proposal was made for reform, but the difficult question is about its connection with the passage of time.[28] Should time limits affect the claims of victims of Nazi persecution and their heirs at all? The relationship that is developing between international law and statutory limitations continues to be topical indeed, considering that the lifespan of remaining generations of Holocaust survivors is fast nearing its end.

From a legal point of view, disputes involving Nazi spoliated art are complex. The work itself is always highly specific. If a legal-technical perspective that derives from a property rights framework determines the issue, the claimant may have lost legal title due to a legal technicality

---

legal-issues-complicate-munich-art-treasure-trove-find-a-934071.html> accessed 24 February 2014. *Der Spiegel* predicted that every piece with uncertain provenance would take years to solve. Competing claims in respect of 'Seated Woman' have already delayed the restitution of that work.

24 AFP, 'Jewish Council Criticizes Gurlitt Nazi Art Return' (*The Local,* 21 November 2013).

25 A task force of six provenance researchers was established and a list of works suspected of having been looted was posted on <www.lostart.de> accessed 24 February 2014 (the lost art internet database of the central office for documentation of lost cultural property administered by the Koordinierungsstelle Magdeburg). More works have since been added to the list.

26 O Aderet, 'German Collector Wants to Return Art Looted by Nazis', Haaretz, 28 March 2014, <http://www.haaretz.com/jewish-world/jewish-world-news/.premium-1.582291>.

27 S 197 BGB.

28 W Veraart and L Winkel, 'An Introduction to Dilemmas of Post-War Restitution in Europe' in W Veraart and L Winkel (eds), *The Post-war Restitution of Property Rights in Europe* (Rvp Press 2011) 7.

such as the time constraints in respect of bringing a claim.[29] The claimant has to locate the art, establish the right to claim, and deal with the effect of the passage of time. Several non-legal dimensions intrude on contractual and non-contractual disputes.[30]

Whereas only about ten Nazi spoliated art claims were filed in the US before 1995,[31] the availability of information has more recently sparked an unprecedented number of claims in state courts.[32] Precedent and the role of technical defences based on statutory limitations and prescription in shaping precedent count among the reasons for the dramatic increase.[33]

Obstacles to restitution may inhere in the law itself. They may escape attention altogether for this very reason, or worse, the justification of being a legal standard serves as a sure-fire justification for non-restitution. The legal requirements for the transmission of ownership are frequently the most difficult obstacle to counter. The very rule that is supposed to govern the problematic behaviour creates the opportunity for non-restitution. The decision of whether restitution is justified necessarily invites a confrontation between facts, law and ethics.

This chapter starts with the legal basis for restitution claims in international law so that domestic legal developments can be viewed in a wider international context. Consideration is given to the post-war restitution of property rights as well as the more open policy-based restitution post 1989. In exploring their options, claimants may engage in

---

29 S Shapiro, 'Note: How Republic of Austria v. Altmann and United States v. Portrait of Wally Relay the Past and Forecast the Future of Nazi Looted-Art Restitution Litigation' (2008) 34 William Mitchell Law Review 1147, 1149; N Murphy, 'Splitting Images: Shared-Value Settlements in Nazi-Era Art Restitution Claims' (2009) 3 Florida Entertainment Law Review 1 (*Social Science Research Network*, 25 February 2010) <http://ssrn.com/abstract=1559373> accessed 25 February 2014.

30 S Theurich, 'Update on Alternative Dispute Resolution in the Art and Cultural Heritage Sector' (*International Bar Association*, August 2009) <http://www.ibanet.org/Article/Detail.aspx?ArticleUid=c93cf2fa-f5f6-4a64-a7d1-8bd907fdf3dd> accessed 24 February 2014.

31 Bazyler (n 11) 165.

32 Demarsin (n 22) 121; I Stamatoudi, *Cultural Property Law and Restitution* (Edward Elgar 2011) 190–92.

33 E.g. *Orkin v Taylor*, 487 F3d 734 (9th Circuit 2007); 128 S Ct 491(claim to 'Vue de l'Asile et de la Chapelle de St. Remy'); In general LF Redman, 'The Foreign Sovereign Immunities Act: Using a "Shield" Statute as a "Sword" for Obtaining Federal Jurisdiction in Art and Antiquities Cases' (2008) 31 Fordham Int'l LJ 781, 784–85.

jurisdictional trade when immunity legislation does not prevent them from doing so. There is an inexorable link between process and substance in this area. A hearing on the substantive merits of the case may be precluded on technical or procedural grounds. This factor may be attractive to a claimant, who may choose the venue for proceedings on this position. Domestic and applicable law arguments continue to provide justification for non-restitution. Arbitration and negotiation will not be given detailed treatment,[34] but it is worth noting that justice pluralism[35] is unavoidable. Policy-based restitution has implications for choice of law argument, and private international law cannot be ignored, therefore. This chapter considers the scope of the definition of a 'forced sale' and the limits of the contribution which multilateral conflicts rules such as the *lex situs* rule can make in this context. Specific consideration is given to forced sales concluded in Switzerland at the time, and the implications of these sales for restitution claims today.

2. LEGAL BASIS OF RESTITUTION CLAIMS TO NAZI SPOLIATED ART IN INTERNATIONAL LAW[36]

The international community recognised a need to prohibit wartime plunder by international agreement. The 1907 Hague Convention on the Laws and Customs of War on Land[37] reaffirmed and expanded on the principle without an attempt to regulate the return of stolen property. Most peace treaties contain clauses on restitution of war booty, of which cultural objects were a popular kind, but they find no application in the context of Nazi spoliated art claims. With the Declaration of London in 1943, the Allies publicly disavowed the protection of anyone who acquired looted works of art in good faith, on the basis that no one ought to benefit from unlawful acts.[38] Important elements of US executive policy on the validity of the acts of Nazi officials are contained in the

[34] On arbitration, see Chapter 4 sub 7.4. Negotiation has not proved popular in the context of Nazi spoliated art disputes.

[35] For a definition, see Chapter 3.

[36] This section is based on C Roodt, 'State Courts or ADR in Nazi-era Art Disputes: A Choice "More Apparent Than Real?"' (2012) 3 Cardozo Journal of Conflict Resolution 421, 426–30.

[37] Art 23 of the Convention (IV) Respecting the Laws and Customs of War on Land and its Annex of Regulations, The Hague, 18 October 1907, The Hague, 18 October 1907, TS 539; entry into force 26 January 1910.

[38] K Chamberlain, 'Holocaust Art Claims and Public International Law' (2008) 13 Art Antiquity and Law 351, 353.

1943 London Declaration.[39] The policy was applied with great enthusiasm at first. A number of legal instruments subsequently reinforced these measures,[40] but enthusiasm dwindled as time passed.[41] Claims eventually stalled.

World War II was the first time an army had fought a war with a conservation corps in charge of a front-line monuments protection programme. Between 1943 and 1951, the Monuments, Fine Arts and Archives Section of the Allied Forces – known as 'Monuments Men' – saved many fine objects from harm. Most of the early volunteers had some experience as museum directors, curators, art scholars, artists, archivists or architects. They aspired to constrain attacks on significant archaeological sites and museums and to mitigate combat damage.[42] Towards the end of the war they started searching for art stolen or looted by the Nazis and restored them to their true owners.[43] The corps fulfilled their mission despite the inadequacy of transportation, supplies and personnel.[44] They knew about Hildebrand Gurlitt's connection to high-level Nazi circles, and although they did not regard him as a serious criminal, they referred to him as the Führer's art dealer.[45]

The International Military Tribunal at Nuremberg declared the plunder and spoliation of art a war crime.[46] The definition of 'war crimes' in the Charter of the Nuremberg Tribunal conformed with the customary international law prohibition against the 'confiscation of private property by aggressive occupying powers'. The same idea appeared in Article 46

---

[39] Inter-Allied Declaration against Acts of Dispossession Committed in Territories under Enemy Occupation and Control, 5 January 1943.

[40] E.g. Final Act of the Bretton Woods Conference in 1944 and the Final Act of the Paris Conference on Reparations in 1945.

[41] KA Falconer, 'When Honour Will Not Suffice' (2000) 21 University of Pennsylvania Journal of International Economic Law 383, 387.

[42] Edsel (n 7) 2.

[43] Edsel (n 7) xiv.

[44] Edsel (n 7) 2.

[45] F Bohr, L Gorris, U Knöfel, S Röbel and M Sontheimer, 'Art Dealer to the Führer: Hildebrand Gurlitt's Deep Nazi Ties' *Spiegel Online* (23 December 2013).

[46] Art 6 of the Charter of the International Military Tribunal at Nuremberg annexed to the London Agreement on War Criminals, 8 August 1945, 82 (no 251) UNTS 279; Inter-Allied Declaration of 1943; Various Different Treaties of Peace, including Treaty of Peace with Finland, 10 February 1947, vol 48 No 746 UNTS 183, Art 25.

of the 1907 Hague Convention and the Kellogg-Briand Pact of 1928.[47] It has been suggested that states can, at best, act as custodians of property tainted by a war crime;[48] they cannot impede the ownership interests of original owners.[49] However, in the absence of state practice, the duty of third states to ensure restitution of looted cultural objects remains contested.[50] This has important implications for entities in possession of Nazi loot or degenerate art that represent third state governments and that may yet have live claims against them. Whether the spoliation also qualifies as a 'crime against humanity' is a more controversial issue, because this concept did not exist prior to the Charter of the International Military Tribunal at Nuremberg.[51]

The Second Protocol to the 1954 Hague Convention for the Protection of Cultural Property in the Event of Armed Conflict[52] sets a start point for the obligation to return, and establishes the principle that cultural objects removed during armed conflict shall never be retained as war reparations. Unfortunately, this instrument applies to military action, not

---

47 Dissenting opinion by Wald J in *Princz v Federal Republic of Germany* 26 F3d 116, 1176–1185 (DC Circuit 1994), followed in *Altmann v Republic of Austria* 317 F3d 954, 964 (9th Circuit 2002); Nuremberg Decision 6 FRD 69, 110 (1946–1947) <http://www.uniset.ca/other/cs4/6FRD69.html> accessed 24 February 2014. MD Murray, 'Stolen Art and Sovereign Immunity: The Case of Altmann v Austria' (2003–2004) 27 Columbia Journal of Law and Arts 301, 316, 319.

48 Art 6(b) of the Charter of the International Military Tribunal, Nuremberg Trial Proceedings vol 1; H Hartung, 'The Holocaust and World War II Looted Art: Arbitrated between Great Dreams and Reality' in The International Bureau of the Permanent Court of Arbitration (ed), *Resolution of Cultural Property Disputes* (The Hague 2004) 327, 333.

49 C Pell, 'Using Arbitral Tribunals to Resolve Disputes Relating to Holocaust-Looted Art' in International Bureau of the Permanent Court of Arbitration (ed), *Resolution of Cultural Property Disputes* (The Hague 2004) 307, 315.

50 Henckaerts and Doswald-Beck (n 18) 136–37; Chamberlain (n 38) 355.

51 A Kaczorowska, *Public International Law* (4th edn, Routledge 2010) 212. A Rosenberg, head of the ERR, was convicted for the war crime of plunder at Nuremberg.

52 The Hague, 26 March 1999; entry into force in 2004. For status table see <http://www.icrc.org/ihl.nsf/INTRO/590> accessed 24 February 2014. The US and the UK have not ratified it.

restitution.[53] Moreover, it applies to a very limited category of cultural objects with a view only to preventing their damage, destruction and pillaging in future conflicts.

Convention claims for restitution may be brought under both the UNESCO and UNIDROIT Conventions,[54] which apply in peacetime and to situations of military occupation. However, cultural heritage conventions do not present options for settling Nazi spoliated art claims at this stage.[55] The UNESCO Convention simply requires the recovering state to compensate an innocent purchaser without providing for private parties' claims. The UNDROIT Convention considers claims for restitution brought by private individuals,[56] providing that '[t]he possessor of a cultural object which has been stolen shall return it.'[57] There are technical complications with claims in terms of the UNIDROIT Convention because no opportunity exists to claim objects looted prior to 1963. The absolute limitation is 50 years since the theft occurred.

3. RESTITUTION IN THE POST-WAR ERA

The post-war restitution of the '40s and '50s was based on Allied restitution laws. During this period, the successor state was prevented by law from inheriting heirless property, or from profiting from Nazi extermination policies. Post-war laws in Germany and Austria repudiated all spurious 'transactions' of the Nazi era, including art 'deals' that were just made to appear legal. In Germany, the seizure of Jewish property by the Nazi regime has been regarded as null and void since the end of World War II.[58] Austria also declared all transactions motivated by Nazi ideology null and void.[59] Allied lawmakers required new clauses to be

---

[53] LJ Borodkin, 'The Economics of Antiquities Looting and a Proposed Legal Alternative' (1995) 95 Columbia Law Review 377, 388.

[54] See Art 7(b)(ii) of the 1970 UNESCO Convention on the Means of Prohibiting and Preventing the Illicit Import, Export and Transfer of Ownership of Cultural Property; Art 3 of the 1995 UNIDROIT Convention on Stolen or Illegally Exported Cultural Objects respectively.

[55] Falconer (n 41) 389.

[56] Arts 1 and 2 of the UNIDROIT Convention.

[57] Art 3(1) of the UNIDROIT Convention.

[58] Military Government Law No 59, 12 Fed. Reg. 7983 (29 November 1947).

[59] *Republic of Austria v Altmann*, 541 US 677, 682 (2004); *Majken Hofmann, Anna Lokrantz, Maria Müller, Andreas Müller Hofmann und Lena Müller Hofmann v Republic of Austria* (21 November 2005) (Arbitral award in

added to the German Civil Code which were unknown to German civil law. Among these was that good faith enjoyed no legal protection even if the purchaser in good faith did not know about the previous Aryanisation. Also, organisations that were entitled to claim heirless property had to be set up.[60] In the end, however, even these far-reaching changes proved inadequate.[61]

Ever since 1989, restitution has become more policy-based and ethics-driven.[62] When the Berlin Wall fell and the Eastern Bloc disintegrated, government records documenting Nazi operations against Jewish culture in the Third Reich and catalogues became accessible. Access to these records has helped claimants to meet the evidentiary burden associated with proving title. Various organisations, commissions and task forces were set up for purposes of restitution of spoliated art. Several initiatives focus on US museum collections,[63] but some also include data from non-US museum collections.[64] No database is comprehensive or operates

German) <www.bslaw.com/altmann/Zuckerkandl/Klage/284724.doc> accessed 24 February 2014.

60 Veraart and Winkel (n 28) 81, 84ff.

61 Veraart and Winkel (n 28) 81.

62 Veraart and Winkel (n 28) 2.

63 E.g. the New York Holocaust Claims Processing Office <http://www.dfs.ny.gov/consumer/holocaust/hcpoindex.htm>; the Interagency Working Group (IWG) on Nazi War Crimes and Japanese Imperial Government Records established in terms of the Nazi War Crimes Records Disclosure Act of 1998 <http://www.archives.gov/iwg/>; and the Nazi-Era Provenance Internet Portal <http://www.nepip.org/> which provides a searchable online registry of objects, which is a single point of contact to US museum collections. All sites accessed 24 February 2014.

64 E.g. Digitisation is being used by IFAR (since 1969) and the Art Loss Register. The ALR operates as a not for profit company with a permanent international database of stolen and missing works of art, antiques and valuables. The Claims Conference set up a comprehensive programme together with the World Jewish Restitution Organization (WJRO), to perform checks on the provenance of current museum collections and on claims made by individual survivors and heirs of owners. It supported the imaging of the *Einsatzstab Reichsleiter Rosenberg* (ERR) files in Kiev, Moscow, Vilnius, Berlin, Koblenz, Amsterdam, Paris, New York, and Washington with a view to making the ERR records generally available. It joined forces with the US Holocaust Memorial Museum to create a database of art objects processed at the Jeu de Paume in Paris between 1940 and 1944. *Cultural Plunder by the Einsatzstab Reichsleiter Rosenberg: Database of Art Objects at the Jeu de Paume* <http://www.errproject.org/jeudepaume/about/> accessed 24 February 2014, comprises micro-form records of the Holocaust from archives all over the world. PK Grimsted, *Reconstructing the Record of Nazi Cultural Plunder: A Survey of the Dispersed*

with worldwide governmental support. The legal obstacles standing in the way of claimants and heirs keen to recover ancestral property attracted more attention.[65] This led to greater willingness to reassess the relationship between the law and the passage of time. The relationship between prescription and international law has now become more visible in Europe. Commentators anticipate changes in prize law and in respect of spoliation rules.[66]

Commentators have argued in favour of international solutions and common international standards to help quantify the original owner's search after confiscation of the object in question.[67] Proposals have not yielded any common rules or uniform procedure as an outcome,[68] and public international law has not progressed in the direction of a single unified efficient mechanism for the resolution of these claims. In fact, some of the proposals for a single international body are highly problematical (as was indicated in Chapter 4).[69] A new international arbitration agreement with limited but exclusive jurisdiction is equally unlikely.[70] Private international law could play a definite role if a property claim is held to have been extinguished by prescription, however. Private international law could permit the claim to be brought either by way of

---

Archives of the Einsatzstab Reichsleiter Rosenberg (ERR) (International Institute of Social History IISH-IISG, Amsterdam, 2010, at <http://www.iisg.nl/publications/errsurvey/> accessed 24 February 2014) provides links to many dispersed materials now available on the Internet with additional digital contributions. The Getty Provenance Index is also worth mentioning.

65 Veraart and Winkel (n 28) 2; B Schönenberger, *The Restitution of Cultural Assets* (Eleven 2009) 228.

66 Veraart and Winkel (n 28) 10.

67 A Tompkins, 'A Permanent International Art Crime Tribunal?' (2009) 2 The Journal of Art Crime 35. See also RE Lerner, 'The Nazi Art Theft Problem and the Role of the Museum: A Proposed Solution to Disputes over Title' (1998) 31 New York University Journal of International Law and Policy 15, 36–37; A O'Connell, 'Immunity from Seizure Study' (30 September 2005) <http://www.lending-for-europe.eu/fileadmin/CM/public/training/Antwerp/Immunity_from_Seizure_Paper_Anna_O_Connell.pdf> accessed 24 February 2014.

68 Murphy (n 29) 9ff.

69 Pell (n 49) 307ff; OC Pell, 'The Potential for Mediation/Arbitration Commission to Resolve Disputes Relating to Artworks Stolen or Looted during World War II' (1999) 10 *De Paul-LCA Journal of Art and Entertainment Law* 10. Also A Tompkins, 'A Permanent International Art Crime Tribunal?' (2009) 2 The Journal of Art Crime 35.

70 Pell (n 49) 310; Falconer (n 41) 383; JA Kreder, 'Reconciling Individual and Group Justice with the Need for Repose in Nazi-Looted Art Disputes: Creation of an International Tribunal' (2007) 73 Brooklyn Law Review 155.

classification or by way of the public policy exception. The painting 'The Holy Family with Saints John and Elizabeth with Angels' (1603) by Joachim Wtewael (1566–1638) was ordered to be restituted to the City of Gotha and the Federal Republic of Germany in the *Gotha* case.[71] The case was heard in England, but it concerned looting from a German museum during the Soviet occupation of Germany, in January 1946. The location of the work between 1946 and the mid-1980s did not prevent the court from referring to the public policy embodied in the English 1980 Limitation Act. If the statutory limitations of the applicable law were short, public policy could prevent them running in favour of a thief and any transferee that did not purchase in good faith.[72]

4. CLAIMANTS' OPTIONS – THE JURISDICTIONAL TRADE

The factors that favour a non-forensic approach to provenance and dispute settlement in claims involving Nazi spoliated art are not limited to a less legalistic treatment of passage of time. First, these claims implicate more than property interests, and frequently the claimant is after more than the material value of the object in question.[73] Secondly, the legal framework can be unyielding,[74] and litigation time-consuming, costly and complex. Parties either compete for all-or-nothing in court or in arbitration, or they consent to a non-judicial dispute resolution mechanism[75] by way of tailored ADR clauses, submission agreements, and ADR mechanisms in normative instruments. Cultural institutions may pledge themselves to ADR and submit to administrative bodies or permanent mediation commissions instead of courts and specialist courts.[76] The recovery rate in litigation is low, and the burden and standard of proof onerous. Because the situation cannot be improved

---

71 *City of Gotha and the Federal Republic of Germany v Sotheby's and Cobert Finance SA* transcript, unreported case no 1997/G/185, 9 September 1998, QBD.

72 Transcript at 57.

73 Schönenberger (n 65) 51–52; 236–37.

74 Lerner (n 67) 36.

75 E.g. *Rosenberg v Seattle Art Museum (Rosenberg I)*, 70 F Supp 2d 1163, 1165 (D Wash 1999), *vacated*, 124 F Supp 2d 1207 (D Wash 2000)(Odalisque).

76 S Theurich, 'Alternative Dispute Resolution in Art and Cultural Heritage – Explored in the Context of the World Intellectual Property Organization's Work' in K Odendahl and PJ Weber (eds), *Kulturgüterschutz – Kunstrecht – Kulturrecht: Festschrift für Kurt Siehr* (Baden-Baden 2010) 569, 575, 580.

simply by moving claims more quickly through the court system,[77] commentators are reluctant to recognise the role of law and litigation in the settlement of claims.[78] The International Law Association considers ADR as desirable, preferable and ideal.[79] Non-binding declarations of intent also exhort states to co-operate and provide ADR mechanisms to resolve ownership disputes. Instruments of 'soft law' call for 'just and fair' solutions of claims.[80] The proliferation of soft law appears to be linked to the difficulties in the way of comprehensive binding agreements for the international community.

None of the declarations of intent contains overriding criteria and procedures for uniform, speedy, cost-effective recovery or indicates how to realise this aim. The Principles associated with the 1998 Washington

---

77 Murphy (n 29) 19.

78 N Palmer, 'Spoliation and Holocaust-related Cultural Objects: Legal and Ethical Models for the Resolution of Claims' (2007) 12 Art Antiquity and Law 1, 8; EI Gegas, 'International Arbitration and Resolution of Cultural Property Disputes' (1997) 13 Ohio State Journal on Dispute Resolution 129, 156.

79 E.g. International Law Association, Cultural Heritage Law Committee Report, Berlin Conference 2004, 6 <www.ila-hq.org/> accessed 24 February 2014.

80 Principle VIII, IX and XI *Washington Conference Principles on Nazi-Confiscated Art*, 30 November–3 December 1998; Parliamentary Assembly of the Council of Europe, Resolution No 1205 on Looted Jewish Cultural Property of 4 November 1999, clause 16 <http://assembly.coe.int/main.asp?Link=/documents/adoptedtext/ta99/eres1205.htm> accessed 24 February 2014; *Vilnius Forum Declaration on Holocaust Era Looted Cultural Assets*, Vilnius, Lithuania, 3–5 October 2000 <http://www.lootedartcommission.com/vilnius-forum> accessed 24 February 2014; ICOM's new mediation programme for museums; *Terezín Declaration* adopted at the Holocaust Era Assets Conference in Prague, 30 June 2009 <http://www.holocausteraassets.eu/program/conference-proceedings/declarations> accessed 24 February 2014 or <http://www.state.gov/p/eur/rls/or/126162.htm> accessed 24 February 2014; Unesco Intergovernmental Committee for Promoting the Return of Cultural Property to its Countries of Origin or its Restitution in case of Illicit Appropriation, *Declaration of Principles Relating to Cultural Objects Displaced in Connection with the Second World War* (2009) and new rules for mediation and conciliation to facilitate restitution of cultural property (ICPRCP, July 2010, CLT-2010/CONF.203/COM.16/2 Rev. <http://unesdoc.unesco.org/images/0018/001875/187506e.pdf> accessed 28 June 2012); Basic Principles and Guidelines on the Right to a Remedy and Reparation for Victims of Gross Violations of International Human Rights Law and Serious Violations of International Humanitarian Law, General Assembly Resolution 60/147 of 16 December 2005 <http://legal.un.org/avl/ha/ga_60-147/ga_60-147.html> accessed 24 February 2014.

Conference on Holocaust-Era Assets[81] set general goals and guidance to encourage claimants to step forward, but they lack definition and clarity.[82] The Parliamentary Assembly of the Council of Europe adopted Resolution 1205[83] does not close any of the gaps in the Washington Conference Principles.[84] The 2000 Vilnius International Forum on Holocaust Era Looted Cultural Assets and the 2009 Terezín Declaration[85] do not create a cause of action for third parties either. Neither instrument improves the legal position of a claimant in actual terms. State-run mediation commissions are slowly but surely making headway. These national commissions respond to 'soft law' and exhortations favouring ADR, and align the legal position with the policy shift in respect of restitution and the current restitution cycle. The extra-legal setting of the mediation commission tends to be backed by the moral conviction of broader society.[86] They offer mediation in one form or another but do not always bear the name of 'mediation commission'.[87]

The Spoliation Advisory Panel in the UK (SAP) offers a particularly strong example of a state mediator.[88] The SAP was established in the Department of Culture, Media and Sport in 2000 to give effect to the Washington Conference Principles in the UK. Its objective is to 'achieve

---

[81] 1998 Washington Conference on Holocaust-Era Assets (*U.S. State Department*) <http://1997-2001.state.gov/www/regions/eur/wash_conf_material.html> accessed 24 February 2014.

[82] JF Sawka, 'Reconciling Policy and Equity: The Ability of the Internal Revenue Code to Resolve Disputes Regarding Nazi-Looted Art' (2009) 17 University of Miami International and Comparative Law Review 1, 14.

[83] Parliamentary Assembly of the Council of Europe, Resolution No 1205 on Looted Jewish Cultural Property of 4 November 1999 § 16.

[84] In particular clauses 12 and 13. D Range, 'Deaccessioning and Its Costs in the Holocaust Art Context: The United States and Great Britain' (2003–2004) 39 Texas International Law Journal 655, 658.

[85] *Vilnius Forum Declaration on Holocaust Era Looted Cultural Assets*, Vilnius, Lithuania, 3–5 October 2000; *Terezín Declaration* adopted at the Holocaust Era Assets Conference in Prague, 30 June 2009.

[86] C Woodhead, 'Nazi Era Spoliation: Establishing Procedural and Substantive Principles' (2013) 18 Art Antiquity and Law 167, 172 points out that this much was apparent when the Holocaust (Stolen Art) Restitution Bill was debated in the House of Commons.

[87] K Kuprecht and K Siehr, 'International Trade in Moveable Tangible Cultural Heritage of Indigenous Peoples: A European Perspective' in CB Graber, K Kuprecht and JC Lai (eds), *International Trade in Indigenous Cultural Heritage* (Edward Elgar 2012) 246, 268–69. See also Hartung (n 48) 335; Woodhead (n 86) 171.

[88] It is not an 'arbitrator' in the European meaning of the term.

a solution which is fair and just both to the claimant and to the institution' in the event of disputes.[89] It discharges its UK-wide mandate within the framework of the Holocaust (Return of Cultural Objects) Act 2009, which applies in respect of art held in seventeen named public collections in England and three in Scotland. In the case of Scotland, the Scottish Ministers have to agree with the recommendation of the Panel and no condition must apply to the object concerned. The Act foresees that property may be restituted upon the recommendation of the SAP,[90] and removes lengthy bars to de-accessioning cultural objects lost during the Nazi era up until November 2019.[91] Prior to its promulgation, all national museums in the UK were statutorily barred from restitution, but this legal obstacle has now been removed. Technical defences such as statutory limitations are applied less strictly in the light of the historic background and special circumstances of Holocaust-related claims.[92] Not only has state-run mediation brought closure in a significant number of cases in England, but the SAP also remains open to making recommendations in the event of disputes involving entities in Scotland and private disputants, or responding to governmental requests for consultation.[93]

A number of states in Europe have benefited greatly from state mediation panels.[94] Examples include the advisory committees or special restitution commissions that operate in Germany (*Beratende Kommission* or Advisory Commission for the Return of Cultural Property Seized by the Nazis, especially from Jewish Owners[95]); the French Commission for

---

[89] Constitution and ToR [6].

[90] Holocaust (Return of Cultural Property) Act 2009, s 3.

[91] *Her Majesty's Attorney-General v Trustees of the British Museum* [2005] EWHC 1089 (Ch) triggered the change in the statutory framework for the restitution of Holocaust-era art.

[92] But see Woodhead (n 86) 171 arguing that in all claims brought before the SAP the legal claim was extinguished, making the SAP the only body suitable to resolve the dispute.

[93] Kuprecht and Siehr (n 87) 269.

[94] Meeting of Five European Committees, Symposium in the Peace Palace in The Hague, 26/27 November 2012 <http://www.restitutiecommissie.nl/en/committees.html> accessed 24 February 2014.

[95] The *Beratende Kommission im Zusammenhang mit der Ruckgabe NS-verfolgungsbedingt Entzogener Kulturgüter, Insbesondere aus Judischem Besitz* was established in 2003 to give effect to pledges that efforts will be made to find a fair and just solution for art held in public collections but lost from private ownership due to Nazi persecution. The pledges are contained in the 1998 Washington Conference Principles; and the 1999 Common Statement issued by

Compensation of Victims of Spoliation (which deals with the implications of anti-Semitic legislation) and the *Dutch Restitutie Commissie* or Advisory Committee on the Assessment of Restitution Applications for Items of Cultural Value and the Second World War (which combines art, historical and legal research).[96]

In the event of restitution claims, amicable settlement is favoured by both the Allied restitution laws that were established and administered by the occupational forces in post-war Germany,[97] and the Property Settlement Act of 1990 (*Vermögensgesetz*) in terms of which a Federal Office is established to deal with Restitution Affairs and Unsolved Property Questions (BADV) and with indemnification in Eastern Germany. The *Beratende Kommission* deals with instances where both parties actively desire a moral recommendation after having exhausted traditional legal remedies or where statutory limitations take effect. Its advice in regard to the possible return of a cultural object kept in a museum does not rely on restitution laws (referred to under 3. above), nor on case law based on such laws.[98] The resolution of disputes in Austria continues to be affected by the post-war restitution initiatives today.[99] The Austrian Art Restitution Committee assesses the claims brought by victims of Nazi persecution on the basis of the *Kunstrückgabegesetz* of 1998 (Art Restitution

---

the Federal Government, Länder and Municipal Associations Common Statement on the Tracing and Return of Nazi-confiscated Art, Especially from Jewish Property, <http://www.lostart.de/Webs/DE/Kommission/Index.html> accessed 24 February 2014. It is located at the Central Office for the Documentation of Lost Cultural Property.

[96] Commonalities and differences were discussed at a meeting of Five European Committees, Symposium in the Peace Palace in The Hague, 26/27 November 2012, <http://www.restitutiecommissie.nl/en/committees.html> accessed 24 February 2014.

[97] E.g. Art 15 USREG; Art 12.2 BrREG; § 31 Abs. 1a and 5 VermG.

[98] E.g. Military Government Regulations and Restitution Laws in the three Western occupied zones in Germany included Law No 59, US Military Government for Germany, 10 November 1947 – Amerikanisches Kontrollgebiet – ABl. (Amtsblatt der Militarregierung Deutschland) Ausgabe G, S. 1; Gesetz No 59 der Militarregierung – Britisches Kontrollgebiet – ABl. No 28, S.1169; and Regulation No 120 of the French High Command in Germany, 10 November 1947, *Amtsblatt des Französischen Oberkommandos in Deutschland* No 119 of 14 November 1947.

[99] *Bakalar v Vavra*, 619 F3d 146 (2nd Circuit 2010) (Austrian Nullification Act rendering forced sales null and void elapsed in 1956 for claims instituted against Austrian citizens, but claim was not against an Austrian citizen in this case).

Law of 1998).[100] This Act does not contain a cause of action for the return of artworks, but refers to the Nullification Act of 1946. The Committee interprets the scope of the Act as imposing a duty on Austria to make restitution.[101] The Committee also refers to the findings of the Commission of Provenance Research.

None of the US institutions that are active in this area[102] have terms of reference even vaguely comparable to those of any state-run mediator. The guidelines of both the American Association of Museums (AAM)[103] and the Association of Art Museum Directors (AAMD)[104] encourage the use of mediation to resolve claims regarding Nazi spoliated art. As voluntary associations without regulating authority, their guidelines cannot be read as a waiver of technical, legal defences or be taken to signal non-enforceability of legal claims. Consequently, the incentive for US museums to pursue mediation is not huge.

5. PRIVATE PARTIES AND MEDIATION

The advice of the permanent bodies that operate across European countries is non-binding and advisory. A party who does not wish to adhere to the advice given is free, in principle, to institute court proceedings to test a legal claim to Nazi spoliated art if the mediation does not satisfy the claim. The Dutch Restitution Commission constitutes an exception. It is competent to issue binding opinions. The SAP can

---

[100] *Bundesgesetz über die Rückgabe von Kunstgegenständen aus den Österreichischen Bundesmuseen und Sammlungen* (Austria) BGBl I 181/1998, amended in 2009.

[101] Information on the Five Advisory Committees, <http://www.restitutiecommissie.nl/en/committees.html> accessed 24 February 2014.

[102] These include: foreign arbitration organisations; auction houses; IFAR (since 1969). The Conference on Jewish Material Claims against Germany (or Jewish Claims Conference <http://www.claimscon.org/> accessed 24 February 2014) has been active for 60 years, among other things to recover unclaimed Jewish property in the former East Germany.

[103] See AAM Guidelines Concerning the Unlawful Appropriation of Objects during the Nazi Era of November 1999, amended in 2001 <http://aamus.org/museumresources/ethics/upload/ethicsguidelines.naziera.pdf> accessed 28 June 2012.

[104] See 'AAMD Report of the Task Force on Spoliation of Art in the Nazi/World War II Era (1933–1945)' (4 June 1998) <https://aamd.org/sites/default/files/document/Report%20on%20the%20Spoliation%20of%20Nazi%20Era%20Art.docx> accessed 25 February 2014.

hear claims regarding objects in private collections where both parties agree.[105] Private parties may opt for independent mediation, but it would offer nothing more 'than a tentative moratorium that neither precludes nor prejudices subsequent litigation or arbitration'.[106] The SAP functions as part of a public framework that makes recourse to litigation unlikely. National collections submit to mediation by virtue of the administrative control and oversight role of the Department for Culture, Media and Sport (DCMS) in respect of these collections and the SAP.[107] This enables the DCMS to ensure that public collections comply with the recommendations,[108] even if SAP recommendations do not constitute legally binding determinations as to legal rights and their observation is but a matter of convention.[109] The institutions listed in the Holocaust (Return of Cultural Property) Act 2009 cannot 'contract out' of a SAP recommendation to the effect that an object must be restituted. A SAP recommendation is likely to prevail despite the lack of enforceability. A court ruling that conflicts with the recommendation made by the SAP is also unlikely on account of the relationship between the SAP, national collections and public galleries. The relationship is not predicated on consent in the way that claims against private collections are. Bodies that operate in terms of the enabling legislation are likely to wish to avoid the moral dilemmas that technical defences might introduce when ethical considerations are skirted in proceedings that turn on the validity of transfer of ownership or an appeal of a ruling in respect of transfer. As a body with national jurisdiction, the SAP takes moral factors into account by virtue of its national mandate. There is no need for it to invoke the public policy exception to determine the outcome of a dispute at the cross-over between private international law and public international law.

---

[105] SAP ToR [6].

[106] IF Gazzini, *Cultural Property Disputes: The Role of Arbitration in Resolving Non-Contractual Disputes* (Transnational Publishers 2004) 63.

[107] Response of UK to Questionnaire, Information on the Five Advisory Committees, <http://www.restitutiecommissie.nl/en/committees.html> accessed 24 February 2014.

[108] P Ward, Holocaust (Return of Cultural Objects) Bill: Committee Stage Report, Research Paper 09/05, June 2009, 5.

[109] Range (n 84) 670.

6. JUSTICE PLURALISM VERSUS A UNIFORM BODY OF LAW

While it has been argued that justice demands coherence across cases that share commonalities and that are settled by the same body, regardless of type,[110] a uniform set of norms (a *lex culturalis*[111]) will be hard to achieve. The legal profession prefers legal certainty, obtained when legal questions concerning proof, title, prescription, estoppel and good faith are ventilated.[112] Ethical approaches are congruent with a plurality of methods by which justice is delivered, however. Consequently, justice pluralism is a more realistic starting point.[113] Justice requires simply a commitment to help heal the past and prevent recurrence in the future. Neither a single worldwide forum nor a uniform body of law is a prerequisite.

State courts do not necessarily make rulings that are easily reconciled with the recommendations of non-judicial or quasi-judicial bodies that operate unconstrained by adversarial procedure and by precedent. Conflicting results are possible where more than one domestic forum becomes involved in the same case and actions run in parallel. Similar cases are not necessarily resolved along similar lines. In Germany, different adjudicators reached different conclusions concerning whether and how compensation payments received after World War II ought to be taken into account when restitution is demanded. For example, the government panel involved with the fate of the Sachs collection (the *Beratende Kommission*) reached a decision that the claim for physical restitution of the poster collection had to be rebuffed.[114] Earlier compensation payments were taken into account when the works were returned.[115] The heir, Peter Sachs, rejected the recommendation and

---

110 Woodhead (n 86) makes this argument in respect of the SAP.

111 A Chechi, *The Settlement of International Cultural Heritage Disputes: Towards a Lex Culturalis?* (unpublished PhD Thesis EUI 2011) 202.

112 JM Carruthers, *The Transfer of Property in the Conflict of Laws* (OUP 2005) § 5.18.

113 See Chapter 1 3.4.

114 Recommendation of 25 January 2007, <http://www.lootedart.com/MFEU4E88305_print;Y> accessed on 24 February 2014; see also § 2 (dd) of *Peter Sachs v Stiftung Deutches Historisches Museum*, Berlin Higher Regional Court, 28 January 2010, 8 U 56/09.

115 The *Beratende Kommission* rebuffed the claim brought by Peter Sachs in the light of earlier restitution payment made by the government. Hartung (n 48) 335; H König, 'Claims for the Restitution of Holocaust-era Cultural Assets and Their Resolution in Germany' (2007) 12 Art Antiquity and Law 59, 62.

decided to test his claim in a legal action. The trial court (*Landgericht*)[116] ruled that the collection had to be returned to him. However, when the museum appealed, the Berlin Higher Regional Court (*Kammergericht*)[117] overturned the decision of the trial court.[118] The German Federal Court of Justice (*Bundesgerichtshof*) clarified the complex legal relationship between special restitution law and general civil law (including prescription rules). It held that general civil law prevails over Allied restitution law and the compensation payable thereunder.[119] This provoked debate about procedure, forum and finality.[120] In cases of conflicting norms in the area of restitution, the Property Settlement Act of 1990 (*Vermögensgesetz*), the German Law on the Regulation of Unsolved Property Questions, would usually receive priority because it takes procedural precedence over restitution claims asserted under the civil law and regulated by the German Civil Code.[121] In this particular instance, however, the trial court was found to lack authority to compel the German Historical Museum to return the collection under the Property Settlement Act. The reason was that restitution claims based on the Allied restitution laws and the Property Settlement Act of 1990[122] could not be enforced in civil proceedings in Germany. Recourse to ordinary courts is precluded[123] even if the case has great merit.[124] Property settlement has to be challenged in the administrative courts that have been authorised to interpret the Property Settlement Act.[125] The Berlin Higher Regional Court was only prepared to recognise the collective restitution claim of the Conference on Jewish Material Claims against Germany (the JCC) in New York. It disapproved of the ruling of the trial court, warning that it

---

116 *Landgericht* (trial court) Berlin, 10 February 2009, 19 O 116/08.

117 *Peter Sachs v Stiftung Deutsches Historisches Museum* Berlin Higher Regional Court 28 January 2010, 8 U 56/09.

118 The Kammergericht Berlin followed the recommendation of the Advisory Commission not to return the posters.

119 *Rückerstattungsanordnung* BK/O (49) 180 *der Alliierten Kommandantur Berlin Betreffend die Rückerstattung Feststellbarer Vermögensgegenstände an Opfer der Nationalsozialistischen Unterdrückungsmaßnahmen* (vom 26. Juli 1949, VOBl. für Groß-Berlin I S. 221).

120 Commission for Art Recovery <http://www.comartrecovery.org/cases/hans-sachs-poster-collection> accessed 24 February 2014; Roodt (n 36) 448–50.

121 §§ 1(a)–(l). Cf BGH NJW 1953, 1909; BVerwGE 98, 261; König (n 115) 60–61.

122 1 (e)–(g).

123 § 1(6) VermG.

124 § (d) and § (h).

125 König (n 115) 60–61.

invites double claims and nullifies, for Germany, the Principles of the 1989 Washington Conference on works of art seized by the Nazis. At the time of the appeal to the Higher Regional Court, parallel appeal proceedings were also pending before the Federal Administrative Court.[126] This ruling was overturned by the Federal Court of Justice and on the basis of general principles of property law contained in § 985 of the German Civil Code. The Federal Court of Justice ordered the return of the posters to the collector's heir[127] despite the expiry of the statutory limitation which commenced to run on re-unification,[128] and notwithstanding earlier payment of compensation by the government. Compensation did not extinguish the claim.[129] The Allied restitution laws could not apply where restitution was not claimed in time because the objects had disappeared after the war and were only found after the period during which claims were permitted had lapsed.[130] The Property Settlement Act could not apply either, because the posters were confiscated in West Berlin. After the Federal Court had spoken, Peter Sachs undertook of his own accord to repay the compensation that his father received upon return of the posters.[131] Thus the restitution of the poster collection to Peter Sachs did not pose a fundamental problem of double compensation for the Federal Court of Justice.[132]

It is not a foregone conclusion that mediation commissions can do more to promote internal consistency and to ensure consistent application of a recognised set of norms domestically.[133] Moreover, no mediation commission can ensure consistency in a global context. The spatial operation of their mandate is per definition territorially limited so that the jurisdictional reach of permanent mediation bodies is confined to the

---

126 BVermG 8 C 12/09; see the remark in § 1 (i).

127 *Peter Sachs v Stiftung Deutsches Historisches Museum*, BGH 16 March 2012, v. ZR 279/10; Press release <http://juris.bundesgerichtshof.de/cgi-bin/rechtsprechung/document.py?Gericht=bgh&Art=en&Datum=Aktuell&Sort=12288&nr=59597&linked=pm&Blank=1> accessed 28 June 2012.

128 *Peter Sachs v Stiftung Deutsches Historisches Museum* (n 127) § 33.

129 *Peter Sachs v Stiftung Deutsches Historisches Museum* (n 127) § 26.

130 *Peter Sachs v Stiftung Deutsches Historisches Museum* (n 127) §§ 15, 21.

131 D Rising, 'Nazi-seized Art Ordered Returned to American Man' (*The Journal*, 16 March 2012).

132 M Weller, 'Key Elements of Just and Fair Solutions' (*de Restitutiecommissie*) <http://www.restitutiecommissie.nl/en/system/files/Weller%20Key%20Elements%20of%20Fair%20and%20Just%20Solutions.pdf> accessed 24 February 2014.

133 Woodhead (n 86) 173ff recommends that the SAP should base its recommendations on codified principles; but see Range (n 84) 665.

state they operate in. As a consequence, different permanent bodies have reached different conclusions in respect of compensation payments.[134] The deprived party could receive double compensation in one venue while remaining uncompensated in another. Whereas the SAP was careful to avoid unjust enrichment and double recompense to the claimants for being deprived of the Glaser collection now in possession of the Courtauld Trust,[135] the Dutch Restitutie Commissie awarded compensation in recognition of an underlying tort, and did not treat the compensation paid by Germany as cause for unjustified enrichment.[136] Many sellers were unable to access payment for the art they had sold and could not dispose of the proceeds freely. The Dutch Restitutie Commissie acknowledged that the claimant had to be given the benefit of the doubt as to whether the proceeds were in fact obtained, and conceded that Glaser could probably not dispose freely of the proceeds. Glaser is likely to have used the proceeds to fund his escape to the US and to pay exit taxes. Repayment of the compensation received was considered to be a matter between Germany and the claimants.[137]

7. PROCESS AND SUBSTANCE INEXORABLY LINKED

To make the best of the options available for settling disputes, the connection between process and outcome must be understood. Technical defences based on jurisdiction, choice of law, clear title to stolen goods, or a 'prohibition on disposal objection' (de-accessioning provisions that

---

[134] E.g. *Vineberg v Bissonnette*, 529 F Supp 2d 300, 305–6, 311 (DRI 2007), *aff'd* 548 F 3d 50 (1st Circuit 2008); *The University of Leipzig v Germany represented by the Federal Office that deals with Restitution Affairs and Unsolved Property Questions* Berlin Administrative Court 26 May 2011, VG 29 K 126.09; C Hickley, 'Jewish Heir Fights Restitution, Wants Museum to Keep Art', *Bloomberg* (31 May 2011); also K Lubina and H Schneider, 'Pringsheim, Provenance and Principles: A Case Study on the Restitution of Nazi Looted Art and Compensatory Payments' in K Odendahl and PJ Weber (eds), *Kulturgüterschutz – Kunstrecht – Kulturrecht: Festschrift für Kurt Siehr* (Baden-Baden 2010) 161, 171.

[135] *Spoliation Advisory Panel Report in Respect of Eight Drawings Now in the Possession of the Samuel Courtauld Trust* (The Stationery Office 24 June 2009) (2009 HC 757) [4].

[136] Recommendation regarding Glaser, Case No RC 1.99, 4 October 2010, 50 <http://www.restitutiecommissie.nl/en/publications.html> [9] accessed 24 February 2014.

[137] Lubina and Schneider (n 134) 174; Woodhead (n 86) 186.

impose the inalienability of collections deriving from museum statutes) may present obstacles to restitution. The technical classification of rules that control the application of a domestic legal system's concepts of time bars or extinction of action may block even voluntary return and restitution, despite the general nature and aim of such rules.

Whereas the European model considers all forms of limitation and liberative prescription to be governed by the law of the cause on account of a substantive classification,[138] US courts frequently apply foreign substantive private law as the exception rather than as the rule.[139] In Scots law, a decision on the merits of the case is not barred[140] because prescription extinguishes the action. If the lapse of time extinguishes the existence of a right and therefore also the action, the court will apply the limitation period of the *lex causae*.[141] In English law, this is the position even if the choice of law rules of the law of the cause, the foreign law, classifies the provision as procedural.[142] SAP mediation excludes an assessment of the legal rights of the parties. Arguably, therefore, the claims that have come before the SAP cannot necessarily be classed as claims that would have been extinguished by a successful limitations plea.[143] Prior to the promulgation of the 2009 Act, the SAP postponed hearing a claim when a legal claim for return remained open. This provided an opportunity for the heir to exhaust the pursuit of legal claims in court.[144] A legal claim remained open also in the very first case the SAP dealt with.[145]

---

[138] E.g. Art 148(1) of the Swiss private international law code; Art 1208 of the Russian Civil Code; and Art 7 of the Turkish private international law code.

[139] See Chapter 3 subsection 3.3. Kreder, 'The New Battleground of Museum Ethics and Holocaust-Era Claims: Technicalities Trumping Justice or Responsible Stewardship for the Public Trust?' (2009) Oregon Law Review 37, 82 declares that local law applies to limitations questions.

[140] E.g. Prescription and Limitation (Scotland) Act 1973.

[141] E.g. *Ersitzung* § 937 BGB (German Civil Code). Contrast legal systems that do not permit acquisitive prescription e.g. s 11 of the Conservation of Cultural and Natural Property Law No 2863, Official Gazette 23/07/1983 no 18113 (Turkey).

[142] S 4(2) of the Foreign Limitation Periods Act 1984.

[143] Argument advanced by Woodhead (n 86) 171.

[144] The Feldmann heirs lodged their claim in 2002, but the SAP issued its recommendation in 2006. *Spoliation Advisory Panel Report in Respect of Four Drawings Now in the Possession of the British Museum* (The Stationery Office 27 April 2006) 10.

[145] *Spoliation Advisory Panel Report in Respect of a Painting Now in the Possession of the Tate Gallery* (The Stationery Office 18 January 2001).

A court may apply the *lex fori* to procedural aspects of the case if the underlying obligation continues to exist even after the statutory limitation period has lapsed. In this case, the limitation only provides a defence to the action.[146] A court may seek to classify the question of limitations or time bars as pertaining to procedure. The readiness to define 'procedure' in such expansive terms compromises consistency among the outcomes achieved in international cases. A claimant may forum-shop on the basis of the wide interpretation which a court adheres to, making it more likely that the merits of the claim will not be investigated. On the other hand, the possessor who defends the claim may use the certainty that legal time limits provide the avoidance of a judicial ruling.[147] US courts have imposed 'absolute deadlines', extended the time limits, unified the point of accrual of the action, and suspended statutory limitations for a limited or an extended period of time.[148] Technical legal defences against a claim for restitution are more likely to succeed in court than in front of a permanent state mediator.

Substance and procedure are interwoven, and possessors choose their strategy accordingly. That museums favour litigation does not come as a surprise. US courts have ruled that the choice between mediation and the technical defences associated with formal litigation is entirely up to museums.[149] Public and private cultural institutions in the US rely on statutory limitations in Nazi spoliated art cases even when ADR is clearly more appropriate.[150] Museums have been particularly successful with

---

146 S Wilson, 'Prescription and Limitation of Actions in Scotland and England in Relation to Dispute Resolution in Construction Contracts' (2001) 15 ELR 122, 123.

147 E.g. the overturned ruling in *Peter Sachs v Stiftung Deutsches Historisches Museum*, Berlin Higher Regional Court, 28 January 2010, 8 U 56/09, § 1(d).

148 E.g. S Cuba, 'Stop the Clock: The Case to Suspend the Statute of Limitations on Claims for Nazi-Looted Art' (1999) 17 Cardozo Arts and Entertainment Law Journal 447; DJ Rowland, 'Nazi-Era Art Claims in the United States: 10 Years after the Washington Conference' [2009] Art and Cultural Heritage Law Newsletter 30, 34; LM Kaye, 'Looted Art: What Can and Should Be Done' (1998) 20 Cardozo Law Review 657, 659.

149 *Toledo Museum of Art v Ullin*, 477 F Supp 2d 802 (ND Ohio 2006); *Detroit Institute of Arts v Ullin* No 06-10333 2007 US Dist LEXIS 28364 (ED Michigan 2007).

150 *Museum of Modern Art and Guggenheim Foundation v Schoeps*, 603 F Supp 2d 273 (SDNY 2009) and *Schoeps v Museum of Modern Art*, 594 F Supp 2d 461 (SDNY 2009). Conversely, in *Vineberg v Bissonnette*, 529 F Supp 2d 300,

statutory limitations pleas in cases involving 'degenerate art'.[151] In this category, *Grosz v Museum of Modern Art* is a particularly unsettling ruling.[152] A cause of action was allowed to accrue during amicable negotiations. The court held that the contestation of possession was an implicit refusal of the demand. In effect, efforts to reconcile differences before submitting to litigation (or arbitration) may lead to a claimant losing the opportunity to argue the merits in court. If this is the legal position, claimants would refuse to attempt to negotiate. Moral and policy factors did not seem to prompt the court to relax their application statutory limitations so as to enable the merits of a case to be heard.

The reluctance to hear arguments on fact and merits is linked to the procedural advantages features of the US court system, which made modern Holocaust litigation possible in the first instance.[153] These features include the scope of jurisdiction, jury trials, discovery rules, class actions, the kind and extent of damages, contingency fees, the approach to human rights abuses and restitution efforts.[154]

The reluctance of US courts to find clear evidence of a federal policy disfavouring statute of limitations in Holocaust claims on account of general and vague language in the *Washington Conference Principles on Nazi-Confiscated Art* (1998) and *Terezín Declaration* (2009)[155] is problematical. It has been US government policy ever since 1949 to undo

---

305–6, 311 (DRI 2007), *aff'd* 548 F3d 50 (1st Circuit 2008), the plaintiff prevailed when the defendant waived the statute of limitations defence.

151 E.g. *Museum of Fine Arts, Boston v Claudia Seger-Tomschitz*, 623 F3d 1 (1st Circuit 2010)(declaratory judgment action, letter of demand sent four years after discovery of the whereabouts of 'Two Nudes (Lovers)' by Kokoschka; Massachusetts statute of limitations barred claim); *Dunbar v Seger-Tomschitz*, 615 F3d 574 (5th Circuit 2010)(acquisitive prescription ran in respect of 'Portrait of a Youth' by Kokoschka under Louisiana law); *Grosz v The Museum of Modern Art*, 772 F Supp 2d 473 (SDNY 2010), *aff'd* 403 Fed Appx 575 (2nd Circuit 2010), *cert denied* 132 S Ct 102; 181 L Ed 2d 30 (2011) (the issue of laches on the part of the artist, an anti-totalitarian painter who was declared an enemy of the state).

152 *Grosz v The Museum of Modern Art*, 772 F Supp 2d 473 (SDNY 2010), *aff'd* 403 Fed Appx 575 (2nd Circuit 2010), *cert denied* 132 S Ct 102; 181 L Ed 2d 30 (2011).

153 *In re Holocaust Victim Assets Litigation I*, 105 F Supp 2d 154–63 (first successful class action delineating several classes of claimants eligible under the settlement).

154 MO Wantuch and A Niethammer, 'Compensation for Nazi Wrongdoing: The Case for an Integrated Approach' (2007) 12 Art Antiquity and Law 46–47.

155 Also *Toledo Museum of Art v Ullin*, 477 Supp 2d 802 (ND Ohio 2006)(claim dismissed under four-year Ohio statute of limitations); *Detroit*

forced transfers and to restitute identifiable property to those who were persecuted and deprived of their property.[156] The hands of state legislatures are tied under the US Constitution, which reserves the power to legislate restitution and reparation claims in respect of losses caused by war as an exclusive reserved foreign affairs power of the federal government. For instance, the most recent state legislation in California amends the statute of limitations applicable to all lawsuits brought to recover works of fine art as a general category.[157]

The power to legislate restitution and reparation claims remains the exclusive preserve of the federal government.[158] As long as no action is taken, possessors will tend to prefer court proceedings over private mediation. It may be possible to end the impasse in US law by suspending statutory limitations at the federal level, implemented via the Holocaust Victims Redress Act 1998.[159]

In order to ensure that cases are decided on their merit, it was proposed that mandatory jurisdiction be conferred on a mediation body,[160] but to date, no permanent mediation commission has been established for the US.[161] The Special Envoy for Holocaust Issues, Bureau of European and Eurasian Affairs, Douglas Davidson, has pleaded for the creation of

---

Institute of Arts v Ullin, No 06-10333 2007 US Dist LEXIS 28364 (ED Michigan 2007) (Institute brought a successful action to quiet title to a Van Gogh, 'The Diggers', claimed by the heirs of Martha Nathan).

[156] *Menzel v List*, 267 NYS 2d 804, 818 note 5 (NY Sup Ct 1966); see also Holocaust Victims Redress Act 1998 (no right to sue for return of confiscated property); Nazi War Crimes Disclosure Act 1998; and Holocaust Assets Commission Act 1998 (does not authorise return of stolen art; merely the authoring of a report).

[157] *Von Saher v Norton Simon Museum of Art at Pasadena*, 592 F3d 954 (9th Circuit 2010) held unconstitutional Cal. Code. Civ. Proc. § 354.3, which took effect on 1 January 2003. Von Saher's petition for review was declined on 27 June 2011, but the decision was reversed. A Adler, 'The Lubomirski Dürers: A Case for Legal and Moral Restitution' (2010) 1 Cultural Heritage and Arts Review 11 <http://www.lootedart.com/web_images/pdf2/CHAReviewII%20Fall%20Winter%202010.pdf> accessed 24 February 2014.

[158] *Von Saher v Norton Simon Museum of Art at Pasadena*, 592 F3d 954 (9th Circuit 2010) (foreign affairs doctrine pre-empted California's extension of statutes of limitations to 31 December 2010).

[159] Cuba (n 148) 488.

[160] As proposed by Gegas (n 78) 155–58, for instance.

[161] Establishment of a US Nazi Loot Restitution Panel was first proposed at the Prague Holocaust Era Assets Conference in 2009. C Hickley, 'Eizenstat Favours US Nazi Loot Panel to Advise on Disputed Art' *Bloomberg* (28 June 2009).

impartial mediation that would 'aid rightful owners or their heirs, still provide attorneys with a decent living, and allow art museums to live up to commitments they willingly assumed fifteen years ago', or deliver a binding opinion similar to the Dutch Restitutions Committee model in respect of private party disputes.[162]

The integration of law and ethics seems difficult to achieve. Time bars are there because evidence may have disappeared and memory may have faded. On the other hand, their application encourages claimants to forget rather than ensure access to justice.

Decisions that are based on formal rationality as opposed to value rationality leave an important prerequisite for achieving global solidarity unfulfilled. This prerequisite lodges in the ethical dimension of society.[163]

8. 'FORCED SALE' IN A TRANSNATIONAL CONTEXT

8.1 Definition

'Forced sales' refer to items acquired by 'Aryans' as defined by Nazi law under circumstances of duress – through pressure and threats. The definition of a 'forced sale' or of 'spoliation' determines the outcome, affects the terms of reference of a body considering claims for restitution, and informs the argument advanced by government when refusing to make restitution. The SAP adopted a general concept of spoliation that covers deprivation of a cultural object post 30 January 1933 by a variety of means, including theft, forced sale, sale at undervalue or otherwise.[164] Finding that a sale was negotiated freely rather than sold at a compulsory Jewish auction will prevent the rightful heirs from claiming ownership successfully. The recommendation by the SAP released in December 2010 concerning 'The Coronation of the Virgin' by Sir Peter Paul Rubens was controversial for this reason. The heirs of the Jewish banker who originally owned it had failed with their ownership claim despite the fact

---

162 D Davidson, 'The View from the State Department' Symposium on 'Should Stolen Holocaust Art Be Returned?' (*New York County Law Association*, 25 March 2013) <http://www.state.gov/p/eur/rls/rm/2013/mar/206719.htm> accessed 24 February 2014.

163 L Wilde, *Global Solidarity* (Edinburgh University Press 2013) 119–20, 191ff.

164 ToR [1]; ToR [12(c)].

that it was widely known that Dresdner Bank routinely implemented anti-Jewish and Nazi policies against its own staff.[165]

Vague definitions may complicate matters considerably for the members of families who had received warnings of confiscation and who are claiming restitution. Members of the Goudstikker family had received warning in 1940 that, if the shares in their family's gallery were not sold to Göring at an undervalue, their property would be confiscated. The question arises whether the concept of 'confiscation' in the AAMD Guidelines was meant to include forced sales or not[166] for purposes of the claim brought by the Goudstikker family.[167]

8.2 Private International Law Can Respond to the Ethical Dimension

Private international law devices are called upon to assist when one norm interferes with the intended functioning of another norm at an international level. The *lex situs* approach continues to receive attention in the literature on stolen art disputes in the US.[168] The public policy exception applies in respect of the *lex situs*[169] if the state expropriates the property owned by non-citizens without compensation within its territory.[170] Arguably, it applies also to forced sales or where sales were for an undervalue.

Nazi spoliated art claims present neither a typical thief/victim or good-faith/bad-faith purchaser scenario. The rules of property stand awkwardly alongside the restitution cycles in international law.[171] An ethics-based recommendation that is attuned to the cycles of restitution

---

165 B Grosvenor, 'Courtauld Defeats Jewish Heirs to Keep Rubens' *Art History News* (20 December 2010).

166 DCMS *Restitution of Objects Spoliated in the Nazi-Era: A Consultation Document* (July 2006) § 3.5 20.

167 Also the *Von Saher* case (n 157) which was litigated in the US. LM Kaye, 'Avoidance and Resolution of Cultural Heritage Disputes: Recovery of Art Looted during the Holocaust' [2006] Willamette Journal of International Law and Dispute Resolution 245–52.

168 L Frey, 'Bakalar v Vavra and the Art of Conflicts Analysis in New York: Framing a Choice of Law Approach for Moveable Property' (2012) 112 Columbia Law Review 1055, 1066–71.

169 C Staker, 'Public International Law and the *Lex Situs* Principle in Property Conflicts and Foreign Expropriations' (1987) 58 BYBIL 151, 219–20.

170 Staker (n 169) 221.

171 J Parker, 'World War II and Heirless Art: Unleashing the Final Prisoners of War' (2005) 13 Cardozo Journal of International and Competition Law 661, 692; RK Paterson, 'Resolving Material Cultural Disputes: Human Rights,

will not necessarily be congruent with a ruling that relies on the *situs* rule of private international law and the property rights framework it is premised upon.[172] In fact, a legal argument based on the *lex situs* rule could mute the moral and emotive considerations that support restitution to a victim of persecution whose loss of the art in question is linked to the persecution. Nonetheless, classification, the underlying policy interests of different laws, and the public policy exception create opportunities to account for ethics. They also create opportunities for steering the emerging relationship between statutory limitations and international law in the direction of value-based decision-making, and for control of impediments to states' restitution obligations. For example, classification may block the application of forum law if it weakens the position of the claimant, and the public policy exception may block statutory limitations under foreign law that have this effect.

8.3 Private International Law in a Belotto-type Scenario

Germany generally refuses Jewish refugees who sold their art in Switzerland from taking advantage of German restitution law. The appellate court in Hamm ruled in 1954 that individuals who lived outside the area under Nazi control were not at risk from the intention of the Nazis to eliminate the Jews.[173] Jews who lived abroad could take advantage of the rebuttable presumption only if they had emigrated and still owned assets in Germany which they left behind.[174]

Germany repeatedly refuses to make restitution of paintings if persecuted families escaped and sold their paintings in Switzerland for an income.[175] It was reported in 2013 that two works by Bernardo Belotto[176] will not be restituted to the heirs of the Jewish businessman, Max Emden, who maintain that their grandfather sold the paintings because the Nazis had seized his businesses. The works were sold in Switzerland after the owners had fled Nazi persecution in 1933. Having fled with the works,

---

Property Rights and Crimes against Humanity' [2006] Willamette Journal of International Law & Dispute Resolution 154, 158.

172 E.g. Government compensation of £125 000 ordered to be paid to the owners of 'View of Hampton Court Palace' by Jan Griffier the Elder (c 1645–1718); Carruthers (n 112) § 5.41.

173 Upper Regional Court (Oberlandesgericht) Hamm, Rechtsprechung zum Wiedergutmachungsrecht 1954, 41; König (n 115) 63.

174 BVerwG VIZ 2000, 94; König (n 115) 63.

175 F Jordans, 'Germany Denies Jewish Heirs: Cologne Returns Art' *AP* (18 December 2013).

176 'Panorama of Vienna' and 'The Zwinger Moat in Dresden'.

Germany does not consider the works looted, does not recognise the sale as a 'forced' sale, and has declined to let the case go before a special expert commission.[177]

This category of case makes a direct appeal to policy and ethics. For instance, the position which Germany adopts might be questioned on the basis of Washington Principle No 8, which requires steps 'to achieve a just and fair solution', based on ethics.

The quality of the causal link between persecution and loss affects the fairness of the solution reached. German restitution laws provide that property lost during the Nazi era can be claimed where a direct link can be shown to exist between the pressure of the persecution and the loss, and there was a rebuttable presumption in favour of this direct link.[178] If the sale was concluded in Switzerland, such a direct link with the persecution in Germany cannot be established. Allied Restitution laws[179] contain a rebuttable presumption to the effect that transfers of ownership from persecuted groups had occurred by way of confiscation. The presumption can be displaced if the purchaser can demonstrate that fair market value was paid and the seller had free access to the payment and could freely dispose thereof.[180] Germany never consented to the binding effect of these provisions.[181]

The tension between conflicts rules and ethics in the international dimension is striking in the circumstances of 'Belotto-type' international cases. What contribution can conflicts rules and approaches make, if any?

It may be asked on what basis any state could insist on the application of its own law, if that law gives effect to transfers of ownership in the unusual circumstances of persecution on ideological and other grounds.[182] Does scope remain for a public policy argument – even if persecuted individuals succeeded in selling valuable works of art in Switzerland?

---

177 F Jordans, 'Germany Denies Jewish Heirs: Cologne Returns Art' AP, 18 December 2013.

178 König (n 115) 63.

179 British Military Law No 59. Cf also *Handreichung* of the Commissioner to the German Federal Government for Culture and Media (*Beauftragter der Bundesregierung für Kultur und Medien*), which seeks to build on the old post-war legislation of the Allied Forces on the indemnification of victims of persecution.

180 Veraart and Winkel (n 28) 80–81.

181 Veraart and Winkel (n 28) 80ff.

182 Hartung (n 48) 334.

Global justice may be understandably difficult to achieve. Justice in respect of ordering, norms and rights of individuals who were being prosecuted is challenged by various components of the 'lock' mechanism that combined with the role of Swiss law in 'lock' formation. The systemic justice which private international law as a whole seeks to achieve,[183] points away from the application of a legal system that offered protection to purchasers. Systemic justice would be alive to the fact that unscrupulous dealers who were doing business with, or on behalf of, Nazi officials, represented an important component of the 'lock' mechanism. At the same time, Swiss soil offered greater physical safety to those who fled. Must it be accepted that the absence of Germany's consent to the Allied Restitution Laws will make material justice hard to secure, and that different outcomes in different states will always flout global justice?

8.4 Material Consistency

The 'Belotto matter' pits older court rulings against more recent rulings of the advisory committee. The very first recommendation issued by the *Beratende Kommission* in January 2005 concerned the case of Julius Freund who had transferred paintings to Switzerland in 1933 and had emigrated to London in 1939.[184] He died there in 1941 and his family sold the paintings at an auction in Switzerland in 1942 for income. The *Beratende Kommission* recommended the restitution of the paintings to the heirs, without providing a reason. The federal authority responsible for ruling on open questions about assets had ruled differently. The most recent ruling of the *Beratende Kommission* concerning a Kokoschka painting in the Ludwig Museum Cologne follows the *Kommission*'s ruling in Freund. On 9 April 2013 the *Beratende Kommission* ruled that it should be returned to the heirs of Alfred Flectheim.[185] Flechtheim fled Germany in 1933 and his gallery in Dusseldorf was taken over by the Nazis. Whereas the heirs claimed the painting on the grounds that the

---

183 A Mills, *The Confluence of Public and Private International Law* (CUP 2010) 17ff, 303.

184 Press Release Nr 19/05 on the first recommendation issued by the *Beratende Kommission*, dated 12 January 2005 (that the Federal Government return three paintings by Karl Blechen and a watercolour by Anselm Feuerbach to the community of heirs of Julius and Clara Freund), <http://www.lootedart.com/MFEU4E88305_print;Y> accessed 24 February 2014. For more, see Weller (n 132) 4–5.

185 Press Release of 9 April 2013 <http://www.lootedart.com/web_images/pdf2/13-04-09%20BerKomm%20zu%20Flechtheim-Koln.pdf> accessed 24 February 2014.

sale only took place because of persecution by the Nazis, the museum claimed that Flechtheim was in financial difficulties before the Nazis came to power. Ruling solely on moral and ethical grounds, the *Beratende Kommission* proceeded on the assumption that Flechtheim was forced to sell the disputed painting because he was subject to persecution.

The question is what substantive principle of justice did the *Beratende Kommission* base its 2005 recommendation on when it recommended that restitution was justified in the Freund case? Does any causal link between Nazi persecution and a sale suffice, provided only that the conditions for restitution under Military Law No. 59 were fulfilled?[186] Which restitution law is to be applied – the British Military Law or German restitution law? Why would the *Beratende Kommission* apply the principles of justice laid down in Military Law No. 59 to sales concluded in 'safe' states outside Germany? On the other hand, it is conceivable that some sales concluded outside Germany could indeed be linked to the pressure of persecution, as is required by German restitution law. Claims for physical restitution of cultural objects and art that were subjected to a forced sale include involuntary transfers. The theory that the place of the event will indicate the applicable law in the case of forced transfer, whereas the legal system with which the unjust factor has its closest and most real connection is supposed to apply when it considers restitution appropriate,[187] does not indicate what choice must be made between German, Allied and Swiss law. Any definition of national law identified as the applicable law would impose a geographical limit on the ethics associated with owners who were forced to sell cultural objects and art after having left Germany. The ownership link could be a secondary factor in a claim involving Nazi spoliated art.[188] In fact, the event of a forced transfer does not call for the application of a conflicts rule as much as for an ethics-based 'anti-conflict' rule. Ethical considerations

---

186 Weller (n 132) 5 refers to the Guidelines (Handreichung) on how to deal with claims. The guidelines seek to extend the principles of the old post-war legislation by the Allied Forces.

187 G Panagopoulos, *Restitution in Private International Law* (Hart 2000) 168.

188 Schönenberger (n 65) 90–91. He refers to three examples: the anti-smuggling initiatives that provide for repatriation of cultural objects and implement Art 9 of the UNESCO Convention and Chapter III of the UNIDROIT Convention; restitution claims brought under Art 5 of the UNIDROIT Convention which extends the interests to be weighed beyond mere territorial links, to cultural, preservation, affiliation and emotive interests in the case of indigenous and tribal communities; and claims in respect of the repatriation of human remains where preservation interests have no role.

cannot be limited by the applicable law; nor ought they to shift in accordance with it. They certainly cannot be strictly confined to sales concluded in Germany.

8.5 Global Justice

There is no global consistency in the recommendations of adjudicatory bodies. The SAP made a recommendation that the sale of the objects at auction at Christie's in 1939 amounted to a forced sale because Nazi persecution caused the sale, but that the gravity was at the lower end of the scale and not comparable to the gravity of sales made in occupied Belgium to pay for food.[189] Expert advice obtained at the time revealed that the prices obtained at the auction were fair. The SAP held that the Nazi era impacted on the claimant's circumstances, but that the moral strength of the claim was insufficiently strong to warrant either a return of the objects or an ex gratia payment. The recommendation was that, whenever one or more of the objects were on display at the British Museum, it should be accompanied by a description of the history and provenance of the object(s) during and since the Nazi era, with special reference to the claimants' interest therein. The approach adopted by the SAP can be commended, because ethics, cultural policy and the exigencies of justice go beyond the territorial scope of a legal definition.

Commentators have already made the point that the SAP ought to base its recommendations on codified principles to promote internal consistency,[190] and that the *Beratende Kommission* has to start work on a restatement of restitution principles and rules.[191]

The conflict of normative principles that is evident in the inconsistencies between the respective approaches of the *Beratende Kommission* and the SAP arises because settled principles of substantive justice are yet to be established. Formal and procedural justice assumes greater significance where material (substantive) justice is so hard to achieve.[192] It goes without saying that procedural conflicts do manifest, and call on legal standards to meet basic moral standards, just as moral standards can be

---

189 *Spoliation Advisory Panel Report in Respect of Fourteen Clocks and Watches Now in the Possession of the British Museum, London* (The Stationery Office 7 March 2012).

190 Woodhead (n 86) 173ff.

191 Weller (n 132) 7.

192 Weller (n 132) 1.

refined with reference to a comparison with carefully selected legal principle.[193] Finality may turn out to be elusive, however.

8.6 Elusiveness of Finality

Proving that a sale was for fair market value and voluntarily concluded can be difficult in civil cases. *University of Leipzig v Germany*[194] offers a striking example of the substantive problem involving the classification of artefacts in the Egyptian collection built up by the Egyptologist Professor Georg Steindorff (1861–1951).[195] It took 16 years to reach finality in an out-of-court settlement. The collection was not spoliated. The university acquired it for fair market value in a pre-April 1938 transaction. Steindorff exported and assembled his collection with the permission of the Antiquities Service in Egypt. Although his freedom to teach was curtailed in 1934 due to his Jewish ancestry, he was treated as a German national until he emigrated in March 1939. British Military Law No. 59 required, for a presumption of a forced sale (i.e. for restitution), only persecution and the transfer of property in a sale. This presumption could be rebutted by showing that (a) the seller received a fair market price; (b) he or she could access the purchase price and dispose of it freely; and (c) in case of sales after 15 September 1935 (entry date for the Nuremberg laws), the sale would have taken place in normal circumstances, without the Nazi regime in power, and that the seller's interests had been taken into account. British Law No. 59 did not displace German law, however. The legal question thus turned on the effect of the 1935 Nuremberg laws on the sale and the presumption.[196] The university bore the onus of proving that the Nazi laws played no part in the sale. Steindorff had compromised on the price and accepted less that he would have received had he sold to another purchaser. Without considering that Steindorff wanted the collection to remain with the university and that comparable prices were paid for similar sales at the

---

[193] Schönenberger (n 65) 228 and N Palmer, 'Spoliation and Holocaust-related Cultural Objects: Legal and Ethical Models for the Resolution of Claims' (2007) 12 Art Antiquity and Law 1, 11 support a more integrated approach.

[194] *University of Leipzig v Germany represented by the Federal Office that deals with Restitution Affairs and Unsolved Property Questions*, Berlin administrative court 26 May 2011, VG 29 K 126.09.

[195] Roodt (n 36) 460–62.

[196] Veraart and Winkel (n 28) 81.

time, the Berlin Court concluded that it was a forced sale.[197] Steindorff's only surviving legal heir, his grandson Thomas Hemer, also wished for the collection to be left in the care of the university. Hemer was unaware that, as a former Jewish citizen of East Germany, he could apply for restitution of the collection between 1990 and 1992. The JCC staked a claim based on information obtained about the history of the university in 1995. Between 2006 and 2011, Hemer declined to be represented by the JCC. During this period, the Federal Office requested details about the museum's acquisition in 2006 from Hemer and requested the JCC to withdraw their claim because Hemer wished for the collection to remain where it was. However, when Hemer claimed the collection from the Federal Office, he was informed that his claim came too late, and that the JCC was the legal owner. The collection had been sold before Steindorff's death, and as such, it was not part of Hemer's inheritance.[198] If the sale had been forced, Hemer would have been entitled as the lawful heir. The JCC denied having had any knowledge about Hemer when it staked its claim and declared itself willing to sell the artefacts to the Steindorff Museum at the current market value of the objects. The objects had to be handed to the JCC under the terms of the court order. Public protests ensued and the Egyptian Minister for Antiquities demanded that the JCC return the objects to Egypt. Only then was a mutually agreeable settlement found. The university and the JCC agreed that the university could keep the collection, and instead devote the compensation that would have been paid to the JCC to documenting Steindorff's life and work.

The irony was that the university initially lost the collection to the JCC on account of maintaining that the sale by Steindorff was voluntary. The German Civil Code could not undo the chaotic property transfer or Aryanisation of property during the Nazi era, but neither could legal presumptions. Since the JCC defined and exercised jurisdiction, Hemer was prevented from asserting a right.

German law was the only law pertinent to the classification of the transaction in the *University of Leipzig* case, but in international cases, the argument for restitution can be weakened if jurisdiction and applicable law run in tandem.[199]

In the multi-level apparatus of civil justice in the German legal system, decisions taken at first and even second instance are readily treated as

---

[197] D Raue, 'Georg Steindorff and His Collection' <www.iae-egyptology.org/uploads/Facts%20about%20the%20case.pdf> accessed 24 February 2014.

[198] Raue (n 197).

[199] Roodt (n 36) 462.

tentative and may be revisited at any point.[200] This is the position on account of the very narrow conception of *res judicata*. Parties who are dissatisfied with judicial findings have numerous appellate remedies at almost every stage of the proceedings. Ordinarily, an appellant has at least two potential levels of resort beyond the first instance local or district court proceeding.[201] German law reserves conclusive 'formal legal authority' for judgments that are subject to no further appeal. Decisional stability is reached only after the Federal Court of Justice has ruled.[202] In *Sachs v German Historical Museum*[203] the German Federal High Court successfully challenged the jurisdiction of restitution bodies and demonstrated its willingness to take full account of the moral dimension of art disputes. It overruled the *Beratende Kommission* on both jurisdiction and the norms applied during the mediation. The ruling by the highest authority had *res judicata* effect; the other rulings did not. In Germany, rights are settled only when the highest court has ruled. In the UK, however, competing conclusions reached in different fora remain a theoretical possibility; it may undermine the mediated settlement of private claims by the Spoliation Advisory Panel if the *lex situs* trump card is played and rights that existed under the applicable law are not neutralised by the public policy exception. When private parties request advice from the SAP, the SAP recommendation could leave legal ownership acquired under the *situs* rule in limbo. Recommending non-restitution where courts may find that the *situs* rule corroborates title, would be an invitation to proceed in court, where the *situs* rule could trump the advice.[204]

Regardless of who the disputants are, finality may be unattainable when the original owner chooses to remain anonymous in a case in which the SAP is requested to make a recommendation. Unless the SAP investigates all potential title claims made by third parties, rival third party claims may be brought after restitution was ordered.[205] One could

---

200 Y Sinai, 'Reconsidering Res Judicata: A Comparative Perspective' (2011) 21 Duke Journal of Comparative and International Law 353, 384.

201 Sinai (n 200) 386.

202 Sinai (n 200) 384.

203 *Peter Sachs v Stiftung Deutsches Historisches Museum*, Berlin Higher Regional Court 28 January 2010, 8 U 56/09; *Peter Sachs v Stiftung Deutsches Historisches Museum*, BGH 16 March 2012, v. ZR 279/10.

204 Carruthers (n 112) §§ 5.37–5.40; T O'Donnell, 'The Restitution of Holocaust Looted Art and Transitional Justice: The Perfect Storm or the Raft of Medusa?' (2011) 22 Eur J Int Law 49, 78.

205 Woodhead (n 86) 179.

also conceive of parallel conflicting decisions taken by two different advisory bodies in two different states.

The Germanic conception of *res judicata* contrasts strongly with that found in common law jurisdictions. In common law legal systems, finality is much broader in scope. A court may ignore previous rulings if no one complains of being vexed or harassed by the re-ventilation of the same claim (or issue).[206] Finality may still be elusive. At least the likelihood for competing conclusions in different fora in the UK is less if the defendant is one of the public collections listed in the enabling legislation.

9. CONCLUSION

This chapter considered the legal basis for restitution claims in international law. Reference was made to the post-war restitution of property rights, and the changes in the pattern in 1989. The elusiveness of a workable framework for compulsory international settlement was highlighted. Without a new treaty setting out the *modus operandi*, procedure and effects of the rulings of this body, courts, arbitral tribunals, special permanent mediators, independent mediators, negotiators and counsellors may all assume and exercise jurisdiction. Justice pluralism is here to stay.

Private international law has the capacity to support and strengthen the ethical dimension of Nazi spoliated art claims. It can steer the emerging relationship between statutory limitations and international law in the direction of value-based decision-making. It can offer control of the impediments to states' restitution obligations. Classification may block the application of forum law if it weakens the position of the claimant, and the public policy exception may block statutory limitations under foreign law that have this effect.

The close link between process, substance and outcome is inescapable in this category of claims. Formal and procedural justice assume greater relevance where material (substantive) justice is so hard to achieve. This makes it more difficult to ensure that rationality is value-based and substantive. Technical procedure-based defences deserve continual challenge for this reason.

State-run mediation is successful in several European states. In the UK, both state-run mediation and litigation support the restitution movement.

---

206 Sinai (n 200) 363.

Several cases litigated in Germany demonstrate that courts are willing to integrate moral interests in claims for restitution.

The tension between conflicts rules and ethics in the international dimension is striking in the circumstances of 'Belotto-type' international cases. This chapter explored whether private international law can ensure systemic justice. The definition of a forced sale is not uniform in the Belotto-type scenario. The definition may shift in accordance with the context, adjudicatory function and the willingness of the adjudicator to break the lock. Legal closure cannot be guaranteed in every Holocaust-related case.

7. Towards the equalisation of claims based on public and private law

1. INTRODUCTION

A 'vesting law' asserts state ownership in the vestiges of the past.[1] Source nations may benefit from having a measure of control over the dispersion of creative works and artefacts that lie in the ground or under water inside their territory. Laws that intend to control theft, looting and illicit excavation and export of antiquities and cultural objects which source states identify as theirs, enable states to institute claims to artefacts underneath the soil that have been removed, and to safeguard their interests as the natural and original 'home' of the object in question.

Rules of common law in respect of ownerless property may have a comparable effect.[2]

Extending respect to foreign law is an important element of international understanding which Rabel considered important in private international law.[3] Ultimately, this respect impacts on the success of civil claims for restitution against traffickers, dealers and middlemen. These laws can curb the global illicit trade of antiquities and archaeological material only when market states extend their application rather than confine it to the territory of the enacting state.

This perspective on the treatment of foreign law transcends the polarised national–international debates about ownership of cultural heritage. The internationalist ideal that national laws ought to be

---

[1] E.g. Law 117 on the Protection of Antiquities of 1983 (Egypt); Legal Bill regarding Prevention of Unauthorized Excavations and Diggings of 1979 (Iran); Protection of Items of Artistic or Historical Interest, Law No 1089 of 1939 (Italy). More examples are to be found among the 'new' states of the post-war world.

[2] E.g. *bona vacantia* principle, as applied in *Lord Advocate v University of Aberdeen and Budge* [1963] SC 533 (Scotland); A Saville, 'Treasure Trove in Scotland' [2002] Antiquity 796, 797.

[3] See Chapter 1.

employed for the good of all[4] certainly sounds simple enough, but restitution claims by source states are frustrated if they are instituted when export took place long before it became illegal to do so.[5] Claims may flounder once courts in market states have scrutinised assertions of state ownership.[6] The non-application of foreign law also hinders restitution. The good faith purchaser frustrated France in its bid for the return of seventeenth-century tapestries depicting scenes from the Odyssey (the 'Riom Tapestries') when they were stolen from a public building in Lyon in 1975.[7] The French government sued in Italian courts (France had not ratified the UNESCO Convention at the time[8]), arguing that the tapestries were unmerchantable, but the Italian courts held that the quality of unmerchantability was a question reserved for Italian state property, not for foreign property. Since Italian law was applied, valid transfer to a purchaser in good faith was permitted in the absence of a certificate of provenance or importation certificate, and despite the fact that the French public law provisions were comparable to Italian inalienability provisions. The French export prohibition does not automatically invalidate a sales contract governed by Italian law as the *lex contractus* of the sale.

Non-application of foreign law may have implications for the culture in question and for humanity inasmuch as it affects the access of the inhabitants of poor nations to their own cultural heritage and to world culture.[9]

In this chapter, the private law effect given to state claims to cultural objects in courts in the US, England and Germany is investigated. A thief, receiver of stolen property, or lawful owner may smuggle a cultural

---

[4] M Papa-Sokal, 'Beyond the Nationalist-Internationalist Polarisation in the Protection of the Archaeological Heritage' (2009) 14 Art Antiquity and Law 237, 265.

[5] *Greece v British Museum* is now pending in the 1978 UNESCO Intergovernmental Committee for Promoting the Return of Cultural Property to Its Countries of Origin. N Mealy, 'Mediation's Potential Role in International Cultural Property Disputes' (2011) 26 Ohio State Journal on Dispute Resolution 169, 173.

[6] C Forrest, 'Strengthening the International Regime for the Prevention of the Illicit Trade in Cultural Heritage' (2003) 4 Melbourne Journal of International Law 592 at IV.

[7] *Stato Francese v Ministero Italiano per i beni culturali e ambientali e De Contessini Livio*, Decision of the Tribunale di Roma on 27 June 1987, aff'd in the Corte d'Appello di Roma on 6 July 1992, upheld by the Corte di Cass (Sez I) 24 November 1995, No 12166. In general Papa-Sokal (n 4) 273.

[8] Ratification took place in 1997.

[9] Papa-Sokal (n 4) 248, 273.

object out of the state where it was found. Smuggled objects may end up in public or private collections after having been exported illegally, and source states may base claims on private law or on public law. As a general proposition, the judicial enforcement of foreign private law rights is not contentious, but there is considerable variation in state practice in regard to claims that are accessory to private law.[10] No neat distinctions can be drawn between the civil law and common law legal systems in this area. Differentiation between public and private interests has affected the level of protection which adjudicators have extended to cultural objects.

The application of foreign public law has long courted controversy.[11] Foreign public law potentially includes state ownership law and export control regulations, but there is no concept of public law that applies uniformly across states. The line between state ownership rules and export control regulations is drawn in different places in different legal families and cultures. The 1970 UNESCO Convention on the Means of Prohibiting and Preventing the Illicit Import, Export and Transfer of Ownership of Cultural Property[12] seeks to define international standards for export controls before international consensus has developed about what those standards should be.[13] This means that the distinction between stolen objects and illegally imported or exported objects, as well as the quality of the domestic support that is extended to export and import regulation schemes[14] and to the 1970 UNESCO Convention, assume relevance and can determine the outcome. A broad (and over-applied) axiom – to the effect that states are under no duty to enforce a foreign public law as opposed to foreign private law rights – has made it difficult for private international law to fulfil its co-ordinating function.

---

[10] IF Gazzini, *Cultural Property Disputes: The Role of Arbitration in Resolving Non-Contractual Disputes* (Transnational Publishers Inc. 2004) 31.

[11] A Jakubowski, 'Return of Illicitly Trafficked Cultural Objects Pursuant to Private International Law: Current Developments' in The Illicit Traffic of Cultural Objects in the Mediterranean (EUI Working Papers 2009) 137, 140.

[12] 14 November 1970, 823 UNTS 231; 10 ILM 289; entry into force on 24 April 1972.

[13] RK Paterson, 'The Legal Dynamics of Cultural Property' [1995] UBC Law Review 243, 257.

[14] E.g. Scheme for the Protection of the Material Cultural Heritage within the Commonwealth, for illegal exports from Commonwealth states, adopted at a triennial meeting of Law Ministers in Mauritius in November 1993.

The axiom originated as far back as the dispute involving the Medici family papers in 1918.[15] It featured prominently in the remarks by Lord Denning in *Attorney-General of New Zealand v Ortiz* in the Court of Appeal.[16] Not too long ago it featured in a Swiss Federal court case.[17] States may also refuse to recognise or enforce the cultural property export controls of other states based on concepts of sovereignty, territoriality of law and public policy, or with reference to international liberalisation of trade and freedom of movement arguments.[18]

The assumption that it would necessarily be contrary to the interests of the forum state if its courts were to apply the public law of another foreign sovereign state in areas where public interests call for protection, thereby serving the aims of that state, is persistent. It cannot be accepted uncritically, however. Recognition of punishment imposed by a foreign criminal court and foreign income can be justifiably denied,[19] and it does not pose a problem when states deny recognition or enforcement of foreign revenue and other taxes on this basis,[20] but the broad inclusion of all foreign public law in the non-application rule applied in civil proceedings is unjustifiable. Importing and exporting states may share similar interests in restricting the movement of cultural objects when the illicit trade is set in motion in the state that is deprived of its cultural heritage.

Despite stark differences among the devices that are employed, practice in respect of recognition and application of foreign public law has converged in the US and the UK. This is an encouraging development, considering the acrimony[21] that differences may cause, and the link between the legal diversity factor, legal uncertainty, illegal practices and forum-shopping.[22] Conceptual distinctions between state and private claims predisposes trafficked cultural materials to further exploitation. When attempting to vindicate a property right in a foreign court, a state

---

[15] *King of Italy v Marquis Cosimo de Medici Tornaquincy* 34 TLR 623 (Ch 1918); Gazzini (n 10) 34.

[16] *Attorney-General of New Zealand v Ortiz* [1982] 3 All ER 451–60.

[17] *India v Credit Agricole Indosuez (Switzerland) SA*, Decision of 8 April 2005, BGE 131 III 418.

[18] JH Merryman, 'Cultural Property, International Trade and Human Rights' (2001) 19 Cardozo Arts and Entertainment 51, 64–65.

[19] International Law Association, Cultural Heritage Law Committee Report, Berlin Conference 2004, 3 <www.ila-hq.org/> accessed 24 February 2014.

[20] *Attorney-General of New Zealand v Ortiz* [1982] 3 All ER (CA) 432, 433; *Huntington v Attrill* [1893] AC 150.

[21] Paterson (n 13) 258.

[22] Gazzini (n 10) 37.

plaintiff ought to stand on equal terms with its private claimant subjects.[23] The chapter highlights the most encouraging signs of equalising the treatment of state and private claims and developments that have weakened the public law taboo.

2. INTERNATIONAL LAW AND DOMESTIC REGULATIONS

2.1 No General Customary Law Rule

Most jurisdictions prohibit the exportation of broad classes of cultural objects without a special permit, yet illegal export does not bar an object from being lawfully imported elsewhere. The fact that export has taken place without a permit does not automatically mean the object in question is contraband when imported at destination. A mechanism at the level of international law would be required, and there is no general rule of customary international law that states need to restitute cultural objects when other states claim them. This is why the repeated confirmations of the confiscation order by Italian courts in respect of the Atleta di Fano (Getty Bronze)[24] has not taken the matter forward. No source nation can, on its own, create an international obligation for other nations to recognise and enforce its export control measures. The criminal law of Italy does not apply extra-territorially and its public law does not automatically apply abroad. Absent a negotiated settlement, the case will turn on private international law rules, so that the question becomes whether Italian public law will be applied in a US court, or whether an Italian court order will be enforced in the US.

---

[23] TW Pecoraro, 'Choice of Law in Litigation to Recover National Cultural Property: Efforts at Harmonization in Private International Law' [1990] Virginia Journal of International Law 1, 12.

[24] Including, but not limited to Tribunal of Pesaro, Order of 12 June 2009, No 2042/07 RGNR; Tribunal of Pesaro, Order of 10 February 2010, No 2042/07 RGNR; Court of Cassation, 18 January 2011, No 6558; Third Criminal Chamber of the Supreme Court 3 May 2012.

2.2 Regional and International Instruments Contain Mostly Uneven Export/Import Restrictions

It is important to understand the position under treaty law.[25] The main ethos of the 1970 UNESCO Convention is to stop the illicit import and export of illegally removed cultural property.[26] While export certificates are prescribed, the Convention does not require signatories to require those certificates for import. This can present an issue for a private owner who finds himself without recourse when the state concerned does not wish to take action or does not designate the object.[27] The 1995 UNIDROIT Convention supports the enforcement of state ownership laws (vesting laws) in the event of unlawful excavation and trade. Illegally exported cultural objects must be physically returned to the requesting state if the removal from its territory has been shown to have significantly impaired certain cultural interests. Non-parties to the UNIDROIT Convention such as the US will apply ordinary civil law rules.

The EU Council Directive 93/7/EEC of 15 March 1993[28] does not differentiate between stolen property (which could include objects removed in breach of a state ownership or vesting law) and illegal exports.[29] Nonetheless, it permits and regulates the extra-territorial enforcement of national law provisions designed to counter unlawful exports of national treasures of artistic, historic or archaeological value from Member States. To date, English courts have not elaborated on how the Directive subverts the axiom on the non-recognition of foreign public

---

[25] A Lanciotti, 'The Dilemma of the Right to Ownership of Underwater Cultural Heritage: The Case of the "Getty Bronze"' in S Borelli and F Lenzerini (eds), *Cultural Heritage, Cultural Rights, Cultural Diversity: New Developments in International Law* (Nijhoff Publishers 2012) 301, 317.

[26] See Art 2(1) of the UNESCO Convention.

[27] SO Forbes, 'Securing the Future of Our Past: Current Efforts to Protect Cultural Property' (1996) 9 Transnational Law 235, 246.

[28] Council Directive 93/7/EEC of 15 March 1993 on the Return of Cultural Objects Unlawfully Removed from the Territory of a Member State, OJ L 74/74, 27.3.93 with amendment of the annex by Directive 96/100/EC of the European Parliament and of the Council of 17 February 1997 (L 60/59, 1.3.1997), and by Directive 2001/38/EC of the European Parliament and of the Council of 5 June 2001, OJ L 187/43, 10.7.2001.

[29] A Biondi, 'The Merchant, the Thief and the Citizen: The Circulation of Works of Art within the European Union' (1997) 34 Common Market Law Review 216.

law in the form of export controls.[30] Directive 2014/60/EU supports the objectives of the EU in respect of preventing and combating unlawful trafficking in cultural objects. Recital 9 refers in express terms to objects originating from clandestine and regular excavations. Similar to Directive 93/7/EEC, the ownership of the cultural object is to be ascertained in accordance with the law (including the public law) of the requesting Member State.[31]

The 1984 Consultative Document on the Commonwealth Scheme for the Protection of the Material Cultural Heritage raised the possibility of an import prohibition scheme which became known as the 'Commonwealth' or 'Mauritius Scheme'.[32] The Scheme prohibits the import of items that were exported without a permit as required by the country of export. An operative event (transgression of the laws of the exporting state) triggers the import controls that apply in the 'country of location' (the place where the object is located when the return provisions of the Scheme are invoked by the country of export). The phrase 'country of location' is likely to be more precise than 'state of origin' or *situs*. The country of location does not enforce the laws of the country of export; the operative event brings the laws of the country of location into play, so that the court of the place where the object is located can enforce its own laws. The Scheme avoids the direct application of the laws of the exporting state, but its intended operation qualifies and challenges the axiom of non-enforcement of foreign public law. While the Scheme has attracted criticism,[33] its procedures for recovery are attractive because they do not derogate from any existing means of recovery of items of cultural heritage, nor do they interfere with the status of existing owners. The Scheme complements the 1995 UNIDROIT Convention without exacerbating the problem of human and financial resources for Commonwealth courts.[34]

---

30 This aspect was not commented on in *Government of the Islamic Republic of Iran v The Barakat Galleries Ltd* [2009] 1 QB 22 (CA) at §§ [128] and [130].

31 Among others Art 13 of Directive 2014/60/EU of the European Parliament and of the Council of 15 May 2014 on the Return of Cultural Objects Unlawfully Removed from the Territory of a Member State and amending Regulation (EU) No 1024/2012 (Recast) OJ EU L159/1, 28.5.2014.

32 See n 14 above.

33 LV Prott and PJ O'Keefe, *Law and the Cultural Heritage Vol. 3 Movement* (1989) 588, 606, 625; PJ O'Keefe, 'Protection of the Material Cultural Heritage: The Commonwealth Scheme' [1995] ICLQ 147, 153.

34 P O'Keefe, *Commentary on the UNESCO Convention 1970* (Institute of Art and Law 2000) 153.

Unfortunately, the Scheme has not resulted in concrete action.[35] It is up to individual Commonwealth countries to pass legislation to bring the principles of the Scheme into operation. A country that wishes to add its weight to the Scheme would have to restrict its export controls to heritage of real national importance, since these are the only items that would justify the time and expense of preparing a request for return.

Since the Commonwealth Scheme is not operational and the Schengen Area[36] is being enlarged in a borderless Europe, the level and standards of import and export controls raise concern. In the Schengen Area, border checks are abolished and may be re-instituted in exceptional circumstances only.[37] This tempts art thieves, corrupt dealers and collectors operating a black market within the Area. British and Irish nationals travel freely in the Common Travel Area of the British Isles. The UK opted out of the Schengen Agreement. Consequently, Scotland is an external border with non-Schengen countries. Regulation 116/2009 imposes uniform controls on the export of protected goods to non-member countries in the EU. It specifically requires export licences for the export of national cultural assets from Member States to a third state. It does not apply intra-EU. Intra-Schengen movement is conducted subject to Member States' right of return in respect of 'national treasures possessing artistic, historic or archaeological value', but export permits are not required. A comparison of imports recorded by customs authorities in the US and the records kept by customs authorities in exporting countries has revealed a reporting gap that correlates directly with the corruption level of the exporting country.[38] Customs officials and border patrols can be amenable to bribery and corruption[39] and are implicated in criminal markets.[40] They require ongoing training, among other things,

---

35 *Government of the Islamic Republic of Iran v The Barakat Galleries Ltd* [2009] 1 QB 22 (CA) at § [162].

36 Created in 1985 with 5 members, but now encompassing 25 EU states and 4 non-EU states. See EC Regulation 562/2006 of the European Parliament and of the Council of 15 March 2006 establishing a Community Code on the rules governing the movement of persons across borders (Schengen Borders Code). The UK, Ireland, Romania, Bulgaria and Cyprus are not participating.

37 Art 23 of the Schengen Borders Code (n 36).

38 R Fishman and S Wai, 'The Smuggling of Art, and the Art of Smuggling: Uncovering the Illicit Trade in Cultural Property and Antiques' (2009) 1 American Economic Journal: Applied Economics 82.

39 E.g. the poor reputation of Italian customs police at the time of the Medici Conspiracy. P Watson and S Todeschini, *The Medici Conspiracy* (Public Affairs 2006) 12.

40 E.g. human trafficking.

with regard to the types and appearance of objects in order to identify these during border checks.

2.3 Standard of Implementation of Treaty Obligations under UNESCO Convention

2.3.1 Flexible and narrow models

Most of the states party to the UNESCO Convention prohibit the import of illegally exported cultural objects from other nations that are party to the Convention, and do not require a bilateral treaty for the operation of import controls in respect of objects that have been stolen from museums or undocumented objects stolen from sites. Canadian and Australian law recognise the export laws of reciprocating states by way of a bilateral or a multilateral treaty.[41] Progressive import restriction models such as the Swiss model can respond to future cultural heritage crisis in another state party.[42] Swiss law authorises the Swiss Federal Council to enter into agreements with other states party to UNESCO to secure cultural heritage; additional measures may be adopted when exceptional events threaten the cultural heritage. This model is more flexible than the Canadian and Australian models.

2.3.2 US model

Before the US ratified the 1970 UNESCO Convention in 1982, it demanded that several changes be made. The US delegation opposed the commitment to enforce foreign export controls that was included in the revised draft prepared by the Secretariat, and counter-proposed more limited procedures for such recognition.[43] The alternative proposal affected the final form of both Articles 7(b) and 9 of the UNESCO

---

41 Cultural Property Export and Import Act, Consolidated Statutes of Canada, Chapter c 51, s 37(1), (2) RSC 1985; Protection of Movable Cultural Heritage Act 1986 (Australia), s 14(3). <www.unesco.org/culture/natlaws> accessed 24 February 2014.

42 Federal law on the International Transfer of Cultural Goods of 20 June 2003 (LTBC; No 444.1); P Gerstenblith, 'Recent Developments in the Legal Protection of Cultural Heritage' in N Brodie, MM Kersel, C Luke and K Walker Tubb (eds), *Archaeology, Cultural Heritage and the Antiquities* Trade (University Press of Florida 2006) 68, 77, 83.

43 Senate report No 27.925 27.

Convention. The US has treated Article 9 as an agreement to make further agreements.[44]

The US adheres to a restrictive, non-self-executing approach. It does not prohibit the import of cultural objects that are not stolen, unless another state party has requested the US to impose import restrictions on designated categories of materials;[45] import restrictions are in place by virtue of a bilateral agreement;[46] or emergency action has been taken under the Cultural Property Implementation Act (CCPIA).[47] A mechanism was set up for the negotiation of bilateral and multilateral agreements involving import restrictions in respect of cultural objects. Import controls can be established at the request of another signatory nation and after a determination by the President that: (a) the cultural patrimony of the requesting nation is in jeopardy from the pillage of its archaeological or ethnological materials; (b) the requesting nation has taken measures to protect its cultural patrimony; (c) import restrictions are necessary and would be effective in dealing with the problem; and (d) the restrictions are in the general interest of the international community.[48] China concluded a bilateral agreement with the US in January 2009 in respect of Chinese archaeological items dating from between 75 000 BCE to 907 CE, for instance.[49] Tibetan and Taiwanese archaeological finds must be certified for import into the US under this Agreement.[50]

Furthermore, the President may deny entry to archaeological or ethnological material to which an emergency condition applies;[51] and may refuse entry to any stolen items from museums or public monuments (which takes account of Article 7(b)(1) of the UNESCO Convention).[52]

---

[44] M Papa-Sokal, 'The US Legal Response to the Protection of the World Cultural Heritage' in N Brodie, MM Kersel, C Luke and K Walker Tubb (eds), *Archaeology, Cultural Heritage and the Antiquities Trade* (University Press of Florida 2006) 36, 37.

[45] Bilateral agreements that apply to designated cultural materials will only last for a maximum of five years.

[46] O'Keefe (n 34) 102–6.

[47] CCPIA, 19 US Code 2602–2603.

[48] CCPIA, 19 US Code 2602(a)(1)(A)–(D) (2003). *United States v Schultz*, 333 F3d 393 at 440–41.

[49] R Schechter, 'Preventing Pillage and Promoting Politics: The Dual Goals of the 2009 US–China Bilateral Agreement to Restrict Imports of Chinese Cultural Property' (2009) 14 Art Antiquity and Law 317, 322–25.

[50] For more, see Schechter (n 49) 322ff, 235ff.

[51] Emergency Implementation of Import Restrictions, 19 US Code 2603(a) and (b).

[52] Stolen Cultural Property, 19 US Code 2607.

The Cultural Property Advisory Committee reviews the requests for import bans, and recommends action to the US Department of State.

This implementation model gives scope to museums to argue that the US does not enforce foreign public laws absent a treaty.[53] In order to qualify to bring a request in the first place, diplomatic relations with the US must exist. Iraq was unable to present a request for this reason.[54]

The CCPIA defines how the UNESCO Convention applies in the US.[55] It regulates import controls over cultural objects and assists states parties to the 1970 UNESCO Convention in the recovery of cultural property. Property that enters the US in violation of the CCPIA is subject to seizure, forfeiture and repatriation.[56] Provision is made only for civil forfeiture of cultural materials belonging to limited classes of stolen cultural objects mentioned in Article 7(b) of the UNESCO Convention.[57] No criminal penalties are provided for. The CCPIA relieves the country of origin from the burden of proving ownership. If foreign export controls have been breached, restitution can be achieved on the basis of these agreements with other States Parties to the UNESCO Convention, even in the absence of a foreign law that assigns ownership to the foreign state.

Because the UNESCO Convention is not retroactive and the CCPIA entered into force only in 1983, materials illegally exported into US territory before 1983 remain unaffected regardless of their problematic provenance.[58] For instance, having been imported into the US between 1974 and 1978, the claim for return of the Atleta di Fano (Getty Bronze) will not be within the scope of the Convention.[59]

2.3.3 Position in the UK

It took the UK altogether 32 years to accede to the UNESCO Convention. Significantly, when the Commonwealth Scheme was proposed in 1993, the UK declared that it would not be in a position to apply it. In

---

53 Compare the Getty's non-return argument in respect of the Atleta di Fano ('Victorious Youth').

54 Executive Order 70 Fed Reg 29435, 2005 WL1243182 extended the declaration of emergency and import prohibition in respect of materials removed from Iraq after August 1990; see Gerstenblith (n 42) 82.

55 Mealy (n 5) 178.

56 CCPIA, 19 US Code 2600(a), (b)(1) and (c)(A)(2006).

57 CCPIA, 19 US Code 2601–2613. 308–11 are the sections of the bill that originally enacted the CCPIA.

58 Art 7(a) of the UNESCO Convention refers to the undertaking to take measures that are consistent with national legislation.

59 Lanciotti (n 25) 319.

1999, prior to the enactment of any formal legislation to implement the UNESCO Convention in the UK, the English court decided *R v Tokeley-Parry*.[60] Police were alerted when Tokeley-Parry, a British conservator, arranged for the British Museum to translate a number of Egyptian papyri, which were identified as stolen from a government store in Egypt. Investigations began in 1994. The search uncovered a network of individuals who contributed to the criminal excavations and exportation of ancient Egyptian artefacts, as well as the regular shipments to the duty-free zone at Zürich Airport before bringing objects to the UK. Tokeley-Parry kept meticulous journal accounts of his smuggling and of the false provenance created for this purpose.[61] In an effort to make the head of Amenhotep III appear like a cheap souvenir, Tokeley-Parry had crassly disguised it with clear liquid plastic, gold leaf and black paint. Four legal trials on three different continents followed: two in Britain, one in Cairo and one in New York.[62] Tokeley-Parry freely admitted to smuggling looted antiquities out of Egypt, but claimed that it was not a crime in the UK to import looted objects. He was found guilty on two counts of dishonestly handling antiquities under section 22(1) of the Theft Act 1968.[63] Section 22(1) provides that a crime is committed if a person handles stolen goods, knowing or believing them to be stolen goods, dishonestly receives the goods, or dishonestly undertakes or assists in their retention, removal, disposal or realisation by or for the benefit of another person, or if he arranges to do so. He was also convicted of making a false statement to procure a passport, and received a jail sentence of six years.

This case demonstrated how English law dealt with the activities that breached the Theft Act, but the case also involved criminal activities resulting in the depletion of another country's cultural heritage.

On 9 February 2000, the government announced that it had decided against signing the UNESCO Convention because 'significant practical difficulties remain in implementing its provisions into UK law'.[64] The nature of these practical difficulties was not made clear at the time.[65]

---

[60] *R v Tokeley-Parry* [1999] Crim LR 578.

[61] Gerstenblith (n 42) 71.

[62] P Watson, 'The Investigation of Frederick Schultz' (*McDonald Institute for Archaeological Research*) <http://www2.mcdonald.cam.ac.uk/projects/iarc/culturewithoutcontext/issue10/watson.htm> accessed 24 February 2014.

[63] S 22(1) of the Theft Act 1968 c 60 (Eng).

[64] Hansard, 9 February 2000.

[65] N Brodie, J Doole and P Watson, *Stealing History: The Illicit Trade in Cultural Material* (McDonald Institute for Archaeological Research 2000) 40.

Accession by the UK was achieved, at last, when the crisis in Iraq assumed disastrous proportions, on 1 November 2002.[66] The UK registered a number of reservations to counter what it considered to be the main weaknesses of the instrument. The reservations were to the effect that the UK: will interpret the term 'cultural property' in Article 1 in accordance with the Annex to EU Regulation 3911/1992 and Directive 1993/7; will apply relevant EC instruments as between EU Member States to the extent that the legislation covers matters to which the Convention applies; and will interpret Article 7(b)(ii) so as to permit application of its existing rules on limitation to claims for the recovery and return of cultural objects.[67]

Ever since 2002, the UK has been bound by the weak provisions on import controls contained in the UNESCO Convention.[68] Cultural property may enter the UK unless the Theft Act 1968 or the Dealing in Cultural Objects (Offences) Act 2003 precludes entry.[69] Neither one of these domestic laws responds to import control as the Commonwealth Scheme suggests, or takes proper account of import and export controls.

An offence is committed under the Theft Act 1968 if an accused dishonestly receives, retains, removes stolen goods or otherwise arranges to do so for the benefit of another. The Act requires only that the theft amount to an offence where it occurs at the time it is committed.[70] In other words, an offence is committed regardless of where the theft took place, whether it took place before or after the Act was promulgated,[71] or whether foreign law applies.[72] In several other respects, however, the Theft Act of 1968 is ill-equipped to respond to the contemporary challenges associated with the illicit antiquities trade. On the face of the Theft Act, it seems that looted property exported to England and Wales may be claimed by the source nation,[73] but the definition of property excludes whatever forms part of the land. Consequently, buried artefacts are considered excluded and illegal excavation does not automatically

---

[66] House of Commons Written Answers, 13 March 2001, col 569w.

[67] § 61 of the Report of the Ministerial Advisory Panel on Illicit Trade (2000); K Chamberlain, 'UK Accession to the 1970 UNESCO Convention' (2002) 7 Art Antiquity and Law 231, 239.

[68] 2195 UNTS 443.

[69] Open General Import Licence declared by the Department of Trade and Industry; SRM MacKenzie, *Going, Going, Gone: Regulating the Market in Illicit Antiquities* (Institute of Art and Law 2005) 69.

[70] S 24(1) of the Theft Act 1968 c 60 (Eng).

[71] S 24 of the Theft Act 1968.

[72] *R v Tokeley-Parry* [1999] Crim LR 578.

[73] Mealy (n 5) 187.

constitute theft.[74] In addition, where a dealer bought an item in good faith but realised afterwards that it had been stolen and decides to sell it on without reporting the crime, section 22 of the Theft Act precludes prosecution. The handler must either have received the goods dishonestly or arranged for their disposal dishonestly and for the benefit of another.[75] Because the Act applies only to stolen property handled 'for the benefit of another person', it holds only the middlemen to account.[76] Prosecution for handling is not feasible when the middleman has broken the transaction chain.

The discovery of Tokeley-Parry's activities incriminated Schultz, who was a prominent and successful art dealer in New York City. Between them, they misappropriated approximately two thousand items belonging to the cultural heritage of Egypt. Schultz had provided the money for both the excavations and the smuggling of Egyptian objects, and was deeply involved in the subsequent dealing of the illicitly acquired antiquities. Schultz never anticipated that Tokeley-Parry's arrest would have any repercussions for himself, and he even presented Scotland Yard with a fraudulent receipt to 'prove' his ownership to 'The Offerer', which had been seized during a raid on Tokeley-Parry's residences.[77]

The Dealing in Cultural Objects (Offences) Act 2003 codified the criminal law under which Tokeley-Parry had previously been convicted.[78] General legislative provision had been made elsewhere for restitution of property stolen by the accused to the deprived owner. For instance, in 2000 the Crown was granted the power to order an accused to return stolen property to the rightful owner, and so to combat the illicit trade in antiquities.[79] The 2003 Act did not put in place any system of return for the objects in respect of which an offence had been committed. Seizure or forfeiture was not provided for. Because the implications of the Egyptian state ownership law were not highlighted in *R v Tokeley-Parry*,[80] nothing prompted the legislature to consider this aspect. In fact, the UK government was satisfied that existing law was sufficient. There were gaps in the context of illegal excavation and goods handled for personal benefit, and consequently the main impetus for the Act was the

---

74 S 4(2) of the Theft Act 1968.

75 *R v Bloxham* [1983] 1 AC 109.

76 S 22(1) of the Theft Act 1968; Mealy (n 5) 187.

77 <http://www2.mcdonald.cam.ac.uk/projects/iarc/culturewithoutcontext/issue10/watson.htm> accessed 24 February 2014.

78 Gerstenblith (n 42) 76.

79 S 148 of the Powers of Criminal Courts (Sentencing) Act 2000.

80 *R v Tokeley-Parry* [1999] Crim LR 578.

opportunity it presented to Parliament to demonstrate that it was serious about implementing the UNESCO Convention.

The 2003 Act created a new 'tainted cultural object offence', which relies on an expansive definition of 'tainted' objects as those illegally excavated and those that are stolen. There is no age threshold for cultural objects or for the buildings or monuments from which an object has been removed, and nothing is automatically included or excluded on account of age. A person is guilty of an offence under the 2003 Act if he dishonestly[81] deals in a cultural object that is tainted. It is immaterial whether he knows or believes that the object is a cultural object,[82] but he must know or believe that the object is tainted in the sense that it was excavated illegally or removed from a building, monument or structure of historical, architectural or archaeological interest, and the excavation or removal contravened the law of any jurisdiction at the time of the activity.[83] The unlicensed excavation or the removal (which may or may not constitute theft or criminal damage, but which has to constitute an offence under the local law to qualify) must have occurred after 30 December 2003.

In order to commit an offence under this Act, the accused must have had knowledge or belief that he was damaging a protected monument or that he was dealing with a tainted object.[84] The 'knowing', 'believing' and 'dishonesty' requirements complicate proof of the offence, because a plea of unawareness of provenance can be entered. No consequences attach to conscious avoidance of knowledge or wilful ignorance under the 2003 Act. Anyone who claims ignorance of the nature of a vesting law and the local status of the artefacts in England can escape conviction. Dealers desist from asking questions about provenance rather than report suspicions to the police or expose themselves to uncovering organised crime in the market.[85] This leniency in respect of effective due diligence

---

[81] The standard is likely that in *R v Ghosh* [1982] QB 1053.

[82] S 1(1) and (2) of the Dealing in Cultural Objects (Offences) Act 2003.

[83] S 2(1) and (2) of the Dealing in Cultural Objects (Offences) Act 2003. Contrast s 28 of the Ancient Monuments Act, in terms of which the accused has to have knowledge or must believe that he is damaging a protected monument to qualify for an offence.

[84] Art 1(1); in contrast, the defence of mistaken belief that the excavation took place on private land would only be available under ARPA, 16 US Code 470aa–470mm (2000), if the permission of the landowner had been obtained.

[85] S MacKenzie, 'The Market as Criminal and Criminals in the Market: Reducing Opportunities for Organised Crime in the International Antiquities Market' in S Manacorda and D Chappell (eds), *Crime in the Art and Antiquities World* ((2011 Springer) 69, 74.

in relation to object provenance appeals to a handful of commentators,[86] but critics realise that the likelihood of successful legal action is limited when failure to run adequate checks on the provenance of an object does not constitute knowledge or belief.[87]

This stopgap measure has not worked. The scope of the Act is limited by the date of enactment and the exclusion of fine art. It is particularly striking that the Act does not include illegally exported objects within its definition of 'tainted objects',[88] despite the frequency of illegal export, the ease with which illegal export can be proved compared to illegal excavation, and the difficulty involved in obtaining evidence of the 'taint'.

While dealers do seem to be more aware of circumstances surrounding items with suspicious provenance, the value of this Act is considered to be principally cosmetic or symbolic.[89]

2.4 State Ownership Rules and Export Control Regulations

National laws usually vest title of antiquities of a specified type or age that are within the national territory, but that are undiscovered as of the effective date of the statute, in the state.[90] Patrimonial rights could be established also if finders are statutorily required to declare their finds to the state or if unreported finds are declared forfeit to the state.

Export control measures prevent the outflow of works of art and antiquities or prohibit the unlicensed export of designated classes of national artistic treasures, even by the rightful owner.[91] These measures are not necessarily confined to objects situated in their original home state, nor do they apply exclusively to the most valuable national treasures.[92] Compared to vesting laws, they cover a much broader category comprising all classes of art and antiquities and affecting a variety of different sub-categories.[93] Controls range from the most liberal permission to export broad categories of works subject only to the right

---

86 WG Pearlstein, 'Buying and Selling in Today's Market' (2012) 3 Spencer's Art Law Journal 1, 8.

87 MacKenzie (n 85) 73.

88 MacKenzie (n 85) 73.

89 MacKenzie (n 85) 71.

90 Papa-Sokal (n 4) 259.

91 Papa-Sokal (n 4) 259.

92 Jakubowski (n 11) 146.

93 A Chechi, *The Settlement of International Cultural Heritage Disputes: Towards a Lex Culturalis?* (unpublished PhD Thesis EUI 2011) 74.

to purchase national treasures or to grant a temporary export permit,[94] to more restrictive controls which include: (a) embargo laws that render the object *extra commercium* (the right of state pre-emption may be included) or imprescriptible (exempting it from the effects of time); (b) consequences of a breach of customs regulations (which may entail pre-emption of legal transfer, or automatic transfer of title to the state by means of forfeiture, which confines the object to its territory); and (c) total bans of certain exports in the absence of permits. Both the legal basis and the means of recovery are different from cases in which sovereign claims derive from state ownership laws. If export controls are considered to be excessively broad in scope or stringent in their operation, non-enforcement is likely.[95] The practice of non-recognition may extend to: (a) export restrictions in force in the state of origin as a ground for refusing import;[96] (b) criminal sanctions associated with illicit import and trade in stolen and illegally imported or excavated objects;[97] and (c) restitution of illegally exported objects.[98]

The extraterritorial application of foreign export controls that apply in the absence of any assertion of state ownership has met with resistance before[99] and remains contentious.[100] The UNESCO Convention does not

---

94 Temporary export permit granted by the South African Heritage Resources Agency in 2012 in respect of 'Arab Priest' by Irma Stern (classed as a work of national importance older than 50 years in terms of the National Heritage Resources Act, No 25 of 1999). Bonhams did not inform the purchaser, the Qatar Orientalist Museum, that export permission is not automatically granted.

95 Chechi (n 93) 89; Papa-Sokal (n 4) 260–61.

96 *US v An Antique Platter of Gold* 991 F Supp 222 (SDNY 1997), aff'd [1999] USCA2 301; 184 F3d 131 (2nd Circuit 1999)(seizure and forfeiture of ancient gold phiale originating and stolen from Sicily); Gazzini (n 10) 30.

97 *US v Hollinshead*, 495 F2d 1154 (9th Circuit 1974); *US v McClain*, 545 F2d 658 (1978), *US v McClain*, 593 F2d 658 (1979), *cert denied*, 444 US 918 (1979) 671 (civil forfeiture based on violation of criminal statute); Gazzini (n 10) 30.

98 *Bumper Development Corporation v Commissioner of Police for the Metropolis* [1991] 1 WLR 1362; [1991] 4 All ER 638 (CA); *Republic of Ecuador v Danusso Civil and District Court of Turin*, First Civil Section 4410/79; Court of Appeal of Turin Second Civil Section 593/82; 18 Rev dir int priv proc 625 (1982); Gazzini (n 10) 30.

99 *Attorney-General of New Zealand v Ortiz* [1982] 3 All ER 451ff; *Attorney-General of New Zealand v Ortiz* [1983] 2 All ER 93 (HL); *US v McClain* 545 F2d 997–1004.

100 J Ulph and I Smith, *The Illicit Trade in Art and Antiquities* (Hart 2012) 28.

enable the systematic enforcement of all export controls. A broad blanket ban on the exportation of cultural objects in the absence of a valid certificate[101] stands in the way of trade; it could confine the movement of art and cultural objects to the contemporary art trade and museum exchanges. Owners have a right to fair compensation when an export permit is denied. When state authorities delay their exercise of a right of pre-emption in respect of a cultural object, human rights arguments would support a claim in respect of the legal effect of the delay.[102] Clearly, the liberalisation of export controls implies a careful balancing of the public interest in retaining the most significant items and rights of private owners.[103]

With regard to the effect of vesting laws and export controls in foreign jurisdictions, national courts do not necessarily consider justiciable a claim brought by a foreign sovereign, directly or indirectly, to enforce its export laws, nor do they always regard the violation of foreign export controls as a ground for restitution in the courts of the importing state.[104] Export prohibitions or controls are generally treated independently of the question of title or ownership,[105] unless illegal exportation qualifies as theft in the state of origin for purposes of the application of domestic law. If a state has established patrimonial rights in regard to undiscovered objects in its territory, removal without permission means the object is

---

[101] A Koush, 'Fight against the Illegal Antiquities' Traffic in the EU: Bridging the Legislative Gaps' (Bruges Political Research Papers Series 2011) 22. Contrast the 1973 Convention on International Trade in Endangered Species of Wild Fauna and Flora, 3 March 1973; entry into force 1 July 1975 (CITES). CITES requires countries to sight export documentation before allowing import. <http://www.cites.org/eng/disc/text.php> accessed 24 February 2014.

[102] *Beyeler v Italy* (Application no 33202/96), 2002 ECHR 462, 28 May 2002 (Italian authorities took longer than four years to exercise a right of pre-emption in respect of 'Portrait of a Young Peasant' by Van Gogh under Italian export control regulations. A statutory two-month period was supposed to have applied. This administrative inertia violated Art I of the First Protocol to the European Convention for the Protection of Human Rights and Fundamental Freedoms); *Sud Fondi Srl c Italia* (Application no 75909/01), 20 January 2009.

[103] See the 'Virgin Adoring the Sleeping Christ Child' by Botticelli, which was acquired for the Scottish National Gallery in 1999 after a museum in Texas had tried to buy it. Jakubowski (n 11) 147–48.

[104] Gazzini (n 10) xxvi.

[105] In the definitions section in Art 1 of the 1995 UNIDROIT Convention on Stolen or Illegally Exported Cultural Objects, 'restitution' refers to stolen objects, whereas 'return' relates to objects removed from the territory of a Contracting State in breach of its export restrictions.

stolen and the deprived nation may then allege that the remover is a thief in the event of illegal export.

There is no denying that vesting laws can serve a political construction of cultural property that is remote from any cultural interest. In this form, they could provide backing for modern national retentionist policies in respect of the antiquities found underneath the soil. This aspect has caused some scepticism in relation to blanket claims of state ownership.[106] Some commentators disapprove of conferring exclusive power on source states to determine which movement is legitimate and which is not.[107] Scepticism is bolstered further by utilitarian arguments that indicate how national restrictions on the sale and export of cultural materials contribute to the growing black market in art and antiquities.[108]

Vesting statutes and export controls can be difficult to distinguish for private international law purposes, and this may complicate a state's claim based on theft. A vesting law enables a nation to allege theft in the event of illegal export,[109] but the distinction between export controls and vesting laws blurs when the law ordains forfeiture upon illegal export. In addition, a vesting statute might mask a simple regulatory export control measure. New Zealand brought the claim in the *Ortiz* case because the Maori group that had been deprived was not in a position to establish their claim to ownership. The trial court and the Court of Appeal differed on the question of whether cultural objects that leave the territory without having been seized can be forfeited. The exporter legally owned the Taranaki Panels whilst in New Zealand; the panels were forfeit to the state under the Historic Articles Act of 1962 only when they left the territory. The trial court ruled that the forfeiture occurs automatically upon illegal export, but the Court of Appeal held that it occurs only upon seizure; since the Taranaki Panels were not seized, New Zealand was neither the owner nor was it entitled to possession. An English court could not adjudicate on the enforcement of a statute that grants title to

---

106 JH Merryman, 'Cultural Property Internationalism' [2005] IJCP 11, 32; JH Merryman, 'A Licit International Trade in Cultural Objects' (1995) 4 IJCP 13, 34.

107 JH Merryman and JAR Nafziger, 'The Private International Law of Cultural Property in the United States' (1994) 42 AJCL Supplement 221, 237.

108 PM Bator, 'An Essay on the International Trade in Art' (1982) 34 Stanford Law Review 275, 315, 318.

109 As the Appeal Court did in *Attorney-General of New Zealand v Ortiz* [1982] 3 All ER 451; JH Merryman, 'The Public Interest in Cultural Property' [1989] California Law Review 339, 363; Bator (n 108) 348–9; KE Yasaitis, 'National Ownership Laws as Cultural Property Protection Policy: The Emerging Trend in United States v Schultz' (2005) 12 IJCP 95, 99.

the Crown at the moment of unlicensed export.[110] The House of Lords upheld the Court of Appeal on the narrower ground that the law fell short of automatic forfeiture,[111] but New Zealand's restitution claim was still denied. Legislative amendments have since followed to prevent such a result in future,[112] but new interpretations of vesting laws and up-to-date legislation are not guaranteed. Maori material culture continues to be highly sought after by private collectors and cultural institutions alike.[113]

The ghost of the non-application default rule still remains alive in many national frameworks that remain averse to the recognition of foreign public law in the absence of treaty and legislation. Courts may be drawn to scrutinise the wording of the national legislation rather than the foreign vesting statute in question. If a vesting statute is regarded to be a front for export regulations or blanket enforcement of state ownership legislation is resisted unless enforcement serves local policy interests, non-application is likely.[114]

3. EQUALISING THE TREATMENT OF CLAIMS BASED ON PUBLIC AND PRIVATE LAW: ROLE OF PRIVATE INTERNATIONAL LAW

While criminal proceedings and co-operation treaties in criminal matters can result in the return of objects to their state of origin, there is no automatic application of foreign criminal sanctions associated with illicit import and trade in stolen and illegally imported or excavated objects.[115] Similarly, there is no rule requiring the enforcement of foreign public law in private international law. Rules and doctrines that pose as a 'public law

---

[110] *Attorney-General of New Zealand v Ortiz* [1982] 3 All ER 432.

[111] *Attorney-General of New Zealand v Ortiz* [1983] 2 All ER 93.

[112] The Antiquities Act 1975 contains provisions on export restriction (e.g. s 5) and on the vesting of title in the Crown (s 11).

[113] <http://www.webbs.co.nz/department/oceanic-and-african-art> accessed 24 February 2014.

[114] The debate continues among the ranks of scholars in the US, e.g. Merryman and Nafziger (n 107) 236; Papa-Sokal (n 4) 237; the non-application rule still has support in the UK, see L Collins et al. (gen eds), *Dicey, Morris and Collins on The Conflict of Laws* (14th edn, Sweet & Maxwell 2006) S 5-033; S 24-012, S25-012 and Chapter 25.

[115] See Treaty on Mutual Assistance in Criminal Matters, US–Italy, 24 ILM 1536; signed 9 November 1982; entry into force 13 November 1985.

taboo' or 'axiom' of non-application of foreign public law in private international law may have the opportunity to assert themselves, therefore.

Contrasting approaches prevail across different legal cultures and families with regard to recognition and application of foreign public law. While the doctrine of non-application is perennially challenged, it is also remarkably persistent.[116]

3.1 Non-application by Default: The Public Law Taboo as Articulated in *Ortiz*

English legal doctrine propounds that courts lack jurisdiction to try a claim based on foreign public law[117] or to enforce foreign penal, revenue and other public laws or an act of state, either directly or indirectly.[118] Lord Denning's remarks in *Attorney-General of New Zealand v Ortiz* in the Court of Appeal are the classic example of the axiom at work in the context of cultural objects.[119] His definition of the category that will not be recognised and enforced in an English forum was expansive; it covered *acta jure imperii*, namely penal and revenue laws, and extended to other public laws, including export controls.[120] Because the forfeiture provision in question formed part of a statute that took effect at the moment of illegal export, he classified it as a public law with a penal character. In his opinion, English courts could not entertain a suit brought by a foreign sovereign, directly or indirectly, to enforce its public laws, if that state purported to exercise sovereignty beyond the limits of its authority.[121] He posited that the enactment of a forfeiture provision was an exercise of sovereign authority and that no state had sovereignty beyond its own frontiers. Legislation prohibiting the exportation of works

---

[116] The litigation on the Atleta di Fano or 'Getty' Bronze demonstrates the application of this axiom in Italian courts; for more, see Lanciotti (n 25) 308. In respect of the position in the UK, see the re-iteration by Ulph and Smith (n 100) § 6.12, § 6.32 and § 6.33. *Government of the Islamic Republic of Iran v The Barakat Galleries Ltd* [2007] EWHC 705 (QB)(Iranian ownership declaration a foreign public and penal law and therefore unenforceable in England) has now been reversed by *Government of the Islamic Republic of Iran v The Barakat Galleries Ltd* [2008] 1 All ER 1177 (CA) (axiom of non-enforcement of foreign penal law not applicable).

[117] Ulph and Smith (n 100) § 6.12, § 6.32 and § 6.33.

[118] Collins (n 114) 5R-019-054.

[119] *Attorney-General of New Zealand v Ortiz* [1982] 3 All ER 451.

[120] *Attorney-General of New Zealand v Ortiz* [1982] 3 All ER 451 at 457b.

[121] *Attorney-General of New Zealand v Ortiz* [1982] 3 All ER 451 at 457a, e.

of art, and providing for their automatic forfeiture if they were to be exported, was included in this category because it is an act done in the execution of sovereign authority. The principles of the sovereign equality of states and the territorial authority of sovereign states[122] prevent a foreign state from enforcing its own law extraterritorially.[123] These principles are reflected in state immunity. The courts of one state are in no position to adjudicate on the actions of another state, nor exercise jurisdiction to aid a foreign state to act in excess of its jurisdiction.[124] If courts were to rule on the actions of another state, the courts of that state could be tempted to retaliate. In addition, the act of state doctrine implies that courts will not question the validity of a foreign state's public acts and that states have no right to perform acts of sovereignty within the territory of other states.[125] These rules can have a bearing on the litigation venue when the defendant is a foreign state.

Had the UNIDROIT Convention been in force between the UK and New Zealand at the time of the *Ortiz* ruling, New Zealand could have requested the return of the Taranaki Panels and resisted the payment of compensation to Ortiz on the basis that he should have known, given the circumstances of the purchase, that their exportation would be illegal.[126]

That title could vest independently of seizure was a possibility which Lord Brightman contemplated in the House of Lords,[127] but vesting was only considered possible while the antiquities are located within the country because the vesting law cannot be given retroactive or extraterritorial effect.[128]

While Lord Denning thought that diplomatic means ought to be used to effect restitution until such time as an international convention could be concluded, this approach was fundamentally inconsistent with the co-operation that nations ought to develop in their relations with one another. As Staughton J remarked in the Court of Appeal:

---

122 M Anton, *Handbuch Kulturgüterschutz und Kunstrestitutionsrecht/ Illegaler Kulturgüterverkehr: (Handbuch Kulturguterschutz und Kunstrestitutionsrecht)* (De Gruyter 2010), Vol 3, 107–9; Jakubowski (n 11) 144.

123 *Attorney-General of New Zealand v Ortiz* [1982] 3 All ER 451 at 459j.

124 *Government of the Islamic Republic of Iran v The Barakat Galleries Ltd* [2007] EWHC 705 (QB) § 97.

125 Gazzini (n 10) 31.

126 BT Hoffman (ed), *Art and Cultural Heritage: Law, Policy and Practice* (CUP 2006) 147.

127 *Attorney-General of New Zealand v Ortiz* [1983] 2 All ER 93 (HL) at 100f–g.

128 P Gerstenblith, 'Schultz and Barakat: Universal Recognition of National Ownership of Antiquities' (2009) XIV Art Antiquity and Law 21, 34.

> Comity requires that we should respect the national heritage of other countries, by according both recognition and enforcement to their laws, which affect the title to property while it is within their territory. The hope of reciprocity is an additional ground of public policy leading to the same conclusion.[129]

The development of co-ordination among diverse legal systems is a common function of private and public international law.[130] Private international law can provide a neutral framework for co-ordination of divergent expressions of regulatory authority.[131] In an interdependent world, mutual courtesy based on justice and convenience – or rather, the inconvenience, injustice and confusion that would result if the application of foreign law were always refused[132] – is a factor to be considered.[133] Mutual refusal to take foreign rules into account encourages cross-border illicit trafficking;[134] it will contribute to the formation of 'locks', which do not serve the interest of global welfare.[135]

Respect for the national heritage of other countries, and the mutual courtesy that this implies, resonates with the elements that underpinned the conception of comity in the Roman-Dutch School: *aequitas*, *humanitas* and *utilitas*.[136] Arguably, in international claims to cultural objects, these elements deserve to be given full expression. The need to foster comity of nations in claims for return of cultural objects has also been

---

[129] *Attorney-General of New Zealand v Ortiz* [1982] 3 All ER 432 at 451b–c. A contrasting view of comity was espoused in *Spiliada Maritime Corporation v Cansulex Ltd* in the context of *forum conveniens*.

[130] *Hunt v T&N plc* [1993] 4 SCR 289 per La Forest J.

[131] H Muir Watt, 'Choice of Law in Integrated and Interconnected Markets: A Matter of Political Economy' (2003) 9 Columbian Journal of European Law 383, 405–6.

[132] P Voet, *De Statutis et eorum Concursu Liber Singularis* trs AB Edwards and DM Kriel under the title *The Selective Paul Voet* (University of South Africa 2007) 4.2.7; 4.2.17 (*Summarium*); J Voet, *Commentarius ad Pandectas* tr P Gane as *The Selective Voet: Being Selections on the Pandects* (Butterworths 1829) 1.4.12 Appendix.

[133] LV Prott, 'Problems of Private International Law for the Protection of the Cultural Heritage' V *Recueil des Cours* (The Hague 1989) 215, 267; I Stamatoudi, *Cultural Property Law and Restitution* (Edward Elgar 2011) 96 n 210.

[134] Pecoraro (n 23) 30.

[135] For more on private international law and global welfare, see Muir Watt (n 131) 405ff.

[136] AB Edwards and DM Kriel, *The Selective Paul Voet* (University of South Africa 2007) 349.

recognised in England.[137] For this reason, the weighing of foreign rules on a case to case basis seems to be the appropriate course of action. Opportunities arise to build global solidarity[138] in situations where provisions designed for the protection of cultural objects are found in both forum law and foreign law; the foreign provision claims application; its application is internationally acceptable; and its application does not encroach on any cognisable interest of the forum.[139]

3.2 The Position in Civil Law Systems

Many civil law systems recognise foreign public law as suggested by the Institute of International Law in the Wiesbaden Resolution of 1975[140] and the Oslo Resolution of 1977.[141] The Resolutions advance liberal propositions concerning the application of foreign public law. The Wiesbaden Resolution provides that, subject to the public policy reservation, the public law character of a provision of foreign law does not prevent its application in the context of either the main or the preliminary (incidental) question *a priori*. Incidental question theory[142] enables a court to determine ownership under foreign public law before deciding upon a restitution claim. The theft poses an incidental question or functions as an independent connecting factor. An independent determination enables the conflicts rules of the forum to determine it, unlike in the case of so-called dependent application, which enables the conflicts rules of the law that governs the main question to determine the incidental question. Selecting

---

137 *Bumper Development Corporation Ltd. v Commissioner of Police of the Metropolis and Others* [1991] 1 WLR 1362 CA (1991) (right of Indian temple is superior to title acquired by Bumper Corporation; artificial procedural considerations should not prevent recognition and enforcement of legitimate legal right).

138 For more on the connection between global solidarity and humanism, see L Wilde, *Global Solidarity* (Edinburgh University Press 2013) 106ff.

139 H Kronke, 'Capital Markets and Conflict of Laws' V (286) *Recueil des Cours* (The Hague 2000) 245, 288.

140 *Institute of International Law Yearbook Vol. 56 Session of Wiesbaden 1975*, 20th Commission, Res. 4: The Application of Foreign Public Law, 551–53.

141 *Institute of International Law Yearbook Vol. 57 Session of Oslo1977*, 20th Commission, 'Public Law Claims Instituted by a Foreign Authority or a Foreign Public Body' <http://www.idi-iil.org/idiE/resolutionsE/1977_oslo_01_en.pdf> accessed 24 February 2014.

142 R Schuz, *A Modern Approach to the Incidental Question* (Kluwer Law International 1997); M Weller, 'Iran v Barakat: Some Observations of the Application of Foreign Public Law by Domestic Courts from a Comparative Perspective' (2007) 12 Art Antiquity and Law 279, 288.

the result based on forum policy offers another alternative.[143] Under the Wiesbaden Resolution, courts are supposed to consider the potential consequences of the exclusion of such norms. The Oslo Resolution declares that the application of foreign public law in claims instituted by a foreign claimant state depends on the subject-matter of the claim, the needs of international co-operation, and the interests of the states concerned.[144] Foreign public law claims that are 'consequential or accessory to private law claims' may be admitted if 'the convergence of the interests of the states concerned' justifies this. Sovereign claims that are accessory to private law entitlements may fit into standard categories such as contract or property. Even if they relate to objects that were not in the possession of the claimant state, these claims are to be considered admissible.[145] Most civil law systems adhere to these guidelines provided forum policy is not contradicted by doing so,[146] with courts being willing to conceive of public and private ownership on equal terms.[147] Swiss law recognises that there are no *de jure* impediments to the application of public law, but 2005 saw the Federal Supreme court apply the axiom of non-application.[148] Import restrictions can be adopted on the basis of the Swiss Federal Act on the International Transfer of Cultural Property of 2003 (CPTA). Liberal approaches that void transfers of cultural property in violation of foreign export rules have been adopted in Portuguese[149] and Dutch rulings.[150] Direct application of foreign public law[151] means

---

[143] Schuz (n 142).

[144] *Session of Oslo 1977* (n 141) IIa; Weller (n 142) 282.

[145] *Session of Oslo 1977* (n 141).

[146] Jakubowski (n 11) 145.

[147] *Arnamagnaean Institute v Ministry of Education* 1966 UfR 22; 1971 UfR 299 (Denmark); *Republic of Ecuador v Danusso* Civil and District Court of Turin, First Civil Section 4410/79; Court of Appeal of Turin Second Civil Section 593/82; 18 *Rev dir int priv proc* 625 (1982) (Italian court recognised a type of property intermediate between public and private property, on a continuum between mere assertion of ownership and actual possession).

[148] Decision of 8 April 2005, BGE 131 III 418.

[149] In Portuguese law, the condition of reciprocity applies. See G Carducci, 'The Growing Complexity of International Art Law: Conflict of Laws, Uniform Law, Mandatory Rules, UNSC Resolutions and EU Regulations' in BT Hoffman (ed), *Art and Cultural Heritage: Law, Policy and Practice* (CUP 2006) 68, 69.

[150] *Batz-sur-Mer Madonna with Child Re Raad v OvJ*, Hoge Raad (Criminal Division) 18 January 1983, NJ (1983) 1402, Nr 445 (restitution by a Dutch court).

[151] Art 13 of the Private International Law Act of 1987 (Switzerland); *Türkische Republik v Kanton Basel-Stadt*, Basel Trial Court judgment 16 August

that precedent is steadily building in favour of the restitution of wrongfully removed cultural objects.[152] The German model (investigated under 5.2.2 below) has reached an advanced stage in respect of the application, recognition and enforcement of foreign public law, even if export in violation of foreign export prohibitions is not always considered for purposes of establishing good faith.[153]

Notwithstanding the advances with regard to the recognition of foreign public law, practices in regard to the recognition and enforcement of inalienability and indefeasibility provisions differ at times within one and the same civil law state. Internal inconsistencies have been evident in Italy.[154]

3.3 Involvement of Private International Law in the Challenge to the Doctrinal Obstacle to Restitution

In Anglo-American common law systems, forum conceptions and standards remain significant. Non-application of foreign public law stands in the way of restitution of cultural objects as a matter of legal doctrine[155] rather than an obstacle that relates to ownership. While it is a popular conception that it reflects the public international law restrictions on the jurisdiction to enforce, the better view is that public international law does not prohibit courts from enforcing foreign public law, but rather authorises states to refuse enforcement without requiring as much.[156] The method and structure of private international law does not block the application and recognition of foreign public law. The application of a

---

1993, aff'd Basel Court of Appeal, 18 August 1995, aff'd Swiss Supreme Court, 22 May 1996.

[152] Chechi (n 93) 106.

[153] *N de N c/N et al*, Swiss Federal Supreme Court, 28 May 1998 SJ 1999 I 1, ground 4d/cc.

[154] Contrast the Riom Tapestries case (n 7 above) with *Republic of Ecuador v Danusso* Civil and District Court of Turin, First Civil Section 4410/79; Court of Appeal of Turin Second Civil Section 593/82; 18 *Rev dir int priv proc* 625 (1982) (Ecuadorian export ban in respect of a cultural item acquired in Ecuador recognised; the sales contract was governed by the law that imposed special protections on national property). Gazzini (n 10) 36; K Siehr, 'International Art Trade and the Law' VI (243) *Recueil des Cours* (The Hague 1993) 9, 188–90; Prott (n 133) 265–66.

[155] B Schönenberger, *The Restitution of Cultural Assets* (Eleven International Publishing, 2009) 146–49.

[156] A Mills, *The Confluence of Public and Private International Law* (CUP 2010) 65, 228; Siehr (n 154) 51, 187.

foreign public law provision that does not contradict forum public policy is permissible if that provision belongs to the applicable law and there is not impediment to its application.[157] In addition, foreign public law may be taken into account as a *datum* irrespective of whether domestic or foreign law applies.[158] It may constitute an operative element in the articulation of a rule that denies enforcement to transactions tainted by illegality or immorality. Progressive scholars have long been calling for the abandonment of the public law taboo, among other things to permit the displacement of forum public law.[159] A few scholars have categorically declared that foreign public law is capable of international application.[160]

Lowenfeld was particularly disturbed by Lord Denning's ruling in *Ortiz*, which he thought subjected New Zealand to the literalism of the 'revenue rule'. Lowenfeld spelt out the consequences[161] and predicted that *Ortiz* would encourage smuggling and theft since it lent 'comfort to swindlers, organisers of cartels, tax evaders, and others whom the law ought not to stretch its principles to protect.'[162] He expressed his disenchantment with a general, elastic category of rules that qualified for non-application, and that enlarged to include practically any legislation that went beyond the traditional common law.[163] His criticisms are fully justified, but the source state may be unable to prove the illegal export of the objects in question. While his views were unpopular, he deserves

---

[157] Jakubowski (n 11) 144.

[158] AA Ehrenzweig, *Private International Law* (Sijthoff 1967) 83–84 on 'foreign rule by nonchoice'; HW Baade 'Operation of Foreign Public Law' in *International Encyclopedia of Comparative Law Vol. III* Chapter 12, 16ff; K Lipstein, *Principles of the Conflict of Laws, National and International* (Nijhoff 1981) 69, 111–12.

[159] Muir Watt (n 131) 401–2; WS Dodge, 'Breaking the Public Law Taboo' (2002) 43 Harvard International Law Journal 161; AF Lowenfeld, 'Public Law and the International Arena: Conflict of Laws, International Law, and Some Suggestions for Their Interaction' II (163) *Recueil des Cours* (Sijthoff & Noordhoff 1980) 311, 322 (on the 'public law tabu').

[160] G Droz, 'The International Protection of Cultural Property from the Standpoint of Private International Law' in Council of Europe, *International Legal Protection of Cultural Property: Proceedings of the 13th Colloquy on European Law* Delphi 20–22 September 1983 (1984) 115; C Staker, 'Public International Law and the *Lex Situs* Principle in Property Conflicts and Foreign Expropriations' (1987) 58 BYBIL 151, 152.

[161] AF Lowenfeld, 'Conflict of Laws English Style' (1989) 37 AJCL 353.

[162] Lowenfeld (n 161) 394.

[163] L Collins, 'Professor Lowenfeld and the Enforcement of Foreign Public Law' (2009) 42 International Law and Politics 125, 133.

credit for realising the importance of considering the effect of 'crimes of global reach'[164] on discrete domestic legal systems.

The axiom of non-application derives from doctrine, and could also be neutralised by it. Reported cases are sparse, but there have been encouraging signs that indicate that public law controls in respect of objects of outstanding cultural significance can be applied. English courts are becoming increasingly more attuned to the nature of state ownership and the implications of regulations designed to protect it, considering that the Court of Appeal in England permitted a sovereign claim by Iran to recover antiquities that form part of its national heritage and which complied with the requirements of private international law.[165] Iran asserted its title to fourth millennium BCE antiquities against a Bond Street art dealer in *Iran v Barakat Galleries Ltd.*[166] The antiquities were allegedly excavated, taken and unlawfully exported from cemeteries in the Jiroft region in 2001. The relics were undiscovered when the vesting provisions of Iran law took effect. Iran claimed conversion, but Barakat Galleries disputed the origin of the objects. This meant that the claim turned on the factual question of the origin and find spot of the allegedly looted antiquities. The parties agreed that the question of title had to be settled with reference to the *lex situs* of the antiquities at the time title was created.

The court at first instance held that the Iranian ownership declaration was a foreign public and penal law which was unenforceable in England.[167] It did not enforce Iran's immediate right of possession. It held that the 1979 Legal Bill regarding Prevention of Unauthorised Excavations and Diggings did not make a clear statement of national ownership that vests title to undiscovered antiquities in the state. It was found to be criminal in nature and thus could not establish a proprietary right when Iran had no actual possession of the antiquities.[168]

The ruling of the court at first instance was overturned on appeal[169] and the claim in conversion held to be tenable. The Court of Appeal took

---

[164] Lowenfeld (n 161) 325.

[165] *Government of the Islamic Republic of Iran v The Barakat Galleries Ltd* [2009] 1 QB 22 (CA) at § [154].

[166] *Iran v Barakat* (n 165).

[167] *Government of the Islamic Republic of Iran v The Barakat Galleries Ltd* [2007] EWHC 705 § 81.

[168] *Iran v Barakat* (n 165) §§ [89] and [90]. In this respect, the ruling was based on the view adopted in respect of justiciability in *Ortiz*.

[169] *Iran v Barakat* (n 165) (axiom of non-enforcement of foreign penal law not applicable). For a critical analysis of the case, see A Briggs, 'Decisions of

account of the law of the place where the rights claimed by Iran originated. It adopted a purposive interpretation to the relevant statutes and allowed special provisions dealing with antiquities to take precedence over general provisions.[170] It ruled that Iran's title was conferred by legislation and that actual possession is not required in order for it to enforce its patrimonial claim in England.[171] In any event, the court was of the view that a claimant could bring an action in conversion without having a proprietary right. English law would treat a right to immediate possession on the part of a state as a patrimonial claim equivalent to a declaration of ownership. While the claim was unique to a state and could only be brought by a state,[172] the court did not equate this to an assertion of sovereign rights,[173] nor did it view the claim as based on a pure governmental interest. Iran was found to regulate its ownership of antiquities and to enjoy all the incidents of that ownership under the terms of the 1979 Legal Bill,[174] unlike an accidental finder. A functional view of the nature of property ownership as a bundle of rights was the preferred view, which was held to include both ownership and an immediate right to possession. It is encouraging that the court adopted a restrictive approach to the non-enforceable category of public law, limiting it to penal and revenue laws (e.g. exchange controls). The court did not characterise its approach as the judicial recognition of foreign public law by an English court.[175] While some parts of the 1979 Legal Bill were penal, other parts vested ownership in the state without depriving anyone who was already an owner of artefacts of an interest. Significantly, no definitive position was adopted in respect of export controls and the list of laws that will not be enforced.[176] The ruling is silent on whether a foreign state's claim for recovery of possession of its public property would be enforced.

British Courts in 2007' in *British Year Book of International Law* (OUP 2008) 588, 630ff.

[170] *Iran v Barakat* (n 165) § [54].

[171] *Iran v Barakat* (n 165) § [143]–[150].

[172] Briggs (n 169) 631–33 indicates that the court in fact failed to respond to this question. He avers that it responded only to a carefully selected question it was prepared to answer, namely whether the state claimed as owner.

[173] *Iran v Barakat* (n 165) § [149].

[174] *Iran v Barakat* (n 165) § [68]–[72].

[175] *Iran v Barakat* (n 165) § [90] where the court commented on the ruling of the court at first instance that a claim for enforcement is not justiciable in England; Ulph and Smith (n 100) 252; Schönenberger (n 155) 215; Weller (n 142) 292–95.

[176] *Iran v Barakat* (n 165) § [128].

Iran's interest may have been a sovereign act pure and simple had the acquisition of ownership been compulsory, such as through seizure of the items or through confiscation or expropriation.[177] Seizure or confiscation would require prosecutorial assistance from the English court to complete the claim on behalf of Iran[178] if Iran had not completed the acquisition by reducing the items to possession. In the circumstances of the *Barakat* case, however, Iran's ownership was complete. Iran invoked a rule of a private law nature in the service of its claim, and did not need assistance.

The appellate ruling stated that it would be contrary to public policy to shut out a state claim to recover antiquities that form part of its national heritage and which otherwise complied with the requirements of private international law.[179] Reference was made to a number of legal instruments which indicated international acceptance that protection of national heritage was desirable and mutual assistance among nations needed for this purpose. None of these instruments affected the outcome of the appeal directly,[180] but it is particularly encouraging that the court recognised the duty states have internationally to assist one another to prevent the unlawful removal of cultural objects. Shutting out the claim that public interests call for protection would not comply with this duty and would contravene public policy.[181] Thus, the strict public policy objection to an international claim for recovery was relaxed in the light of the indication given by international instruments that the international community accepted the desirability of protecting national cultural heritage. That the policy choice made by the court was based on international instruments conforms to the vision of Rabel for private international law,[182] and the ideas Lowenfeld had about the intersection of private international law and cultural heritage law.[183]

---

177 *Princess Paley Olga v Weisz* [1929] 1 KB 718 (CA).
178 Collins (n 163) 144.
179 *Iran v Barakat* (n 165) § [154].
180 *Iran v Barakat* (n 165) §§ [156]–[163].
181 *Iran v Barakat* (n 165) §§ [154]–[155].
182 E Rabel, *The Conflict of Laws: A Comparative Study Vol. 4* (Ann Arbor, U Mich 1958) 40.
183 Lowenfeld (n 161).

4. QUALIFYING THE DOCTRINAL OBSTACLE TO RESTITUTION AND THE PUBLIC LAW TABOO

4.1 By Legislative Initiative

Courts in the Member States of the EU are competent under European rules to return an object in recognition of foreign state law protecting cultural treasures, and to enforce a judgment involving a cultural object in respect of which another EU Member State or third state has asserted ownership. This competence derives from the Council Directive (EEC) 93/7 of 15 March 1993 on the return of cultural objects unlawfully removed from the territory of a Member State[184] and from domestic legislation that gives effect thereto.[185] In similar vein, Directive 2014/60/EU counters the axiom of non-enforcement of foreign public law by means of procedures and criteria for the return of objects that were removed unlawfully from any of the Member States' territories.

Anti-money laundering laws, such as the Proceeds of Crime Act 2002, have also circumvented the axiom of non-enforcement of foreign export controls.[186] Anti-money laundering and forfeiture laws create offences for knowing or suspecting that the handling of antiquities in one country represents proceeds of a predicate crime (theft) in another.[187] Cash sales of valuable property with poor records, sold under the rubric of no-questions-asked, already expose dealers to prosecution.[188] Proceeds of these sales are recoverable as proceeds of crime. Objects can be taken into custody or seized if there is evidence of criminal conduct or if the

---

184 OJ L 74/74, 27.3.93 amended 1997 and 2001.

185 E.g. the Return of Cultural Objects Regulations 1994, which transposes the Directive into UK law; *Gesetz zur Ausführung des UNESCO-Übereinkommens vom 14. November 1970 über Maßnahmen zum Verbot und zur Verhütung der Rechtswidrigen Einfuhr, Ausfuhr und Übereignung von Kulturgut und zur Umsetzung der Richtlinie 93/7/EWG des Rates vom 15. März 1993 über die Rückgabe von Unrechtmäßig aus dem Hoheitsgebiet eines Mitgliedstaats Verbrachten Kulturgütern* 18. Mai 2007 (BGBl. I 757, No 21 2547), which transposes the Directive into German law.

186 D Chappell and K Polk, 'Unravelling the "Cordata": Just How Organized Is the International Traffic in Cultural Objects?' in S Manacorda and D Chappell (eds), *Crime in the Art and Antiquities World* (Springer 2011) 99, 110.

187 S MacKenzie, 'Illicit Deals in Cultural Objects as Crimes of the Powerful' (2011) 56 Crime Law Social Change 133, 135.

188 Ulph and Smith (n 100) 267, 270.

accused benefited from his or her 'criminal lifestyle',[189] without the need to prove either dishonesty or that the property was stolen.

The non-application default rule has been modified by legislation and by treaty in Canada and Australia.[190] The same is true for the US, where conflicts doctrine precludes the application of foreign penal and revenue law.[191] The unique position adopted by courts in the US differs from the growing readiness in the UK to admit positive reasons of policy to allow claims based on foreign state ownership laws where title must be determined.[192] The position adopted by US courts receives more detailed treatment in the next section.

4.2 By Judicial Recognition of Foreign Law Categories of Ownership

US courts apply foreign public law only when this is accommodated in the law, and they check whether the restitution of illegally exported objects is backed up by a treaty or bilateral agreements on import controls.[193] The question of the direct application and enforcement of foreign cultural heritage laws is avoided, but in terms of the *McClain/Schulz* doctrine, the *lex situs* after illegal import of an object – even if dogmatically applied – can recognise categories of ownership which the foreign law in question is based on. US courts repatriate smuggled cultural objects[194] to source states on the basis of its federal crime statute, the National Stolen Property Act (NSPA).[195] Originally enacted to enable criminal federal prosecution for stolen cars taken across state borders, the NSPA carries both financial and incarceration penalties for receipt and interstate transportation of stolen goods. The general features of the

---

[189] S 6(4); convictions for money laundering under ss 327 and 328 attract the use of the lifestyle assumptions under s 75 and schedule 2 of the Proceeds of Crime Act 2002.

[190] Consolidated Statutes of Canada, Chapter C-51, s 37(1), (2); Protection of Movable Cultural Heritage Act 1986 (Australia), s 14(3).

[191] EF Scoles, P Hay et al., *Conflict of Laws* (St Paul, Minn 2000) 142; Weller (n 142) 290.

[192] Ulph and Smith (n 100) 51; Collins (n 114) S 5-033; S 24-012; S25-012, and Chapter 25.

[193] 19 US Code 2091–2095 (1972) (certain pre-Columbian sculpture or murals to be seised and returned at the expense of the country of origin); 19 US Code 2602–2611 (agreements to implement Art 9 of the UNESCO Convention); agreements that designate groups of cultural property (http://exchanges.state.gov/culprop/chart.html); Schönenberger (n 155) 75–76; Pearlstein (n 86) 3.

[194] Schönenberger (n 155) 214–15.

[195] National Stolen Property Act, 18 US Code 2314–2315.

NSPA coincidentally also enabled the courts to prosecute for the handling of goods known to be stolen from an owner who lives abroad.[196] The NSPA soon became a tool in the repatriation of foreign cultural objects that have been transported, transmitted, transferred, received, possessed, or sold by anyone who knew that they had been stolen. The NSPA applies to both discovered and undiscovered archaeological finds.

The actual legal grounds for seizures in terms of the NSPA are found in US customs regulations and not in the NSPA itself.[197]

The core question is whether property that had been sold or discovered qualifies as 'stolen' for purposes of the NSPA when claimed, and whether a declaration of national ownership is a prerequisite for the application of the Act.[198] The knowing violation of a foreign ownership law may result in criminal liability under this Act.[199] The state ownership laws in the states where the objects were excavated and exported from, was recognised as having private law effect in *US v Hollinshead*,[200] *US v McClain*[201] and *US v Schultz*.[202] The property category of the foreign legislation was recognised, and the objects were considered 'stolen' for purposes of the NSPA.[203] 'Stolen property' is given broad scope.[204] Regardless of where the property was stolen, US authorities can do what the state ownership law authorises the foreign state to do.[205]

The *McClain* ruling defined the international dimension of claims to cultural objects for the Second Circuit, which encompasses New York. The defendants planned to smuggle Mexican pre-Columbian ceramic

---

196 E.g. *US v Schultz* 333 F3d 402–3.

197 Schönenberger (n 155) 68.

198 *US v McClain*, 545 F2d 988 (5th Circuit 1977) at 992, 996, 1000–1001; *US v McClain*, 593 F2d 658 (5th Circuit 1979) 670–71.

199 18 US Code 2314, 2315; Weller (n 142) 290.

200 *US v Hollinshead* No 10970 (SD Cal 14 March 1973); 495 F2d 1154 (9th Circuit 1974) (taking of well-documented Maya stele in Guatemala constitutes theft for NSPA purposes).

201 *US v McClain*, 545 F2d 988 (5th Circuit 1977) reh'g denied, 551 F2d 52 (5th Circuit 1977) aff'd in part, rev'd in part, 593 F2d 658 (5th Circuit 1979) *cert denied*, 444 US 918 (1979).

202 *US v Schultz*, 178 F Supp 2d 445 (2002); 333 F2d 393 (2nd Circuit 2003) *cert denied US v Schultz*, 540 US 1106.

203 A Goldberg, 'Reaffirming McClain' [2006] UCLA L Review 1031, 1041; MBG Lufkin, 'End of the Era of Denial for Buyers of State-Owned Antiquities: United States v Schultz' (2002) 11 IJCP 305.

204 *US v McClain*, 545 F2d 988 (5th Circuit 1977) 994–97; *US v Schultz*, 333 F3d 393 (2nd Circuit 2003) 402–3.

205 Yasaitis (n 109) 97.

articles and jewellery across state lines. Export of pre-Columbian items became forbidden when the Mexican Federal Law on Archaeological, Artistic and Historic Monuments and Zones Act extended public control over previously privately owned property. Consequently, illegally exported items would be considered 'stolen' from Mexico. The Act, which took effect in 1972, contained terms that were sufficiently clear for a US citizen to understand.[206] Having deliberately ignored the clear and unambiguous state ownership, the defendants were convicted on the substantive counts of dealing in stolen property that was already in the US. These convictions were reversed because it was not conclusively established that the articles were removed from Mexico after the vesting law took effect in 1972. The conviction for conspiracy to continue removing antiquities was allowed to stand.[207] This conviction clarified that the NSPA applies when smugglers are aware that a foreign state ownership law exists, and that it applies to the antiquities in question, because smugglers know then that the items are stolen.[208] When the case was appealed a second time, the requirement was formulated as that the defendant must either have known that the objects were stolen, or that removal of the objects violated the law that confers national ownership on the source state.[209]

For a restitution claim to succeed and a conviction for theft to be obtained under the NSPA, actual possession of the objects by the source state is not necessary. All that is required to avoid giving retroactive and extraterritorial effect to national legislation[210] is proof: (a) that the provision that vests ownership is sufficiently clear to give notice of what conduct is prohibited (foreign judges cannot be expected to solve interpretational problems); (b) that the cultural objects concerned were found within the borders of the modern political unit after the date of its commencement;[211] and (c) that the conversion had taken place after the

---

[206] *US v McClain*, 545 F2d 988 (5th Circuit 1977) 997–1004.

[207] *US v McClain*, 593 F2d 658 (5th Circuit 1979) 670–72.

[208] *US v McClain*, 545 F2d 988 (5th Circuit 1977) 1002.

[209] *US v McClain*, 593 F2d 658 (5th Circuit 1979) 660–63.

[210] Gerstenblith (n 128) 25.

[211] The object must be documented and catalogued by the source state. Any undocumented material from an earlier civilisation found inside the geographic territory inhabited by lineal descendants of that civilisation cannot found a conviction. E.g. *Peru v Johnson*, 720 F Supp 810 (CD Cal 1989 aff'd sub nom *Peru v Wendt*, 933 F2d 1013 (9th Circuit 1991) (recovery of Inca antiquities failed in California partly due to erratic domestic application); *Republic of Croatia v The Marquess of Northampton 1987 Settlement*, 610 NYS2d 263 (NY App Div 1994), *cert denied*, 84 NY2d 805 (NY 1994) (Hungary and Croatia laid

effective date of the vesting law.[212] The *McClain* doctrine was successfully applied in several civil claims for the recovery of stolen archaeological objects and restitution was made where the prerequisites of the doctrine were satisfied.[213] Courts check whether a foreign provision that aims to achieve prevention and control, sanction, forfeiture and restitution based on ownership or conversion, lives up to the court's own standards of unambiguous title and vigorous local enforcement against nationals and foreigners.[214] Evidence of consistent domestic enforcement is required before courts will consider the application of such a provision locally.[215]

It is now accepted that the CCPIA and the NSPA are not mutually exclusive in the international movement of undocumented objects. They operate in respect of different aspects of US public policy and in different contexts.[216]

Twenty-five years after the decision in *McClain*, a court in New York confronted head-on the issue of whether illegally exported objects constituted stolen property in *United States v Schultz*.[217] Schultz was a prominent and successful art dealer in New York City who misappropriated approximately two thousand items belonging to the cultural heritage of Egypt in the course of his dealings with British conservator, Tokeley-Parry. Among the Egyptian artefacts that were smuggled into the US were the head of a statue of the 18th dynasty of Egypt dating from 1580 BC (Amenhotep III), and a depiction of a kneeling king on the tomb of Hetepka at Saqqara, known as 'The Offeror'. The statue head had an estimated value of around £850 000. Egypt had made a legislative

---

claim to the Sevso Treasure but failed on this point among others). Mealy (n 5) 169, 174, 185; Ulph and Smith (n 100) 264.

212 An act of conversion such as unauthorised import or export after the effective date of the law in question.

213 *Republic of Turkey v Metropolitan Museum*, 762 F Supp 44 (SDNY 1990) (Statute of limitations in respect of Lydian Hoard claim decided in favour of Turkey); *US v Pre-Columbian Artifacts and the Republic of Guatemala*, 845 F Supp 544 (ND Ill 1993)(civil forfeiture of antiquities on basis that they were stolen); *Turkey v OKS Partners*, 1994 US Dist LEXIS 17032 (D Mass 1994). Gerstenblith (n 42) 68, 69.

214 *Ortiz/McClain* doctrine. Cf Papa-Sokal (n 4) 264; Forrest (n 6).

215 E.g. *Peru v Johnson* 720 F Supp 810 (CD Cal 1989); *US v Schultz* 333 F3d 393 (2nd Circuit 2003) 400–402.

216 Gerstenblith (n 42) 68, 69; P Gerstenblith, 'The Public Interest in the Restitution of Cultural Objects' (2001) 16 Conn J Int L 197, 221–22.

217 *US v Schultz*, 178 F Supp 2d 445 (2002), 333 F3d 393 (2003), 540 US 1106, 157 L Ed 2d 891 (2004).

declaration in Law 117 to the effect that after 1983, all antiquities belonged to the Egyptian government. The illicit trade in cultural objects was not criminalised at the time.

Schultz was charged with conspiracy to violate the NSPA by conspiring to deal in antiquities that were found in Egypt and taken in violation of Law 117.[218] Egypt proved that the artefacts which Schultz conspired to receive were discovered after 1983. Schultz was convicted of conspiracy to receive stolen goods under § 2315 of the NSPA.[219] He received a $50 000 fine and was sentenced to a 33-month prison sentence for having transported Egyptian antiquities in interstate and foreign commerce. He also had to return antiquities in his possession. The fine did not correlate with the amount of money that would be made from the trade in the antiquities involved in the crime in question. Whether the punishment was sufficient to deter wrongdoing, remains debatable.

Both the trial court and the appellate court investigated first whether the foreign law was, on its face, an ownership law, to determine if the objects qualified as stolen; and secondly, whether the Egyptian authorities enforced the law domestically within Egypt as an ownership law.[220] Both courts considered the criteria satisfied, and it became clear that antiquities subject to a national ownership law and removed without permission continued to be stolen property after leaving Egypt and entering the US. The broad purpose of the NSPA encompassed property stolen in another country and owners who are foreign.[221]

Because Law 117 is not an export control regulation, the court dismissed the argument premised on the non-enforcement of foreign export controls without further ado.[222] The argument advanced by Schultz, that the NSPA was never intended to 'reach ownership claims based on national vesting laws when the object in question has not been reduced to possession of the foreign state', failed.[223] The basic underlying principle of the NSPA, to deter theft, was considered more suitable for application in the case than the CCPIA,[224] and conduct that came

---

218 *US v Schultz*, 178 F Supp 2d 445 (2002) at 446.

219 *US v Schultz*, 333 F3d 393 (2nd Circuit 2003) 410.

220 *US v Schultz*, 178 F Supp 2d 445 (2002) at 447–48; 333 F3d 393 (2003) at 399–402.

221 *US v Schultz*, 333 F3d 393 (2nd Circuit 2003) at 402–3.

222 *US v Schultz*, 333 F3d 393 (2nd Circuit 2003) at 407–8.

223 *US v Schultz*, 178 F Supp 2d 445 (2002) at 449; 333 F3d 393 (2nd Circuit 2003) at 403.

224 The CCPIA is a civil customs statute that supplements existing civil and penal remedies involving stolen objects with civil forfeiture.

within the purview of both statutes could not limit the scope of the NSPA. This made nonsense of Schultz's claim that the CCPIA superseded the NSPA in relation to cultural property and, since the CCPIA was supposed to return the NSPA to aiding state governments in the recovery of stolen vehicles, the CCPIA was the only law competent to deal with theft of cultural property. His argument that the application of the Egyptian law would destroy the art trade,[225] was also found to be weak.

In response to his argument that the antiquities in question did not fit the common law definition of 'stolen property', the court pointed out that there is no single commonly accepted definition, and therefore it could not confine itself to a common law definition. All felonious takings are included[226] and property stolen from a foreign sovereign had to be treated the same as any stolen property.[227]

An effort not to know more was sufficient to hold Schultz culpably knowledgeable and open to prosecution. The case has significant implications for dealers and collectors in the US antiquities market who make a conscious effort to not want to know more. A country seeking return would need to prove that the defendant both knew of, and understood, the national ownership law, and knew that his actions would result in theft under that law.[228] If a defendant chooses to remain purposefully and deliberately ignorant of either the facts or the law in order to escape the consequences of the law, the avoidance is equivalent to knowledge.[229] Auction house employees who deal knowingly in illegally exported antiquities can be criminally liable under the NSPA since *mens rea* would be present. It has been argued that this may motivate them not to make enquiries about provenance.[230] It makes sense to submit auction houses to a strict duty of diligence because they profit from a trade that entails risk on the part of the true owner and may deprive a nation of its heritage.

---

[225] *US v Schultz*, 333 F3d 393 (2nd Circuit 2003) at 410.
[226] *US v Schultz*, 333 F3d 393 (2nd Circuit 2003) at 409–10.
[227] *US v Schultz*, 333 F3d 393 (2nd Circuit 2003) at 410.
[228] *US v Schultz*, 333 F3d 393 (2nd Circuit 2003) at 402.
[229] *US v Schultz*, 333 F3d 393 (2nd Circuit 2003) at 413; [2003] USCA2 238 (endorsed by Court of Appeals for Second Circuit).
[230] K Alderman, 'The Ethical Trade in Cultural Property: Ethics and Law in the Antiquity Auction Industry' [2008] ILSA Journal of International and Comparative Law 1, 9–10.

The decision in *Schultz* affirms *United States v Hollinshead*[231] and *United States v McClain*.[232] In fact, the *McClain* doctrine made all the difference in the prosecution of Schultz. The application of the NSPA to contracts to smuggle or transfer tainted objects purportedly belonging to a foreign sovereign is now governed by the '*McClain/Schultz* doctrine'. US courts will apply it as the method of enforcement in civil recovery actions in future.[233]

5. INTERNATIONAL UNDERSTANDING

5.1 Surveying Progress

The vesting of ownership of buried or undiscovered antiquities by means of legislation is an attribute of sovereignty. Nations can establish and alter the relationship between public and private ownership through statute.[234] The *McClain/Schultz* method of enforcement which US courts apply does not exclude the foreign law from application *a priori*,[235] nor is restitution premised on the application of foreign law. The NSPA, which finds application as domestic law, requires that the object in question must have been stolen, and permits the foreign statute to define *when* the object is considered stolen. Egypt's assertion of its patrimonial interest as custodian of the public interest in cultural objects discovered after the effective date in the *Schultz* case fitted in with the 'property' category of the local US law.

After the judgment, a coalition of dealers wrote a brief requesting that the court reverse Schultz's conviction. The dealers claimed that, by enforcing patrimony laws, the court relinquished control over the US antiquities trade to foreign states, and that this contradicted the limited import ban envisioned by the CCPIA.[236] This appeal did not succeed.

The *Schultz* ruling displays awareness of the distinction between theft and illegal export,[237] but it does not set the distinction up as a barrier

---

231 *US v Hollinshead*, No 10970 (SD Cal 14 March 1973); 495 F2d 1154 (9th Circuit 1974).

232 *US v McClain*, 545 F2d 988 (5th Circuit 1977); 593 F2d 658 (5th Circuit 1979), *cert denied*, 444 US 918 (1979) 671.

233 Gerstenblith (n 42) 73.

234 Gerstenblith (n 128) 46.

235 Carducci (n 149) 77; Weller (n 142) 290.

236 19 US Code 2601–2613 (2006).

237 *US v Schultz*, 333 F3d 393 (2nd Circuit 2003) at 407–8.

against restitution. This treatment of the property category will serve the best interest of states with archaeological finds that appeal to the US antiquities market. It has special importance for those source states that have no bilateral agreement with the US.[238] Bilateral trade agreements are not needed when the NSPA achieves the same aims.[239] This approach also offers hope that the NSPA will apply to undocumented archaeological objects from states in a similar position to Iraq, provided the foreign law meets the requisite standard of internal enforcement.[240] Article 3(2) of the UNIDROIT Convention has provided the necessary backing for the practice since it entered into force.[241] To require vigorous domestic enforcement of state ownership in respect of artefacts subject to indigenous title before their title can be defended poses more of a problem.[242]

The Dealing in Cultural Objects (Offences) Act 2003 takes the *McClain/Schultz* doctrine further. The Act does not impose any requirement that the excavation or the removal has to take place within England and Wales, and it does not matter if domestic or foreign law has been infringed. The 2003 Act applies even when no foreign state ownership law is applicable: when a state of origin seeks application or enforcement of its own law, a detailed analysis of the relevant provisions of foreign law is not required to determine its true nature.[243] The removal of the archaeological object does not even have to amount to theft under local law; the unlicensed excavation or the removal only needs to constitute 'an offence' under the local law to qualify.[244] This aspect of the Act could potentially tame the public law taboo in state claims accessory to private law. Such claims are highly unlikely, however, given that the 2003 Act does not confirm that return to a foreign nation in a civil suit is feasible if a criminal conviction cannot be obtained. It also remains an open question whether antiquities looted directly from the ground or from a monument are forfeit to the state or can be returned to a foreign nation in a civil suit if no criminal prosecution has taken place under the 2003 Act.

The approach in *Barakat* bears some resemblance to the recognition of foreign state ownership laws by US courts, but the theory is clearly

---

[238] Forrest (n 6) sub IV; Chechi (n 93) 79.

[239] Mealy (n 5) 184.

[240] Gerstenblith (n 42) 82.

[241] Schönenberger (n 155) 195.

[242] LV Prott, 'The International Movement of Cultural Objects' (2005) 12 IJCP 225, 242; Paterson (n 13).

[243] Gerstenblith (n 42) 76–77.

[244] Gerstenblith (n 42) 77–78.

different.[245] Compared to the ruling in *Schultz*, the *Barakat* ruling was more interested in the fundamental nature of ownership and less concerned with the 'face' of the state ownership law.[246] The level of domestic enforcement played no role. In contrast to the legal position under the Dealing in Cultural Objects (Offences) Act 2003, the *Barakat* ruling calls for investigation of the nature of foreign laws and the time and place of discovery.[247] The *Barakat* ruling does not impose a separate enforcement limitation in the way the Act does. As far as the Act is concerned, it is insufficient that the objects were taken after the date on which the relevant vesting law took effect. The Act introduced double non-retrospectivity (one time requirement extends to the offence, and another applies to the object), and yet a third requirement in respect of time may apply if a vesting law has been breached. While no one may be held guilty of a criminal offence on account of an act or omission which did not constitute a criminal offence under the national or international law that applied when the offense was committed,[248] it is problematic to require that the tainted object must be stolen or looted after 30 December 2003. If objects were tainted before the relevant date, conviction cannot follow. This position requires proving precisely when the object was stolen. The *Barakat* ruling avoids the worst flaws of the 2003 Act, as it applies to antiquities stolen at any time after the enactment of a vesting statute. When criminal prosecution fails, the *Barakat* ruling provides for greater flexibility; if the criminal trial succeeds, the *Barakat* ruling will complement the 2003 Act.[249]

The weakest points of the 2003 Act will need to be improved before Scotland could gain anything from emulating this model. It would be necessary to extend the definition of 'tainted', reverse the burden of proof, increase the penalty, and remove the double non-retrospectivity, i.e. the time requirement in respect of the taint. It may be argued that there are sufficient safeguards against the negative effects of the illicit import of cultural property in place for Scotland. First, the position in respect of *bona vacantia*[250] covers undiscovered archaeological finds. Secondly, Scots law criminalises the handling of or retaining possession of goods obtained by theft, robbery, fraud, or embezzlement, with the

---

[245] Ulph and Smith (n 100) 51; 253.

[246] Gerstenblith (n 128) 43–44.

[247] Gerstenblith (n 128) 43.

[248] Art 7 of the Convention for the Protection of Human Rights and Fundamental Freedoms.

[249] Gerstenblith (n 128) 47–48.

[250] Ss 67–73 of the Civic Government (Scotland) Act 1982.

intention of keeping the goods from their true owner (reset). These aspects combine well with money laundering legislation that enables authorities to recover tainted cultural artefacts in the possession of the accused. Border checks and export permits on the external border of the Schengen Area depend on both national rules[251] and EU legislation.[252] Loopholes exist in practice.[253] Movement from the Schengen Area into Scotland, a non-Schengen state, faces tougher regulation, but no offence is committed under the Dealing in Cultural Objects (Offences) Act of 2003 if an object is taken into Scotland.

The next section considers how international understanding can be strengthened.

5.2 Cultivating Deeper International Understanding

A comprehensive and multi-pronged approach that combines a robust criminal justice and criminological approach with import control, direct application of foreign public law rules where the conflicts method permits this, and recognition of foreign public law as a standard has the best chance of improving the level of protection of art and cultural objects against theft and looting. It is seldom helpful to prejudge the issue based on whether the claim is predicated on public or private law.

A useful initiative was launched when UNESCO and UNIDROIT joined forces to develop the Model Provisions on State Ownership of Undiscovered Cultural Objects, among other things to facilitate the enforcement of the 1995 UNIDROIT Convention by national courts.[254] No state approval has been sought for the provisions, since they are not part of an international convention. States interested in drafting new provisions establishing ownership of undiscovered cultural objects and

---

[251] In the UK, see the Export Control Act of 2002; Export of Objects of Cultural Interest (Control) Order 2003; Customs and Excise Management Act 1979 (penalities in the event of criminal prosecution). There is a Reviewing Committee on the Export of Works of Art and Objects of Cultural Interest which was established in 1952, and which applies the Waverley Criteria when called upon to advise on the export of objects of cultural interest. Waverley Committee Report, RA Butler 6 September 1952, Report of a Committee appointed by the Chancellor of the Exchequer HMSO 1952.

[252] Schengen Borders Code (n 36).

[253] For instance, in 2013 it was still possible to board the Eurostar in Brussels with a ticket to Lille (Belgium and France are Schengen states) and travel into London without passing any passport checks.

[254] M Frigo, 'Model Provisions on State Ownership of Undiscovered Cultural Objects – Introduction' [2011] Uniform Law Review 1044, 1048.

archaeological heritage, or in replacing existing provisions at the national level, may model their legislation on these provisions.[255] The next section takes a closer look at the way in which the Model Provisions accommodate foreign public law.

5.2.1 Model Provisions that accommodate the application of foreign public law

The Model Provisions on State Ownership of Undiscovered Cultural Objects cover objects that are of importance for prehistory, history, literature, art or science, and are located in the soil or underwater.[256] Source states have a duty and a responsibility to protect and preserve their undiscovered cultural objects, but the notion of 'protection' is left undefined so that it can be construed on a case-by-case basis.[257] The Model Provisions consider cultural objects excavated contrary to the law or retained illicitly to be stolen objects.[258] If domestic laws qualify 'illicit excavation and retention' of a cultural object as theft, national theft provisions are also triggered and there is less chance that a problematic characterisation of the claim can neutralise their application. Transfer of ownership of a cultural object deemed to be stolen is null and void, unless it can be established that the transferor had a valid title to the object at the time of the transfer.[259] An undiscovered archaeological object that is deemed to be stolen is prevented from being the object of a private right.[260] This is the function of inalienability provisions, for they are designed to prevent objects crossing the boundary of public to private ownership. A similar provision in place in domestic law would mean that a transfer abroad of an undiscovered object taken from the state that has declared its ownership of such an object will be null and void. If international judicial co-operation in criminal matters enables the return

---

[255] Pearlstein (n 86) 2.

[256] Clause 2 – Definition. Reproduced in Frigo (n 254).

[257] Clause 1 – General Duty.

[258] Clause 4 – Illicit excavation or retention; Art 3(2) UNIDROIT Convention.

[259] Clause 5 – Inalienability. The burden of proof is on the defence, not the source state.

[260] Clause 5 – Inalienability. This provision does not cover antiquities that have long been in circulation and that have never been 'undiscovered', and that have been sold in contravention of an inalienability clause in the donation (*Frias v Pinchon* 1886 Clunet 593).

of an object that is considered stolen to the country where it was discovered,[261] domestic law need not set out guidelines to facilitate return.[262]

The Model Provisions on State Ownership offer some inspiration and guidance to source nations that wish to fortify their chances to reclaim objects successfully. As long as these laws operate prospectively, they do not affect the substance of the takings clause or its underlying policies, thereby guarding against any constitutional question arising in the US.[263] While it is too early to assess the impact of the Model Provisions in practice, they promise to contribute to overcoming practical difficulties in the application of foreign public law. Wide support for the Model Provisions would strengthen the moral underpinning of both the UNESCO and UNIDROIT Conventions.

5.2.2 The multi-pronged approach of German law

German law and practice offers a good illustration of a multi-pronged approach.[264] First of all, German law does not require a treaty for the operation of import control, and the non-application default rule has already been modified by legislation,[265] with the result that it has limited scope under German law. Norms with an indirect effect on private law must be applied.[266]

Secondly, the distinction between public and private property is handled skilfully. While domestic courts are not allowed to hear claims based on foreign revenue or penal law, courts do hear claims based on private law. This includes sovereign claims that rely on and are conditioned by private law. If another state seeks to rely on its state ownership,

---

261 Clause 6 – International enforcement.

262 E.g. the proposal made in respect of the NSPA by JE Morrow, 'The National Stolen Property Act and the Return of Stolen Cultural Property to Its Rightful Foreign Owners' (2007) 30 Boston College International and Comparative Law Review 249, 260.

263 Gerstenblith (n 216) 239.

264 Weller (n 142) 283 ff.

265 *Gesetz zur Ausführung des UNESCO-Übereinkommens vom 14. November 1970 über Maßnahmen zum Verbot und zur Verhütung der Rechtswidrigen Einfuhr, Ausfuhr und Übereignung von Kulturgut und zur Umsetzung der Richtlinie 93/7/EWG des Rates vom 15. März 1993 über die Rückgabe von Unrechtmäßig aus dem Hoheitsgebiet eines Mitgliedstaats Verbrachten Kul-Turgütern* 18. Mai 2007 (BGBl. I 757, No 21 2547).

266 K Odendahl, *Kulturgüterschutz: Entwicklung, Struktur und Dogmatik eines Ebenübergreifenden Normsystems* (Mohr Siebeck 2005) 622–23; Schönenberger (n 155) 147.

the claim is classified as pertaining to private property. If a foreign state institutes proceedings in Germany and German law applies, the category 'public property' would be transposed into private property even if that state acquired the property by an act of state, because private property represents the closest legal analogy in German law.[267] Ownership is ownership, whether public or private. Commentators are aware that classifying property as 'public property' could mean that a claim in respect thereof may be regarded as based on public law, and that the issue would then be about the enforcement of foreign public law.[268]

Thirdly, the private international law framework is particularly well developed. Claims for the recovery of antiquities are permissible if the application of foreign public law is necessary to determine preliminary issues (such as ownership) relating to these claims.[269] Both the factual and the legal effects of foreign public law are taken into account. The public policy control applies to any application or recognition of effect of foreign public law by a German court.[270] The courts also take account of foreign public law in the context of the law applicable to contract. A German court famously applied a foreign export prohibition in cultural objects *via* German law, which was the applicable law, in *Allgemeine Versicherungsgesellschaft v E.K.* (the Nigerian masks case).[271] A Nigerian company wanted to transport three containers with African masks and statues from Nigeria to Hamburg. Nigerian law prohibited the unlicensed export of cultural objects. The Nigerian company contracted with a German insurance company to cover the risk of shipping the masks to Germany. When several masks disappeared during the shipment, the insurance paid out in respect of the losses. The insurer sued the ship-owner for compensation. The court had to determine whether the insurance contract for the transportation of the artefacts, which was governed by German law, was valid – the insurance was intended to protect the Nigerian company against a loss that would be ruled to be

[267] Weller (n 142) 295.

[268] Weller (n 142) 292–94.

[269] *Arabic Republic of Egypt v Antiques Dealer*, Higher Regional Court of Berlin, judgment of 16 October 2006, 10 U 286/05, NJW 2007 705 applied Egyptian Law No 117 of 1983 on the Protection of Antiquities.

[270] 'Land Reform' case, Federal Constitutional Court, judgment of 23 April 1991, 1 BvR 1170/90, 1174/90, 1145/90, NJW 1991 1597ff.

[271] BGH, 22 June 1972 0 II ZR 113/70; BGHZ 59, 82, 83. The case was decided prior to the 1980 Rome Convention on the Law Applicable to Contractual Obligations, Consolidated version [2005] OJ C334/1.

contrary to public policy.[272] The UNESCO Convention had been in force in Nigeria since 1972, but it was not effective in Germany at the time[273] and no immediate public interest of Germany was affected by the violation of Nigerian export controls. Regardless of these potential limitations however, the court used Nigerian public law as a standard against which to measure the legitimacy of the insured interest.[274] The fact that the Nigerian law pursues policies concerning which the international community has reached consensus, namely to protect cultural property, was sufficient to annul the contract.[275] The German court did not enforce the Nigerian export control directly,[276] but its public law was taken into account,[277] and this led to a refusal to uphold a contract in breach of the public law.

German commentators recognise that the axiom of non-application of foreign public law is no longer current and has ceased to be a guiding principle of international law. Their work focuses on defining the requirements for the application of foreign public law.[278] Weller indicates that 'public policy' and the conditions for validity and morality represent open conditions which may be concretised in a specific case.[279] The conditions for the validity of the insurance contract, such as morality, were framed in an open way in the Nigerian masks case. Concretisation is a crucial step in art and cultural heritage claims. The court took account of the public law that invalidated the contract when it was concluded.[280] Weller suggests that the conception of open conditions be restricted to: (a) foreign public laws that pursue policies that conform with the policies of the *lex contractus*; and (b) policies that do not violate the public policy of the forum. Armbrüster considers foreign laws that

---

[272] C Armbrüster, 'Private Law as an Instrument for the Protection of Cultural Property' (2013) 10 TDM Special Issue 1, 6.

[273] Germany has now acceded and incorporated the Convention; see n 258. J Dolinger, 'World Public Policy: Real International Public Policy in the Conflict of Laws' (1982) 17 Texas International Law Journal 167, 188.

[274] Weller (n 142) 287.

[275] See Art 138 § 1 of the BGB (German Civil Code); A Chong, 'The Public Policy and Mandatory Rules of Third Countries in International Contracts' (2006) 2 JPIL 27, 42–3.

[276] Siehr (n 154) 53.

[277] Chong (n 275) 41, 59.

[278] B von Hoffmann and K Thorn, *Internationales Privatrecht: Einschließlich der Grundzüge des Internationalen Zivilverfahrensrechts* (8th edn, CH Beck München 2005) 471ff (Chapter 3).

[279] Weller (n 142) 286.

[280] Weller (n 142) 287–88.

establish limits to the possibility to transfer cultural objects where the transfer itself is governed by the law of a different jurisdiction. He argues in favour of respecting state ownership of undiscovered materials based on a vesting law, and suggests that the law of the place that first prohibited the export of a work of art should govern property rights in respect of that work because a special connection exists between a work of art and an export ban. While he concedes that exceptions apply, he argues that comity and international harmony of decision support such a choice.[281]

5.2.3 An export ban can affect the validity of a contract of sale, once an artefact has been transferred abroad

One way of enforcing export controls indirectly is the stigmatisation of an object moved contrary to an export prohibition in order that it may lose value.[282] Case law in the US and the UK confirm that the value of an antiquity that is exported contrary to export control or inalienability rules could indeed be affected. Italy's claim in respect of the Atleta di Fano (Getty Bronze) is a topical case in point.[283] An older case, *Jeanneret v Vichey*,[284] has relevance in as far as several art dealers testified that the marketability of the painting was impaired by Italy's claims and threats of confiscation, and reputable dealers and auction houses would be reluctant to handle the painting in the circumstances. The appeal court still denied Jeanneret a remedy for the illegal export of the painting she bought. The court reasoned that the painting would not be confiscated and no monetary liability would be incurred if it never reentered Italy.[285] In *Kingdom of Spain v Christie's*[286] an English court granted a declaration that the export permit for Goya's 'La Marquesa de Santa Cruz' had been forged. The declaration confirmed the expectation that, without export documents, the value of the work would decrease. It was an alternative way of ensuring that the painting was dealt with in accordance with the UK Code of Practice for the Control of International Trading in Works of Art, of denigrating its value and preventing its continued circulation.

---

281 Armbrüster (n 272) 5.
282 Siehr (n 154) 190, 196.
283 Lanciotti (n 25) 311.
284 *Jeanneret v Vichey*, 693 F2d 259 (2nd Circuit 1982).
285 At 267–68.
286 *Kingdom of Spain v Christie's*, 1986 WLR 1120.

5.2.4 An 'international public policy for export control' in respect of the most significant items of cultural heritage?

While comity is frequently dismissed as a plausible basis for the recognition and enforcement of foreign law, the critics cannot explain away the link between basic respect for foreign law and its recognition. As Staughton J remarked in *Attorney-General of New Zealand v Ortiz*, an international aspiration to counter the illicit trade in cultural objects is built, in part, on respect for the cultural heritage of other countries.[287] International public policy, in the sense of what promotes respect for the law, could conceivably preclude the application of a conflicts rule (and a legal system) that would undermine international cultural heritage conventions and accelerate the illicit trade of cultural objects and works of art. The Arbitral Tribunal constituted in *Inceysa Vallisoletana v El Salvador*[288] held that it is impossible to

> recognize the existence of rights arising from illegal acts, because it would violate the respect for the law which … is a principle of international public policy.[289]

This concept has been used in international investment arbitration ever since the award rendered in October 2006 in *World Duty Free v Kenya*.[290] Considering that signing the UNESCO Convention signals a readiness to accept a universal repatriation standard,[291] export controls that are sufficiently limited in scope can be recognised on the basis of supporting the moral underpinning of international conventions, when illegality or immorality taints transactions.

The Nigerian masks case demonstrates how international public policy can be taken into account when German law governs a contract. The relationship between international public policy and the common law is more uncertain, however. Comity has featured as the reason why effect should be given to the public policy of a third state that coincides with international conceptions of morality, where the argument concerns non-enforceability of an immoral contract.[292] Nonetheless, it lacks broad EU support. The final text of the Rome I Regulation on the law

---

[287] Per Staughton J in *Attorney-General of New Zealand v Ortiz* [1982] 3 All ER 436 at 451.

[288] ARB/03/26.

[289] At § 249.

[290] *World Duty Free v Kenya* ICSID Case No ARB/00/7.

[291] Paterson (n 13) 250.

[292] Chong (n 275) 37, 59–60, 70 (in support of direct application of foreign mandatory rules).

applicable to contractual obligations[293] has not taken this development forward either. Article 9(3) points to the law of the place where performance is to take place, which may be different from the place where the law limits trade in such items. A contract to supply cultural objects from a country that has banned export to safeguard its own cultural interests cannot be refused enforcement, unless the mandatory provisions in the place of performance render it unlawful. Complex title laundering does not require the identification of the place of performance as much as it requires widening the lens to include the overriding mandatory rules of every state along the laundering chain. If a cultural object has been traded illicitly, it would be located outside the jurisdiction that has the strongest interest in limiting trade. The overriding mandatory provisions in every intermediate jurisdiction (where part of the 'performance' takes place), ought to be taken into account.

That the EU does not use every opportunity to strengthen the scope for private international methods to curb the illicit trade, puts obstacles in the way of a durable multi-pronged approach.

6. CONCLUSION

States must achieve a balance between protection of their cultural heritage and the free movement of cultural material. This balance varies according to the volume of outflow of cultural material.[294] Source nations face many challenges to their claims for repatriation or restitution of undiscovered antiquities taken from their territories. Their own domestic legislative frameworks may complicate their recognition and application. International conventions do not provide watertight protection: implementation may lack the requisite level of conviction, and codes of conduct may also chip away at ethical standards of acquisition. Well-resourced collectors and institutions in market states rely on classification and the commercial imperative that attracts good-faith purchaser protections and statutory limitations that prevent return. In addition to what import control schemes and forfeiture of proceeds of crime can accomplish, restitution can ultimately be facilitated by the direct application of foreign public law and by permitting the standard of protection found in foreign public law to inform the open conditions in the law of the forum.

[293] Regulation (EC) No 593/2008 of the European Parliament and of the Council of 17 June 2008 on the law applicable to contractual obligations (Rome I) OJ L 177, 04.07.2008, 6.

[294] Prott (n 133) 236.

The respective methods and strategies of UK and US law differ greatly. In the US, courts recognise categories of ownership which the foreign law in question is based on and which trigger remedies which are available domestically. They apply the category 'stolen' under the NSPA in a civil claim. Import restrictions and criminal prosecution have had an effect on art museums. The UK has not made a significant investment either in terms of criminal law or restrictions on the movement of cultural objects.[295] The persistence of the public law taboo may stand in the way of restitution at the judicial level unless the procedures and criteria for the return of objects that were removed unlawfully from any of the Member States' territories are utilised in terms of Directive 2014/60/EU, and private international law method is deployed to dismantle it where third states institute claims for return. English law has not yet reached the stage where public law claims accessory to private law claims qualify for recognition, but the courts are aware that the public policy exclusion may subdue a claim in conversion. As a result, the relaxation of the strict public policy objection to an international claim for recovery based on a foreign vesting statute has been an option. The readiness of German law to facilitate the recognition and application of foreign public law serves as an inspiration in this area. German law relies on a multi-pronged approach comprising import control and skilful handling of foreign public law. It does not draw sharp distinctions between the recognition of vesting laws and export laws.

No doubt wider recognition of an international public policy on export control will upset the very delicate balance between source nations and market nations, and could come at a high cost for many museums and private collections.At the same time, the capacity to respect the concepts, categories, and objectives of another legal system is the capacity to promote the coexistence of different cultures. International co-operation can be strengthened to improve consistency and efficiency in respect of export and import permits, reliant on a database and templates used throughout the EU. Export controls combined with an inalienability provision that prevents an object deemed to be stolen from being the object of a private right can strengthen the legal position of a source

---

295 A Efrat, 'Getting Governments to Co-operate against Looting: Insights from the American and British Experience' [2012] Journal of Art Crime Electronic Issue 31, 41 <http://portal.idc.ac.il/facultypublication.publication?PublicationID=2874&FacultyUserName=YXNpZg==>; accessed 25 March 2014.

state. The Model Provisions on State Ownership can contribute to more regularity in the occasional recognition of the status of inalienability, prohibition on disposal status, or restrictions on transfer.

8. Realising the potential of private international law to settle claims to art and cultural heritage

1. INTRODUCTION

Private international law and cultural heritage law are both in search of comprehensive models and guiding principles to counter the illicit trade of art and antiquities and to reconcile radically opposing interests. Preservation, protection, access, free movement, and the 'public good' count among the public interests that clash and clamour for attention in claims for restitution. These claims call forth tensions between public and private, between law and ethics. Criminal activities involving art have several aspects in common with clandestine excavation of antiquities. Those who are motivated by economic gain are attracted to these crimes; revolution, war, conflict and state repression provide fuel for these activities; and once committed, title laundering is likely.

The relationship between private international law and cultural heritage law is at an interim rather than a final stage. The capacity of private international law to accommodate cultural heritage law, and to promote international understanding, is not a foregone conclusion. Continuous adjustment is required to enable this to happen as their interaction becomes more frequent and more intense.

2. GLOBAL LEGAL DIVERSITY AND THE INTERNATIONAL DIMENSION OF PRIVATE INTERNATIONAL LAW IN CIVIL LITIGATION

Looters, dealers and middlemen use or avoid the law in cross-border deals to advance their position in the market, but the true owner or the source state can institute a civil claim to obtain restitution or return of an object that has been traded after it has been stolen, looted, excavated or smuggled into another jurisdiction. These claims will frequently be brought in a market state or in an intermediary (transit) jurisdiction, where the nature of the claim will be determined and where private international law will supply jurisdiction rules and choice of law rules.

The global legal diversity factor that characterises the search is particularly defined in respect of the acquisition and loss of title at the national level, and in respect of standards for acquisition. It affects the art market, creates opportunities for trafficking, and increases the risk of litigation. The diversity factor is not confined to legal systems but extends also to the fora available within a single jurisdictional unit or area. Rules, norms and standards may diverge even if public interest and structures overlap.

Due to the assumption that the scope of the criminal and private international law of the forum state must be clearly distinguished, the mutual effect of the two disciplines is rarely explored together. Yet, there are civil remedies by which wrongs can be rectified. For instance, civil forfeiture could rectify a violation of a criminal statute. Private international law offers other strategies and tools in claims based on ownership or restitution of cultural objects, but a doctrinal conception of private international law as part of national law is bound to nullify their effect. A 'national' straitjacket can make it difficult for adjudicators to do justice to rules that derive from other levels and spheres of law (e.g. rules that reflect the implications of sovereignty, the public acts of other states, and the express and tacit consent of nations).

Private international law can better support cultural heritage law when it operates in the international dimension. As a global lens, its aspiration is to overcome the horizontal competition among states that makes for unevenness in adjudicated outcomes. From this vantage point it offers help with identifying when legal systems are involved in 'lock' formation, and which comparative jurisdiction and choice of law approaches keep pace with the value judgements that underpin cultural heritage law. Methodological pluralism supports the relationship between private international law and cultural heritage law.

It would be counterproductive to assume that private international law devices are superfluous. The ideal of a uniform law, or a universal language understood and embraced by centralised structures, is too remote from the reality to make a meaningful difference in practice. At the same time, international instruments designed to counter the cultural losses which the world is suffering can accomplish little on their own. Private international law can help identify gaps in the implementation and execution of existing international instruments. It can support interpretations of the sources of public international law that would contribute to international understanding and promote appropriate forms of justice.

It may also enable more informed decision-making with regard to the options available for dispute resolution.

2.1 Jurisdictional Aspects

Once the object has been identified and the whereabouts of the possessor have been established, proceedings can commence. Jurisdictional rules and challenges control the venue in which a case brought by a state, a private actor, or a non-state entity can proceed. Seising a national court is one of the pathways to justice that are available to claimants. Jurisdiction in respect of confiscation or expropriation actions by the state within its own territory comes within the purview of the act of state doctrine and foreign immunity laws. A narrow interpretation of the exceptions to foreign immunity can preclude a hearing on the merits. Regardless of whether the act of state doctrine derives from domestic or international law, its relationship with private international law bears on claims for restitution because it may affect the application of foreign law. Ultimately, it is more important to safeguard access to justice than to promote any single form of dispute resolution above others. Chapter 4 demonstrates that a significant state interest in the application of mandatory rules may result in the establishment and exercise of jurisdiction. The EU has now supported access to justice by adding to the jurisdictional bases contained in the Brussels regime. When more than one venue is seised with a case, there is potential for one norm to interfere with the intended functioning of another norm. Domestic or regional conditioning plays an important role in how *compétence-compétence*, *lis pendens* and *res judicata* function across jurisdictions. There is considerable scope for parties to address the implications of *res judicata* in their agreement or terms of reference in order to foreclose relitigation of the subject matter of the dispute. Whether a court can be seised to give effect to an existing legal right depends on how it construes the negative effect of *compétence-compétence* or waiver of access to court.

No state has adopted a 'default' arbitration model. There is scope for the argument that arbitration simplifies choice of law in dispute resolution, but procedurally it offers the respondent an extended choice of delaying tactics. Indeed, arbitration can be more onerous than litigation, and it does not guarantee the achievement of neutrality and speed. As such, it is unlikely to emerge as a superior mechanism that simplifies dispute resolution when ownership and restitution claims are instituted in respect of stolen or illegally exported objects.

2.2 The Choice of Law Stage

The adjudicator requires an opportunity to receive and consider, on its merits, a request for return or restitution of an object that was retained or removed unlawfully. Depending on how a court deploys mechanisms such as classification and the public policy exception, choice of law method can grant (or preclude) an opportunity to rule on the merits of the case and to employ value-rationality. The potentially applicable legal systems may enable the adjudicator to select the one that protects the rights of the owner and interrupts the formation of a lock. The application of a legal system that recognises that crime voids the title transfer, or that the object bears an indelible taint until it is restored, disrupts lock formation and the expectations of traffickers. Chapter 5 dealt with this aspect.

An aspect that was not pursued in this work, for reasons of scope, is the safekeeping of a cultural object for the duration of the trial, pending the outcome. The object will be detained and prevented from being removed, unless anti-seisure legislation demands application. The circumstances of the cases frequently involve art on loan, and the borrowing state, where the art is located, would be interested to give effect to its own mandatory civil and criminal law provisions. This topic presents many opportunities for future research.

Reaching wide agreement on substantive principles by which to resolve disputes involving Nazi spoliated art has proved difficult. Much hesitation has accompanied international policies in this area. The difficulty of designing and implementing general substantive rules of uniform application and specific norms for Nazi spoliated art has put the focus on procedural aspects and the issue of legal access. Adjudicators have opportunity to apply a value-based rationality nonetheless. Classification may enable non-enforcement of time bars that encourage claimants to forget rather than ensure legal access.

The general implications of government expropriation and Nazi expropriation were set out in Chapters 2 and 3. Chapter 6 considered the definition of a 'forced sale' and the implications of the *lex situs* rule for restitution claims. Procedural arguments and classification may preclude a hearing on the merits in court, but in state-run mediation such arguments will not have much impact. ADR processes may have to be followed as a condition precedent to litigation, or it may be the case that a state mediator is answerable to a state department that is compelled by legislation to administer it. Procedures followed by commissions in France, Germany, and the Netherlands do not distinguish between ownership by public bodies and private parties, whereas in the UK they do. State-run mediation in the UK and Germany has surmounted legal and non-legal obstacles to restitution on several occasions.

The tension between conflicts rules and ethics in the international dimension becomes acute in the circumstances of 'Belotto-type' international cases, where global justice and finality may be understandably difficult to achieve. Can conflicts rules and approaches offer any contribution? If the circumstances of individuals were life-threatening, there remains scope for a public policy argument – even if persecuted individuals succeeded in selling valuable works of art in Switzerland. The circumstances of the individual case will indicate the severity of the threat while the escapee was still in Germany, the degree of hardship faced with and without the involuntary transfer, and the various components of the 'lock' mechanism that accompanied the flight.

The success of a restitution claim may depend on the recognition and application of provisions of public law designed to safeguard access to the object in question, e.g. provisions that regulate accession for purposes of public display, or provisions that prohibit export. In these situations foreign prevention and control measures and criminal sanctions cannot be applied directly. The recognition by domestic courts of a public law category has long been a controversial issue in private international law. Accessory claims to trafficked cultural objects are likely to invite judicial consideration of the legal nature of state claims for the return of illicitly trafficked cultural objects. Such claims may be based on private or public law. The axiom of non-enforcement of foreign export law encourages the illicit trafficking of cultural objects, but international understanding and mutual assistance call for the application of foreign public law in sovereign claims that are accessory to private law. When the foreign provision asserts its application, the adjudicator requires an opportunity to check if mutual recognition would encroach on any forum interest and whether it would be internationally acceptable. Chapter 7 investigates the role of the values of mutuality and co-operation in the enforcement of foreign public law that safeguards cultural objects against physical damage, dismemberment and decontextualisation. The enforcement of foreign public law has reached an advanced stage in Germany. In the US and the UK, state ownership claims to undiscovered cultural objects are enforced not on the basis of general choice of law method, but rather on the basis of defining 'stolen' in a way that goes beyond the Anglo-American common law definition. Recognising the category of property that applies in the state in which the theft occurred, and by whose law restitution would be justified, facilitates restitution. Novel ways of applying domestic law and the willingness to relax the strict public policy objection to a claim can disrupt lock formation and trafficking.

3. SURMOUNTING THE GREATEST OBSTACLES TO CLAIMS BASED ON OWNERSHIP AND RESTITUTION

The greatest obstacles in the way of success of claims based on ownership and restitution appear when the cultural significance of an object, the commercial imperative, and the formation of locks go unidentified and unchallenged. Moreover, an inadequate appreciation of the implications of global solidarity, ethics and cultural diplomacy will make for poor, instrumentalist decisions.

The EU plays a valuable role in encouraging co-operation between Member States with a view to protecting cultural heritage of European significance, to which such national treasures belong. Even so, Member States have exclusive competence in classifying cultural objects as national treasures. The special nature and elusive definition of art and cultural objects raise questions concerning the status and category of the object itself. If the special nature of cultural objects is under-estimated, adjudicators will also miss the opportunity to exercise the value choices that underlie their protection and the preservation of the historical record.

The commercial imperative is insensitive to the importance of transmission of culture to current and future generations. It does not pay attention to the need to control the free movement of objects whose preservation is under threat. It does not seek to prevent the outflow of cultural materials. It can be readily agreed, as the *lex culturalis* intends, that the mechanical application of general ordinary choice of law rules designed for commerce and trade deserves to be countered. It is worthwhile, therefore, to identify the ways in which private international law can support cultural heritage law to counter the illicit trade of art and antiquities.

The greatest risks of private international law argument and method arise in the absence of a clear conception of the scope it can give for broader criminal objectives and aims. Consigners of stolen or smuggled works of art are tempted to hide behind the good-faith purchase laws of certain European countries. Powerful dealers and middlemen are able to negotiate the interface of civil law and private international law aspects to advance their position in the market. A global lens helps the adjudicator to take account of the implications of activities that interlock with the features of a legal system, because a particular jurisdiction can be studied as a setting in the organised market or as a component in a wider criminological system. A global lens puts policy-makers in a better position to evaluate law reforms that promise much, but which do not prevent 'locks' from forming. For instance, the conflicts rules advanced in the Belgian Code of Private International Law does not disable title laundering.

Ignorance prevails concerning the harm which forum-shopping and conflicts rules can do as part of a 'lock' system. The special nature of cultural heritage may go unrecognised as a result of forum-shopping. A wider lens can prevent this from happening. A wider lens also enables the mechanisms of international dispute resolution involving claims to art and cultural objects to be studied alongside the substantive protections. Such an umbrella approach highlights the adverse effects of *ad hoc* approaches to dispute settlement in cultural heritage disputes and of suppressing arguments that go to the merits of a claim.

The true measure of the success of any method that purports to have something to contribute to cultural heritage law, is its ability to control the spillover effects of the market demand onto source states; promote impeccable, clear acquisition standards; foster a deeper commitment to value-based rationality; and foster a deeper commitment to the aspirations embodied in instruments of international policy. While the normative ideal that represents a yardstick for these criteria is hard to identify amidst various different ideologies, the relationship between private international law and the broader ethical framework is capable of being defined more closely. It is found in global solidarity, which requires every role occupant and every state official to step up to the challenge posed by art crime and illicit trafficking. The way in which claims for restitution are dealt with can strengthen global solidarity or exacerbate the problems associated with the ethics deficit in acquisition practices and the lack of cultural diplomacy.

3.1 Hypothesis

Demand-and-supply economics is suitable when the provenance of a cultural object is complete. It is inadequate in the context of cultural tensions, conflict, war and confiscation. Market failures heighten the need for more security in a market that allows the exchange of irreplaceable cultural objects. As a global lens on lock formation, and a building block in global solidarity, private international law can help 're-script' the demand-and-supply cycles of the illicit trade in cultural objects and Nazi looted art. Global solidarity is built on mutuality and value-rationality among other key human potentials. Both potentials demand a step-up in the approaches and methods that prevail today with regard to ownership and restitution claims.

While this hypothesis resonates with many aspects of the *lex culturalis*, it seeks to recast the mould rather than to identify 'common rules of adjudication' that demonstrate cultural sensitivity.

3.2 Recasting the Mould: An Example

This book suggests a way of thinking that prevents the dogmatic underpinnings of conflicts rules and approaches from clouding the issue before policy considerations and ethical concerns have been ventilated. This mould makes it harder for the law to shield criminals, thieves, robbers and embezzlers.

Restitution claims frequently present a new problem of characterisation, which directly impacts the outcome of the litigation. Multilateral conflicts rules must accommodate a potentially limitless number of foreign causes of action, but they are limited in number. These choice of law rules generally enjoy more pre-eminence in international disputes compared to causes of action or underlying legal categories. Courts frequently default to the property transaction as a basis for classification when art has crossed jurisdictional lines after having been stolen. Classification also determines the effect of the passage of time on the claim. Classified as a matter of substance, the same connecting factor and the same law will govern as was indicated by the *lex situs* rule. While purchasers always have an opportunity to verify the provenance and conveyance history of an art object, the *lex situs* rule requires them to investigate only one law before proceeding with a transaction, and advances an uncritical acceptance that title is cleared in a single sale. The rule fortifies the interests of the market; it thwarts the objective of many protective rules in source states and the aims of pertinent international instruments.

Ideally, the structure and method of private international law ought to help mark the fact of theft or the context of smuggling. The category and the connecting factor associated with the relevant choice of law rule must be responsive to the ethics deficit of the illicit trafficking and trade of cultural objects. For instance, if the inherent taint or defect in a title to property attaches to stolen goods until they are returned to the original owner (e.g. *vitium reale* in Scots law), the commercial imperative is halted. If the applicable law is selected on the basis of a policy choice in favour of the party who lost possession on account of the vice of theft, then lock formation is countered. If the cause of action is barred by statutory limitations, the public policy exception (or classification) can preclude them from having effect. The figure-ground perception of multilateral choice of law rules and the public policy exception helps to explain that the policy choice can take precedence in restitution claims and procedures for return. To lean in the direction of domestic law (often based on the view that courts apply their own law more effectively, accurately and justly than any foreign law) can take on fresh meaning in this context.

The structure and method of private international law provides ways and means that enable adjudicators to compensate for the oversimplification of the problems that arise in art transactions on account of the *lex situs* rule, and to ease tensions between private law and criminal law in the art markets in New York and London.

There are several other mechanisms by which clashing interests can be managed. These mechanisms are highlighted throughout the book.

3.3 Expectations and Results

If the application of the method and structure of private international law were guided by mutuality and value-rationality in cases involving the restitution or recovery of looted and trafficked objects, it would ultimately simplify the complex choices associated with international claims for restitution of art and cultural objects for parties, their advisors and their adjudicators. More specifically, this approach can help:

(a) to identify legal systems that form locks or participate as components of 'lock' mechanisms that support title laundering;
(b) to gain perspective on classification, including simple, rough classifications;
(c) to engage in a nuanced analysis of the hidden abodes of civil claims based on ownership of a thing or its restitution without having to design more choice of law rules;
(d) to gain perspective on the procedural treatment of foreign law;
(e) to clarify the role of policy interests that support restitution;
(f) to make room for the distinctness of the legal traditions and ways of life of those who have overlapping interests in art and cultural objects unless tolerance puts cultural objects at risk (thereby helping to clarify the limits of tolerance);
(g) to gain perspective on the importance of recognition of foreign public law, in order to counter illicit trafficking practices; demonstrate how recognition of foreign public law is connected to global solidarity and comity (in the sense of *aequitas*, *humanitas* and *utilitas*); and show that crime can be taken into account in the context of a private claim if the definition of theft extends to

antiquities found in the ground and appropriated in contravention of state ownership laws;

(h) to demonstrate where and how private international law complements ethics; and

(i) to indicate that justice pluralism is unavoidable, but that conflicts justice, material justice or systemic justice can contribute to greater global understanding and welfare.

Private international law can pave the way for cultural diplomacy. Locally and globally speaking, our welfare depends on the level of respect we are willing to accord everyone's 'being in the world' – to the very conditions of human life, the very means of union among those who have different cultures and histories, and to that which helps us relate more wholeheartedly to one another.

The 'provenance' of private international law is deserving of our trust. It is hoped that a different mould of thinking will soon raise the expectations of private international law in claims to art and cultural objects.

Bibliography

Books

Adorno TW, *Minima Moralia: Reflections from Damaged Life* (tr D Redmond 2005) (Suhrkamp Verlag 1951).

Akinsha K and Kozlov G with S Hochfield, *Beautiful Loot: The Soviet Plunder of Europe's Art Treasures* (Random House 1995).

Andrews N, *The Three Paths of Justice: Court Proceedings, Arbitration and Mediation in England* (Cambridge 2012).

Anton AE, *Private International Law* (2nd edn, W Green 1990).

Anton M, *Handbuch Kulturgüterschutz und Kunstrestitutionsrecht/Illegaler Kulturgüterverkehr: (Handbuch Kulturguterschutz und Kunstrestitutionsrecht)* (De Gruyter 2010), 3 vols.

Arendt H, *Between Past and Present* (The Viking Press 1961).

Arnold M, *Culture and Anarchy* (Cambridge 1935).

Aust A, *Handbook of International Law* (2nd edn, CUP 2010).

Baudrillard J, *The Conspiracy of Art* (tr A Hodges) (The MIT Press 2005).

Bell B, *Forum-shopping and Venue in Transnational Litigation* (OUP 2003).

Brodie FN, Doole J and Watson P, *Stealing History: The Illicit Trade in Cultural Material* (McDonald Institute for Archaeological Research 2000).

Bühring-Uhle C, Kirchhoff L and Scherer G, *Arbitration and Mediation in International Business* (2nd revised edn, Kluwer Law International 2006).

Carducci G, *La Restitution Internationale des Biens Culturel et des Object d'Art: Droit Commun, Directive CEE, Conventions de l'Unesco et d'Unidroit* (LGDJ 1997).

Carey Miller DL, *The Acquisition and Protection of Ownership* (Juta 1986).

Carruthers JM, *The Transfer of Property in the Conflict of Laws* (OUP 2005).

Carty A, *Philosophy of International Law* (Columbia University Press 2007).

Clarkson CMV and Hill J, *The Conflict of Laws* (4th edn, Oxford 2011).

Collins L et al. (gen eds), *Dicey, Morris and Collins on The Conflict of Laws* (14th edn, Sweet & Maxwell 2006) with Second Cumulative Supplement (Sweet and Maxwell 2008).

Crawford EB and Carruthers JM, *International Private Law: A Scots Perspective* (3rd edn, W Green 2010).

De Vattel E, *The Law of Nations* (1758) (tr J Chitty) (Philadelphia 1852).

Droz D, *Compétences Judiciaires et Effets des Jugements dans le Marché Commun* (Dalloz 1972).

Edsel R, *The Monuments Men: Allied Heroes, Nazi Thieves, and the Greatest Treasure Hunt in History* (Center Street 2009).

Edwards AB et al., *The Selective Paulus Voet*, Editio Specialis Fundamina (University of South Africa 2007).

Ehrenzweig AA, *Private International Law* (Sijthoff 1967).

Fawcett JJ and Carruthers JM, *Cheshire, North & Fawcett Private International Law* (14th edn, OUP 2008).

Feliciano H, *The Lost Museum: The Nazi Conspiracy to Steal the World's Greatest Works of Art* (Basic Books 1997).

Forrest C, *International Law and the Protection of Cultural Heritage* (Routledge 2010).

Forsyth CF, *Private International Law* (5th edn, Juta 2012).

Fromm E, *To Have or To Be?* (Continuum 2002).

Garnett R, *Substance and Procedure in Private International Law* (OUP 2012).

Gazzini IF, *Cultural Property Disputes: The Role of Arbitration in Resolving Non-Contractual Disputes* (Transnational Publishers Inc. 2004).

Grossfeld B, *The Strength and Weakness of Comparative Law* (Oxford 1990).

Hartman GH, *The Fateful Question of Culture* (Columbia University Press 1997).

Henckaerts JM and Doswald-Beck L, *Customary International Humanitarian Law Vol I Rules* (International Committee of the Red Cross 2005).

Hopkirk P, *Foreign Devils on the Silk Road: The Search for the Lost Cities and Treasures of Chinese Central Asia* (OUP 1980).

Hugonis Grotii, *De Iure Belli et Pacis* 1625 Book III Section XVI (John W Parker 1853).

Kaczorowska A, *Public International Law* (4th edn, Routledge 2010).

Keenan DJ and Riches S, *Business Law* (10th edn, Longman 2005).

Lalani S, *Doubt Develops Where Certainty Ceases: Foreign Law in Domestic Courts* (PhD Thesis, University of Lausanne 2011).

Lalive PA, *The Transfer of Chattels in the Conflict of Laws* (Clarendon Press 1955).

Levontin AV, *Choice of Law and Conflict of Laws* (AW Sijthoff 1976).
Lipstein K, *Principles of the Conflict of Laws, National and International* (Nijhoff 1981).
MacKenzie SRM, *Going, Going, Gone: Regulating the Market in Illicit Antiquities* (Institute of Art and Law Leicester 2005).
Maher G and Rodger B, *Civil Jurisdiction in the Scottish Courts* (W Green 2010).
Mann FA, *Foreign Affairs in English Courts* (Clarendon Press, 1986).
McLachlan C, *Lis Pendens in International Litigation* (Hague Academy of International Law 2009).
Merryman JH, *Thinking about the Elgin Marbles* (2nd edn, Kluwer 2009).
Mihan G, *Looted Treasure: Germany's Raid on Art* (Alliance Press 1944).
Miles MM, *Art as Plunder: The Ancient Origins of Debate about Cultural Property* (CUP 2008).
Mills A, *The Confluence of Public and Private International Law* (CUP 2010).
Muscarella OW, *The Lie Became Great: The Forgery of Ancient Near Eastern Cultures* (Styx 2000).
Nafziger JA and Nicgorski AM, *Cultural Heritage Issues: The Legacy of Conquest, Colonization and Commerce* (Martinus Nijhoff 2009).
Nicholas LH, *The Rape of Europa: The Fate of Europe's Treasures in the Third Reich and the Second World War* (Alfred Knopf 1994).
O'Keefe P, *Commentary on the UNESCO Convention 1970* (Institute of Art and Law 2000).
Odendahl K, *Kulturgüterschutz: Entwicklung, Struktur und Dogmatik eines Ebenübergreifenden Normsystems* (Mohr Siebeck 2005).
Palmer N, *Museums and the Holocaust: Law, Principles and Practice* (Institute of Art and Law Ltd 2000).
Panagopoulos G, *Restitution in Private International Law* (Hart 2000).
Pannikar R, *Cultural Disarmament: The Way to Peace* (John Knox Press 1995).
Prott LV and O'Keefe PJ, *Law and the Cultural Heritage Vol. 3 Movement* (Butterworth 1989).
Prowda JB, *Visual Arts and the Law* (Lund Humphries 2013).
Raape L, *Internationales Privatrecht* (5th edn, Verlag Franz Vahlen 1961).
Rabel E, *The Conflict of Laws: A Comparative Study Vol. 4* (Ann Arbor, University of Michigan 1958).
Rabinbach A and Gilman SL, *Third Reich Sourcebook* (University of California Press 2013).
Robertson I, *A New Art from Emerging Markets* (Lund Humphries 2011).

Schick J, *The Gods Are Leaving the Country* (Orchid Press 1999).

Schönenberger B, *The Restitution of Cultural Assets* (Eleven International Publishing 2009).

Schuz R, *A Modern Approach to the Incidental Question* (Kluwer Law International 1997).

Scoles EF, Hay P, Borchers PJ and Symeonides SC, *Conflict of Laws* (St Paul Minn 2000).

Scovazzi T, Ubertazzi B and Zagato L (eds), *Il Patrimonio Culturale Intangibile nelle sue Diverse Dimensioni* (Guiffre 2012).

Shiu-Hing Lo S, *The Politics of Cross-Border Crime in Greater China: Case Studies of Mainland China, Macao and Hong Kong* (ME Sharpe 2009).

Stamatoudi I, *Cultural Property Law and Restitution* (Edward Elgar 2011).

Steiner HJ and Vagts DF, *Transnational Legal Problems: Materials and Text* (The Foundation Press Inc. 1986).

Study Group on a European Civil Code and the Research Group on EC Private Law (C von Bar et al. eds.) *Principles, Definitions and Model Rules of European Private Law: Draft Common Frame of Reference* (Sellier 2009).

Symeonides SC, *The American Choice-of-Law Revolution: Past, Present and Future* (Martinus Niijhof 2006).

Tijhuis AJG, *Transnational Crime and the Interface between Legal and Illegal Actors: The Case of the Illicit Art and Antiquities Trade* (Wolf Legal Publishers 2006).

Tolstoy L, *What Is Art?* (tr A Maude) (The Brotherhood Publishing Company 1898).

Ulph J and Smith I, *The Illicit Trade in Art and Antiquities* (Hart 2012).

Ulpian, *Commentary on the Praetor's Edict.*

Vadi V, *Cultural Heritage in International Investment Law and Arbitration* (CUP 2014).

Van Woudenberg N, *State Immunity and Cultural Objects on Loan* (Martinus Nijhoff 2012).

Verhagen HLE, *Conflit Mobile bij Roerende Zaken: Assimilatie of Transformatie* (Kluwer 2007).

Voet J, *Commentarius ad Pandectas* (tr P Gane) under the title *The Selective Voet: Being Selections on the Pandects* (Butterworths 1829).

Voet P, *De Statutis et eorum Concursu Liber Singularis* tr AB Edwards and DM Kriel under the title *The Selective Paul Voet* (University of South Africa 2007).

Von Hoffmann B and Thorn K, *Internationales Privatrecht: Einschließlich der Grundzüge des Internationalen Zivilverfahrensrechts* (8th edn, CH Beck München 2005).

Von Savigny FK, *Private International Law, and the Retrospective Operation of Statutes: A Treatise on the Conflict of Laws, and the Limits of their Operation in Respect of Place and Time* (Guthrie tr) (2nd rev edn, T & T Clark 1880).
Watson P and Todeschini S, *The Medici Conspiracy* (Public Affairs 2006).
Watson P, *From Manet to Manhattan* (Random House UK 1992).
Weil S, *The Need for Roots* (Routledge 2002).
Whincop MJ and Keyes M, *Policy and Pragmatism in the Conflict of Laws* (Ashgate 2001).
Wilde L, *Global Solidarity* (Edinburgh University Press 2013).
Yeide NH, *Beyond the Dreams of Avarice: The Hermann Goering Collection* (Laurel Publishing 2009).

Recueil des Cours

Juenger FK, 'General Course on Private International Law' IV (193) *Recueil des Cours* (The Hague 1985) 123.
Kegel G, 'The Crisis of Conflict of Laws' II *Recueil des Cours* (The Hague 1964) 95.
Kowalski WW, 'Restitution of Works of Art Pursuant to Private and Public International Law' (2001) 288 *Recueil des Cours* (The Hague 2002) 212.
Kronke H, 'Capital Markets and Conflict of Laws' V (286) *Recueil des Cours* (The Hague 2000) 245.
Lowenfeld AF, 'Public Law and the International Arena: Conflict of Laws, International Law, and Some Suggestions for their Interaction' II (163) *Recueil des Cours* (Sijthoff & Noordhoff 1980) 311.
Mann FA, 'The Doctrine of Jurisdiction in International Law' I (111) *Recueil des Cours* (The Hague 1964) 1.
Mann FA, 'The Doctrine of International Jurisdiction Revisited after Twenty Years' III (186) *Recueil des Cours* (The Hague 1984) 9.
Prott LV, 'Problems of Private International Law for the Protection of the Cultural Heritage' V *Recueil des Cours* (The Hague 1989) 214.
Siehr K, 'International Art Trade and the Law' VI (243) *Recueil des Cours* (The Hague 1993) 9.
Symeonides SC, 'The American Choice-of-Law Revolution in the Courts' 298 *Recueil des Cours* (The Hague 2002) 431.

Contributions in Composite Works

Alder C and Polk K, 'The Illicit Traffic in Plundered Antiquities' in P Reichel (ed), *Handbook of Transnational Crime and Justice* (Sage Publications 2005) 96.

Appiah A, 'Cosmopolitanism: Ethics in a World of Strangers' in LV Prott (ed), *Witnesses to History: A Compendium of Documents and Writings on the Return of Cultural Objects* (Unesco Publications 2009) 95.

Baade HW, 'Operation of Foreign Public Law' in *International Encyclopedia of Comparative Law Vol. III* Chapter 12.

Barker I, 'Thoughts of an Alternative Dispute Resolution Practitioner on an International ADR Regime for Repatriation of Cultural Property and Works of Art' in BT Hoffman (ed), *Art and Cultural Heritage: Law, Policy and Practice* (CUP 2006) 483.

Carducci G, 'The Growing Complexity of International Art Law: Conflict of Laws, Uniform Law, Mandatory Rules, UNSC Resolutions and EU Regulations' in BT Hoffman (ed), *Art and Cultural Heritage: Law, Policy and Practice* (CUP 2006) 68.

Chappell D and Polk K, 'Unravelling the "Cordata": Just How Organized is the International Traffic in Cultural Objects?' in S Manacorda and D Chappell (eds), *Crime in the Art and Antiquities World* (Springer 2011) 99.

Curtis NGW, 'Thinking about the Right Home: Repatriation and Marischal Museum, University of Aberdeen' in M Gabriel and J Dahl (eds), *UTIMUT – Past Heritage Future Partnerships: Discussions on Repatriation in the 21st Century* (IWGIA/NKA 2008) 44.

De Ly F, 'Conflicts of Law in International Arbitration – an Overview' in F Ferrari and S Kroll (eds), *Conflicts of Law in International Arbitration – an Overview* (Sellier 2011) 3.

Dittrich-von Wehring K, 'Introduction' in R Fisher (ed), *A Cultural Dimension to the EU's External Policies – from Policy Statements to Practice and Potential* (Amsterdam 2007) 3.

Droz G, 'The International Protection of Cultural Property from the Standpoint of Private International Law' in Council of Europe, *International Legal Protection of Cultural Property: Proceedings of the 13th Colloquy on European Law* (Strasbourg 1984) 538.

Elia R, 'Analysis of the Looting, Selling, and Collecting of Apulian Red-figure Vases: A Quantitative Approach' in N Brodie, J Doole and C Renfrew (eds), *Trade in Illicit Antiquities: the Destruction of the World's Archaeological Heritage* (Cambridge 2001) 145.

Feliciano H, 'The Great Culture Robbery: The Plunder of Jewish-Owned Art' in A Beker (ed), *The Plunder of Jewish Property during the Holocaust: Confronting European History* (NY University Press 2001) 164.

Fleckner U, 'Marketing the Defamed: On the Contradictory Use of Provenances in the Third Reich' in G Feigenbaum and I Reist (eds), *Provenance: An Alternative History of Art* (Getty Research Institute 2012) 137.

Francioni F, 'Culture, Heritage and Human Rights: An Introduction' in F Francioni and M Scheinin (eds), *Cultural Human Rights* (Martinus Nijhoff 2008) 1.

Gaillard E and Banifatemi Y, 'Negative Effect of Competence-Competence: The Rule of Priority in Favour of the Arbitrators' in E Gaillard and D di Pietro (eds), *Enforcement of Arbitration Agreements and International Arbitral Awards: The New York Convention in Practice* (Cameron 2008) 257.

Gerstenblith P, 'Recent Developments in the Legal Protection of Cultural Heritage' in N Brodie, MM Kersel, C Luke and K Walker Tubb (eds), *Archaeology, Cultural Heritage and the Antiquities Trade* (University Press of Florida 2006) 68.

Gilkey LB, 'Can Art Fill the Vacuum?' in D Apostolos-Cappadona (ed), *Art, Creativity and the Sacred* (Continuum 1996) 187.

Graber CB, Kuprecht K and Lai JC, 'The Trade and Development of Indigenous Cultural Heritage: Completing the Picture and a Possible Way Forward' in CB Graber, K Kuprecht K and JC Lai (eds), *International Trade in Indigenous Cultural Heritage* (Edward Elgar 2012) 463.

Graham JL, 'Art Exchange: How the International Art Market Lacks a Clear Regulatory Framework' in V Vadi and HEGS Schneider (eds), *Art, Cultural Heritage and the Market: Legal and Ethical Issues* (Springer 2014) 323.

Hanisch H, 'Internationalprivatrechtliche Fragen im Kunsthandel', in A Dieckmann et al., *Festschrift für Wolfram Müller-Freienfels* (Schulthess 1986) 193.

Hartung H, 'The Holocaust and World War II Looted Art: Arbitrated between Great Dreams and Reality' in The International Bureau of the Permanent Court of Arbitration (ed), *Resolution of Cultural Property Disputes* (The Hague 2004) 327.

Hoffman BT, 'European Union Legislation Pertaining to Cultural Goods' in BT Hoffman (ed), *Art and Cultural Heritage: Law, Policy and Practice* (CUP 2006) 191.

Hutt S, 'Cultural Property Law Theory' in JR Richman and MP Forsyth (eds), *Legal Perspectives on Cultural Resources* (AltaMira Press 2004) 17.

Jakubowski A, 'Return of Illicitly Trafficked Cultural Objects Pursuant to Private International Law: Current Developments' in The Illicit Traffic of Cultural Objects in the Mediterranean (EUI Working Papers 2009) 137.

Jayme E, 'Die Nationalität des Kunswerkes als Rechtsfrage' in G Reichelt (ed), *Internationaler Kulturgüterschutz* (Wien 1992) 7.

Jayme E, 'Neueste Entwicklungen im Internationalen Kunstrecht' in *Kunst im Recht* (Graz Jurisprudential Faculty 2004) 15.

Jennings RY, 'Universal International Law in a Multicultural World' in M Bos and I Brownlie (eds), *Liber Amicorum for the Rt Hon Lord Wilberforce* (Clarendon Press 1987) 39.

Jokela H, 'Internationalism in Private International Law' in DS Clark (ed), *Comparative and Private International Law Essays in Honor of John Henry Merryman on His Seventieth Birthday* (Duncker & Humblot 1990) 395.

Juenger FK, 'The Problem with Private International Law' in J Basedow et al. (eds), *Private Law in the International Arena: From National Conflict Rules Towards Harmonization and Unification: Liber Amicorum Kurt Siehr* (TMC Asser Press 2000) 289.

Keyes M, 'The Suppression of State Interests in International Litigation' in S McVeigh (ed), *Jurisprudence of Jurisdiction* (Routledge-Cavendish 2007) 123.

Kowalski WW, 'General Observations: Claims for Works of Art and Their Legal Nature' in International Bureau of the Permanent Court of Arbitration (ed), *Resolution of Cultural Property Disputes* (Kluwer Law International 2004) 31.

Kuprecht K and Siehr K, 'International Trade in Moveable Tangible Cultural Heritage of Indigenous Peoples: A European Perspective' in CB Graber, K Kuprecht and JC Lai (eds), *International Trade in Indigenous Cultural Heritage* (Edward Elgar 2012) 246.

Kuprecht K, 'Human Rights Aspects of Indigenous Cultural Property Repatriation' in K Odendahl and PJ Weber (eds), *Kulturgüterschutz – Kunstrecht – Kulturrecht: Festschrift für Kurt Siehr* (Baden-Baden 2010) 191.

Lalive P, 'A Disturbing International Convention: The UNIDROIT Convention on Cultural Objects' in LV Prott (ed), *Witnesses to History: A Compendium of Documents and Writings on the Return of Cultural Objects* (Unesco Publications 2009) 29.

Lanciotti A, 'The Dilemma of the Right to Ownership of Underwater Cultural Heritage: The Case of the "Getty Bronze"' in S Borelli and F

Lenzerini (eds), *Cultural Heritage, Cultural Rights, Cultural Diversity: New Developments in International Law* (Nijhoff Publishers 2012) 301.

Last K, 'Cultural Pluralism and the Return of Cultural Heritage' in S Tierney (ed), *Accommodating Cultural Diversity* (Ashgate 2007) 123.

Lubina K and Schneider H, 'Pringsheim, Provenance and Principles: A Case Study on the Restitution of Nazi Looted Art and Compensatory Payments' in K Odendahl and PJ Weber (eds), *Kulturgüterschutz – Kunstrecht – Kulturrecht: Festschrift für Kurt Siehr* (Baden-Baden 2010) 161.

MacKenzie S, 'Identifying and Preventing Opportunities for Organized Crime in the International Antiquities Market' in S Manacorda (ed), *Organized Crime in Art and Antiquities* (2009 International Scientific and Professional Advisory Council of the UN Crime Prevention and Criminal Justice Programme) 41.

MacKenzie S, 'The Market as Criminal and Criminals in the Market: Reducing Opportunities for Organised Crime in the International Antiquities Market' in S Manacorda and D Chappell (eds), *Crime in the Art and Antiquities World* (Springer 2011) 69.

Nafziger JAR, 'The Protection and Repatriation of Indigenous Cultural Heritage in the United States' in C Bell and RK Paterson (eds), *Protection of First Nations Cultural Heritage: Laws, Policy, and Reform* (UBC Press 2009) 110.

O'Neill M, 'Repatriation and Its Discontents: The Glasgow Experience' in E Robson, L Treadwell and C Gosden (eds), *Who Owns Objects?: The Ethics of Collecting Cultural Property* (Oxbow 2006) 105.

Palmer N, 'Arbitration and the Applicable Law' in International Bureau of the Permanent Court of Arbitration (ed), *Resolution of Cultural Property Disputes* (The Hague 2004) 291.

Palmer N, 'Litigation: The Best Remedy?' in International Bureau of the Permanent Court of Arbitration (Hrsg.) (ed), *Resolution of Cultural Property Disputes* (The Hague 2004) 113.

Papa-Sokal M, 'The US Legal Response to the Protection of the World Cultural Heritage' in N Brodie, MM Kersel, C Luke and K Walker Tubb (eds), *Archaeology, Cultural Heritage and the Antiquities Trade* (University Press of Florida 2006) 36.

Parkhouse A, 'The Illicit Trade in Cultural Objects: Recent Developments in the United Kingdom' in BT Hoffman (ed), *Art and Cultural Heritage: Law, Policy and Practice* (CUP 2006) 178.

Pell C, 'Using Arbitral Tribunals to Resolve Disputes Relating to Holocaust-Looted Art' in International Bureau of the Permanent Court of Arbitration (ed), *Resolution of Cultural Property Disputes* (The Hague 2004) 307.

Radicati di Brozolo LG, 'Interference by National Courts with International Arbitration: The Situation after Saipem v Bangladesh' in C Müller and A Rigozzi (eds), *New Developments in International Commercial Arbitration* (Schultess 2009) 1.

Radicati di Brozolo LG, 'Res Judicata' in *Post Award Issues* ASA Special Series no 38 2011, Chapter 7.

Reimann M, 'Comparative Law and Private International Law' in M Reimann and R Zimmermann (eds), *The Oxford Handbook of Comparative Law* (Oxford 2006) 1363.

Renold MA, 'Stolen Art: The Ubiquitous Question of Good Faith' in The International Bureau of the Permanent Court of Arbitration (ed), *Resolution of Cultural Property Disputes* (The Hague 2004) 251.

Rödl F, 'Regime-Collisions, Proceduralised Conflict of Laws and the Unity of the Law: On the Form of Constitutionalism Beyond the State' in R Nickel (ed), *Conflict of Laws and Laws of Conflict in Europe and Beyond* (Intersentia 2010) 263.

Theurich S, 'Alternative Dispute Resolution in Art and Cultural Heritage – Explored in the Context of the World Intellectual Property Organization's Work' in K Odendahl and PJ Weber (eds), *Kulturgüterschutz – Kunstrecht – Kulturrecht: Festschrift für Kurt Siehr* (Baden-Baden 2010) 569.

Veraart W and Winkel L, 'An Introduction to Dilemmas of Post-War Restitution in Europe' in W Veraart and L Winkel (eds), *The Post-war Restitution of Property Rights in Europe* (Rvp Press 2011) 7.

Vitale C, 'The Protection of Cultural Heritage between the EU Legal Order and the Global Legal Space' in E Chite and BG Mattarella (eds), *Global Administrative Law and EU Administrative Law: Relationships, Legal Issues and Comparison* (Springer Verlag 2011) 211.

Von Stockhausen T, 'The Failure of Provenance Research in Germany' in G Feigenbaum and I Reist (eds), *Provenance: An Alternative History of Art* (Getty Research Institute 2012) 124.

Warren KJ, 'Perspectives of the Victims: Case Studies' in PM Messenger (ed), *The Ethics of Collecting Cultural Property* (University of New Mexico Press 1989) 17.

Watson P, 'Convicted Dealers: What We Can Learn' in N Brodie, MM Kersel, C Luke and K Walker Tubb (eds), *Archaeology, Cultural Heritage and the Antiquities Trade* (University Press of Florida 2006) 93.

Wichard JC and Wendland WB, 'Mediation as an Option for Resolving Disputes between Indigenous/Traditional Communities and Industry Concerning Traditional Knowledge' in BT Hoffman (ed), *Art and Cultural Heritage: Law, Policy and Practice* (CUP 2006) 477.

Journals

Adler A, 'The Lubomirski Dürers: A Case for Legal and Moral Restitution' (2010) 1 Cultural Heritage and Arts Review 11.

Alderman K, 'The Ethical Trade in Cultural Property: Ethics and Law in the Antiquity Auction Industry' [2008] ILSA Journal of International and Comparative Law 1.

Alderman K, 'The Human Right to Cultural Property' [2011] Michigan Journal of International Law 69.

Alderton M, 'The Act of State Doctrine: Questions from Validity to Abstention from Underhill to Habib' [2011] Melbourne Journal of International Law 1.

Armbrüster C, 'Private Law as an Instrument for the Protection of Cultural Property' (2013) 10 TDM Special Issue 1.

Arroyo DPF, 'Private International Law and Comparative Law: A Relationship Challenged by International and Supranational Law' (2009) XI Yearbook of Private International Law 31.

Bandle AL and Theurich S, 'Alternative Dispute Resolution and Art-Law – A New Research Project of the Geneva Art-Law Centre' (2011) 6 Journal of International Commercial Law and Technology 28.

Basedow J, 'Internal and External Conflicts, Federalism and Market Regulation: Federal Choice of Law in Europe and the US – a Comparative Account of Interstate Conflicts' (2008) 82 Tulane Law Review 2119.

Bator PM, 'An Essay on the International Trade in Art' (1982) 34 Stanford Law Review 275.

Bazyler MJ, 'Nuremberg in America: Litigating the Holocaust in United States Courts' (2000) 34 University of Richmond Law Review 1.

Bennett TW, 'Choice of Law Rules in Claims of Unjust Enrichment' (1990) 39 ICLQ 136.

Biondi A,'The Merchant, the Thief and the Citizen: The Circulation of Works of Art within the European Union' (1997) 34 Common Market Law Review 1173.

Bogdanons M, 'The Casualties of War: The Truth about the Iraq Museum' (2005) 109 American Journal of Archaeology 477.

Borodkin LJ, 'The Economics of Antiquities Looting and a Proposed Legal Alternative' (1995) 95 Columbia Law Review 377.

Bowman B, 'Transnational Crimes against Culture: Looting at Archaeological Sites and the "Grey" market in Antiquities' (2008) 24 Journal of Contemporary Criminal Justice 225.

Brekoulakis S, 'The Negative Effect of Compétence-Compétence: The Verdict Has to Be Negative' (2009) 2 Austrian Arbitration Review 237.

Brodie N, 'Pity the Poor Middlemen' (1998) 3 Culture Without Context 7.

Brodie N, 'Congenial Bedfellows? The Academy and the Antiquities Trade' (2011) 27 Journal of Contemporary Criminal Justice 408.

Brown MF, 'Heritage Trouble: Recent Work on the Protection of the Intangible Cultural Property' (2005) 12 IJCP 40.

Bush SE, 'The Protection of British Heritage: Woburn Abbey and The Three Graces' (1996) 5 IJCP 269.

Byrne-Sutton Q, 'The Goldberg Case' (1992) 1 IJCP 151.

Caprio CA, 'Artwork, Cultural Heritage Property, and the Foreign Sovereign Immunities Act' [2006] Uniform Law Review 285.

Carbonneau TE, 'Judicial Approbation in Building the Civilization of Arbitration' (2009) 113 Penn State Law Review 1343.

Carey Miller DL, 'Title to Art: Developments in the USA' (1995) 1 Scottish Law and Practice Quarterly 115.

Carey Miller DL, Meyers DW and Cowe AL, 'Restitution of Art and Cultural Objects: A Re-Assessment of the Role of Limitation' [2001] Art Antiquity and Law 1.

Chamberlain K, 'Holocaust Art Claims and Public International Law' (2008) 13 Art Antiquity and Law 351.

Chamberlain K, 'UK Accession to the 1970 UNESCO Convention' (2002) 7 Art Antiquity and Law 231.

Chechi A, 'Some Reflections on International Adjudication of Cultural Heritage-Related Cases' (2013) 10 TDM Special Issue 1.

Church J 'Evolving US Case Law on Cultural Property Disputes' [1993] IJCP 47.

Church J, 'Evaluating the Effectiveness of Foreign Laws on National Ownership of Cultural Property in US Courts' [1992] Columbia Journal of Transnational Law 179.

Coggins CC, 'A Licit International Traffic in Ancient Art: Let There Be Light' (1995) 4 IJCP 61.

Cohen L and Felson M, 'Social Change and Crime Rate Trends: A Routine Activity Approach' (1979) 44 American Sociological Review 588.

Collin RM, 'The Law and Stolen Art, Artifacts, and Antiquities' (1993) 36 Howard Law Journal 17.

Collins L, 'Professor Lowenfeld and the Enforcement of Foreign Public Law' (2009) 42 International Law and Politics 125.

Cook WW, 'Characterization in the Conflict of Laws' (1941) 51 Yale Law Journal 191.

Cornu M and Renold M, 'New Developments in the Restitution of Cultural Property: Alternative Means of Dispute Resolution' (2010) 17 IJCP 1.

Cremades BM and Madalena I, 'Parallel Proceedings in International Arbitration' (2008) 24 Arbitration International 3.

Crowell DL, 'Autocephalous Greek-Orthodox Church of Cyprus v Goldberg & Feldman Fine Arts Inc: Choice of Law in the Protection of Cultural Property' (1992) 27 Texas International Law Journal 173.

Cuba S, 'Stop the Clock: The Case to Suspend the Statute of Limitations on Claims for Nazi-Looted Art' (1999) 17 Cardozo Arts and Entertainment Law Journal 447.

Cuniberti G, 'Beyond Contract – The Case for Default Arbitration in International Commercial Disputes' (2008) 32 Fordham Int'l LJ 417.

Cuniberti G, 'Parallel Litigation and Foreign Investment Dispute Settlement' (2006) 21 ICSID Review Foreign Investment Law Journal 381.

Czigler TD and Takacs I, 'The Law Applicable to Contracts in the European Union' (2012) 20 The California International Law Journal 21.

Daly BW, 'The Potential for Arbitration of Cultural Property Disputes; Recent Developments at the Permanent Court of Arbitration' [2005] Law and Practice of International Courts and Tribunals 261.

Davis M, 'Time to Change the Federal Forum Non Conveniens Analysis' (2002) 77 Tulane Law Review 309.

Davis T, 'Supply and Demand: Exposing the Illicit Trade of Cambodian Antiquities through a Study of Sotheby's Auction House' (2011) 56 Crime Law and Social Change 155.

Demarsin B, 'Let's Not Talk about Terezín: Restitution of Nazi Era Looted Art and the Tenuousness of Public International Law' (2011) 37 Brooklyn Journal of International Law 117.

Demarsin B, 'The Third Time Is Not Always a Charm: The Troublesome Legacy of a Dutch Art Dealer: The Limitation and Act of State Defences in Looted Art Cases' (2010) 28 Cardozo Art and Entertainment Law Journal 255.

Dietzler J, 'On "Organized Crime" in the Illicit Antiquities Trade: Moving Beyond the Definitional Debate' (2013) 16 Trends in Organized Crime 329.

Dodge WS, 'Breaking the Public Law Taboo' (2002) 43 Harvard International Law Journal 161.

Dolinger J, 'World Public Policy: Real International Public Policy in the Conflict of Laws' (1982) 17 Texas International Law Journal 167.

Douglas S, 'The Nature of Conversion' (2009) 68 Cambridge LJ 198.

Durney M and Proulx B, 'Art Crime: A Brief Introduction' (2011) 56 Crime Law and Social Change 115.

Durney M et al. 'Art and Antiquities Trafficking News Notes for May 2010–October 2010' (2010) 1 Cultural Heritage and Arts Review 57.

Ehrenzweig AA, 'A Counter-revolution in Conflicts Law? From Beale to Cavers' (1966) 80 Harvard Law Review 377.
Falconer KA, 'When Honour Will Not Suffice' (2000) 21 University of Pennsylvania Journal of International Economic Law 383.
Falkoff S, 'Mutually Beneficial Repatriation Agreements: Returning Cultural Patrimony, Perpetuating the Illicit Antiquities Market' (2008) 16 JL & Pol 165.
Fauvarque-Cosson B, 'Comparative Law and Conflict of Laws – Allies or Enemies?' (2001) 49 AJCL 407.
Fielder Redman L, 'The Foreign Sovereign Immunities Act: Using a "Shield" Statute as a "Sword" for Obtaining Federal Jurisdiction in Art and Antiquities Cases' (2008) 31 Fordham Int'l LJ 781.
Fincham D, 'How Adopting the Lex Originis Rule Can Impede the Flow of Illicit Cultural Property' (2008) 32 Columbia Journal of Law and the Arts 111.
Fishman JP, 'Locating the International Interest in Intranational Cultural Property Disputes' (2010) 35 The Yale Journal of International Law 347.
Fishman R and Wai S, 'The Smuggling of Art, and the Art of Smuggling: Uncovering the Illicit Trade in Cultural Property and Antiques' (2009) 1 American Economic Journal: Applied Economics 82.
Forbes SO, 'Securing the Future of Our Past: Current Efforts to Protect Cultural Property' (1996) 9 Transnational Law 235.
Forrest C, 'Art on Loan: The Role of Immunity in Dispute Resolution' (2013) 10 TDM 1.
Forrest C, 'Strengthening the International Regime for the Prevention of the Illicit Trade in Cultural Heritage' (2003) 4 Melbourne Journal of International Law 592.
Forrest C and Fletcher-Tomenius P, 'The Protection of the Underwater Cultural Heritage and the Challenge to UNCLOS' (2000) 5 Art Antiquity and Law 125.
Fox C, 'The UNIDROIT Convention on Stolen or Illegally Exported Cultural Objects: An Answer to the World Problem of Illicit Trade in Cultural Property' [1993] American University International Law Review 225.
Francioni F, 'Beyond State Sovereignty: The Protection of Cultural Heritage as a Shared Interest of Humanity' [2004] Michigan JIL 1209.
Francioni F, 'The Human Dimension of International Cultural Heritage Law: An Introduction' (2011) 22 EJIL 9.
Franzina P, 'The Proposed New Rule of Special Jurisdiction Regarding Rights In Rem in Moveable Property: A Good Option for a Reformed Brussels I Regulation?' (2011) 3 Diritto de Commercio Internazionale 789.

Frey L, 'Bakalar v Vavra and the Art of Conflicts Analysis in New York: Framing a Choice of Law Approach for Moveable Property' (2012) 112 Columbia Law Review 1055.

Frigo M, 'Ethical Rules and Codes of Honor Related to Museum Activities: A Complementary Support to the Private International Law Approach Concerning the Circulation of Cultural Property' [2009] IJCP 49.

Frigo M, 'Model Provisions on State Ownership of Undiscovered Cultural Objects – Introduction' [2011] Uniform Law Review 1044.

Gegas EI, 'International Arbitration and Resolution of Cultural Property Disputes' (1997) 13 Ohio State Journal on Dispute Resolution 129.

Gerstenblith P, 'Identity and Cultural Property: The Protection of Cultural Property in the United States' (1995) 75 Boston University Law Review 559.

Gerstenblith P, 'Schultz and Barakat: Universal Recognition of National Ownership of Antiquities' (2009) XIV Art Antiquity and Law 21.

Gerstenblith P, 'The Public Interest in the Restitution of Cultural Objects' (2001) 16 Conn J Int L 197.

Gillies L, 'The Conflict of Laws as a Technique of Demand Side Regulation in Claims for the Recovery of Cultural Objects' [2015] JPIL (forthcoming).

Gillies P and Dahdal A, 'Waiver of a Right to Arbitrate by Resort to Litigation, in the Context of International Commercial Arbitration' (2007) 2 Journal of International Commercial Law and Technology 221.

Granovsky M, 'A Permanent Resolution Mechanism of Cultural Property Disputes' (2008) 8 Pepperdine Dispute Resolution Law Journal 25.

Guedj TG, 'The Theory of the Lois de Police, A Functional Trend in Continental Private International Law – A Comparative Analysis with Modern American Theories' (1991) 34 AJCL 661.

Harris MJ, 'Who Owns the Pot of Gold at the End of the Rainbow? A Review of the Impact of Cultural Property on Finders and Salvage Laws' (1997) 14 Arizona Journal of International and Comparative Law 224.

Hartley TC, 'Pleading and Proof of Foreign Law: The Major EU Systems Compared' (1996) 45 ICLQ 271.

Hawkins A, 'A Tale of Two Innocents: Creating an Equitable Balance between the Rights of Former Owners and Good Faith Purchasers of Stolen Art' (1995) 64 Fordham Law Review 49.

Hay P, 'Comments on Self-Limited Rules of Law in Conflicts Methodology' (1982) 30 AJCL Supplement 129.

Heiskanen V, 'Forbidding *Dépeçage*: Law Governing Investment Treaty Arbitration' (2009) 32 Suffolk Transnational Law Review 367.

Jayme E, 'Globalization in Art Law: Clash of Interests and International Tendencies' (2005) 38 Vanderbilt Journal of Transnational Law 937.

Juenger FK, 'Conflict of Laws: A Critique of Interest Analysis' (1984) 32 American Journal of Comparative Law 1.

Kaye LM, 'Avoidance and Resolution of Cultural Heritage Disputes: Recovery of Art Looted during the Holocaust' [2006] Willamette Journal of International Law and Dispute Resolution 243.

Kaye LM, 'Looted Art: What Can and Should Be Done' (1998) 20 Cardozo Law Review 657.

Keim R, 'Filling the Gap Between Morality and Jurisprudence: The Use of Binding Arbitration to Resolve Claims of Restitution Regarding Nazi-Stolen Art' (2003) 3 Pepperdine Dispute Resolution Law Journal 295.

Kelly MJ, 'Conflicting Trends in the Flourishing International Trade of Art and Antiquities: Restitutio in Integrum and Possessio Animo Ferungi/Lucrandi' [1995] Dickinson Journal of International Law 31.

Kenyon A and MacKenzie S, 'Recovering Stolen Art – Australian, English and US Law on Limitations of Action' (2001–2002) 30 Western Australian Law Review 233.

Kessedjian C, 'Public Order in European Law' [2007] Erasmus Law Review 25.

Kreder J, 'The New Battleground of Museum Ethics and Holocaust-Era Claims: Technicalities Trumping Justice or Responsible Stewardship for the Public Trust?' [2009] Oregon Law Review 37.

Kreder JA, 'Reconciling Individual and Group Justice with the Need for Repose in Nazi-Looted Art Disputes: Creation of An International Tribunal' (2007) 73 Brooklyn Law Review 155.

Kropholler J, 'Die Vergleichende Methode und das Internationale Privatrecht' (1978) 77 Zeitschrift für Vergleichende Rechtswissenschaft 1.

Lane DC, Bromley DG, Hicks RD and Mohoney JS, 'Time Crime: The Transnational Organization of Art and Antiquities Theft' (2008) 24 Journal of Contemporary Criminal Justice 243.

Lee M, 'A Choice of Law Dilemma: The Conflict and Reconciliation of Laws Governing Cross-Border Transfers of Stolen Art' [2008–2009] Cardozo Public Law Policy and Ethics Journal 719.

Lenzner NR, 'The Illicit International Trade in Cultural Property: Does the UNIDROIT Convention Provide an Effective Remedy for the Shortcomings of the UNESCO Convention?' (1994) 15 University of Pennsylvania Journal of International Business 469.

Lerner RE, 'The Nazi Art Theft Problem and the Role of the Museum: A Proposed Solution to Disputes Over Title' (1998) 31 New York University Journal of International Law and Policy 15.

MacKenzie S, 'Illicit Deals in Cultural Objects as Crimes of the Powerful' (2011) 56 Crime Law Social Change 133.
MacLachlan C, 'A Long Road Home' (2010) XV Art Antiquity and Law 275.
Martinek M, 'The Seven Pillars of Wisdom in Private International Law: The German and the Swiss Experience with the Codification of Conflicts Law Rules' [2001] Chinese Yearbook of Private International Law and Comparative Law 15.
Mealy N, 'Mediation's Potential Role in International Cultural Property Disputes' (2011) 26 Ohio State Journal on Dispute Resolution 169.
Merryman JH and Nafziger JAR, 'The Private International Law of Cultural Property in the United States' (1994) 42 American Journal of Comparative Law Supplement 221.
Merryman JH, 'A Licit International Trade in Cultural Objects' (1995) 4 IJCP 13.
Merryman JH, 'Cultural Property Internationalism' [2005] IJCP 11.
Merryman JH, 'Cultural Property, International Trade and Human Rights' (2001) 19 Cardozo Arts and Entertainment 51.
Merryman JH, 'The Public Interest in Cultural Property' [1989] California Law Review 339.
Merryman JH, 'Thinking About the Elgin Marbles' [1985] Michigan Law Review 1881.
Merryman JH, 'Two Ways of Thinking about Cultural Property' [1986] AJIL 831.
Michaels R, 'The New European Choice-of-Law Revolution' (2008) 82 Tulane Law Review 1607.
Muir Watt H, 'Choice of Law in Integrated and Interconnected Markets: A Matter of Political Economy' (2003) 9 Columbia Journal of European Law 383.
Mullery J, 'Fulfilling the Washington Principles: A Proposal for Arbitration Panels to Resolve Holocaust-Era Art Claims' [2010] Cardozo Journal of Conflict Resolution 643.
Murphy JD, 'The People's Republic of China and the Illicit Trade in Cultural Property: Is the Embargo Approach the Answer?' [1994] IJCP 227.
Murphy N, 'Splitting Images: Shared-Value Settlements in Nazi-Era Art Restitution Claims' (2009) 3 Florida Entertainment Law Review 1.
Murray MD, 'Stolen Art and Sovereign Immunity: The Case of Altmann v Austria' (2003–2004) 27 Columbia Journal of Law and Arts 301.
O'Donnell T, 'The Restitution of Holocaust Looted Art and Transitional Justice: The Perfect Storm or the Raft of Medusa?' (2011) 22 Eur J Int Law 49.

O'Keefe PJ, 'Protection of the Material Cultural Heritage: The Commonwealth Scheme' [1995] ICLQ 147.
Palmer N, 'Recovering Stolen Art' (1994) 47 Current Legal Problems 215.
Palmer N, 'Spoliation and Holocaust-related Cultural Objects: Legal and Ethical Models for the Resolution of Claims' (2007) 12 Art Antiquity and Law 1.
Papa-Sokal M, 'Beyond the Nationalist-Internationalist Polarisation in the Protection of the Archaeological Heritage' (2009) 14 Art Antiquity and Law 237.
Parker J, 'World War II and Heirless Art: Unleashing the Final Prisoners of War' (2005) 13 Cardozo Journal of International and Competition Law 661.
Passas N, 'Cross-border Crime and the Interface between Legal and Illegal Actors' (2003) 16 Security Journal 19.
Paterson RK, 'Resolving Material Cultural Disputes: Human Rights, Property Rights and Crimes against Humanity' [2006] Willamette Journal of International Law & Dispute Resolution 154.
Paterson RK, 'The Legal Dynamics of Cultural Property' [1995] UBC Law Review 243.
Pearce N, 'From Relic to Relic' [2013] Journal of the History of Collections 1.
Pearlstein WG, 'Buying and Selling in Today's Market' (2012) 3 Spencer's Art Law Journal 2.
Pecoraro TW, 'Choice of Law in Litigation to Recover National Cultural Property: Efforts at Harmonization in Private International Law' [1990] Virginia Journal of International Law 1.
Pell OC, 'The Potential for Mediation/Arbitration Commission to Resolve Disputes Relating to Artworks Stolen or Looted during World War II' (1999) 10 De Paul-LCA Journal of Art and Entertainment Law 10.
Petrus CH, 'Spanish Perspectives on the Doctrines of Kompetenz-Kompetenz and Separability: A Comparative Analysis of Spain's 1988 Arbitration Act' (2000) 11 American Review of International Arbitration 396.
Piers M and Erauw J, 'Application of the UNCITRAL Principles of International Commercial Contracts in Arbitration' (2012) 8 JPIL 441.
Prott LV and O'Keefe PJ, '"Cultural Heritage" or "Cultural Property"?'[1992] IJCP 307.
Prott LV, 'The International Movement of Cultural Objects' (2005) 12 IJCP 225.

Radi Y, 'The "Culture of Balancing" of International Investment Law – Cultural Interests and Investors' Interests in International Investment Treaties and Arbitration' (2013) 10 TDM Special 1.

Range D, 'Deaccessioning and Its Costs in the Holocaust Art Context: The United States and Great Britain' (2003–2004) 39 Texas International Law Journal 655.

Redman LF, 'The Foreign Sovereign Immunities Act: Using a "Shield" Statute as a "Sword" for Obtaining Federal Jurisdiction in Art and Antiquities Cases' (2008) 31 Fordham Int'l LJ 781.

Reed A, 'Venue Resolution and Forum Non Conveniens: Four Models of Jurisdictional Propriety' (2013) 22 Journal of Transnational Law and Contemporary Problems 369.

Reichelt G, 'International Protection of Cultural Property' [1985] Uniform Law Review 42.

Ritchie AM, 'Victorious Youth in Peril: Analyzing Arguments Used in Cultural Property Disputes to Resolve the Case of the Getty Bronze' (2009) 9 Pepperdine Dispute Resolution Law Journal 325.

Roodt C and Carey Miller DL,'Vitium Reale in Private Law and Private International Law' (2013) 10 TDM Special Issue 1.

Roodt C, 'Autonomy and Due Process in Arbitration: Recalibrating the Balance' European Journal of Law Reform [2011–2013] (Special Issue) 413.

Roodt C, 'Border Skirmishes between EU Courts and Arbitral Tribunals: Finality in Conflicts of Competence' (2011) 13 Yearbook of Private International Law 91.

Roodt C, 'Conflicts of Procedure between Courts and Arbitral Tribunals in Africa: An Argument for Harmonization' (2010) 25 Tulane European and Civil Law Forum 65.

Roodt C, 'Reflections on Finality in Arbitration' (2012) 2 De Jure 485.

Roodt C, 'Reflections on Theory, Doctrine and Method in Choice of Law' (2007) XL CILSA 76.

Roodt C, 'Restitution of Art and Cultural Objects and Its Limits' (2013) 46 CILSA 286.

Roodt C, 'State Courts or ADR in Nazi-era Art Disputes: A Choice "More Apparent Than Real?"' (2012) 3 Cardozo Journal of Conflict Resolution 421.

Rowe DW, 'Stolen Property in the Conflict of Laws' [1980] Canterbury Law Review 71.

Rowland DJ, 'Nazi-Era Art Claims in the United States: 10 Years after the Washington Conference' [2009] Art and Cultural Heritage Law Newsletter 30.

Sancho Villa D, 'Jurisdiction over Jurisdiction and Choice of Court Agreements: Views on the Hague Convention of 2005 and Implications for the European Regime' (2010) 12 Yearbook of Private International Law 399.

Sargent AB, 'New Jurisdictional Tools for Displaced Cultural Property in Russia' [2010] Yearbook of Cultural Property Law 167.

Saville A, 'Treasure Trove in Scotland' [2002] Antiquity 796.

Sawka JF, 'Reconciling Policy and Equity: The Ability of the Internal Revenue Code to Resolve Disputes Regarding Nazi-Looted Art' (2009) 17 University of Miami International and Comparative Law Review 1.

Schechter R, 'Preventing Pillage and Promoting Politics: The Dual Goals of the 2009 US-China Bilateral Agreement to Restrict Imports of Chinese Cultural Property' (2009) 14 Art Antiquity & Law 317.

Schultz T, 'Human Rights: A Speed Bump for Arbitral Procedures? An Exploration of Safeguards in the Acceleration of Justice' [2006] IALR 1.

Shapiro D, 'Repatriation: A Modest Proposal' (1998) 31 International Law and Politics 95.

Shapiro S, 'Note: How Republic of Austria v. Altmann and United States v. Portrait of Wally Relay the Past and Forecast the Future of Nazi Looted-Art Restitution Litigation' (2008) 34 William Mitchell Law Review 1147.

Shine P, 'The Treatment of Non-EU Nationals before Domestic Courts of Member States' (2010) 9 Chinese Journal of International Law 451.

Short KA, 'Preventing the Theft and Illegal Export of Art in a Europe without Borders' (1993) 26 VanderBilt Journal of Transnational Law 633.

Sidorsky E, 'The 1995 Unidroit Convention on Stolen or Illegally Exported Cultural Objects: The Role of International Arbitration' (1996) 5 IJCP 19.

Siehr K, 'Chronicles of 1 July 2000–31 December 2000' (2001) 10 IJCP 137.

Siehr K, 'Commercial Transactions and the Forfeiture of State Immunity under Private International Law' (2008) 13 Art Antiquitiy and Law 339.

Siehr K, 'The Protection of Cultural Heritage and International Commerce' [1997] IJCP 304.

Siehr K, 'The Protection of Cultural Property: UNIDROIT Convention and EEC Instruments of 1992/93 Compared' (1998) 3 Uniform Law Review 677.

Sinai Y, 'Reconsidering *Res Judicata*: A Comparative Perspective' (2011) 21 Duke Journal of Comparative and International Law 353.

Spiegler HN, 'Recovering Nazi-Looted Art: Report from the Front Lines' (2001) 16 Connecticut Journal of International Law 297.

Staker C, 'Public International Law and the Lex Situs Principle in Property Conflicts and Foreign Expropriations' (1987) 58 BYBIL 151.
Stein P, 'Jus Commune and Its Demise' (2004) 25 Journal of Legal History 161.
Sternlight JR, 'Creeping Mandatory Arbitration: Is It Just?' (2004/2005) 57 Stan LR 1631.
Stewart DP, 'Recognition and Enforcement of Foreign Judgments in the United States' (2010) 12 Yearbook of Private International Law 180.
Sykes K, 'Recovery of Stolen and Looted Works of Art: London December 10 1998' (1999) 4 Art Antiquity and Law 81.
Symeonides S, 'The American Revolution and the European Evolution in Choice of Law: Reciprocal Lessons' [2008] Tulane Law Review 1741.
Symeonides SC, 'A Choice-of-Law Rule for Conflicts Involving Stolen Cultural Property' (2005) 38 Vanderbilt Journal of Transnational Law 1177.
Symeonides SC, 'Choice of Law in the American Courts in 2010: Twenty-Fourth Annual Survey' (2011) 59 American Journal of Comparative Law 303.
Tompkins A, 'A Permanent International Art Crime Tribunal?' (2009) 2 The Journal of Art Crime 35.
Torsen MA, 'National Reactions to Cultural Property Looting in Nazi Germany: A Window on Individual Effort and International Disarray' [2005] EJCL 1.
Tyler BJ, 'The Stolen Museum: Have United States Art Museums Become Inadvertent Fences for Stolen Art Works Looted by the Nazis in World War II?' (1998–1999) 30 Rutgers Law Journal 464.
Vadi VS, 'Toward a Lex Administrativa Culturalis? The Adjudication of Cultural Disputes before Investment Arbitral Tribunals' (2013) 10 TDM Special 1.
Valentin P, 'The UNIDROIT Convention on the International Return of Stolen or Illegally Exported Cultural Objects' [1999] Art Antiquity and Law 107.
Van Apeldoorn LJ, 'Mobilia non habent sequelam' (1932) 11 Tijdschrift voor Rechtsgeschiedenis 132.
Van Haersolte-van Hof J, 'The Revitalization of the Permanent Court of Arbitration' [2007] NILR 395.
Varner E, 'Arbitrating Cultural Property Disputes' (2012) 14 Cardozo Journal of Conflict Resolution 477.
Wantuch MO and Niethammer A, 'Compensation for Nazi Wrongdoing: The Case for an Integrated Approach' (2007) 12 Art Antiquity and Law 46.

Weller M, 'Iran v Barakat: Some Observations of the Application of Foreign Public Law by Domestic Courts from a Comparative Perspective' (2007) 12 Art Antiquity and Law 279.
Wilson MJ, 'Demystifying the Determination of Foreign Law in US Courts: Opening the Door to a Greater Global Understanding' (2011) 46 Wake Forest Law Review 887.
Wilson S, 'Prescription and Limitation of Actions in Scotland and England in Relation to Dispute Resolution in Construction Contracts' (2001) 15 ELR 122.
Woodhead C, 'Nazi Era Spoliation: Establishing Procedural and Substantive Principles' (2013) 18 Art Antiquity and Law 167.
Yasaitis KE, 'National Ownership Laws as Cultural Property Protection Policy: The Emerging Trend in *United States v Schultz*' (2005) 12 IJCP 95.

Reports, Guidelines and Surveys

'AAMD Report of the Task Force on Spoliation of Art in the Nazi/World War II Era (1933–1945)' (4 June 1998) <https://aamd.org/sites/default/files/document/Report%20on%20the%20Spoliation%20of%20Nazi%20Era%20Art.docx>.
'AAM Guidelines Concerning the Unlawful Appropriation of Objects during the Nazi Era of November 1999, amended in 2001' <http://www.aam-us.org/resources/ethics-standards-and-best-practices/collections-stewardship/objects-during-the-nazi-era>.
Basic Principles and Guidelines on the Right to a Remedy and Reparation for Victims of Gross Violations of International Human Rights Law and Serious Violations of International Humanitarian Law, General Assembly Resolution 60/147 of 16 December 2005 <http://legal.un.org/avl/ha/ga_60-147/ga_60-147.html>.
De Clercq WCEH, *Report on a Legal Framework for Free Movement Within the Internal Market of Goods Whose Ownership Is Likely to be Contested* (2002/2114(Ini) (2003), Eur. Parl. Doc. A5-0408/2003).
European Commission, *Guide to the Application of Treaty Provisions Governing the Free Movement of Goods* (European Union 2010) <http://ec.europa.eu/enterprise/policies/single-market-goods/files/goods/docs/art34-36/new_guide_en.pdf>.
European Commission, *Study Report on Preventing and Fighting Illicit Trafficking in Cultural Goods in the European Union*, 10 October 2011, 190–94, 248–49 <http://ec.europa.eu/home-affairs/doc_centre/crime/docs/Report%20Trafficking%20in%20cultural%20goods%20EN.pdf>.

Grimsted PK, *Reconstructing the Record of Nazi Cultural Plunder: A Survey of the Dispersed Archives of the Einsatzstab Reichsleiter Rosenberg (ERR)* (International Institute of Social History IISH-IISG, Amsterdam, 2010) <http://www.iisg.nl/publications/errsurvey/>.

Legal Services EEIG (2012), sub 'Austria' (D Karollus-Bruner) <http://eguides.cmslegal.com/arbitration>.

Lörcher T, Pendell G and Wilson J (eds), *CMS Guide to Arbitration Vol 1* (4th edn, CMS

Lord Jackson, *Review of Civil Litigation Costs: Final Report* (1st edn, The Stationery Office 2010).

Nuyts A, 'Study on Residual Jurisdiction: General Report' (3 September 2007) <http://ec.europa.eu/civiljustice/news/docs/study_residual_jurisdiction_en.pdf>.

O'Connell A, 'Immunity from Seizure Study' (30 September 2005) <http://www.lending-for-europe.eu/fileadmin/CM/public/training/Antwerp/Immunity_from_Seizure_Paper_ Anna_O_Connell.pdf>.

'The ABCs of Cross-Border Litigation in the United States' (*Crowell Moring*, 2008) <http://www.crowell.com/files/abc-guide-to-cross-border-litigation.pdf>.

Waverley Committee Report, RA Butler 6 September 1952, Report of a Committee appointed by the Chancellor of the Exchequer HMSO 1952.

Recommendations

Spoliation Advisory Panel Report in Respect of a Painting Now in the Possession of the Tate Gallery (The Stationery Office 18 January 2001).

Spoliation Advisory Panel Report in Respect of Four Drawings Now in the Possession of the British Museum (The Stationery Office 27 April 2006).

Spoliation Advisory Panel Report in Respect of Fourteen Clocks and Watches Now in the Possession of the British Museum, London (The Stationery Office 7 March 2012).

Resolutions

Institute of International Law Wiesbaden Resolution, 'The Application of Foreign Public Law' 20th Commission, Res. 4, (1975) 56 *Institute of International Law Yearbook* 551.

Institute of International Law Oslo Session, 'Public Law Claims Instituted by a Foreign Authority or a Foreign Public Body' 20th Commission (1977) 57 *Institute of International Law Yearbook* <http://www.idi-iil.org/idiE/resolutionsE/1977_oslo_01_en.pdf>.
Institute of International Law Basel Resolution, 'International Sale of Works from the Angle of the Protection of the Cultural Heritage' (1992) 64/II *Institute of International Law Yearbook* 403.

Symposia

'Prague Holocaust Era Assets Conference: Terezin Declaration' (*US Department of State*, 30 June 2009) <http://www.state.gov/p/eur/rls/or/126162.htm>.
'1998 Washington Conference on Holocaust-Era Assets' (*US Department of State*) <http://1997-2001.state.gov/www/regions/eur/wash_conf_material.html>.
Campfens E, 'Impression of the Symposium "Fair and Just Solutions?"' (*Advisory Committee on the Assessment of Restitution Applications For Items of Cultural Value and the Second World War*, 3 December 2012) <http://www.restitutiecommissie.nl/en/impression_of_the_day.html>.
Davidson D, 'The View from the State Department' Symposium on 'Should Stolen Holocaust Art be Returned?' (*New York County Law Association*, 25 March 2013) <http://www.state.gov/p/eur/rls/rm/2013/mar/206719.htm>.

Research Papers

Casini L, '"Italian Hours": The Globalization of Cultural Property Law' (Jean Monnet *Working Paper 10*, September 2010) <http://centers.law.nyu.edu/jeanmonnet/papers/10/101101.pdf>.
Chechi A, Contel R and Renold MA, 'Case Victorious Youth – Italy v. J. Paul Getty Museum' Platform ArThemis (http://unige.ch/art-adr), Art-Law Centre, University of Geneva, October 2011.
Contel R, Soldan G and Chechi A, 'Case Euphronios Krater and Other Archaeological Objects – Italy and Metropolitan Museum of Art' (Art-Law Centre, University of Geneva, June 2012) <https://plone.unige.ch/art-adr/cases-affaires/euphronios-krater-and-other-archaeological-objects-2013-italy-and-metropolitan-museum-of-art/case-note-2013-euphronios-krater-and-other-archaeological-objects/view>.
Efrat A, 'Getting Governments to Co-operate against Looting: Insights from the American and British Experience' [2012] Journal of Art Crime Electronic Issue <http://portal.idc.ac.il/facultypublication.publication?PublicationID=2874&FacultyUserName=YXNpZg==>31.

Felson M, 'The Ecosystem for Organized Crime' (*HEUNI Paper No. 26*, 20 October 2006) <http://www.heuni.fi/material/attachments/heuni/papers/6Ktmwqur9/HEUNI_papers_26.pdf>.

Juenger FK, 'The Problem with Private International Law', Centro di studi e ricerche di diritto comparato e straniero: saggi, conferenze e seminari, No 37 (Rome 1999), <http://www.cisg.law.pace.edu/cisg/biblio/juenger1.html>.

Koush A, 'Fight against the Illegal Antiquities' Traffic in the EU: Bridging the Legislative Gaps' (Bruges Political Research Papers Series 2011).

MacKenzie C, 'Auktion 392, Reclaiming the Galerie Stern in Dusseldorf' <http://portico.concordia.ca/www/auktion392/html/03essay.html>.

Orford T, '"Sending it Back" – the Role of Law and the Cultural Patrimony Debate' <http://www.artright.co.za/media/cms_page_media/37/Sending%20Art%20Back%20by%20Toby%20Orford.pdf>.

Pell OC, 'Holocaust-Looted Art: Lost But Not Forgotten' (*UVA Lawyer*, Fall 2002) <http://www.law.virginia.edu/html/alumni/uvalawyer/f02/opinion.htm>.

Radicati di Brozolo LG, 'Res Judicata in International Arbitral Awards' (*SSRN* 15 April 2011) <http://ssrn.com/abstract=1842685>.

Rassool C, 'Human Remains, the Disciplines of the Dead and the South African Memorial Complex' <http://sitemaker.umich.edu/politics.of.heritage/files/rassool_human_remains.doc>.

Raue D, 'Georg Steindorff and his Collection' <www.iae-egyptology.org/uploads/Facts%20about%20the%20case.pdf>.

Renold MA, 'The International Protection of Archaeological Heritage: Questions of Private International Law and of Legal Harmonization' <http://biblio.juridicas.unam.mx/libros/7/3457/18.pdf> 297.

Stipanovic TJ and Lamare JR, 'Living with ADR: Evolving Perceptions and Use of Mediation, Arbitration and Conflict Management in Fortune 1,000 Corporations' (*SSRN working paper*, 19 February 2013) <http://ssrn.com/abstract=2221471>.

Theurich S, 'Update on Alternative Dispute Resolution in the Art and Cultural Heritage Sector' (*International Bar Association*, August 2009) <http://www.ibanet.org/Article/Detail.aspx?ArticleUid=c93cf2fa-f5f6-4a64-a7d1-8bd907fdf3dd>.

Watson P, 'The Investigation of Frederick Schultz' (*McDonald Institute for Archaeological Research*) <http://www2.mcdonald.cam.ac.uk/projects/iarc/culturewithoutcontext/issue10/watson.htm>.

Weller M, 'Key Elements of Just and Fair Solutions' (*de Restitutie-commissie*) <http://www.restitutiecommissie.nl/en/system/files/Weller%20Key%20Elements%20of%20Fair%20and%20Just%20Solutions.pdf>.

Webpages

<http://www.artresolve.org/>
<http://www.comartrecovery.org/cases/hans-sachs-poster-collection>
<http://www.getty.edu/art/gettyguide/artObjectDetails?artobj=8912>
<http://www.bbc.co.uk/news/uk-england-cumbria-11287093>
<https://www.gov.uk/government/news/painting-deemed-national-treasure-may-leave-uk>
<http://www.britishmuseum.org/explore/highlights/highlight_objects/aoa/b/benin_plaque_oba__europeans.aspx>
<http://www.expo2010.cn/expo/english/eu/nc/ct/userobject1ai12652.html>
<http://www.pca-cpa.org/showfile.asp?fil_id=2054>

Newspaper Articles

AFP, 'Looted Nigerian Art Returned to Traditional Ruler' *South African Courier* (23 June 2014).

AFP, 'Jewish Council Criticizes Gurlitt Nazi Art Return' *The Local* (21 November 2013).

AFP, 'Missing Matisse Thieves, a Cuban American Man and a Mexican Woman, Plead Guilty in Miami' <http://artdaily.com/news/58676/Missing-Matisse-thieves–a-Cuban-American-man-and-a-Mexican-woman–plead-guilty-in-Miami>.

Alberge D, 'Stolen Ivory Miniatures Attract Pounds 15,000 Reward' *The Independent* (4 August 1993).

Barboza D, Bowley G and Cox A, 'A Culture of Bidding: Forging an Art Market in China' *The New York Times* (28 October 2013).

Blanc S, 'New Fronts Open in Chinese Art Market as Records Fall' *API* (11 October 2013).

Bohr F, Gorris L, Knöfel U, Röbel S and Sontheimer M, 'Art Dealer to the Führer: Hildebrand Gurlitt's Deep Nazi Ties' *Spiegel Online* (23 December 2013).

Carvajal D, 'Wooing the Public to Recover' *The New York Times* (19 March 2014).

Clarke A, 'The Future of Civil Mediation' *Tribunals Judiciary* (8 May 2008).

Evans S, 'Merkl and Putin View Exhibition of Disputed Art' *BBC News Europe* (22 June 2013).

Ghose T, 'Syria's Civil War Imperils Nation's Rich Archaeological Treasures' *NBC News* (4 September 2013).

Grandell T, 'Ransom Demand for Stolen Pictures' *The Guardian* (2 January 2001).

Grosvenor B,'Courtauld Defeats Jewish Heirs to Keep Rubens' *Art History News* (20 December 2010).

Halperin J, 'Egypt's Malawi Museum Ransacked' *The Art Newspaper* (21 August 2013).

Hickley C, 'Eizenstat Favours US Nazi Loot Panel to Advise on Disputed Art' *Bloomberg* (28 June 2009).

Hickley C, 'Jewish Heir Fights Restitution, Wants Museum to Keep Art' *Bloomberg* (31 May 2011).

Holligan A, 'Dutch Art Theft Suspects Offer Paintings for Deal' *BBC News Europe* (13 August 2013).

Jordans F, 'Germany Denies Jewish Heirs: Cologne Returns Art' *AP* (18 December 2013).

Knapton S, 'Smuggled Ancient Sculpture Returns to Egypt' *The Telegraph* (19 December 2008).

'Legal Issues Complicate Munich Art Treasure Trove Find' *Spiegel Online International* (18 November 2013) <http://www.spiegel.de/international/germany/legal-issues-complicate-munich-art-treasure-trove-find-a-934071.html>.

Lightman LJ, 'Mediation: An Approximation of Justice' *Tribunals Judiciary* (28 June 2007).

'Meisterwerke zwischen Müll – Fahnder entdecken in München Nazi-Schatz in Milliardenhöhe' *Focus Online* (4 November 2013) <http://www.focus.de/kultur/kunst/nazi-raubkunst-meisterwerke-zwischen-muell-fahnder-entdecken-kunstschatz-in-milliardenhoehe_aid_1147066.html>.

Mostrous A, 'The Murky World of the Art Detective' *The Times* (9 August 2014).

Oliver A and Baker D, 'Pictured: The Dramatic Moment Police Stopped Suspected Art Thief at Gunpoint and Recovered a Stolen £68.3 million Cezanne' *Mail Online* (12 April 2012).

Platoni K, 'The Ten Million Dollar Woman' *East Bay Express* (4 August 2004).

Preston A, 'Art Theft: Who's in the Frame? Why Steal a Priceless Masterpiece When It's Almost Impossible to Sell?' *Daily Mail Online* (9 February 2013).

Rayner G, 'Lord Myners Faced Questions over £3m Ransom for Stolen Turners' *The Telegraph* (28 February 2009).

Rising D, 'Nazi-seized Art Ordered Returned to American Man' *The Journal* (16 March 2012).

Seelye KQ and Mashberg T, 'A New Effort in Boston to Catch 1990 Art Thieves' *New York Times* (18 March 2013).

Stengle J, 'Photo Albums Related to Nazi Art Theft Unveiled' *Yahoo News* (28 March 2012).

Vincent A, '10 Most Wanted Missing Paintings' *The Telegraph* (4 November 2013).

Index

Aderet, O 254
adjudicatory authority 161–4, 219–23
  arbitration *see separate entry*
  jurisdiction 161–4, 220
    1995 UNIDROIT Convention 168–9
    EU rules on civil and commercial 167–78, 220
    US courts 162, 168–9, 173, 177–83
  jurisdiction declined 163, 183–4
    common law and civil law systems 184–7
    US courts 187–8
  Nazi spoliated art 164, 211–7, 221
  out-of-court settlements 190–1, 284
  parallel proceedings 147, 165–7, 174, 187, 189, 210, 217–9, 221–3, 269, 271, 287
  private international law rules 'out-manoeuvred' 164–8
  res judicata 181, 188–90, 218, 221, 286–7, 341
    and enforcement of arbitral award 207–11, 221
    Nazi spoliated art 213
Adler, A 276
Adorno, TW 1
adverse possession 28, 50
Afghanistan 21, 47
Akinsha, K 252
Alberge, D 229
Alder, C 19
Alderman, K 47, 109, 325
Alderton, M 103
alternative dispute resolution 52–6, 70, 149–52, 160, 216–7, 262–8
  mediation 50–1, 53–4, 149, 151, 193–4, 216, 262, 264–8, 271–2, 274, 276–7, 287, 342–3
  Spoliation Advisory Panel (SAP) 65, 264–5, 267–8, 272–3, 277, 283, 286
Andrews, N 183, 190
anti-suit injunctions 206–7
Anton, AE 184
Anton, M 34, 36, 310
Appiah, A 3
applicable law 37, 98, 151, 315, 346
  arbitration 153, 156–9
  choice of law 26, 41–5, 49–50, 73, 83–90, 92–3, 106, 109–10, 127, 236–7, 340, 342–4, 346
    deter title laundering: structure and method of 237–48
  lex causae 38–9, 97
  lex fori 38–9, 43–4, 50, 89, 101
  multilateral choice of law rules (conflicts rules) 43–4, 83–4, 86, 88, 93, 231–2, 346–7
  see also classification
arbitration 54–5, 58, 72, 151–5, 160, 163, 191–2, 220–1, 223, 341
  anti-suit injunctions 206–7
  breach of waiver of right to court hearing 202–5
  choice of law 156–9, 223, 341
  choice of procedural law 202
  complexities 198–211
  consent 167, 194, 199–201, 205, 222
  default model 201
  European Union 154, 158
    secondary EU law 196
  expertise 198, 220
  global instruments and systems for 193–5
  investment 335
  jurisdiction 203–5
  Nazi spoliated art 212–5, 261

non-contractual nature of dispute 193, 196, 198–201
non-legal factors 196–8
parallel proceedings: court and 166–7, 217–9, 221–3
res judicata and enforcement of award 207–11, 221
speed and fairness 155
state immunity 214–5
Arendt, H 2
Armbrüster, C 234, 238, 240, 333–4
armed conflict *see* war
Arnold, M 3
Arroyo, DPF 61, 68, 110, 169
art and antiquities trade 12, 112, 307
co-mingling of licit and illicit 21–2, 28–9
art crime 17, 24, 27, 71–2
co-mingling of licit and illicit trade 21–2, 28–9
demand, supply and regulation 23–5
looting 47, 61, 73, 118, 122–3, 199, 212, 250, 258
theft *see separate entry*
trafficking in illicitly obtained antiquities 19–21
art market 9, 11–6
co-mingling of licit and illicit trade 21–2, 28–9
art-napping 18
ArtResolve 193
Aryanisation 114, 260, 277, 285
Atleta di Fano (Getty Bronze) 34, 75, 293, 299, 309, 334
auctioneers 100, 213, 229
Aust, A 105
Australia 81, 162, 165, 185, 297, 320
Austria 38, 50, 76, 173, 185–6, 191–2, 214
Nazi spoliated art 259, 266–7
repatriation 79

Baade, HW 315
Bandle, AL 52, 152, 199
Barboza, D 19
Barker, I 212, 214
Basedow, J 42
Bator, PM 48, 112, 114, 307
Baudrillard, J 1
Bazyler, MJ 70, 251, 255
Belgium 130, 150–1, 242–3, 249, 345
Bell, A 180, 185–7
Bell, C 77
Bennett, TW 91, 93
Biondi, A 144, 294
Blanc, S 12
Bogdanons, M 47
Bohr, F 257
bona fide purchasers *see* good faith purchasers
bona vacantia 86, 289, 328
Borodkin, LJ 4, 259
Bos, M 189
Bowman, B 22, 24
Brekoulakis, S 204
bribery: customs officials and border patrols 296–7
Briggs, A 316–7
Brodie, FN 62, 135, 300
Brodie, NJ 23, 29
Brown, MF 60, 74
Bühring-Uhle, C 197
Bush, SE 1
Byrne-Sutton, Q 99

Cambodia 21, 120
Campfens, E 215
Canada 4, 116–7, 297, 320
Caprio, CA 164, 183
Carducci, G 18, 27–8, 92, 108, 119, 124, 143, 148, 231, 234–6, 238, 313, 326
Carey Miller, DL 8–9, 92, 94, 124–5, 144, 230
Carruthers, JM 41, 69, 80, 94, 133, 148, 228–9, 231, 233, 236–7, 239, 241, 269, 279, 286
Carty, A 49
Carvajal, D 252
Casini, L 6
Chamberlain, K 117, 122, 130, 164, 256, 301
Chappell, D 11, 20–1, 23, 319

Chechi, A 5, 26, 35, 54–6, 60, 71, 75, 82–3, 90, 107, 116, 120–1, 132, 140, 151, 193–4, 225, 227, 232, 236–7, 245, 247, 269, 304–5, 314, 327
China 11–3, 19, 298
  see also Dunhuang
Chong, A 333, 335
Church, J 125
civil law systems 37, 39, 95, 226, 291
  arbitration 204
  choice of law 89
  due diligence 97
  foreign public law 312–4
  jurisdiction 183–4, 186
  res judicata 189
  territoriality 102–4
  UNESCO 132
  UNIDROIT 127, 130
Clarke, A 151
Clarkson, CMV 162, 174, 184
classification (categorisation) 26, 33, 37–9, 90–101, 228, 336, 342, 346–7
  conceptual device 100–1, 106
  European Union 172–3, 177
  lex originis 147, 234–5, 238, 242
  lex situs 40, 42, 44, 56, 93–5, 97, 104, 148, 228, 230–3, 236, 244, 247, 248–9, 278–9, 346–7
  Nazi spoliated art 39, 50, 261–2, 272–7, 287, 342
  substance and procedure 38–9, 50, 96, 272–7
  see also public policy exception
codes of conduct 45, 135, 216, 334, 336
Coggins, CC 12, 20, 112
Cohen, L 24
Collin, RM 243
Collins, L 94, 228, 308–9, 315, 318, 320
comity 44, 82, 103, 206, 240, 310–2, 335, 347
commercial imperative 11–6, 224, 227, 346
commercial law 11, 29, 64, 73, 129, 225, 236
common law 39–40, 59, 85, 87, 89, 92–3, 226, 289
  act of state doctrine 102–5
  anti-suit injunctions 206
  foreign public law 291, 314
  forum non conveniens 82
  good faith 97
  issue estoppel 209–10
  jurisdiction 162, 164–5, 183–6
  nemo dat quod non habet 126, 229, 233, 241
  ownerless property 289
  res judicata 189–90
  UNIDROIT 130
comparative law 61, 127
compensation 68, 70, 76–7, 104, 306
  arbitration 154, 198, 210
  degenerate art 104
  EU 144–8
  Nazi spoliated art 73, 104, 253, 269–72
  UNESCO 129, 235–6, 259
  UNIDROIT 127, 129, 233
conciliation 151
confiscation 10, 17, 26, 32–3, 43, 50, 57, 68, 73, 104, 341, 345
  International Court of Justice (ICJ) 120–1
  Nazi spoliated art *see separate entry*
conflict *see* war
connecting factor 38, 56, 81, 83, 93–4, 97, 228, 232, 234, 239–40, 346
consistency of decisions 83, 154, 269–72, 274
Contel, R 72, 106, 191
conversion 58, 67, 91–2, 96, 100, 172, 199, 231, 244, 247–8, 316–7, 322–3, 337
Cook, WW 39
Cornu, M 15, 22, 53, 67, 69, 76, 79, 88, 150–1, 198, 234
Council of Europe 264
Craddock, P 45
Crawford, EB 94, 228
Cremades, BM 186, 189, 218
crime against humanity 258
criminal law 28–9, 33–4, 68, 73, 128, 144, 147, 226, 299, 305, 340
  arbitration 199–200
  money laundering 319–20

theft *see separate entry*
UNIDROIT 129
United Kingdom 97, 337
tainted cultural object offence 303–4, 327–8
Theft Act 1968 300–2
United States 71–2, 199–200, 299, 320–7, 337
Crowell, DL 99, 243
Cuba, S 274, 276
cultural diplomacy 52, 344–5, 348
cultural heritage law 5–6, 55–6, 61, 269, 318
context: private international law meets 16–25
practical control offered to 36, 339–43
choice of law method 41–2
classification 37–9
ethics 45–8
foreign public law 40–1
global solidarity 48–52
international dimension 36–7, 340
public policy exception 42–5
surmounting greatest obstacles 344–8
cultural objects 2–5, 129, 225–6
Cuniberti, G 165, 201
Curtis, NGW 78
Cyprus 69
Czigler, TD 58

Daly, BW 54, 152, 199
Davidson, D 276–7
Davis, M 185
Davis, T 22
De Clercq, WCEH 212
De Ly, F 156, 221
dealers 9, 12, 18, 20–3, 30, 32, 213, 302, 334, 344
Nazi spoliated art 251–2, 253–4, 257, 281
Schultz case 325–6
tainted cultural object offence 303–4
UNESCO 124
vesting laws 25
degenerate art 72–3, 104, 251–2, 258, 275
delict 37, 91, 98–9
demand, supply and regulation 23–5, 72
Demarsin, B 8, 102, 214, 253, 255
Denmark 170
designer theft 18
Dietzler, J 21, 27, 30, 32
Dikman, Aydin 69
dispute settlement 11, 148–9, 221, 345
alternative dispute resolution *see separate entry*
arbitration *see separate entry*
out-of-court settlements 190–1, 284
Dittrich-von Wehring, K 136
Dodge, WS 315
Dolinger, J 333
Douglas, S 100
Droz, G 174, 315
due diligence 46, 64, 96–8, 100, 132, 160, 239, 241, 303–4, 325
arbitration 154
EU 146–7
Iraq 120
UNESCO 236
UNIDROIT 126–7, 129, 233
due process 166–7, 179–80, 247
Dunhuang
Mogao caves 11
Durney, M 17–9, 24, 29, 36

Edsel, R 251, 257
Edwards, AB 311
Efrat, A 10, 12, 129, 337
Egypt 47, 300, 302, 323–4, 326
Ehrenzweig, AA 85, 315
Elia, R 21
Emden, Max 279
equitable principles 73–4, 153
estoppel 28, 209–10, 213, 269
ethics 16, 43, 90, 109, 150–1, 268–9, 275, 336, 343–4, 346, 348
arbitration 195–6
classification and public policy exception 278–9
ethical aspirations 45–8
forced sales 280, 282–3, 286
restitution 50–1, 69–71, 74, 79–80, 260
value-rationality 29, 48–50, 277, 279, 287, 342, 345, 347

Ethiopia 52
European Union 14, 28, 44, 50–1, 57, 62, 89, 110, 344
  arbitration 154, 158, 196, 217
    anti-suit injunctions 206–7
  cultural priorities 7–8
  Directives 8, 143–8, 160, 176, 196, 225–6, 235, 294–5, 301, 319, 337
  export controls 291
  foreign public law 294–5, 296, 301, 319, 329, 335–7
  free movement 7–8, 135–7, 159, 170
    'goods' 137–8
    restrictions 138–40
  jurisdiction 81–2, 147, 167–9, 206, 220
    Brussels/Lugano regime 170–1, 183–4, 186, 341
    courts of Member States 170–3, 177–8
    new Judgments Regulation (Recast) 173, 176–7, 186–7, 206–7
    prorogated 173–4
    revising Judgments Regulation 174–6
  Nazi spoliated art 50–1, 212, 215
  Regulations 58, 81–2, 119, 141–2, 147, 167, 169, 170–8, 206, 296, 301, 335–6
  repatriation 136–7, 143–8
  Schengen Area 296, 329
Evans, S 252
evasion of the law (*fraus legis*) 101, 246
evidentiary law 29, 39
export control 6–9, 15, 25, 40, 43, 51, 72, 111–2, 119, 131, 134, 290, 292–3, 337, 343
  civil law systems 313–4
  Commonwealth Scheme 295–6
  connecting factor 240
  EU 137–9, 141–2, 144, 159, 294–6, 319
  international understanding
    Germany 332–5, 337
    public policy 335–6
    validity of contract of sale 334
  internationalists 114
  no general customary law rule 293
  state ownership rules and regulations on 304–8
  UK 139, 142, 294–5, 301, 309–10, 317
  UNESCO 125–6, 128–9, 131, 134, 291, 294, 305–6
    standard of implementation 297–9, 301
  UNIDROIT 113
expropriation 10–11, 26, 32–3, 43, 68, 73, 102–5, 341
  US courts 181–2, 187–8

fair trial/hearing 151, 155, 185, 202–3, 215
Falconer, KA 73, 122, 213, 217, 257, 259
Falkoff, S 128
Fauvarque-Cosson, B 43, 61, 62, 108
Fawcett, JJ 94, 184, 228
Feliciano, H 250, 253
Felson, M 31, 226
Fielder Redman, L 164, 182, 185
finality of judgments (*res judicata*) 181, 188–90, 218, 221, 286–7, 341
  and enforcement of the arbitral award 207–11, 221
  Nazi spoliated art 213
Fincham, D 232
Finland 76, 130, 173
Fishman, JP 48, 109, 164, 182
Fishman, R 296
Flechtheim, Alfred 281–2
Fleckner, U 251
Forbes, SO 294
forced sales 33, 47, 73, 277–88, 343
  definition 277–8
foreign public law 40–41, 51, 88, 289–93, 336–8, 343, 347–8
  civil law systems 312–4
  equalisation 308–18
  international law and domestic relations 293–308
    no general customary law rule 293
    regional and international instruments 294–7

state ownership rules and export controls 304–8
UNESCO Convention: standard of implementation 297–304
international understanding 326–36
public law taboo 291–5, 308–9, 327, 333, 337, 343
challenge to doctrinal obstacle to restitution 314–8
non-application by default 309–12
qualifying doctrinal obstacle to restitution and 319–26
UNIDROIT 113, 127, 294–5, 310, 327, 329, 331
forfeiture 34, 88, 128, 299, 302, 305, 307–10, 319, 336, 340
Forrest, C 36, 51, 60, 77, 114, 290, 323, 327
Forsyth, CF 84
forum non conveniens 82, 183–6
forum-shopping 82, 169, 173, 182–3, 274, 292, 345
Fox, C 126
France 33, 71, 130, 173, 252, 290, 342
arbitration 201, 204
Nazi spoliated art: mediation 265–6
repatriation 79
Francioni, F 2, 5, 62, 113, 119
Franzina, P 175
fraus legis 101, 246
free movement 13, 292, 336, 344
in EU *see under* European Union
Freund, Julius 281
Frey, L 94, 238, 278
Frigo, M 10, 114, 240, 329
Fromm, E 13

Gaillard, E 158, 204
Garnett, R 38–9, 245
Gazzini, IF 14, 48, 54, 58–9, 65, 68, 82, 95, 109, 116, 120, 124–5, 128–9, 133, 142, 148, 151–2, 154–7, 159, 166–8, 190, 193–4, 197–9, 201–3, 207, 210, 214–5, 217–22, 228, 240, 268, 291–2, 305–6, 310, 314
Gegas, EI 54, 152, 199, 263, 276
Germany 4, 9, 33, 36–7, 50, 76–7, 130, 342–3
classification 91, 172–3
foreign public law 314, 331–5, 337
good faith 97, 260
import control 331, 337
jurisdiction 172–3
limitation period 245, 254, 271
Nazi spoliated art *see separate entry*
res judicata 189, 286–7
'stolen' 237
title laundering 237
UNESCO 333
UNIDROIT 130
Gerstenblith, P 2, 6, 12, 20, 47, 61, 86, 92, 100, 104, 117, 119, 297, 300, 302, 310, 322–3, 326–8, 331
Ghose, T 47
Gilkey, LB 1
Gillies, L 17, 26, 35, 177
Gillies, P 204
global justice 281, 283–4, 343
global solidarity 11, 36, 44, 48–52, 130, 135, 277, 312, 344–5, 347
Goko, C 79
Goldberg, A 321
good faith purchasers 13, 20, 262, 290, 302, 336, 344
common v civil law 97, 259–60
due diligence *see separate entry*
EU 148
London Declaration of 1943 256
market overt 229
Nazi spoliated art 50, 73–4, 256, 260, 269
parallel proceedings 166
Swiss law 33, 50, 252
title laundering *see separate entry*
UNESCO 132, 235–6
UNIDROIT 126–7, 129
Goudstikker, Jacques 102, 278
governmental interest analysis 42
Graber, CB 14, 56
Graham, JL 12
Grandell, T 18
Granovsky, M 52, 152
Greece 74, 75, 97, 150–1
Grimsted, PK 260
Grosvenor, B 278
Grotius, H 116

Guatemala 131
Guedj, TG 84
Gurlitt, Hildebrand 251, 253–4, 257

Hague Convention on the Laws and Customs of War on Land 117, 122, 256, 258
Hague Convention for the Protection of Cultural Property 32, 47–8, 117–8, 122, 258–9
Halperin, J 47
Hanisch, H 237
Harris, MJ 70, 114
Hartley, TC 89
Hartman, GH 2
Hartung, H 109, 122, 214, 258, 264, 280
Hawkins, A 8
Hay, P 84–5
Heiskanen, V 156
Hemer, Thomas 285
Henckaerts, JM 252, 258
Hickley, C 272, 276
Hoffman, BT 142, 310
Holligan, A 17
Holocaust 15–7, 65
  Nazi spoliated art *see separate entry*
Hong Kong 12
Hopkirk, P 11
human potential 48, 51, 345
human remains 59, 77–9
  objects removed from 80
human rights 14, 29
  fair trial/hearing 151, 155, 185, 202–3, 215
  pre-emption right, exercise of 306
  self-determination 77
Hungary 173
Hutt, S 23

Iceland 170
illegal export 19–21, 34, 47, 72–3, 135, 226, 291, 293–4, 299, 304, 306–10, 315, 322–3, 326–7, 334
illicit excavation 19–21, 27, 34, 47, 72–3, 126, 129, 132, 226, 301–4, 330
import control 15, 40, 43, 51, 69, 88, 119, 134, 336–7
  Commonwealth Scheme 295–6, 299, 301
  EU 138–9, 296
  Germany 331, 337
  Swiss law 313
  UK 301
  UNESCO 124–5, 128, 134, 291, 294
    standard of implementation 297–9, 301–2
  US 298–9, 320, 337
India 12
indigenous peoples 13–4, 27, 56–9, 130, 132, 327
  arbitration 197
  human remains 59, 77–9
    objects removed from 80
  Maori material culture 307–8
  Native Americans 78, 80, 86–7, 178–9
International Chamber of Commerce (ICC) 72, 195, 208
international co-operation 337, 344
  see also global solidarity
International Council of Museums (ICOM) 135
International Court of Justice (ICJ) 120–1
International Law Association (ILA) 57, 74, 193, 202, 263
Iran 12, 316–8
Iraq 47, 118–20, 299, 301
Ireland 174, 296
Italy 4, 52, 76, 130, 226, 229, 233, 252, 290
  Atleta di Fano (Getty Bronze) 34, 75, 293, 299, 309, 334
  foreign public law 314
  Medici conspiracy 22, 28, 72, 296

Jackson Review (2010) 54
Jakubowski, A 14, 35, 37, 65–6, 225, 236, 242–3, 291, 304, 306, 310, 313, 315
Japan 130
Jayme, E 35, 48, 107, 234–5, 237
Jennings, RY 115
Jokela, H 115
Jordans, F 279–80

Juenger, FK 35, 83, 85
jurisdiction 17, 26, 80–3, 147, 161–7, 340, 341
  1995 UNIDROIT Convention 168–9
  arbitral tribunal 203–5
  declined 163, 183–4
    common law and civil law systems 184–7
    US courts 187–8
  European Union 81–2, 147, 167–9, 206, 220
    Brussels/Lugano regime 170–1, 183–4, 186, 341
    courts of Member States 170–3, 177–8
    new Judgments Regulation (Recast) 173, 176–7, 186–7, 206–7
    prorogated 173–4
    revising Judgments Regulation 174–6
  exclusive 82, 173
  forum non conveniens 82, 183, 184–6
  forum originis 235
  parallel 83
  United States 82, 85, 162, 165, 168–9, 173
    challenges 187–8
    forum non conveniens 184–6
    FSIA and IFSA 181–3, 187–8
    minimum contacts 178–81
    museums: immunity regime 177–8
    recognition and enforcement 181
jurisdictional trade 190–1, 256, 262–7
justice 26–7, 69, 154
  conflicts 90, 107, 227, 348
  global 281, 283–4, 343
  just and fair solutions 70, 263, 265, 280
  material or substantive 90, 107, 110, 185, 227, 249, 283, 348
  pluralism 43, 62, 90, 256, 269–72, 348
  systemic 281, 288, 348

Kaczorowska, A 258
Kanakariá mosaics 98–9
Kaye, LM 164, 247, 274, 278
Keenan, DJ 229
Kegel, G 90
Keim, R 211
Kelly, MJ 131
Kenyon, A 227, 231, 239, 245
Kessedjian, C 138
Keyes, M 161–5
Knapton, S 52
König, H 269–70, 279–80
Koush, A 14, 28, 242, 306
Kowalski, WW 34, 69, 228–9
Kreder, JA 73, 213, 261, 273
Kronke, H 312
Kropholler, J 62
Kuprecht, K 13, 52, 59, 151, 197, 264–5
Kuwait 118

laches defence 28, 239
Lalani, S 89
Lalive, P 95, 127, 130, 232, 246
Lanciotti, A 34, 75, 225–6, 294, 299, 309, 334
Lane, DC 21, 24–5
Last, K 2, 35, 77–8, 101, 133
Le Brun, C 9
Lee, M 35, 232, 247
Lenzner, NR 123, 133
Lerner, RE 261–2
Levontin, AV 39, 84, 91
lex culturalis see cultural heritage law
lex mercatoria 158
Lipstein, K 315
lis pendens 167, 186–7, 210, 218–9, 341
loans, art 52–3, 58, 67, 75, 178, 183, 192, 198, 342
lock formation 29–33, 148, 226, 243, 246, 248, 311, 340, 342–3, 345–6
'lock' jurisdictions 30–3, 36, 142, 224–49, 252, 281, 343, 347
London Declaration of 1943 256–7
looting 47, 61, 73, 118, 122–3, 199, 212, 250, 258
Lörcher, T 202
Lowenfeld, AF 66, 315–6, 318
Lubina, K 73, 104, 272
Luxembourg 173

MacKenzie, S 15–6, 22, 24, 95, 301, 303–4, 319
McLachlan, C 80, 184, 189, 207
McVeigh, S 161
Maher, G 91, 172, 177
Mann, FA 103, 161
market reduction approach 24
market state 10, 16, 25, 28, 51, 132, 159, 289, 290, 336–7, 339–40
  internationalists 114
Martinek, M 241
Mealy, N 114, 131, 290, 299, 301, 323, 327
mediation 50–1, 53–4, 149, 151, 193–4, 216, 262, 264–8, 271–2, 274, 276–7, 287, 342–3
Medici conspiracy 22, 28, 72, 296
Merryman, JH 74, 100, 111–2, 131, 238, 292, 307–8
Mexico 208–9, 321–2
Michaels, R 85
Mihan, G 114
Miles, MM 45
military necessity 117
Mills, A 26, 36–7, 43, 60, 62, 110, 115–6, 161, 281, 314
money laundering 43, 97, 319–20, 329
Monuments Men 257
morality *see* ethics
Morrow, JE 331
Mostrous, A 18
Muir Watt, H 49, 311, 315
Mullery, J 212–3
Murphy, JD 23, 133, 234
Murphy, N 70, 190, 213, 217, 255, 261, 263
Muscarella, OW 22

Nafziger, JAR 77, 183
national treasures 9, 234, 304–5
  EU law 7–8, 138–40, 143–6, 225–6, 235, 294–6, 344
  UK 8–9, 139, 329
  Waverley Criteria 8–9, 329
Nazi spoliated art 33, 58–9, 72–4, 121–3, 221, 250–6, 342, 345
  adjudicatory authority 211–7
  categories 72–3
  claimants' options: jurisdictional trade 262–7
  ethical/moral grounds for restitution 50–1, 69–70, 74, 79–80, 260
  forced sales 33, 73, 277–88, 343
  justice pluralism vs uniform body of law 269–72
  legal basis of restitution claims 69–70, 256–9
  policy-based restitution 50–1, 99, 255–6, 260
  private parties and mediation 267–8
  process and substance 39, 50, 272–7
  public policy exception and sovereign acts 104–5
  restitution in post-war era 259–62
  United States 182, 188, 211, 215, 217, 246
nemo dat quod non habet 126, 229, 233, 241
Netherlands 3, 17, 69, 97, 130, 173, 188–9, 342
  foreign public law 313
  Nazi spoliated art 266–7, 272
New York Convention (1958) 154–5, 194, 205–8, 211–3
New Zealand 78–9, 307–8, 315
Nicholas, LH 253
Nigeria 51
non-contractual disputes 37, 91, 98–9, 193, 196, 198–201, 255
non-contractual obligations 92
non-legal factors 16, 45, 149, 151, 196–8
non-retroactivity/non-retrospectivity 132–3, 299, 310, 328
Norway 130, 170
Nuremberg Laws 104, 284
Nuyts, A 170, 173

O'Connell, A 178, 261
Odendahl, K 128, 331
O'Donnell, T 59, 286
O'Keefe, PJ 4–5, 295, 298
Oliver, A 18
O'Neill, M 80
Orford, T 196
orphan works 238

out-of-court settlements 190–1, 284
ownership claims 9, 113–4
market overt exception 229
nemo dat quod non habet 126, 229, 233, 241
transfer of ownership 30, 37–8, 40, 230, 232, 234, 342
Nazi spoliated art 255, 268, 280
UNIDROIT 127, 233, 330
undiscovered objects 25, 40, 114, 128, 240, 245, 306–7, 316, 321, 329–31, 334, 343

Palestine 47
Palmer, N 18, 54, 95, 148, 152–3, 192, 196, 199, 232, 251, 263, 284
Panagopoulos, G 92–3, 239–40, 282
Pannikar, R 3
Papa-Sokal, M 7, 74, 113, 115, 133–4, 290, 298, 304–5, 308, 323
Papua New Guinea 74
parallel proceedings 147, 165–7, 174, 187, 189, 210, 217–9, 221–3, 269, 271, 287
Parker, J 278
Parkhouse, A 132
Passas, N 30
Paterson, RK 149, 194, 197, 278, 291–2, 327, 335
peace-time solutions: UNESCO and UNIDROIT Treaties 123–35
Pearce, N 22
Pearlstein, WG 112, 134–5, 149, 304, 320, 330
Pecoraro, TW 99, 238, 240, 293, 311
Pell, OC 211–3, 258, 261
Permanent Court of Arbitration (PCA) 157–8, 195, 201, 211, 213
Petrus, CH 204
Piers, M 156–9, 221
Platoni, K 250
pluralism, justice 43, 62, 90, 256, 269–72, 348
Poland 173
Portugal 130, 173, 313
pre-emption right, exercise of 306
Preston, A 23
Pretelli, I 174
private international law 15–6, 311, 318
context: cultural heritage law meets 16–25
control of cross-border movement and trade 25–36
domestic law interacts with 111–5
practical control offered by 36, 339–43
choice of law method 41–2
classification 37–9
ethics 45–8
foreign public law 40–1
global solidarity 48–52
international dimension 36–7, 340
public policy exception 42–5
public international law meets 115–6
surmounting greatest obstacles 344–8
procedure 38–9, 50, 80–3, 88–90, 96, 155, 272–7
arbitration 202, 214, 220, 223
property law 29, 59, 70–1, 110, 224–5, 254–5, 271, 278
Prott, LV 4–5, 9, 28, 35, 61, 94, 110, 227, 232, 236, 240, 295, 311, 327, 336
provenance/provenience 13, 20–1, 23–4, 30–1, 45, 88, 224, 228, 241, 247
choice of law rules and context 236–7
due diligence *see separate entry*
fact-finding establishing 70–1
museum displays: description of 283
Nazi spoliated art 251
purchaser: opportunity to ascertain 247, 346
tainted cultural object offence: unawareness of 303–4
Prowda, JB 57
public international law 15, 29–30, 41, 43, 73, 77, 102–5, 340
adjudicatory authority 161, 187–8
customary law 117–8, 132, 257, 293
foreign public law 314
jus cogens 122
Nazi spoliated art 213–4, 257, 261
private international law meets 115–6
state immunity *see separate entry*
UNESCO 133

public policy exception 26, 42–5, 50, 62, 73, 85, 107, 218, 342, 346–7
criminal conduct 101
Nazi spoliated art 261–2, 278–9, 287
safety valve 43, 90, 106
sovereign acts 102–5

Raape, L 241
Rabel, E 60, 93, 289, 318
Rabinbach, A 250
Radicati di Brozolo, LG 188, 207, 221
Range, D 264, 268
Rassool, C 79
Raue, D 285
Rayner, G 18
recognition and enforcement
of arbitral awards 207–11, 213
of judgments 83, 177, 181, 213
reconciliation 55–6, 79, 160
Redman, LF 255
Reed, A 81
Reichelt, G 28, 224, 232, 237
Reimann, M 62
religious law systems 190
Renold, MA 40, 134, 239
repatriation 77–80, 132, 136–7, 143–8, 299, 320–1, 335
res judicata 181, 188–90, 218, 221, 286–7, 341
and enforcement of the arbitral award 207–11, 221
Nazi spoliated art 213
restitution 14–5, 26–7, 32–3, 40–1, 67–7, 305–6, 310
doctrinal obstacles to 74–7, 314–26
legal grounds for 68–71, 256–9
moral grounds for/ethics-driven 50–1, 69–71, 74, 79–80, 260
Nazi spoliated art *see separate entry*
policy-based 50–1, 99, 255–6, 260
trophy art 252
UNESCO 129, 133
UNIDROIT 125–6, 129–30
retrospectivity/retroactivity 119, 132–3, 209
Rising, D 271
Ritchie, AM 69
Robertson, I 12
Rödl, F 36
Romania 173
Roodt, C 13, 22, 60, 95, 108, 167, 191, 208, 210, 217–8, 224, 256, 284–5
routine activity theory 24
Rowe, DW 232
Rowland, DJ 274
Russia 32–3, 76–7, 130, 187–8

Sancho Villa, D 82
Sargent, AB 33, 76–7, 182, 188, 252
Saville, A 289
Sawka, JF 214–5, 217, 264
Schechter, R 298
Schick, J 11
Schönenberger, B 8, 12, 22, 32–3, 50, 61, 70, 72, 80, 92, 96, 102–4, 118, 120, 129, 144, 148, 150, 153, 182, 262, 282, 284, 314, 317, 320–1, 327, 331
Schultz, T 155, 205
Schuz, R 312–3
Scoles, EF 320
Scotland 8, 40, 59, 81–2, 296, 328–9
arbitration 205
bona vacantia 86, 328
classification 91, 97, 172
jurisdiction 169, 172–3, 184
Law Commission 148, 230
Nazi spoliated art 265, 273
vitium reale 230–1
Scovazzi, T 60
sector vulnerability 24
Seelye, KQ 71
self-determination 77
Shapiro, D 37, 91
Shapiro, S 255
Shine, P 207
Shiu-Hing Lo, S 19
Shore, L 209
Short, KA 142
Sidorsky, E 54, 129, 152, 193, 195, 199, 222
Siehr, K 35, 47, 61, 81, 95, 101, 143, 152, 164, 191, 237–8, 240, 314, 333–4
Silk Road 11
Sinai, Y 189–90, 286–7

soft law 61, 63, 70, 115, 137, 157, 159, 216, 263–4
source state 10, 25, 28, 51, 72, 291, 307, 315, 322, 327, 336–40, 345–6
  economic benefits of cultural objects 24
  export control 293, 337–8
  historical record 20–1
  nationalists and internationalists 111–5, 289–90
  restitution: interests 27
  undiscovered cultural objects: Model provisions 25, 329–31
South Africa 79
sovereign act 26, 32–3, 50, 102–5, 183
Soviet Union 15, 188, 252
Spain 130, 173
Spiegler, HN 253
Staker, C 104, 239, 278, 315
Stamatoudi, I 137, 140, 144, 168, 217, 232, 255, 311
state immunity 26, 103, 105, 107, 122–3, 214–5, 310
  US courts 181–3
state ownership, declaration of (vesting law) 25, 40–1, 112–5, 120, 245, 289, 291, 322–5, 348
  export control regulations and 304–8
  Germany 331–2, 334, 337
  Model Provisions: undiscovered cultural objects 25, 329–31
  UNIDROIT 294, 329–31
statutory limitations/prescription 25, 27–9, 33–4, 39, 50, 74, 95–8, 101, 192, 221, 228, 336
  Belgium 242–3
  EU 146
  Germany 245, 254, 271
  lex originis 238
  Nazi spoliated art 211, 254–5, 261–2, 265–6, 271, 273–7, 342
  public policy exception 346
  public policy status 244–5, 262
  repatriation 78
  UNESCO 129
  UNIDROIT 126, 211, 259
  United Kingdom 96–7, 231, 244–5, 262, 265, 273
  United States 96–7, 192, 247–8, 274–6
Stein, P 224
Steindorff, Georg 284–5
Steiner, HJ 70, 104
Stengle, J 251
Sternlight, JR 201
Stewart, DP 181
Stipanovic, TJ 191, 216
supply, demand and regulation 23–5
Sweden 173
Switzerland 20, 33, 38, 50, 130, 170, 208, 218–9, 252, 281
  foreign public law 313
  implementation of UNESCO treaty obligations 297
Sykes, K 148
Symeonides, S 35, 42, 85, 97, 232, 234, 237, 247
Syria 47

Taiwan 218–9
theft 17–9, 27, 29, 33, 47, 71–2, 100–1, 128, 147, 306–7, 315, 330–1, 346–8
  arbitration 199–200
  Scotland 328–9
  title laundering 230–1, 235–7, 241, 244 – 8
  UK: Theft Act 1968 300–2
  UNIDROIT 126–8
  US: National Stolen Property Act (NSPA) 320–7
Theurich, S 60, 154, 255, 262
Tijhuis, AJG 10, 15, 18–9, 21–2, 27–30, 50, 226, 246
time limits 25, 27–9, 33–4, 39, 50, 74, 95–8, 101, 192, 221, 228, 336
  Belgium 242–3
  EU 146
  Germany 245, 254, 271
  ILA draft principles (2004) 193
  lex originis 238
  Nazi spoliated art 211, 254–5, 261–2, 265–6, 271, 273–7, 342
  public policy exception 346
  public policy status 244–5, 262
  repatriation 78

UNESCO 129
UNIDROIT 126, 211, 259
United Kingdom 96–7, 231, 244–5, 262, 265, 273
United States 96–7, 192, 247–8, 274–6
title 260, 269
title laundering 20, 27–33, 72, 95, 99, 106, 148, 224–49, 336, 347
choice of law rules and context 236–7
deterring 237–48
Belgium 242–3, 345
English courts 244–5
New York courts 246–8
menace of 227–36
Tolstoy, L 1, 48, 51
Tompkins, A 261
Torsen, MA 250
tort 37, 91, 98–9, 199
conversion 58, 67, 91–2, 96, 100, 172, 199, 231, 244, 247–8, 316–7, 322–3, 337
detinue 92
replevin 92
trafficking in cultural objects 9–10, 19–21
transfer of ownership 30, 37–8, 40, 230, 232, 234, 342
Nazi spoliated art 255, 268, 280
UNIDROIT 127, 233, 330
transit state/intermediary state 28, 95, 142, 233, 236, 339–40
trophy art 15, 73, 252
Turkey 4
Tyler, BJ 127

Ulph, J 16, 20, 47, 51, 58, 91, 95, 100, 114, 126, 136, 139, 305, 309, 317, 319–20, 323, 328
Ulpian 224
UNCITRAL Rules 157–8, 193, 195
UNESCO 7, 123–4, 131–6, 160, 196, 333, 335
good faith 97
mediation and arbitral panels 193–4
Nazi spoliated art 259
Parthenon Marbles 74
prevention and control 124–5
export controls 125–6, 128–9, 131, 134, 291, 294, 305–6
standard of implementation 297–304
sanctions 128
status 130
title laundering 28, 235–6
undiscovered cultural objects 25, 329–31, 338
UNIDROIT 26–7, 123–4, 131–2, 160, 211, 295, 310, 327
arbitration 153, 156–7, 158–9, 193
burden of proof 127
foreign public law 113, 127, 294–5, 310, 327, 329, 331
jurisdiction (signatory states of 1995 Convention) 168–9
Nazi spoliated art 259
prevention and control 125–8
sanctions 128–9
state ownership (vesting laws) 25, 294
status 130
title laundering 232–3
undiscovered cultural objects 25, 329–31, 338
United Kingdom 4, 12, 21, 59, 115, 130, 199–200, 287, 342–3
ADR 151–2
Spoliation Advisory Panel 65, 264–5, 267–8, 272–3, 277, 283, 286
arbitration and courts 200–1, 204–5
anti-suit injunctions 206
choice of law 88–9, 244–5, 273
buried ownerless property 86
classification 38, 91–2, 96–7, 100, 172
public policy exception 103, 105, 262, 286
Common Travel Area 296
criminal law 97, 337
tainted cultural object offence 303–4, 327–8
Theft Act 1968 300–2
cultural priorities 8–9
EU: free movement 139

export control 139, 142, 294–5, 301, 334
foreign public law 292, 294–5, 299–304, 320, 327–8, 334, 337, 343
challenge to doctrinal obstacle to restitution 314–8
non-application by default 309–12
Iraq 119
jurisdiction 81, 85, 162, 165, 169–72, 174
forum non conveniens 184–6
limitation periods 96–7, 231, 244–5, 262, 265, 273
looter cannot pass good title 212
Museums Association 135
repatriation 78, 80
Spoliation Advisory Panel 65, 264–5, 267–8, 272–3, 277, 283, 286
title laundering 227, 229–33, 235, 244–5, 249
UNESCO 299, 300–1, 303
United Nations
General Assembly 113, 120
Security Council 118–9
United States 12, 34, 41–2, 44, 59, 115
ADR agreement 151
arbitration 151, 154
anti-suit injunctions 206–7
mandatory 201
res judicata 208–9
choice of law 89, 246–8
archaeological sites 86–7
classification 92, 99
public policy exception 102, 105
criminal law 71–2, 199–200, 299, 320–7, 337
cultural priorities 6–7
discovery 97
foreign public law 292–5, 297–9, 320–7, 331, 334, 337, 343
import control 296, 298–9, 337
Iraq 118–9
jurisdiction 82, 85, 162, 165, 168–9, 173
challenges 187–8
forum non conveniens 184–6
FSIA and IFSA 181–3, 187–8
minimum contacts 178–81
museums: immunity regime 177–8
recognition and enforcement 181
limitation periods 96–7, 192, 247–8, 274–6
looter cannot pass good title 212
mediation 151
Native Americans 78, 80, 86–7, 178–9
Nazi spoliated art 182, 188, 211, 215, 217, 246, 255–7, 260, 273–7
mediation 267, 274, 276–7
res judicata 190
title laundering 227, 241, 246–9
UNESCO 131, 133–5, 297–9
UNIDROIT 130, 294
unjust enrichment 91–2, 199, 240, 272

Vadi, V 5, 14
Valentin, P 127, 131
value-rationality 29, 48–50, 277, 279, 287, 342, 345, 347
Van Apeldoorn, LJ 224
Van Haersolte-van Hof, J 120, 195
Van Vliet, LPW 37–8
Van Woudenberg, N 2, 26, 118, 136
Varner, E 55, 153, 195, 198–9
Venice Court of National and International Arbitration (VENCA) 193
Veraart, W 50, 59, 69, 74, 254, 260–1, 280, 284
Verhagen, HLE 94
Vincent, A 18
Vitale, C 112, 140, 144
vitium reale 227, 230–1, 233, 236–7, 248–9, 346
Voet, P 311
Von Hoffmann, B 333
Von Savigny, FK 83, 85
Von Stockhausen, T 251

waivers 209, 218, 267
access to court 201–5, 341
state immunity 214–5
Wantuch, MO 152, 275
war/armed conflict 21, 27, 47–8, 69, 76–7, 112, 116–8, 345

ad hoc measures adopted in modern conflicts 118–20
Gulf Conflict 47, 118–20
war crimes 257–8
Ward, P 268
Warren, KJ 125
Watson, P 12, 15, 20, 22, 296, 300
Weil, S 2
Weller, M 271, 282–3, 312–3, 317, 320–1, 326, 331–3
Whincop, M 35, 89, 95, 190, 217
Wichard, JC 53
Wilde, L 13, 48, 52, 277, 312
Wilson, MJ 89–90
Wilson, S 274
Woodhead, C 264–5, 269, 271–3, 283, 286
World Customs Organization (WCO) 142
World Trade Organization (WTO) 14

Yasaitis, KE 112, 307, 321
Yeide, NH 251–2